JANE PETTIGREW'S
WORLD OF TEA

83Press
1900 International Park Drive, Suite 50
Birmingham, Alabama 35243
USA

ISBN: 978-1-940772-51-6
Printed in Hong Kong

Gong Fu tea wares. Photograph by David Collen; courtesy of *essenceoftea.com*

CONTENTS

CONTENTS

New growth on bushes in Darjeeling at Risheehat Tea Estate, whose name means "Home of Holy Saints." The snow-covered peaks of Mount Kanchenjunga lie beyond. Photograph by John O'Hagan; © Hoffman Media

FOREWORD

Lovers of tea's social history and its culture will already know Jane Pettigrew's many previous tea books, but this, her *World of Tea*, is exploring a new field entirely.

To record and describe all the known tea-growing origins across the globe is a daunting task. I know this from my 40 years in the tea industry working on countless gardens scattered across six of the world's continents. Often, while relaxing with a cold beer at sundown, I have idly thought of, and just as often swiftly rejected, writing such a difficult book. Jane, however, with her customary patience and diligence and eye for detail, has managed to contact, collect, collate, and record many hundreds of tea growers who have been active for decades as well as the rapidly increasing number who are just beginning to make a mark in tea production. So, I heartily welcome and endorse Jane's *World of Tea* and feel particularly involved with it as I have met and advised many of the growers mentioned, both professionally and on an informal tea fraternity basis. Tea growers, established or new, are largely hidden from the tea-consuming world, but they fully deserve the recognition that Jane's book accords them.

I challenge any tea devotee, be they hobbyist or professional, not to spend many happy hours poring in delight over the scores of enticing country maps with their iconic green tea-tips location markers and not be amazed by some of the new tea origins. I know many of these, but some are entirely new, even to me. Tea growing in Togo and Mali; on Réunion; in the Netherlands, Wales, and Switzerland; or in Michigan and Mississippi in the United States? Who would have thought it? Such new origins deserve our scrutiny and attention. With climate volatility beginning to adversely affect many traditional tea origins, some of these new contenders could well become traditional origins in the future.

A word is deserved also for the innate flexibility of the single tea species *Camellia sinensis* that, in its early wild days, evolved in a tropical south-east Asian forest but now thrives as an agricultural crop across all those six continents in climatic conditions ranging from humid tropics to distinctly chilly northern zones. This book demonstrates and celebrates tea's amazing journey from shy tropical forest dweller to a seasoned world traveller.

—NIGEL MELICAN, *Teacraft Ltd*

INTRODUCTION

My journey through the world of tea has been long, eventful, and exciting. I began working in tea in 1983, and my early travels took me more often to tea-consuming countries than to the regions of the world that actually produce the leaves we brew. In the early 1990s, France and Russia wanted to understand the history and traditions of our British way of tea; Americans on cruise liners and Brazilians in Rio de Janeiro were fascinated by our afternoon-tea rituals and etiquette, and so I was invited to explain and elaborate. But then, the Japanese also began to enquire about finger sandwiches, scones, clotted cream, and British tea history and invited me to British fairs in Japan's major cities. Happily, those trips, of course, also involved visits to the country's tea gardens and gave me a new insight into the cultivation and processing of teas such as sencha, gyokuro, and matcha. In the mid-1990s came visits to long-established tea-producing countries such as Sri Lanka, India, and Malaysia, and my tours of factories and discussions with tea pickers and tea makers helped me understand the mass production of black tea. But China's tea factories were not open to visitors at that time, so we could not learn from them. And—it's hard to imagine this now—there was no Internet, no Google, no blogs, few books, and no access to knowledge of individual tea countries unless we actually travelled there and saw everything for ourselves. My early books on tea were an attempt at helping other tea lovers understand the industry a little better, but they were full of mistakes and were shamefully ignorant of China's white, yellow, oolong, and dark teas and of Taiwan's oolongs—for we knew nothing of those at that time.

Through the 1990s, there were hints of a new interest in tea, small bubbles of activity that rose to the surface from time to time, but it was not until the turn of the new millennium that we began to see more evidence of a real tea renaissance. I found myself on a wave that has since been gathering strength and speed all around the world. And as the tide has turned in favour of good tea and interest has grown, we have seen not just an increase in the number of passionate tea drinkers but a surge in the number of people who now grow tea. People all around the world seem to love growing tea. They develop an attachment to their plants that is akin to a parent's feelings for his or her children. Tea plants are not just grown; they are raised, nurtured, protected, supported, and nourished so that they can give of their best. Tea grows happily in subtropical conditions, but it takes courage, patience, knowledge, and tenacity to grow tea successfully in the harsh conditions of, for example, Canada,

My aim in writing this book was to give readers an insight into every tea-growing region of the world, both established and new, and to provide ready access to all the details of the different locations, the types of tea made, the methods of manufacture, and the character of those teas. I hope that this book helps tea lovers everywhere learn and understand more easily and feel more connected to our fascinating world of tea. I apologise to any growers I have missed and would love to hear from them so that they can be included in the next edition.

I would like to express my heartfelt gratitude to the wonderful team at Hoffman Media—Brian Hart Hoffman, Cailyn Haynes, Meg Lundberg, Karissa Brown, Samantha Sullivan, and cartographer Melissa Langston, among others— who have worked with me on this project with such patience, support, and understanding and have helped me pull so much information, so many facts, and so many images and detailed maps together to create a work that I hope everyone finds engaging, enlightening, and helpful in their work in tea. And I'd like to say a very special thank-you to my editor, Lorna Reeves, with whom I have worked for a number of years on *TeaTime* magazine, and who has been a wonderfully kind, thoughtful, constant, and steady guide throughout the many months it has taken to complete the book.

Sincere thanks also go to the following people who have been so helpful and generous with information, photographs, and translations: Nigel Melican of Tea Craft, UK; Eva Lee of Tea Hawaii & Company, USA; Victoria Bisogno of El Club del Té, Argentina; Juyan Webster of The Chinese Tea Company, UK; Asako Steward of Infuse Tea, Japan and UK; Dr. Tim Bond of AVT Tea Services Ltd., and the Tea Advisory Panel, UK; Thomas Shu of JT & Tea, USA and Taiwan; Indi Khanna of Tea 'n' Teas and Tea Studio, India; Leo Kwan of Tea Hong and Tea Guardian, Hong Kong; Manoj Jalan of Jalan Tea Group, India; Iris Qiu, Certified Chinese Tea Master, London and China; Dan Robertson of The Tea House and World Tea Tours, USA; David Collen of The Essence of Tea, Malaysia; Dani Lieuthier of Caminho do Chá, Brazil; Thomas Kasper of Siam Teas, Germany.

Alabama, New York State, Wales, Scotland, Switzerland, or Togo. And yet, the plants seem to respond to the love and care they are shown, and they survive. The new growers bring astonishing dedication, imagination, and skill to their processing and are making some extraordinary teas that are now becoming available on the world market. And the sharing of knowledge and understanding between tea makers all over the world is inspirational to us all.

Sri Lankan pluckers at work on Mattekelle Tea Estate, one of Dilmah's gardens at the heart of the island's Dimbula region.
Photograph courtesy of Dilmah Tea

The mountains of Yunnan Province, China, where tea first grew.

Photograph by David Collen; courtesy of *essenceoftea.com*

CHAPTER 1

THE ORIGINS OF TEA

FOR THOUSANDS OF YEARS, THE BEVERAGE
CALLED TEA HAS BEEN MADE FROM THE
LEAVES OF THE *CAMELLIA SINENSIS*,
A MEMBER OF THE *CAMELLIA* GENUS.

During the Han dynasty (206 B.C. to A.D. 220), the Chinese character *cha* was first used to refer to both the plant and the drink, and the first study of the plant in Europe appeared in 1678 when Dutch physician and botanist Wilhelm ten Rhyne published his text on tea (in Latin) in an appendix to Jacob Breyn's *Exoticum plantarum centuria prima* (First Century of Exotic Plants). In 1712, German botanist and physician Englebert Kaempfer published his study of tea in Japan, referring to the plant as *Theae Japonensis* in his *Amoenitates Exoticae* (Exotic Pleasures). He wrote, "Tea, called Tsjaa by the Japanese and Theh by the Chinese, still has no character of its own accepted and approved by the universities." In 1753, following Kaempfer's lead, Swedish botanist Carl Linnaeus suggested naming the plant *Thea sinensis*. Also in 1753, English writer John Hill declared in his *Treatise on Tea* that black tea and green tea were made from different plants (a belief commonly held at the time), and in the second edition of his *Species Plantarum*, (1762 to 63), Linnaeus reclassified *Thea sinensis* as *Thea viridis*, used to make green tea, and *Thea bohea*, used for black tea.

Linnaeus was also responsible for naming the *Camellia* genus in honour of the work of Georg Josef Kamel (or Camellus), a Czech Jesuit priest and botanist who, in 1704, published works on plants found in the Philippines. However, Linnaeus made no connection between *Thea* and *Camellia*, and it was English botanist Robert Sweet who, in 1818, reclassified the tea plant and moved all *Thea* species plants into the *Camellia* genus. In 1905, the International Code of Botanical Nomenclature settled on *Camellia sinensis* (L.) O. Kuntze as the correct name for the tea plant, the letter *L* referring to Carl Linnaeus, and O. Kuntze for the German apothecary Otto Kuntze, who, in 1881, first gave the tea plant the name we use today. In 1907, Scottish botanist Sir George Watt clarified the fact that green tea and black tea were made from the same plant and that it was manufacture that determined the different types.

Other outdated names once used for the plant include *Thea viridis*, *Thea bohea*, *Camellia Thea*, *Thea sinensis*, and *Camellia Theifera*.

Yi people, one of China's minority ethnic groups, at Tashan Tea Company in Yinjing County, Ya'an, Sichuan, China. Photograph courtesy of Camellia Sichuanesis

TEA OR CHA

The more common names for tea used around the world today can be traced back to Chinese origins. The Chinese word for tea, meaning "a bitter herb," was originally written 茶 and was pronounced "tu." During the Han dynasty, the character became 茶 and was pronounced differently in different dialects—in Mandarin, "chá"; in Min Chinese in southern China, "ta" or "te"; in the Amoy dialect of Fujian Province, "tê." Depending on which version of the word early foreign traders came into contact with, the name for tea was absorbed into different languages and was adjusted accordingly. In almost all languages today, words for tea derive from the original Chinese pronunciations used in different parts of the country.

THE LOCATION OF TEA'S ORIGINS

It is impossible to know the exact location where the tea plant first appeared, but most researchers agree that it has its origins in the corridor of biodiversity that runs along the foothills of the Himalayas and stretches from Assam to south-west China. Some botanists believe that it originated along the banks of the Irrawaddy River in Burma (now Myanmar) and then spread north into south-east China, northern Burma, and Assam; some say that it first grew in Yunnan Province in the south-west of China; and a third group believes that the plant had two separate places of origin, one in eastern and south-eastern China, the other in Yunnan Province in the south-west of

LEFT: Ancient tea trees in Yunnan Province, where some tea trees are thought to be at least 3,000 years old. Photograph by David Collen; courtesy of *essenceoftea.com*
RIGHT: Ancient trees in northern Laos, where they grow in similar conditions to those of Yunnan. Photograph courtesy of Dominic Smith

the country. This idea of two origins stems from the fact that two main variations of the plant were found—the small-leafed variety in the temperate regions of south-eastern China, and the large-leafed plant in the tropical regions of Yunnan, Vietnam, Laos, Myanmar, and Assam. In 1935, Takashi Shimura reported in his article "Cytological Investigations in Tea Plants" (published in the *Japanese Journal of Crop Science*) that the Chinese and Assam varieties had the same chromosome number and, therefore, did not differ in their cell structure, suggesting that the two varieties, commonly referred to today as the Chinese variety (*Camellia sinensis* var. *sinensis*) and the Assam variety (*Camellia sinensis* var. *assamica*), did not have separate origins.

The difficulty in defining one single birthplace for tea is made more complicated by the existence of other varieties of the tea plant. The *Camellia irrawadiensis* was first found growing in the Irrawaddy Basin in Myanmar and is thought by some to be the original tea plant. The *Camellia taliensis* (or *daliensis*, a close relative of the tea plant found growing in Dali Prefecture in Yunnan) is indigenous to western and south-western Yunnan Province and to northern Myanmar, and is thought by others to be the ancestor of modern cultivated varieties. Its presence in Yunnan's dense forests again suggests that this region is tea's true home and that the majority of the original trees may have been destroyed over the centuries by agricultural development in the region or by overfelling or overpicking. *Camellia taliensis* is considered to be a hybrid of *Camellia sinensis* and *Camellia irrawadiensis*. Local villagers still process leaves from wild or semiwild *taliensis* trees today to make high-grade Puerh dark teas and white teas, but western commercial cultivators rejected both the *irrawadiensis* and *taliensis* varieties because their leaves were found to contain less caffeine and did not produce a suitable flavour profile. Both types are, however, extremely important to the conservation of the *Camellia sinensis* gene pool.

Although no one location has been categorically defined as tea's birthplace, the majority view appears to be that the plant first appeared in China's Yunnan Province, and possibly also in Sichuan and Guizhou provinces, during Earth's tertiary geological period from 66 million to 2.58 million years ago. Glaciers that formed during the following Quaternary period (earth's current geological period) destroyed many types of plants. But regions such as Simao and Xishuangbanna in south-western Yunnan were free from glaciers, so ancient plant families there survived in the mountain forests of southern China and Assam in north-eastern India. In 1958, English botanist Joseph Robert Sealy estimated in his *Revision of the Genus Camellia* that Yunnan was the origin of tea, and in his 1985 paper *The Origin of The Tea Plant*, Minoru Hashimoto of the Faculty of Agriculture at Meijo University, Japan, wrote: "Specialists in China … support the idea of a single origin for tea. Chen Chuan and Chen Cheng-kou (1979), for example, studied the genetic character of wild tea plants and made biochemical analyses which suggested that tea's origins lay in Yunnan where a large-leaf variety is produced." Hashimoto also explained that "giant wild tea trees have been found one after another deep in the mountains and woods of Yunnan, Sichuan and Guizhou areas." He concludes, "The origin of the tea plant would seem to be centered in the area identified by most Chinese tea specialists; that is Yun-gui Kaoyuan. In addition, the fact that this south-western district is the world center of Theaceae also seems to confirm it as the tea plant's origin." What Hashimoto refers to as Yun-gui Kaoyuan is more commonly called Yungui Gaoyuan but is also called the Yunnan–Guizhou Plateau, Yungui Plateau, Plateau of Yunnan, Yun-kuei Kao-yuan, and Yunkwei Plateau. It is a plateau that runs through most of Yunnan Province at an altitude of around 2,000 metres (6,562 feet) and extends eastward into Guizhou Province.

CAMELLIA SINENSIS AND ITS SUBSPECIES

The tea plant is classified scientifically as *Camellia sinensis* (L.) O. Kuntze, family Theaceae, genus *Camellia*, species *sinensis*. The evergreen plant thrives in the shade or semishade of woodlands and forests and prefers deep, light sandy or loamy soils with an acidic pH of between 4.5 and 5.5. The roots need plenty of water, but the ground must be well drained. Its white flowers are hermaphrodite and have fragile white petals that are sometimes tinged with hints of pale pink and surround a whorl of bright yellow stamens. The bushes need between 1,140 to 1,270 millimetres (45 to 50 inches) of rain distributed evenly throughout the year. The different types of *Camellia sinensis* need varying temperatures for successful growth. The hardier types are happiest at temperatures between 12.5°C (55°F) and 32°C (90°F) and can survive snow—which acts as an insulator to the bush—but suffer badly in frost. Temperatures over 35°C (95°F) also stress the plants.

> **Within *Camellia sinensis*, three natural subspecies are recognised, of which two are cultivated:**
>
> 1. *Camellia sinensis* var. *sinensis*, sometimes referred to as *Camellia sinensis* (L) and commonly known as the Chinese variety.
> 2. *Camellia sinensis* var. *assamica*, sometimes referred to in the industry as *Camellia assamica* (Masters) and commonly known as the Assam variety.
> 3. *Camellia sinensis assamica* ssp. *lasiocalyx*, sometimes referred to in the industry as *Camellia assamica* (Planch. MS) or *Camellia cambodiensis*, and commonly known as the Cambod variety. This third type is rarely used for commercial cultivation.

CAMELLIA SINENSIS VAR. *SINENSIS*

The Chinese subspecies is a large shrub that produces numerous erect stems from the base of the plant and grows to a height of 3 to 4 metres (10 to 13 feet) and when mature forms a dome shape. Its narrow, thick, matte leaves are usually 1 to 6 centimetres (0.4 to 2.4 inches) long and 1.5 to 2 centimetres (0.6 to 0.8 inches) wide. The small flowers form singly or in pairs, and the three-lobed ovary contains 1 to 3 spherical seeds. The plant is hardy and prefers the cool temperatures of high mountain slopes and can survive at altitudes of up to 2,700 metres (8,858 feet). During colder seasons, the plant is dormant and starts forming new leaf shoots only when spring brings warm sunshine and the first early rain showers. The plant is indigenous to China and Japan.

CAMELLIA SINENSIS VAR. *ASSAMICA*

The Assam subspecies is so called because it was first found there by Europeans in the early 19th century. It is taller than the Chinese plant and, if left to grow without human intervention, can reach heights of 18 metres (59 feet). It generally has one stem or trunk from which sturdy branches develop. The leaves are much larger than those of the Chinese plant, and the plant is often referred to as the big-leafed variety. The shiny leaves can be between 8 and 30 centimetres (3 and 12 inches) long, especially on older wild trees, and have distinct veins throughout each leaf and prominent marginal veins. The creamy-white flowers often have hints of yellow at the base of each petal. The plant likes low-lying locations in subtropical regions and thrives in high temperatures and high humidity. In general, the leaves of the assamica variety contain higher levels of caffeine and polyphenols than those of the Chinese variety. The plant is indigenous to Assam, China, Myanmar, Thailand, Laos, and Vietnam.

CAMELLIA SINENSIS ASSAMICA SSP. *LASIOCALYX*

The Cambod subspecies, or *Camellia sinensis* var. *cambodiensis* (also known as *Camellia sinensis parvifolia*, or the Java bush), is a hybrid of *Camellia sinensis* var. *sinensis* and *Camellia sinensis* var. *assamica*. It grows as a sturdy and very productive small tree with several upright stems and a network of equal-length branches. The glossy, erect leaves are larger than those of the China type but smaller than those of the Assam plant, and the flower petals show hints of pinkish-red at the base. It is indigenous to Assam, Myanmar, and Vietnam, and because of its ability to easily hybridise, it is sometimes used in the creation of new cultivars.

OTHER THEACEAE FAMILY TEA SPECIES

Other tea species that are also classified as members of the Theaceae family include *Camellia taliensis* (also known as *daliensis* and *Polyspora yunnanensis*), found in Yunnan Province, Myanmar, Laos, and Thailand; *Camellia irrawadiensis* (also called Wilson's Camellia and *Camellia irrawadiensis Barua*) found in Myanmar, Laos, and southern China; and *Camellia sinensis* var. *pubilimba*, found in the Chinese provinces of Guangdong, Guangxi, Hainan, and Yunnan.

BELOW LEFT: Tea blossom at Charleston Tea Plantation in South Carolina, United States. BELOW RIGHT: Assamica plants at Belseri Tea Estate, Assam, India. Photographs by John O'Hagan; ©Hoffman Media BOTTOM LEFT: New shoots on tea bushes in Kakegawa, Japan. Photograph courtesy of Asako Steward, City of Kakegawa

CAMELLIA SINENSIS: VARIETALS AND CULTIVARS

Within the three main subspecies of the tea plant discussed on the previous pages, thousands of varietals and cultivars grow around the world, each one with its own individual properties, such as leaf size, leaf colour, flower size, tannin content, caffeine level, and polyphenols. Some people would argue that the word *varietal* is an adjective rather than a noun and that *variety* is the correct word to use in this context, but *variety* is often used to mean type or category of manufactured tea (black, oolong, green, and so on), and to avoid confusion, we tend now to use *varietal*. The word *jat*, originally from the Indian tea industry, is also used to mean a particular varietal, for example, China jat or Assam jat.

In discussing different tea plants, *varietal* (or *variety*) and *cultivar* are often used as interchangeable terms, and some languages have only one word or character for both. However, in strict botanical terms, *varietal* refers to a plant that has developed by natural selection or mutation, and *cultivar* (from "cultivated variety") refers to a plant that has been created on purpose by scientists or botanists. So, for example, the subspecies *Camellia sinensis* var. *assamica* found growing just in Yunnan Province includes a long list of more than 20 natural varietals, such as Yiwu Green Bud from Mengla County in Xishuangbanna, Tengchong Broad Leaf from Tengchong County in Baoshan, and Mingfeng Mountain Broad Leaf from Yongde County in Lincang. Examples of cultivars developed in Japan in recent years include Sayamamidori, registered in 1953 for the production of *sencha*; Kyoumidori, registered in 1954 for the production of *tencha* and *gyokuro*; and Benikaori, registered in 1960 for black tea manufacture.

New cultivars are created by crossbreeding plants that have been selected for their ability to thrive in particular conditions and give tea liquors that have the desired aroma and flavour profile. Cultivars may be bred for their high yield; their resistance to pest attack; their ability to withstand hotter, drier weather; their antioxidant content; the strength of flavour they give to black tea; or the floral aroma and taste expected from, for example, jade oolongs. New cultivars are released for planting by research institutes only after the relevant government authorities have given their approval.

New tea plants for cultivation can be grown from seed or can be created by layering or grafting. Seeds are planted after having first been soaked in water. Seedling plants take between 12 and 18 months to reach a height of around 15 centimetres (6 inches), when they can be transplanted out into the tea field. Layering involves making a small incision in a branch of a healthy bush and then training the branch down into the ground where it is left to form roots. Grafting takes the rootstock of one plant and the stems, leaves, flowers, and fruits of another and fuses them to make a new plant. Today, the most widely used method of producing new stock is to create clonal plants by vegetative propagation. By this method, leaf cuttings are taken from mother plants that have been carefully selected for their ability to thrive in particular conditions. Each cutting is planted in sheltered conditions, forms roots within six to eight weeks, and grows a substantial new shoot in four to five months.

Although vegetative propagation gives tea farmers greater control over the stock of new plants they grow, plants developed in this way have a much weaker root system than plants grown from seed and also have a shorter productive life than do seed-grown plants. Clonal plants produce leaf successfully for approximately 50 years, whereas seed-grown plants go on flushing for well over 100 years.

To have control over plants grown from seed, some tea estates dedicate an orchard of selected tea plants purely for the production of seeds. The seed orchard plants are allowed to grow freely, are not plucked or pruned, and so produce flowers and seeds as they would if they were growing in the wild.

TOP LEFT: Steep slopes covered with tea bushes at Risheehat Tea Estate in Darjeeling, India. BOTTOM LEFT: Garden marker at Risheehat Tea Estate in Darjeeling, India, which states that the division is planted with "China jat" sinensis plants. Photographs by John O'Hagan; ©Hoffman Media TOP RIGHT: On the left, a new plant grown from a leaf cutting with a weak root system; on the right, a plant grown from seed with a much stronger root system. © Ambootia Tea Group BOTTOM RIGHT: Close-up of a strong study bush at Agrícola Himalaya's Bitaco Tea Estate in Colombia. Photograph courtesy of Bitaco Tea Estate

TERROIR

Just as wine producers use the word *terroir* to explain why certain wines develop a specific character in a particular location, so tea lovers also use the term to define the individual and sometimes unique natural factors that play an essential role in developing the character of a particular tea. Terroir distills the very essence of the place in which a specific tea is grown and processed, and includes geographic position, climate and weather patterns, altitude, terrain, soil, the local ecosystem, and other plants growing around and amongst the tea.

Geographic position, that is, the proximity of a tea estate to the equator, has a direct influence on climate and weather and on how the bushes grow through the year. Tea plants that grow in gardens on or very near the equator flush all year in constant warm temperatures. So, in countries such as Kenya, Uganda, Ecuador, Colombia, and Indonesia, the plants push out their new leaf shoots throughout the year, and the character of the teas varies little from month to month. But even these equatorial regions experience slight fluctuations in rainfall and temperature, and drier, cooler periods slow the plant's growth and give quality "peak season" teas. In Kenya, for example, the best teas are harvested during the drier periods in January and February and again in July and August. But tea bushes that grow more than 16 degrees north or south of the equator are affected by marked seasonal changes, stop growing during cold months, but flush vigorously in the summer's soaring heat and heavy rain. In Darjeeling, for example, slow tentative growth in spring after a period of winter dormancy gives the First Flush teas a delicacy and refined subtlety that disappear once the summer monsoon brings faster growth and plainer teas.

All aspects of climate and weather—temperature, sunshine, wind, mist, humidity, and cloud cover—play their part in contributing to the aroma and flavour profile of a tea. Most varietals of the tea plant, for example, cannot survive temperatures below 5°C (41°F), but in the Nilgiri Hills in January and February

each year, a brief snap of very low temperatures allows the tea growers to make their special "frost teas." The contrast of very cold nights and strong sunshine during the day stresses the plants and causes them to accumulate metabolites (such as pyruvate, acetaldehyde, and ethanol) in the leaves, giving the teas a light, fragrant character that is quite different from that of Nilgiri teas produced at other times of the year.

Altitude is, of course, directly linked to weather conditions, and in many mountainous situations, the higher the elevation, the cooler and mistier the weather, the slower the growth of the plants, and the lighter and more delicate the teas. Plentiful cloud cover (or shading of any kind) results in less photosynthesis in the leaf cells; higher quantities of chlorophyll, essential oils, and amino acids such as L-theanine; and lower levels of bitter-tasting catechins. So, tea liquors are milder, sweeter, less astringent, and sometimes have an umami, brothy character.

The terrain of a tea garden influences its exposure to weather patterns, the composition of the soil and the way in which it drains, the depth to which tea roots can penetrate to find nutrients and water, and the chemistry of the water from springs, rivers, and rainfall that nurtures the plants. The tea may also absorb the perfume of trees and flowers growing nearby or may draw a hint of flavour from the hidden roots of other plants. Even insects can interfere with the plants' behaviour, and in Taiwan, the sweet, fruity flavour of Oriental Beauty depends entirely upon the arrival each summer of small leafhoppers that bite the leaves as they grow in the hot sun, causing the plants to produce enzymes to defend themselves and provoking oxidation in the leaves before they have been plucked.

Tea producers have learned to appreciate everything nature contributes and to work in harmony with natural influences to produce teas that are unique in character and quality.

OPPOSITE PAGE, TOP: The rolling Nilgiri Hills of southern India, shrouded in mist. Photograph courtesy of *camellia-sinensis.com* MIDDLE: Neat rows of tea growing at high altitude on steep slopes in West Java, Indonesia. Photograph courtesy of Harendong Tea Estate BOTTOM: Tea fields in Kenya where the bushes grow at high altitude on rolling plains. Photograph courtesy of James Finlay Limited ABOVE: Bois Chéri tea estate in Mauritius. © Saint Aubin Loisirs Ltée

TEA HARVESTING

To make tea, tender young leaf shoots are removed from the bush. Traditionally, this is done by hand, but in many parts of the world, where too few people are available to pluck the tea, the leaf is removed by machine. The plucked leaf is processed to make one of six categories of tea—white, green, yellow, oolong, black, or dark—and the tea category to be made determines when and how the leaf is plucked.

The way young tea shoots are harvested from the plant has a direct influence on the health and productivity of the plant. Without photosynthesis (the chemical process during which the plants use energy from the sun to convert water, carbon dioxide, and minerals into oxygen and organic compounds), the plant cannot produce new leaves and will, therefore, die. Because older tea leaves hidden below the outer layer of new growth do not contribute to the plant's photosynthesis, a healthy outer layer of leaves is essential for adequate photosynthesis to take place; therefore, only a percentage of new leaves should be picked. This "selective plucking" removes new shoots consisting of only two young leaves and a bud, leaving other leaves on the lower stem to nourish the next generation of leaf shoots. If shoots of three or four leaves and a bud are harvested too frequently, the plant's health can be compromised, and yields will be reduced.

When and how tea shoots are harvested also affects the quality of the made tea. For the best teas, the leaves and buds must be plucked when they contain the correct balance of chemical compounds, enzymes, water, and fibre. Young leaves contain the highest concentration of aroma and flavour, but if they are picked when too young and too small, the quantity gathered will be diminished. If the leaves contain too much water, they are difficult to process. Too much stalk and fibre in the shoots reduces quality and makes coarser teas. Too much bright sunlight can reduce the amount of chlorophyll and amino acids in the leaves, thus producing teas that lack sweetness and intensity of flavour.

Ambootia Tea Estate in Darjeeling, where all the tea in the different gardens is harvested by hand to ensure high-quality leaf. © Ambootia Tea Group

Once the leaf shoots have been collected from the plant, they must be very carefully handled since damage to the fresh shoots before they are processed negatively affects the quality of the made tea. Baskets and bags that pluckers carry should never be overfilled, and when loaded onto trucks or tractors for transportation to the factory, the leaves should be loosely packed into crates or bags that allow air to circulate around them. Pressure causes a buildup of heat in the leaves, reduces the chances of making good tea, and increases losses at the factory.

The frequency of harvesting, known as the "plucking round," depends on the speed at which the plants develop new shoots. This, in turn, depends on the tea garden's proximity to the equator and local weather patterns. In hot, humid regions, plucking may take place every few days; in very cold regions, the bushes may only flush four times a year.

The finest teas are hand plucked, as here in Darjeeling, but many estates around the world now have to use mechanical harvesters of various types because of a lack of labour or high labour costs. Photograph by John O'Hagan; ©Hoffman Media

PLUCKING BY HAND

To make the finest teas, the new leaf shoots are plucked by hand, and the size, age, and number of leaves on each shoot depends on the type of tea to be made. The young shoot is snapped off carefully in order to break the stem cleanly and allow the plant to produce another new shoot.

There are four internationally recognised plucking standards:

1. *Imperial plucking* takes one bud and one leaf.
2. *Fine plucking* takes one bud and two leaves.
3. *Medium plucking* takes one bud and three leaves.
4. *Coarse plucking* (sometimes known as souchong plucking) removes more than three leaves with each bud.

In all of the above, the buds and leaves remain attached to the stem.

For needle-style white teas such as Yin Zhen (Silver Needles), only the tightly furled bud is plucked while it is still covered with a layer of tiny white hairs, called in Chinese the *Bai Hao* or *Pekoe*, in French the *duvet*, and in English the downy covering or pubescence. For peony-style white teas such as Bai Mu Dan or Shou Mei, one bud and one or two open leaves are plucked.

The finest yellow teas and some green teas are made from just the furled bud, while other green teas demand imperial or fine plucking. For dark, large-leafed oolongs such as Mi Lan Dan Cong or Da Hong Pao, shoots consisting of three or four open leaves are harvested. For balled oolongs such as Ali Shan or Ti Kuan Yin, a stem with a bud and three or four leaves attached is used. And Taiwan's Oriental Beauty is made from fine-plucked shoots of one bud and two leaves. For the best-quality black teas, fine plucking is employed, but in some countries, medium plucking is more common. For Puerh and other dark teas, pickers take one bud and three or four leaves. The older leaves on each shoot are rich in polyphenols and minerals and give an increased astringency and bitterness to the young Puerh, but they add to the sweet, fruity flavours that develop in the tea as it ages.

SHEAR PLUCKING

Japan was the first to use shears to harvest tea at the end of the 19th century, and India and Malaysia followed in the first half of the 20th century. Shear plucking can harvest three times more fresh leaf than can hand plucking, and because of a lack of labour or the high cost of wages in many countries today, shear plucking is common in Indonesia, Malaysia, southern India, Assam, Turkey, Central Africa, Chile, Malawi, Kenya, and elsewhere. Shear plucking does not allow fine or selective plucking, and the scissorlike blades cut whatever is in their range as they chop. Operatives need careful training, and it is important not to stress the plants by harvesting too frequently and too hard as this can reduce yield and give poor-quality teas. The best shear-plucking machines have a hopper that is stepped above the level of the blades by between 1 and 1.25 centimetres (0.4 and 0.5 inches) and raises the machine above the layer of fragile young shoots that are still growing and might otherwise be damaged. Some regions of the world combine hand and shear plucking, depending on the season and the type of tea being made.

MECHANICAL HARVESTING

A variety of mechanical harvesters is available to tea farmers in countries with high labour costs or a severe lack of labour. One- and two-man-operated handheld machines cut the tea shoots with blades similar to those in a hedge trimmer, and the leaves are blown into a large bag attached to the machine on a stream of motor-generated air. Wheel-mounted machines straddle rows of tea bushes. The tea shoots are severed by a cutter bar running under the harvester and are then blown up a wide tube into a collection container. The disadvantage of most mechanical harvesting is the rough cutting of the tea stems, the uneven quality of the harvested leaf, and the negative effect on the health of the bushes due to very frequent coarse plucking.

A lightweight "magic carpet" hovercraft-style machine, the T1000 created by Australian inventor Geoff Williames, conveys itself over the bushes and, with one operator, can harvest up to 1 hectare per hour. Williames has also invented a "selective harvesting machine," which is designed to simulate

hand plucking. By means of a sensitive paddle, it harvests only shoots of the right age and length, while leaving immature buds and shoots on the bush. This type of machine requires four to six operatives, can do the job of 50 pluckers, can be hand held or wheel mounted, and can increase yields by 30 percent over hedge-trimmer machines. Terrain and soil conditions control which, if any, of these machines is appropriate for a particular region. Steep slopes are not suitable for mechanical harvesting, and soft, uneven ground creates problems for tractors and wheel-mounted harvesters. In 2017, Williames also patented a mechanical Hand Plucker that can selectively "hand pluck" at a rate of 92,000 times per hour.

TOP: A mechanical harvester in use in Japan. Photograph courtesy of Sasuki Green Tea , Co., Ltd. BOTTOM: The world's only selective, mechanical hand plucker, designed and manufactured by Williames Tea Pty Ltd, Australia, *williamestea.com*. Photograph courtesy of Geoff Williames

COMPONENTS OF FRESH TEA LEAVES

POLYPHENOLS

Polyphenols are natural plant compounds, which add flavour and mouthfeel to tea. They are subdivided into various groups (flavonoids, phenolic acids, and tannins, for example), and of these, flavonoids are the largest group. Flavonoids are thought to be produced by plants as a defense against fungus, bacteria, insects, and other predators, and in tea, these give the liquor an astringent and bitter taste. They are formed in sunlight from the amino acids in the leaves—plants growing in full sunlight contain higher levels, while teas grown in shady conditions retain more of their amino acids and therefore taste sweeter and smoother. The new buds and the first one or two new leaves on each shoot contain higher levels of flavonoids. Within the group of flavonoids found in tea, flavanols make up the largest proportion. The most important of these are the catechins epigallocatechin-3-gallate (EGCG), epicatechin (EC), epicatachin-3-gallate (ECG), epigallocatechin (EGC), and gallocatechin (GC). The highest levels of EGCG are found in green tea. Tea's flavonoids are thought to have a beneficial antioxidant effect in the human body, and research suggests that they help protect against age-related diseases such as heart attack, stroke, thrombosis, and atherosclerosis as well as against certain forms of cancer. The levels of polyphenols found in different tea categories vary according to the manufacturing process of each category and the amount of oxidation that takes place in the leaves. The more oxidation in the leaves, the lower the level of polyphenols. Scientists now prefer to use the term *aeration* instead of *oxidation* to refer to parts of the process, such as withering, during which some chemical changes occur in the leaf. *Oxidation* is, of course, a specific term for some processes but does not refer to all the changes that happen in the leaf during aeration.

TANNINS

The historic use of the word *tannin*—connected in the past with wood tannins extracted from the oak tree for use in the tanning of animal skins—has led today to a misunderstanding of what tannins are. They are, in fact, a subclass of astringent, bitter polyphenols found in almost all plants. Indeed, tannin levels in tea are very low, and the bulk of polyphenols in green and black teas are actually flavonoids, not tannins.

ENZYMES

The most important enzymes in tea are polyphenol oxidase (PPO) and peroxidase (POD). As the leaf cells begin to break down during withering and oxidation, these enzymes mediate changes in the polyphenols, turning the leaves from green to brown, just as happens when apples, potatoes, avocados, and pears, for example, are cut and the flesh is left exposed to oxygen in the air. In tea, the enzymes cause the conversion of simple polyphenols, forming theaflavins, which are responsible for the brightness and quality of the tea's liquor, and thearubigins, which give tea its rich red or reddy-orange colour, its depth, and its body. To stop oxidation during the processing of tea, enzymatic activity in the leaves is inhibited or stopped by applying heat. The earlier in the processing this enzyme inactivation takes place, the higher the level of polyphenols retained in the tea.

AMINO ACIDS

Amino acids are nitrogen-containing chemical compounds that play an important role in developing aromas in tea during manufacture. The most abundant amino acid in tea (approximately 50 percent) is L-theanine, which was discovered in green tea in 1949. It gives green tea a sweet, umami, brothy character and is found in higher levels in teas that have been grown in shaded conditions. This is because lower levels of light mean that fewer of the sweet amino acids are converted to bitter polyphenols. The amount of L-theanine in specific teas varies according to plant varietal, terroir, cultivation methods, etcetera. To date, L-theanine has been found in only three plants in the entire universe: *Camellia sinensis*; the edible bay bolete mushroom found in North America and Europe; and *Ilex guayusa*, a member of the holly family native to the Amazon rainforest. L-theanine is believed to promote the activity of alpha waves in the brain, resulting in reduced mental and physical stress, reduced blood pressure, and a greater ability to relax. The combination of L-theanine and caffeine in tea is thought to help promote faster reaction times in the brain and to keep us focused and alert but calm. The European Food Safety Authority (EFSA) has not approved this claim, however, and says that cause and effect has not been sufficiently proven.

VOLATILES

Aroma and flavour compounds in tea can be classified into primary compounds and secondary compounds. Plants emit primary volatile compounds as a defense mechanism when the plants are diseased, attacked by insects, or damaged in some way. These compounds are found in the fresh leaves and vary according to plant varietal, region, harvest times, and so on. Secondary compounds develop in the tea during processing and are derived from carotenoids, amino acids, terpene glycosides, and lipids, among other things. More than 600 volatile compounds have to date been identified in different teas, including hexanal (fruity and grassy), hexenol (herbaceous and woody), linalool (floral, sweet, woody, lavender), geraniol (rosy, floral, geranium), pentanal (pungent, almond, malt), and benzeneacetaldehyde (hyacinth, lilac), but further research is required to identify all the volatile compounds in all different categories of tea.

CAFFEINE

Caffeine in tea is a natural insecticide and is lethal to most insects. To protect the new shoots, it is concentrated in the new leaf buds and young leaves. All teas contain caffeine, and any teas made from the new buds (white tea) and very young leaves (gyokuro, matcha, First Flush Darjeeling, Long Jing, for example) may contain a higher level of caffeine.

OPPOSITE PAGE: Freshly harvested tea at Westholme Tea Company, Vancouver Island, Canada. Photograph courtesy of Victor Vesely, Westhome Tea Farm ABOVE: A selection of Bitaco teas made by Agrícola Himalaya in Colombia. Photograph courtesy of Bitaco Tea Estate

Preparing tea in the South Korean style, which is less strictly ritualistic than the Japanese Tea Ceremony and focuses on brewing and serving tea in a more informal and relaxed way. Photograph courtesy of Ryu Seunghoo

When we drink caffeinated beverages, the caffeine acts as a stimulant to the central nervous system, increases stamina, reduces fatigue, and keeps us awake and alert. L-theanine moderates the speed at which the body absorbs caffeine in tea, which is slower than the speed of caffeine absorption from coffee. Instead of immediately affecting our heart rate and pulse (as happens when we drink coffee), the caffeine in tea affects our central nervous system and heightens our responses. Once in our systems, the half-life of caffeine is independent of the source, so the level of caffeine from tea should be the same as the level of caffeine from coffee, but the slower absorption of caffeine from tea means slower release and, therefore, a longer-lasting effect in the body.

Decaffeinated teas contain small quantities of caffeine and yield an average of 3 milligrams per 3-gram serving.

The amount of caffeine found in different types of tea depends partly on the individual tea but more on the way in which it is brewed. When tea is brewed in boiling water, more caffeine is drawn out of the leaf into the liquor; when brewed in cooler water, less caffeine is drawn out. When tea is brewed for a longer time, more caffeine is drawn out, and when brewed for a shorter time, less caffeine is drawn out. So, because we usually brew black, dark oolongs, and dark teas in near-boiling water, the liquors from those teas usually contain more caffeine. And because jade oolongs and green and white teas are brewed in cooler water, their liquors usually contain less caffeine. Small tea particles release their caffeine more quickly than larger pieces of leaf or whole leaf.

In the past, there have been worries about the harmful effects of caffeine for pregnant women and children, but the latest report from the European Food Safety Authority advises that 400 milligrams (0.014 ounces) of caffeine a day (approximately 8 mugs) do not pose any danger to nonpregnant adults; pregnant and lactating women are advised to drink up to 200 milligrams (4 mugs) daily; and children aged 4 years or over can safely drink 1 to 2 mugs of milky, unsweetened tea per day.

FLUORIDE

Fluoride is a natural mineral found in the soil, and the tea plant readily absorbs it and deposits most of it in the leaves. In low doses, fluoride reduces tooth decay. At much higher doses and frequent exposure, fluoride can cause health complications. Dry tea leaves contain between 103 and 839 milligrams per kilogram (.0016 to .0134 ounces per pound). Brewed tea infusions contain much less, ranging between 0.43 and 8.85 milligrams per kilogram (.0000068 to .000142 ounces per pound). The longer the leaves are steeped, the more fluoride is released.

OTHER NUTRIENTS

Tea's fresh leaves contain manganese (essential for bone growth and body development); zinc (important for cell growth and immunity); potassium (vital for maintaining body fluid levels); beta-carotene (a precursor of vitamin A, essential for night vision); thiamine (vitamin B1); riboflavin (vitamin B2); niacin acid (vitamin B3); pantothenic acid (vitamin B5); vitamin B6; folic acid (vitamin B12, essential for the formation of red blood cells, for foetal development, and for prevention of arterial sclerosis; all the B vitamins help our bodies convert food to energy, metabolise fats and proteins, and are important for the general health of our bodies); ascorbic acid (vitamin C, required for the maintenance of healthy skin and mucus membrane); and vitamin E (an antioxidant).

OTHER INGREDIENTS

Tea also contains carbohydrates in the form of starches and sugars (mainly glucose, fructose, and sucrose). Other components include chlorophyll (antioxidant, encourages healing, helps control hunger, controls body odour); pigments (the most important are green chlorophylls and orange and yellow carotenoids); and saponins (which give tea a bitterness and astringency and have anti-inflammatory and anti-allergy properties).

OXIDATION AND FERMENTATION

All tea categories (white, green, yellow, oolong, black, and dark) are made from the leaves of the *Camellia sinensis*. Different categories vary according to manufacturing methods and different levels of oxidation or fermentation that take place in the leaves during processing. The terms *oxidation* and *fermentation* are often used interchangeably to explain the chemical reactions that take place during manufacture, but the two words are not interchangeable as the two processes are different.

Oxidation is an enzymatic process that converts the smaller molecular weight polyphenols (e.g., catechins in tea) to larger molecular weight species such as theaflavins and thearubigins, reactions mediated by enzymes such as polyphenol oxidase (PPO) and peroxidase (POD). This causes the green leaves to turn brown and changes the tea's chemical makeup, aroma, flavour, and appearance. (The same happens when the flesh of an apple or a pear is exposed to oxygen.) During tea manufacture, the enzymes in tea can be deactivated by applying heat to the leaves, and the sooner the enzymatic activity is stopped, the less oxidised the tea will be. The more bruised, broken, or cut the tea leaves are before the enzymes are deactivated, the more quickly the tea will oxidise. Oxidation is an aerobic process that requires the presence of oxygen.

Microbial fermentation is the result of microbial and/or bacterial (not enzymatic) activity and is often provoked by humidity and warmth. It takes place in yellow teas when steam is purposely trapped in the tea during manufacture. It takes place in dark teas (Puerh and other types) where fermentation is the result of humidity, warmth, and the activity of molds such as *Aspergillus niger* and *Aspergillus luchuensis* in the tea. Fermentation in tea is an anaerobic process that takes place without the presence of oxygen.

TOP LEFT: Leaf withering in troughs at a biodynamic organic tea estate in the Nilgiri Hills, India. Photograph by Indi Khanna; ©Tea 'n' Teas TOP RIGHT: Turning the leaf in withering troughs at Rukeri Tea Estate in Rwanda. Photograph courtesy of Sorwathe Ltd., Rwanda BOTTOM: Leaf oxidising on bamboo baskets in China. Photograph courtesy of The Chinese Tea Company, London

OXIDATION IN TEA

When the cells of freshly plucked tea leaves are bruised, broken, or cut, tea's various components react with the oxygen in the air surrounding the tea, and a chemical reaction begins. The polyphenols (which include catechins) are converted to theaflavins (giving briskness and yellow colour) and thearubigins (giving body and a reddish colour). The green chlorophyll in the leaves changes to brown pigments called pheophytyns and pheophorbides, and aroma and flavour begin to develop as the amino acids, carotenoids, and lipids also undergo a change. The higher the level of oxidation, the fewer the polyphenols left in the tea. Heavily oxidised teas such as black and dark oolongs, therefore, contain fewer polyphenols, and nonoxidised or lightly oxidised teas such as white, green, and greener oolongs contain more.

WITHERING

When the fresh leaf shoots are gathered from the tea bushes, they are full of water. As soon as they have been picked off the plant, they start to lose water or "wither." Before manufacture starts, the tea is often allowed to wither for a certain amount of time to allow more of that water to evaporate, and the length of the wither depends on what sort of tea is to be made. For white tea, withering is long and slow; for green and yellow teas, there is a short wither for a few hours or no withering at all; for oolong teas, the leaves wither first in the sun and then indoors, and the length of time depends on how oxidised the leaf is to be; black teas are withered for between 12 and 22 hours; and for dark teas, there is a short wither before the base green tea (*maocha*) is made. As the leaves lose water, they become flaccid while, at the same time, the chemical makeup of the tea begins to change. Enzyme activity is increased; proteins break down to become amino acids; the concentration of caffeine increases as water is reduced; carbohydrates break down to form simple sugars; volatile flavour components develop; and chlorophyll is reduced. The various chemical reactions depend on the length of the wither, and the longer the wither, the more flavour and aroma develop.

DIFFERENT CATEGORIES OF TEA

WHITE TEA

White tea is the least processed of all tea categories. It is very gently handled so that leaf cells are not ruptured or bruised, and the buds in the finished tea are usually still covered with a silky layer of tiny silver-white hairs. These hairs (in Chinese, the *Bai Hao* or *Pekoe*) protect the new bud from the harmful effects of insect attacks, cold winds, bright sun, heavy rain, and so on. The bud also contains a high level of caffeine, which acts as an insecticide to protect the new shoots as they develop.

White teas, originally from China's Fujian Province, can be made from single buds or young shoots consisting of one new bud and one or two young open leaves. Once these have been carefully picked, they are spread on bamboo matting or trays and allowed to wither in gentle sunlight. The tea is then brought indoors to continue drying slowly over a few days. The length of time required for this stage of the process depends on the ambient temperature and humidity. Bright sun and high temperatures cause the tea to dry too quickly, and this inhibits the development of flavour.

As the leaves and buds dry, very light spontaneous oxidation takes place in the leaf cells, and some parts of the buds and leaves may turn yellow or brown. Tightly furled buds oxidise very little or not at all and so remain silvery white. Open leaves oxidise more, so the dry tea may mingle silvery buds with green-brown or brown leaves.

In cool, damp climates, the tea sometimes undergoes a final "baking" in a room where a very gentle ambient temperature slowly removes any excess moisture. This final drying is sometimes carried out in a bamboo basket over a smouldering smokefree fire, but too much heat applied too quickly can spoil the final appearance and flavour. During all stages of processing, the tea must be very gently handled.

MANUFACTURE OF WHITE TEA

careful plucking so that leaf cells are not bruised or broken	withering in gentle sunlight	indoor withering	final baking or drying	sorting into different grades

LEFT: Picking tea in Fujian Province, China. Photograph courtesy of Angela Pryce TOP: Because these tiny buds for white tea are not heat treated but allowed to dry slowly outdoors and then indoors, each shows a little oxidation on the stem. BOTTOM: Withering leaf outdoors in Fujian Province, China. Photographs courtesy of The Chinese Tea Company, London

Green tea, the oldest of all the tea categories, can be made from single buds or from young shoots that consist of one new bud and one, two, or three leaves. Once picked, the leaves are usually withered for a few hours to allow a small quantity of their water content to evaporate. If the wither is too long, oxidation will start to take place in the leaves.

To stop any oxidation, dry heat or steam is applied to the leaf to fix the green colour and flavour. In Chinese, this is called *shaqing* or "kill-green." We also refer to it as "fixing," "de-enzyming," or "denaturing." The longer it takes to deactivate all the enzymes, the more flavour and aroma develop in the tea. Dry heat tends to take longer than steaming, so panned teas often have more complex flavours than do steamed varieties.

Dry heat is applied in a hot, dry wok or a panning machine. If a hot wok is used, the lightly withered tea leaves are turned and tumbled against the hot metal. Panning machines were developed to do the job of the wok and allow the more efficient handling of larger quantities of leaf. The machine consists of a large cylinder inside, which is a rotating metal drum, and the tea is tumbled inside the hot drum for approximately two minutes. The dry leaves of panned green teas are often yellow-green or olive-green in appearance and give liquors that are gold-green or amber-green. To apply steam, the leaf is placed inside a cylinder or drum in which steam is injected. The leaves are tumbled for approximately 20 seconds to ensure that they are all evenly heat-treated. The dry leaf is often quite a dark green, and liquors are lime-green in colour.

After heating, the leaves are usually rolled or pressed to develop flavour. This can be done in many different ways. The most common method is to roll a small heap of leaves on a bamboo basket or mat by hand or in a small rolling machine. Or leaves and buds are consecutively dried and rolled in a wok, and different hand movements give each tea its individual shape. The little bud sets of Long Jing (Dragon Well) are pressed into small flat needles in a hot wok; Taiping Houkui (Taiping Monkey King) is rolled between two layers of wire mesh to become long flat needles that bear tiny crisscross patterns from the wires; Bi Lo Chun (Green Snail Spring) is rolled between the palms of the hands while being processed in the wok; Ping Shui Ri Zhu (Green Pearl) is formed into little curls by a woklike machine in which a curved paddle twists and coils the drying leaf; and Zhu Cha (Gunpowder) is rolled into tight pellets between the palms of the hands or in machines with paddles inside. Machine-rolled gunpowder teas are never as neat and tidy as those rolled by hand, and the best grades are still rolled by hand. Steamed teas such as Japanese sencha are rolled and dried by automated machines, while high-quality gyokuro and shincha are processed using the traditional temomi method, during which the tea is rolled by tea masters into long thin needles on a hoiro table.

Many of these processes dry the tea while it is being rolled or pressed, but if the leaves still contain water after rolling, they must be dried to reduce the water content to 2 to 3 percent. This can be carried out in a wok, where the tea is constantly turned with a brush or a gloved hand, or the tea can be dried in baskets set over gently smouldering charcoal or in the sun or an oven. The temperature and timing are very important since extra layers of flavour can be developed during this last stage or manufacturing.

MANUFACTURE OF GREEN TEA

withering to reduce the leaves' water content	application of heat to stop oxidation	rolling or pressing to develop flavour	drying to reduce water content to 2 to 3 percent	sorting into different grades

TOP LEFT: Processing Taiping Huo Kui green tea in Anhui Province, China. Photograph courtesy of Wenli Guo TOP RIGHT: Bi Luo Chun (Green Snail Spring) green tea, made in Jiangsu Province, China. MIDDLE LEFT: Long Jing Dragon Well green tea from Zhejiang Province, China. Photograph courtesy of The Chinese Tea Company, London MIDDLE RIGHT: Sorting tea in Kakegawa, Shizuoka, Japan. Photograph courtesy of Asako Steward, City of Kakegawa BOTTOM: Processing green tea in Huo Shan, Anhui Province, China. Photograph courtesy of Wenli Guo

The processing of yellow tea is complicated and long and demands the skills of an experienced tea master. The finest yellow teas are made from single buds plucked in the early spring. Perfect undamaged buds must be a specific length and shape and must never be picked after rain or when morning dew is on the leaves. Lower grades of yellow tea are produced using leaves or buds gathered later in the year.

The first two stages of yellow tea processing (withering and panning) are the same as those for green tea, but the initial panning is done at a lower temperature. As the buds are tumbled in the wok to stop oxidation, the heat is gradually increased and then reduced again. By the time the tea is taken out of the wok, most of the enzymes have been deactivated. To reduce the water content to 40 to 50 percent, the tea is dried over strong heat, cooled slightly, and then wrapped in paper or heaped in baskets; this may be repeated once more or several times. This stage is called *Men-huang* or "smothering" (sometimes referred to as "yellowing" or "sweltering"), and because the tea is warm, the water in the leaves begins to turn to steam, which is trapped in the tea. This causes slight microbial fermentation and reduces the tea's grassy astringency, giving it a mellower, less-vibrant flavour than that of green tea. In the classification of teas, we think of oolongs as being on the scale somewhere between green teas and black teas with regard to the oxidation that takes place in the leaves. Yellow teas fall between green teas and dark teas as concerns the microbial fermentation that happens in the tea while being "smothered" in warm, humid conditions.

After the first wrapping or heaping, the tea is heated again to reduce the water content to 20 percent. While still warm and damp, it is wrapped or heaped for a second time and then dried to reduce the water content to less than 5 percent. The tea master determines the time required for the entire process, which can last for four or five days.

Some Chinese producers today skip the wrapping or heaping stage (which is what makes the tea a yellow tea and without which the tea is quite simply a green tea).

LEFT: Making yellow tea in Huo Shan, Anhui Province, China. RIGHT: Little buds ready for picking to make yellow tea in Huo Shan, Anhui Province, China. ©Dan Robertson-Used with permission

MANUFACTURE OF YELLOW TEA

withering to reduce the leaves' water content	panning over low heat to stop oxidation and reduce water content	reduction of water content to 40 to 50 percent	slight cooling

wrapping or heaping	panning to reduce more of water content	second wrapping or heaping (may be repeated several times)	drying	sorting into different grades

Oolong means "black dragon," and these teas are named for the brown-black, twisted leaves of dark oolongs that often have the appearance of snarling dragons or writhing serpents. Whereas green teas undergo no oxidation and black teas undergo a long oxidation, the oxidation in oolong teas ranges from 10 percent to almost 80 percent, and so the teas are referred to as partially oxidised teas. There are three styles of oolong:

1. The more traditional have twisted open leaves that are 40 to 60 percent oxidised and are, therefore, very dark brown. These are usually referred to as dark, open-leafed oolongs or dark, unfurled oolongs.
2. Bao Zhongs (Pouchongs) are so lightly oxidised—only 10 to 18 percent—that they are sometimes classified as green teas.
3. The more modern oolongs are only 20 to 30 percent oxidised, and the leaf shoots are rolled into tight pellets. Because of their colour, which ranges from pale to dark green, they are often called jade oolongs; because of their shape, they are also known as balled oolongs.

Dark Oolongs

Most dark oolongs are made from more mature shoots of three or four open leaves. The harvested leaves are laid out in gentle or shaded sunlight for approximately two hours, during which time they slowly begin to dry and lightly oxidise. They are then taken indoors where the leaves are laid out on large round bamboo baskets to continue drying and oxidising. The leaves must oxidise to between 40 and 60 percent (sometimes more), and to accelerate the natural process, they are tossed and shaken on the bamboo baskets and placed inside rotating bamboo drums. This helps bruise the leaves and break the leaf cells, and so provokes faster oxidation.

As the leaves oxidise, their colour changes from bright green to a darker brown-green or red-green, and a flowery or fruity aroma begins to develop. This partial oxidation takes between seven and nine hours, depending on the ambient temperature and humidity. The tea master judges when the tea is ready by smelling, feeling, and assessing the appearance of the leaf. The leaf is then transferred to a panning machine, where the rotating hot metal drum kills the active enzymes and halts any further oxidation. Next, the tea is gently rolled to work the juices in the leaves and intensify the flavour; this also gives the leaves their twisted shape. The tea is then dried in a hot oven, a panning machine, or in the sun to remove all but 2 to 3 percent of the water content.

In China, stalks and stems are then removed from the tea by hand so that all you should see in the dry leaf is individual whole, twisted leaves.

Tea withering on bamboo baskets inside a factory in Yunnan Province, China. Photograph by David Collen; courtesy of *essenceoftea.com*

MANUFACTURE OF DARK OOLONG TEA

sun withering for two hours	indoor withering for up to nine hours during which the leaf is shaken on bamboo baskets and tumbled in a bamboo drum to bruise the leaf		partial oxidation (50 to 60 percent, sometimes more)

panning to stop oxidation	rolling	drying	in China, removal of stalks and stems	in China and Taiwan, roasting over charcoal	sorting into different grades

Most dark oolongs in China and Taiwan are also given a final roasting in baskets set over glowing charcoal. This adds complex layers of darker notes reminiscent of charcoal, chocolate, and toasted nuts. Different levels of roasting develop different flavours in the tea. A low fire (*qing huo*) brings out the tea's floral notes; a medium fire (*chung huo*) develops more fruity notes; and a high fire (*gao huo*) develops toasty caramel and burnt sugar notes. Finally, the teas are sorted for packing.

Bao Zhong (Pouchong)

To make Bao Zhong, the leaf is processed in the same way as for dark oolongs, but the oxidation process is very short—between 10 and 18 percent—and the leaf is only lightly rolled to develop the flavour. The lightly twisted leaves are an intense dark green, and the flavour is of sweet peas with a hint of ripe apricots and a very slight suggestion of toasted biscuits (cookies). Bao Zhong teas are made in the Wenshan area near Taipei in northern Taiwan.

Jade (Balled) Oolongs

For jade oolong, longer shoots of three or four leaves and a bud are nipped off the plant and remain intact throughout processing. The best teas are plucked by hand, but some leaf shoots for oolong tea are harvested by machine. The leaves go through exactly the same stages as described above for dark oolongs, but the tea is only 20 to 30 percent oxidised and so remains very green. After sun withering, indoor withering, bruising, shaking, and tumbling in the bamboo drum, the leaves are panned to arrest the oxidation, lightly rolled to develop the flavour, and dried briefly to remove a little more of the water in the leaves. The second stage, often carried out the following day, rolls the tea shoots into tight green nuggets. The first part of this stage is to drape a large square cotton or muslin cloth into a deep basket and to fill the cloth with 9 or 10 kilos (20 or 22 pounds) of the leaf that was made earlier or the day

before. The bag is then formed into a large ball, which is tightened on a machine that rotates the bag while the corners at the top of the bag are held tightly. This begins to squeeze the tea shoots into smaller pellets. The tight bag is then rolled for approximately 20 minutes on a machine that presses down on the bag, squeezing the juices in the tea and intensifying the flavour and aroma. The bag is then removed from the roller and opened, and the tea is turned briefly in the warm panning machine to reduce the water content and break up the tea. The process of wrapping the tea in the cloth, tightening the bag, rolling, and panning is repeated—sometimes 30 or 40 times—until each shoot has become a tightly rolled nugget of tea. The tea is then dried to remove most of the remaining moisture and sorted for packing. In some cases, particularly if the teas are being entered for competitions, any visible stalks are removed. Balled oolongs often have deliciously sweet, sappy notes that hint at spring flowers such as hyacinths, lilies of the valley, narcissus, and orchids.

MANUFACTURE OF JADE OOLONG TEAS

sun withering for two hours	indoor withering for up to nine hours	bruising, shaking, and tumbling to provoke oxidation	partial oxidation (20 to 30 percent)	panning to stop oxidation

rolling	partial drying	repeated wrapping, rolling, panning	drying	in China, removal of visible stalks	sorting into different grades

Baked (Amber) Oolongs

After jade oolongs have been finished in the factory, they are sometimes put through a secondary baking (or roasting) process, either over charcoal or in special baking ovens. This sometimes takes place at the tea factory under the supervision of the tea master, or it is carried out by retail merchants who buy the finished jade oolongs from the factory and then bake the teas in an oven in their store. Or consumers bake their own teas at home or in the office using a small bamboo baking oven.

This secondary slow baking dries more water from the tea, giving the tea a green-brown or dark brown colour, and the longer the baking, the darker the little pellets of tea become. The roasting intensifies the tea's floral and fruity notes and also develops a rich, deep flavour, adding extra layers of nutty, toasty complexity. Baking also reduces the amount of caffeine in the tea, and deposits of white caffeine powder can be seen around the door of the baking oven. Sometimes the teas are stored after baking and are repeatedly baked and stored over several years. The baking process was originally developed because the roasted flavours and lower levels of caffeine made the teas popular amongst older people, but today, many younger tea drinkers enjoy the teas' layered and toasty character. Bao Zhongs may also be baked to give a browner leaf and an intense floral sweetness.

GABA Oolongs

GABA teas are made by exposing the tea to nitrogen during processing to increase the GABA (gamma aminobutyric acid) content. This is said to boost the activity of alpha brain waves, which, in turn, improves mental function, reduces stress and anxiety, lowers blood pressure, improves memory, and alleviates depression. Most GABA teas are made as oolongs, but they can also be processed as black or green tea.

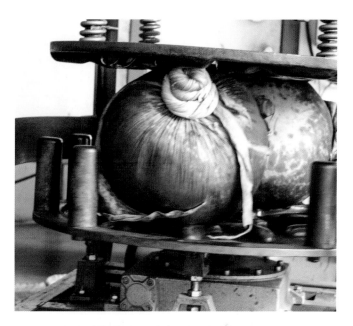

OPPOSITE PAGE: Organic balled oolong made at Harendong Tea Estate in West Java, Indonesia. TOP: Rolling balled oolong tea inside cotton cloths at Harendong Tea Estate in Indonesia. Photographs courtesy of Harendong Tea Estate ABOVE: Roasting dark oolong over charcoal to bring out the top notes of ripe stone fruit and develop complex, toasty, slightly caramelised lower notes. Photograph by David Collen; courtesy of essenceoftea.com

During the manufacture of black tea (known as "red tea" by the Chinese), the leaves go through the longest oxidation of all six categories. The finest black teas are made from tender leaf shoots consisting of two leaves and a bud, and once harvested, these are laid out in a cool room to "wither," during which they lose between 30 and 40 percent of their water content. This slow drying can take 12 to 22 hours, depending on the ambient temperature and humidity and on the style of tea to be made. As the tea loses moisture, it becomes limp and begins to oxidise and develop aroma compounds. The speed and length of the wither directly affect the brightness, briskness, colour, and strength of the made tea. After withering, the leaves are rolled or cut to break the leaf cells and expose the juices in the leaf to oxygen, thus provoking oxidation.

Two processing methods are available—orthodox and CTC (cut, tear, and curl or crush, tear, and curl). The orthodox method rolls the tea in large rolling machines that were designed in the 19th century to replicate the action previously carried out in China using hands or feet. The withered leaf is fed into a cylinder that rotates over a metal table where raised metal ribs bruise and break the leaf cells. The amount of pressure exerted on the tea and the length of the rolling process are adjusted according to the size and style of leaf required. The longer and heavier the roll, the smaller the leaves will become and the stronger the tea flavour will be. In some parts of the world, tea is still rolled by hand, but a good deal of time and effort is required to rupture the leaf cells enough to provoke full oxidation. After rolling, the tea is spread out in tubs or on slabs or trays in a cool part of the factory and left to oxidise. The tea is then dried in ovens, panning machines, or baskets set over smouldering charcoal.

The CTC method was developed in the 1930s to meet a growing demand for smaller particles of tea to pack into paper tea bags, which had been developed through the first decades of the 20th century. The tea bag was designed to brew strong tea quickly, and the particles, therefore, needed to be as small as possible. During the CTC process, the withered leaves are often first put through a Rotorvane machine, which minces and shreds the leaf before it is fed into the CTC cutters. The CTC machine consists of two rotating cylindrical rollers with hundreds of very sharp teeth that cut, tear, and curl the leaf into small, similar-size particles. After rolling or cutting, the tea is allowed to oxidise, and in a fully automated CTC factory, oxidation takes place as the tea travels on a conveyor belt from the cutters at one end to the oven at the other. The time required for oxidation depends on the ambient temperature and humidity and on the size of the leaf particles. Larger pieces of leaf may take several hours to fully oxidise, whereas CTC particles need only 15 to 30 minutes. After oxidation, the tea must be dried to remove all but 2 to 3 percent of the remaining water content. This can take place in a tray dryer, which moves the tea slowly through hot air for approximately 20 minutes on connected trays, or in a fluid bed dryer (FBD), which blows the tea through the dryer on a moving stream of hot air. Or tea can be dried in baskets set over glowing charcoal, or in a panning machine, or in the sun.

Orthodox manufacture produces different leaf sizes ranging from whole or large pieces of leaf to medium-size "broken" grades and small particles classified as "fannings" and "dust." The larger pieces are sold loose as speciality teas, and the fannings and dust grades are used mainly for tea bags. CTC manufacture produces particles that can vary in size from pellets that look like freeze-dried coffee granules to small powdery pieces.

At the end of the production process of both orthodox and CTC tea, the different-size pieces of leaf must be separated out. (Different-size particles of tea brew at different speeds, and uneven pieces mean uneven brewing. And when tea is blended, the blend should consist of uniform particles. That's because large particles blended with small particles will separate out in the packet, and the whole purpose of blending will be lost.) This is done through a mechanical sorting machine that passes the tea through a series of sieves with different-size meshes so that large pieces are caught by the large mesh, the medium pieces pass through and are caught by the medium mesh, and the small particles pass through to smaller meshes. At each level, the teas are drawn off into containers and then bulked in large bins that bear the name of the tea grade.

TOP: Samples of tea ready for tasting prior to the Colombo auction, Sri Lanka. Photograph by John O'Hagan; ©Hoffman Media BOTTOM LEFT: Black tea from the high-grown Uva district of Sri Lanka. BOTTOM RIGHT: Sorting made black tea in the Uva Highlands, Sri Lanka. Photographs courtesy of Dilmah Tea

MANUFACTURE OF BLACK TEA

withering to reduce the water in the leaves by 30 to 40 percent	rolling or cutting to rupture the leaf cells and provoke oxidation	full oxidation	drying	sorting into different grades

Dark teas (known by the Chinese as "black teas") were originally made more than 1,000 years ago for transportation to Tibet and other remote regions of China, where the local people drank large quantities of tea but could not grow their own because of the high altitude. To satisfy their demands, tea from other provinces was carried—by porters or on the backs of mules, horses, or yaks—up to the high plains of those isolated areas and traded for other goods. The teas drunk in Tibet were made in southern Yunnan Province, marketed in the town of Puerh (after which the teas are named), and then transported through northern Yunnan and Sichuan provinces to Lhasa on a dangerous and difficult journey that took eight to 10 months. Each year, thousands of kilograms of Puerh tea were exchanged for hundreds of Tibetan horses, renowned for their speed, strength, and endurance, for the Chinese army.

The teas sold to Tibet were green teas made in Yunnan from the native, large-leafed Da Ye (big leaf) assamica varietal. To ensure that they travelled safely and took up as little room as possible, the teas were compressed into cakes or blocks and wrapped in grasses or leaves before being transported and, once in Lhasa, were often stored for long periods of time until needed. The southern regions of Yunnan are very forested and humid, and the air carries a variety of microflora, fungi, bacteria, and yeasts that found their way onto the leaves of the tea trees. On the journey from Puerh to Tibet, humidity, rainwater, and changes in temperature activated those microbes and caused a very slow continuous fermentation to change the character of the tea. The assamica varietal tends to give green teas a rather bitter, astringent character, but the slow microbial activity was found to gradually change that to a milder, mellower flavour, and the longer the tea was stored and fermented, the sweeter and more honeyed the tea became.

TOP LEFT: Compressed Puerh cakes in a factory in Yunnan Province, China. TOP RIGHT: Shaping a Puerh cake inside a cotton bag; the twisted bag is used to press down on the tea and leaves a round indentation in the middle of the surface of the cake. BOTTOM: The traditional stones used for compressing Puerh cakes in Yunnan Province, China. Photographs by David Collen; courtesy of essenceoftea.com

The Use of the Puerh Name

In December 2008, the Agriculture Department of Yunnan introduced a ruling that Puerh tea should only be so called if it meets certain geographical and technical specifications. The tea can be called Puerh only if it has been produced in 11 prefectures of the province. It must be made from the Da Ye broad-leafed variety of the tea plant (the *Camellia sinensis* var. *assamica*) by the specified traditional methodology. Teas made outside the designated areas, in Guizhou Province, for example, or using leaf harvested in Vietnam or Laos cannot now legally be called Puerh tea.

Two Types of Puerh

As the character of these aged teas became more popular, not just in Tibet but in Hong Kong and other parts of China, the tea producers in southern Yunnan began processing teas that replicated the microbial fermentation that had previously happened by chance because of nature's intervention. These teas are known as *sheng* or raw Puerh. Because they have to be stored for a number of years for the mellowing process to change the flavour profile, in 1972, the Menghai Tea Factory and Kunming Tea Factory in Yunnan Province developed the *wo dui* method of Puerh manufacture, which speeds up the fermentation and mellowing process by wetting and heaping the teas. Puerh teas made by this modern method are known as *shou*, or cooked, ripened, or ripe Puerh teas.

The age of the tea tree or plant and the time of plucking affect the quality and the value of Puerh teas. Old trees are considered the best since their leaves give deeper, more complex flavours and aromas and have less bitterness and astringency than young bushes. Leaves harvested in the spring are considered better than autumn-picked leaves, which in turn are preferred to those picked during the summer months. Both raw and ripened Puerh teas undergo microbial fermentation and mild oxidation during the aging process. The most important of the microbial agents is *Aspergillus niger*, a fungus widely found in soil.

Manufacture of Sheng (Raw) Puerh

Once harvested, the leaves are withered briefly in shaded sunlight to evaporate some of the water content. Next, they are tumbled in a hot wok or panning machine to inhibit oxidation and then rolled by hand on bamboo baskets or by machine and dried in the sun. Drying in the sun takes longer than in a hot pan or over charcoal. Thus, the small quantity of enzymes that remain in the tea (panning does not kill them all at the fixing stage) are deactivated more slowly, and slight oxidation takes place in the tea as it dries, slowly turning the vibrant green leaves to a dark sage-green or brown. The made green tea is called *maocha* or raw green tea.

The tea can then be aged as loose tea or compressed into cakes of different shapes and sizes. The most common are round disks. Depending on the size of cake to be made, the required quantity of maocha is weighed and steamed in a cylindrical colander-like can to lightly dampen the leaves. The leaf is then placed inside a cotton bag, and the tea is worked down into the base of the bag. As the top of the bag is twisted and coiled tightly to push down on the tea, the knot of fabric creates a small indentation in the middle of the tea, which is always apparent on the underside of the dried cake. Still inside its bag, the tea is then pressed beneath a heavy, flat-bottomed stone or hydraulic press. Other shapes are pressed into moulds to make square, rectangular, pumpkin- or nest-shaped cakes of different sizes. Once the tea has been shaped and pressed, bags or moulds are removed, and the compressed teas are stored in a room where temperature and humidity are carefully regulated to encourage and control the aging process. The microbial degradation that takes place very slowly over a number of years gradually changes the chemical composition of the tea, increasing the amount of vanillin (which gives the tea a sweet vanilla flavour), phenylacetic acid (a sweet, honey flavour), and dihydroactinidiolide (which develops a fruity flavour in the tea). The more loosely the tea is packed in the compressed cake, the more quickly it will ferment, and cakes that have been more tightly compressed in hydraulic machines take longer to age.

Manufacture of Shou (Ripened) Puerh

The first stages of shou Puerh processing are exactly the same as for sheng Puerh. Green maocha is made from assamica leaves and buds, but instead of being gently steamed and compressed, the tea is heaped in warm, humid conditions and sprayed with water that contains selected microflora such as *Aspergillus niger*, *Penicillium*, and yeasts. The type and variety of microflora directly affects the quality of the ripened tea. The pile of tea is turned and mixed to ensure an even spread of water and microbes and is then covered. The microbial activity in the tea causes a rise in temperature (just as happens in a compost heap), and from time to time, the tea is uncovered and turned again to evenly distribute the heat and the microbial activity. This covering, uncovering, and turning is repeated during a period of several weeks or months until the required level of fermentation has been achieved. When ready, the tea is dried and then compressed in the same way as for raw Puerh, or it is left loose. The microbial activity that takes place in good ripened Puerh gives the tea a woody, slightly earthy character, and most ripened cakes are stored for a few years to lose their typical musty character. However, the flavour and aroma of a good ripened Puerh is never the same as that of a good aged raw Puerh, and whereas raw Puerhs continue to improve the longer they are stored, ripened Puerhs change little after the first few years.

MANUFACTURE OF SHENG (RAW) PUERH			
manufacture of maocha (raw green tea)	dampening by steam	compressing or left loose	aging in temperature- and humidity-controlled conditions

A selection of Puerh tea cakes from Yunnan Province, China.
Photograph courtesy of The Chinese Tea Company, London

MANUFACTURE OF SHOU (RIPENED) PUERH

manufacture of maocha (raw green tea)	wetting, heaping, and covering	repeated turning and covering	drying	compressing or storing as loose tea	aging in temperature- and humidity-controlled conditions

Dark teas, or *hei cha*, are teas that go through secondary processing that provokes or encourages microbial fermentation in the tea. Puerh tea is the best known of Chinese dark teas, but Hubei, Hunan, Guangxi, Shaanxi, and Sichuan provinces also make their own types. Laos, Vietnam, and Myanmar make Puerh-type teas. South Korea makes small coinlike rounds of Ddok Cha from fresh leaves that are steamed, pounded to a pulp, compressed into little cakes, dried, stored, pierced, and strung on a cord. Japanese Puerh-style tea is made from unrefined *aracha* green tea, which is moistened, pasteurised, cooled, mixed with selected microbes, pasteurised, left while aromas develop, pasteurised again, and dried. Japanese *awabancha* is made from leaves that are boiled and then fermented with lactic-acid bacteria, and Japanese *goishicha* is made by heaping steamed green leaves, fermenting them under a mat, packing them into a barrel for further fermentation, and drying them in the sun.

Malawi's loose Puerh-style tea is made at Satemwa Tea Estate.

The character and style of these teas vary from place to place according to the tea varietal used, the manufacturing process, and the microbes in the tea. The manufacture of most dark teas starts with green tea and involves dampening, heaping, covering, compressing, and ageing, but the order of these stages may vary, and certain steps may be repeated. For example, for Hunan Hei Cha, dried maocha is heaped and stored for a year, then steamed, compressed, and stored again in warm, humid conditions. During maturation, the yellow spores of the *Eurotium cristatum* mold grow in the tea, creating little colonies of Jin Hua (Golden Flower), and quality is judged on the quantity of these spores. Other microbes often found in dark teas are *Aspergillus luchuensis*, *Aspergillus glaucus*, and *Aspergillus niger*. When they are young, many of these dark teas are astringent and bitter, but as with Puerh, a thicker, milder, more mellow taste develops with age.

Logs of Anhua dark tea made in Hunan Province, China.
Photographs ©2018 William Waddington, TeaSource LLC

THE STORAGE OF TEA

As soon as tea has been processed in the factory, it must be carefully stored to protect it from contamination by humidity, light, and other smells. Tea is very hygroscopic and easily absorbs moisture from the air and other odours from its surroundings, for example, smoke, industrial oil, spices, herbs, essential oils, fruit flavours, or the perfume of flower blossoms. To maintain tea's quality, it must be stored in foil or foil-lined bags or in tin, porcelain, or pottery containers with airtight lids. Glass jars are not suitable as they allow sunlight to filter through and damage the tea's quality; wooden boxes are not acceptable unless the tea is stored in a foil or cellophane bag inside the box; and cardboard does not provide an adequate barrier. Any materials used must be food safe, and containers must be stored in a cool, dry place.

Japanese matcha, which loses its freshness very quickly once opened, is usually kept in the refrigerator, and in some very humid places around the world, people sometimes prefer to store their tea in the refrigerator or freezer. But in this case, containers must be as airtight as possible so as not to allow any humidity into the tea.

ALL ABOUT BREWING

Tea is prepared in many different ways around the world, but the majority is prepared by steeping teabags or loose tea in water, in a teapot, gaiwan, or glass. Here are a few guidelines to ensure that this style of brewing achieves the best possible results:

Choose quality tea that has been carefully stored in an airtight container.

Choose water that has been filtered to remove impurities and contains plenty of oxygen. (Japanese green teas do not require high levels of oxygen.)

Heat the water to the appropriate temperature for the type of tea.

Use a brewing vessel that allows the tea plenty of room to infuse.

Use an appropriate quantity of tea for the volume of water used.

Time the brew according to tea type, water temperature, and required taste.

Separate the leaf from the liquor when the optimum taste has been achieved.

ESSENTIAL EQUIPMENT

A filter jug or water-filtration system

An airtight container for the tea

Digital scales to measure the tea
(Scoops are suitable only if their capacity for a particular tea has already been calculated.)

A kettle or water heater

A vessel in which to brew (teapot, jug, or mug with an infuser basket, gaiwan, or glass, for example)

Thermometer

Timer, showing minutes and seconds

Dish for the used infuser basket containing wet leaves

Bowl, cup, or glass from which to drink the tea

Photograph courtesy of Ryu Seunghoo

TEABAGS OR LOOSE TEA

In the days when only paper teabags were available, tea lovers spurned them and chose to brew with quality loose-leaf tea. Paper teabags are extremely unattractive, have no romance or elegance, contain chopped up pieces of tea, dusty particles, and pieces of fibre and stalk that give colour and strength but poor flavour. The tea inside has often been selected for its low price rather than for quality, and offers only a poor substitute for quality, speciality tea.

However, since the Japanese invention of pyramid Fuso teabags (variously called gourmet pyramids, crystal teabags, silk pyramids, and tea temples), which contain large pieces of tea, the attitude toward the teabag has changed, and even tea companies that declared they would never sell them now find that, to meet customers' demands, they need to offer a range of their teas in these bags. These are popular both in the service industry, where they make fast brewing and portion control more manageable, and for home use, where many people do not feel confident enough and often do not have the necessary equipment to brew loose-leaf tea.

In all discussions about the merits and demerits of teabags and loose tea, it is important to remember that not all loose-leaf tea is necessarily good and not all teabags are bad. Everyone must judge for themselves and choose accordingly.

Every cup or bowl of tea we brew is made up of 98 percent water, and the quality of the water we use brings out the very best, or overwhelms, corrupts, or spoils the true character of the tea liquor. And to bring out the vibrancy of the tea's flavour, the water must contain plenty of oxygen (although this is not true for Japanese green teas). In his *Cha Ching* (*Tea Classic*), Lu Yu wrote of the importance of choosing the right sort of water for tea and advised that the best was taken from a mountain stream (gathering oxygen as it tumbles on its way), the second best was from a river, and the worst option was well water. He explained that the best mountain water was scooped from "slow-flowing streams, stone-lined pools, or milk-pure springs." Because few of us have the choice of collecting water from a nearby spring, we obviously have to depend on tap or bottled mineral water.

In some parts of the world, professional tea tasters use distilled water for checking the quality of teas, but distilled water is so neutral that the true character of the tea can be lost in it. If relying on bottled water, choose brands that offer total dissolved solids of between 100 and 200 milligrams per litre (.0033 and .0067 ounces per quart) and a neutral pH of between 6 and 8. And beware of any mineral waters that carry added salts. However, using bottled water is an expensive and environmentally unfriendly approach because of the inevitable transportation involved and the amount of glass or plastic required. So wherever possible, it is better to use tap water. But in most places around the world, the water that pours from our taps contains calcium and other minerals, chlorine, dissolved heavy metals, sand, clay, dust, rust, bacteria, pollens, insecticides, chemicals, and other pollutants that affect the taste of the tea we brew. The best solution to this problem is to use water that has been passed through a filtration system designed to remove as many of these unwanted ingredients as possible. This can be achieved by fitting a filter to the main water inlet coming into the home or catering outlet, fitting a filter system to the cold water tap in the kitchen, using an industrial countertop or wall-mounted water-delivery system that filters the water before heating it, or, in a domestic situation, by using a worktop filter jug. The best of these are made by Brita.

To draw out the best from each tea we brew, a certain balance of minerals in the water is required, and the filtration system we choose can affect this. Carbon and resin ion-exchange filters remove calcium, chlorine, heavy metals, sand, and dust but leave in the water the minerals that brew the best tea. Caterers usually choose reverse osmosis systems, which remove all the ingredients but then put back selected minerals via a cartridge fitted to the system. However, every situation is different and requires professional, local advice.

If water is not filtered, particularly in areas where the water contains high levels of limescale, the colour, aroma, and taste of every tea will be spoiled. The liquor will quickly become cloudy, dull, and lifeless and will develop an unattractive chalky layer on the top of the tea. To understand the importance of this, carry out a comparative brew test with unfiltered tap water and filtered tap water to check the way the water affects the character of the tea.

HEATING THE WATER

A growing number of temperature-controlled kettles are now available around the world. These are extremely helpful for home brewing, for teaching, and for brewing at small tea-tasting events. On a larger scale, in hotels, restaurants, coffee bars, and tearooms, an industrial-scale water delivery system is essential for both speed and safety. The best systems, such as the Marco Uber-boiler, allow the delivery of water at the correct temperature every time tea is brewed. For stills and other boilers, many outlets install at least two, each set at a different temperature, for example, 95°C (203°F) and 70°C (158°F). To brew teas that require cooler temperatures, add cold filtered water to a jug of hotter water, and then check the water with a thermometer before pouring onto the tea.

HOW MUCH TEA?

It is crucial to know how much water a brewing vessel holds before deciding how much tea to use. For western-style brewing, use 2.5 to 3 grams (.088 to .106 ounces) per 200 millilitres (7 fluid ounces) of water. But keep in mind that this is only a guide, and quantities can be adjusted to suit personal preference or the individual tea. For complete accuracy, use digital scales to weigh the tea. (Pocket-size scales are easily available, cost very little, and allow accurate weighing in grams or ounces.)

WATER TEMPERATURES FOR BREWING

Tea lovers around the world recognise that different teas taste better when brewed in water heated to different temperatures. There are no hard and fast rules, but usually teas brew better at the temperatures listed in the table below.

Tea can also be infused successfully in cold or iced water over a number of hours, and the resulting liquor has none of the bitter astringency that hot water sometimes draws out. This is because bitter polyphenols are hardly soluble in water, so the tea will contain floral and fruity compounds but not the astringency of the catechins.

TYPE OF TEA	RECOMMENDED BREWING TEMPERATURE
Most blacks, dark	90 to 98°C (194 to 208°F)
Dark oolongs, hojicha	85 to 95°C (185 to 203°F)
More delicate blacks such as Darjeeling and Nilgiri Frost, and jade oolongs	85 to 90°C (185 to 194°F)
Genmaicha	80 to 90°C (176 to 194°F)
White	75 to 90°C (167 to 194°F)
Yellow, kukicha	80°C (176°F)
Bancha	near boiling
Karigane	70 to 80°C (158 to 176°F)
Chinese greens	70 to 75°C (158 to 167°F)
High-grade sencha	70°C (158°F)
Normal-grade sencha	90°C (194°F)
Fukamushi (deep steamed) sencha	70 to 80°C (158 to 176°F)
Gyokuro	50 to 60°C (122 to 140°F)

TIMING THE BREW

In general, the lower the temperature, the longer the tea can steep without becoming bitter and unpleasant. This varies according to tea type and brewing method (see below), and brewing times can be varied to suit personal preference.

TYPE OF TEA	RECOMMENDED STEEPING TIME
Large-leaf or whole-leaf blacks	4 to 5 minutes
Dark	3 to 4 minutes (or multiple short brews of 30 seconds each)
White	3 to 5 minutes
Dark oolongs, baked oolongs	3 to 5 minutes (or multiple short brews)
Chinese greens	3 to 4 minutes
Yellow	3 minutes
Jade oolongs	3 minutes (or multiple short brews of 20 to 30 seconds each)
Medium-size-leaf blacks	2 to 3 minutes
Small-leaf and CTC blacks and greens	1 to 2 minutes
Kukicha	50 seconds
Bancha, genmaicha, hojicha	30 seconds
Karigane	1 minute
High-grade sencha	1 minute
Normal-grade sencha	1 minute
Fukamushi (deep-steamed) sencha	1 minute
Gyokuro	2.5 minutes

The best materials for teapots and other brewing vessels are clays (such as those from Yixing in China), porcelain, bone china, and glass. Metal pots (silver, iron, and so on) should be avoided unless they have a coating inside to prevent the flavour of the metal from tainting the tea. The ideal shape is squat and round to allow the leaves to swirl and dance in the water to release their colour and flavour.

The best brewing vessels are designed to allow easy removal or separation of the tea leaves from the water once the tea has brewed. The old-fashioned method of allowing tea leaves to remain in the water beyond the optimum steeping time is not acceptable since most teas become bitter, too strong, and unpalatable after five or six minutes, sometimes less. Infuser baskets should be as deep and wide as possible to allow the leaves to absorb water and infuse properly. If the vessel does not have its own infuser basket, choose a suitable infuser in stainless steel, nylon, porcelain, or glass to fit the pot. Alternatively, brew in one pot, and when the tea is ready, pour the liquor through a strainer into a second clean, warmed pot. Other design features to check on all teapots are how easy the pot is to lift and hold, how well the spout pours, whether the lid stays in place, and whether there is a small hole in the lid that allows air to pass into the pot as the tea is poured and, hence, prevent dribbles running down the spout.

The pot or infuser mug should be rinsed with hot water before being used to ensure that it is spotlessly clean and so that when the leaves are measured in, they respond to the warmth and open more quickly in the hot water poured on. Before brewing, gather the chosen pot; the tea to be brewed; a scoop (if its capacity is known) or little digital scales for measuring the tea; a kettle that has been filled with cold, filtered water containing plenty of oxygen; a tea thermometer; a timer; and a cup, bowl, or mug from which to drink the tea. If the teapot has an infuser basket inside, a little dish is also required to hold the used infuser when it is lifted out of the pot. It is crucial that the leaves do not stay in the water for longer than the recommended brewing time, so choose an effective way to easily separate them.

Bring the water in the kettle to the required temperature. A temperature-controlled kettle will switch itself off when the water reaches the chosen temperature, or the water temperature can be checked with a thermometer. When the water is almost ready, pour a little into the pot to cleanse and warm it in preparation for the dry tea, swirl it around, and tip the water away. Measure the correct quantity of tea into the pot or infuser basket and, when the water is at the correct temperature, pour it onto the tea. Replace the lid of the pot or infuser mug, and immediately set the timer to the recommended number of seconds or minutes. After the correct time, separate the leaves from the liquor. With some teas, the wet leaves in the infuser basket can be returned to the pot for further subsequent steepings.

Photograph by John O'Hagan; © Hoffman Media.

Yixing pots are best suited to oolong and dark teas. The traditional way of brewing tea using a Yixing pot is called the Gong Fu ceremony. To brew in the Gong Fu style, you will need a wooden tray that allows water to drain away, a kettle, a Yixing pot, a glass or porcelain jug, a dish or caddy to hold the loose-leaf tea, Gong Fu utensils for scooping the tea leaves into the pot, small tea bowls from which to drink the tea, and little saucers.

First, place all the utensils on the tray. Pour some hot water into the pot to warm and cleanse it. Put on the lid, and pour more hot water over the lid to ensure that it is full. Pour more hot water into the jug. Then pour the water from the jug into the little bowls, pouring away any excess water from the jug. Lift the teapot carefully, placing the index finger over the lid to hold it in place, and pour the water from the teapot into the jug. Leave this water in the jug to keep it warm. Remove the teapot lid, and measure the tea into the pot, using a larger quantity of leaf than you would use in a Western-style teapot (between one-half and two-thirds of the pot's capacity). Replace the lid and, while holding the lid in place, gently shake the teapot to wake up the leaves. Remove the teapot lid, and allow those taking part in the ceremony to smell the leaves in the pot. Next, pour hot water from the kettle onto the leaves in the pot, replace the teapot lid, and pour more water over the top of the pot to ensure no air is trapped inside and that the pot is completely full. While the tea is brewing, pour away the water from the jug. Lift the teapot carefully, holding the lid in place with the index finger, and pour the tea into the empty warm jug. Pour away the hot water that has been sitting in the little bowls, and pour the tea from the jug into the bowls, being careful to share the tea out equally, a little at a time, to ensure that the colour and flavour of the tea is equally balanced. Then place the little bowls of tea on saucers, and present to the guests. While they sip the tea, brew a second pot of tea in exactly the same way. The second and subsequent steepings vary slightly, depending on the tea, with each infusion lasting a little longer than the previous brew.

LEFT: Shaping an unglazed, hand-built teapot from clay produced in Yixing in Jiangsu Province, China. TOP: To build a Yixing teapot, the clay is hand-cut and skillfully assembled using a selection of traditional wooden tools. BOTTOM: Raw Yixing clay lies deep underground; to prepare it for use, the mined clay is pulverised into fine particles, refined, mixed with water to a thick paste, and vacuum-processed to remove bubbles and some of the moisture. *Photographs by David Collen; courtesy of essenceoftea.com*

To brew in a gaiwan, first warm the bowl with a little hot water from the kettle, swirl the water, then tip it away, and scoop in the tea. For oolongs or Puerh teas, rinse the leaves and wake them up by pouring on hot water at the correct temperature in a circular movement. Place the lid over the bowl, leaving a narrow gap between lid and bowl, and immediately pour away the water. Then, lift off the lid, pour more water onto the leaves (repeating the circular movement), replace the lid, and allow the leaves to steep for 15 to 30 seconds, depending on the type of tea. As the tea brews, use the edge of the lid to gently stir the top layer of leaves to ensure they are fully immersed in the water, and then place the lid back over the bowl.

When the tea has brewed for the correct time, place the lid at an angle to allow a very narrow gap between it and the bowl, pick up the bowl with the thumb and middle finger, hold the lid on firmly with the index finger, and pour the tea into a small jug. From the jug, pour the tea into small bowls, sharing the liquor equally so that the colour and flavour is the same in each bowl. To enjoy the aroma of the brewed leaves, lift the gaiwan to the nose, tilt the lid slightly open, and breathe in the wonderful perfume. When required, add water to the gaiwan, and brew the tea a second time, allowing the leaves to steep a little longer. Again, use the lid to ensure that all the leaves are immersed. Pour as before.

To use the gaiwan as a drinking vessel, when the tea is ready, tip the lid to a slight angle to create a gap just wide enough to allow the tea to be sipped from the bowl; lift the saucer, cup, and lid together, holding them firmly together; and drink carefully. Using a gaiwan for drinking rather than brewing is suitable only for teas that do not become bitter after steeping for 2 or 3 minutes (for example Long Jing green, jasmine green, white tea, Chinese Keemun, and some oolongs). To avoid spoiling a tea by oversteeping, use the gaiwan for brewing, pour off the liquor, and drink the tea from small bowls.

Gaiwans—three-piece brewing and drinking vessels consisting of lid, bowl, and saucer—have been used to brew tea in China for 800 years or more. In Mandarin, *gai* means "lid" and *wan* means "bowl"; in Cantonese, the name is *chazhong*; and in English, these beautiful porcelain or glass vessels are usually referred to as "covered cups" or "covered bowls." The bowl provides ample room for the tea to dance and unfurl in the hot water, and it allows multiple steepings. The brewed liquor can be poured into a jug or a cup, using the lid to separate the liquor from the leaves, or it can be sipped directly from the gaiwan while the lid is held at an angle over the top of the cup to hold back the leaves.

In China and elsewhere, tea is often brewed in tall straight glasses. As with the gaiwan, this is successful only for brewing teas that do not become bitter after several minutes in the water. When brewing in a glass, measure the leaves into the empty glass, and add water in a steady, slow stream so that the water runs down the inside of the glass and sets the leaves swirling. Bud teas look beautiful brewed in this way. The leaves and buds rise to the top of the glass, slowly absorb water, and then gracefully drift down through the clear water, with the tip of each bud pointing up and the stems pointing down until they come to rest on the bottom of the glass, where they sway gently from side to side like slender ballerinas balancing on pointe shoes.

BREWING MACHINES

New inventions to make brewing easier appear all the time—some successful, other less so. Inventors of machines for use in catering outlets have realised that tea brewing always requires a certain amount of time and cannot be hurried, but aim to make the process more consistently accurate. The best new machines add a little theatre to what happens at the counter and so attract more interest from potential tea drinkers who can see the shape, style, and colour of the tea and can watch the leaves opening up as they brew.

The Teapresso, very popular in Taiwan, works by the same methodology as a coffee espresso machine, injecting steam through a pod of tea leaves and delivering a shot of tea that can be blended into a tea latte, frappe, or bubble tea mix.

The Alpha Dominche Steampunk, which consists of glass cylinders mounted in a steel frame, offers adjustable water volume, temperature, and steep times, which are all controlled on an iPad. Water is heated by steam in the top cylinder, then drops into a lower compartment. Tea leaves are added to the top compartment, and the water is then forced up from below to brew the tea and is agitated by steam to accelerate extraction of flavour and colour. After the required time, the tea liquor drops down into the lower compartment ready to be served.

The BKON's Craft Brewer uses negative vacuum pressure to extract flavour and colour in about 60 seconds from leaves that would normally take four or five minutes to infuse.

OPPOSITE PAGE: Photograph by William Dickey; © Hoffman Media. ABOVE: The Steampunk brewing machine at the retail counter in Fortnum & Mason, Piccadilly, London, United Kingdom. Photograph courtesy of Fortnum & Mason Plc

Acres of tea bushes and the famous Angel Oak Tree at Charleston Tea Plantation, Wadmalaw Island, South Carolina, USA. Photograph by John O'Hagan; ©Hoffman Media

CHAPTER 2

NORTH AMERICA

TEA REACHED AMERICA WITH THE DUTCH IN THE

17TH CENTURY, AND WHEN PETER STUYVESANT,

GOVERNOR OF NEW AMSTERDAM, SURRENDERED

DUTCH SETTLEMENTS TO THE BRITISH IN 1664,

THE NEW RESIDENTS OF RENAMED NEW YORK

FOUND TEA WELL ESTABLISHED AMONGST

THE TOWN'S UPPER CLASSES.

After the quarrel with Britain over taxes that led to the Boston Tea Party in 1773, Americans vowed to give up tea, but instead, they established their own trade with China. On the 22nd of February 1784, *The Empress of China*, the first American vessel to be directly involved in that trade, set sail from New York for Canton. And with a burgeoning demand for green tea, merchants also began importing large amounts from Japan. French botanist André Michaux planted North America's first Chinese tea seeds in South Carolina in 1795, and in the 1840s, Junius Smith planted bushes in South Carolina. In the late 1850s, the United States government hired Scottish botanist Robert Fortune to acquire more seed from China, and in 1858 and 1859, he dispatched seed from Hong Kong to the U.S.A. An experimental plot of five acres was established in Washington D.C., and trial plantings of the new seedlings were carried out in the Carolinas, Georgia, and Florida but were abandoned because of poor management and the disruption of the American Civil War (1861 to 1865). In the 1890s, seeds from China, India, and Japan and cuttings from Washington were planted in Georgia and at Summerville, South Carolina. The estate was eventually sold to Charles Shepherd, who farmed 89 acres of tea there until he died in 1915.

Tea found its way into what is today Canada with the Hudson Bay Company in the 18th century. Granted a royal charter by England's King Charles II in 1670, the company traded fur from Hudson Bay to customers in London and Europe. As commercial operations grew, the company started selling coffee, tea, alcohol, and food through its trading posts. Canada's first tea was planted in the mid-1950s at St. Vincent's Tea Plantation in the Fraser Valley, British Columbia. The plants did not survive, and horticulturalists have always maintained that Canada's west coast is too cold and damp for tea. However, Van Dusen Botanical Gardens in Vancouver has grown tea plants since 1983, and Canada has one established tea farm on Vancouver Island and another experimental plot on Denman Island that lies between mainland Vancouver and Vancouver Island.

With an increasing number of tea farmers across North America, the United States League of Tea Growers was formed in 2013 to connect those involved and to work together to share resources, research, and information. The league's aim is to raise public awareness of tea production in the United States and to support farmers in their individual growing programs.

Tea bushes sparkle with frost at Westholme Tea Company, North Cowichan, Vancouver Island, Canada. Photograph courtesy of Victor Vesely, Westholme Tea Farm

Labrador Sea

Hudson Bay

British Columbia

CANADA

Victoria ★

Olympia ★ **Washington**

Columbia River

★ Salem

Oregon **Idaho**

★ Boise

Snake River

Lake Superior

Lake Huron

Lake Michigan

Lake Ontario

Lake Erie

Hudson River

Michigan
★ Lansing

★ Albany **New York**

Missouri River

Mississippi River

★ Sacramento

UNITED STATES

★ Annapolis

Maryland

★ Richmond

James River

Virginia

★ Raleigh

R O C K Y M O U N T A I N S

Colorado River

A P P A L A C H I A N M O U N T A I N S

California

North Carolina

★ Columbia

Savannah River

Mississippi

Alabama

★ Atlanta

South Carolina

Brazos River

Chattahoochee River

Louisiana

Montgomery ★

★ Jackson

Georgia

Pecos River

Colorado River

Austin ★

Baton Rouge ★

Tallahassee ★

ATLANTIC OCEAN

Rio Grande

Texas

Gulf of Mexico

Florida

PACIFIC OCEAN

Tropic of Cancer

MEXICO

CUBA

Honolulu ★

Hawaii

Caribbean Sea

🌱 Tea grower

🌱🌱 Multiple growers

| 0 | 125 | 250 | | 500 Miles |

| 0 | 125 250 | | 500 Kilometres |

N

W E

S

The tea is gathered from the bushes at Charleston Tea Plantation,
South Carolina, using a converted mechanical tobacco harvester.
Photograph courtesy of Charleston Tea Plantation, Wadmalaw Island, SC

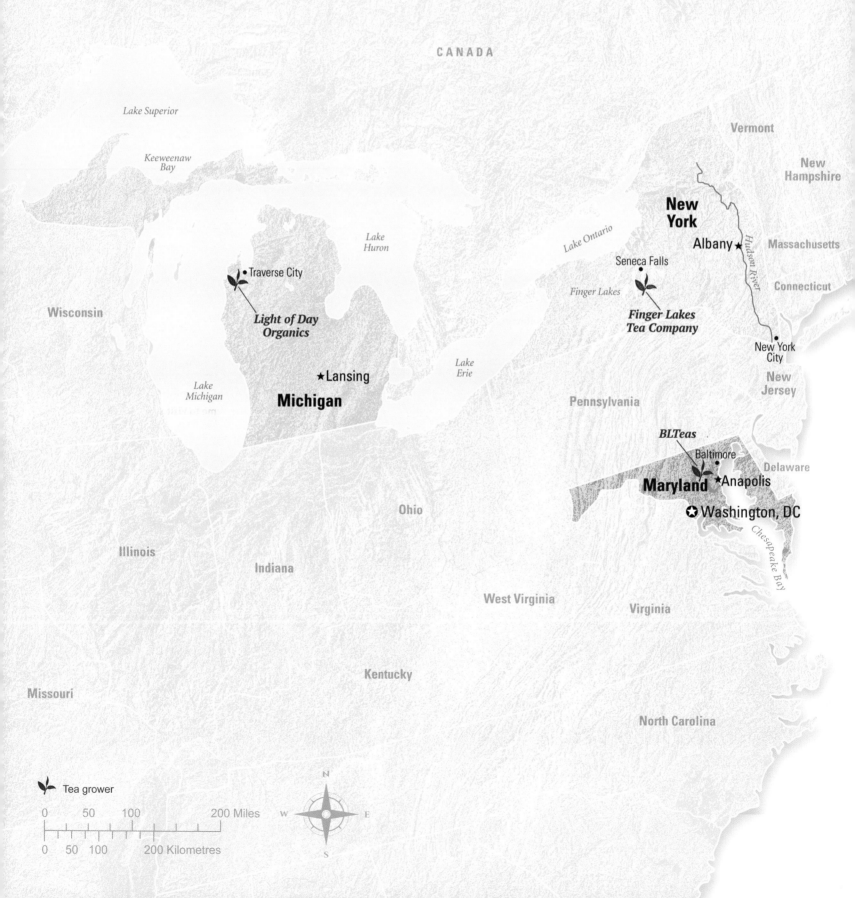

CANADA

Lake Superior

Keeweenaw Bay

Wisconsin

Lake Huron

• Traverse City

Light of Day Organics

★ Lansing

Michigan

Lake Michigan

Lake Erie

Ohio

Illinois

Indiana

West Virginia

Kentucky

Missouri

Vermont

New York

New Hampshire

Albany ★

Seneca Falls •

Lake Ontario

Finger Lakes

Finger Lakes Tea Company

Massachusetts

Hudson River

Connecticut

New York City •

New Jersey

Pennsylvania

BLTeas

Baltimore •

Delaware

Maryland ★ Anapolis

✪ Washington, DC

Chesapeake Bay

Virginia

North Carolina

🌱 Tea grower

0   50   100   200 Miles

0   50 100   200 Kilometres

N
W   E
S

MARYLAND

(USA)

BLTEAS | *Woodbine*

In 2013, Lori and Bob Baker purchased Heron's Meadow Farm on Daisy Road, Woodbine, and planted their first 100 tea plants in spring 2014. Despite the cold temperatures, the baby bushes survived the harsh winter. But to try to deal with the challenge of Maryland's cold winters, the Bakers have been sourcing seeds from robust plants that survive in the colder regions of the world. In April 2015, another 350 plants went into the ground, and in spring 2016, 5,000 hardy Georgian (the country, not the state) tea seeds were planted. The hope is that they will be able to develop a regional varietal that naturally adapts itself to the local environment. Meanwhile, they sell black and green teas from other origins flavored with herbs grown in a pesticide-free environment at the farm.

BLTeas' first harvest. Photograph by Lori Baker

Country, State, or Province
Maryland

Number of Gardens
1

Main Districts or Gardens
BLTeas, Woodbine

Area Under Tea
3 acres with approximately 5,500 plants

Average Annual Production (Kilograms)
Not yet known

Terrain
Gently sloping land

Altitude
212 metres (696 feet)

Production Period
Not yet known

Best Time to Visit
April, May, June, September, October

Main Varietals/ Cultivars
Hardy Georgian varietals

Types of Tea Made
Not yet known

Predominant Flavours; Tasting Notes
Not yet known

MICHIGAN

(USA)

LIGHT OF DAY ORGANICS | *Traverse City*

Registered nurse and horticulturalist Angela Macke started growing tea and other botanicals on the shores of Lake Michigan in 1999, using a combination of Hawaiian and Darjeeling biodynamic tea seed. The farm now houses more than 2,000 plants that grow inside hoophouses where classical music is played constantly. In winter, the tunnels protect the tea from breakage and subzero damage caused by heavy snow; in summer, the sides of the tunnels are covered with shade tarp and are rolled up for ventilation. Farming methods are certified Demeter Biodynamic, and cultivation is very labour intensive. Macke makes white, dark oolong, green, and black teas, some of which she blends with other botanicals.

Angela Macke grows a range of botanicals and blends them with some of her teas. Photograph courtesy of Light of Day Organics

Country, State, or Province
Michigan

Number of Gardens
1

Main Districts or Gardens
Light of Day Organics, Traverse City

Area Under Tea
400 plants on 0.028 hectare of organic/ Biodynamic farm

Average Annual Production (Kilograms)
38.5

Terrain
Open, mostly flat surrounded by pine stand, pastures, and protected woodlands

Altitude
152.4 metres (500 feet)

Production Period
Late March and early August

Best Time to Visit
May to September

Main Varietals/ Cultivars
Assamica, sinensis, Sochi (Russia)

Types of Tea Made
WHITE: Silver Needle, Pai Mu Tan

Predominant Flavours; Tasting Notes
WHITE: delicate, lightly floral

NEW YORK

(USA)

FINGER LAKES TEA COMPANY | *Seneca Falls*

The Finger Lakes Tea Company farm was established in 2012 by the Lin family who are originally from Qingtian in China's Zhejiang Province. Seed was imported from China, and 55,000 plants were in the ground by 2012. A very severe winter that year killed most of them. In 2014, another 5,000 plants went into the ground but could not withstand the shock of sudden frost in the autumn of that year combined with very hot days. Now, only 500 plants remain, and these need time to mature slowly in the region's cold climate. Once the bushes are more established, the Lin family's plan is to make black and dark teas and a Mao Feng–style green.

Blended teas flavoured with other botanicals sold by Finger Lakes Tea Company. Photograph courtesy of Benjamin Lin

Country, State, or Province
New York

Number of Gardens
1

Main Districts or Gardens
Finger Lakes Tea Company, Seneca Falls

Area Under Tea
12 hectares

Average Annual Production (Kilograms)
Not yet known

Terrain
A region of glacial valleys, rivers, streams, and lakes

Altitude
137 metres (449 feet)

Production Period
Not yet known

Best Time to Visit
May, June, October

Main Varietals/ Cultivars
Chinese varietals

Types of Tea Made
Black, dark, green

Predominant Flavours; Tasting Notes
Not yet known

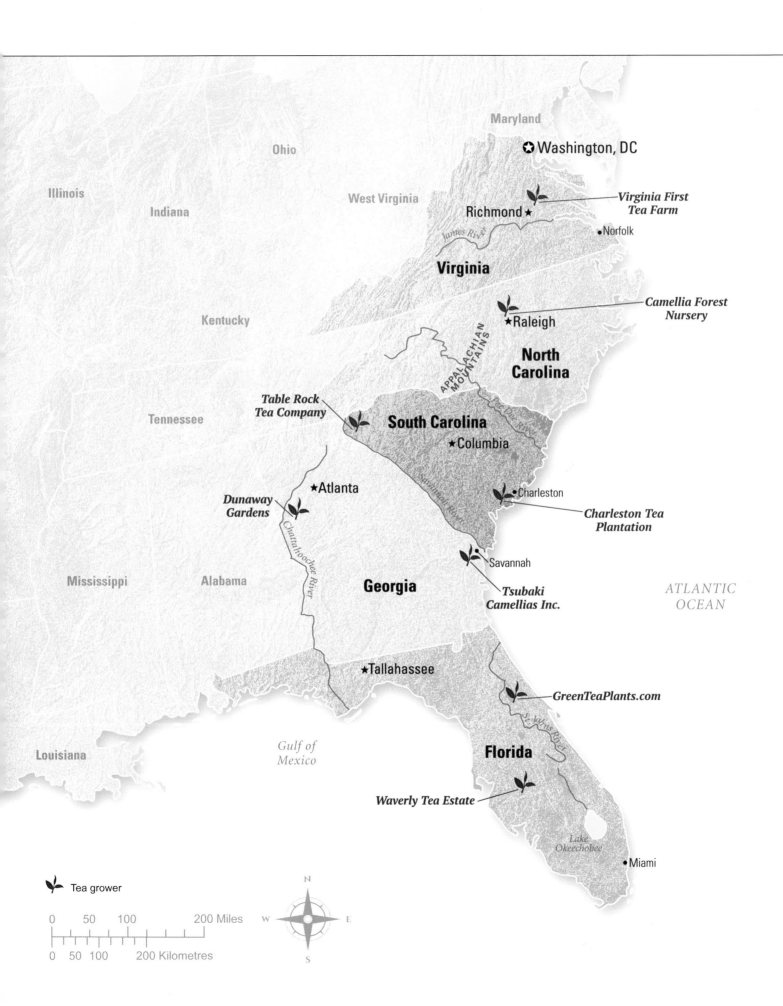

Maryland

Ohio

Illinois

Indiana

West Virginia

✪ Washington, DC

Virginia First
Tea Farm

Richmond ★

James River

• Norfolk

Kentucky

Virginia

Camellia Forest
Nursery

★ Raleigh

**North
Carolina**

*APPALACHIAN
MOUNTAINS*

Tennessee

Table Rock
Tea Company

South Carolina

Pee Dee River

★ Columbia

★ Atlanta

Dunaway
Gardens

Chattahoochee River

Savannah River

• Charleston

Charleston Tea
Plantation

Savannah

ATLANTIC
OCEAN

Mississippi

Alabama

Georgia

Tsubaki
Camellias Inc.

Louisiana

★ Tallahassee

GreenTeaPlants.com

*Gulf of
Mexico*

Florida

St. Johns River

Waverly Tea Estate

*Lake
Okeechobee*

• Miami

🌱 Tea grower

0   50   100   200 Miles

0   50 100   200 Kilometres

N
W   E
S

FLORIDA

(USA)

GREENTEAPLANTS.COM | *Eustis*

Steven Behncke has travelled all over the tea-growing world to find seeds and young plants for his family tea nursery in Eustis, where he grows and sells his stock to new tea farmers. In the past, he has imported seed from Korea, India, and Nepal but now aims to bring in more from China. He is also the founder of Peace Trail International, the community service and training arm of Logos Academy Inc., which has the goal of uniting local communities and empowering them through education to live in a sustainable way. His company has plans to part-sponsor a new tea-growing project at Llano Brenes in the highlands of Costa Rica.

WAVERLY TEA ESTATE | *Waverly, Polk County*

Fourth-generation citrus grower James Orrock has been growing tea since 2011 with help from Donnie Barrett of Fairhope Tea Plantation, and now owns a 10-acre plot in Waverly, Polk County, that is planted with more than 5,000 tea plants. The estate lies at an altitude of between 85 and 88 metres (279 and 289 feet), where temperatures range from around freezing in winter to 35°C (95°F) in summer. The plants like the region's natural humidity, although the moist air can cause fungal diseases on the plants. Orrock is working with the University of Florida on projects related to such problems. Depending on the rains, the plucking season usually begins in late February or early March and continues to October or November; the fresh shoots are processed to make black, green, and white teas. The green tea has a character similar to that of Long Jing with hints of bok choy and buttered asparagus, while the black tea has a mild stonefruit flavour.

Country, State, or Province
Florida

Number of Gardens 2

Main Districts or Gardens
GreenTeaPlants.com, Eustis

Waverly Tea Estate,
Waverly, Polk County

Area Under Tea
Waverly Tea Estate:
10 acres with 5,000 plants

**Average Annual
Production (Kilograms)**
Waverly Tea Estate:
Not yet known

Terrain
Waverly Tea Estate:
Hilly landscape

Altitude
Waverly Tea Estate:
85 and 88 metres (280 and 290 feet)

Production Period
Waverly Tea Estate:
Late February/early March to October/November

Best Time to Visit
April to May; September to November

Main Varietals/Cultivars
GreenTeaPlants.com: Korea, India, Nepal, and China

Waverly Tea Estate: Plants from Fairhope Tea Plantation in Alabama

Types of Tea Made
Waverly Tea Estate: Black, green, and white teas

**Predominant Flavours;
Tasting Notes**
Waverly Tea Estate:
BLACK: mild stonefruit flavour
GREEN: similar character to Long Jing with hints of bok choy, buttered asparagus, seafood, and fresh-mown grass

GEORGIA

(USA)

DUNAWAY GARDENS | *Newnan*

Dunaway Gardens, at the heart of Georgia's Piedmont region, once surrounded the home of actress Hetty Jane Dunaway (1879–1961). The gardens fell into a state of neglect in the 20th century, however, and for almost 50 years lay hidden beneath vines and kudzu. Restoration began in 2000. While working there, Josh Fisher and Zach Bigham found abandoned tea plants that were planted in the 1920s. In 2011, they set out to create a working organic tea farm, planting seedlings around and beneath existing plants. They also started growing cuttings by vegetative propagation to produce a hardy plant that gives an even yield. The tea is cultivated organically (USDA certified) at an altitude of 260 metres (853 feet), and Georgia's climate, with good annual rainfall and good temperatures during the harvesting season, suits the plants well. Now, 15,000 tea plants are growing on three plots that cover a total of 2 to 3 acres. The harvested leaf is processed by hand to make limited small lots of a fragrant, full-bodied, robust black; a sweet, floral oolong with a long finish; a light, astringent green with a vegetal aroma; and a light, silky white tea.

TSUBAKI CAMELLIAS, INC. | *Savannah*

Tsubaki Camellias, Inc. was established in 1959 as a specialist camellia nursery. Today, in addition to growing camellias, owners Ben and Debbie Odom and their daughter Lindsey breed and grow tea plants in a greenhouse/nursery to supply tea growers and farmers. When they started growing tea, they became aware that seedling plants varied widely in leaf size, growth patterns, flower colour, etcetera, and from 1,500 baby plants, they selected about 40 they believed were unique. These were then used for growing more plants by vegetative propagation, and over the years, the Odoms have developed many different tea varietals, including *Camellia sinensis* var. *Rosea*, which has pale pink blossoms instead of the usual white flowers. Tsubaki has enough space to grow 15,000 tea plants per year, and with the growing interest and demand around the United States, the company plans to expand further.

Country, State, or Province
Georgia

Number of Gardens
2

Main Districts or Gardens
Dunaway Gardens,
Newnan

Tsubaki Camellias, Inc.,
Savannah

Area Under Tea
Dunaway Gardens:
15,000 on 3 plots that total 2 to 3 acres

Tsubaki Camellias, Inc.:
1.214 hectares, 4 more being developed

Average Annual Production (Kilograms)
Dunaway Gardens: Not yet known

Tsubaki Camellias, Inc.:
Not applicable

Terrain
Dunaway Gardens: One original south-facing field in full sunlight planted with first cloned plants, located in a low, flat sandy field at the base of Cedar Creek. Second field of sandy loam on pre-existing terraces also southerly facing, partly shaded. Test field of seedlings in clay soil, facing south-west, partly shaded in the mornings.

Tsubaki Camellias, Inc.:
Surrounded by the wide open plains of Savannah.

Altitude
Dunaway Gardens:
260 metres (850 feet)

Tsubaki Camellias, Inc.:
15.5 to 28 metres (50 to 92 feet)

Production Period
Dunaway Gardens:
Late April to late September

Tsubaki Camellias Inc.:
May to September

Best Time to Visit
May to August

Main Varietals/ Cultivars
Dunaway Gardens:
Unknown

Tsubaki Camellias, Inc.:
Number of different varietals and cultivars

Types of Tea Made
Dunaway Gardens:
White, green, and black

Predominant Flavours; Tasting Notes
Dunaway Gardens:
BLACK: fragrant, full-bodied, robust
OOLONG: sweet, floral with a long finish
GREEN: light, astringent with a vegetal aroma
WHITE: light, silky

NORTH CAROLINA

(USA)

CAMELLIA FOREST NURSERY | *Chapel Hill*

Camellia Forest Nursery has been collecting and cultivating tea plants since the 1970s. Owners Christine and David Parks have selected cultivars that thrive in cool regions of the world and have crossbred them to create plants that are well suited to cold North American weather patterns. They also nurture "tender" cultivars that grow better in the warmer, more southerly regions of the United States and that will adapt to possible climate change in the future. Because of a steady increase in demand from new tea farmers in the United States, Camellia Forest now produces plants wholesale and, at the end of 2016, had more than 30,000 new plants ready for sale.

Camellia sinensis var *sinensis small leaf* and 'Rosea' pink flowering tea growing alongside each other at Camellia Forest Garden. Photograph courtesy of Christine Parks

Country, State, or Province
North Carolina

Number of Gardens
1

Main Districts or Gardens
Camellia Forest Nursery, Chapel Hill

Area Under Tea
Tea plants grown with other camellias on 9.3-hectare site

Average Annual Production (Kilograms)
Not applicable

Terrain
The nursery lies amongst the undulating plains and hills of the Piedmont plateau.

Altitude
148 metres (486 feet)

Production Period
March/April to September/October

Best Time to Visit
April to November

Main Varietals/Cultivars
Many types including *Camellia sinensis* 'Rosea' (pink flowering)

Types of Tea Made
Not applicable

Predominant Flavours; Tasting Notes
Not applicable

SOUTH CAROLINA

(USA)

CHARLESTON TEA PLANTATION | *Wadmalaw Island*

In 1963, the Lipton Tea Company took cuttings and rootstock from abandoned plants at Pinehurst to establish an experimental tea garden on Wadmalaw Island and another in Summerville. When Lipton abandoned the program in 1987, Mack Fleming, former head of Lipton's research team, and tea taster William Barclay (Bill) Hall purchased the Wadmalaw Island farm and renamed it Charleston Tea Plantation. In 2003, the plantation was sold to Bigelow Tea Company, which now runs it in partnership with Hall as a tea estate and visitor centre. The 150,000 bushes are harvested using a converted tobacco harvester. The estate's American Classic Tea, which Hall created in the 1980s, has been the official tea of the White House since 1987.

TABLE ROCK TEA COMPANY | *Upstate*

Jennifer and Steve Lorch were inspired to grow tea while working in Kenya on a clean-water project and have been farming tea in the Cherokee Foothills in Upstate since 2008. They have more than 17 acres of land and thousands of tea plants, some of which are used for cuttings to extend their crop. They make oolong teas and a unique "cold-harvest" green from leaf harvested in the winter. They are also planning to increase the size of their farm and build a small-scale processing facility.

Country, State, or Province
South Carolina

Number of Gardens
2

Main Districts or Gardens
Charleston Tea Plantation, Wadmalaw Island

Table Rock Tea Company, Upstate

Area Under Tea
Charleston Tea Plantation:
51.4 hectares

Table Rock Tea Company:
3.1 hectares

Average Annual Production (Kilograms)
Charleston Tea Plantation:
Not known

Table Rock Tea Company:
Not yet known

Terrain
Charleston Tea Plantation:
Low-lying flat field on Wadmalaw Island

Table Rock Tea Company:
Steep, heavily wooded, rolling hills with red clay, along the Cherokee Foothills at the base of Table Rock Mountain

Altitude
Charleston Tea Plantation:
Sea level

Table Rock Tea Company:
333 metres (1,100 feet)

Production Period
Charleston Tea Plantation:
May to October

Table Rock Tea Company:
May to September

Best Time to Visit
Charleston Tea Plantation:
May to October

Table Rock Tea Company:
March to May, September, October

Main Varietals/Cultivars
Charleston Tea Plantation:
More than 320 varietals and cultivars

Table Rock Tea Company:
Sinensis and assamica

Types of Tea Made
Charleston Tea Plantation:
Black, green

Table Rock Tea Company:
Oolong, green, plans for black

Predominant Flavours; Tasting Notes
Charleston Tea Plantation:
FIRST FLUSH BLACK: smooth, mellow
BLACK: fresh, bright, smooth
GREEN: light, delicate, clean, a hint of earthiness

Table Rock Tea Company:
WHITE: clean, light floral
GREEN: soft, floral with grassy notes and hints of hay and honey
OOLONG: floral with suggestions of roasted vegetables, toasted caramel, and chocolate

VIRGINIA

(USA)

VIRGINIA FIRST TEA FARM | *Spotsylvania*

The Ramos family has been growing tea on the family farm since 2012. They propagated their plants from Korean tea seeds, and daughter Joanna made several trips to her home region of Kumsan, South Korea, to learn how to cultivate tea. Although the farm has not yet received organic certification, the tea is grown organically, with weeds pulled up by hand and no use of chemical pesticides or fertilisers. The family manufactures products such as laundry detergent, soap, and shampoo using green tea extract. At first, they used imported Korean green tea. Now, their own home-grown tea is included in the recipe, which, unlike that of most soaps, uses non-animal ingredients such as cucumbers and dried berries sourced from local organic farms. As soon as the farm has equipment for panning and drying the fresh tea leaves, they will make tea for drinking as well.

Young tea bushes planted out in Spotsylvania.
Photograph ©2015 Allison Apperson Goulding

Country, State, or Province
Virgina

Number of Gardens
1

Main Districts or Gardens
Virginia First Tea Farm, Spotsylvania

Area Under Tea
9 hectares

Average Annual Production (Kilograms)
Not yet known

Terrain
Sweeping flat field

Altitude
4.5 metres (15 feet)

Production Period
Not yet known

Best Time to Visit
April, May, September, October

Main Varietals/ Cultivars
Grown from seeds from South Korea

Types of Tea Made
Green

Predominant Flavours; Tasting Notes
Not yet known

Wyoming

Nebraska

Iowa

Ohio

Indiana

Illinois

Colorado

Kansas

Missouri

Kentucky

New Mexico

Oklahoma

Arkansas

Tennessee

Tennessee River

Georgia

East Texas Tea Company, Inc.

The Great Mississippi Tea Company

Alabama

Mississippi River

Mississippi

Pearl River

• Dallas

Brazos River

★ Jackson

★ Montgomery

Colorado River

Louisiana

Alabama River

Mobile

Andalusia Tea, LLC

Pecos River

Texas

Baton Rouge ★

New Orleans

Fairhope Tea Plantation

Rio Grande River

★ Austin

Robert MacArthur

Bill Luer

Pearl River Tea Estate

MEXICO

Gulf of Mexico

🌱 Tea grower

0   50   100   200 Miles

0 50 100   200 Kilometres

ALABAMA

(USA)

ANDALUSIA TEA, LLC | *Andalusia*

Bob Sims first researched the possibility of growing tea in his native Alabama during the late 1990s and, in 2014, found a suitable piece of land (once a peanut farm) in Covington County. He hired international technical consultant Nigel Melican to help him prepare the site before planting thousands of young bushes grown from seed. The last 1,000 plants went into the ground in early 2014 after delays caused by extremely cold temperatures and constant rain. Since going into the ground, the plants have had to cope with drought, very heavy rain, and extreme fluctuations in temperature, which led to the loss of the weakest plants and the survival of the strongest. The plan is for steady expansion of the tea field and construction of a small factory.

FAIRHOPE TEA PLANTATION | *Baldwin County*

Fairhope Tea Plantation sits in a remote spot beside the calm waters of Weeks Bay in southern Baldwin County, just inland from the Gulf of Mexico. Tea has been grown here since 1977 when Lipton planted a trial plot, but a hurricane destroyed the crop two years later. Donnie Barrett, whose father was in charge of that experimental program, rescued three different varietals and started crossbreeding them to create his own local cultivar. He has more than 60,000 bushes growing along the western banks of the bay and makes green, black, and oolong teas.

ROBERT MACARTHUR | *Mobile*

Robert MacArthur has been growing tea on half an acre since 2005. He planted a dozen mail-order plants from various sources and then gathered seeds and cuttings to extend the plot to the current 300 bushes. He has recently introduced a few olive trees to the tea garden as they like the same soil and fertilisation regime and provide some shade for the tea. He makes both green and black teas, which are sold in his gift shop.

ABOVE, TOP RIGHT, AND BOTTOM RIGHT: Hardy new
seedlings from Georgia, East Europe, stored in polytunnels
before going into the ground at Andalusia Tea, LLC.
BOTTOM FAR RIGHT: Preparing the land for the new plants
at Bob Sims's Andalusia tea farm. Photographs by Bob Sims

Country, State, or Province
Alabama

Number of Gardens
3

Main Districts or Gardens
Andalusia Tea, LLC, Andalusia

Fairhope Tea Plantation, Baldwin County

Robert MacArthur, Mobile

Area Under Tea
Andalusia Tea, LLC:
4.45 hectares

Fairhope Tea Plantation:
4 hectares

Robery MacArthur:
0.38 acre

Average Annual Production (Kilograms)
Andalusia Tea, LLC:
Not yet known

Fairhope Tea Plantation:
45.5

Robery MacArthur:
Not yet known

Terrain
Andalusia Tea, LLC:
Gentle sloping fields surrounded by woodlands, lakes, and wetlands

Fairhope Tea Plantation:
Flat, well-drained land near Mobile Bay

Robery MacArthur:
Suburban plot where olive trees also grow

Altitude
Andalusia Tea, LLC:
97.25 metres (319 feet)

Fairhope Tea Plantation:
15.5 metres (50 feet)

Robery MacArthur:
3 metres (9.8 feet)

Production Period
Andalusia Tea, LLC:
March to November

Fairhope Tea Plantation:
May to October

Robery MacArthur:
March to October

Best Time to Visit
Andalusia Tea, LLC:
February to April;
October to December

Fairhope Tea Plantation:
March, April,
September, October

Robery MacArthur:
Not yet known

Main Varietals/ Cultivars
Andalusia Tea, LLC:
Hardy, drought resistant Georgian varietals

Fairhope Tea Plantation:
Hybrid from three different varietals

Robery MacArthur:
Various varietals and cultivars

Types of Tea Made
Andalusia Tea, LLC:
Not yet known

Fairhope Tea Plantation:
A little black, some white, mostly green and oolong

Robery MacArthur:
Green and black teas

Predominant Flavours; Tasting Notes
Andalusia Tea, LLC:
Not yet known

Fairhope Tea Plantation:
HURRICANE BLEND
BLACK: smooth, mellow
BLACK: rich, full of flavour, powerfully floral, with no bitterness

Robery MacArthur:
Not yet known

LOUISIANA

(USA)

BILL LUER | *New Orleans*

Bill Luer has been growing and making tea in New Orleans since 2003 after he realised that camellias grow everywhere in his area. He has a total of about 35 plants, which are a mix of different varietals acquired from Camellia Forest Nursery in North Carolina. His garden is low lying, and the plentiful rain and high humidity suit the plants well, although winters can be very cold. He processes the leaves by hand to make white, green, oolong, black, and even a Puerh-style tea throughout the season—from March or April to September or October. He named his range 30/90 Tea from the latitude and longitude of New Orleans.

Tea plants growing at the front of Bill Luer's house in New Orleans.
Photograph by William Luer

Country, State, or Province
Louisiana

Number of Gardens
1

Main Districts or Gardens
Bill Luer, New Orleans

Area Under Tea
35 plants

Average Annual Production (Kilograms)
Small quantities for home consumption

Terrain
Garden around house in Uptown New Orleans, growing among olive and citrus trees

Altitude
0.6 metres (2 feet)

Production Period
March/April to September/October

Best Time to Visit
December to May

Main Varietals/ Cultivars
Sinensis, assamica, Guangzhou, Tea Breeze, Sochi (Russia), Darjeeling, and Louisiana

Types of Tea Made
White, green, oolong, black, Puerh-style dark tea

Predominant Flavours; Tasting Notes
Not yet known

MISSISSIPPI

(USA)

THE GREAT MISSISSIPPI TEA COMPANY | *Brookhaven*

When Hurricane Katrina destroyed Jason McDonald's timber stand in 2005, he decided that tea—low growing, resistant to storm damage, and sustainable—was a suitable alternative. He planted his first 250 bushes in autumn 2013 and an additional 60,000 plants in late 2014. It is possible that some of the plants, sourced from around the United States, relate to the original seeds André Michaux planted in 1795 and those Robert Fortune sent in 1859. By summer 2017, 6 acres had been planted, but climate change and consequent unpredictable weather patterns (heavy rain in early summer 2016, drought at the end of summer, and very cold temperatures in winter) have made it quite difficult to establish the plants on a wide scale. However, by summer 2017, McDonald was producing both black and green teas, and had also started growing tea on the Big Island, Hawaii, where the climate is kinder to tea growers.

PEARL RIVER TEA ESTATE | *Poplarville*

In November 2008, Jeff Brown and Donald Van Der Werken acquired tea cuttings and seedlings from North and South Carolina and planted them in a greenhouse at their blueberry farm. (Blueberries and tea like the same type of acidic soil.) As the young plants became sturdier, they were transplanted to shaded raised beds irrigated by a spring from the Pearl River that runs through the farm. Now, 9,000 tea plants are established in canopied raised beds and planted out in the farm's rolling hills. Processing began in 2016, and Brown and Van Der Werken have acquired rolling, oxidising, and drying machinery that helps them produce black teas with floral, peachy notes and a smooth finish and green teas with citrus and earthy characteristics. They also make a fruity blend by adding dried blueberry leaves to their black tea. The teas are sold at a farmers' market in New Orleans, Louisiana, and there are plans to offer educational farm tours to anyone interested in learning more about tea.

Country, State, or Province
Mississippi

Number of Gardens
2

Main Districts or Gardens
The Great Mississippi Tea Company, Brookhaven

Pearl River Tea Company, Poplarville

Area Under Tea
The Great Mississippi Tea Company: 60 hectares

Pearl River Tea Company: 0.404 hectares with plans to expand

Average Annual Production (Kilograms)
The Great Mississippi Tea Company: Not yet known

Pearl River Tea Company: Not yet known

Terrain
The Great Mississippi Tea Company: South-facing, gently sloping hills and rolling valleys.

Pearl River Tea Company: Gently rolling hills and valleys in the Pearl River and Delta Valley area

Altitude
The Great Mississippi Tea Company: 127 metres (416 feet)

Pearl River Tea Company: 95 metres (312 feet)

Production Period
The Great Mississippi Tea Company: March to October

Pearl River Tea Company: April to May, August to September

Best Time to Visit
April, May, October

Main Varietals/ Cultivars
The Great Mississippi Tea Company: Mixed varietals and cultivars from U.S. sources

Pearl River Tea Company: Varietals and cultivars from North and South Carolina

Types of Tea Made
The Great Mississippi Tea Company: Machine-and hand-plucked black

Pearl River Tea Company: Black, blueberry leaf black, oolong, green

Predominant Flavours; Tasting Notes
The Great Mississippi Tea Company: Not yet known

Pearl River Tea Company:
BLACK: earthy, with hints of fresh sage and oak
BLUEBERRY LEAF BLACK: subtle fruity hints of blueberry
OOLONG: slight hints of citrus and chamomile, with buttery overtones
GREEN: freshly cut grass, flowery aroma

Young tea bushes at The Great Mississippi Tea Company's farm at Brookhaven, Lincoln County. Photograph courtesy of Jason McDonald/ The Great Mississippi Tea Company

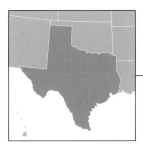

TEXAS

(USA)

EAST TEXAS TEA COMPANY | *Dallas*

Josephie Dean Jackson, an Australian with an agricultural background, grows tea on her ranch that lies amongst rolling hills on the edge of the great Piney Woods of the Southern United States. The subtropical conditions, plentiful rain, high humidity, and acidic, well-draining soil suit the tea plants well. The initial 500 bushes were planted in 2008, and more Darjeeling seedlings, assamicas, and seeds from Japan and Mississippi went into the soil in 2014. The tea plants do not seem to mind the snow that falls twice a year and the very high summer temperatures. The tea grows surrounded by loblolly pines and white and water oaks. And as the plot developed, other plants—quince, pomegranate, osmanthus, jujube, almond, peach, pear, apricot, lilac, and rose—were established amongst the tea bushes. The long-term goal is to have 200 acres of tea and a 5,000-square-foot (465-square-metre) tea resource centre with meeting rooms, display areas, a stage, a tea bar overlooking a pond with a gazebo and willows, and a small factory and laboratory with tea-making machinery from China. The white, green, oolong, and black teas—including a smoked black with pecan, mesquite, and sage—are all hand-processed. Since 2016, Josephie has also had more than 2,000 tea plants, mostly from Georgia (the country, not the state), growing in an urban tea garden in Dallas, using pots, raised beds, and berms (artificial ridges or banks). She also grows tea at her Coeur d'Thé tea garden in Idaho.

Country, State, or Province
Texas

Number of Gardens
1

Main Districts or Gardens
East Texas Tea Company, Dallas

Area Under Tea
Long-term goal of 500 acres, plus 2,000 plants in pots in urban Dallas garden

Average Annual Production (Kilograms)
Not yet known

Terrain
Rolling hills on the edge of the thick Piney Woods forest

Altitude
158 metres (520 feet)

Production Period
April to mid-June and September to October

Best Time to Visit
February to April; September to November

Main Varietals/Cultivars
Seeds from Darjeeling, Japan, and the Great Mississippi Tea Company

Types of Tea Made
White; green; oolong; black teas; smoked black with pecan, mesquite, and sage

Predominant Flavours; Tasting Notes
BLACK: highly floral, honeyed, malty, nutty
GREEN: buttery and honeyed

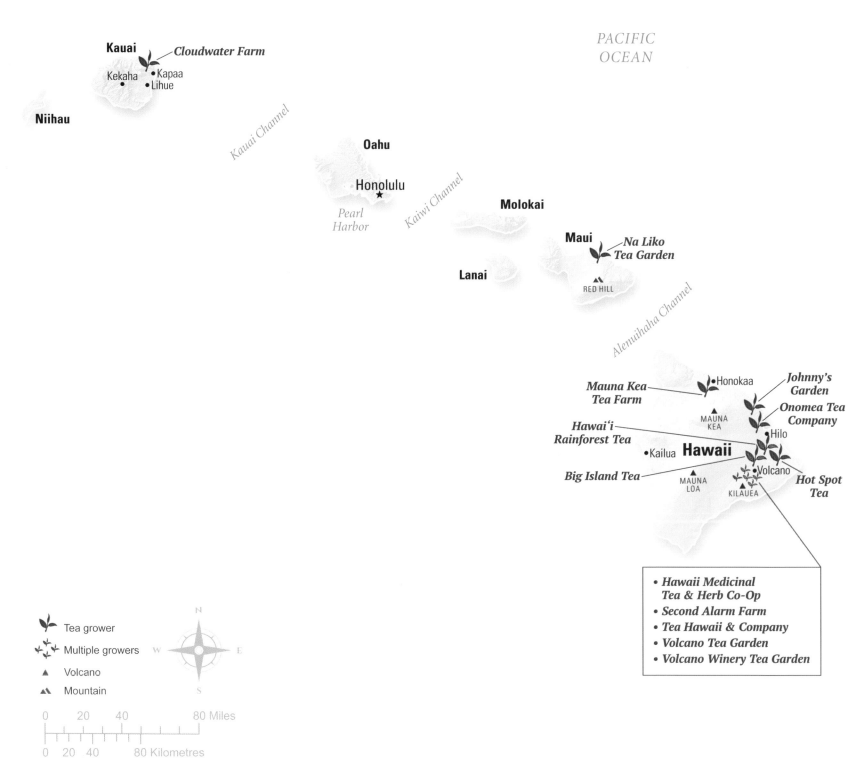

PACIFIC
OCEAN

Kauai — *Cloudwater Farm*

Kekaha • Kapaa
• Lihue

Niihau

Kauai Channel

Oahu

Honolulu
★

Pearl
Harbor

Kaiwi Channel

Molokai

Maui — *Na Liko Tea Garden*

Lanai

RED HILL

Alenuihaha Channel

Mauna Kea Tea Farm — •Honokaa

Johnny's Garden

Onomea Tea Company

MAUNA KEA

Hawai'i Rainforest Tea

Hilo

Hawaii

•Kailua

•Volcano

Big Island Tea — MAUNA LOA

KILAUEA

Hot Spot Tea

- *Hawaii Medicinal Tea & Herb Co-Op*
- *Second Alarm Farm*
- *Tea Hawaii & Company*
- *Volcano Tea Garden*
- *Volcano Winery Tea Garden*

Tea grower

Multiple growers

Volcano

Mountain

N
W   E
S

0   20   40   80 Miles

0   20   40   80 Kilometres

HAWAII

(USA)

Hawaii's first tea was planted in 1887 on a 5-acre plot in Kona on Hawaii Island, but it was abandoned because of high production costs. In the 1960s, Lipton considered growing tea here but decided costs were too high. In the late '70s, Japanese varietals were planted at the Lyon Arboretum on Oahu, and in the 1980s, when the sugarcane industry declined, Francis Zee of the U.S. Department of Agriculture, Pacific Basin Agricultural Research Center (USDA PBARC), suggested tea as an alternative crop. Zee is often now referred to as the grandfather of tea growing and processing on the Big Island. From 1999 to 2001, cuttings from the Lyon Arboretum, seedlings from Taiwan and Japan, and more clonal cultivars were introduced. Trials were carried out in different ecoclimates at various elevations on Hawaii Island—at Waiakea, 183 metres (600 feet); Mealani, 853 metres (2,799 feet); and Volcano, 1,219 metres (3,999 feet)—and a processing unit was set up at Mealani Research Station in 2004. Hawaii's wide-ranging altitudes, rainfall, and tropical conditions make it ideal for tea cultivation. The weather is a benevolent mix of abundant sunshine, cool breezes from the Pacific Ocean, and trade winds that bring mild temperatures and plentiful rainfall. In many areas, mineral-rich volcanic ash has been covered over time with layers of humus, creating a soil that tea plants love.

BIG ISLAND TEA | *Glenwood, Hawaii Island*

Eliah Halpenny and Cam Muir nurture 6,000 tea plants on the northeastern slopes of Mauna Loa Volcano and maintain mixed varietals to manage harvesting at different periods throughout the season. To balance the ecosystem here, oil palms grow alongside koa, maile, kukui, ohia lehua, and hapu'u trees, and rainwater catchment provides water for irrigation. The farm uses no machinery, no pesticides, and no herbicides, and the teas are all hand-picked and hand-rolled. Eliah and Cam have created a farm co-operative with five other local tea growers, and Eliah processes the leaf they grow. The co-op works with fair-trade relationships that benefit the community, help the development of new farmers, and enable their economic success. The company's teas include a complex black tea that has bright citrus flavour with suggestions of apples, dried cherry, butter, and caramel, and a Chinese-style green tea that carries complex hints of flowers, fresh-cut grass, and citrus fruits.

CLOUDWATER FARM | *Near Kilauea, Kauai Island*

In 2002, after learning about tea cultivation and processing in Japan, Michelle Rose bought a plot of land at the edge of a nature reserve on a jungle-covered ridge below Mount Namahana on Kauai Island. She planted tea amongst clumps of bamboo and native lau hala screw pines whose leaves will eventually be woven into tea mats and packaging for the hand-crafted teas. The farm covers 20 acres, and the teas include a full-bodied, smooth, slightly woody Twisted Black; a Golden Assamic Black with apricot notes; a Wok Roasted Green with grassy, vegetal notes; a delicate, sweet Wai Mani white that tastes of sweet peas, honey, and bamboo shoots; and a honeyed Walking Stick Wulong with hints of ginger, nutmeg, and sweet potato.

HOT SPOT TEA | *Fern Forest, Hawaii Island*

Patrick Woody has been growing tea for 10 years in an ohia forest on the slopes of Kilauea Volcano at an altitude of 762 metres (2,500 feet). His 4,000 bushes are a mix of Yabukita, Benikaori, Yutaka Midori, Bohea, Darjeeling, and Kilinoensis (a new strain of tea resulting from a breeding program at Big Island Tea involving several Asian varietals and cultivars). Growing in pockets of land where existing soil has been built up with mulch and natural fertiliser, they thrive amongst mixed ornamentals and newly planted native trees that add diversity to the forest canopy. Hot Spot's white tea has notes of fragrant puakinikini and gardenia with just the slightest suggestion of roasted marshmallow.

JOHNNY'S GARDEN | *Hakalau, Hawaii Island*

John Cross's tea garden, established in 1993 on the lower slopes of Mauna Kea Volcano on the Hāmākua Coast, is the oldest in Hawaii. Previously in charge of sugarcane production, Cross was tasked in the 1980s with finding suitable replacement crops and planted two different tea varietals. His crop is harvested and processed as Makai ("facing the ocean") black tea by Tea Hawaii, and the name captures the image of vibrant green bushes set against a backdrop of the shimmering azure waters of the

Pacific. The tea is clean, smooth, and refined with delicate notes of roasted barley, sweet potatoes, caramel, malt, and rice syrup.

HAWAII MEDICINAL TEA & HERB CO-OP | *Volcano, Hawaii Island*

Jason McDonald set up this consumer cooperative at the 30-acre Akatsuka Orchid Farm in Volcano Village to offer a full range of tea services to tea growers with a minimum of 1 acre of plants. McDonald (who established The Great Mississippi Tea Company in 2013 and now spends time both there and in Hawaii) planted a trial quarter acre of tea here in 2016 and has enough tea bushes in greenhouses for another 10 acres.

TOP: Brewing one of Big Island Tea Company's teas at Glenwood, Hawaii Island. Photograph courtesy of Cam Muir ABOVE: Tea Hawaii & Company tea bushes growing beneath rainforest trees at Eva Lee and Chiu Leong's farm in Volcano, Hawaii Island. Photograph courtesy of Eva Lee, *TeaHawaii.com*

HAWAI'I RAINFOREST TEA | *Kurtistown, Hawaii Island*

Bob Jacobson's 9-acre tea farm lies at an altitude of about 305 metres (1,001 feet) in Kurtistown, on the south-eastern tip of Hawaii Island. It was established in 2008 with cuttings from the Hawaii College of Tropical Agriculture and received organic certification in 2013. The plants grow in native rainforest, alongside orchids and ferns, beneath the shade of ohia lehua trees. Jacobson has to protect the garden from huge wild pigs that roam the area and have, in the past, torn up thousands of his plants. Each year, he makes just a few kilos of white tea from shoots of one bud and two leaves harvested from a mix of cultivars that includes Yutaka Midori, Bohea, Benikaori, and Yabukita.

MAUNA KEA TEA FARM | *Honokaa, Hawaii Island*

Kimberly and Takahiro Ino grow tea using natural and organic methods on the high slopes of their Mauna Kea tea farm. They pluck mainly by hand and machine, and make approximately 454 kilos (1,000 pounds) of both pure pan-fired and blended green teas each year. Production is certified organic and relies on techniques developed through study of the Hawaii terroir and the preferences of the Western palate. The Inos' green tea is fresh, vegetal, grassy, and floral, and their flavoured blends reflect a dedication to supporting other farms that produce such high-quality crops as ginger, turmeric, and coconut. The teas, harvested through the year, are labelled by quality and season of harvest. They are sold through the Mauna Kea Tea website and local restaurants, natural food stores, and gift shops.

NA LIKO TEA GARDEN | *Kaupakalua, Maui Island*

More than 1,000 tea bushes grow in sweeping curves in a sunny field at Liam Ball's Haiku tea garden where the lush valley enjoys shade from the east and plentiful rainfall through the year. Ball first planted in 2008 and spent five years nurturing the plants and harvesting very small experimental quantities of green leaf. He subsequently acquired more seedlings from nearby Big Island Tea and is constantly expanding the planted area. *Na Liko* means "newly opened leaves," and the teas are floral with a hint of tannin.

ONOMEA TEA COMPANY | *Papaikou, Hawaii Island*

Since 2003, Rob Nunally and Mike Longo have been growing certified organic tea on a ridge that extends into the ocean along the Hamakua Coast overlooking Onomea Bay. Their first 40 plants went into the ground amongst citrus trees and banana palms and thrived in well-drained acid soil and abundant rainfall. The garden is now home to 3,000 plants. The Onomea black tea has a toffee, chocolate, and malt character; the green tea brews a light liquor with hints of walnut and sweet corn with delicious umami notes; the oolong is sweet, complex, floral, and creamy; and the aged, fermented, and baked KoKo Ki has notes of chocolate, malt, caramel, and dried fruit.

SECOND ALARM FARM | *Volcano, Hawaii Island*

Jim Chestnut and Edna Arawaka have a 3-acre farm at an altitude of 868 metres (2,848 feet) in Volcano Village where the tea bushes love the volcanic soil, generous rainfall, and humid forest climate. The plants are grown organically amongst coffee bushes and orchids. The teas are handpicked, hand-processed, and sold through local shops. In 2015, the farm's Orchid Isle Oolong won third place in the Non Commercial Division of the first TOTUS (Tea of the United States) awards. Visitors can stay in the farm's small guesthouse.

Fresh leaves carefully gathered by Eva Lee of Tea Hawaii & Company, Volcano, Hawaii Island. Photograph courtesy of Eva Lee, *TeaHawaii.com*

TEA HAWAII & COMPANY | *Volcano, Hawaii Island*

Eva Lee and Chiu Leong grow tea on the summit of Kilauea Volcano. They acquired their first plants in 2001 and planted them along the contours of their forest garden under the shade of native ohia trees and hapu'u ferns. Lee worked closely with Francis Zee of the U.S. Pacific Basin Agricultural Research Center and has been a driving force in the development of tea cultivation in Hawaii. She established the Hawaii Tea Society and instigated and organises America's domestic tea production competition TOTUS (Tea of the United States) awards. Lee and Leong propagate and grow new plants as well as advise and teach others how to grow and process. Working both by hand and with machinery, they process their own green, white, and black teas, and also process leaf from Johnny's Garden and Volcano Winery. Tea Hawaii's Forest White is floral, sweet, and smooth, and the farm's Chinese-style green tea is exotic and clean with a lingering fresh, bright aftertaste.

VOLCANO TEA GARDEN | *Volcano, Hawaii Island*

Mike Riley started growing tea in 1995 and now has 0.25 acres of plants on the windward side of the Big Island's Kilauea Volcano. The bushes, originating from specific cultivars from China, Taiwan, and Japan, thrive at an altitude of 1,097 metres (3,600 feet) on sloping terrain under the shade of native forest trees and tree ferns. Riley produces white, green, and black teas and specialises in hand-processed, flinty, crisp, smooth Mauka ("facing the mountain") Oolong that has mild tropical notes of green papaya and honey. Mike sells his teas through his neighbours Eva Lee and Chiu Leong who live just up the road at Tea Hawaii.

VOLCANO WINERY TEA GARDEN | *Volcano, Hawaii Island*

In 2006, Alex Wood planted tea alongside his vines in trenches that he dug in the lava rock. More than 1,000 bushes now thrive on a flat field on the south-eastern slopes of Mauna Loa Volcano on the south side of the island. The Winery's delicate white teas have citrus and lavender notes; the smooth black tea that is processed by Eva Lee of Tea Hawaii has hints of vanilla, caramel, and truffle. A coarser black grade is used to flavour the Winery's Infusion Tea Wine.

Eva Lee of Tea Hawaii & Company carrying a basket of freshly picked leaves at Johnny's Garden, Hakelau, Hawaii Island. (OPPOSITE PAGE) TOP: Johnny's Garden at Hakelau was the first to grow tea in Hawaii. BOTTOM: Tea grows under a canopy of native trees and ferns in the Tea Hawaii forest garden in Volcano. Photographs courtesy of Eva Lee, *TeaHawaii.com*

Country, State, or Province
Hawaii

Number of Gardens
14 + new grower collectives

Main Districts or Gardens
See text for individual growers.

Area Under Tea
In 2014, between 10 and 20 hectares, with plans to increase the total to several hundred hectares

Average Annual Production (Kilograms)
See text for individual growers.

Terrain
Volcanic mountains and undulating slopes

Altitude
From sea level to 1,219 metres (4,000 feet)

Production Period
All year

Best Time to Visit
Any time, but early June is best

Main Varietals/Cultivars
Different varietals and cultivars: mainly Darjeeling, Bohea, Yabukita, Yutaka Midori, Chin Shin, Benikaori, Kilinoensis

Types of Tea Made
Black, green, white, oolong

Predominant Flavours; Tasting Notes
Various depending on location and altitude (See text for details.)

PACIFIC
OCEAN

Yukon
Territory

Northwest Territories

Nunavut

British
Columbia

Alberta

Manitoba

Saskatchewan

Vancouver
Island

TG Tea Farm

Denman Island
•Vancouver

Westholme
Tea Company

Victoria ★

Sakuma Brothers
Farms

Olympia ★

Washington

Coeur
d'Alene

Coeur d'Thé

Minto Island
Tea Company

Columbia River

★ Salem

Montana

North Dakota

Oregon

Idaho

★ Boise

South Dakota

Wyoming

Nebraska

Golden Feather
Tea

Imperial
Tea Court
Tea Garden

★ Sacramento

Nevada

Utah

Colorado

Kansas

California

Arizona

New Mexico

Texas

🌱 Tea grower

0   50 100   200 Miles

0 50 100 200 Kilometres

BRITISH COLUMBIA

(CANADA)

WESTHOLME TEA COMPANY | *North Cowichan*

In 2003, Victor Vesely and Margit Nellemann bought a farm (previously used for cattle and horses) in the Cowichan Valley on Vancouver Island and started growing herbs, flowers, fruits, and vegetables. With a passion for tea, they also decided to import organic speciality teas from various world origins. They created more than 30 flavoured teas and herbal infusions using the imported teas and home-grown flowers and herbs such as lavender, lemongrass, and calendula. In 2010, they decided to grow their own tea organically, so they obtained Chinese tea seeds from U.S. nurseries and planted out two terraces of new seedlings on the contours of a well-drained, south-facing slope. Despite the severe frost of the harsh winter months and temperatures that fall as low as -15°C (5°F), the young bushes survived uncovered, and a further 400 seedlings were planted in 2014. While the bushes were gaining strength during the first five years, some of the new leaves were processed as matcha, which was used to flavour the chocolate cake served in the farm tearoom. Nellemann and Vesely now have 1,200 tea plants, and the range of teas includes Tree Frog Green, Island Green, Island Green Winter Bloom (blended with tea flowers), Quail's Plume (roasted green), Quail's Nest (roasted twig tea), Maple Quail's Nest (twig tea), and Swallow Tail Oolong. The farm's converted barn provides a venue for tea tastings, tango demonstrations, tea and food pairings, themed tea parties, and performances of world tea ceremonies.

TG TEA FARM | *Denman Island*

Brendan Waye nurtured young sinensis varietals from Hawaii and Kenya seed under glass in Vancouver. Then, in spring 2017, he transplanted 5,000 baby plants to a 6-acre sloping plot on Denman Island, which nestles in a bay halfway down the east coast of Vancouver Island. Waye expects the warm air that currently touches the southern tip of the island to gradually move north because of climate change, and he is optimistic for tea's future here. The island has a unique Mediterranean-like microclimate that supports the cultivation of plants that are more difficult to grow in mainland Canada. Over the next five years, Waye plans to establish 30,000 to 50,000 plants here.

Country, State, or Province
British Columbia

Number of Gardens
2

Main Districts or Gardens
Westholme Tea Company,
North Cowichan

TG Tea Farm,
Denman Island

Area Under Tea
Westholme Tea Company:
Small plot on 4.45-hectare farm

TG Tea Farm:
5,000 plants on 6 acres

Average Annual Production (Kilograms)
Not yet known

Terrain
Westholme Tea Company:
Hillside in fertile glacial valley, very suitable for agriculture

TG Tea Farm: Sheltered sloping plot in a bay between Vancouver Island and Texada Island, off the coast of mainland Vancouver

Altitude
Westholme Tea Company:
60 metres (197 feet)

TG Tea Farm:
58 metres (191 feet)

Production Period
Westholme Tea Company: May to October or November

TG Tea Farm:
May to late September

Best Time to Visit
March to May;
September to November

Main Varietals/ Cultivars
Westholme Tea Company: Sochi (Russia)

TG Tea Farm: Chinese varietals from Darjeeling

Types of Tea Made
Westholme Tea Company: Steamed and panned greens, hojicha, lightly oxidized oolong, maple-smoked highly oxidized whole leaf, broken leaf and ground oolong for cooking and garnish

TG Tea Farm:
Plans for green teas

Predominant Flavours; Tasting Notes
Westholme Tea Company:
GREEN: evocative of summer rain on hay
ROASTED HOJICHA: notes of cacao
OOLONG: floral with hints of muscatel

TG Tea Farm:
Not yet known

Westholme Tea Company, North Cowichan, Vancouver Island, where the tea bushes have been thriving, despite harsh winter temperatures, since 2010. Photographs courtesy of Victor Vesely, Westholme Tea Farm

CALIFORNIA

(USA)

IMPERIAL TEA COURT TEA GARDEN | *Yolo County*

Roy Fong chose the location for his 23-acre plot in California's Bay Area because the state is one of America's most prolific camellia-growing regions. But the hot, dry climate presents a serious challenge, and irrigation, water filtration, and solar netting for shade are essential here. The first 20 plants, grown hydroponically from leaf cuttings, were transplanted into the ground in spring 2016 to see how they fared against rainstorms and wind. More cuttings have since been planted as Fong finds answers to the difficulties the weather causes. He has a tea-growing partner in Mexico and also plans a Chinese-style teahouse and school in California where soil management, hydroponic systems, tea plant hybridization, and production of different types of tea can be taught.

GOLDEN FEATHER TEA | *Concow*

Mike Fritts started growing tea in 2010 and now has more than 600 tea plants of unknown origin on half an acre at his Northern California farm in Concow, which lies in a region not unlike the high tea regions of Taiwan. He makes a Golden Oolong that won second place in the 2015 TOTUS (Tea of the United States) awards. Fritts is also consultant on growing *Camellia sinensis* in California to the Global Tea Initiative for the Study of Tea Culture and Science run by the University of California–Davis. And he is a member of Veteran Farmers, a program that offers jobs to military veterans.

Country, State, or Province
California

Number of Gardens 2

Main Districts or Gardens
Imperial Tea Court Tea Garden,
Yolo County

Golden Feather Tea, Concow

Area Under Tea
Imperial Tea Court Tea Garden:
9.3 hectares

Golden Feather Tea: 600 plants
on half an acre

Average Annual Production (Kilograms)
Not yet known

Terrain
Imperial Tea Court Tea Garden:
Open hilly land

Golden Feather Tea:
Hilly, forested land
around Concow Reservoir

Altitude
Imperial Tea Court Tea Garden:
Approximately
30.5 metres (100 feet)

Golden Feather Tea:
611 metres (2,005 feet)

Production Period
Imperial Tea Court Tea Garden:
Spring to autumn

Golden Feather Tea:
Spring to autumn

Best Time to Visit
March to November

Main Varietals/Cultivars
Imperial Tea Court Tea Garden:
Mixed varietals and hybrids

Golden Feather Tea:
Not known

Types of Tea Made
Not yet known

Predominant Flavours; Tasting Notes
Not yet known

IDAHO

(USA)

COEUR D'THÉ | *Coeur d'Alene*

After successfully growing tea in Texas since 2008, Josephie Dean Jackson planted tea seedlings from Nepal, Sochi, and Georgia (the country, not the state), on Fernan Hill, Coeur d'Alene, in 2015. The first plantings were established amongst fruit and nut trees, while new seedlings grow under a canopy of thinned-out forest. The bushes best survive the extremely heavy snow here when densely planted, and they are protected from deer by a 2.1-metre (7-foot) perimeter fence. They benefit from the high iron content of the local water, good drainage, gentle and evenly distributed rainfall, frequent fogs, and long, gently sunny summer days. The first made teas are expected in 2022 as the growth in the cool temperatures here is slow.

Hoarfrost on seedlings from Nepal at Coeur d'Thé in Coeur d'Alene where temperatures can drop to -26°C (-15°F) in the middle of winter.
Photograph courtesy of Josephie Dean Jackson

Country, State, or Province
Idaho

Number of Gardens
1

Main Districts or Gardens
Coeur d'Thé, Fernan Hill, Coeur d'Alene

Area Under Tea
3 acres

Average Annual Production (Kilograms)
Not yet known

Terrain
Deep alluvial soil in glacial area

Altitude
667 metres (2,188 feet)

Production Period
Early May to late July, and late August to late September

Best Time to Visit
May to August

Main Varietals/ Cultivars
Sinensis varietals from Nepal and Sochi (Russia), and sinensis "rosea" varietal from Camellia Forest, North Carolina

Types of Tea Made
Not yet known

Predominant Flavours; Tasting Notes
Trial plucking gave a fragrant, buttery tea

OREGON

(USA)

MINTO ISLAND TEA COMPANY | *Willamette Valley, Salem*

Tea cuttings were introduced to Oregon from South Carolina in the 1800s, but the project was abandoned. The plot, then called Minto Tea Growers, was developed in 1988 by agriculturalist Rob Miller and agricultural consultant John Vendeland. They planted an experimental half acre with imported seeds and cuttings from Japan, Hawaii, and South Carolina, choosing six varietals for their flavour, aroma, and ability to thrive in local conditions. Since 2008, Miller's daughter Elizabeth and her husband, Chris Jenkins, have been running the organic farm where they produce between 36 and 45 kilos (80 and 100 pounds) of tea each year from 12.5 acres, and in 2016, more than 60,000 young plants were established on several more acres. The small-batch organic teas include blacks, greens, and oolongs, which are sold online and at the Portland State Saturday Market from April to September. The company is strongly committed to sustainably growing quality organic tea and has also started offering tours to interested tea lovers.

Chris Jenkins tending new plants at Minto Island Tea Company where he and his wife, Elizabeth, make organic black, oolong, and green teas.
Photograph courtesy of Minto Island Tea Company

Country, State, or Province
Oregon

Number of Gardens 1

Main Districts or Gardens
Minto Island Growers,
Willamette Valley,
south of Salem City

Area Under Tea
0.2 hectare, with plans
for several more hectares
to be developed in 2016

**Average Annual
Production (Kilograms)**
36 to 45

Terrain
Gentle slopes rising from
the Willamette Valley

Altitude
47 metres (154 feet)

Production Period
April to September

Best Time to Visit
April to October

Main Varietals/Cultivars
Seeds and cuttings from
Japan, Hawaii, and South
Carolina

Types of Tea Made
Whole-leaf black, green,
oolong

**Predominant Flavours;
Tasting Notes**
BLACK: brisk, roasty, nutty,
with hints of pine, citrus
fruits, and cinnamon
OOLONG: nutty and sweet
GREEN: light, vegetal, sweet

WASHINGTON

(USA)

SAKUMA BROTHERS FARMS | *Burlington*

Richard and Steve Sakuma started growing tea in the early 21st century at their berry farm in Skagit Valley. They planted 5 acres with varietals they hoped would withstand chilly winter temperatures, but they lost 15,000 seedlings to harsh weather, pests, and fungus. The first harvest was gathered in 2007, and new plants have been propagated from the few remaining varietals. In 2017, the project was on hold because of the pressure of the work from berry production, but it is hoped that other family members will take over the tea farm and be able to start producing tea again in 2018.

The Sakuma brothers' field of tea at their berry farm in Burlington.
Photograph courtesy of Richard Sakuma

Country, State, or Province
Washington

Number of Gardens 1

Main Districts or Gardens
Sakuma Brothers Farms,
Burlington

Area Under Tea
0.6 hectare

Average Annual Production (Kilograms)
113.3

Terrain
Flat, alluvial river bottom

Altitude
9 metres (30 feet)

Production Period
Mid-June to mid-September

Best Time to Visit
May to September

Main Varietals/Vultivars
6 different hardy varietals and cultivars

Types of Tea Made
Green, white, oolong

Predominant Flavours; Tasting Notes
WHITE: light, creamy with berry sweetness and spicy aftertaste
OOLONG: sweet, syrupy
GREEN: complex, nutty, spicy, and citrus with hints of dried cherries, brown sugar, raw hulled barley, and brown rice

Los Andes Nature Reserve in Guatemala where
tea was first planted on Atitlán Volcano in 1956.

Photograph by Kenneth Hazard

CHAPTER 3

CENTRAL
and
SOUTH AMERICA

THE BEST-KNOWN TEA-GROWING COUNTRY
OF SOUTH AMERICA IS ARGENTINA, WHERE
THE TEA ESTATES DATE BACK TO THE 1920S.

Local priest Tijon Hnatiuk brought Georgian tea seeds from Ukraine and planted them on 4.5 hectares of land in Misiones Province in Argentina. When tea trials were carried out in a number of locations in the north of Argentina during the 1930s, only Misiones and Corrientes proved suitable. But even in those two successful areas, pioneer growers were discouraged by low prices and because their homegrown tea was not as good as imported varieties. But, during the financial crisis of the 1950s, the government banned all imports of tea, and this spurred local farmers to increase production and to improve the quality of what was by now a popular beverage.

European and Japanese settlers to Brazil in the 19th century brought their tea cultures with them. This gave the beverage an important place in the daily lives of some families, although coffee and yerba mate have always been more popular. Tea was first grown in Brazil in 1812. The country was an important producer until the early 21st century when an increase in wages made cultivation unviable and farmers turned to more profitable crops. Four growers produce green tea today. As in Argentina, there is a growing interest in speciality tea, particularly among young consumers, and new retail businesses and tearooms are opening in the more southerly regions where cold weather makes hot tea a welcome beverage.

Guatemala's first tea estate dates back more than 120 years to the days when German immigrants grew both coffee and tea there. Peru's tea history started in 1918, but other South American countries started growing tea much more recently. Bolivia established tea gardens in the late 1930s; the only tea estate in Colombia dates back to 1946; Ecuador started growing tea in 1964; and Chile first grew tea in the 1990s.

Agrícola Himalaya, Colombia. BOTTOM, FROM LEFT: Agrícola Himalaya tea factory; a crimson-rumped toucanet (*Aulacorhynchus haematopygus*) found in Colombia's humid forests and amongst the tea bushes; plucked leaves ready to go to the factory. Photographs courtesy of Bitaco Tea Estate

Guatemala

Gulf of Mexico

MEXICO

Caribbean Sea

★Guatemala City

CENTRAL AMERICA

NORTH ATLANTIC OCEAN

Tropic of Cancer

Equator

Galápagos Islands

★Bogotá

Colombia

Lake Maracaibo

LLANOS

Orinoco River

SOUTH AMERICA

GUIANA HIGHLANDS

Magdalena River

ANDES MOUNTAINS

Rio Negro

Amazon (Solimões) River

Amazon River

★Quito

Ecuador

SANGAY VOLCANO

Marañón River

Peru

AMAZON BASIN

Madeira River

Tapajós River

Xingu River

Tocantins River

Araguaia River

MATO GROSSO PLATEAU

BRAZILIAN HIGHLANDS

San Francisco River

Purus River

Parus River

ANDES MOUNTAINS

★Lima

Lake Titicaca

★La Paz

Bolivia

Mamoré River

★Brasilia

Brazil

SOUTH PACIFIC OCEAN

Lake Poopó

GRAN CHACO

Serra do Mar

Tropic of Capricorn

Iguazu Falls

Uruguay River

Paraguay River

Paraná River

Chile

ANDES MOUNTAINS

Santiago★

Argentina

Buenos Aires★

PAMPAS

Colorado River

SOUTH ATLANTIC OCEAN

PATAGONIA

Santa Cruz River

Tea grower

Multiple growers

Volcano

N

W

E

S

0   250   500   1,000 Miles

0   500   1,000 Kilometres

Los Andes tea farm and nature reserve set against the backdrop of Atitlán Volcano, Guatemala. Photograph by ANACAFE

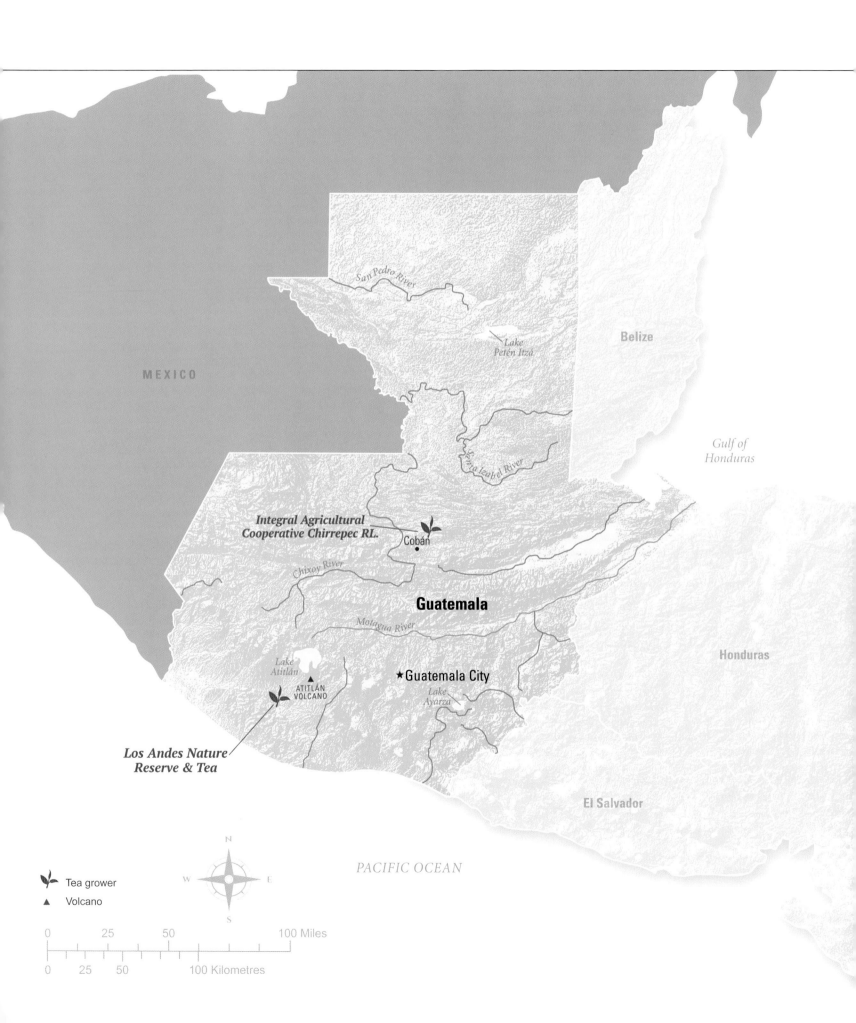

MEXICO

San Pedro River

Lake Petén Itzá

Belize

Gulf of Honduras

Izabel River

Integral Agricultural Cooperative Chirrepec RL.
Cobán

Chixoy River

Guatemala

Motagua River

Honduras

Lake Atitlán
▲ ATITLÁN VOLCANO

★Guatemala City

Lake Ayarza

Los Andes Nature Reserve & Tea

El Salvador

PACIFIC OCEAN

🌱 Tea grower

▲ Volcano

0	25	50	100 Miles

0	25	50	100 Kilometres

GUATEMALA

In the 1880s and 1890s, a number of Germans settled around the city of Cobán and established coffee plantations in the surrounding Central Highlands. Some realised that the region's humid tropical climate, plentiful rainfall, and cool high elevations were also ideal for tea. They established a tea plantation called Finca Chirrepec, built a tea factory, and commercialised the tea. During World War II, the Germans' property was taken into government hands, but the bushes were left to grow wild and were quickly overgrown by dense jungle. In the mid-1950s, a British couple, Mark Oliver and his wife, Hellen, planted tea at their Los Andes Estate on the southern slopes of Atitlán Volcano, part of Guatemala's Volcanic Ring of Fire, in the south of the country, overlooking the Pacific Ocean. However, regional tea consumption in this coffee-consuming country has not increased over the years, and producers have always depended heavily on foreign markets. Both of Guatemala's tea estates grow some of their tea organically, and in the late 1990s, they had to reduce output because of high costs of production, a drop in organic tea prices, and a world oversupply of cheap tea from places such as Indonesia, Africa, and India. But since 2006, the value of Guatemalan tea has increased in the United States, and so production and exports may rise once again.

Tea, coffee, rubber, quinine, avocados, and macadamia nuts grow happily together on Atitlán Volcano. Photograph by Kenneth Hazard

In 1956 and 1957, Mark Oliver, then the English owner of the Los Andes Nature Reserve, planted tea seeds from India and Africa here and built a factory to manufacture black tea. In 1985, the Hazard family acquired the estate, and they now grow rubber, quinine, organic coffee, avocados, and macadamia nuts, as well as tea. Of the 630 hectares, 202 are cultivated, 23 are planted with tea, and 400 (65 percent) are virgin cloud forest where brightly coloured birds, including the quetzal, Guatemala's national bird, fly amongst the tall trees. The Hazards' priority is to create a harmonious and sustainable relationship between agricultural production, human development, and environmental conservation. Fifty families live on the reserve, and the Hazards provide health care, a preschool facility, a primary school, and a secondary school with a library. Inside the Los Andes factory, Rotorvane machines process fresh leaf from the farm's own bushes and from three small neighbouring farms. Most of the organic teas are sold into the Central American market, and approximately 15 percent is shipped to the United Kingdom and the United States.

INTEGRAL AGRICULTURAL COOPERATIVE CHIRREPEC RL | *Cobán*

In 1967, with the help of the government, a group of Mayan families from the Chirrepec community formed a cooperative of 83 settlers to grow tea on the mountain slopes near the Mayan village of San Juan Chamelco, close to the city of Cobán. *Chirrepec* means "beside a cave," and the local Mayan people tell of the rituals that were performed in a nearby cave during the days of their ancestors and that still take place today. The tea-making skills of the farmers were handed down from earlier generations who worked here for the original German settlers, and more tea bushes have been propagated from the original 19th-century plants. Today, 300 families are members of the Chirrepec Cooperative Tea Garden. They work together to ensure the smooth running of this agricultural enterprise, where the tea grows alongside pine trees, vegetables, spices, and various fruits. The work of the individual farmers is technically supervised by the board. Both men and women pluck the fresh leaf and deliver it to the Chirrepec factory, where Taiwanese machinery is used to produce an organic black tea. Some of the teas are sold in local supermarkets under the brand name Chirrepec Maya Organic Plantation Tea, and approximately 91 kilos (201 pounds) are exported each week to Italy and the United States. There are plans to extend the tea area and to export up to 20,000 kilos (44,092 pounds) per year. The cooperative recently created a small retail shop, museum, and café at the garden and offers guided ecotours of the estate to explain the planting, nurturing, harvesting, processing, and marketing of the Chirrepec tea.

Country, State, or Province
Guatemala

Number of Gardens 2

Main Districts or Gardens
Los Andes: Atitlán Volcano

Chirrepec Cooperative:
Tea Garden, Cobán

Area Under Tea
Los Andes: 23 hectares

Chirrepec Cooperative:
37 hectares

Average Annual Production (Kilograms)
Los Andes: 81,646.65, of which 41,730.5 are certified organic

Chirrepec Cooperative: 90,000

Terrain
Los Andes: Richly fertile, well-drained volcanic soil of Atitlán Volcano

Chirrepec Cooperative: Steep mountain slopes around the city of Cobán

Altitude
Los Andes: 762 to 1829 metres (2,500 to 6,000 feet)

Chirrepec Cooperative: 1,310 metres (4,300 feet)

Production Period
May to December

Best Time to Visit
November to April

Main Varietals/Cultivars
Los Andes: Assamica and sinensis hybrids from plants originally brought from India and Africa

Chirrepec Cooperative: Not known

Types of Tea Made
Los Andes: Black

Chirrepec Cooperative: Black

Predominant Flavours; Tasting Notes
Los Andes:
BLACK: full-bodied, strong, smooth with malty notes and light astringency

Chirrepec Cooperative:
BLACK: medium-bodied, smooth

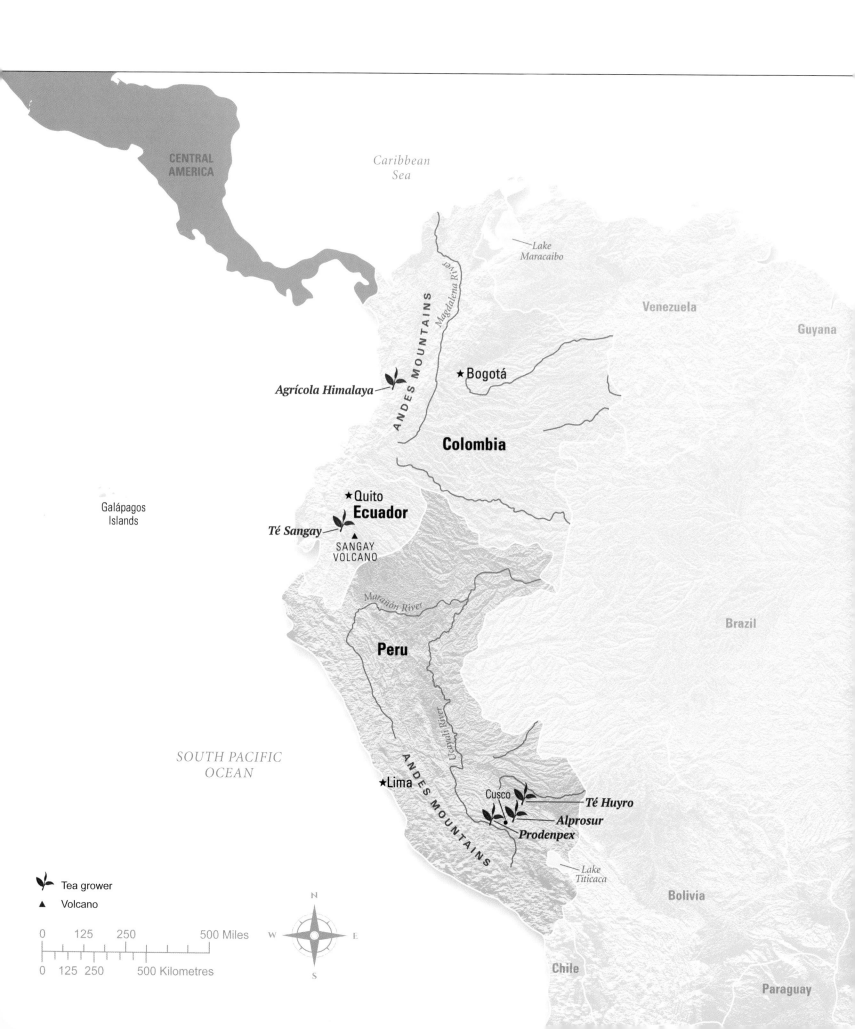

CENTRAL
AMERICA

*Caribbean
Sea*

ANDES MOUNTAINS

Magdalena River

*Lake
Maracaibo*

Venezuela

Guyana

★Bogotá

Agrícola Himalaya

Colombia

★Quito
Ecuador

Té Sangay

▲
SANGAY
VOLCANO

Galápagos
Islands

Marañón River

Peru

Ucayali River

Brazil

SOUTH PACIFIC
OCEAN

ANDES MOUNTAINS

★Lima

Cusco

Té Huyro

Alprosur

Prodenpex

*Lake
Titicaca*

Bolivia

Chile

Paraguay

Tea grower

▲ Volcano

0   125   250   500 Miles

W ⊹ E
N
S

0   125 250   500 Kilometres

COLOMBIA

AGRÍCOLA HIMALAYA | *Bitaco*

Colombia has one tea garden, high up in the western hills of the Colombian Andes, near the small town of Bitaco, and Agrícola Himalaya's UTZ-certified farm is part of the Chocó biogeographical area. The first tea seeds were introduced to Colombia from Brazil in the late 1800s but did not survive. In 1946, in a program with the Ministry of Agriculture to find suitable locations for tea, Joaquín Llano planted Ceylon tea seeds (from a farm near Bogotá where bushes from the 1800s grew wild) at his farm, La Sofía, in Bitaco. When the tea thrived, the ministry sent 900 additional plants, and in 1954, the first handcrafted tea was sold as Té la Sofía. In the 1960s, Joaquin's son, Alberto, carried out further trials and established a new garden, Hacienda Himalaya, next to his father's farm. He travelled to Peru to learn about tea production, imported machinery from the United Kingdom, Ecuador, and Argentina, and the first Té Hindú teas were produced. In the late 1970s, political conflict disrupted the country, the hacienda workers went on strike from 1978 to 1982, and the farm went bankrupt and closed down. In 1984, Alberto's sons rehabilitated the garden, introduced rolling machines and other equipment from India, increased productivity, and also started cultivating herbs such as mint and chamomile.

The tea shoots are hand-plucked, and until 2015, the leaf was processed as 82,000 kilos (180,779 pounds) of CTC black tea and 37,000 kilos (81,571 pounds) of CTC green. The factory, which employs 200 people, has been transformed to manufacture orthodox black and green teas, which are packed under the Bitaco brand and sold locally, in other parts of Latin America, the United Kingdom, Germany, France, the United States, and Canada. The company also sponsors the Agricultural Himalaya Foundation, which supports kindergartens, rural education, music education, theatre, and tae kwon do groups for local children. Director María Carlota de Llano ensures that the company works for the protection of the environment and supports local culture, business, and the progress of the community.

photographs on pages 94 and 95

Country, State, or Province
Colombia

Number of Gardens
1

Main Districts or Gardens
Agrícola Himalaya, Bitaco, Valle del Cauca Department

Area Under Tea
51 hectares

Average Annual Production (Kilograms)
63,503

Terrain
Hilly slopes in the Andes

Altitude
1,800 and 2,050 metres (5,906 and 6,726 feet)

Production Period
All year

Best Time to Visit
All year, but for the dryer season, December to March

Main Varietals/Cultivars
Mostly Cambodian, plus assamica varietals from Ceylon, and Chinese varietals

Types of Tea Made
Orthodox black, green, and flavoured black and green teas sold as Bitaco brand; teabag products sold as Té Hindú brand

Predominant Flavours; Tasting Notes
BLACK: mild, sweet, woodsy
GREEN: delicate, clean, smooth

ECUADOR

TÉ SANGAY | *Morona Santiago Province*

There is just one tea estate in Ecuador, planted in 1960 by Swiss agriculturalist Leo Hamburger. He acquired from the government 5,000 hectares of land in Morona Santiago Province and propagated tea seeds that he had collected in Africa. In 1962, British tea planter Mitchell Cotts bought 2,000 hectares of Hamburger's land and founded Compañía Ecuatoriana del Té C.A. (CETCA), established the Sangay Tea Estate, and shipped bulk black tea to London. In 1975, the company began selling black tea into the domestic market under the brand name Hornimans. In 1984, CETCA and Té Sangay were acquired by the British Inchcape Group, which sold them in 2007 to Fernando Castillo. In 2010, the company started exporting Hornimans black teas to the United States, Puerto Rico, Germany, Holland, and Malaysia. Castillo died in 2012, and his son Fernando Castillo Cruz now manages the company.

Named after the snowcapped Sangay Volcano 80 kilometres (50 miles) away, the 946-hectare estate sits up at 914 metres (2,999 feet) amongst the volcanic peaks of the Andes. Because of its location on the equator, the assamica bushes flush all year on 530 hectares and are plucked using mechanical harvesters powered by locally produced palm oil. Until the 1990s, the leaf was transported to the factory in trolleys running along a cable, but today, it travels by road. Inside the factory, the leaf is turned into both CTC and orthodox black teas, some of which are sold locally as Sangay, Hornimans, or El Estado del Té brands. Total production is 700,000 kilos (1.54 million pounds) of tea and herbs each year, the majority of which is exported to other South American countries, the United States, Europe, and Malaysia.

The estate workers, originally from remote villages high in the Andes, live in nearby Palora, a small town that developed as a result of Té Sangay. The Sangay estate is committed to sustainable farming, maintains 339 hectares of primary forest, has its own hydroelectric plant, is Rainforest Alliance Certified, and offers training in farming practices. Since reducing its use of agrochemicals, tea yields have increased fivefold over the past 15 years, and many native birds and animals have returned to the tea garden.

Country, State, or Province
Ecuador

Number of Gardens
1

Main Districts or Gardens
Té Sangay, Morona Santiago Province

Area Under Tea
946 hectares

Average Annual Production (Kilograms)
700,000

Terrain
Volcanic high mountain slopes in the Andes

Altitude
914 metres (3,000 feet)

Production Period
All year

Best Time to Visit
June to September

Main Varietals/ Cultivars
Assamicas from African seeds

Types of Tea Made
CTC and orthodox black tea

Predominant Flavours; Tasting Notes
BLACK: rounded and strong with a lightly bitter dark chocolate note

TOP: Sangay Volcano, after which Sangay Tea Estate is named. BOTTOM LEFT: Neatly harvested rows of bushes at Té Sangay. BOTTOM RIGHT: Withering troughs in the Té Sangay factory. Photographs courtesy of Compañía Ecuatoriana del Té C.A.

PERU

Peru's tea history dates back to 1913 when Dr. Benjamín de la Torre propagated Japanese seeds at his farm in Huyro, La Convención, but the project was abandoned with his death in 1915. In 1928, the government hired Sri Lankan consultants, and in 1928, 16,000 mixed varietals were planted in Huanuco, Chinchao, and Cayumba in central Peru. By 1941, 800,000 bushes were also well established in Huanuco, in the south, and a factory had been built there. The construction of another factory in Huyro followed in 1943. Between 1977, when 2,700 hectares of land were planted with tea, and 1985, a rehabilitation program with the Dutch agency for international cooperation (DGIS) introduced African clones, improved two estates (Jardines de Té and Té-Café del Perú in Tingo María), and built another factory in Amaybamba in Huyro. Peru's internal conflict from 1980 to 2000 ended most tea cultivation in Huanuco (farmers turned instead to other crops, such as oranges and bananas, for the domestic market), and the main tea areas today are in the Cusco region in the south. The original rolling machines, oxidation equipment, and dryers are still in use, but with inefficient agricultural practices, poor plucking standards, and long distances from the fields to the factories, yield and quality are lower than they could be. The best-known packers include Hornimans, Lipton, Volcán, Único, Yanayaco, and Té Huyro. They mostly produce tea bags, but some larger-leaf, coarser tea is sold loose.

Pluckers working in the fields in the Huyro Region. Photograph courtesy of Buenmundo Tea and Coffee Company E.I.R.L.

PRODENPEX | *Cusco*

Prodenpex, established in Cusco in the 1930s, has been manufacturing mainly green tea since 1991 and buys fresh leaf from thousands of smallholders.

ALPROSUR | *Cusco*

Alprosur, also based in Cusco, grows its own tea and buys fresh leaf from smallholders. The green and black teas produced here are packed into tea bags.

TÉ HUYRO | *Cusco*

During agrarian reforms of the 1970s, the tea fields were abandoned, but many smallholders started growing tea on their own land, and the Huyro Amaybamba factory was handed over to the Central Cooperative Té Huyro, a group of seven outgrower cooperatives. The factory, which uses Rotorvane technology to process the tea, is the biggest in the country.

BUENMUNDO TEA & COFFEE COMPANY E.I.R.L | *Lima*

This company's owner, Thomas Johansson, has been working with a small group of farmers in the Huyro area to help them improve the quality of their tea. They pluck only two leaves and a bud instead of three or four leaves and then process the leaf more carefully, using old equipment from abandoned factories. The first experimental batches of black tea were of good quality, sweet, smooth, and full-bodied, but the project was difficult to manage because of troubles within the cooperative, lack of suitable machinery, unsuitable plant varietals, resistance from landowners, the remote nature of the tea farms, and unreliable communications. Johansson had hoped to help the farmers reach a quality suitable for the international market and still believes in the potential of Peruvian tea. His future plans include setting up his own tea-growing operation in the Huyro area.

Country, State, or Province Peru

Number of Gardens
3 + smallholder farmers

Main Districts or Gardens
Cusco (*Prodenpex, Alprosur, Té Huyro*)

Area Under Tea
2,500 hectares

Average Annual Production (Kilograms)
1.45 million

Terrain
Rich fertile soil on the gentle slopes in the Watanay River Valley

Altitude
1,800 to 1,853 metres (5,905 to 6,079 feet)

Production Period
November to May

Best Time to Visit
All year; for dry weather, May to October

Main Varietals/Cultivars
Japanese cultivars, other mixed varietals and hybrids

Types of Tea Made
Rotorvane orthodox black and green tea, mainly dust grades for teabags

Predominant Flavours; Tasting Notes
BLACK: plain, fibrous, rather bitter, a little sour
GREEN: plain, metallic notes

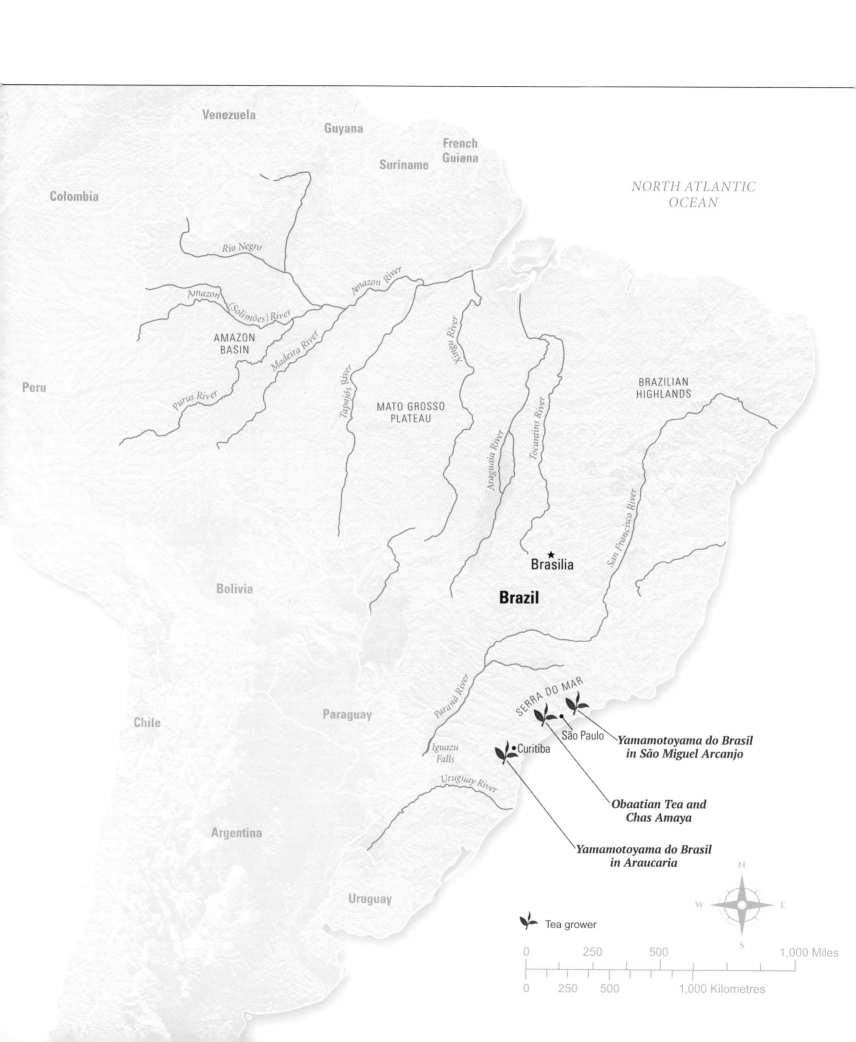

Venezuela

Colombia

Guyana

Suriname

French
Guiana

NORTH ATLANTIC
OCEAN

Rio Negro

*Amazon
(Solimões) River*

Amazon River

AMAZON
BASIN

Madeira River

Peru

Purus River

Tapajós River

Xingu River

MATO GROSSO
PLATEAU

Araguaia River

Tocantins River

BRAZILIAN
HIGHLANDS

San Francisco River

★ Brasilia

Brazil

Bolivia

Paraguay

Paraná River

SERRA DO MAR

São Paulo

*Yamamotoyama do Brasil
in São Miguel Arcanjo*

Chile

•Curitiba

*Obaatian Tea and
Chas Amaya*

*Iguazu
Falls*

Uruguay River

*Yamamotoyama do Brasil
in Araucaria*

Argentina

Tea grower

Uruguay

N

W   E

S

0   250   500   1,000 Miles

0   250   500   1,000 Kilometres

BRAZIL

The first experiments in tea cultivation took place in Brazil in 1812, four years after Dom Joao VI ordered the establishment of the new botanical gardens in Rio de Janeiro. The regent brought in both Chinese tea seeds and Chinese growers to teach the Brazilians how to grow and manufacture tea, and new gardens were planted out and run using mainly slave labour. When slavery was abolished in Brazil in 1888, the industry collapsed. No more tea was produced until Japanese immigrants settled in Registro in the Brazilian Central Highlands in the 1920s, introduced assamica seeds from Ceylon and India, and revived the country's tea-growing activities. One man in particular, Torazo Okamoto, was responsible for importing seeds and factory machinery and for developing successful processing techniques. The peak years for Brazilian tea were the 1970s when the country produced approximately 11 million kilos (24.25 million pounds). But after that, the rather plain character of the black teas, low prices, poor yields, competition from coffee and yerba mate, increased wages, and costs of production brought about a decline, and by 2014, Yamamotoyama do Brasil was the only large company in the country producing tea on an industrial scale. Chas Amaya, Obaatian Tea, and at least one other small company grow tea in or near the town of Registro.

YAMAMOTOYAMA DO BRASIL | *São Miguel Arcanjo* and *Araucaria*

This Japanese tea-growing company, founded in Japan in 1690, started growing tea in Brazil in 1970. In 1960, the family had started looking for locations outside Japan where tea would grow successfully and found that Brazil's state of São Paulo, with the right soil, plenty of rain, and a tropical climate, provided suitable conditions. Today, the company has two estates in mountainous coastal regions—one at São Miguel Arcanjo, São Paulo, and another at Araucaria, Paraná, where the teas are mechanically harvested and processed as green sencha teas, using Japanese technology and machinery. Some of the teas are exported to Japan and the United States.; early spring shincha, sencha, bancha, genmaicha (blended with popped rice), and white teas are sold into the Brazilian domestic market.

CHAS AMAYA | *Registro*

The Amaya family arrived in Brazil from Japan in 1919, settled in Registro near the Atlantic coast in São Paulo, and started farming sugar cane, rice, beans, and coffee, but in the 1930s, switched to tea. The company was first called Irmos Amaya and then changed its name to Helio Amaya Cia. Ltda. Today, the third generation of the family runs the company as Chas Amaya and produces black and green teas for the Brazilian specialty market.

OBAATIAN TEA | *Registro*

In 2014, 87-year-old Elizabete Ume Shimada and her daughter Teresinha Eiko established a small tea garden, Shimada Farm, in the Ribeira Valley in the southern part of the state of São Paulo. Shimada had worked in the Registro tea estates since the age of 5, and as she watched the industry collapse in the early years of the 21st century, she decided to establish a small company on 2.5 hectares of land. Her handpicked tea, marketed as Obaatian Tea, is grown at an altitude of 25 metres (82 feet) and processed, using refurbished machinery, to make a high-quality orthodox black tea.

Sweeping fields of tea at Yamamotoyama do Brasil's farm in São Miguel. Photograph courtesy of Yamamotoyama

Country, State, or Province
Brazil

Number of Gardens
4 + smallholders

Main Districts or Gardens
States of São Paulo and Paraná

Yamamotoyama do Brasil
in São Paulo and Paraná

Chas Amaya, Registro,
São Paulo

Obaatian Tea,
Registro, São Paulo

Area Under Tea
Yamamotoyama do Brasil:
200 hectares

Chas Amaya: 50 hectares (Chas
Amaya owns 150 hectares, but
100 are not currently in use.)

Obaatian Tea:
2.5 hectares

**Average Annual
Production (Kilograms)**
Yamamotoyama do Brasil:
7.2 million

Chas Amaya: 70,000 black tea,
10,000 green tea

Obaatian Tea: 240

Terrain
Yamamotoyama do Brasil:
Sweeping, gently
undulating fields

Chas Amaya: Flat fertile land
on the outskirts of the town
of Registro, and close to
Brazil's Atlantic coast

Obaatian Tea: Located in the
centre of the town of Registro;
flat land with fertile soil and
a misty humid climate

Altitude
Yamamotoyama do Brasil:
700 metres (2,296 feet)

Chas Amaya:
Approximately 25 metres
(82 feet)

Obaatian Tea:
Approximately 25 metres
(82 feet)

Production Period
Yamamotoyama do Brasil:
September to April

Chas Amaya:
September to May

Obaatian Tea:
September to May

Best Time to Visit
September to May

**Main Varietals
/Cultivars**
Yamamotoyama do Brasil:
Mainly Japanese cultivars
Yabukita and Yutaka Midori

Chas Amaya:
Original assamicas

Obaatian Tea:
Original assamicas,
cultivar number 259

Types of Tea Made
Yamamotoyama do Brasil:
Japanese-style sencha
and small quantities
of white

Chas Amaya: Black,
First Flush green teas

Obaatian Tea:
Orthodox black tea

**Predominant Flavours;
Tasting Notes**
Yamamotoyama do Brasil:
GREEN: aromatic, subtle,
sweet
WHITE: mild, delicate

Chas Amaya:
SMALL, BROKEN BLACK:
strong, full-bodied, rich
coppery liquor with
light floral notes and
hints of honey
GREEN: herbal aroma and
a toasty character with a
slightly bitter aftertaste

Obaatian Tea:
BLACK: Curly, golden-tipped
leaves give a rich, amber,
sweet, malty liquor with
hints of caramel, chocolate,
almonds, and molasses

Peru

Sarampiuai Canton,
Larecaja Province

★La Paz

Bolivia

Lake Poopó

Mamore River

Brazil

SOUTH PACIFIC
OCEAN

Chile

A N D E S   M O U N T A I N S

Paraguay

Argentina

Misiones
Province

Corrientes
Province

Uruguay

Santiago★

Buenos Aires ★

Salado River

Salus Chile

Colorado River

Negro River

SOUTH ATLANTIC
OCEAN

PATAGONIA

*Santa Cruz
River*

Tea grower

Multiple growers

N
W   E
S

0   250   500   1,000 Miles

0   250   500   1,000 Kilometres

ARGENTINA

Argentina's tea estates are located in Misiones and Corrientes in the north-east corner of the country. Its black teas became popular in Chile in the 1960s, and as production in Argentina increased, hand plucking became too expensive. Manual mechanical harvesters were therefore developed to reduce the cost of production, and in 1973, machine harvesters mounted on tractors were introduced at Las Marias estate in Corrientes. The vast, gently undulating fields are well suited to this fast mass collection of new leaf shoots. But huge tractors cannot perform the fine plucking of hand-pickers, so the quality of the tea is affected. It is not so much the taste but the clarity of the teas that matters to the country's most important customers in the United States. The teas do not become cloudy as they cool after brewing and so are very suitable for the American market, where 85 percent of the tea consumed is cold or iced. Most Argentinians drink yerba mate rather than tea (although more do now drink green and white teas because of their perceived health benefits), so 95 percent of the country's black teas are exported. The United States buys 65 percent of Argentina's annual production, while the rest is sold to Chile, Germany, the Netherlands, the UK, and Poland.

Private companies in both regions grow and process their own tea as well as buy fresh leaf from smallholder farmers. They produce mainly black teas, using Rotorvane, Vertical Sniechowski Tea Processor (VSTP) (developed in Misiones and introduced in 1999), Lawrie Tea Processor (LTP), and a few CTC machines. Almost all the teas are small broken black grades, but some factories now manufacture small quantities of Japanese-style steamed green teas.

Establecimiento Las Marías, tea growers in Corrientes since the 1960s. Photographs courtesy of Establecimiento Las Marías

CORRIENTES PROVINCE

Large-scale cultivation of tea in Corrientes began in the 1950s, and it was during this period that Victor Navajas Centeno extended his yerba mate farm at Las Marias to include tea. Assam varietals were planted, and in the 1960s, the estate started a program of clonal selection and vegetative reproduction to expand the tea area. In this extreme southern part of the country's north-eastern tea zone, the climate is subtropical and humid, with very hot summers and very cold, sometimes freezing, winters. The rich red soil of the flat plains and gently sloping hills is concealed beneath vast, dense fields of tea. From October to May, the harvesting tractors sweep through the bushes every 12 days to collect the fresh shoots and deliver them quickly into the factory for processing. Corrientes accounts for only 5 percent of Argentina's tea production, and Las Marias is one of the largest companies. It sells its teas and herbals into the domestic market under the brand name Taragüi.

MISIONES PROVINCE

The name of this important tea region dates back to the arrival in the 17th century of Jesuit missionaries who worked to convert the local Guaraní people to Christianity. It is today Argentina's largest tea-growing region and, like Corrientes, is an area of subtropical rainforest where the rolling landscape of vast plains of tea and yerba mate is punctuated by jungles and pine forests, canyons, rivers, and waterfalls. A little to the north are the spectacular cataracts of Iguazú Falls on the border with Brazil and Paraguay. As in Corrientes, the weather can be hot and humid in summer but very chilly during the winter months with occasional frosts, and the tea-growing season lasts only from October to April. The most important processing companies in the area are Las Treinta, Casa Fuentes, Don Basilio, and El Vasco, which manufacture mainly small-particle strong black tea for tea bags and iced tea. Don Basilio Tea also produces large-leaf orthodox black and green teas at its 692-acre SRL Estate Campos de Té. It won first place with its Green Loose Leaf and second place with its FBOP black in the Gold Medal Tea Competition at the Annual North American Tea Conference in 2016. Helmuth Otto Kummritz of HM Hebras Misioneras and Kaori Kairiyama of Tea Wind also make orthodox teas. Helmuth makes large-leaf black orthodox, oolong, and large-leaf green teas. Kaori's family makes black, oolong, green, and hojicha teas.

Country, State, or Province
Argentina

Number of Gardens
8,000 smallholder farmers; 60 private estates

Main Districts or Gardens
Corrientes Province and Misiones Province in the north-east of the country

Area Under Tea
45,000 hectares

Average Annual Production (Kilograms)
83 million

Terrain
Corrientes: Undulating hills and plains; red clay soil

Misiones: Irregular plains with canyons, rivers, jungles and forests, iron-rich soil

Altitude
300 to 600 metres
(985 to 1968 feet)

Production Period
Corrientes: October to May
Misiones: October to April

Best Tme to Visit
October to December;
April to June

Main Varietals/Cultivars
Sinensis and assamica and locally developed clones from INTA (National Institute of Agrotechnology)

Corrientes: Mostly assamica and locally produced clones

Misiones: Chinese varietal, locally developed clones from INTA

Types of Tea Made
90% black broken orthodox; 2% broken green; small amounts of large-leaf black and green orthodox teas

Corrientes: VSTP and Rotorvane orthodox broken black

Misiones: Predominantly black Rotorvane; Don Basilio SRL Estate, Campos de Te, makes specialty blacks and greens; Helmuth Kummritz's tea company HM Hebras Misioneras makes orthodox black, green, and dark teas; the Kairiyama family's company, Tea Wind, produces handcrafted black and green teas

Predominant Flavours; Tasting Notes
Corrientes:
BLACK: plain, slightly earthy, but quite strong; a little like Assam CTC teas but without the sweet malty notes; excellent clarity

Misiones:
BLACK: plain, slightly earthy, but quite strong; good colour and excellent clarity

Don Basilio SRL Estate Campos de Te:
ORTHODOX BLACK: neat curled dry leaf, clear bright reddish liquor, quite astringent and a sweetish finish
GREEN: bright amber liquor that is light, sweet, full-bodied, and very floral

BOLIVIA

Tea cultivation began here in the late 1930s with plants brought in by Dutch and German planters. After an agreement in 1976 between the Bolivian and Taiwanese governments, more land was planted, and factories were built at Caranavi, Chimate, and Chapare. But by 1993, the factory at Chimate had closed down because of administrative changes and a lack of finance but was privatised and continued to operate until 2001. In May 2005, with funding from the United States Agency for International Development (USAID), Empresa Boliviana de Tes Especiales SA – Chai Mate SA was established. With more than 200 farmers involved, bushes were rehabilitated, new machinery for making green tea was purchased, farmer field schools were organised, tea nurseries were set up, and organic certification was acquired. The orthodox green and black teas were well received in Europe and the United States, but the project collapsed a few years later.

Farmers in Larecaja Province still grow tea in Sarampiuni Canton on the high slopes of the Yungas, a tropical and subtropical band of forest that runs through central Bolivia and into Peru to the north and Argentina to the south. The leaf is processed and packed by Bolivian tea packers Hansa LTDA, whose main brand is Windsor Tea. The company's organic tea range, which includes green and black tea and a black tea blend mixed with cinnamon and cloves, is sold in Europe and Latin America.

Country, State, or Province
Bolivia

Number of Gardens
Smallholder farmers

Main Districts or Gardens
Larecaja Province, La Paz Department

Area Under Tea
Not yet known

Average Annual Production (Kilograms)
Not yet known

Terrain
Tropical and subtropical forest on high slopes

Altitude
687 metres (2254 feet)

Production Period
November to May

Best Time to Visit
May to October

Main Varietals/ Cultivars
Mostly assamicas

Types of Tea Made
Black and green

Predominant Flavours; Tasting Notes
Not yet known

CHILE

SALUS CHILE | *Cautín Province*

When the Chernobyl nuclear disaster happened in Ukraine in 1986, it had an immediate effect on the German herb company Salus Haus, which until then had been buying a variety of herbal ingredients from Eastern Europe. Since these were now contaminated, owner Otto Greither and his team had to start looking for other locations for the cultivation of their herbs. In 1991, they found a perfect region near the town of Villarrica in the province of Cautín set amongst the volcanic peaks of the Andes in southern Chile. Although the area previously had never been intensively farmed, before establishing the new organic Salus Chile farm, the soil and air were thoroughly tested to check for pollutants such as chemical fertilisers. This part of the Chilean Andes is protected from contamination by the Pacific Ocean to the west, the Antarctic to the south, and the high Andes Mountains to the east, so it was decided that the climate, clean air, good soil, and readily available workforce made it an excellent location. The 600-hectare farm now grows fruit crops, linseed, medicinal plants (such as arnica, yellow gentian, red clover, eucalyptus, and cowslip), and tea.

When Salus decided to grow tea, the plan was to produce a high-quality Japanese-style green tea. So, in 2003, 5,000 seedlings, selected for their ability to withstand temperatures below -10°C, were imported from the United States, quarantined, and eventually planted in Villarrica. More plants have since been grown from seed and by vegetative propagation. A herd of 400 ewes provides the organic fertiliser that feeds the soil, and the company is regulated by European Union, U.S., and Japanese organic programs. The new shoots are harvested both manually and mechanically and transported to the factory, where they are steamed, rolled in orthodox rollers, and dried. Production is limited during these early years of cultivation, but the available tea is packed into tea bags and sold in Chile and abroad under the brand name Salus Flora.

Country, State, or Province
Chile

Number of Gardens
1

Main Districts or Gardens
Salus Chile, Araucanía region, Cautín Province

Area Under Tea
1.5 hectares

Average Annual Production (Kilograms)
7,000 to 8,000

Terrain
Steep hillsides in volcanic mountain region of Chilean Andes

Altitude
349 metres (1,145 feet)

Production Period
November to March

Best Time to Visit
All year

Main Varietals/ Cultivars
Varietals imported from the USA

Types of Tea Made
Green

Predominant Flavours; Tasting Notes
GREEN: fresh and vegetal, similar to a Japanese sencha

Acres of tea fields in Rwanda.
Photograph courtesy of Sorwathe Ltd., Rwanda

CHAPTER 4

AFRICA

THE DEVELOPMENT OF TEA CULTIVATION

IN AFRICA RUNS PARALLEL TO THE HISTORY

OF THE COLONISATION OF THE CONTINENT

BY EUROPEAN POWERS.

TOP: Emrok Tea's Ogirgir Estate in Nandi County, Kenya. Photograph courtesy of Emrok Tea Factory (EP2) Ltd.
ABOVE LEFT: Range of black teas ready for tasting at Rukeri Tea Estate, Rwanda. ABOVE RIGHT: Tea plucker at Rukeri Tea Estate, Rwanda. Photographs courtesy of Sorwathe Ltd., Rwanda

Settlers from Germany, France, Belgium, Holland, and Britain often acquired land in the countries their governments had taken over, and established new estates and farms. The most successful tea-growing areas proved to be in East Africa, and countries such as Kenya, Malawi, Rwanda, Burundi, Tanzania, and Zimbabwe continue to supply vast quantities of black tea to the world market today.

Although tea was first grown in many of these countries at the beginning of the 20th century when tea was still processed by the orthodox manufacturing method, most are now better known for their CTC black teas. With the gradual development of the teabag at the beginning of the 20th century and the invention of the first machines that packed paper teabags in the 1930s, the CTC machine was developed to produce small tea particles specifically for those bags. Because the increasing demand for teabags through the 1950s and '60s meant that larger quantities of tea were required, production in East Africa was expanded, and most factories were equipped with CTC machines to feed the growing teabag industry. A few factories now produce small quantities of orthodox black and other specialty teas, but most continue to manufacture CTC black teas for the teabag market.

Whereas initially it was the large estates in these countries that were cultivated, the smallholder sector has today become much more important, and farmers who grow tea on their own plots of 0.5 to 2 hectares sell their fresh leaf into factories owned by governments, joint ventures, or foreign companies. In Kenya, more than 500,000 smallholders produce approximately 62 percent of the country's tea; Rwanda's 30,000 small-scale farmers produce 65 percent of the country's output; the leaf processed by Burundi's factories is supplied by 300,000 outgrowers; Tanzania has 30,000 tea smallholders; and in Malawi, 12,000 small farms grow tea. But although these independent farmers are crucial to the industry, the low prices paid by the processing factories upon which they have had to rely have often trapped them in poverty. Today, schemes run by tea associations, various non-profit organisations, and ethical certification bodies are changing the way the industry operates and are helping smallholder farmers increase their yields, improve the quality of their leaf, and receive a profit share of factory prices on top of the price paid for the fresh leaf. The investment of money and increased expertise have also helped upgrade facilities and machinery, replace old bushes with new cultivars, improve agricultural practices, and develop essential infrastructure such as roads and reliable power supplies.

Like many other world regions, Africa faces the challenging problem of climate change. Significant shifts in traditional weather patterns have meant that wetter weather in the normally dry period at the beginning of each year has affected East Africa by provoking faster growth of the tea plants and, therefore, higher crop figures in equatorial countries such as Kenya, Rwanda, and Burundi. But in more southerly countries, dryer, warmer weather has had a negative impact on production. These changes have important implications for soil condition, pest infestation, production figures, quality, prices, and earnings.

In 2014, in recognition of the challenges the global tea industry faced, especially Africa, a group of tea organisations launched the Tea 2030 project. These included the Ethical Tea Partnership (ETP); Fairtrade International; Finlays; IDH, the Sustainable Trade Initiative; Rainforest Alliance; S&D Coffee & Tea; Tata Global Beverages; Twinings; Unilever; and Yorkshire Tea. Its launch report stated, "It needs the legitimate co-operation of all parts of the value chain—consumer, retailer, packer, trader, processor, grower, and worker—working together as part of a sustainable value network to create an economically viable industry that delivers healthy and sustainable products."

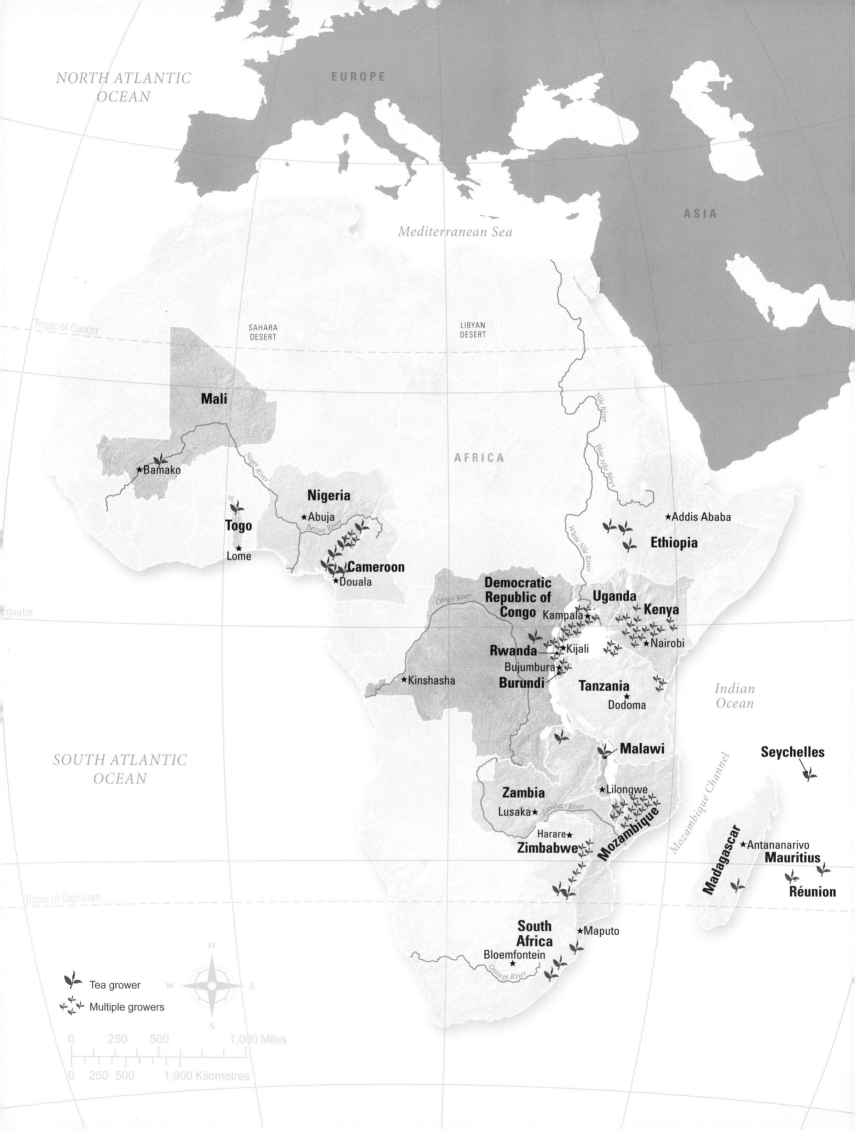

NORTH ATLANTIC
OCEAN

EUROPE

ASIA

Mediterranean Sea

Tropic of Cancer

SAHARA
DESERT

LIBYAN
DESERT

AFRICA

Mali

★Bamako

Nigeria

★Abuja

Togo

★Lome

Cameroon

★Douala

**Democratic
Republic of
Congo**

Kampala★

Uganda

Kenya

★Addis Ababa

Ethiopia

★Kijali

Rwanda

Bujumbura★

Burundi

★Nairobi

Equator

★Kinshasha

Tanzania

★Dodoma

*Indian
Ocean*

Malawi

★Lilongwe

Zambia

Lusaka★

Harare★

Zimbabwe

Mozambique

Seychelles

★Antananarivo

Mauritius

Madagascar

Réunion

Tropic of Capricorn

**South
Africa**

★Maputo

Bloemfontein★

SOUTH ATLANTIC
OCEAN

Mozambique Channel

0   250   500   1,000 Miles

0   250 500   1,000 Kilometres

Rukeri Tea Estate, Rwanda, makes a range of quality orthodox teas as well as CTC black. Photograph courtesy of Sorwathé Ltd., Rwanda

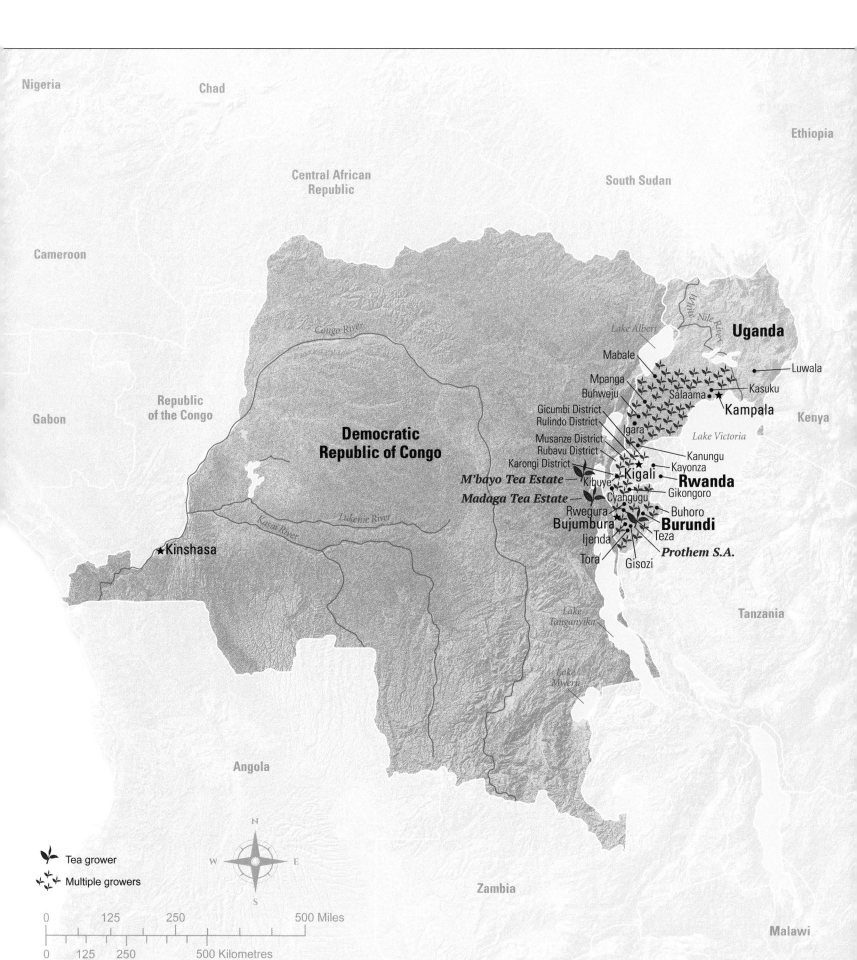

Nigeria

Chad

Central African
Republic

Cameroon

Ethiopia

South Sudan

Uganda

Gabon

Republic
of the Congo

Democratic
Republic of Congo

Congo River

Lake Albert

White Nile River

Mabale

Mpanga
Buhweju

Gicumbi District
Rulindo District

Igara

Musanze District
Rubavu District

Karongi District

M'bayo Tea Estate
Kibuye

Madaga Tea Estate

Cyangugu

Rwegura

Bujumbura

Ijenda

Tora

Gisozi

Salaama

Kanungu

Kigali

Gikongoro

Buhoro

Teza

Prothem S.A.

Kayonza

Rwanda

Burundi

Luwala

Kasuku

Kampala

Lake Victoria

Kenya

Kasai River

Lukenie River

★Kinshasa

Lake
Tanganyika

Lake
Mweru

Tanzania

Angola

Zambia

Malawi

Zimbabwe

🌿 Tea grower

🌿🌿 Multiple growers

N
W   E
S

0   125   250   500 Miles

0   125   250   500 Kilometres

BURUNDI

Tea production in Burundi dates back to 1931 when Gisozi Tea Research Station carried out the first trail plantings. Following the success of that research, Institut de Sciences Agronomiques du Burundi (ISABU) established the first plantation at Teza and a second at Rwegura. In the 1970s and '80s, smallholders began to grow tea, and five factories were built—four were funded by the European Investment Bank and a fifth by the French agency Caisse Centrale de Coopération Economique (CCCE). By the early 1990s, production had reached a total of 6 million kilograms (13.2 million pounds), but the civil war, which started in 1993 and ended in 2005, led to a drop in output to 4.2 million kilograms (9.3 million pounds). Since then, the situation has improved. Production has gradually increased, and tea is Burundi's second most important crop after coffee, accounting for approximately 10 to 15 percent of the country's revenue. Some 300,000 smallholder farmers own 78 percent of the tea land, with individual plots of around 0.8 hectares. The country exports roughly 95 percent of its tea, with 80 percent of that being sold through the Mombasa auctions and 20 percent to private buyers.

Like Rwanda and Kenya, Burundi's proximity to the equator means that the crop can be grown year-round and benefits from a moderate climate, good rainfall, and few pests. Tea is cultivated in six regions: Teza, in the north, established in 1967; Rwegura, also in the north, approximately 20 kilometres (12 miles) from the border with Rwanda, developed in 1972; Tora, in the south-west, set up in 1976; Ijenda, developed in 1984 in the central part of the country close to the capital Bujumbura and the border with Congo; Buhoro (Mabayi), established in 1992 in the north-east, 45 miles from the border with Rwanda and Congo; and Gisozi (also called Mwaro) in the centre of the country. Since 1990, all the factories except Gisozi have been controlled by the Office du Thé Burundais (OTB), which has been in charge of the industry since 1971 and provides seedlings, fertilisers, and technical support. Since 2013, improvements in machinery and engineering support at Rwegura and Ijenda have enhanced tea quality. OTB is planning to distribute new cultivars to farmers to help them improve yield and quality and is planning to extend its own plantations. Manufacture is mainly of CTC black teas that are very useful in breakfast blends.

Long before the civil war, the government recognised that changes were required to strengthen the tea industry, and its policy at that time was to gradually reduce the role of the state and offer the tea factories and state-owned plantations for sale to private companies. This did not take place, but the government now sees privatisation as a priority to improve efficiency and tea quality. Until that happens, Gisozi, established by Prothem S.A. (Promotion de la Théiculture en Province de Mwaro) in 2006 and operational since 2011, is the only private tea company in the country. Prothem established the factory with the goal of fighting poverty in the region by increasing tea production, creating more jobs, assisting farmers financially, improving facilities, raising the price paid to growers for fresh leaf, and protecting the environment through a program of reforestation. The Prothem factory buys leaf from 10,000 local farmers, manufactures 1.8 million kilograms (4 million pounds) of CTC and orthodox black teas each year, and runs tea nurseries and planting programs. In the first quarter of 2015, because of a decline in production in neighbouring Kenya, Burundi's tea export revenues rose by 5 percent compared with the same period in 2014. In 2016, political disruption adversely affected growth of the industry, but improving local conditions are expected to lead to better prices in the future. Meanwhile, Burundi faces all the same challenges that affect other African tea regions—drought, climate change, lack of regular power supplies, poor roads, lack of land on which to expand tea cultivation, deforestation, and soil erosion.

TOP: Mabayi Tea Estate. MIDDLE: An automated CTC black tea production line. BOTTOM: Tora tea factory. Photographs courtesy of Thomas NKeshimana

Country, State, or Province
Burundi

Number of Gardens
300,000 smallholders

Main Districts or Gardens
Teza, Rwegura, Tora, Ijenda, Buhoro, Gisozi

Area Under Tea
900 hectares of tea estates plus 2,000 hectares of smallholder land

Average Annual Production (Kilograms)
9 million

Terrain
Rolling fields of tea with very fertile soil in steeply sloping highlands

Altitude
1,500 to 2,000 metres (4,921 to 6,561 feet)

Production Period
All year

Best Time to Visit
October to December

Main Varietals/Cultivars
Not yet known

Types of Tea Made
Black CTC, and small quantities of orthodox black

Predominant Flavours; Tasting Notes
BLACK CTC: good strength and flavour, robust
BLACK ORTHODOX: woody, with hints of spice

DEMOCRATIC REPUBLIC OF CONGO

This Central African country was colonised in the late 19th century by King Leopold of Belgium, who ruthlessly exploited it for his own economic gain. In 1908, the Belgian government took it over and renamed it Belgian Congo, and in 1960, the country became the independent Democratic Republic of Congo. Tea estates were established in the 1940s, and by the 1970s, Congo was one of the largest tea-producing regions of Central Africa. However, decades of conflict caused a steady decline in production, and by 2015, almost all the estates in North Kivu had been abandoned. A few in South Kivu were still operational but unprofitable and made very poor, fibrous teas to compete with imported low-grade Ugandan teas.

M K SHAH EXPORTS LIMITED | *Bakavu*

In February 2014, a ray of hope lit up two estates when M K Shah Exports Limited (owners of 12 gardens in Assam and West Bengal) purchased M'bayo and Madaga estates in Bakavu, a subtropical region that lies between the shores of Lake Kivu and the forested mountains of the East African Rift. This was the first time an Indian company had invested in Congo. Great Lakes Plantations, M K Shah's African arm, now owns the two factories, the tea estate, a timber plantation, and a *Cinchona* trees plantation, used for quinine production. Shah decided to buy here because of the compost-rich, volcanic soil and the beneficially warm climate, but he faces numerous challenges such as high costs, lack of electricity, and lack of government support. The company has renewed CTC equipment, introduced orthodox machinery, doubled the size of the factory, installed new equipment, acquired ISO 22000 and HACCP certification, rehabilitated abandoned tea, trained staff, developed farmer co-operatives to supply green leaf, and now employs 1,500 people from the local villages. Propagation of new plants in the nursery has had almost 95 percent success, and so the speed of extending the estates is now faster. Some of the teas are sold privately to customers in Europe and the United States, and approximately 40 percent goes through the Mombasa auctions. The company is also now growing *Cinchona* bark at M'bayo and is exploring the possibility of cultivating other low-volume, high-value crops. Shah is committed to improving local standards of living, providing medical and sanitary facilities, and increasing education in the local community.

Country, State, or Province
Democratic Republic of Congo

Number of Gardens
2

Main Districts or Gardens
M K Shah Exports Limited, Bakavu

Area Under Tea
1,550 hectares; an additional 100 to 120 hectares expected by 2020

Average Annual Production (Kilograms)
1 million; 1.2 million expected by 2020

Terrain
Rich volcanic soil in rolling hills close to the Rwandan border

Altitude
1,950 to 2,150 metres (6,000 to 6,200 feet)

Production Period
All year

Best Time to Visit
June to September

Main Varietals/Cultivars
African clones originally from Indian stock, and assamica varietals from Assam

Types of Tea Made
Black CTC and orthodox black teas

Predominant Flavours; Tasting Notes
BLACK CTC: very bright, sweet, and slightly spicy
BLACK ORTHODOX: light and fruity

LEFT: Shade trees at M'bayo Tea Estate, Democratic Republic of Congo. RIGHT: Training factory staff at M'bayo tea factory.
Photographs courtesy of Jaydeep Shah

RWANDA

The first tea in Rwanda was planted in the early 1920s, but it was not a success; the government tried again in 1952 and 1958, when it introduced tea to the Mulindi Valley. In 1964, the parastatal Office des Cultures Industrielles du Rwanda (OCIR) was established to oversee the tea industry, and in the late 1960s, cultivation was expanded into the Cyohoha region. Since the mountainsides were too densely populated and already given over to subsistence farming, the marshland in the Cyohoha Valley was drained and planted with tea. The plants grew extremely well, but the harvested leaf had to be transported to the Mulindi factory 80 kilometres (50 miles) away. So, in 1975, Joseph Wertheim, founder of the U.S. company Tea Importers and already involved in the Rwandan tea industry, entered into a joint-venture agreement with the Rwandan government to build a processing factory at Kinihira. This venture was the first private tea business in Rwanda, and Wertheim founded Sorwathé (Société Rwandaise pour la Production et la Commercialisation du Thé), which today grows its own tea on 285.24 hectares in Northern Province and buys 75 percent of its leaf from 4,527 smallholders who cultivate 925 hectares on plots averaging 0.23 hectares.

Because the expansion of Rwanda in the 1960s coincided with a growing demand for teabags, the industry here was set up to manufacture CTC black tea, and the teas are today one of the country's most important cash crops. From the beginning, Rwanda produced quality tea, and once the devastating effects of the 1994 genocide had been overcome, the industry continued to produce good-quality black CTC tea for teabags. To realise the country's full potential, the government introduced a New Tea Sector Strategy for Rwanda 2005 to 2010, which encouraged an increase in the total area under tea; created five new estates and three new factories; improved infrastructure, equipment, and facilities; developed better-yielding clones; increased output; and organised a program of marketing and promotion. The tea expansion program of 2012 to 2017 aimed to plant a further 18,000 hectares, build nine more factories, and distribute 43 million seedling plants by the end of 2017. The areas under development are in Nyaruguru District in the south-west and the Gatare project, a partnership between the COTHEGA tea cooperative and Rwanda Tea Trading Ltd, which is planting another 2,200 hectares in Western Province. Until 2004, except for Sorwathé, all other factories and plantations were state owned, but today all of them have been privatised. The industry recognises the need to invest further in factories in order to increase processing capacity and to facilitate the manufacture of a wider range of speciality teas.

Small-scale farmers cultivate most of the tea land, and each smallholder co-operative sells fresh leaf to an allocated factory. There are 14 factories at present in Rulindo, Gicumbi, Musanze, Rubavu, Karongi, Rusizi, and Gikongoro districts, and each one also grows tea on an industrial block near the factory. Tea is planted in drained marshland (Valley Tea) and on mountain slopes (Hill Tea) in the western and central regions. Valley Tea and Hill Tea each have a distinct character, reflecting the different agricultural conditions under which the tea is grown. Yields are higher in the warm, humid climate of the lower elevations, but the quality of the tea is better in the mountain regions, where the plants grow more slowly amongst the cool, misty peaks.

The industry provides employment for approximately 53,000 people, and approximately 99 percent of the tea is exported, mostly to Pakistan. In 2011, Pfunda in Western Province was the first estate to become Rainforest Alliance Certified, and Sorwathé was the first company to acquire organic certification. In addition to producing approximately 3 million kilograms (6.6 million pounds) of black CTC teas annually (approximately 14 percent of Rwanda's production), Sorwathé now makes black orthodox, steamed green, and white Silver Tip teas.

TOP: The Sorwathé Tea Factory, Northern Province. ABOVE LEFT: Tea processing at Rukeri Tea Factory. ABOVE RIGHT: At Sorwathé Tea Factory, small particles of leaf come out of the CTC cutting machines and are spread onto the conveyor belt where the tea oxidises before going into the dryer at the far end of the processing line. Photographs courtesy of Sorwathé Ltd., Rwanda

Country, State, or Province
Rwanda

Number of Gardens
14 and 30,334 smallholders

Main Districts or Gardens
Northern Province: (Rulindo, Gicumbi and Musanze districts)
Western Province: (Rusizi, Karongi, and Rubavu districts)
Southern Province: (Gikongoro District)

Area Under Tea
21,500 hectares, including 8,600 hectares of smallholder farms

Average Annual Production (Kilograms) 25 million

Terrain
Fertile soil in drained marshland and well-drained, fertile, sandy-clay in hilly areas

Altitude
Valley Tea: 1,550 to 1,800 metres (5,085 to 5,905 feet)
Hill Tea: 1,900 to 2,500 metres (6,233 to 8,202 feet)

Production Period
All year

Best Time to Visit
June to mid-September

Main Varietals/Cultivars
Not yet known

Types of Tea Made
Black CTC, Black orthodox, white, green orthodox

Predominant Flavours; Tasting Notes
Valley Tea:
CTC BLACK: bright and coppery with a rich, smooth, full-bodied character
Hill Tea: better quality because of elevation; rich, smooth, and full-bodied with added hints of malt, molasses, and red wine
BLACK ORTHODOX FROM RUKERI TEA ESTATE: tippy, quite brisk, rounded, sweet, nutty, with hints of caramel and spice
WHITE SILVER TIP: light and floral
GREEN: mildly

UGANDA

Uganda's first tea plants were raised at Entebbe's botanic gardens in 1900; small-scale commercial cultivation began in the late 1920s; and the industry was expanded, mainly by Europeans and Asians, in the mid-1950s. By 1966, the government had established four smallholder estates at Igara, Mpanga, Mabale, and Kayonza in Western Uganda. Also, more private companies had started growing tea, and the crop had become an important foreign-exchange earner. During the political turmoil from 1974 to 1985 when Idi Amin was in power and expelled all Asians, the tea industry almost collapsed entirely. From 1986 to 1990, major rehabilitation brought the government's four factories back to full production, and many abandoned estates were acquired by private companies. Between 1995 and 2000, the state-owned factories were privatised, and Uganda Tea Growers Corporation set up the Small-holder Tea Development Programme to sell fresh green leaf into the four factories. The farmers can choose to become shareholders in exchange for green leaf; fair prices are guaranteed; and extension services such as seeds, fertilisers, and technical advice are provided. Since privatisation, the factories have all increased their output, and this has encouraged government to start providing social services, better roads, and electricity from the national grid. But the tea areas still face challenges from poor infrastructure, high costs, low tea prices, a dependence on international markets, and a lack of research facilities.

Uganda is today the third-largest producer in East Africa (after Kenya and Malawi); tea is the country's third most important foreign earner; and the industry employs more than 60,000 people. Since the country sits just north of the equator, there is abundant sunshine and plentiful rain during two wet seasons each year (although this pattern is changing, and in recent years, the rains have come less frequently, causing concern for the industry's future). The bushes flush all year and are mostly harvested with shears. The large private estates account for 46 percent of harvested leaf, with the rest being grown by smallholders.

Of the many companies that grow tea in Uganda, which include Madhvani Group of Companies, McLeod Russel (U) Ltd, and Toro & Mityana Tea Co. Ltd. (TAMTECO), the biggest are Uganda Tea Development Agency Ltd (UTDAL) and Uganda Tea Corporation Limited (UTCL).

UGANDA TEA DEVELOPMENT AGENCY LTD (UTDAL)

UTDAL owns three factories at Kayonza, Igara, and Buhweju. Kayonza Growers Tea Factory in Kanungu District sits at an altitude of 1,072 metres (3,517 feet) and was opened in 1964. It was privatised in 2000 and buys approximately 15 million kilos (33 million pounds) of fresh leaf annually—15 percent from its own fields and 85 percent from 6,200 smallholders. Igara Growers Tea Factory, located at 1,767 metres (5,797 feet) in Bushenyi District, was built in 1969 to process the increasing amount of leaf that local smallholders were producing. Each year, the factory processes 34 million kilos (75 million pounds) of leaf grown by 6,880 outgrowers, some of whom cultivate their own land, while others work eight Igara-owned plots that cover 229 hectares and supply 5 to 7 percent of the green leaf. The large modern Buhweju Factory was built in 2010 to process the increasing amount of leaf smallholders in the area were producing. Tea has been grown here since 1961 but with no factory—all the leaf had to be transported to Igara. Now the new factory produces black CTC teas that fetch very good prices at the Mombasa auction.

UGANDA TEA CORPORATION LIMITED (UTCL)

UTCL has been growing tea since the 1990s and today has three estates at Kasuku, Luwala, and Salaama, which employ 2,600 people. These cover a total of 1,200 hectares of land in Mukono and Jinja districts. Kasuku and Salaama also have factories where their own crop and leaf bought in from smallholders is processed to produce more than 3.5 million kilos (7.7 million pounds) of black tea per year, approximately 10 percent of the country's total output.

Country, State, or Province
Uganda

Number of Gardens
28 factories, plus around 15,000 smallholders

Main Districts or Gardens
Southwest Uganda between Lake Victoria and the Rwandan and Congolese borders

Area Under Tea
21,000 hectares, including smallholder; 200,000 hectares more have been identified as suitable for cultivation

Average Annual Production (Kilograms)
52 million

Terrain
Rich, well-drained, fertile soils on the slopes of Mount Rwenzori and along the crescent of Lake Victoria

Altitude
792 to 1,767 metres (2,600 to 5,800 feet)

Production Period
All year

Best Time to Visit
December to February, or June to August

Main Varietals/Cultivars
Original plants from Kenya; new clones developed by Ugandan scientists

Types of Tea Made
Black CTC

Predominant Flavours; Tasting Notes
BLACK CTC: medium quality

Libya

Algeria

Mauritania

Mali

Niger River

Niger

Faragо
•

Farako Tea Company

Chad

★**Bamako**

•Sikasso

Burkina Faso

Guinea

***Noar Foundation
Tea Project***

Benin

•Kaduna

Nigeria

Niger River

Côte d'Ivoire

Ghana

Togo

★**Abuja**

Benue River

MAMBILLA
PLATEAU

Liberia

Lome
★

Ndu Tea Estate

•Kakara
•Ndu

***Mambilla
Beverage Company***

Central
African
Republic

***Ndawara Highland
Tea Estate***

•Djuttitsa

Cameroon

Tole Tea Estate

Liko Tea Estate

MOUNT
CAMEROON

★**Douala**

Djuttitsa Tea Estate

*SOUTH ATLANTIC
OCEAN*

Equatorial
Guinea

Gabon

Republic of
the Congo

Tea grower

Multiple growers

Mountain

N
W   E
S

0   125   250   500 Miles

0   125   250   500 Kilometres

CAMEROON

From 1884, Cameroon was a German protectorate, but in 1919, the country was divided between Britain and France. In 1960, it became the independent Federal Republic of Cameroon. The Germans planted the first tea in 1928 at Tole in South-West Region. In 1952, the Cameroon government established the Tole Tea Estate and handed management to the Cameroon Development Corporation (CDC), formed in 1946–47, to oversee the cultivation of tropical crops. A CTC factory was built there in 1954. In 1957, the Estates and Agency Company laid out a second estate at Ndu in North-West Region, and an orthodox factory was constructed in 1962. In 1977, Ndu was taken over by CDC. In 1985–86, a third garden was opened on 444 hectares at Djuttitsa in West Region. Smallholder schemes were suggested but never took off because the government offered little help with essential financial inputs, and farmers saw tea cultivation as too labour-intensive and an unwelcome competitor to their other cash crops.

In 1994, CDC sold its three estates to Cameroon Tea Estates (CTE), owned by Alhadji Baba Ahmanou Danpullo. Workers became unhappy with their living and working conditions and engaged in several years of strikes and blockades, while tea quality and production suffered. Tole is still unsettled. Ndu is recovering under a new manager, and the European Union is supporting a smallholder scheme. Djuttitsa has remained relatively calm throughout. In 2002, Danpullo established the 2,000-hectare Ndawara Highland Tea Estate with a CTC factory in North-West Region, and Liko Tea Estate has recently been established in the forested zone of Mount Cameroon and buys its leaf from local smallholders. Most Cameroon tea is consumed locally or is sold to other African countries.

Country, State, or Province
Cameroon

Number of Gardens 5

Main Districts or Gardens
South-West Region:
Tole Tea Estate; Liko Tea Estate
North-West Region: Ndu Tea Estate; Ndawara Tea Estate
West Cameroon:
Djuttitsa Tea Estate

Area Under Tea
8,000 hectares, plus smallholders

Average Annual Production (Kilograms)
5 million to 7 million, expected to rise to 9 million by 2020

Terrain
South-West Region: Rich volcanic soil on the lower, slopes of Mount Cameroon
North-West Region: Fields of tea set amongst rolling hills and steep grasslands
West Cameroon: Volcanic soil on eastern slopes of Mount Cameroon, surrounded by eucalyptus trees

Altitude
South-West Region: 600 to 750 metres (2,000 to 2,500 feet)
North-West Region: 2,133 metres (7,000 feet)
West Cameroon: 1,800 metres (5,900 feet)

Production Period
All year

Best Time to Visit
November to February

Main Varietals/Cultivars
Clones from Kenya, originally from Indian stock

Types of Tea Made
Black CTC

Predominant Flavours; Tasting Notes
BLACK: bright, strong

MALI

In 1962, China entered into an agreement with the government of Mali to financially support the development of a new 100-hectare estate, and build a green tea factory at Farako, south of Sikasso, on the northern banks of the River Niger. Sikasso, the most southerly region of the country, was selected for this new tea project because of its plentiful rainfall, tropical climate, and fertile soil. Mali consumes approximately 100 million kilograms (220.4 million pounds) of tea a year, and the government was keen to increase domestic production and reduce the high quantities of tea imported each year. The Sino-Malinese scheme established the Farako Tea Company, trained new tea growers and factory workers, and supported ongoing field training and plantation management. In 2011, the Malian government and the public-owned Tea Company of Mali (SOGETM-SA) signed a deal to boost activities at the Farako tea farm. The plan was to cultivate a total of 302 hectares and to install an irrigation scheme and power plant. There are also plans to extend tea cultivation to other parts of the country.

The tea plants grow well in the tropical climate of southern Mali.
Photograph by John O'Hagan; ©Hoffman Media LLC

Country, State, or Province
Mali

Number of Gardens
1

Main Districts or Gardens
Sikasso

Area Under Tea
102 hectares

Average Annual Production (Kilograms)
90,719

Terrain
Fertile soil in lowland valleys and flat plateaux where savannah meets rain-fed forest

Altitude
410 metres (1,350 feet)

Production Period
Not yet known, possibly all year

Best Time to Visit
January, February, October, November, and December

Main Varietals/Cultivars
Not yet known

Types of Tea Made
Chinese Chun Mee–style green tea

Predominant Flavours; Tasting Notes
Strong, robust

NIGERIA

In 1975, the country's first tea estate was established on 450 hectares at Kakara Village in the grassy highlands of the Mambilla Plateau where cool temperatures, plentiful rainfall, and countless rivers and waterfalls provide excellent conditions for tea growing.

In 1982, Nigeria's Cocoa Research Institute selected five tea clones to release to farmers, and the Nigerian Beverages Production Company was incorporated to manage the project. It introduced a smallholder scheme; increased the number of tea growers; and provided plants, fertiliser, technical support, and transportation. Eucalyptus trees were planted amongst the tea to help stabilise production during the October to March dry season, and yields and quality slowly improved. From 1993 to 1997, Dutch management and consultancy company HVA International provided technical assistance. When the program ended in 1997 due to political problems, the tea area had been rehabilitated and extended to 850 hectares, the factory had been modernised, a 500-hectare irrigation system had been installed, the smallholders association had been strengthened, and quality and output had improved. Today, the Mambilla Beverage Company, producers of Highland Tea, cultivates 600 hectares, and smallholder farmers grow tea on a further 600 hectares. Harvesting is both manual and mechanical.

However, the industry faces many challenges, including ongoing political unrest, high costs, out-of-date farming techniques, low yields, unreliable power supplies, and low processing capacity. This means that farmers sometimes process their tea by pounding the fresh leaves, then oxidising and drying them in the sun. Mambilla Plateau has more than 50,000 hectares of available land, and in 2010, after two tea companies had ceased production and amidst fears that the industry was collapsing, there were calls for a government tea policy, the establishment of a tea council, and greater investment in production, processing, research, infrastructure, and finance for smallholders. In April 2017, there were further calls for the enactment of such a policy from Abel Diah, Speaker of the Taraba House of Assembly, who said that it would create jobs and make tea production a sustainable source of foreign-exchange earnings.

Country, State, or Province
Nigeria

Number of Gardens
1

Main Districts or Gardens
Mambilla Beverage Company, Mambilla Plateau, Taraba State

Area Under Tea
1,200 hectares including smallholders

Average Annual Production (Kilograms)
1.6 million

Terrain
Hilly, grassy highland plateau—Nigeria's highest and coldest

Altitude
1,800 metres (5,906 feet)

Production Period
All year

Best Time to Visit
November to March

Main Varietals/ Cultivars
Original varietals from early planting, plus 5 new high-yielding clones

Types of Tea Made
Black CTC

Predominant Flavours; Tasting Notes
BLACK CTC: quite plain

TOGO

In 1884, Togoland became a German colony, and coffee, cocoa, and cotton estates were established. Since it gained its independence in 1960, 65 percent of workers have been employed in agriculture, but tea was never a major crop. In 2010, in an effort to help subsistence farmers, the Noar Foundation for Global Community Development, a Dutch NGO, established the country's first tea nursery to raise new plants for cultivation in northern Togo, where the acidic soil, warm climate, and plentiful rainfall are very suitable. For the Togolese, tea offers work for both men and women, year-round earnings, opportunities for smallholder farmers, and green, sustainable farming. The aims of the foundation are to deliver economic empowerment, education, and health care while respecting the environment and cultural diversity.

Between 10,000 and 20,000 assamica seeds from India were germinated in the nursery, and in 2012, hundreds of young plants were moved out into the lush black soil of the steep hills. Initially, many died because of the cruel dry season from late November to mid-March, called the Harmattan, during which no rain falls, wells and other sources of water dry up, and dense dust storms sweep across the land. But farmers here are skilled cultivators, and they developed a technique to protect and nurture the bushes, using palm leaves, cloth, and a system of regular watering, and almost all the plants are now growing sturdily. Seeds collected from the bushes are germinated in the nursery to raise the next generation of hardy, drought-resistant plants, and seeds have been placed with the Agricultural Ministry for seed banking and experimentation.

Forty young workers are employed to care for the plants, and in 2015, harvesting and processing techniques were developed to make the first black teas by hand. As production increases, a factory is planned, and the Noar Foundation will sponsor an exchange program with Indian and African tea growers to share technology and experience.

TOP: Sturdy new plants at the Noar Foundation project. ABOVE: Germinating tea seeds at Kwude Tea Nursery. Photographs courtesy of M. Noar, Noar Foundation

Country, State, or Province
Togo

Number of Gardens
1

Main Districts or Gardens
Northern Togo

Area Under Tea
4 hectares, with plans for several hundred

Average Annual Production (Kilograms)
Not yet known

Terrain
Plateau region of rolling savannah north of the Togo Mountains

Altitude
900 metres (2,950 feet)

Production Period
All year, depending on the effects of the Harmattan dry period

Best Time to Visit
November to February

Main Varietals/ Cultivars
Indian varietals

Types of Tea Made
To date, handmade black teas; will change when a factory is built

Predominant Flavours; Tasting Notes
Not yet known

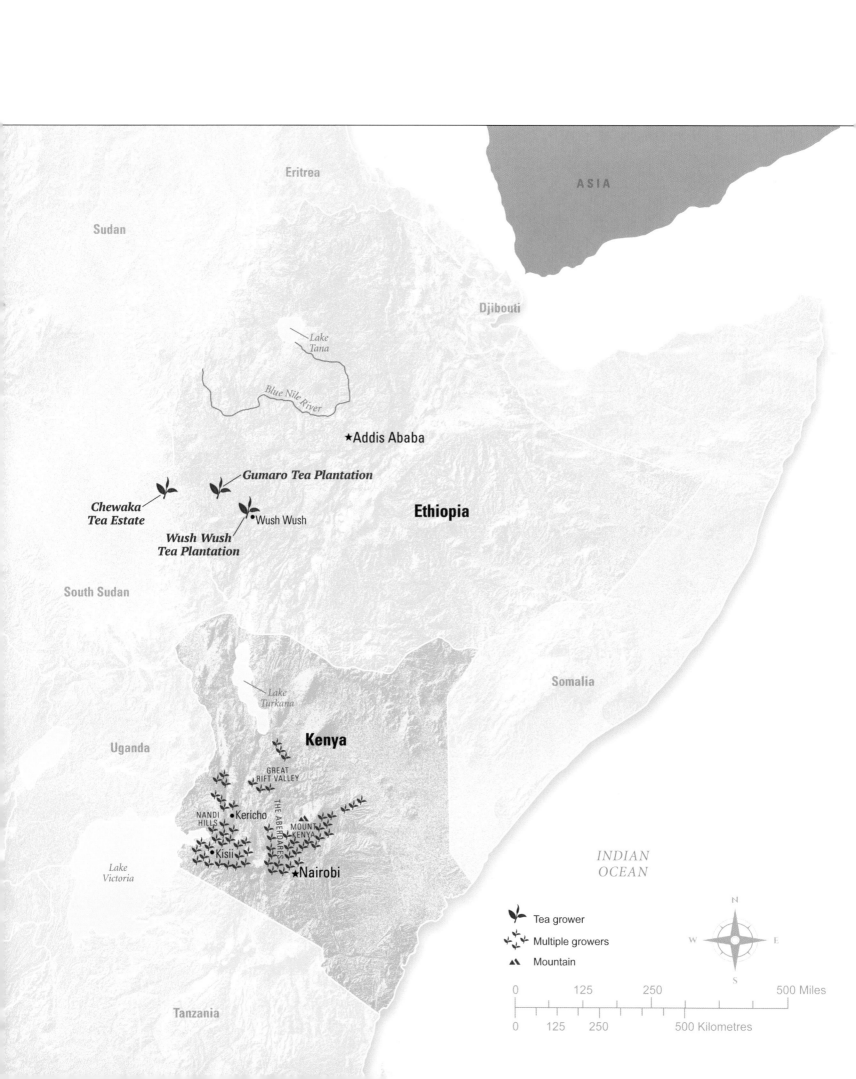

Eritrea

ASIA

Sudan

Djibouti

Lake Tana

Blue Nile River

★Addis Ababa

Gumaro Tea Plantation

Chewaka Tea Estate

Ethiopia

•Wush Wush

Wush Wush Tea Plantation

South Sudan

Somalia

Lake Turkana

Kenya

Uganda

GREAT RIFT VALLEY

NANDI HILLS

•Kericho

THE ABERDARES

MOUNT KENYA

•Kisii

★Nairobi

Lake Victoria

INDIAN OCEAN

Tanzania

Tea grower

Multiple growers

Mountain

N
W   E
S

0   125   250   500 Miles

0   125   250   500 Kilometres

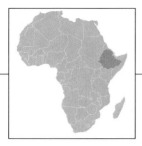

ETHIOPIA

Tea seeds from India were brought into Gumaro in south-western Ethiopia by a British diplomatic mission in 1928. They were distributed to local farmers, and in 1957, one of those pioneer growers expanded his tea farm to 25 hectares. In 1973, trials were also carried out at Wush Wush in the south-west of the country, and in 1981, the government encouraged the expansion of the tea industry in both regions. Since the 1990s, the industry has benefited from technical assistance and training funded by HVA International, Dutch Management & Consultancy Company, and the African Development Bank, and strong economic growth has resulted from increased agricultural productivity. In 2000, Ethio Agri-CEFT plc, with interests in Ethiopian coffee, flowers, cereal, and vegetables, as well as tea, acquired the estates and factories at Gumaro and Wush Wush, and in April 2016, invested large sums in the expansion of a tea processing and packaging factory in the Huajan Industrial Zone on the outskirts of Addis Ababa, in Lebu.

Ethiopia's geographical position, just north of the equator, means that the country can grow tea year-round. In the lower areas, the climate is very warm all year, but in the higher elevations, where the tea grows, temperatures rarely rise above 25°C (77°F), and the tea estates benefit from plentiful rainfall from June to the end of September and again in March. In 2014, the Ministry of Agriculture identified 129,499 square kilometres (50,000 square miles) of land that is suitable for tea production, and it is now offering subsidies and tax exemptions to interested investors. Improved management and processing are leading to an increase in both outturn and quality, and the country's total annual production is expected to soon reach 7 million kilograms (15.4 million pounds).

GUMARO TEA PLANTATION | *Illubabor*

During the 1980s, Gumaro's tea area was increased using clonal plants raised from tissue culture in the United Kingdom. A smallholder farmer scheme was set up in 2004 with owners Ethio Agri-CEFT, and the factory processes Gumaro's own leaf and that of local outgrowers who are provided with tea seedlings and technical advice by Ethio Agri-CEFT. The smallholders' fresh leaf is sold to the factory at an agreed price.

WUSH WUSH TEA PLANTATION | *Southern Kaffa Zone*

Wush Wush was also extended to its present size during the 1980s with clones from the United Kingdom and, like Gumaro, was taken over in 2000 by Ethio Agri-CEFT plc. Wush Wush has two factories and an outgrower scheme like the one at Gumaro, which encourages local farmers to cultivate good-quality tea and sell it to the factory to boost their cash earnings. Once processed, the black CTC tea is transported to a packing facility in Addis Ababa for grading and packing for the domestic market and for export. Wush Wush also makes small quantities of green tea. The teas are sold straight or flavoured with herbs and spices, such as ginger, mint, thyme, and cinnamon, under the brand names Gumaro, Wush Wush, and Addis.

CHEWAKA TEA ESTATE | *Chewaka*

In 1995, East African Agri-Business bought 870 hectares of land at Chewaka in the south-west of the country, and it has plans to eventually grow tea on 1,250 hectares. Chewaka Tea Estate was laid out with 10 different varietals chosen for their high-quality liquors, good yields, and resistance to pests. The garden and factory were launched in 2001. The company now has 45 to 50 percent of the country's market share, and Chewaka's teas sell as Black Lion and Good Morning brands in Dubai (UAE), Egypt, Sudan, Djibouti, Pakistan, and other countries in the Middle East.

Country, State, or Province
Ethiopia

Number of Gardens
3

Main Districts or Gardens
Gumaro Tea Plantation, Illubabor, south-western Ethiopia

Wush Wush Tea Plantation, Southern Kaffa Zone

Chewaka Tea Estate, Chewaka, South-west highlands

Area Under Tea
Gumaro Tea Plantation: 860 hectares

Wush Wush Tea Plantation: 1,249 hectares

Chewaka Tea Estate: 600 hectares, with plans to increase to 1,250 hectares

Average Annual Production (Kilograms)
6.35 million (expected to reach 7 million soon)

Terrain
Gumaro Tea Plantation: Rich, red-brown, well-drained soil

Wush Wush Tea Plantation: Fertile, well-drained soil

Chewaka Tea Estate: Gently sloping fields in south-west highlands

Altitude
Gumaro Tea Plantation: 1,718 metres (5,636 feet)

Wush Wush Tea Plantation: 1,900 metres (6,233 feet)

Chewaka Tea Estate: 1,828 metres (6,000 feet)

Production Period
All year

Best Time to Visit
September to April

Main Varietals/ Cultivars
Plants grown from Indian seeds

Chewaka Tea Estate: 10 different varietals; 4 from Gumaro; 6 from Kenya

Types of Tea Made
Black CTC

Predominant Flavours; Tasting Notes
BLACK CTC: bright, brisk, strong, sometimes slightly spicy

KENYA

During the first decade of the 20th century, the British government encouraged migration of British citizens to Kenya, and by 1905, some 3,000 people had started farming here. In 1903, one of the new settlers, G. W. L. Caine, planted the first of Kenya's tea bushes on his land at Limuru, not for commercial cultivation but simply because he found the plants very attractive. Those bushes are now tall trees at what is today Unilever's Mabroukie Tea Estate in the Ngong Hills. In 1904, Arnold Butler McDonnell purchased 140 hectares at Kiambethu near Nairobi and tried to grow flax, corn, and coffee, but all the crops failed because of the high altitude. So instead, in 1918, he planted 9 hectares of tea bushes, which grew well, and by 1926, he had become the country's first commercial producer. Other farmers followed suit, the industry grew rapidly, and by 1933, black Kenya tea was being exported to London.

In 1950, the Kenya Tea Board was established to regulate the industry and to co-ordinate research and promotion. In the 1960s, the Ministry of Agriculture encouraged Kenyans to grow tea, and after independence in 1963, the industry expanded further. By the late 1990s, production had increased from 18 million kilos (39.7 million pounds) in 1963 to 294 million kilos (648 million pounds). The Special Crops Development Authority, established by the colonial government, was replaced by the Kenya Tea Development Authority (KTDA), which was set up to promote smallholder tea farming. The Tea Research Institute opened in 1980 to address such issues as yield, quality, climate change, new clones, and tea promotion. In 2000, the KTDA became a private organisation, the Kenya

Pickers at Emrok Tea's Ogirgir Tea Estate. Photograph courtesy of Emrok Tea Factory (EP2) Ltd.

Tea Development Agency. Today, the agency manages 67 factories that process smallholders' leaf as mostly black CTC as well as an increasing quantity of impressive orthodox black along with some green tea. Kangaita, a Fair Trade–certified factory, is particularly noted for its aromatic, spicy, fruity orthodox black teas that often have a malty note. And Emrok Tea Factory, in the Nandi Hills, also makes orthodox black teas as well as white and green teas.

The tea grows in the Kenyan Highlands, west of the Rift Valley at Kisii, in the Aberdares, in Nandi, and around Mount Kenya. The climate is hot and humid with plentiful, well-distributed rainfall, and since the growing regions straddle the equator, the tea flushes throughout the year. The shoots are harvested by hand, with shear pluckers, or with hedge-trimmer machines. During the busiest rainy seasons, the factories run 24 hours a day, six days a week. The best-quality teas, which have more flavour and strength, are harvested during the drier months of January, February, and July. Smallholder farmers produce 60 percent of total output, with the remaining 40 percent grown by large private companies.

PURPLE TEA

An important trend in Kenya in recent years has been the widespread planting of TRFK 306, a new purple cultivar thought to have originated in Assam, developed over more than 25 years by the Tea Research Foundation of Kenya (TRFK), and released to farmers in 2011. The crimson-purple leaf is high in anthocyanin, the same polyphenol found in superfoods, such as blueberries, purple sweet potatoes, and blackcurrants, and which acts as an antioxidant in our bodies. Purple teas are marketed as offering higher levels of antioxidants than other black and green teas, but the high level of polyphenols in the leaves means that the teas can be very bitter and astringent. The first purple teas, made in the first decade of the 21st century, were so bitter that they were often blended with sweet berries to give them a more palatable character. But the factories have experimented with different processing techniques, and instead of manufacturing black teas from the leaves, some companies

now make a Chinese-style green tea. Emrok Tea Factory pans the fresh leaf as soon as it comes into the factory before cooling, then rolling it in orthodox rollers, and drying it for approximately 20 minutes. Tea made from the purple leaves is also being turned into ready-to-drink flavoured, bottled beverages as well as capsules intended to be taken as a food supplement.

THE KERICHO HIGHLANDS

Some of Kenya's largest tea estates are situated in the Rift Valley Highlands, west of Kericho. The tea fields cover 10,000 hectares and sweep across the high plains that are also home to eucalyptus plantations, flower farms, and dense forest. Many of the factories here are owned by private companies, such as Unilever, James Finlay, and Williamsons. Unilever Tea Kenya Ltd, which started as Brooke Bond, has grown tea here since 1924 and now owns 28 tea estates and eight factories. Its Kimugu Factory makes green tea for export to Japan and China. James Finlay Kenya established its first garden here in 1925 and now operates nine estates and four factories at Kitumbe, Chomogonday, Changana, and Kymulot. Williamson Tea Kenya Ltd, with connections here that date back to the 1950s, today owns four estates with factories—Changoi, Kapchorua, Kaimosi, and Tinderet. Other private companies include Sotik Tea, Kikebe Estates, Mua Tea, Kapchebet, and Kaisugu. Kericho is also home to the Kenya Tea Development Agency whose 11 factories buy fresh leaf from smallholders and process it as mainly black CTC teas.

KISII HIGHLANDS

In Kisii, Western Province, the tea plants flourish on 10,585 hectares of highland in fertile volcanic soil that is generously watered by a long rainy season from March until June, and shorter rains from October to December. Smallholders deliver their crop into 12 KTDA factories where they are shareholders as well. The region is also home to several private companies, including Sotik Tea Companies and Kikebe Ltd. In 2012, the KTDA launched a scheme to plant 1.8 million trees annually on the tea estates in the region to help combat the effects of climate change.

TOP LEFT: Withered leaf being gathered into bags ready to go to the rolling room. TOP RIGHT: A patchwork of tea fields. ABOVE LEFT: CTC cutting machines. ABOVE RIGHT: Orthodox rollers used to make speciality green tea at Emrok Tea's factory in the Nandi Hills. Photographs courtesy of Emrok Tea Factory (EP2) Ltd.

THE NANDI HILLS

Nandi has for many years been an important foreign-exchange earner, but lower tea prices, declining exchange rates, higher production costs, and reduced profits in the second decade of the 21st century meant that some tea smallholders uprooted their bushes and turned to other crops. However, big companies such as Eastern Produce Kenya Ltd (EPK) and Nandi Tea Estates continue to do well here. EPK, a large international company that was originally established in Sri Lanka in the 19th century and then expanded into East Africa, has seven estates and five factories and manages two client factories with three large associated estates. The company buys fresh leaf from 7,500 smallholders and turns it into high-quality black CTC teas. Nandi Tea Estates grows tea on 1,047 hectares and processes its own and smallholders' leaf to make black CTC grades for export. The recently built Emrok Tea factory is one of only two in Kenya that has installed a fully automated production line and that manufactures fresh leaf from its own Ogirgir estate and from neighbouring smallholder farmers. It produces both CTC black tea and a range of orthodox black, green, white, and purple teas.

MOUNT KENYA

Tea grows in the cool, misty climate of the steep southern slopes of Mount Kenya, Kenya's second-highest mountain. Kangaita Tea Factory was built here in 1965 at an altitude of 2,036 metres (6,680 feet) and is the best known in the region. It buys leaf from 5,730 smallholders and manufactures black CTC teas and a range of delicate white teas and large-leaf orthodox blacks. Growers here have also begun to cultivate the purple tea cultivar.

THE ABERDARES

Tea is cultivated on the eastern slopes of the Aberdares, an area of forests, bamboo stands, mountain peaks, and open moorland north of Nairobi. As well as CTC blacks, orthodox blacks are also produced here and have sweet citrus notes or hints of apricots and peaches.

Emrok Tea's Ogirgir Tea Estate in the Nandi Hills.
Photograph courtesy of Emrok Tea Factory (EP2) Ltd.

Country, State, or Province
Kenya

Number of Gardens
More than 100 factories and more than 500,000 smallholder farmers

Main Districts or Gardens
Kericho, Mount Kenya, Kisii Highlands, the Nandi Hills, the Aberdares

Area Under Tea
More than 180,000 hectares, including 100,00 hectares of smallholder growers

Average Annual Production (Kilograms)
Approximately 430 million

Terrain
Wide-open fields of red volcanic soils in the highlands

Altitude
1,524 to 2,743 metres (5,000 to 9,000 feet)

Production Period
All year

Best Time to Visit
All year

Main Varietals/Cultivars
Assamicas from original Indian stock; new cultivars and clones developed by the Tea Research Foundation of Kenya (TRFK)

Types of Tea Made
Black CTC, small amounts of black orthodox, white (needle-style and peony-style), and green tea from purple clone

Predominant Flavours; Tasting Notes
BLACK CTC: bright, coppery liquors that are brisk and strong, an important ingredient in robust English Breakfast-style blends
BLACK ORTHODOX: complex, full-bodied, smooth, sometimes malty, sometimes fruity
NEEDLE-STYLE WHITE TEAS: subtle, fruity, with a hints of grapefruit
PEONY-STYLE WHITE TEAS: bolder, with fresh fruity and grassy notes
GREEN TEA FROM PURPLE CLONE: plain, grassy, slightly astringent

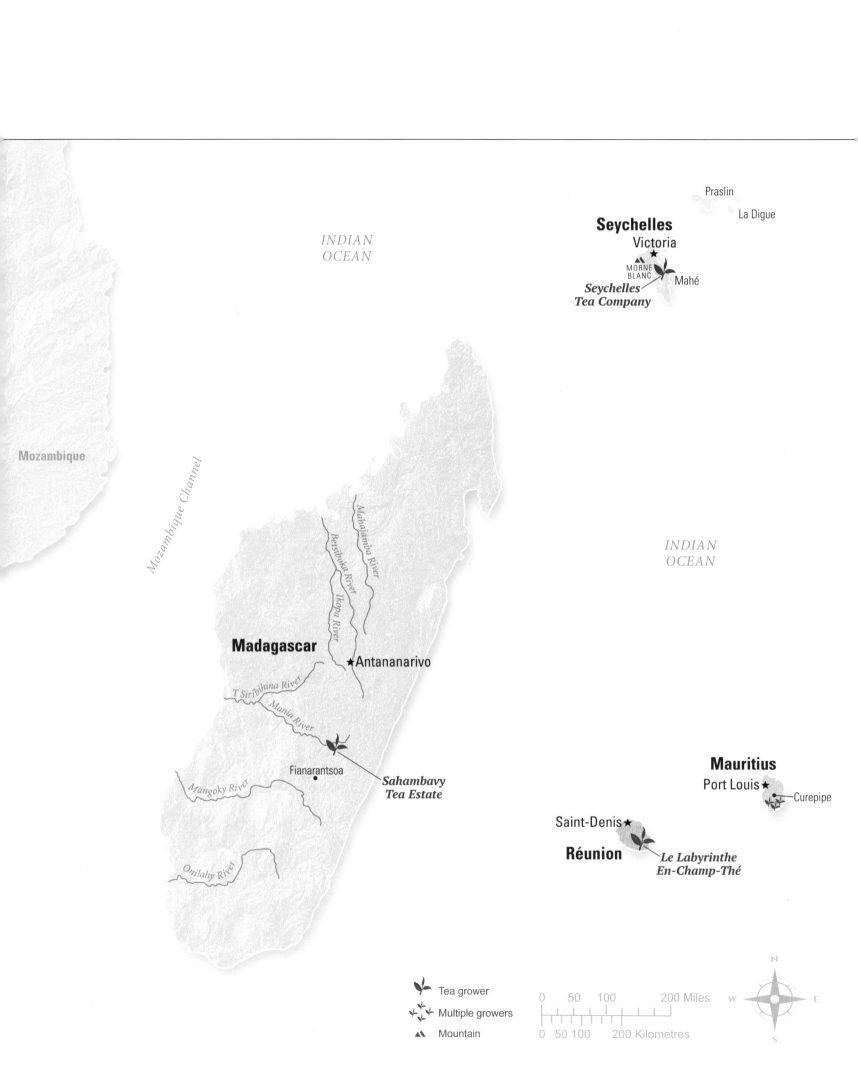

INDIAN
OCEAN

Praslin

La Digue

Seychelles

Victoria

MORNE
BLANC

Mahé

*Seychelles
Tea Company*

Mozambique

Mozambique Channel

INDIAN
OCEAN

Mahajamba River

Betsiboka River

Ikopa River

Madagascar

★Antananarivo

T Siribihina River

Mania River

*Sahambavy
Tea Estate*

Fianarantsoa

Mauritius

Port Louis★

Curepipe

Mangoky River

Saint-Denis★

Réunion

*Le Labyrinthe
En-Champ-Thé*

Onilahy River

Tea grower

Multiple growers

Mountain

0   50   100   200 Miles

0   50 100   200 Kilometres

N

W   E

S

MADAGASCAR

The first tea seedlings, brought in from Kenya, were planted in the 1970s in the hills near Fianarantsoa, south-central Madagascar, in a new project that was partly financed by the European Economic Community to help introduce tea into the Malagasy economy. The lower areas here enjoy a subtropical, hot, and humid climate, but up in the cooler temperatures of the higher slopes, the plants thrived, and a 500-hectare estate was prepared for planting. In 1978, the first state-owned factory was built, and in 1996, the garden was privatised. Today, the Sahambavy Tea Estate covers only approximately 150 hectares, one-third of which is cultivated and managed by small-scale farmers. The tea bushes cover the gently rolling slopes against a backdrop of thick forests of eucalyptus trees. Rice paddy fields spread across the valley below, and on the higher slopes, terraced vineyards surround Fianarantsoa town, an old royal city that in the 19th century was the administrative capital of the region.

The fresh shoots are harvested manually by 250 pluckers. Their busiest time is from November to April, when the season of warm, wet weather makes the bushes flush faster. But from May to October, the growth slows down during the dryer, cooler weather, and the pluckers' baskets take longer to fill. Since 2004, the estate has been producing a little green tea, as well as CTC black of which 80 percent is exported to Kenya for sale into the international markets through the Mombasa auctions. The black teas are often blended locally with dried pieces of locally grown Bourbon vanilla pods and packed for sale in the local market and abroad. Local consumers love to drink the teas strong, mixed with condensed milk and brown sugar.

Country, State, or Province
Madagascar

Number of Gardens
1

Main Districts or Gardens
Fianarantsoa: south-central region

Area Under Tea
150 hectares

Average Annual Production (Kilograms)
453,592

Terrain
Gentle slopes in rolling green hills above Sahambavy Lake

Altitude
1,250 metres (4,100 feet)

Production Period
All year

Best Time to Visit
April to October

Main Varietals/Cultivars
Assamicas via Kenya

Types of Tea Made
Black CTC and a very small amount of green

Predominant Flavours; Tasting Notes
BLACK CTC: warm amber liquors with an intense aroma and a strong full-bodied flavour

MAURITIUS

Because Mauritius was a Dutch colony from 1638 to 1710, it is possible that the local people became aware of tea during that period. Certainly, black tea is today more widely drunk than coffee and plays an important part in the island's everyday life. The idea of growing tea was initiated under French rule in the 1760s, and production increased briefly when the British took control in 1810. But it was not until the end of the 19th century that tea cultivation began in earnest. In 1948–49, the Tea Research Station was established at Wootoon, and in 1955, the government initiated a tea smallholder scheme to encourage farmers to lease land and grow tea close to the new tea factories.

Today, tea is grown in the south of the country in Bois Chéri, Grand Bois, La Flora, and New France, as well as in the central highlands, around Curepipe. The tea is cultivated by smallholders, eight larger growers, and three private producers, who have factories at Bois Chéri, La Chartreuse, and Corson Tea Estate. The last of the state-owned factories closed in 1999, and some of the land has subsequently been leased to smallholders. Current problems include an aging workforce, high costs for fertilisers, and the replacement of tea by sugarcane, which matures faster and yields profits more quickly.

The Mauritian *sinensis* varietal bushes are harvested manually or with shears, and the leaf is sold to the factories by smallholder co-operatives. The black CTC teas are exported to France and Australia, and in 2015, discussions were taking place with China with a view to exporting to the market there. There were hopes of also finding buyers in Japan and South Africa. With annual production between 1.3 million and 1.6 million kilograms (2.9 and 3.5 million pounds) and domestic consumption of approximately 1.5 million kilograms (3.3 million pounds), the government limits the importation of other teas for blending in order to protect the industry. Importers are charged very high prices for import licenses and pay heavy duties on all imported teas.

TOP AND ABOVE LEFT: Bois Chéri, the oldest tea estate in Mauritius, was planted in 1892. ABOVE RIGHT: An old boiler in the Bois Chéri tea museum. © Saint Aubin Loisirs Ltée

Country, State, or Province
Mauritius

Number of Gardens
11, plus 1,340 smallholder farmers

Main Districts or Gardens
Southern region and central Midlands

Area Under Tea
672 hectares

Average Annual Production (Kilograms)
1.5 million

Terrain
Open, undulating fields and steeper slopes

Altitude
203 to 609 metres (666 to 2,000 feet)

Production Period
October to May

Best Time to Visit
All year

Main Varietals/Cultivars
Sinensis varietals from China

Types of Tea Made
Black CTC and steamed greens

Predominant Flavours; Tasting Notes
BLACK CTC: bright, coppery, strong liquors that have a vanilla character
GREEN: golden-green liquors with full flavour and an astringent bite

RÉUNION

LE LABYRINTHE EN-CHAMP-THÉ | *Saint-Joseph, Grand Coude*

From 1955 to 1972, Réunion was well known for its tea production, and in the 1960s, 350 hectares of tea were cultivated on the island. Today, only 3 hectares are farmed by Johny Guichard (known locally as Jojo), a Frenchman who had always wanted to be a farmer but had no land. In 2002, he found a piece of land close to his house and started to grow geraniums, but in order to survive financially, he needed to diversify. He realised that tea had once been a major crop on Réunion, and in 2005, he began to grow tea organically and sell what he made at local farmers' markets. He then decided to combine farming with agritourism and created a "tea labyrinth" that offers guided tours to visitors to allow them to discover the story of agriculture in the area and of traditional organic farming in the village. The charming play on words means that the tea garden's name sounds like *Labyrinthe enchanté*.

Guichard grows tobacco plants amongst the tea bushes to trap insects, and plants pumpkins as groundcover to control weeds. He harvests the tea shoots between 6 a.m. and 9 a.m. to make white and green teas that are sold to visitors, to organic shops and tourist locations around the island, and in France. He also cultivates geraniums, which are used to make aromatic oils and to flavour a tea syrup and a white tea jelly. The tea farm and labyrinth have become so popular that Guichard plans to build a tea house with a larger reception area for the growing number of visitors.

Johny (Jojo) Guichard gathering the crop at Le Labyrinthe En-Champ-Thé.
© Michaël Duchemann MD

Country, State, or Province
Réunion

Number of Gardens
1

Main Districts or Gardens
Le Labyrinthe En-Champ-Thé, Saint-Joseph, Grand Coude

Area Under Tea
10 hectares

Average Annual Production (Kilograms)
1,400

Terrain
Gentle slope on high volcanic plateau of fertile farmland

Altitude
1,100 metres (3,609 feet)

Production Period
Late September to June

Best Time to Visit
May to October

Main Varietals/ Cultivars
Assamicas grown from old plants on an abandoned, 1950s tea garden

Types of Tea Made
White and green

Predominant Flavours; Tasting Notes
WHITE: light, subtle, and sweet
GREEN: stronger and more exciting than the white, with a more pronounced flavor

SEYCHELLES

SEYCHELLES TEA | *Mahé Island*

The rocky hillsides of the granite peaks running down the centre of Mahé Island are covered with abandoned cinnamon, cloves, ginger, and tea bushes that were perhaps planted by early traders and settlers on this, the largest of the Republic of Seychelles islands. Commercial cultivation of tea was pioneered in 1961 by two Kenyan planters, Bill Handerson and Francis Drybrough, who imported 1,000 kilograms (2,205 pounds) of seed and established a tea nursery at Port Glaud. They then planted 120 hectares of tea on terraced slopes in the hills of Morne Blanc, where the original nursery is today "Field Number 4" of the organic farm. By 1966, the Seychelles Tea Company was exporting its SeyTé brand to the United Kingdom, Germany, and Japan from the Tea Factory, which has breathtaking views over the western slopes of Mahé and out over the Indian Ocean.

Over the years, the planted area gradually diminished, and when the Seychelles Marketing Board took over the garden in 1988, only 44 hectares were still being cultivated. Local women pick approximately 30 kilograms (66 pounds) of fresh shoots by hand every day, and the leaves are processed to make orthodox broken black tea, small quantities of green tea, and a white "Silver Tea" made from just the new buds. Some of the black tea is sold unblended as pure Seychelles tea, while most is blended with imported Ceylon tea and flavoured with vanilla, cinnamon, orange, strawberry, mint, lemon, or lemongrass. In the past, small quantities of the teas were exported to Germany, the United Kingdom, Japan, and France, and the company is hoping to export again in the future. At the moment, however, all the teas are sold locally under the SeyTé brand in supermarkets and tourist venues on the islands.

The Tea Factory is open to visitors every day except Sundays and public holidays, and there are plans to expand the factory and upgrade the surrounding area for increased eco-tourism.

Country, State, or Province
Seychelles

Number of Gardens 1

Main Districts or Gardens
Seychelles Tea, Morne Blanc, Mahé

Area Under Tea
Less than 40 hectares

Average Annual Production (Kilograms)
50,000 to 80,000

Terrain
Lower slopes of steep Morne Blanc Mountain with panoramic views of the western slopes of Mahé and the Indian Ocean

Altitude
500 metres (1,640 feet)

Production Period
All year

Best Time to Visit
April, May, October, November

Main Varietals/Cultivars
Assamica seeds from Kenya

Types of Tea Made
Black orthodox, mostly blended with Ceylon tea and flavoured; small quantities of silver-needle white tea

Predominant Flavours; Tasting Notes
BLACK ORTHODOX BROKEN: blended with Ceylon black tea and additional ingredients to make 6 flavoured black teas (black, orange, mint, lemon, vanilla, and cinnamon)
WHITE: elegant and delicate, locally often lightly brewed with cardamoms and cloves

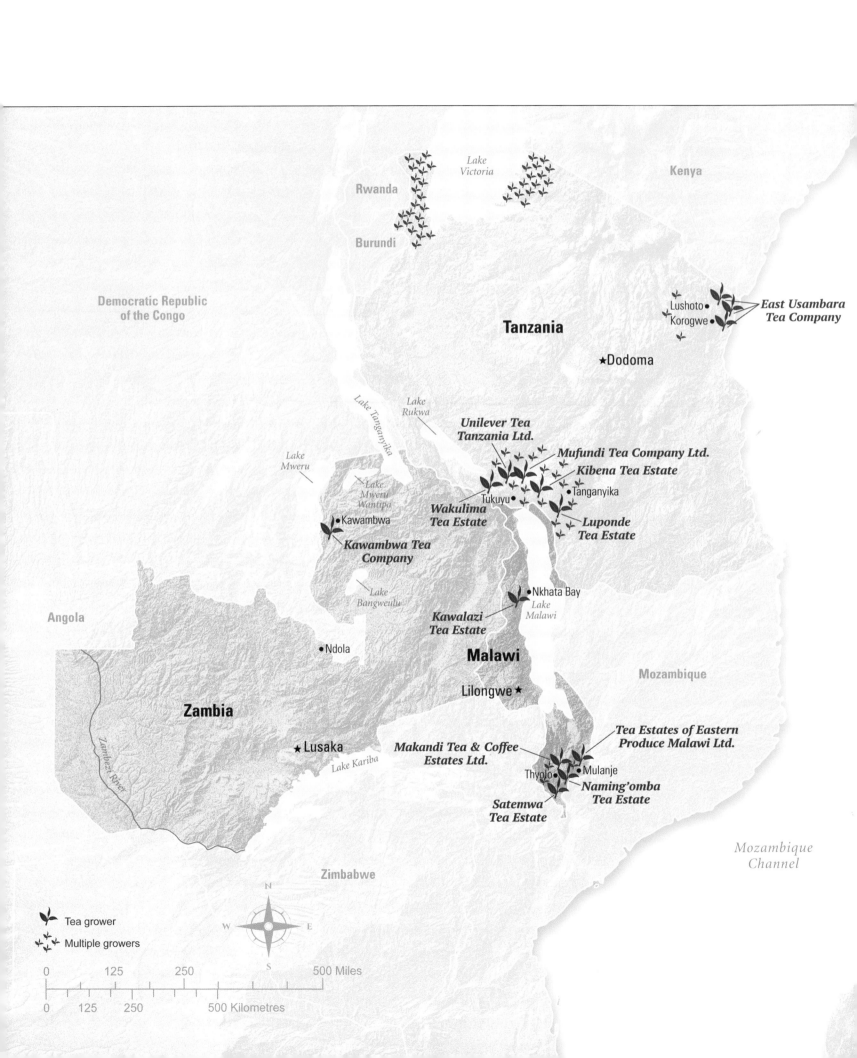

Rwanda

Lake
Victoria

Kenya

Burundi

Democratic Republic
of the Congo

Tanzania

Lushoto •
Korogwe •

***East Usambara
Tea Company***

★Dodoma

Lake
Rukwa

Lake
Tanganyika

***Unilever Tea
Tanzania Ltd.***

Mufundi Tea Company Ltd.

Kibena Tea Estate

Lake
Mweru

Lake
Mweru
Wantipa

• Tanganyika

Tukuyu •

***Wakulima
Tea Estate***

***Luponde
Tea Estate***

• Kawambwa

***Kawambwa Tea
Company***

Lake
Bangweulu

• Nkhata Bay

Lake
Malawi

***Kawalazi
Tea Estate***

Angola

• Ndola

Malawi

Mozambique

Zambia

Lilongwe ★

★ Lusaka

Lake Kariba

***Makandi Tea & Coffee
Estates Ltd.***

***Tea Estates of Eastern
Produce Malawi Ltd.***

Thyolo •

• Mulanje

***Naming'omba
Tea Estate***

***Satemwa
Tea Estate***

Zimbabwe

Mozambique
Channel

Tea grower

Multiple growers

N
W   E
S

0   125   250   500 Miles

0   125   250   500 Kilometres

MALAWI

Malawi was the first of the East African countries to grow tea commercially and is today the second most important producer after Kenya. Until 1964, when the country gained its independence from Britain, it was known as Nyasaland, and the first British settlers, mainly missionaries, traders, hunters, and planters, arrived in the 1860s and '70s. Most of the new farmers chose to plant tobacco and coffee but also experimented with tea, wheat, ginger, and various fruits. The first trials with tea were made by Jonathan Dunce, one of the new planters, in 1878. Scottish missionary Dr. Walter Angus Elmslie also grew plants from seeds he had acquired at Edinburgh's botanical gardens, and two of those bushes are still growing at the Blantyre Mission. Large-scale cultivation started in 1891 when coffee planter Henry Brown arrived from Ceylon, acquired 20 tea seeds from the Blantyre Mission bushes, and planted them at his new Thornwood Estate in Mulanje. In 1893, tea was also planted at Lauderdale Estate in Mulanje, as well as in Limbe. Further trials were run in Limbe, Zomba, Mwanza, Mangochi, Karonga, and Michiru, but the tea did not do well. So it was in Mulanje and Thyolo that new estates, factories, and packing facilities were developed. As the tobacco market collapsed during the first half of the 20th century, more and more land was given over to tea, and by 1918, the total area under tea was 1,830 hectares.

Today, the main growing regions are Mulanje and Thyolo in the south and a smaller area in Nkhata Bay District in the north. More than 93 percent of tea is produced by private companies, and the remainder is grown by small-scale farmers, who cultivate plots of approximately half a hectare. Tea is the most important export after tobacco and sugar and accounts for 8 percent of export earnings. The plucking season is during the rainy season from December to May, but climate change in the first years of the 21st century has meant a longer, hotter period, and erratic rainfall and hotter temperatures have led to a reduced crop and a greater likelihood of more frequent insect attacks. The Tea Research Foundation (Central Africa), set up in Mulanje in the 1960s, carries out research into these and other problems such as the development of new cultivars, yield levels, and the use of irrigation. Since 1996, a Tea Replanting Programme, with funding from the European Union, has replaced old plants with the new, higher-yielding clones on more than 1,800 hectares of land.

Most of the teas produced are CTC blacks, which are sold through the Limbe auctions and by private contract to the United Kingdom, Europe, South Africa, Botswana, Kenya, Zambia, the United States, Canada, Pakistan, Japan, and Australia.

THYOLO

Malawi's southern province of Thyolo (pronounced cho-lo) developed as a tea-growing region in the 1920s and '30s as more and more planters converted from rubber and tobacco production. The best-known companies are Satemwa Tea Estate, Naming'omba Tea Estate, Eastern Produce Malawi Ltd., and Makandi Tea & Coffee Estates Limited.

Maclean Kay, a rubber planter from Malaya (now Malaysia), established Satemwa Tea Estate in 1923 on the slopes of Mount Thyolo in the Shire Highlands. He planted his first tea in 1926. In 1928, he was also responsible for importing Indian assamica seeds, which were used to expand the country's tea industry. The company is today owned and managed by Maclean's grandson Alexander Cathcart Kay, employs 2,600 workers, and produces 2.5 million kilograms (5.5 million pounds) of tea each year. Satemwa produces black CTC teas for the global market, along with a range of excellent orthodox black, white, green, oolong, dark, and flavoured teas for the specialty market.

Naming'omba Tea Estate was established in 1927 by Malcolm Barrow, who bought land that had been used to grow tobacco. He converted it to tea using seeds imported from India, and by 1929, the estate covered 450 acres. In 1934, he acquired two neighbouring tea estates, constructed a factory at Naming'omba, and consolidated his holdings as Nyasa Tea Estates Limited. As well as owning the leading tea estate in Thyolo, Barrow also served as a member of the country's legislative council from 1941 to 1953 and as deputy prime minister of the Federation of Rhodesia and Nyasaland, which existed from 1953 to 1963. In the 1960s, ownership of the estate passed to Christopher Barrow, who renamed it Naming'omba Tea Estates Limited in 1966 and sold it to a local company in 2012. As well as producing black CTC teas, it also makes strong, malty, decaffeinated black teas by stripping out the caffeine at the green leaf stage instead of removing it after the tea has been processed.

In 1995, Eastern Produce Malawi Ltd absorbed estates previously owned by Blantyre & East Africa Limited, founded in 1898 to grow tobacco and tea. Today, Eastern Produce has estates, each with a factory, to the south-west of Blantyre at Makwasa, Mianga, Kasembereka, and Gotha, and the fresh leaf they process is grown by 3,500 smallholder members of the Eastern Outgrowers Trust. Makandi Tea Estates, owned by Dhunseri Petrochem & Tea Pte Ltd., has two estates, Chisunga and Mindale.

MULANJE

Mulanje lies in the south-eastern corner of Malawi, where Mount Mulanje, a towering rocky massif, dominates the countryside. The mountain is home to black eagles, buzzards, vervet monkeys, and klipspringer antelopes, and from the craggy peaks, fast-flowing waterfalls and rivers pour down to the tea fields in the foothills below. The estates here include Lujeri Tea Estate and those of Eastern Produce Malawi, Ltd., at Esperanza, Lauderdale, Mini Mini, Ruo, Glenorchy, Likanga, Eldorado, Thornwood, Phwazi, Chisambo, and Limbuli. Lujeri is one of the oldest colonial tea estates in the area and buys its fresh leaf from Sukambizi Association Trust (SAT). This organisation of small-scale tea producers was formed in 2003 to give the farmers more power when negotiating prices and payment terms. Today, 5,700 members grow 8 million kilos (17.6 million pounds) of green leaf, which the Lujeri factory turns into 1.7 million kilos (3.7 million pounds) of black CTC tea. Lujeri provides training in good farming practices and has developed a nursery to propagate high-quality seedlings.

Lujeri Tea Factory, which sits at the foot of Mount Mulanje.
Photograph courtesy of Teacraft Ltd.

NKHATA BAY

From the 1950s to the 1980s, Nkhata Bay, to the west of Lake Malawi in the north of the country, was one of the main tea-producing regions of Malawi, but most of the tea has now been replaced by rubber. The once famous Chombe estate was abandoned in the early 1990s, and the main producer today is the Kawalazi Tea Estate, acquired in 2012–13 by Dhunseri Petrochem & Tea Pte Limited. The tea is sold under the Kavuzi and Kawalazi brand names.

TOP: Satemwa Tea Estate in Thyolo makes a range of high-quality speciality teas as well as CTC black. MIDDLE: Employees at Satemwa Tea Estate. Photographs courtesy of Anette Kay/Fruitcake Media BOTTOM: Mount Mulanje rises sharply from the tea fields in southern Malawi. Photograph courtesy of Teacraft Ltd.

Country, State, or Province
Malawi

Number of Gardens
Approximately 40 and 12,000 smallholder farmers

Main Districts or Gardens
Thyolo Province, Mulanje, Nkhata Bay

Area Under Tea
18,000 hectares, including 12,000 smallholders

Thyolo Province: 9,000 hectares

Mulanje: 6,220 hectares

Nkhata Bay: 652 hectares

Average Annual Production (Kilograms)
39 million

Terrain
Thyolo Province: Undulating plains and hillsides covered with woodland and ancient mahogany forest

Mulanje: Sloping fields at the foot of Mount Mulanje

Nkhata Bay: Undulating fields surrounded by gentle hills

Altitude
Thyolo Province: 900 to 1,300 metres (2,952 to 4,265 feet)

Mulanje: 600 to 700 metres (1,969 to 2,297 feet)

Nkhata Bay: 566 metres (1,856 feet)

Production Period
December to May

Best Time to Visit
Early May, late June to early July, late September

Main Varietals/ Cultivars
Some original plants grown from seed from Edinburgh Botanical Garden, assamicas from India, and new cultivars developed by the Malawi Tea Research Station

Types of Tea Made
Mostly black CTC teas

Thyolo Province: Black CTC, orthodox black, white, green, oolong, and dark teas from Satemwa Tea Estate; black decaffeinated tea from Naming'omba

Mulanje: Black CTC

Nkhata Bay: Black CTC

Predominant Flavours; Tasting Notes
BLACK CTC: plain but bright, useful in breakfast blends

Naming'omba, Thyolo Province:
BLACK DECAFFEINATED: bright, full-bodied, malty

Satemwa, Thyolo Province:
BLACK ORTHODOX: sweet, malty, spicy, or fruity
WHITE: delicate with citrus or caramel notes, or buttery with floral hints, or fruity with suggestions of apricots and kumquats
GREEN: smooth, soft, with hints of nuts or seaweed
OOLONG: grassy with peppery notes
DARK: earthy, woody with hints of damp moss and autumn forests

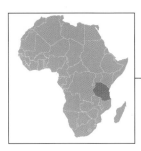

TANZANIA

Tea was introduced to Tanganyika in 1902 by German settlers and was planted at the Agricultural Research Station at Amani in the north-east of the country. In 1904, plants were established at Kyimbila in Rungwe District, and commercial production began in 1926, with tea replacing some of the coffee crop. Free seed was distributed to planters, factories were built, and by 1934, 1,000 hectares of land had been planted. By 1960, production of black tea had reached 3.75 million kilograms (8.27 million pounds). In 1964, the country gained its independence from Britain and was renamed Tanzania. Up to this point, large foreign companies had grown tea, with the Tanganyika Tea Board overseeing all tea-related matters. The government now introduced a program of smallholder tea farming and changed the Tea Board to the Tanzania Tea Authority, which became responsible for the trade and the marketing of smallholder tea. By the 1980s, outgrowers' share of total production stood at almost 30 percent. However, by the mid-1990s, that had dropped to less than 10 percent, and in 1994, the Tanzania Smallholder Tea Farmers Development Agency was created to promote and increase the outgrower sector.

The three main growing regions are today located in the Southern Highlands, in the north-east, and in the north-west of the country. With the regions lying close to the equator, the year does not divide into seasons, but the different regions have dry periods at different times of the year during which the bushes do not flush. In the north-west, the months of June and July are very dry; in the north-east, Lushoto is very dry in January, June, July, September, and October; Korogwe is dry in January, February, and July; and Muheza has no dry months, so the bushes are harvested all year. In the south, most areas have dry periods from May or June to October, but when the weather is wetter and cooler, the teas are better quality and fetch higher prices than those produced in the north. Most of the harvesting is done by hand, but since 2013, some Japanese-style hedge-trimmer harvesters have also been in use. The industry provides employment for approximately 50,000 families, and tea is the fifth most important export crop after cashew nuts, coffee, cotton, and tobacco. The bulk of the black CTC teas are exported to the United Kingdom, Kenya, and Pakistan, with smaller quantities going to the United States and Canada, Somalia, South Africa, and Sudan.

In areas where investor/smallholder partnerships do not operate, yields and green leaf quality remain well below those of Kenya. Farmers often receive low prices for their leaf. They, therefore, have little incentive to invest in fertilisers, and their yields remain low. The industry is also held back by inadequate infrastructure, unpredictable power supplies, poor roads, and unreliable vehicles. In addition, climate change is presenting new difficulties, and the Tea Research Institute of Tanzania (TRIT) is carrying out research into soil and water conservation, irrigation, mechanised harvesting, soil fertility management, crop responses to fertiliser regimes, and the development of new cultivars that will help the farmers produce a better crop. In 2014, TRIT released four new clones for commercial production, and it is hoped these will help increase output and quality.

The largest producers are Mufindi Tea Company, Unilever, East Usambara Tea Company, and TATEPA. Other companies include Metl, Watco, Dhow Merchantile, Tanwat, Kisigo Tea Company, Kagera Tea Company, New Mponde Tea Factory Ltd., and Bombay Burmah.

MUFINDI TEA COMPANY LTD

Owned by Rift Valley Corporation, Mufindi Tea Company has three estates in the Southern Highlands at Mufindi, Luponde, and Kibena; manufactures approximately 10 million kilos (22 million pounds) per year; and employs 2,500 people. In 2012, the company built a new factory at Ikanga in Lupembe to process smallholders' leaf, and the farmers own a 25 percent share. The company provides extension services, technical support, and transportation and sells fertiliser to the farmers at cost price.

To increase earnings in the specialty market, Luponde Tea Estate in the Livingstonia Mountains now produces large-leaf orthodox black teas, an organic steamed green, a silver-needle white, two Earl Greys (one green, one black), and various organic herbs as well as 20 million kilos (44 million pounds) of black CTC tea annually.

UNILEVER

Unilever's tea estates were established in Mufindi in the 1940s as the Tanganyika Tea Company, became Brooke Bond in the '70s, and in 1984, were acquired by Unilever. The tea grown here is used in Unilever blends for the world market. The Mufindi estate produces approximately 10 million kilos (22 million pounds) of tea every year and employs 6,000 people. In 2013, it entered into a partnership with the government to create 5,000 sustainable jobs at Mufindi and to develop a further 6,000 hectares of smallholder farms. The company is investing in new factories, local infrastructure, research, and support programs for the smallholders.

EAST USAMBARA TEA COMPANY

East Usambara Tea Company is owned by UK company Global Tea & Commodities Ltd and has three factories in Muheza in the East Usambara Mountains in the north-east. The company is Tanzania's third-largest producer, employs 3,500 people, and makes 3.2 million kilos (7.1 million pounds) of black tea annually.

TATEPA

Tanzania Tea Packers Limited (TATEPA) was established in 1995 as a blending and packing company and became involved in tea production when it acquired the Kibena and Wakulima tea estates and factories near Mbeya in southern Tanzania. Most of the green leaf is supplied by 14,000 smallholders, and in collaboration with the Rungwe Smallholders Tea Growers Association, Wakulima provides local farmers with inputs, technical assistance, collection of fresh leaf, and support with marketing and distribution. In Tukuyu, TATEPA and the UK Government Department for International Development have set up a successful partnership whereby the farmers own more than 25 percent of the factory. Wakulima is also planning a joint venture to pack value-added teas for the domestic market.

Although Tanzania now makes small quantities of orthodox teas, the majority of the country's production is strong, spicy black CTC. Photograph by John O'Hagan; © Hoffman Media

Country, State, or Province
Tanzania

Number of Gardens
20 factories

Main Districts or Gardens
Southern Highlands:
Mufindi, Njombe,
and Rungwe districts

North-east Zone:
Lushoto, Korogwe,
and Muheza districts

North-west Zone: Bukoba
and Muleba districts

Area Under Tea
22,700 hectares, half of
which are cultivated by
30,000 smallholders on plots
of less than half a hectare

**Average Annual
Production (Kilograms)**
32 million

Terrain
Southern Highlands: Flat
terrain and steep slopes in
rolling hills surrounded by
ancient rainforest

North-east Zone: Fertile
highland valley in the
East Usambara Mountains;
slopes covered with tea,
pine trees, eucalyptus trees,
and banana palms

North-west Zone: Hilly
terrain with thick tropical
vegetation, forests, and
open grassland

Altitude
Southern Highlands:
1,200 to 2,134 metres
(4,000 to 7,000 feet)

North-east Zone:
1,000 to 2,200 metres
(3,280 to 7,217 feet)

North-west Zone:
1,400 and 2,200 metres
(4,693 and 7,217 feet)

Production Period
Seasonally or all year,
depending on region

Best Time to Visit
Southern Highlands:
May to November

North-east Zone:
February, August,
September

North-west zone:
July, August, February,
March

Main Varietals/Cultivars
Origin of first seeds not
known; clones imported
from Kenya and Malawi
in 1970s and clones from
selected local plants

Types of Tea Made
Southern Highlands:
Black CTC

North-east Zone:
Black CTC and small
quantities of orthodox
black, steamed greens,
and white teas made at
Luponde Tea Estate

North-west Zone:
Black CTC

**Predominant Flavours;
Tasting Notes**
BLACK CTC: dark, robust
liquors with a malty, spicy
character and sometimes
a citrus note
BLACK ORTHODOX: rich, crisp
GREEN: fresh and light
WHITE SILVER NEEDLE:
delicate and aromatic

ZAMBIA

Tea-growing in Zambia started on a trial basis in the 1960s when the colonial British government decided to develop the country's own tea industry rather than continue to import tea from neighbouring producers. There was also a need to create employment in rural areas, and trials indicated that Kawambwa District of Luapula Province in the north-east of the country was the most suitable location for the first tea estate. In 1970, the Kawambwa Tea Scheme was established on 22.26 hectares under the control of the Ministry of Rural Development. In 1974, the ministry renamed it Kawambwa Tea Company (KTC), the area under tea was expanded, and a factory was built. After the ministry was closed down in 1984, KTC was bought and sold several times and at one point in 2014 was run by the managers who tried to keep production going. The government eventually stepped in, and by November 2014, the factory was operating again, and the black CTC tea being produced showed improvement. Government also allocated another 20,000 hectares to be developed as a new tea estate and tree plantation. But by May 2015, promises to save Kawambwa had not been fulfilled, and the workers were once again calling for help from the government. The quantity and quality of tea have fluctuated in this unstable situation.

Some of Kawambwa's tea is sold to Yatu Tea, a small Zambian company set up in 1999 by Miriam and Modi Chapotamos with the support of the United States Agency for International Development (USAID). The factory at Ndola in the centre of the country (where the Chapotamoses make a point of employing more women than men) packs the Zambian-grown black CTC tea into tea bags for sale throughout southern Africa. The Tea Association of Malawi would also like to see Zambia's tea being sold through the Limbe auction in Blantyre, and it is hoped that this will attract new buyers to the auctions and make Malawi's tea market more lucrative.

Country, State, or Province
Zambia

Number of Gardens 1

Main Districts or Gardens
Kawambwa Tea Company, Kawambwa District of Luapula Province in the north-east of the country

Area Under Tea
500 hectares

Average Annual Production (Kilograms)
Capacity of 1 million, but not being achieved because of breakdown of ownership and management

Terrain
Rolling hills on the edge of the northern Zambian Plateau above the Luapula Valley

Altitude
1,300 metres (4,265 feet)

Production Period
All year

Best Time to Visit
May to October

Main Varietals/ Cultivars
Not yet known

Types of Tea Made
Black CTC

Predominant Flavours; Tasting Notes
BLACK CTC: rich, strong

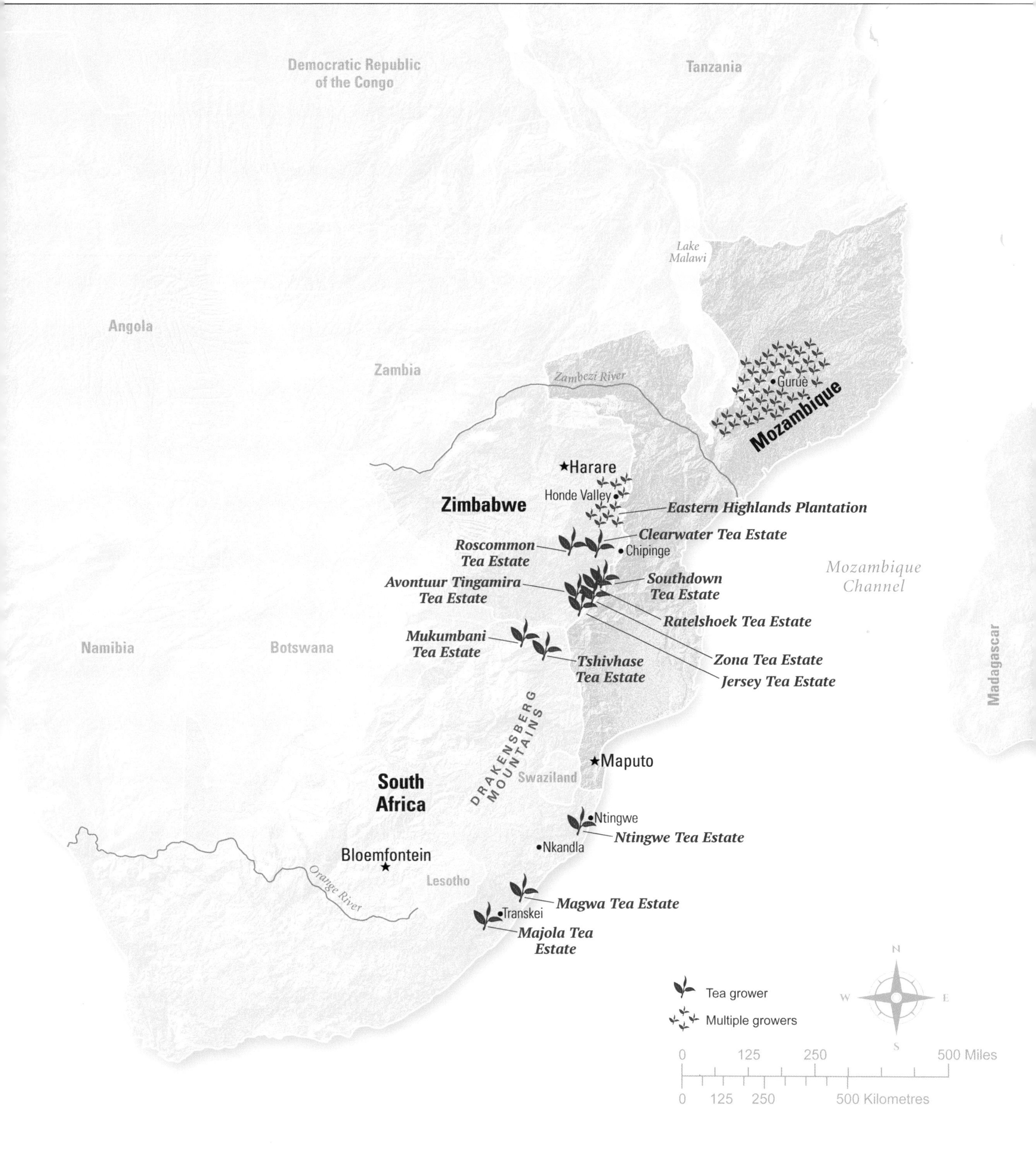

Democratic Republic
of the Congo

Tanzania

Angola

Zambia

*Lake
Malawi*

Zambezi River

Mozambique

• Gurúè

★ Harare

Honde Valley •

Zimbabwe

Eastern Highlands Plantation

Clearwater Tea Estate

*Roscommon
Tea Estate*

• Chipinge

*Mozambique
Channel*

*Avontuur Tingamira
Tea Estate*

*Southdown
Tea Estate*

Ratelshoek Tea Estate

*Mukumbani
Tea Estate*

*Tshivhase
Tea Estate*

Zona Tea Estate

Jersey Tea Estate

Namibia

Botswana

D
R
A
K
E
N
S
B
E
R
G

M
O
U
N
T
A
I
N
S

★ Maputo

Swaziland

**South
Africa**

Bloemfontein
★

Orange River

Lesotho

• Ntingwe

Ntingwe Tea Estate

• Nkandla

Madagascar

Magwa Tea Estate

• Transkei

*Majola Tea
Estate*

Tea grower

Multiple growers

N

W   E

S

0   125   250   500 Miles

0   125   250   500 Kilometres

MOZAMBIQUE

The Portuguese colonised Mozambique in 1505, and the town of Gurúè in Zambezia Province was established during the 19th century. In the 1930s, the mountain slopes around Gurúè were developed as a major tea region, and local companies such as Chá Moçambique and Plantações Manuel Saraiva Junqueiro had estates here. Fifteen factories processed the leaf, the tea was exported all over the world, and the district's economy flourished. By the late 1970s, 9,000 hectares of land had been planted; the industry employed 28,000 workers; and each year the country produced approximately 17 million kilograms (37.5 million pounds) of black tea, which was exported to the United Kingdom and North America. But in 1975, independence brought the departure of the Portuguese, a period of extreme social and economic decline, and civil war from 1977 to 1992, during which time the tea estates and factories were abandoned and destroyed.

Today, only five factories remain, production has dropped to just 13 percent of pre-independence output, and only 3,000 workers are employed during peak seasons. Indian companies now own most of the estates. One is run as an Indian-Mozambican joint venture, while smallholders account for approximately 35 percent of production. Exacerbating the problems of the now sluggish industry are low wages; late payment of wages by some factories; workers who are therefore unmotivated; and low-yielding, poor-quality, old plants that need replacing. However, in 2014, the government held discussions with Indian producers to gain their advice and expertise, and there is hope that the situation may be improved by developing the outgrower sector and giving more control to smallholders.

The country produces mainly black CTC tea, but since 2009, the Cha Luso factory, owned by HK Jalan Group, has been experimenting with the manufacture of orthodox black and green teas. Mozambique teas have traditionally been sold through the Kenya auctions, but in 2014, the industry expressed an interest in selling through Malawi's auctions in the future.

Country, State, or Province
Mozambique

Number of Gardens
5, plus 200,000 smallholders

Main Districts or Gardens
Zambezia Province in the southern Rift Valley in the north of the country

Area Under Tea
5,700 hectares

Average Annual Production (Kilograms)
2.26 million

Terrain
Steep slopes in the fertile foothills with rocky outcrops; sandy soils prone to draining too fast

Altitude
600 to 1,200 metres (1,968 to 3,937 feet)

Production Period
December to May

Best Time to Visit
All year

Main Varietals/ Cultivars
Assamica and sinensis varietals

Types of Tea Made
Black CTC

Predominant Flavours; Tasting Notes
BLACK CTC: quite plain, poor quality

SOUTH AFRICA

Commercial cultivation started here in 1877 with seeds from Assam, and over the following years, estates were established in KwaZulu-Natal in the Drakensberg Mountains, in Transkei, in Limpopo, and in Ntingwe in central Zululand. The industry expanded in the 1970s and '80s to create jobs in the rural areas. But when apartheid ended in 1991, government subsidies were withdrawn, costs went up, and production became too expensive. By 2004, most of the farmers had turned to other activities. Then, in 2008–9 government efforts to revitalise the industry and a number of successful partnerships with the private sector resulted in a substantial increase in production. Today, tea is grown at Ntingwe Tea Estate in the cool, wooded hills of KwaZulu's Nkandla District; at Tshivhase Tea Estate, which owns Tshivhase (established in 1977) and Mukumbani (established in 1987), in the Vhembe District of the northerly province of Limpopo; and at Magwa Tea Estate, a 1,800-hectare farm outside Lusikisiki in Eastern Cape Province. A R116 million rescue package was put in place in 2017 and was intended to save both Magwa and Majola Tea Estate near Port Saint Johns on the Wild Coast of Eastern Cape Province. But, whereas Magwa, whose shares were owned by the Eastern Cape Development Corporation (ECDC), could therefore be saved, Majola was owned by the Majola Workers' Trust and so could not. In late 2017, Majola was provisionally closed down while attempts were made to put a new business plan together.

NTINGWE TEA ESTATE

Ntingwe Tea Estate, originally a research project set up in 1987 by the province's development agency, Ithala Development Corporation Limited, has become a success story for South African tea. Quality clonal bushes grow on 260 of the planned 585 hectares and are mechanically harvested (all other growers pluck by hand). The Ntingwe factory produces approximately 750,035 kilos (1.65 million pounds) of quality black CTC tea annually for export, in particular to the United States and the United Kingdom, where it fetches high prices as a single-origin tea. For many years, UK company Taylors of Harrogate sold it as Zulu Tea and used it in its famous Yorkshire Gold brand. In 2008, Ntingwe explored the possibility of making steamed green tea, and the KwaZulu-Natal Department of Agriculture provided R17 million (more than US$1.2 million) to buy essential Japanese technology. The green teas now fetch higher prices than the black and are already popular in Japan. Ntingwe also hopes to sell the green teas in Europe and the United States.

Country, State, or Province
South Africa

Number of Gardens
5

Main Districts or Gardens
KwaZulu-Natal, Limpopo and the Eastern Cape

Area Under Tea
4,059 hectares

Average Annual Production (Kilograms)
4 million to 7 million

Terrain
Wide, flat fields surrounded by woodland

Altitude
6,00 to 1,000 metres (1,968 to 3,280 feet)

Production Period
October to mid February

Best Time to Visit
All year

Main Varietals/ Cultivars
Clones from assamicas from Assam

Types of Tea Made
Black CTC, steamed green

Predominant Flavours; Tasting Notes
BLACK CTC: robust, dry, crisp, with a tart orange zest aftertaste

TOP: Employees' houses clustered together in the middle of Grenshoek Tea Estate. ABOVE LEFT: An irrigation system. ABOVE RIGHT: Leaf collection into airy crates to prevent damage to the leaves. Photograph courtesy of Angela Pryce

ZIMBABWE

The first tea was planted in southern Rhodesia (known today as Zimbabwe) in 1924 by two Assam planters, Arthur Ward and Grafton Phillips, who established a small plot of Assam varietals on New Year's Gift Estate in Chipinge. The industry grew, and by 1989, production had reached almost 18 million kilos (39.7 million pounds). But during Robert Mugabe's years of "land reform," many of the tea workers fled into South Africa. Abandoned tea bushes and understaffed factories meant that any tea produced was of very poor quality and unpredictable quantity. Compounding those problems were rampant inflation, fuel shortages, unreliable power supplies, lack of capital, and weakening infrastructure. In 2012, only 300 or so of the 3,500 Honde Valley smallholders were still farming tea. Some factories had stopped working altogether, and production had dropped to 10 percent of capacity. However, by 2014, most of the factories were operating again, and production was running at close to 60 percent capacity.

The main growing regions are in the Honde Valley and Chipinge in the east of the country, and the tea fields sweep across vast plains stretching towards the mountains in the hazy distance. Zimbabwe's position close to the Tropic of Capricorn means that production takes place for only eight months of the year. In addition to growing some of their own leaf, the factories buy fresh leaf from thousands of smallholder farmers who live within a radius of 40 kilometres (25 miles) of the factories. More and more of the tea is harvested using shears and motorised machines, but the quality often suffers in the hot temperatures because of delayed delivery to factories, protracted weighing, and slow quality checks. The black CTC teas are sold to the United Kingdom, the Middle East, the United States, and Pakistan for teabag blends.

Lack of availability of credit and slow cash flow in the past made it extremely difficult to instigate necessary improvements to harvesting, supply chain, and infrastructure. Climate change is also having a greater effect on Zimbabwe than on other African countries. Since 1987, six of the warmest years ever have been recorded, with a 40 percent drop in rainfall. This has affected absorption of sprayed fertilisers, yield, and quality. But more available money is now paying for tractors, new machinery, tea-grower union schemes, support and training for farmers, and better roads. Various non-governmental organisations have also become involved in schemes to increase earnings and improve farmers' longer-term prospects. A project run by SNV Zimbabwe, in partnership with World Vision, is helping improve crop productivity and quality by funding new seedling bushes, pruning machines, and fertilisers. It also offers training in credit management, price negotiation, crop viability, and supply chains.

The industry in Zimbabwe is dominated by three major producers—Tanganda Tea Company, Ariston Holdings Ltd., and Eastern Highlands Plantations Limited (EHPL). Family-owned Buzi Tea Estate also grows tea in Chipinge. The 100-hectare Honde Valley ARDA Katiyo Estate, owned by the Agricultural and Rural Development Authority, closed in 2012 as a result of poor prices and a switch by farmers to banana cultivation.

TANGANDA TEA COMPANY | *Chipinge*

Tanganda started growing tea in the 1920s and is today the largest producer. Its four estates at Ratelshoek, Zona, Jersey, and Avontuur Tingamira in the Chipinge District cover a total of 2,000 hectares.

SOUTHDOWN (ARISTON HOLDINGS LTD) | *Chipinge*

Agri-industrial company Ariston is the country's second-largest producer and owns three tea estates in Chipinge—Clearwater, Southdown, and Roscommon (the latter also grows macadamia nuts and bananas).

Tanganda and Ariston are working to develop a further 3,000 hectares of smallholder land, and will provide seedling plants, transport to collect green leaf, financial help, and technical support.

EASTERN HIGHLANDS PLANTATION | *Honde Valley*

The large estate lies at the foot of Mount Nyangani in the Honde Valley and employs 1,300 people. Fresh leaf is processed at the Wambe factory to produce 4.144 million kilos (9.1 million pounds) per year.

Ratelshoek Tea Estate in Chipinge and different harvesting methods.
Photographs courtesy of Teacraft Ltd.

Country, State, or Province
Zimbabwe

Number of Gardens
9, plus 3,500 smallholders

Main Districts or Gardens
Honde Valley and Chipinge in the Eastern Highlands

Area Under Tea
6,800 hectares

Average Annual Production (Kilograms)
13 million

Terrain
Undulating tea fields; red and black fertile soils on vast open plains of agricultural land in the Eastern Highlands Range

Altitude
900 metres (2,953 feet) in Honde Valley; 1,108 metres (3,635 feet) in Chipinge

Production Period
October to May

Best time to visit
April to October

Main Varietals/Cultivars
Assamica varietals from India, and new quality clones

Types of Tea Made
Black CTC

Predominant Flavours; Tasting Notes
CTC BLACK: strong, dark liquors; robust, medium quality, mainly used in blends

Japanese tea garden at Ticino on the slopes of Monte Verità, high above
the city of in Ascona, Switzerland. Photograph courtesy of Peter Oppliger

CHAPTER 5

EUROPE

EUROPE DID NOT BECOME AWARE OF TEA UNTIL
THE 16TH CENTURY WHEN PRIESTS, ENVOYS,
AND MERCHANTS FROM ITALY AND PORTUGAL
WERE THE FIRST TO MENTION THE BEVERAGE
IN ACADEMIC TRACTS AND LETTERS HOME.

TOP: Shear plucking at a tea farm in Turkey. BOTTOM LEFT: A lorry load of freshly plucked leaf ready to go to the factory for processing. BOTTOM RIGHT: View of a tea field from the nearby town of Cayeli, Rize Province, on the Black Sea in Turkey. Photographs courtesy of tea explorer Dani Lieuthier

The Venetian lawyer Giovanni Battista Ramusio learned from Chaggi Memet, a Persian merchant, that "all over the country of Cathay [China], they made use of another plant, or rather of its leaves. This is called by those people Chiai Catai [China tea], and grows in the district of Cathay, which is called Cacianfu [Sichuan]."

In 1557, the Portuguese established a trading base on Macau, and it is possible that Portuguese ships included tea amongst the Oriental goods they carried back to Lisbon. The Dutch joined the quest for spices in the 1590s; created the Dutch East India Company in 1602; and started importing pepper, nutmeg, cloves, silk, and porcelains from Indonesia, Japan, and China. In 1610, the company brought home its first small consignment of tea and began to re-export it to other European countries.

By the 1630s, wealthy French families were drinking tea as a luxury beverage. The letters of the Marquise de Sevigné tell us that the Princesse de Tarente consumed 12 cups of tea a day and that Madame de la Sablière added a little milk to hers. Both King Louis XIV and Cardinal Mazarin drank tea as a cure for gout. Although the French Revolution (1789–1799) discouraged tea drinking as the elite indulgence of the upper classes, many continued to copy what was by then a British fashion.

Tea also reached Germany in the 1630s, but local physician Simon Pauli challenged claims that it was beneficial to the health, and coffee and beer became the preferred beverages. However, in East Frisia, a northern region through which tea was imported in the 17th century, a tea-drinking culture developed that still exists. Black tea is brewed strong, sugar and cream are added but not stirred in, and as the liquid is sipped, the tea blends with the swirling cream to give a smooth, sweet liquor. During the 19th century, a number of tea wholesalers established their warehouses in the ports of Bremen and Hamburg, and Germany today is extremely important to the bulk buying and blending of teas from around the world.

The first tea to arrive in England was delivered into the London docks on a Dutch East Indiaman and was first advertised in 1658 for sale at a coffeehouse in the city. The diarist Samuel Pepys mentioned drinking his first cup in 1660, and London merchant Thomas Garraway declared, "That the Vertues and Excellencies of this Leaf and Drink are many and great is evident and manifest by the high esteem and use of it . . . among the physitians and knowing men in France, Italy, Holland. . . ." When Princess Catherine of Braganza arrived from Portugal to marry Charles II in 1662, she brought with her a small casket of tea and brewed it for her ladies at court, setting a fashion that charmed the upper classes. The East India Company first imported tea directly from China in 1669, and over time, the brew became the preferred beverage across the social spectrum despite the continuing high price. In the 1830s, the East India Company established experimental tea gardens in India, and in 1839, the first black Assam tea was sold in the London auctions. British tea gardens were then developed in other parts of India and in Ceylon. By the 1890s, prices had dropped, and tea had become the drink of the British nation.

Russians first drank tea in the 1690s, but the high cost—due to the long, slow route along which it was carried from China to St. Petersburg and Moscow—meant that only the wealthy could afford it. The country did not grow its own tea until the 20th century.

Plucking shears used in Turkish tea fields. Photograph courtesy of tea explorer Dani Lieuthier

Tea grower
Multiple growers

N
W · E
S

0   250   500   1,000 Miles
0   250   500   1,000 Kilometres

Arctic Circle

Norwegian Sea

Barents Sea

Russia

Volga River

★ Moscow

Kama River

Baltic Sea

North Sea

Tyne River

United Kingdom

Trent River

Amsterdam ★

Netherlands

★ London

Don River

EUROPE

ATLANTIC OCEAN

Paris ★

Loire River

Seine River

Switzerland

Bern ★

ALPS

Po River

Rhône River

Gulf of Biscaya

France

PYRENEES MOUNTAINS

Ebro River

Adige River

Italy

Rome ★

Tiber River

APENNINES MOUNTAINS

Adriatic Sea

Black Sea

Georgia

★ Tbilisi

Kelkit River

Euphrates River

Spain

Douro River

Portugal

★ Madrid

Tagus River

Guadiana River

Lisbon ★

Guadalquivir River

Azores

Sakarya River

★ Ankara

Gediz River

Turkey

Tigris River

Mediterranean Sea

Strait of Gibraltor

AFRICA

A truck loaded with freshly harvested leaf waiting to go to a Turkish factory. Photograph courtesy of tea explorer Dani Lieuthier

Tea grower

0   50 100   200 Miles
0 50 100   200 Kilometres

ATLANTIC
OCEAN

North Sea

Ireland

United Kingdom

★ Amsterdam

Special Plant
Zundert BV •Zundert **Netherlands**

English Channel

Belgium

Germany

Luxembourg

Celtic Sea

Paris★

Seine River

Nantes•

Loire River

Le Parc
du Grand-Blottereau

France

Switzerland

Bay of
Biscay

Rhône River

Italy

PYRENEES
MOUNTAINS

Pazo Quinteiro
da Cruz — •Pontevedra

Ebro River

Chá Camélia —
•Porto

Douro River

Spain

Portugal

★ Madrid

Tagus River

Lisbon ★

Guadiana River

Mediterranean Sea

Azores

Guadalquivir River

Chá Porto Formoso — *Gorreana*
Tea Estate

Strait of —
Gibraltor

AFRICA

FRANCE

The French upper classes developed a taste for tea in the 1630s and, as in other parts of Europe, drank it as a luxury beverage in their grand houses and royal palaces. King Louis XIV had a fondness for it and drank it as a healthy tonic to protect against gout and heart problems. In the 19th century, as the British developed their afternoon-tea ritual, the French, too, indulged in elegant tea gatherings in the middle of the afternoon, and many of France's most successful tea companies were established during this period.

LE PARC DU GRAND-BLOTTEREAU | *Nantes*

For a number of years, Le Parc du Grand-Blottereau in Nantes has been home to a small plot of tea bushes, but the city council never thought of plucking the new shoots to make tea until the idea was suggested in 2002 by the newly formed Brittany/Pays de la Loire Club des Buveurs de Thé. In April of that year, club members decided they would like to share their passion for the beverage, its culture, and its cultivation. In collaboration with Nantes City Council, the club imported a further 100 young tea bushes from Suncheon, Nantes's twin town in South Korea, and planted them behind the pavilion of the park's Korean Garden. In April 2011, tea club members plucked 900 grams (31.5 ounces) of leaf and turned it into 300 grams (10 ounces) of green tea. Each spring, the club regroups here between 10 a.m. and noon to pick the new shoots to make the first-flush tea. The leaves are withered indoors, then tumbled in a wok before being rolled in cloths and dried. Called La Colline de Suncheon, the tea gives a pale green liquor that has the vegetal sweetness of Korean green teas and the savoury seaweed notes of Japanese sencha. The tea harvest festival is open each year to the public, but only tea club members are allowed to actually pick and process the tea.

Country, State, or Province
France

Number of Gardens
1

Main Districts or Gardens
Nantes

Area Under Tea
A small portion of a border behind the Korean pavilion

Average Annual Production (Kilograms)
300 grams

Terrain
Flat borders in Le Parc du Grand-Blottereau

Altitude
7 metres (23 feet)

Production Period
April

Best Time to Visit
April to October

Main Varietals/Cultivars
Korean cultivars

Types of Tea Made
Green

Predominant Flavours; Tasting Notes
GREEN: sweet, vegetal, with hints of seaweed

THE NETHERLANDS

In 1602, the Dutch East India Company (Vereenigde Oost-Indische Compagnie, or Verenigde Oostindische Compagnie) was established as a chartered company. In 1610, the company began to import tea from China via Batavia, its headquarters on the island of Java, Indonesia. As in other parts of Europe at the time, the cost of the dry leaves in the Netherlands was extremely high, so tea was only affordable to the very wealthy. But as quantities coming into the country increased, prices fell, and as demand grew, *Camellia sinensis* var. *sinensis* tea seeds were planted on Java with the intention of producing Dutch-grown tea. The climate proved to be unsuitable for the Chinese varietal, and the plants did not flourish. Commercial cultivation did not begin until the 1830s when the assamica was planted on Java and, in the early 1900s, on Sumatra. Although the Netherlands was responsible for introducing tea to Europe and for shipping the first small quantities into London in the late 1650s, the taste for tea gradually declined over the centuries, and coffee was more widely consumed. But since the turn of the 21st century, the number of tea stores, tea companies, tea education, tea events, and tea competitions has steadily increased.

LEFT: Rolled green leaves just beginning to oxidise at Special Plant Zundert BV. RIGHT: Johan Jansen, owner of Special Plant Zundert BV, in one of his polytunnels of tea. Photographs courtesy of Tea by Me BV

SPECIAL PLANT ZUNDERT BV | *Zundert*

Johan Jansen has been interested in tea since he was a little boy, and while in his final year at university where he studied agricultural management, he decided to spend six months exploring China to learn more about the plant and the beverage. When he returned home 10 years ago, he resolved to try growing tea and spent eight years developing a new cultivar that would thrive in the harsh North European climate, could survive temperatures of -15°C (5°F), and would resist mould. His new hardy plant, which he has named Tea by Me, was developed from plants imported from Japan, China, New Zealand, Canada, the United States, and the UK. This is the first time that a European nursery has developed a new hardy tea cultivar, and other growers around the world are already showing an interest in the plant. At Special Plant Zundert BV (Jansen's modern automated company that specializes in a range of unusual shrubs), 2 hectares of tea plants grow outdoors in polytunnels, and 6 hectares grow in greenhouses. All cultivation parameters, such as light, shade, feeding, and soil, can be controlled to help the plants thrive, and in warmer weather, the sides of the polytunnels are rolled up to let in fresh warm air. As well as selling the plants, Jansen and tea sommelier Anne Geert-Adams are making all types of tea by hand and by machine, but focus particularly on the manufacture of steamed green teas. They plan to develop Tea by Me as a brand that sells not just young tea plants but also a range of loose-leaf teas. They hope to encourage other people to grow tea locally, and will sell freshly plucked green leaf (packed in coolbags inside which the leaf stays fresh and green for several days) to anyone who wants to try making tea but does not actually grow any plants. They are also developing a support network and will offer training workshops, advice about machinery, and expertise to new growers and tea makers.

Country, State, or Province
The Netherlands

Number of Gardens 1

Main Districts or Gardens
Special Plant Zundert BV,
Zundert

Area Under Tea
8 hectares

Average Annual Production (Kilograms)
Not yet known

Terrain
Very flat

Altitude
Sea level

Production Period
Outdoors and in polytunnels, March to December; all year in greenhouses with lighting

Best Time to Visit
March to September

Main Varietals/Cultivars
Camellia sinensis var. *sinensis*, Special Plant Zundert cultivar called Tea by Me

Types of Tea Made
All categories, but mainly steamed green teas

Predominant Flavours; Tasting Notes
THE BEST GREEN: umami and buttery with hints of grass and wet hay, lightly floral with sweet tones of roasted almond

PORTUGAL

AND THE AZORES

In 1557, the Chinese agreed to allow Portuguese merchants to settle on the Island of Macao, just off the south coast of China, and this became the Portuguese base for trade in Chinese silk, Japanese silver, and porcelain. Of course, the resident Portuguese also came across tea and carried samples back to Lisbon. The Jesuit priest Father Jasper de Cruz mentioned tea in a letter home in 1560, and by the beginning of the 17th century, the expensive beverage was becoming popular at court. When Catherine, daughter of King John IV, of the House of Braganza, was sent to England to marry King Charles II, she was already a dedicated tea drinker, having grown up in a noble Portuguese household. Historical records show that a small plantation near Ponte de Lima had been established in the middle of the 19th century but closed down when its owner returned home to Brazil.

Tea cultivation in the Azores, colonized by the Portuguese in the 15th century, dates back to the early 19th century. In 1801, while in Brazil, the king of Portugal received a gift of tea plants from the emperor of China, and these were planted in different parts of Brazil. In 1820, seeds from Rio de Janeiro were taken to São Miguel, the largest of the Azores islands, and tea cultivation gradually took over from the citrus fruit industry. The tea plants thrived here in the volcanic soil and warm, humid climate and seemed not to need shelter from the salty winds off the Atlantic Ocean. In 1874, two Chinese experts were employed to advise on cultivation and the construction of a factory, and on the 27th of July 1879, *The New York Times* wrote that Azores tea was "of good appearance, though perhaps somewhat over-roasted; the smell also is good, and the flavor by no means to be despised." By 1900, 14 estates were producing tea. However, Portugal's policy to protect its tea industry in its Mozambique colony negatively affected production in the Azores, and by 1966, only five factories were still operating. Today, there are only two—Gorreana and Porto Formoso. The bushes are plucked mechanically, and both estates use orthodox rollers. The teas are mostly consumed locally or in mainland Portugal.

CHÁ CAMÉLIA | *Vila do Conde, Norte Region*

The coastal region to the north of Porto on Portugal's Atlantic Coast is known as the land of the camellia trees, and so in 2011, Dirk Niepoort and Nina Gruntkowski planted 200 experimental tea cuttings in their garden in Porto to check whether the climate and conditions would suit *Camellia sinensis*. When the plants flourished, they decided to establish a small tea farm slightly further up the coast, just inland from Vila do Conde, at an abandoned family farm where the soil, humidity, and moderate climate create a perfect home for tea. In 2014, they planted 6,500 Japanese cultivars, acquired from Peter Oppliger's tea garden in southern Switzerland, on an organic and biodynamic 1.24-acre plot at the farm and in 2017 were planning to plant another 1.24 acres over the following two years. The new plants have been grown from seed and leaf cuttings taken from the existing plants, and once the tea bushes have matured, the leaf will be processed as high-quality Japanese-style sencha, some handcrafted and some made by machine. Niepoort and Gruntkowski say that their previous work in wine has helped them understand the complexity of tea cultivation and to appreciate the fascinating layers of culture and traditions of both beverages.

Nina Gruntkowski (centre), with Japanese tea producers Haruyo (right) and Shigeru (left) Morimoto, planting her first tea at Vila do Conde.
Photograph courtesy of Chá Camélia

GORREANA TEA ESTATE | *São Miguel (The Azores)*

Gorreana was established on the north coast of São Miguel in 1883 by Ermelinda Gago da Câmara and is still owned and managed by the Câmara family. The plants in the oldest sections of the garden are Chinese varietals, but in 1948, assamicas were also introduced. The estate has a museum that documents the early years of the Azores tea industry.

CHA PORTO FORMOSO | *São Miguel (The Azores)*

The neighbouring Porto Formosa garden, which dates back to the 19th century, was closed for approximately 20 years and reopened in 2001. It comprises a garden, a processing factory, and a tea museum, and there are plans to double the existing 3 hectares of tea.

TOP: Chá Gorreana Tea factory where fresh leaf harvested by machine is processed as large and broken black and green teas. ABOVE: Steep terraced slopes of bushes that have been growing here at Chá Gorreana in the Azores since 1883. Photographs courtesy of Plantaçoes de Chá Gorreana Ltd.

Country, State, or Province
Portugal and the Azores

Number of Gardens
1 at Vila do Conde in mainland Portugal

2 in the Autonomous Region of the Azores

Main Districts or Gardens
Chá Camélia, Vila do Conde

Gorreana, County of Ribiera Grande, São Miguel Island, the Azores

Chá Porto Formoso, County of Ribiera Grande, São Miguel Island, the Azores

Area Under Tea
Chá Camélia: 6,500 plants on half a hectare

Gorreana: 45 hectares

Chá Porto Formoso: 3 hectares

Average Annual Production (Kilograms)
Chá Camélia: Not yet known

Gorreana: 36,287

Chá Porto Formoso: 5,000

Terrain
Chá Camélia: Low-lying flat land on the Atlantic Coast in northern Portugal, just inland from the town of Vila Do Conde

Gorreana: Steep slopes and undulating fields on rich volcanic soil

Chá Porto Formoso: Steep slopes and undulating fields on rich volcanic soil

Altitude
Chá Camélia: Approximately 100 metres (328 feet)

Gorreana: Up to 610 metres (2,000 feet)

Chá Porto Formoso: 35 metres (115 feet)

Production Period
Chá Camélia: Late April to early May

Gorreana: Late March to September

Chá Porto Formoso: Late March to September

Best Time to Visit
Vila do Conde, Mainland: June to October

Azores: May to early September

Main Varietals/Cultivars
Chá Camélia: Japanese cultivars from Peter Oppliger in Switzerland

Gorreana: Sinensis and assamicas (The local varietal, which has evolved naturally and is resistant to salty winds, is sometimes referred to as *Camellia azorica*.)

Chá Porto Formoso: Sinensis via Brazil

Types of Tea Made
Chá Camélia: Japanese-style green

Gorreana: Black orthodox, green

Chá Porto Formoso: Broken black

Predominant Flavours; Tasting Notes
Chá Camélia: Not yet known

Gorreana:
LARGE-LEAF BLACKS: bold, complex, full-bodied
BROKEN BLACKS: light, aromatic
GREEN: tannic, full-flavoured

Chá Porto Formoso:
BLACK: delicate, aromatic

SPAIN

PAZO QUINTEIRO DA CRUZ | *Ribadumia*

The 18th-century manor house Pazo Quinteiro da Cruz, at Ribadumia, Pontevedra, on the Atlantic Coast of Galicia in north-west Spain, has a small tea garden on its 17-acre farm. Most of the land is planted with wine grapes and more than 500 different species of trees and shrubs from around the world, including more than 1,500 different varieties of ornamental camellia. The temperate, marine climate here is very similar to that of the Azores, so the decision was made to also grow *Camellia sinensis*. The bushes are cultivated organically inside a bamboo enclosure, and the first flush is used to make small quantities of white tea, while the second and third flushes are processed as green tea. The teas are sold in packets and are also served to visitors who come here to enjoy a Spanish-style 7 p.m. "afternoon tea."

The gardens at Pazo Quinteiro da Cruz where tea is grown alongside more than 500 species of trees and shrubs. Photograph courtesy of Pazo Quinteiro da Cruz - Turismo de Galicia

Country, State, or Province
Spain

Number of Gardens
1

Main Districts or Gardens
Pazo Quinteiro da Cruz, Ribadumia

Area Under Tea
Just under 1 acre

Average Annual Production (Kilograms)
Not yet known

Terrain
Flat land exposed to sun and shade; forest area on sloping land with little sun exposure

Altitude
20 metres (65.6 feet)

Production Period
March to early October

Best Time to Visit
June to mid-August

Main Varietals/ Cultivars
Sinensis from China, and some assamicas

Types of Tea Made
Handcrafted green and small quantities of white

Predominant Flavours; Tasting Notes
GREEN: fruity, floral with hints of loquat, apple, and camellia
WHITE: soft and sweet with a hint of fig

ATLANTIC
OCEAN

Spey River

Dee River

**The Wee Tea
Plantation**

Kinnettles Farm

Tummel River

•Kinnettles

Windy Hollow Farm

**Tea Gardens
of Scotland**

★Edinburgh

Tweed River

Scotland

Tyne River

North Sea

**Northern
Ireland**

★Belfast

County Down•

England

Ireland

**Portaferry
Tea Farm**

Trent River

Great Ouse River

Irish Sea

UNITED
KINGDOM

Wales

Thames River

London
★

**The Original
Welsh Tea
Company Ltd.**

Cardiff
★

•West Sandford

Avon River

Celtic Sea

•Tresillian

Hele House

English Channel

**Tregothnan
Tea Estate**

France

Tea grower

0   50   100   200 Miles

0   50   100   200 Kilometres

UNITED KINGDOM

During World War II, when the supply of food to Britain was threatened by the activities of German U-Boats, Prime Minister Winston Churchill and his government debated the possibility of growing tea on home soil instead of having to ship it into the United Kingdom from India and Ceylon. But because newly planted bushes would take four or five years to mature and become sturdy enough to yield their first crop, the idea was quickly abandoned. No tea was grown commercially in Britain until 1999 when Tregothnan Tea Estate, near Truro in Cornwall in the south-west of England, was established.

The Honourable Evelyn Boscawen, owner of Tregothnan Estate in Cornwall, with the Indian High Commissioner during his visit to the United Kingdom's first tea garden. Photograph courtesy of Tregothnan

ENGLAND

(UNITED KINGDOM)

TREGOTHNAN TEA ESTATE | *Tresillian, Truro, Cornwall*

The large house, which stands at the top of a steep hill above the Fal River Estuary (*Tregothnan* is Cornish for "the house at the head of the valley"), has been the seat of the Boscawen family since 1335. It became famous for its ornamental *Camellia japonicas* in the early part of the 19th century. Current owner Evelyn Boscawen, eldest son of the ninth Viscount Falmouth, and his garden director Jonathan Jones started experimenting with *Camellia sinensis* in 1999 when they recognized that the soil pH and the mild, humid Cornish climate might suit the tea plant extremely well. To collect suitable plants and seeds and to learn about the cultivation and processing of tea, Jones travelled to some of the world's most important tea-growing regions. The first seedlings were raised in what was once Tregothnan's kitchen garden, and the first tea was harvested in 2005. Because the original plants were sourced from many different locations, they are a mixture of mostly unidentified varietals, and an important part of Jones's work has been to select plants that thrive best here and to then propagate them in the nursery. The number of plants in the ground has steadily increased, and small quantities are harvested throughout the growing season.

HELE HOUSE | *West Sandford, Devon*

When Alison Johansen decided to grow tea after holidaying in Sri Lanka, she spent some time at Kinnettles Farm in Scotland with Susie Walker-Munro and other members of Tea Gardens of Scotland (TGS), a group of farmers working to diversify into tea growing in old walled gardens and glasshouses. In January 2016, she bought 4,500 of the young plants and hardened them off inside a barn, then in a shady area of the garden, before establishing them in the ground on a very steep slope that was once pastureland. Then, a 1-acre plot was prepared carefully to make it deer and rabbit proof. Once the first plants have settled in, more plants may be added. The plan is to grow organically and to make single-estate black tea.

The Himalayan Garden at Tregothnan Estate in Cornwall where tea grows alongside ornamental species of *Camellia*. Photograph courtesy of Tregothnan

Country, State, or Province
England

Number of Gardens
2

Main Districts or Gardens
Tregothnan Tea Estate, Tresillian, Truro, Cornwall

Hele House, West Sandford, Devon

Area Under Tea
Tregothnan Tea Estate: 25 acres, with plans for a total or 150 acres

Hele House: 1 acre

Average Annual Production (Kilograms)
Tregothnan Tea Estate: 6,096

Hele House: Not yet known

Terrain
Tregothnan Tea Estate: Undulating sections of Tregothnan Estate and south-facing steep slopes running down to the River Fal

Hele House: Very steep slope, red volcanic soil; ancient landscape of rolling hills and meadows; situated in slight rain shadow that gives protection from the area's heavy rain

Altitude
Tregothnan Tea Estate: 5 to 80 metres (16.4 to 262.5 feet)

Hele House: 120 metres (394 feet)

Production Period
Tregothnan Tea Estate: April to October

Hele House: Not yet known

Best Time to Visit
April to October

Main Varietals/Cultivars
Tregothnan Tea Estate: Different varietals and cultivars from many different countries

Hele House: Nepalese and Georgian seedlings from Kinnettles Farm in Scotland

Types of Tea Made
Tregothnan Tea Estate: Black, green, matcha, small amounts of white

Hele House: Not yet known but probably black

Predominant Flavours; Tasting Notes
Tregothnan Tea Estate:
BLACK: dry, slightly astringent, slightly reminiscent of a spring flush Darjeeling
GREEN: light, clean, with no astringency

Hele House: Not yet known

SCOTLAND

(UNITED KINGDOM)

KINNETTLES FARM | *Kinnettles, Forfar, Angus*

Kinnettles is an arable farm on the edge of the Strathmore Valley in Angus on the east coast of Scotland. In 2007, owners Euan and Susie Walker-Munro realised the soil pH of the farm was similar to that of the Cornish Tregothnan Tea Estate, and they decided to try growing tea. They were the first to plant in Scotland, and Susie's tea credentials are strengthened by the fact that her great-great-great-grandfather was Charles Alexander Bruce, employee of the East India Company who made the first assamica black tea shipped to London from India in 1839. The first cuttings to arrive at Kinnettles perished because of their shallow root systems together with the area's chilly temperatures, heavy snow, high winds, and vine weevil attacks. In 2010, however, an additional 300 sinensis varietals went into the ground inside polytunnels on a south-west-facing slope surrounded by rhododendrons, primulas, and snowdrops. In 2015, they had matured enough to start plucking the leaf, and Susie recruited the help of Beverly-Claire Wainwright, award-winning tea maker, to produce just 2 kilograms (4.4 pounds) of stylish, hand-rolled, golden-tipped black tea called Kinnettles Gold, now sold each spring by Pekoe Tea in Edinburgh.

Kinnettles Farm in Angus, where Euan and Susie Walker-Munro were the first to plant tea in Scotland in 2007. Photograph courtesy of Tea Gardens of Scotland

TEA GARDENS OF SCOTLAND

Susie Walker-Munro and Beverly-Claire Wainwright also pioneered Tea Gardens of Scotland (TGS) in 2016, a group of 10 gardeners who have grown tea from seed because this is much more suitable to the Scottish climate than cuttings grown by vegetative propagation. The long taproot of seed-grown plants mines down for its water, draws up different minerals, and better anchors the plant so it can withstand high winds and frosts. Specially selected, cold-tolerant Georgian and Nepalese seeds were grown in glasshouses and polytunnels and then planted outside in the groups' walled gardens and small farms of between 0.25 and 1.25 acres in Angus, Fife, and Perthshire. These cover a total of 5.5 acres densely planted with 4,000 plants per acre, and by 2019, 100 percent pure Scottish teas from the bushes in these various locations will be ready to enjoy. Kinnettles also works with a new tea grower in Devon where 1.25 acres were planted in 2017.

WINDY HOLLOW FARM | *Trinity Gask, By Auchterarder, Perthshire*

Also working with Kinnettles, Monica Griesbaum and her husband, Andy, purchased sinensis seeds from Nepal and Georgia. These germinated well, and between 2,000 and 2,500 young plants went into the ground at their 24-acre organic farm in spring 2017.

Monica started processing samples of her first tea the same year. Each spring, another 2,000 seedlings will be added, depending on space and need. She hopes to make green, white, black, and oolong teas, using machinery powered by solar, wind, and hydro energy. The farm also offers tours to anyone interested in tea cultivation.

THE WEE TEA PLANTATION | *Dalreoch, Perthshire*

This company uses unusual agronomy techniques at Dalreoch Tea Garden in Perth and Kinross to increase yield from the plants. Once established, each plant is stripped of 65 to 80 percent of its mature leaves and surrounded by a guard made of UV light–reflective film. The restriction of light forces the plant to produce new leaves at the top of each shoot. The company sells its own white and blended teas and blends from outgrowers in Dumfries and Galloway.

Country, State, or Province
Scotland

Number of Gardens
3, plus a number of outgrowers cultivating on small farms and in walled gardens.

Main Districts or Gardens
Kinnettles Farm, Angus

Windy Hollow Farm, Perthshire

The Wee Tea Plantation, Perthshire

Area Under Tea
Kinnettles Farm:
Tea growing inside 2 polytunnels covering approximately an eighth of an acre

Windy Hollow Farm:
Between 5 and 7 acres, possibly more in the future

The Wee Tea Plantation:
A few acres

Average Annual Production (Kilograms)
Kinnettles Farm:
Not yet known

Windy Hollow Farm:
Not yet known

The Wee Tea Plantation:
Not yet known

Terrain
Kinnettles Farm:
Steep south-facing slope below main farm house

Windy Hollow Farm:
Gentle slopes on rolling hills; mainly on basalt rock; plants watered by rain and an Artesian spring

The Wee Tea Plantation:
Sloping plot in foothills of Scottish Highlands, originally rough grazing land

---

Altitude
Kinnettles Farm:
300 metres (984 feet)

Windy Hollow Farm:
88 metres (288 feet)

The Wee Tea Plantation:
230 metres (755 feet)

Production Period
Kinnettles Farm:
March to September

Windy Hollow Farm:
April to August

The Wee Tea Plantation:
April to September

Best Time to Visit
May to September

Main Varietals/Cultivars
Kinnettles Farm:
Camellia sinensis sinensis from Darjeeling stock, and a few assamicas

Windy Hollow Farm:
Sinensis from Nepal and Georgia

The Wee Tea Plantation:
Not known

Types of Tea Made
Kinnettles Farm: Black

Windy Hollow Farm:
Not yet known

The Wee Tea Plantation:
White, smoked white

Predominant Flavours; Tasting Notes
Kinnettles Farm:
BLACK: fresh, clean aroma, honey-sweet liquor, with a touch of astringency, an appealing freshness, and apple and citrus notes

Windy Hollow Farm:
Not yet known

The Wee Tea Plantation:
WHITE: hints of pine, vanilla, and grape
SMOKED WHITE: smoky, nutty with hints of peach

NORTHERN IRELAND

(UNITED KINGDOM)

PORTAFERRY TEA FARM | *County Down*

Oscar Woolley and Anne Irwin own and run Suki Tea in Belfast, Northern Ireland. To experience and understand all aspects of the tea industry, they decided to try to grow their own tea plants. Of the 2,000 cuttings acquired from Luponde Tea Estate in southern Tanzania in 2014 and 2015, only 500 survived. These were nurtured inside a polytunnel at Greenmount Agricultural College in County Antrim, and more cuttings were taken to create further stock for the tea garden. Once the plants had matured, they were planted out on a 2-acre plot in Portaferry, County Down, where the soil is ideal, the microclimate virtually frost free, and the south-facing slope catches the sun and provides good drainage. There are also plans for a tearoom and visitor centre.

Fresh leaves plucked from young bushes grown at Portaferry, County Down, by Oscar Woolley and Anne Irwin of Suki Tea, Belfast. Photograph courtesy of Suki Tea

Country, State, or Province
Northern Ireland

Number of Gardens
1

Main Districts or Gardens
Portaferry, County Down

Area Under Tea
2 acres

Average Annual Production (Kilograms)
Not yet known

Terrain
South-facing slope near the coast of Strangford Lough, a large sea loch on the east coast of Northern Ireland

Altitude
A few metres (a few feet)

Production Period
April/May to September/October

Best Time to Visit
April to August

Main Varietals/ Cultivars
Clones imported from Tanzania

Types of Tea Made
Not yet known

Predominant Flavours; Tasting Notes
Not yet known

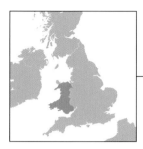

WALES

(UNITED KINGDOM)

THE ORIGINAL WELSH TEA COMPANY LTD | *Peterston Super Ely, Cardiff*

Lucy George and her family have grown fruit here since 1984, but with increasing costs of production, they decided to switch to tea. They bought some 3-year-old sinensis plants, seed-grown assamicas, and other seed-grown varietals from Nepal and Georgia, and from this diverse stock, they hope to select the best characteristics and produce their own cuttings. By spring 2016, 2,000 seedlings had been planted in six polytunnels. The hope was to have at least 5 to 6 acres planted by 2018, with a plan to eventually plant a total of approximately 15 acres. While cultivating inside polytunnels, George experimented with different films and nettings, the best times to cover and vent, irrigation needs, etcetera, in order to discover the best conditions for the tea. But she hopes that the majority of the tea will grow successfully in the open air in the mild, often cloudy, wet, and windy climate. Eventually the teas will be marketed as Peterston Tea Estate teas.

Tea plants share a polytunnel with strawberries at Lucy George's tea farm in Cardiff. Photograph courtesy of Lucy George

Country, State, or Province
Wales

Number of Gardens
1

Main Districts or Gardens
Vale of Glamorgan

Area Under Tea
Planned total of 15 acres

Average Annual Production (Kilograms)
Not yet known

Terrain
Sandy loam, with a clover/rye cover to suppress weeds

Altitude
70 metres (230 feet)

Production Period
April to October

Best Time to Visit
April to October

Main Varietals/ Cultivars
Seed-grown assamicas and seed-grown varietals from Nepal and Georgia

Types of Tea Made
Not yet known

Predominant Flavours; Tasting Notes
Not yet known

Germany

Slovakia

Austria

Hungary

★Bern

Switzerland

Casa del Tè

Rhône River

Adige River

Slovenia

Ascona •

•Monte
Verità

Croatia

*Brisaggo
Islands*

*Lake
Maggiore*

A L P S

Terreni alla Maggia

Po River

Reno River

Adriatic Sea

Serbia

Bosnia and
Herzegovina

France

**Experimental Camellia
Plantation**

Lucca •

Arno River

Tevere River

Italy

Montenegro

★
Rome

APENNINES MOUNTAINS

Albania

*Tyrrhenian
Sea*

*Ionian
Sea*

MOUNT
ETNA

N

Mediterranean Sea

W   E

S

🌱 Tea grower

▲▲ Mountain

0   50   100   200 Miles

AFRICA

0   50   100   200 Kilometres

ITALY

Sometime in the 1550s, Venetian magistrate Giovanni Battista Ramusio learned from a Persian trader that the Chinese boiled the leaves of an herb called Chai Catai in water and drank it to cure headaches, stomach aches, aching joints, and other ailments. During the next 50 years, Italian priests, apothecaries, and philosophers wrote about and possibly tasted tea, but there is no evidence that tea was imported into Italy and consumed as an everyday drink as it was in Holland, Portugal, and eventually England. It is only since the 1990s that tea has started to attract the interest of health journalists and a small number of connoisseur tea drinkers.

EXPERIMENTAL CAMELLIA PLANTATION | *Sant'Andrea di Compito, Tuscany*

The Cattolica family has been growing *Camellia japonica* at Villa Borrini, their family home in northern Tuscany, since 1760, and each year, the Compito region hosts a Camellia Festival that attracts thousands of visitors. Sant'Andrea sits amongst the steep hills of the Compitese National Park where the temperate microclimate and high humidity are well suited to the cultivation of olives, grapes, and camellias. In 1987, Guido Cattolica, botanist, horticulturalist, and head of Tuscany's International Camellia Society, decided to also grow tea. Seeds were brought from China to the Botanical Gardens in nearby Lucca, and 1,000 plants were germinated in greenhouses until they were about 2 years old. They were then planted at the family estate at Sant'Andrea beside the long-established ornamental camellias.

A program of careful propagation and selection eventually led to the development of the special Sant'Andrea varietal grown here today in five sections of the garden on curving terraces. Shade tunnels protect the bushes from the Tuscan sun, and an irrigation system brings fresh mountain water from a nearby stream. The first harvest took place in 1990, and in 2000, a record 25 kilos (55 pounds) of fresh leaf were processed to make 6 kilos (13 pounds) of made tea.

Country, State, or Province
Italy

Number of Gardens
1

Main Districts or Gardens
Experimental Camellia Plantation, Sant'Andrea di Compito, Lucca, Tuscany

Area Under Tea
Small section of family garden

Average Annual Production (Kilograms)
6

Terrain
Gentle sloping hillside on Monte Serra

Altitude
100 metres (328 feet)

Production Period
March to September

Best Time to Visit
May or September

Main Varietals/ Cultivars
Sant'Andrea cultivar developed from Chinese stock

Types of Tea Made
Three Tigers Black, Jade Powder Green, Opal Oolong

Predominant Flavours; Tasting Notes
BLACK: delicate, the subtlety of a Darjeeling with nutty darker notes of a China Keemun
GREEN: very light steamed green character
OOLONG: aromatic, lightly grassy

SWITZERLAND

Switzerland is traditionally a coffee-drinking country, and in the past, the few tea dealers that existed there dealt more in herbal and fruit infusions than in actual tea. Tea drinking was introduced to the country by 19th-century British tourists, and today, a small but growing number of speciality tea stores attracts an increasing connoisseur clientele. The Tea Club Switzerland, founded in 2002, aims to promote tea drinking and provide knowledge for interested consumers.

CASA DEL TÈ | *Monte Verità, Ascona*

In 2002, Peter Oppliger created a small Japanese tea garden at Ticino on Monte Verità to help visitors understand and appreciate tea cultivation and tea culture, but it was never intended to be a commercial venture. Oppliger, a specialist in medicinal plants, carried out his first trials with *Camellia sinensis* on the Isola Grande, one of Lake Maggiore's two Brissago Islands, where the subtropical climate proved perfect for the seedlings. He was then invited to establish a small tea garden at The Centre for Tea Culture on the slopes of Monte Verità above the city of Ascona. Today, the garden is home to 1,400 tea bushes that grow in the tranquil atmosphere of this small experimental garden. The first harvest of Ticino tea took place in 2007, and now, three crops are gathered each year in spring and summer. Later cuttings are gathered for vegetative propagation. The spring flush is the main crop, and skilled Japanese tea makers arrive each year in May to pick and hand-process the tiny shoots to make fresh, sweet, Japanese-style shincha, sencha, and gyokuro green teas. The steaming, hand rolling, and drying of the leaf takes three and a half hours and produces just 500 grams (17.6 ounces) of tea. In 2016, Oppliger retired and sold the tea garden to Katrin and Gerhard Lange from Länggass Tee in Bern.

There are still 120 plants on the Isola Grande and another 1,000 at Terreni alla Maggia at a new garden in Ascona, planted in 2012. These are planned for commercial production, while Monte Verità will continue to be used only for study purposes. Fresh leaf from Terreni alla Maggia is used as one of the essential ingredients of Digestivo Monte Verità, a beneficial digestive wine created by Oppliger at his Laboratorio Casa del Tè. It contains extract of green tea along with medicinal herbs and spices grown on Monte Verità and on nearby Monti di Ronco overlooking Ascona.

Japanese tea master gathering the first spring harvest at Casa del Tè Japanese tea garden on Monte Verità in the Swiss Alps. Photograph courtesy of Peter Oppliger

Country, State, or Province
Switzerland

Number of Gardens
2

Main Districts or Gardens
Casa del Tè,
Monte Verità, Ticino

Terreni alla Maggia,
Ascona

Area Under Tea
Casa del Tè: 2,500 square metres planted with 1,400 plants

Terreni alla Maggia:
1,000 square metres

Average Annual Production (Kilograms)
Casa del Tè: 2

Terreni alla Maggia:
Not yet known

Terrain
Casa del Tè: Steep mountain slopes among the Swiss Alps

Terreni alla Maggia:
Acid soil on flat farmland on the northern banks of Lake Maggiore

Altitude
Casa del Tè:
91.4 metres (300 feet)

Terreni alla Maggia:
200 metres (656 feet)

Production Period
Casa del Tè:
May to August

Terreni alla Maggia:
May to August

Best Time to Visit
May, June, July

Main Varietals/Cultivars
Casa del Tè:
Sinensis via Japan

Terreni alla Maggia:
Sinensis propagated from Japanese plants at Casa del Tè, Monte Verità

Types of Tea Made
Casa del Tè:
Japanese-style green shincha, sencha, gyokuro

Terreni alla Maggia:
Green leaf used to flavour locally made digestive wine

Predominant Flavours; Tasting Notes
Casa del Tè:
GREEN: fresh, sweet, with hints of fresh grass, marine notes

Terreni alla Maggia:
Not applicable

Finland

St. Petersburg

Estonia

Latvia

Lithuania

★Moscow

Belarus

Russia

Poland

Ukraine

ASIA

Slovakia

Hungary

Moldova

Krasnodar

Romania

Serbia

Krasnodar

Abkhazia
Samegrelo

Bulgaria

Sochi

Imereti

Black Sea

Guria —

Georgia

Macedonia

Adjara

Batumi

Albania

Artvin

★Tbilisi

Ordu

Trabzon

★Ankara

Giresun

Rize

Turkey

Greece

Volga River

Don River

Kama River

Kura River

Sakarya River

Kelkit River

Euphrates River

Gediz River

Tigris River

Tea grower

Multiple growers

*Mediterranean
Sea*

0   125   250   500 Miles

0   125   250   500 Kilometres

GEORGIA

Georgia was a part of the Russian Empire from 1800 until 1918, and after a brief period under the protection of the British, Soviet rule was reinstated in the country until the collapse of the USSR in the mid-1990s. The development of the tea industry in Georgia was therefore closely linked to that of Russia, and for many years, the region supplied almost all of the strong black tea that was drunk from teapots kept warm on Russian samovars.

In 1848, the first Chinese tea seeds were propagated at the botanic gardens in Ukraine and Abkhazia, and plants were also established in Zugdidi and Ozurgeti in the west of the country close to the Black Sea. But the industry did not develop commercially until the 1880s when gardens were laid out in Sokhumi and Batumi with more Chinese seeds. In the 1890s, expeditions to China, India, Ceylon, and Java brought back 6,000 seedlings and thousands of seeds, which were planted at new gardens at Batumi in Adjara. By 1914, 900 hectares had been planted and six factories were operating, but the quality of the tea was poor due to a lack of expertise and technological infrastructure. In 1920, the crop was given new status as a special area of economic activity. The Tea and Subtropical Cultures Research Institute was founded in Anaseuli in West Georgia; new cultivars were developed for their quality and aroma; and from 1925, the industry expanded rapidly. By 1932, 125,500 hectares had been planted, and the Russians introduced mechanical harvesters to gather the leaf for processing in 19 state-owned factories. But as volumes increased, tea quality fell. Georgia's black teas were always processed using orthodox machinery, but in the 1980s, a unique technology was introduced to manufacture granulated CTC-type grades. When green tea manufacture was introduced in 1937, the leaf was steamed in the Japanese style, but in 1957, dry heat panning was introduced and is still used today.

Since the demise of the USSR, the industry has stagnated. Only 15,000 hectares of tea gardens remain; only 17 of the previous 150 factories are working; and annual production has dropped from 13 million kilos (28.7 million pounds) in 1999 to between 2 million kilos (4.4 million pounds) and 5 million kilos (11 million pounds) in 2014. The main tea regions today are Adjara, Guria, Imereti, Samegrelo, and Abkhazia, and 90 percent of the industry is privately owned. Some of the larger companies, which own estates of between 50 and 350 hectares, have upgraded equipment and improved the quality of the mass-produced teas for both domestic and international markets. Approximately 20 of the country's 1,496 farm cooperatives grow tea, but many lack machinery and need time to refurbish their plots of tea. The European Neighbourhood Programme for Agriculture and Rural Development (ENPARD) is working to meet the challenges, to assist with the revival of neglected tea estates, and to search for new markets. Most exports currently go to Germany, Ukraine, Mongolia, Belarus, and Tajikistan, where the tea is blended or used to make bottled tea extracts.

In the early years of the 21st century, while the large enterprises began to modernise and improve quality, smaller producers started to purchase smallholder tea plots of between 10 and 50 hectares. Today, those small-scale farmers hand-pluck the tea or use handheld machines and process the tea by hand or using old, modified Soviet equipment or machinery they have built themselves. In 2003, the Georgian Hand-Made Tea Makers Association was founded. This group of local families worked the plantations under the Soviets and have continued to harvest the bushes and manufacture tea in small quantities in their own homes. Because there was no access to machinery, the tea had to be processed by hand, and those who knew how instructed others. The group gradually attracted more farmers and now includes some 700 families who grow tea on small plots of 0.2 to 5 hectares. The only machinery they are allowed to use, according to the association's regulations, is a dryer installed at a nearby Quality Control Centre. They take their tea there when the sun is not strong enough to dry it naturally. With the support of Georgian management consultant Tamaz Mikadze and British technical tea consultant Nigel Melican, association members now produce approximately 25 tons a year and sell their teas to customers in the United Kingdom, the United States, and Europe.

Natela, who picks tea from bushes in a village near Ozurgeti and processes it by hand to make a large-leaf black tea that is sold as Georgian Old Lady tea by Nothing But Tea in the UK. Photograph courtesy of Tamaz Mikadze

Country, State, or Province
Georgia

Number of Gardens
17, plus smallholder farmers

Main Districts or Gardens
Abkhazia Region
Adjara Region (3 working factories)
Guria Region (6 working factories)
Imereti Region (3 working factories)
Samegrelo Region (5 working factories)

Area Under Tea
15,000 hectares planted with tea but only 3,000 to 7,000 hectares operational

Average Annual Production (Kilograms)
Approximately 3 million

Terrain
Steep slopes in the foothills of the Caucasus Mountains

Altitude
500 to 600 metres (1,640 to 1,968 feet)

Production Period
May to September

Best Time to Visit
May, June, or late August and September

Main Varietals/Cultivars
Georgian varietals (known as Kolkhida) that took 60 years to evolve from high-quality, high-yielding plants from China; other varietals include plants originally from India, Sri Lanka, Japan, and Java

Types of Tea Made
Orthodox and CTC-type black (60%) and green (20%), brick green tea (20%)

Predominant Flavours; Tasting Notes
BLACK CTC: rather plain
BLACK ORTHODOX: light, low tannin content so no astringency
HAND-MADE BLACK: mild, light, sweet, floral, woody, sometimes with hints of cinnamon
SMOKED BLACK: rounded and smoky, with hints of apple, citrus, and honey
GREEN: strong, or light and slightly savoury

RUSSIA

The Russian people learned to love tea during the second half of the 17th century after Russia and China had signed the first treaty on the trading of regular supplies of tea from China in 1679. The Chinese ambassador to Moscow gave several chests of tea to Tsar Aleksey Mikhailovich Romanov, and once the Treaty of Nerchinsk of 1689 had facilitated more trade, regular camel caravans, taking 16 months to complete the journey, carried black tea from China through Mongolia to Moscow. The expensive new beverage was at first enjoyed only by the wealthy, but as stocks increased and prices dropped, tea became a staple of Russian life. By 1880, Russia was importing half of China's tea exports. The opening of the Trans-Siberian Railway in 1903 allowed faster access to cheaper teas from elsewhere, and so Russia imported less Chinese tea and more from India and Ceylon as well as from Russia's own newly established gardens in Sochi and Georgia, which were planted in the 1830s.

KRASNODAR

Russia first attempted to grow tea in Sochi in the region of Krasnodar in 1887 but failed because of that year's extremely cold winter. But in 1905, Yuda Koshman, who had learned to grow and manufacture tea in Georgia, established a successful plantation in Solokhaul, and in 1925, seeds from those bushes were used to plant more gardens in the Krasnodar region. Expansion continued, and by 1940, the area under tea had reached 700 hectares, the first factory had been constructed, and green tea was being made for the first time. During the 1990s, production fell back, but in 2013, the Ministry of Agriculture almost doubled state subsidies for tea growing, and this helped facilitate a recovery. Previously abandoned tea bushes amounting to 500 hectares were reclaimed, new processing equipment was purchased, and by 2015, six companies were producing tea. However, it seems unlikely that the target of 900,000 kilograms (1.98 million pounds) per year will be reached in the short term, and quality varies from fine hand-picked teas to plainer machine-picked varieties.

Country, State, or Province
Russia

Number of Gardens
6

Main Districts or Gardens
Krasnodar

Area Under Tea
1,400 hectares

Average Annual Production (Kilograms)
Approximately 400,000

Terrain
Sheltered slopes in the Caucasian Mountains in Sochi

Altitude
400 metres (1,312 feet)

Production Period
May to November

Best Time to Visit
May, June, July

Main Varietals/ Cultivars
Cultivars from Georgia

Types of Tea Made
Black, steamed greens

Predominant Flavours; Tasting Notes
BLACK: bright, brisk, strong, sometimes with hints of chocolate
STEAMED GREEN: vegetal, with slightly fishy, sencha-like notes

TURKEY

Turkey was initially a coffee-consuming country, but with the fall of the Ottoman Empire in 1923, Arabic suppliers stopped selling coffee to Turkey, and black tea became the preferred beverage. Early attempts to grow tea in 1888 were not successful, but in 1937, the Ministry of Agriculture imported from Georgia 20 tons of Chinese seeds that were planted in Rize. The first factory was built at Rize Central Nursery Garden in 1941, and during the 1950s, cultivation expanded rapidly into Giresun and other areas along the Black Sea. State-owned Çay-Kur, the directorate of tea establishments, was founded in 1971 to co-ordinate production and held the monopoly until 1984, when the industry was opened to private enterprise. Today, Çay-Kur owns 47 processing facilities and one packing factory and commands 60 percent of the market.

Rize is home to 65 percent of the tea fields, and there are more gardens in Trabzon (21 percent), Artvin (11 percent), and Giresun and Ordu (3 percent). The tea grows on steep hillsides on a 30-kilometre (18.6-mile) strip of land stretching along the coast to the Georgian border. The plants thrive in the fertile soil, hot and sunny weather, and plentiful rainfall, and are of better quality than teas from the other areas where elevations are much lower, the soil is heavy clay, and rainfall is sparse. Smallholders grow tea on plots of between 2.47 and 37 acres and harvest the shoots, using large shears with nylon bags attached. Plucking methods are not precise, and an unsatisfactory mix of young and old shoots finds its way into the bags. The pluckers often work on rainy days, and leaves are stored wet inside big nylon bags. Sometimes four days' harvest of picked leaf is left inside bags while they await collection and delivery to the factory, and the bags are often packed so tightly into the delivery truck that the leaf is further damaged. Turkey produces approximately 6 percent of the world's tea and would like to export more.

photographs on pages 170, 171, and 173

Country, State, or Province
Turkey

Number of Gardens
202,000 smallholder farmers; 300 processing factories

Main Districts or Gardens
Rize (65%);
Trabzon (21%);
Artvin (11%);
Giresun and Ordu (3%)

Area Under Tea
766,000 hectares

Average Annual Production (Kilograms)
220 million

Terrain
Steep slopes on the northern Black Sea Coast

Altitude
Between 800 and 1,000 metres (2,624 and 3,280 feet)

Production Period
May to October

Best Time to Visit
April to August

Main Varietals/ Cultivars
Various varietals and cultivars from original Chinese seeds

Types of Tea Made
Orthodox, Rotorvane or CTC black

Predominant Flavours; Tasting Notes
BLACK: strong, intense (often blended with spices and drunk with a lot of sugar)

Tea pickers at work at Harendong Tea Estate, set among the misty mountains of West Java, Indonesia. Photograph courtesy of Harendong Tea Estate

CHAPTER 6

ASIA

THE CONSTANT CRISS-CROSSING OF BORDERS AND

SEAS FROM CHINA INTO SURROUNDING COUNTRIES

BY TRAVELLERS, MERCHANTS, AND PRIESTS

HUNDREDS OF YEARS AGO INTRODUCED TEA TO

THE PEOPLE OF JAPAN, KOREA, LAOS, VIETNAM,

MYANMAR, CAMBODIA, TIBET, AND NEPAL.

Freshly picked tea leaves withering in Jiulong County in south-eastern Garzê Tibetan Autonomous Prefecture, Sichuan Province, People's Republic of China. Photographs courtesy of Camellia Sichuanesis

Later, the migration of Chinese groups at various times through China's history carried tea and the skills required to grow it into Thailand and Taiwan. The beverage travelled along trade routes to Iran and Azerbaijan, and tea cultivation in Malaysia, Indonesia, India, Bangladesh, and Sri Lanka was established by European colonizing powers. Other Asian countries, such as the Philippines and Nepal, have started growing tea more recently as a sustainable crop to improve earnings and raise living standards in poorer regions.

The Chinese became one nation for the first time under the Qin dynasty (221 to 206 B.C.), whose first emperor, the Tiger of Qin, employed hundreds of thousands of workers from all over the land to construct the Great Wall, vast royal palaces, and other important civic buildings. The unification of the country and the perpetual movement of a vast labour force from one province to another spread the word about tea and made it more available. When the Han dynasty came to power (206 B.C. to A.D. 220), it expanded into nearby territory, annexing the tea-growing provinces of Fujian, Sichuan, and Yunnan, and began trading along the Silk Road that stretched west as far as Macedonia, then a Roman province. Chinese ships sailed to India and beyond, and their cargoes of silks and other goods were sold into the Middle East and Europe by Indian and Persian middlemen. Gradually, tea found its way into lands along these various trading routes and became part of the local culture in so many diverse places.

The Tea Horse Road, along which tea was transported from southern and western China to Tibet during the Tang dynasty (618 to 907), was expanded and developed under the Song dynasty (960 to 1279) into a network that traded thousands of tons of tea each year into India, Nepal, and western regions of Asia. One route connected the town of Puerh with Lhasa, where the bricks of tea were stored in Tibetan monasteries and then redistributed to India and Nepal; another branch of the Tea Horse Road wound its way into Burma (now Myanmar), Thailand, and Singapore; a third route went south into Vietnam and then connected with Tibet and Europe; and yet another road ran from Puerh through the town of Heshun in western Yunnan into Burma.

Tea trees thrived in Myanmar for centuries, and in the 1930s, ancient assamica bushes and trees were growing in an area estimated to cover more than 337 square kilometres (130 square miles) in the north-eastern Shan state. It's possible that Cambodia learnt about tea from envoys that were sent to the Chinese court in the 8th century. Tea found its way into Laos along two tea caravan trails, which ran south from Yunnan Province through Xieng Khaeng to Thailand. In Vietnam, tea had acquired a Buddhist philosophical and religious significance by 11th century and was mentioned in a poem dedicated to King Tran Anh Tong as a source of purity. The 15th-century Confucian scholar and poet Nguyen Trai is revered for having chosen a hermit life of "tea, poetry, and the moon." To retain and protect the history and culture of this ancient trade route, the Laotian Sustainable Tourism Development Project has recently developed a modern tourist trail that follows the old road through the country's north-western mountains across the country to Chiang Mai in Thailand's northern tea forests.

Chinese migrants who settled in Thailand in the 18th century brought with them a love of tea and the skills to process the leaves that they gathered from the wild assamica tea trees growing in the forest there. And in the 1940s and '50s, more immigrants from China arrived in the region to escape Mao Zedong's Communist reign. They planted tea bushes using cuttings and seeds from Taiwan, and these small beginnings led to larger-scale cultivation in the 1980s with assistance from Taiwan and varietals from the Alishan area.

Taiwan became a tea-producing region after the Chinese Qing dynasty (1644 to 1912) took control of the island in 1683. Until 1662, Formosa, as it was then known, was governed by the Dutch and the Spanish, and from 1662 to 1683, by the local Zheng dynasty (1661 to 1683) that ruled the country as the Kingdom of Tungning. The Chinese then took over the island and made it part of Fujian Province, and as a result, immigrants from the mainland crossed the Taiwan Strait and settled there. Wild tea trees were found growing in the Formosa highlands, and in the 18th century, the new Chinese residents imported tea seeds from the mainland to establish commercial gardens around Taipei in the north of the island.

As tea and other Chinese goods travelled west along the Silk Road and other trade routes, it became popular in the countries along the way, reaching Iran in the 15th century. Today, Iran has its own tea industry, and the beverage is still the most popular drink throughout the country. It is served at home for breakfast, lunch, and dinner, in some houses still brewed using a samovar, and every street has a *chaikhaneh*, or tea house. Black tea is brewed strong, served in little curvaceous glasses, and sipped through a sugar cube held between the teeth. Azerbaijan also learned to love the beverage from travellers selling tea along the old trade routes, and here, too, little pear-shaped *armudu* glasses of *shirin chay*, or sweet tea, are served at all social occasions.

Preparing matcha for the Japanese Tea Ceremony. © Aiya Europe GmbH

In the 6th century, religion became the conduit for tea from China to Japan and Korea. Buddhist monks often travelled to China in order to study and, of course, drank tea and became familiar with the cultivation of the plant. They learnt how to process and brew the leaves and carried dry leaf and tea utensils back to their own temples and monasteries where they taught their fellow monks to perform the tea ceremony. They also brought back seeds for propagation in monastery gardens, and the drinking of Japanese and Korean green tea became part of religious ceremonies, state and royal occasions, and the everyday lives of emperors, scholars, monks, and priests.

Much later, the global tea industry grew as European powers established tea gardens in lands that they had colonized. The Dutch East India Company first planted tea on the island of Java in Indonesia in 1684, expanded the industry there in the 1820s, and established new estates in Sumatra during the 1840s. By this time, the British East India Company had also started growing its own tea to satisfy a growing demand at home. The company first discussed the need to break its expensive dependence on Chinese imports in the 1760s but did little to find suitable locations until the early years of the 19th century. The discovery of tea plants growing wild in the jungles of Assam in the 1820s came just in time because, in 1839, the Chinese government closed the port of Canton to foreign traders in its fury over the sale of opium into the country, and Britain went to war with China in the first of two Opium Wars. Without the development of tea estates in northern India, Britain might very well have had to give up drinking tea. The success of the company's first tea-processing activities in Assam encouraged expansion of Britain's tea industry into other parts of West Bengal, into the neighbouring province of Darjeeling, and the highlands of Tamil Nadu and Kerala in the south of the country, and in the 1870s, to the nearby island of Ceylon. In 1826, Britain took control of Malaya (now Malaysia), and tea estates in the Cameron Highlands were developed a century later. By the end of the 19th century, most of the tea consumed in Britain no longer arrived into the port of London on ships from China but was grown on tea estates in British colonies.

TOP LEFT: Chinese tea picker in Fujian Province. Photograph by David Collen; courtesy of *essenceoftea.com* TOP RIGHT: The tea mountains of West Java, Indonesia. Photograph courtesy of Harendong Tea Estate ABOVE LEFT: A bowl of matcha, rich in all the beneficial ingredients found in tea. © Aiya Europe GmbH
ABOVE RIGHT: Basket of freshly picked leaves at a tea garden on Huang Shan (Yellow Mountain) in Anhui Province, China. Photograph courtesy of Wenli Guo

⚹ Tea-growing area

0   250   500   1,000 Miles

0 250 500   1,000 Kilometres

N
W ✦ E
S

Arctic Circle

ASIA

Azerbaijan ★Baku

★Tehran

Iran

Pakistan

Islamabad★

New Delhi★

Nepal
Kathmandu ★Thimphu

Bhutan
★Dhaka

Bangladesh

India

*Arabian
Sea*

Beijing★

*East Sea
(Sea of Japan)*

Japan

★Seoul
**South
Korea**
★Tokyo

Jeju
Island

*East
China
Sea*

China

Tropic of Cancer

★ Taipei
Taiwan

Myanmar   **Laos**
★Hanoi

★Vientiane

★Rangoon

Thailand

Bangkok★
Cambodia **Vietnam**
★Phnom Penh

Manila ★

*PACIFIC
OCEAN*

Philippines

*Bay of
Bengal*

*Adaman
Sea*

*South
China
Sea*

*Celebes
Sea*

Sri Lanka
Colombo★

Malaysia
★
Kuala
Lumpur

Equa

*INDIAN
OCEAN*

AFRICA

Jakarta

Indonesia

*Timor
Sea*

Tropic of Capricorn

Tea pickers in a Sri Lankan tea garden, set against a backdrop of waterfalls and rocky outcrops. Photograph courtesy of James Finlay Limited

CHINA

China's tea history dates back almost 5,000 years to the time of Shennong, mythical sovereign, father of agriculture and herbal medicine, and honoured as the man who discovered the benefits of tea drinking. He is said to have brewed and tasted hundreds of herbs in order to discover their medicinal properties, and when a few leaves fell from an overhanging branch of a wild tea tree into the pan of water he was heating, he found the liquor both delicious and restorative. Another story suggests that he chewed tea leaves to help him recover from the ill effects of deadly plants. Yet another tells how he fell ill after drinking a poisonous infusion one day, and as he lay unconscious through the night, by chance under a tea tree, the dew that had collected on the tea leaves ran down into his mouth and revived him. And so, tea became known as a healthful tonic that would cure countless everyday ailments, as a refreshing beverage that sustained and refreshed, and as a drink that brought tranquillity and promoted clarity of thought. Shennong is said to have written that tea tasted bitter but that by "drinking it, one can think quicker, sleep less, move lighter, and see clearer." Much later in China's history, during the Tang dynasty (618 to 907), Lu Yu wrote in his *Cha Ching* (*Tea Classic*), "If one is generally moderate but is feeling hot or warm, given to melancholia, suffering from aching of the brain, smarting of the eyes, troubled in the four limbs, or afflicted in the hundred joints, he may take tea four or five times."

Under the Tang, the culture of tea and the way in which it was prepared and drunk acquired new importance. Writers and poets extolled and revered the simplicity of the tea ritual, the beauty of porcelain tea bowls, and the power of tea to inspire and lift the spirits beyond earthly concerns. In his "Tea Song," Lu Tong captures in words the effects of drinking seven cups of tea. The first four quench his thirst, dispel his loneliness, and warm his blood, and:

> *The fifth cup totally refreshes, purifying skin and bone;*
> *At the sixth bowl, I am one with the Immortal Sages,*
> *And before I can even finish the seventh bowl*
> *I feel the fresh breeze stirring beneath my arms.*
> *Where is the peak of Peng-lai, home of the Sages?*
> *Let me ride this fresh breeze and return there now.*

As China flourished during this golden age, so, too, did tea. Production increased, tea gardens were established in 12 of the provinces in which it thrives today, and cultivation, harvesting, and manufacture were formalized. Lu Yu wrote, "One is likely to fall ill if tea is picked in the wrong season," and pre-Qing Ming leaves, picked "before the rains" that come after this Festival of Pure Brightness on the 4th or the 5th of April each year, were considered to make the finest teas. The harvested tea was steamed, pulped, mixed with plum juice, and shaped into bricks or cakes that were then baked until dry. Lu Yu explained, "The beverage that people take may be from coarse, loose, powdered, or cake tea. It can be chopped, boiled, roasted and then tamped down into a bottle or pottery vessel where it awaits only hot water."

The brew was flavoured with sweet onions, ginger, orange peel, dogwood berries, cloves, or peppermint, and Lu Yu dismissed it as "no more than the swill of gutters and ditches." But even he advised that a little salt may be added to tea that had been carefully prepared with water from a mountain stream.

Tea cultivation spread farther during the days of the Song dynasty (960 to 1279), and Emperor Huizong (1100 to 1125) introduced the idea of Imperial Tribute Teas, which ensured that the finest, rarest teas, particularly from Fujian Province, were manufactured especially for him and rushed to the imperial palace as soon as they had been made. Wealthy houses now employed tea masters who chose the teas to be drunk and prepared them for the family and the family's guests. For the rest of the population,

tea was available in teahouses, noisy establishments that served as meeting place, business centre, restaurant, office, gambling shop, and trading post for marriage brokers and money lenders.

To control the quality of Song tea, fresh leaves were now carefully graded before being dampened and pressed into triangular or ball-shaped cakes. But processing and preparation methods began to change. Instead of being steamed and compressed, the fresh leaves were now packed into a sack and stored in an airtight earthenware jar for several months. The dried tea was then ground to a fine powder and whisked in hot water to a frothy jade liquid. In monasteries, the sharing of a bowl of whipped tea developed into a ceremonial ritual. Since it was during the Song dynasty that Japanese Buddhist monks learned to drink tea while studying in China, the whisking of powdered tea became the formalised method of preparation for the Japanese tea ceremony. But just as the Japanese were becoming familiar with powdered tea, the Chinese now turned more to loose-leaf tea, which replaced most other forms during the Ming dynasty (1368 to 1644). Loose leaf was much easier to brew, although the liquor was often bitter, so in order to reduce the harsh astringency, the fresh leaves were dry roasted (instead of steamed) to capture the true flavour of the tea. The disadvantage of this new style of tea was the amount of storage space required and the difficulties of transporting the tea. Trade with Europe was growing at the beginning of the 17th century, and the Chinese were faced with the dilemma of how to pack tea

Landscape of tea in Fujian Province. Photograph by David Collen; courtesy of *essenceoftea.com*

so that it would withstand long sea journeys to the new markets. At first, lidded porcelain jars were found to be suitable, but these were replaced with wooden chests as shipments increased. Chinese tea makers also began to modify their manufacturing processes in order to produce teas that did not lose their flavour and quality during the long sea voyage, and so oxidised teas were developed and the first black and oolong teas became available.

Through the Qing dynasty (1644 to 1912), the range of leaf teas increased, and white, yellow, and black teas, including Keemun from Anhui Province, were widely exported. During the first decade of the 17th century, the Dutch and Portuguese established regular trade with China and introduced tea to other parts of Europe. At some point in the 1640s, the Dutch took tea to America and, in the late 1650s, sailed their ships into the London docks carrying small quantities of the dry leaf. Over the next 300 years, China's tea exports increased steadily. To meet growing demand in the 20th century, the area under tea almost tripled between 1965 and 1976 from 336,000 to 963,000 hectares. Loans were made available to tea farmers to help them buy fertilisers and machinery. National tea conventions in 1966, 1972, and 1974 discussed policy and targets, and production rose from 91.63 million kilos (202 million pounds) in 1965 to 211.4 million kilos (466 million pounds) in 1976. When Deng Xiaoping became leader after the death of Mao in 1976, he introduced competition between private companies and opened the country to foreign trade and investment. Production rose steadily through the 1980s and '90s and has climbed by around 6.6 percent or more each year since 2000. In 2007, the total area planted with tea was 153,000 hectares and production totalled 1.17 million kilos (2.57 million pounds). In 2015, the total area had risen to 287,000 hectares and output had reached 2.27 million kilos (5 million pounds). Green tea accounted for 63.14 percent of that; dark teas, 13.04 percent; white, 11.37 percent; black, 11.33 percent; yellow, 0.96 percent; and

oolong, 0.15 percent. Quality and knowledge have also increased, and while tea drinkers around the world develop their own passion for tea, China, too, is enjoying a new tea culture that values the country's tea history, famous tea mountains and ancient trees, brewing rituals, tea utensils, and tea traditions as well as the teas themselves.

Tea is still made today in village houses by individual families who have passed their skills down through the generations. In some areas, it is made in small manufacturing units the size of a one-car garage, and production also continues in small historical wooden factories in famous mountains. In the past few years, the country has seen the construction of more and more large modern factories that are equipped with the latest technology and automated processing machinery and where even fine specialty teas are processed by machine rather than by hand. Many tea lovers value the heritage and skill involved in the manufacture of artisanal teas and prefer to buy from tea masters who make small quantities by hand or with minimal machinery. Some specialty teas will never be as good when made by machine, and we have all noticed how untidy gunpowder teas have become in recent years simply because machines cannot roll the leaves into such perfect, neat, regular pellets as hands are able to do. But mechanisation is not necessarily a bad thing, and as long as a skilled tea maker oversees and manages the process to ensure that standards are maintained, teas produced on a larger scale in automated factories can also be of very good quality. However, while interest in specialty Chinese teas has been growing steadily since the turn of the new millennium, the export of Chinese teas is often held back by three problems: the overuse of pesticides means that teas often do not comply with maximum residue levels in importing countries; customers outside China are not prepared to pay the high prices that are acceptable to domestic consumers; and rising costs within China have increased tea prices and put the country at a disadvantage in international markets.

Country, State, or Province
China

Main Districts or Gardens
Gansu Province, Shaanxi Province, Sichuan Province, Chongqing Municipality, Tibet Autonomous Region, Yunnan Province, Guizhou Province, Henan Province, Hubei Province, Hunan Province, Anhui Province, Jiangsu Province, Shandong Province, Zhejiang Province, Fujian Province, Guangdong Province, Guangxi Province, Hong Kong, Jiangxi Province, Hainan Province

Area Under Tea
2.877 million hectares

Average Annual Production (Kilograms)
Approximately 2.4 billion

Production Period
March to October/November, depending on region

Best Time to Visit
Eastern provinces: late March, April, September, October

South-western provinces: March to May, September, October

Main Varietals/Cultivars
More than 650 different varietals and cultivars

Withering tea on bamboo baskets. Photograph by David Collen; courtesy of *essenceoftea.com*

CHINA'S TEA-GROWING REGIONS

Tea is grown in 18 of China's provinces: Anhui, Fujian, Gansu, Guangdong, Guangxi, Guizhou, Hainan Island, Henan, Hong Kong, Hubei, Hunan, Jiangsu, Jiangxi, Shaanxi, Shandong, Sichuan, Yunnan, and Zhejiang. It is also cultivated in the autonomous region of Tibet and the provincial municipality of Chongqing (known as Mountain City), a recently formed tea region on the eastern side of Sichuan. Guizhou accounts for approximately 15.8 percent of total area while Fujian produces around 17.46 percent (the largest share) of the total produced each year. China's tea hectares account for around half of all the world's land under tea, and the country's annual production accounts for some 35 percent of world output.

China's tea provinces are generally grouped into four regions, divided by climate and location. The Jiangnan area (which produces two-thirds of all of China's tea) encompasses provinces south of the Yangtze River and includes Zhejiang, Jiangxi, Hunan, and southern parts of Anhui, Hubei, and Jiangsu provinces. The Jiangbei area lies north of the Yangtze and includes Henan, Shaanxi, Gansu, Shandong, and northern parts of Anhui, Hubei, and Jiangsu provinces. The southern region consists of Guangdong, Fujian, Hainan, and Guangxi. And the south-west region includes Sichuan (including Chongqing), Guizhou, Yunnan, and Tibet.

The rocky Wuyi Mountains in Fujian Province, famous for dark oolongs. Photograph by David Collen; courtesy of *essenceoftea.com*

CHINESE TEA SEASONS

Whereas in India teas are categorized as First Flush, Second Flush, etcetera, according to the season when the fresh leaves are harvested, in China, solar dates divide the tea year. These dates vary slightly from year to year. The most commonly used terms are the following:

SPRING HARVESTED TEAS

Pre-Qing Ming Tea (or Ming Qian Tea), picked before Qing Ming Qing Ming is the Festival of Pure Brightness and falls each year on the 4th or 5th of April. It is also Tomb Sweeping Day, a public holiday when families honour their ancestors by making offerings and sweeping the family tombs and graves. Because the date is so early in the spring, teas picked pre-Qing Ming have grown slowly in cool temperatures and dry weather and, therefore, have delicate, sweet flavours.

Qing Ming Tea (or Yu Quan Tea, or Before the Rain Tea) | Tea picked after Qing Ming and before Gu Yu, which falls from the 19th to the 21st of April each year. The Gu Yu (Grain Rain) festival is a traditional Chinese agricultural celebration held to invite the spring rains to fall and water the newly planted crops.

Gu Yu Tea | Tea picked after Gu Yu and before Li Xia, which falls from the 5th to the 7th of May each year and is the official beginning of summer.

SUMMER HARVESTED TEAS

Li Xia Tea | Tea picked after Li Xia and before Xiao Man (Grain Buds). Xiao Man, from the 20th to the 22nd of May, is the second solar term of summer when summer harvest crops such as barley and wheat start to bear seeds.

Xiao Man Tea | Tea picked after Xiao Man and before Mang Zhong. Mang Zhong (Grain in Ear) from the 5th to the 7th of June signifies the ripening of the crops.

Mang Zhong Tea | Tea picked after Mang Zhong and before Xia Zhi, the summer solstice from the 21st to the 22nd of June.

Xia Zhi Tea | Tea picked after Xia Zhi and before Xiao Shu (Minor Heat) from the 6th to the 8th of July. Xiao Shu predicts that the hottest period is coming.

Xiao Shu Tea | Tea picked at the time of "Minor Heat" from the 6th to the 8th of July.

Da Shu Tea | Tea picked at the time of "Major Heat" from the 22nd to the 24th of July.

ABOVE LEFT: Ancient tea bushes growing on Phoenix Mountain, Guangdong Province, where dark Phoenix Dan Cong oolongs are made. Photograph courtesy of The Chinese Tea Company, London ABOVE RIGHT: Withering leaf in the sun in Guangdong Province to develop the famous, sweet, stone-fruit flavours of Dan Cong oolongs. Photograph courtesy of Canton Tea Company

Multiple growers

0   250   500   1,000 Miles
0   250   500   1,000 Kilometres

N
W   E
S

RUSSIA

*Jinan
Gansu   Shandong   Yellow
Sea
CHINA
★Lanzhou   Shaanxi   Zhengzhou   Jiangsu
★Xi'an   Henan   ★Nanjing
★Hefei
Hubei   Anhui
Sichuan   Wuhan★   Hangzhou   East
Tibet   Chengdu★   Chongqing   Nanchang   Zhejiang   China
Autonomous Region   Sea
Jiangxi
★Lhasa   Changsha★ Jiangxi   Fuzhou   TAIWAN
Hunan
Guizhou   Fujian

Yarlung Zangbo (Tsangpo)   Guiyang★   Guangdong
Jinsha River   Guangxi   Guangzhou
Lancang River   Kunming★   Xijang River   ★
Nu River   Hong Kong
Huang (Yellow) River   Special Administrative Region
Yunnan   ★Nanning
Tropic of Cancer
Yangtze River
Haikou★ Hainan

INDIA   SOUTHERN
ASIA

Bay of
Bengal

South
China
Andaman   Sea
Sea

Gulf of
Thailand

Wuyi Mountains in Fujian Province.
Photograph by David Collen; courtesy of *essenceoftea.com*

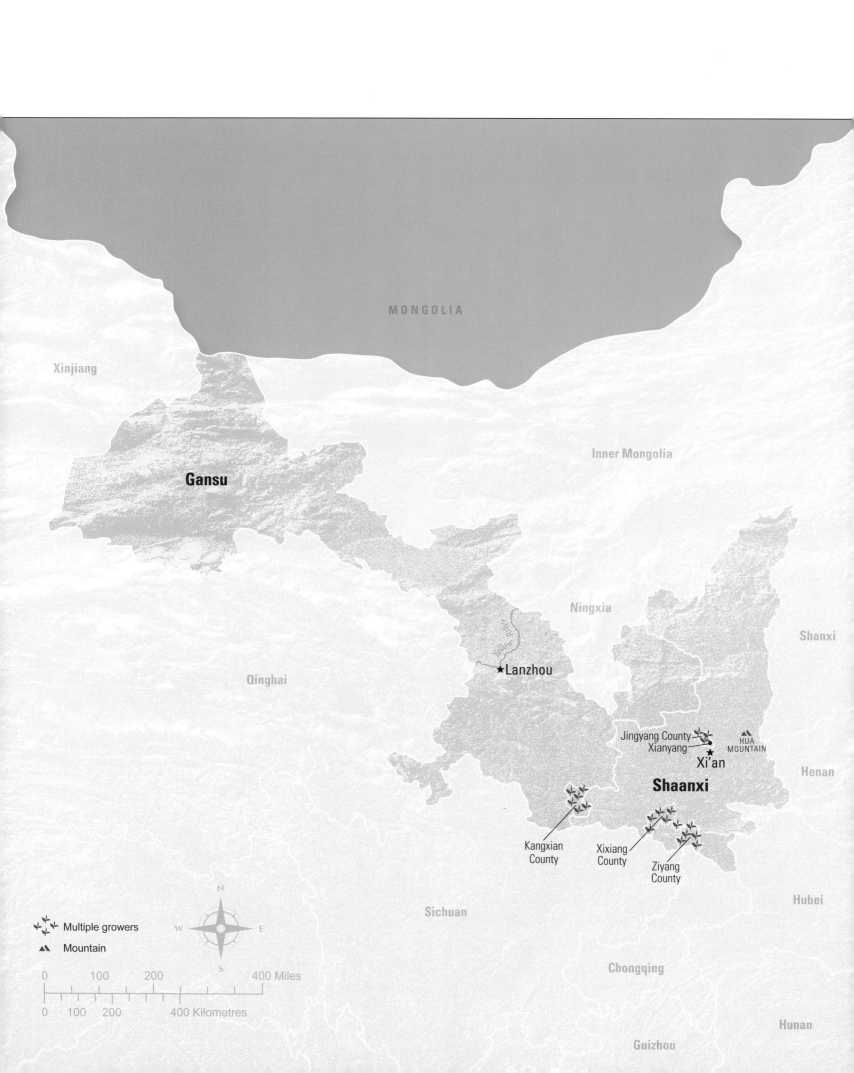

MONGOLIA

Xinjiang

Inner Mongolia

Gansu

Ningxia

Shanxi

Yellow River

★Lanzhou

Qinghai

Jingyang County
Xianyang
▲▲ HUA
MOUNTAIN

Xi'an★

Shaanxi

Henan

Kangxian
County

Xixiang
County

Ziyang
County

Sichuan

Hubei

❦ ❦ Multiple growers

▲▲ Mountain

Chongqing

| 0 | 100 | 200 | 400 Miles |

| 0 | 100 | 200 | 400 Kilometres |

N
W   E
S

Hunan

Guizhou

GANSU

(CHINA)

Gansu is a long, narrow, arid region that lies between the Loess, Mongolian, and Qinghai-Tibet plateaus in the north-west of China and has a long history of trading compressed dark teas from Sichuan, Hunan, Hubei, and Guizhou to the minority groups living in Tibet and Mongolia. Compressed cakes and bricks of tea made in Hunan were conveyed along four routes that ended in Lanzhou on the Yellow River in the central region of Gansu Province. One route ran from Anhua County in Hunan Province to Jingyang in Shaanxi Province and on to Lanzhou; the second ran from Anhua in Hunan to Yiyang in Hunan and Wuhan in Hubei Province, then on to Zhengzhou in Henan Province, ending its journey in Lanzhou; a third route carried the tea from Anhua in Hunan to western Hubei Province, on to Chongqing in Sichuan Province, and finally to Lanzhou; and the fourth route started in Anhua Province in Hunan and went through Xupu in Hunan, Baojing in Hunan, and Chongqing in Sichuan before reaching Lanzhou. Because it was such an important trading route, the province contains many historic temples and grottoes, some of which are World Heritage Sites.

The northern regions are too dry for the cultivation of tea, so Gansu's green teas are produced only in the lower-lying, warmer, wetter region in the south-eastern corner of the province, often described as an oasis in China's dry western region. Native tea bushes were discovered 200 years ago. In 1958, tea seeds from Hunan were imported, and in 1964, more seeds from Anhui, Hunan, and Jiangxi were planted in Kangxian. Green teas made here include Bi Yu teas with curled leaves and Longnan Long Jing, Wenxian Long Jing, or Liziba Long Jing, made in the same way as Long Jing teas to give dried teas with flat-pressed bud sets.

KANGXIAN LONG SHEN *(Dragon God)*

To make this tea, freshly plucked shoots of one to three young leaves are withered briefly, panned, pressed, and dried in the wok to keep the leaves straight and flat like Long Jing tea but with longer leaves. It almost looks like a cross between a Long Jing and a Taiping Hou Kui and has a fresh, clean, slightly nutty character.

LONGNAN BI YU *(Green Jade)*

Grown close to the border with Sichuan and Shaanxi provinces, new shoots are picked in early April before Qing Ming, then withered for two to six hours, panned, pressed, and rolled with the hands to give the tea a curled appearance rather like Bi Luo Chun (Green Spring Snail). The attractive leaves yield a lightly spicy flavour with orchid notes.

Country, State, or Province
Gansu Province

Area Under Tea
10,870 hectares

Average Annual Production (Kilograms)
1.3 million

Terrain
In the south-east, where tea is grown, the landscape is of high mountains and deep valleys; the region lies between the province's higher plateaux in the west and north and the Sichuan Basin to south.

Altitude
600 to 1,200 metres (1,969 to 3,937 feet)

Best Time to Visit
late March, April, September, October

Main Varietals/Cultivars
Several green tea cultivars including Longjing 43, Fuyun No. 6, Mingshan 13, Jiukeng, Yixing, and Ziyang

Types of Tea Made
Green

Predominant Flavours; Tasting Notes
GREEN: *Kangxian Long Shen (Dragon God)*—slightly nutty aroma and fresh, clean taste
Longnan Bi Yu (Green Jade)—light, slightly spicy with hints of orchids

SHAANXI

(CHINA)

Shennong, Father of Tea, is said to have been conceived in Shaanxi's Hua Mountain, which lies just to the north of the ancient capital of Xi'an. The city, then called Chang'an, became the political centre of China during the 11th century B.C. and gradually gained importance as a major trading post for merchants buying and selling silk, cottons, spices, ceramics, metals, scrolls, and tea, and for commodities travelling to and from other parts of China, Mongolia, Siberia, and Russia. Under the Tang (618 to 907), the seat of power was moved east to Luoyang in Henan Province, but Chang'an retained its importance as the terminus of the Silk Road, along which goods were transported from China northwards to Moscow and west to Samarkand, Damascus, and beyond. From the middle of the 14th century, like Hunan and Sichuan, Shaanxi was producing compressed Fu Cha tea cakes in Xianyang, and these became one of the most important products traded along the busy route into Mongolia.

The province is still best known for these dark fermented brick teas but also makes a number of green teas. Lying so far north, most of Shaanxi is too cold for tea cultivation, but the climate of Ziyang and Xixiang counties in the south of the province is less extreme, and these regions produce mild, fragrant green teas that include Zi Yang Cui Feng, Ziyang Mao Feng, and Wu Zi Xian Hao. A number of Shaanxi tea companies offer selenium-rich green teas since the region's soil is particularly rich in zinc and selenium. Selenium is an essential trace mineral that, taken in small quantities, is important for cognitive function, immunity, and fertility, although can be toxic if taken in excess.

SHAANXI DARK TEA | *Shaanxi Fu Cha*

Often referred to as Mongolia Diet Tea, Border Tea, or Official Tea, in the past, Shaanxi Fu Cha was processed in Jingyang County, Xianyang Prefecture, using locally grown green leaf and leaf brought in from Hunan and Sichuan. In 1958, the government shut down the Fu Cha factories, but the industry is now recovering. The tea is made during the summer months when the plants are growing fast and the quality of the leaves is much lower than in the spring. Shoots of three or four leaves and a bud are withered, panned, rolled, and sun-dried to make the base *maocha*. This is then steamed and piled in a warehouse for a year, during which time the tea develops a fruity, flowery aroma. The tea is then roughly cut, steamed again, and compressed into bricks or logs, but must not be packed too tightly because air needs to circulate to activate the bacteria and spores in the tea and provoke fermentation. The compressed tea is stored for three or four weeks at temperatures between 26° and 28°C (78.8° and 82.4°F). During that time, *Eurotium cristatum* mold develops speckles of Jin Hua (Golden Flower) spores on the tea. The storage temperature is then increased to 38° to 42°C (100.4° to 107.6°F) to evaporate the tea's water content, and after cooling, the tea is packed in paper, ready for sale. The more Jin Hua in the tea, the better the quality is considered to be. The teas have a rather woody taste and are said to reduce blood pressure and cholesterol levels and to help the digestion.

Country, State, or Province
Shaanxi Province

Area Under Tea
143,900 hectares

Average Annual Production (Kilograms)
74.2 million

Terrain
90% of the region is made up of mountains and hills, with higher altitudes in the west and lower plains in the east. Steep hills interspersed with canyons and basins

Altitude
1,100 metres (3,609 feet)

Best Time to Visit
late March, April, September, October

Main Varietals/Cultivars
Ziyangzhong

Types of Tea Made
Green, dark teas

Predominant Flavours; Tasting Notes
GREEN: mild fragrance
DARK: *Shaanxi Fu Cha*—smooth, sweet, slightly nutty, with long floral aftertaste

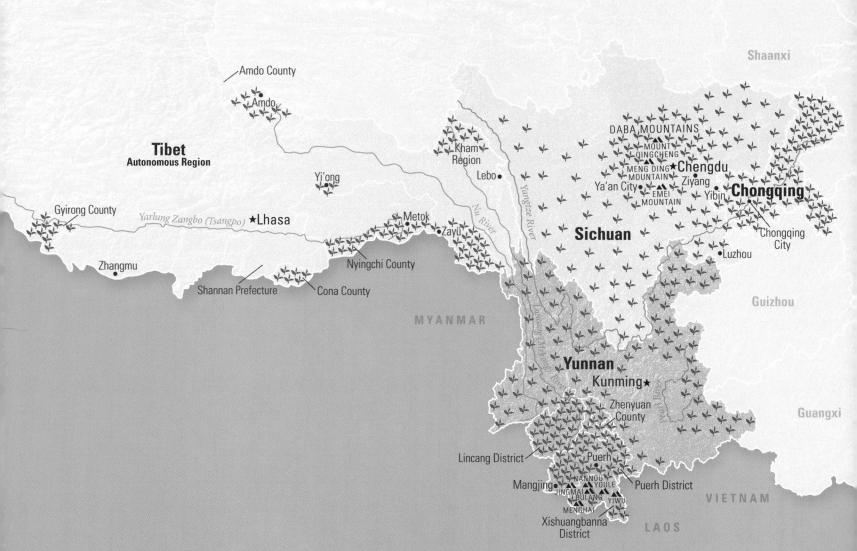

0   50   100   200 Miles

0 50 100   200 Kilometres

N
W   E
S

CHINA

Gansu

Shaanxi

Amdo County

Amdo

Tibet
Autonomous Region

Kham
Region

Lebo

Yi'ong

DABA MOUNTAINS

MOUNT
QINGCHENG

MENG DING
MOUNTAIN
Ya'an City

★Chengdu

Ziyang

Chongqing

Gyirong County

Yarlung Zangbo (Tsangpo)

★Lhasa

Metok

Zayü

Nu River

Yangtze River

EMEI
MOUNTAIN

Yibin

Sichuan

Chongqing
City

Zhangmu

Shannan Prefecture

Nyingchi County

Cona County

Luzhou

MYANMAR

Lancang Mekong River

Guizhou

Yunnan

Kunming★

Zhenyuan
County

Pearl River

Guangxi

Lincang District

Puerh

Mangjing

NANNOU
YOULE

JINGMAI

BULANG

MENGHAI

YIWU

Puerh District

Xishuangbanna
District

VIETNAM

LAOS

SICHUAN

(CHINA)

Sichuan's Meng Ding Mountain is recognised as the birthplace of tea cultivation and tea culture, and during the Zhou dynasty (1122 to 256 B.C.), residents of the province paid a tribute of tea to Emperor Wu of Zhou, the first Zhou emperor who reigned from 1046 to 1043 B.C. An ancient book written at that time, *The Ritual of Zhou*, included references to the protocol of tea at court, and a book written in 59 B.C. by Wang Bao, a resident of Sichuan, gave instructions for buying and brewing tea and mentioned the utensils required. In 53 B.C., the Taoist monk Wu Lizhen advised that tea made from wild tea trees growing on Meng Ding could be used as a medicine, and he began to cultivate bushes from the wild plants. Tribute teas for the emperor were plucked from seven "holy trees" that Wu Lizhen had planted, and the tiny buds were processed to make a green tea that was recorded as having long, thin, yellow-green leaves and a delicate, sweet flavour. Each year, the tea was picked on one day before Qing Ming, and it became a time of great celebration. Local officials dressed in special robes, musicians beat drums and gongs, homage was paid to the seven trees, and firecrackers were set off to celebrate the special spring harvest. Monks then chanted prayers while the tea was processed by a professional tea master, and when it was ready, the tiny amount of tea was packed into two silver bottles that were placed inside a wooden box and sealed with yellow silk printed in red. The precious box was then carried to the imperial palace, escorted through each town on the route by local government officials. During the Qing dynasty, a stone wall was built around the seven trees to create an Imperial Tea Garden, which still exists today and is open to visitors. Sichuan continued to make famous tribute teas, and in his *Cha Ching*, (written between 760 and 762), Lu Yu wrote: "There are Bulk Tea and Tribute Tea in Qingcheng County." Mount Qingcheng, to the north-east of Meng Ding, is one of China's most important Taoist mountains.

Local Sichuan merchants used tea as currency to pay for other commodities, such as yaks required for carrying goods, but after the Tang princess Wenchang married Tibetan king Songstan Gampo in 641 and introduced tea to the Tibetan people, an increase in the transportation of tea to Lhasa, in exchange for Tibetan horses, meant that what was originally known as the Tea Yak Road became the Tea Horse Road. The trail along which Sichuan compressed teas were transported ran almost 2,253 kilometres (approximately 1,400 miles) from Ya'an, in the west of Sichuan, through Luding and Kangding in the west, merged with roads from Yunnan, and continued up to Lhasa.

Sichuan's mountains are dotted with Taoist and Buddhist temples and monasteries that mark the province's ancient tea history, and the high misty peaks leading up to the Qinghai-Tibet Plateau are well suited to the production of excellent teas. Famous green teas include Zhu Ye Qing (Bamboo Green Tea) from Emeishan, one of China's four sacred Buddhist mountains; Emeishan Xueya (Emei Mountain Snow Buds); Emeishan Mao Feng (Emei Mountain Hairy Tips) from Ya'an City; Bashan Queshe (Ba Mountain Bird's Tongue); and Meng Ding Ganlu (Meng Ding Mountain Sweet Dew), also from Ya'an City. Other famous teas include Meng Ding Huang Ya yellow tea, Chuan Hong Gongfu black, orchid-flavoured green teas, and Ya'an brick tea, a dark tea made for hundreds of years for transportation to Tibet.

Drying green tea in a wok using a brush to keep the tea moving against the hot metal so that it does not burn. Photograph by Jane Pettigrew

SICHUAN GREEN TEAS | *Zhu Ye Qing (Bamboo Green Tea)*

Although this tea has been made for centuries by monks living in Emei Mountain (Emeishan), it was given its poetic name in 1964 when Foreign Minister Chen Yi was offered the tea during a visit to The Temple of Ten Thousand Years on Emeishan and remarked that the small green buds resembled young bamboo shoots. The tea bushes grow at high elevations of 1,000 metres (3,281 feet), and little shoots of one bud and one leaf are picked three to five days before Qing Ming. It takes between 30,000 and 35,000 small shoots to produce just 500 grams (17.6 ounces) of dried tea. Some large companies process their teas in automated factories, but the traditional method is to wither the leaves for a short time on bamboo baskets, then turn the tea carefully in a hot wok to prevent oxidation, and with the wok temperature reduced a little, the tea master gently squeezes and presses down on the leaves as they dry. The shoots retain their original shape and look like tiny peapods that are very slightly curved and pointed at both ends.

Emei Xueya (Emei Snow Buds)

This mild, sweet tea grows at altitudes of between 800 and 1,200 metres (2,625 and 3,937 feet) on the cold, misty slopes of Emeishan, where snow wraps the tea gardens in winter and clouds reduce the amount of natural light, increasing the level of sweet amino acids in the new buds that appear slowly in the early spring. Listed as a tribute tea under the Sui (581 to 618) and the Tang (618 to 907) dynasties, it was mentioned by Lu Yu in a poem: "The snow bud tea originated from Emei Mount was so good as the green of Gu Zhuchun." The plump jade buds are harvested in March before Qing Ming and before all the snow has disappeared from the mountain slopes, and the tea is panned and dried in woks. The buds are not rolled but retain their natural shape and look like tiny peapods. The liquor they yield is crystal clear and green, and the aroma and flavour are sweet and fresh.

SICHUAN YELLOW TEA
Meng Ding Huang Ya (Meng Ding Yellow Tea)

This yellow tribute tea from Meng Ding Mountain dates back more than 1,200 years to the Tang dynasty and is made using tiny buds picked in late February or very early March. To make 500 grams (17.6 ounces) of Huang Ya, the pickers need to harvest 45,000 to 50,000 buds. After a three-hour wither, the tea is panned, and the tea master squeezes and presses the buds as they move against the hot metal. Then, while still warm and damp, small quantities are wrapped inside thick yellow paper and stored in a warm, humid room. Every half hour or so, the little parcels are opened, the tea is moved around, and then the parcel is closed up again. After five hours, the panning is repeated until about half the water content has evaporated, and the buds are then wrapped again in paper and stored for one or two hours. The packets are opened again, and the tea is panned for a third time until only 30 percent water remains in the leaves. The tea is spread out on paper in a layer about 5 centimetres (2 inches) thick and left for 36 hours to cool and rest, and it is then roasted to remove all but 4 to 5 percent of the moisture content. The processing demands a great deal of work, day and night, to ensure that it does not spoil.

SICHUAN BLACK TEA | *Chuan Hong Gongfu*

This neat, wiry black tea is produced in the region around Yibin, which lies east of Chengdu and just west of the recently created municipality of Chongqing. While Sichuan's more delicate green and yellow teas benefit from the cloud and mist of the high peaks, this lower-lying, subtropical, humid area is ideal for the production of black teas. Small, downy buds and leaves are picked in the spring and are put through the normal black tea stages of withering, rolling, oxidation, and drying. The finished tea is full of downy golden buds and elegant, neatly twisted leaves and looks a little like a Yunnan Gold or Golden Monkey black.

SICHUAN DARK TEA

At one time, Ya'an was a part of Tibet, but the mountainous region just below the Qinghai-Tibet Plateau now officially lies within western Sichuan. Compressed brick teas are made here today as they were centuries ago for transportation to the minority groups living in Tibet and the more remote regions of Sichuan. Just as Puerh City is the trading center for Yunnan's dark teas, Ya'an City is the main market for Sichuan's brick teas. Less highly regarded than Puerh teas by the Chinese, the Ya'an teas are popular with the Tibetans who like the strong earthy flavour that blends well with the rancid yak's butter and salt that are traditionally added to the brewed tea. In the past, two types of Ya'an brick tea were exported from here to Tibet: Huang Zhuancha (or yellow brick tea), a cheap, strong tea made from powdered leaves and popular with poorer people, and Mengshan (also known as Mingshan or Mingding) brick tea that was, and still is, popular among those who are a little more discerning about the quality of the teas they drink.

Ya'an teas, sometimes referred to simply as *Ya Cha* (Ya teas), are made at different times of the year. In May and June, Tiao Cha is made from shoots of one bud and five mature leaves; from July onwards, Mao Zhuang and Zuo Zhuang teas are made from shoots of a bud and three to five mature leaves. For Tiao tea, the fresh shoots are panned, steamed, rolled, wet piled, and dried. For Mao Zhuang tea, the freshly picked tea is panned, the leaves and stems are separated, and then the leaves are dried, while the stems are blended with other teas for wet piling with other teas. For Zuo Zhuang tea, the fresh shoots are panned, then steamed, rolled and cooled three times, wet piled, and dried. The three different types of raw material are blended in different proportions to make compressed teas for different destinations. Kang Brick, a special blend for Tibet, contains 50 percent Zuo Zhuang grade, 30 percent Tiao grade, 7 percent Mao Zhuang grade, 8 percent stems, and 5 percent Tiao best grade; Jin Jie (Golden Tip) is a blend of higher grade teas for Tibet. Ya Xi (Elegant Tips), sold to China, is one of the best grades and contains fewer stems and a higher proportion of Tiao Cha. Once measured in the correct amounts, the blended maocha is steamed in batches and compressed in bamboo baskets in layers separated by sheets of bamboo leaves, each layer containing 500 grams (17.6 ounces). Each basket holds 20 layers of 500 grams (17.6 ounces) each, a total weight of 10 kilos (22 pounds). The tea is then cooled and left to age. Once matured, it is prepared for transportation to Ya'an by wrapping each layer in thick paper, placing the layers back into the basket, and sealing the basket. In Ya'an, the bricks of tea are prepared for the onward journey by wrapping them in packages of a size suitable for transportation on the backs of yaks or ponies. Teas for imminent consumption are wrapped in bamboo, while bricks that are destined for the long journey up to Lhasa or to other remote regions are packaged inside sun-dried yak hides. Before fitting them around the tea, the hides are soaked in water and then sewn around the blocks of tea so that, as they dry out, they shrink to form a tight, waterproof covering to protect the tea.

Country, State, or Province
Sichuan Province

Area Under Tea
321,100 hectares

Average Annual Production (Kilograms)
262 million

Terrain
The tea mountains in the west of the province border with the foothills of Tibet. The tea grows on vast, high, hilly fields amongst misty clouds and rain. Meng Ding's tea gardens scramble up steep hillsides in the centre of the province.

Altitude
580 to 1,300 metres
(1,903 to 4,265 feet)

Best Time to Visit
March to May,
September, October

Main Varietals/Cultivars
Wu Chuan Da Shu Cha *(Big-Tree-Tea from Wuchuan)*, an old varietal from Wuchuan County, Guizhou, used for dark tea; Zaobaijian; Mingshan Baihao; Shuyong; Yinghong; Nanjing; Nanjiang Dayecha; Gulin Niupicha; Chongqing Pipacha; Beichuan Zhongyezhong; Mengshan; Mingshanzao; Mingshan Tezao; Huaqiu; Tianfu; Chuannong Huangyazao; Chuanmu 28; Mabianlü

Types of Tea Made
Green, orchid-flavoured green, yellow, black, dark

Predominant Flavours; Tasting Notes
GREEN: *Zhu Ye Qing (Bamboo Green Tea)*—sweet, slightly astringent, flinty, with hints of asparagus and young bamboo shoots
Emei Xueya (Emei Snow Buds)— sweet and fresh
YELLOW: *Meng Ding Huang Ya (Meng Ding Yellow Tea)*—sweet, mild, creamy, suggestions of hazelnuts
BLACK: *Chuan Hong Gongfu*— mellow, fresh, and brisk with undertones of caramel
DARK: strong, earthy

CHONGQING (CHINA)

In 1997, Chongqing, a district in the eastern part of Sichuan Province, became a separate tea-growing provincial municipality. Lying on the Qinghai-Tibet Plateau where tea first grew thousands of years ago, the region is thought to have been cultivating tea since around 1100 B.C. It is a land of mountains and rivers, with steep slopes to the north and south of the Yangtze River, which runs from north-east to south-west through the province. Lu Yu mentioned that, deep in the southern Daba Mountains, "there are tea trees that are so thick that it requires two people to embrace them," and tea bushes now cover hectare after hectare throughout the region. Some 40 gardens produce approximately 30 million kilos (66 million pounds) of white, green, jasmine green, orthodox black, CTC black, oolong, and dark teas while some companies have built new automated facilities for the production of steamed green teas as well as making high-quality speciality teas. The best-known teas are Yongchuan Xiuya green, Jinyun Mao Feng green, Bashan Silver Tip White tea, and Chongqing Tuo Cha dark tea.

Yongchuan Xiuya (Yongchuan Elegant Buds)

Yongchuan District lies halfway between Chongqing City and Luzhou in Sichuan Province in the western mountain region of the municipality that is famous for its bamboo as well as for its tea gardens. Before Chongqing was designated a separate area from Sichuan, this famous green tea was once known as a Sichuan tea, but is now classified as a Chongqing green that is made in five of Yongchuan's mountains. The manufacturing process was standardized in the 1960s and has become one of the region's most famous needle-shaped teas. The plucking standard is one bud and one leaf, and processing includes a short wither, panning, rolling to form the elegant buds that give the tea its name, and drying. Some of the teas are made by machine but traditionally this is a hand-made tea. The dry leaves are thin and tight, approximately 1 centimetre (0.39 inches) long, and emerald in colour with a covering of silver hairs. They look wonderful when brewed in a tall glass, and the liquor is fresh, clean, full-bodied, and sweet with hints of almonds.

Country, State, or Province
Chongqing Municipality

Area Under Tea
45,500 hectares

Average Annual Production (Kilograms)
31.1 million

Terrain
Tea gardens here are cultivated in the Daba Mountains, which stretch for hundreds of miles.

Altitude
700 to 2,000 metres (2,297 to 6,562 feet)

Best Time to Visit
March to May, September, October

Main Varietals/Cultivars
Chongpi 71-1, Yucha 1, Yucha 2, Bayu Tezao, and others

Types of Tea Made
White, green, jasmine green, oolong, orthodox and CTC black, dark tea

Predominant Flavours; Tasting Notes
GREEN: *Yongchaun Xiuya (Yongchuan Elegant Buds)*—fresh, clean, full-bodied, and sweet with hints of almonds

Yi people, one of China's ethnic minorities important to the cultivation and manufacture of tea, picking tea in Yinjing County, Ya'an.
Photograph courtesy of Camellia Sichuanesis

TIBET

(CHINA)

Tibet is today China's Tibet Autonomous Region or Xizang Autonomous Region (called Tibet or Xizang for short). Tibetans learned to love tea during the Tang dynasty (618 to 907), and up to 6.4 million tonnes a year of compressed blocks of Chinese Puerh tea were carried to Lhasa and exchanged for horses for the Chinese army. In 1074, the rate was set at 130 pounds (60 kilograms) of tea for one horse. The bricks were wrapped in wet yak skins, which shrank as they dried, creating solid blocks that remained intact on the rough eight- to 10-month journey. One yak carried two 27-kilo (46.3-pound) blocks and caravans of 200 to 300 yaks made their slow, difficult way through forests, open plains, across rope bridges, and up winding mountain tracks where rock falls and vertiginous mountain slopes meant hazardous progress. In 1893, in *My Experiences in Tibet*, Annie R. Taylor described how, in Ke-gu town, "The tea is bartered by the Chinese for wool, hides and furs, gold dust, mercury, and other Tibetan products.... The tea, branches as well as leaves, is packed in compressed bricks about fourteen inches long, ten wide, and four thick."

To drink the tea, the cakes were crushed, boiled in water with a little soda, strained, then churned in a tall wooden cylinder with *tsampa* (barley flour), salt, and rancid yak's butter until emulsified. Today, most Tibetans use electric food mixers to blend the same ingredients and drink the *po cha* (butter tea) for nourishment and to replace salt lost from the body at Tibet's high altitudes.

During the early years of China's Cultural Revolution, Mao Zedong called for the expansion of tea cultivation, and the tea areas spread into Tibet as well as into other parts of China, and since 1956, tea has been grown in various locations in the lower-lying regions of Tibet. Trial plantings showed that the assamica varietal grew well in south-eastern Metok near the border with India; the small-leafed sinensis varietal from Sichuan also grew successfully in Metok and in the southerly regions of Zayü, Yi'ong, Dongqiu, Lebo, Zhangmu, and Gyirong. In 2000, a report by the Tibetan Environment and Development Desk confirmed that tea is today cultivated in Metok, Zayü, Tramo, Nyingchi, and certain parts of Amdo and Kham. The leaves are processed to make green and black tea, some of which is compressed into bricks (in Puerh style) for local consumption.

Yi'ong is home to one of the country's largest estates, and the teas grown in Bomi County, Linzhi Prefecture, in the south-east of the country, are now available in China and in small quantities in the West. Yi'ong Tea Plantation, established in 1966, sits beside Yi'ong Lake in Yi'ong National Geopark on wide, misty plains surrounded by Linzhi's tall mountain peaks. *Yi'ong* means "beautiful place," and the region is famous for its vast forests, glaciers, waterfalls, lakes, and clear rivers that cascade down through gorges, canyons, and wide valleys carved out between the peaks. The tea plants benefit from the altitude and the temperate humid climate, and the garden produces aromatic green teas that are sold internationally as Mount Everest Tea. Locally, the brand uses the Tibetan name for Mount Everest, Qomolangma Tea. The processing of the tea is carried out at the Tibet Taiyang Agricultural Resources Development Company Ltd., whose factory also blends some of the green teas with locally grown herbs, such as snow lotus and saffron, and packs them into tea bags. The finer teas, such as Mao Feng, are sold loose.

More growers are now establishing tea gardens on the lower slopes of the country that run down into Sichuan. And a new garden in Gyirong Town, in the south of the region, lies only 150 kilometres (93.2 miles) from Mount Everest. Surrounded by the snowy peaks of the Himalayas, the tea grows at an altitude of 3,000 metres (9,842 feet), which is very high for the *Camellia sinensis*. Two of the owners are Tibetan and one is from Yunnan, and the bushes were transplanted here to see how they would grow. There was a concern that the climate would prove too cold and that very thick snow and ice in winter would kill the plants, but they were carefully wrapped up to protect them and they survived. They began to push out new buds and leaves as soon as spring returned, and the first harvest was gathered in July and August of the following year.

Country, State, or Province
Tibet Autonomous Region

Number of Gardens
More than 22 gardens and smallholder growers

Main Districts or Gardens
Nyingchi County in south-east (including Bomi, Zayü, Metok); Cona County in Shannan Prefecture; Gyirong Town in the south near the Nepalese border; and in Amdo and Kham along the northern border with Qinghai Province

Area Under Tea
More than 150 hectares

Average Annual Production (Kilograms)
200,000

Terrain
Nyingchi sits in south-east Tibet where the Himalayas extend eastwards to join the Hengduan Mountains that stretch into Sichuan to the east. Most of Tibet's tea-growing areas are very mountainous with snow-capped peaks, flatter land in the valleys, and many lakes, streams, and rivers

Altitude
1,900 to 3,000 metres (6,200 to 9,842 feet)

Production Period
May to October

Best Time to Visit
March to June

Main Varietals/ Cultivars
Sinensis from Sichuan, assamicas from Yunnan; new plantings include Fuding white and Tie Guan Yin varietals

Types of Tea Made
Green, black, and Puerh-style teas

Predominant Flavours; tasting notes
GREEN: very pale liquors, fresh, light, and refined, with a rich, lingering aftertaste
BLACK: Some are rather plain; the best are dark, rich and smooth.
DARK: slightly earthy, smooth and mellow

View of the Snowland Holy Tea Plantation in Tibet. Photographs courtesy of Camellia Sichuanesis

YUNNAN

(CHINA)

If Sichuan's Meng Ding Mountain is revered as the province where tea was first cultivated, Yunnan is recognised as the birthplace of the tree itself, and wild tea trees dating back thousands of years still grow in the forests here. In 1991, the Chinese Academy of Agricultural Sciences and another nine agencies identified a 2,700-year-old wild tea tree in Qianjiazhai, Zhenyuan County. The tree is 25.6 metres (84 feet) tall, and its girth measures 282 centimetres (9.25 feet). In 1992, the Yunnan Academy of Agricultural Sciences and four other agencies identified an 1,800-year-old tree growing in Bangwai Village, Lincang District. The tree stands 11.8 metres (38.7 feet) tall and has a girth of 358 centimetres (11.7 feet). Over the millennia since tea started growing here, the plants have cross-fertilized and adapted to the local conditions. To date, Yunnan has registered 199 varietals, but some surveys have identified as many as 244.

According to ancient Chinese records, the indigenous Pu people sent tribute teas to the Shang emperors more than 3,000 years ago, and their descendants, the Bulangs, are thought to have been the earliest to actually cultivate tea plants in the province some 900 years ago. Bulang families are still guardians of 214 hectares of ancient trees that grow on Bulang Mountain in Menghai County and still produce Puerh teas. By the 7th century, when the Tang came to power, tea from Xishuangbanna on the Laotian border in the south was traded into Dali, some 300 miles to the north, and a stone tablet in the Buddhist Pagoda at Mangjing on Jingmai Mountain records that the ancient tea garden there was created in 696. By the time of the Song emperors (960 to 1126), Puerh City had become the center for the local tea trade, and the teas became known as Puerh teas. Under the Tang and Ming emperors, the trading of tea from Yunnan to Tibet increased, and during the Qing dynasty (1644 to 1912), teas from particular mountain districts, such as Xishuangbanna, became famous. Teas traded here were transported up to Tibet along the Tea Horse Road to be exchanged for Tibetan ponies. In the 1920s and '30s, before the War of Resistance against Japan (1937 to 1945), approximately 5 million kilos (11 million pounds) of Yunnan tea were sold to Sichuan and Tibet every year, and a further 500,000 kilos (1.1 million pounds) were exported elsewhere. When the communists came to power in 1949 and Mao Zedong founded the People's Republic of China, Yunnan started developing new factories, research institutes, and new tea districts.

TOP: Carrying fresh leaf back to a village for processing. ABOVE LEFT: Baskets of maocha (the base tea from which Puerh tea is made) drying on bamboo baskets in the sun. ABOVE RIGHT: Ancient tea trees in Yunnan Province, the birthplace of the tea plant. Photographs by David Collen; courtesy of *essenceoftea.com*

TOP: Weighing maocha ready for steaming and compressing into a cake of puerh. ABOVE: Wrapping Puerh cakes in neat stacks inside dried bamboo leaves. Photographs by David Collen; courtesy of *essenceoftea.com*

Yunnan is today China's second-largest tea-producing region, after Fujian, and data from the Yunnan Provincial Agriculture Department shows that approximately 396,667 hectares produce more than 335.3 million kilos (739 million pounds) of tea every year. Puerh tea accounts for 48.8 percent, 27.2 percent is green tea, 22.4 percent is black, and the rest is jasmine and white. Some 6 million people grow tea in the province, and a total of 11 million are employed in the industry. Production is very diverse, and tea is grown in wild forests where there is little human intervention; in managed agroforests where tea trees and bushes are pruned and thinned to allow the plants more space and to let in light and the natural ecosystem is carefully maintained; in mixed-crop fields where tea grows with other crops such as grains; on huge intensive monoculture terraced plantations planted more recently with new cloned plants propagated from selected leaf cuttings; and in small private gardens that are a mixture of all of the above. The last 50 years have seen huge agricultural intensification and the proliferation of monoculture crops such as tea, rubber, coffee, and other cash crops. The newer terraced estates rely heavily on chemical plant protection agents (PPAs) to boost soil fertility, increase yields, and control pests, and this has caused problems of crop contamination. But many families have recognised the value of agroforests, particularly for the production of Puerh teas, and have transformed areas previously used for the monoculture of rice or tea to carefully managed tea agroforests, and this has increased tea production.

Yunnan is most famous for its aged, fermented dark Puerh teas and also makes greens and jasmine greens, white teas such as Yueguang Bai Cha (Moonlight White), and Yunnan Gold and Tippy Yunnan blacks.

YUNNAN WHITE TEAS

White bud teas made from Yunnan's big-leaf varietals, including *Camellia taliensis*, tend to have more flavour, depth, and sweet fruitiness than white teas made in other provinces from different varietals and cultivars. The teas are often sold with names such as Gu Shu Yinzhen, Yunnan Da Bai Silver Needles, Yunnan Sweet White Threads, and so on.

Since 2005, some Yunnan producers have been compressing white bud teas, picked from ancient or old trees, into Puerh-style cakes, which are intended to be stored and aged. Yueguang Bai Cha (Moonlight White), for example, is made from buds picked from 100- to 300-year-old arbor trees, and the leaf is then withered in the moonlight and pressed into white Puerh cakes. Varieties include needle-style cakes using just the buds, Peony White tea cakes made from buds and open leaves, and Shou Mei White tea cakes made from leaves and buds picked later in the year.

YUNNAN BLACK TEAS

Yunnan's black teas are often referred to as Dianhong teas. *Dian* is the old name for Yunnan and refers to the Dian people who ruled here until the 2nd century B.C. *Hong* means red, the Chinese term for what are known as black teas in the west. The teas are made from the local assamica varietal, but other varietals and cultivars are also used, and some Yunnan blacks are made from ancient wild or semi-wild trees.

Yunnan Gold (Dianhong Gongfu Cha), sometimes called Tippy Yunnan, is made from open leaves and a high proportion of large downy buds, which give the dry leaf its golden appearance. Yunnan Pure Gold (Jinya Dianhong Cha) is made from just the downy buds.

YUNNAN DARK TEAS | *Puerh Tea (Puer, Pu-erh, Pu'erh)*

By the 6th century, tea from Yunnan was being transported to Lhasa where it had become a popular food supplement for the Tibetan people whose diet at the high altitudes was limited. Because the transportation of loose tea caused enormous logistical difficulties, green tea made in Yunnan was compressed into cakes before being loaded onto ponies, yaks, and mules ready for the long journey from Puerh City (renamed Simao in 1950 but reverted to its original name in 2007) north through Yunnan, into Sichuan, and up to Lhasa. The cakes of tea took up less space and were less at risk if bags of tea were dropped or spilled when ponies stumbled on the rough Tea Horse Road. The preferred shape was a round flat disk of approximately 357 grams (12.6 ounces), and these were stacked inside layers of bamboo leaves.

The journey to Tibet took six to eight months through heavy rain, thick and foggy mists, and blazing summer sun. The rough track wound its way through damp forests, dry plains, and open marshland, across swaying rope-and-wood suspension bridges, along crumbling pathways, where loose stones and rocks were often sent hurtling down the perpendicular cliffs to crash hundreds of feet below, and narrow, zigzagging rocky mountain paths just wide enough for the passage of one man or one heavily laden animal at a time. During the laborious journey, the tea absorbed humidity, and this activated the micro-flora in the tea and provoked a slow bacterial fermentation. The micro-organisms found their way into the tea because they were present in the air of Yunnan's dense tea forests, settled on the leaves of the tea trees, and were in the tea after processing. The humidity and warm temperatures on the journey to Tibet activated a natural fermentation process, which continued during storage of the teas in Lhasa. The longer they were stored, the more the character of the teas changed from the astringent grassiness of Yunnan green tea to a mellower, smoother, fruitier flavour. Teas sold to Lhasa at that time were of very poor quality, often made from leftover leaves, twigs, and branches, and if drunk just after processing would have tasted rough and coarse, but the aging process made them more palatable. As the market for these aged teas increased, tea producers in Yunnan started to process teas that replicated the fermentation that had initially started by accident. By 1800, quality was improving, and teas were now categorised according to leaf quality, season, origin, and maker's name, although the year of production was not recorded.

The 1950s saw a burgeoning demand for Puerh teas from Hong Kong because of the number of Chinese refugees displaced there from mainland China during the Nationalist-Communist Civil War (1946 to 1950). At the same time, the foundation of the People's Republic of China in 1949 had prompted the Yunnan state tea industry to modernise and standardise production. In 1972, there was a new development. The best Puerh teas need seven to 10 years to begin to develop their more mellow character, and so, in order to speed up the fermentation process and make more tea available more quickly, the Menghai Tea Factory and the Kunming Tea Factory adapted the method of wet piling, called *wo dui*, used in Guangxi Province since the 18th century. Mass production of this "ripened" tea began in 1975, and most teas made by this method are stored for only two or three years before being ready to drink.

Puerh tea made by the traditional method of slow aging is called Sheng (raw) Puerh; tea made by the modern wet-piled method is called Shu (ripe, ripened, or cooked) Puerh.

Sheng (Raw) Puerh
To make raw Puerh, tea buds and leaves are picked, withered in the shade for a few hours, panned at a low temperature to remove some of the water content and soften the leaves, rolled by hand on bamboo baskets, and dried in the sun. As it dries,

this *maocha* (raw or rough tea) oxidises slowly and darkens from bright green to a mixture of green-brown and downy, silvery buds. This oxidation happens because, although the tea has been panned before rolling, the heat treatment is not enough to kill all the enzymes in the leaf, and those that remain activate slow oxidation as the leaves dry slowly in the sun. During the normal production of green tea, the tea is dried much more quickly in the wok, panning machine, or oven, so no oxidation takes place.

Maocha can be sold and drunk as it is, but to make Puerh, it is steamed in a cylindrical can with holes in the base that allow the steam to pass up through the tea. A linen or cotton bag is slipped over the cylinder and flipped upside down so that the tea falls into the bag and the cylinder is removed. A little paper identity tag, called a *nei fei*, which indicates the factory name and the brand, is placed amongst the leaves, and the bag of tea is placed on a large concave stone. The sides of the bag are twisted and pressed down onto the tea to work it down into the bottom of the bag and form a neat compressed disk that is very even around the edges and round like a biscuit (cookie). As the bag is twisted and tightened, the knot of fabric makes a round indentation in the center of the tea's surface. The bag with the tea inside is then placed on a wooden plank under a very heavy stone, and the tea maker climbs onto the stone and uses body weight to compress the tea. In large factories, the pressing is carried out using hydraulic presses or a mechanically operated heavy stone. The bag is then removed, and the cake of tea is air-dried, then wrapped and stored in temperature-controlled and humidity-controlled conditions. The wrapping paper is printed with the year the tea was made (and sometimes the season), the region, the grade of leaves used, the plant varietal or cultivar, and the name of the factory. Inside the wrapper is a slip of paper called a *nei piao*, which gives further information about the factory, the brand, and the tea itself. Sheng Puerh is most commonly compressed into large or small round cakes, but other shapes, such as rectangles, or birds' nests, are also made.

Shu (Ripe, Ripened, or Cooked) Puerh

Shu Puerh is also made using maocha, which is processed in exactly the same way as for Sheng Puerh. But instead of being lightly steamed, the tea is mixed with water, heaped, covered, and stored in a humid, warm warehouse for several months. Before piling and wetting the maocha, the floor of the warehouse must be cleaned. This is done by covering it with a layer of tea dust from cooked Puerh tea, 1 centimetre (.39 inch) thick. Water is sprayed on the dust until it is completely wet, and more water is sprayed onto the tea dust every one or two days. After two weeks, the dust will have absorbed all the odour and dirt on the floor. The dust is then washed away, and the floor is left to dry. Then the maocha is spread on the floor and sprayed evenly with water. From time to time, the covers are removed, the tea is mixed and turned, and the covers are then replaced. Careful control of the humidity, temperature, and rate of the fermentation are crucial to the production of good Shu Puerh. After about 45 days, the large pile of tea is split into smaller piles to slow down the speed of fermentation. When it is ready, the tea is dried and then sold as a young, loose ripened Puerh; aged, loose ripened Puerh; or compressed ripened Sheng Puerh, in the shape of round cakes, rectangles, pumpkins, birds' nests, or mushrooms. Shu Puerh is rarely aged longer than 10 years.

To compress a Puerh cake, the bag of tea is placed beneath a heavy stone; the tea maker then climbs onto the stone and uses body weight to compress the tea. Photograph by David Collen; courtesy of *essenceoftea.com*

Cakes of Puerh tea ready for the aging process, during which the tea will slowly ferment, changing colour and becoming very slowly sweeter and more mellow over time. Photograph by David Collen; courtesy of *essenceoftea.com*

FERMENTATION IN PUERH TEA

The main micro-organisms involved in the fermentation of dark tea in Yunnan Province are *Aspergillus niger* and *Saccharomyces*, a type of sugar fungus that includes yeasts used in the manufacture of bread, wine, and beer. *Aspergillus niger* helps change fats, proteins, natural fibres, and insoluble carbohydrates into amino acid, hydrated pectin, and soluble carbohydrates. It gives the tea a smoother, mellower character. *Saccharomyces* also helps develop a sweeter, smoother taste in the tea. The balance of microbes found in Puerh tea varies according to the region in which the tea is made. During aging, the storage temperature and humidity must be carefully regulated, and teas will ferment more quickly if the leaves and buds have not been too tightly compressed and, therefore, allow air to circulate freely through the tea. Teas with a large surface area in proportion to the size of the cake also ferment more quickly.

PUERH VARIETALS

Yunnan's indigenous tea varietal is the assamica Da Ye, a big-leaf tea plant, and several sub-varietals have been found growing in ancient forests in different regions of the Yunnan. Puerh teas are classified according to the trees or bushes harvested and can be made from ancient trees (more than 500 years old), old trees (less than 500 years old), small trees (50 to 100 years old), wild arbor trees (semi-cultivated), wild trees (growing without any human intervention), mother trees, tall trees, small-leafed trees, and so on. The best and most expensive teas are made from ancient wild trees that have grown organically, without the application of any fertilisers or pesticides and without pruning, for hundreds or thousands of years. The roots draw up the deepest, richest flavours from the earth in which they grow and from the roots of other plants with which they intertwine. Teas made from semi-wild arbor trees that were planted hundreds of years ago and have been left to grow organically amongst other native vegetation are considered very desirable but are not as valuable as truly wild trees. Teas made from younger cultivated bushes that are less than 50 years old and were grown from seeds or leaf cuttings taken from wild or semi-wild trees give less quality and flavour.

FAMOUS PUERH MOUNTAINS

Three areas of Yunnan are famous for their Puerh teas: Xishuangbanna (Mengla County, Jinghong City, and Menghai County), Puerh District (Jingmai Mountain and Wuliang Mountain) and Lincang District (Mengku County, Fengqing County, and Yongde County). Each region in Yunnan has its own microclimate and ecological balance, and the teas made there have a unique flavour profile. Over the years, the Chinese authorities have designated certain mountains as the most important for the production of Puerh teas. Until 1962, the famous six mountains were Gedeng, Mansa, Mangzhi, Manzhuan, Yibang, and Youle mountains. These are all located in Xishuangbanna Prefecture, which lies in the very south of the province, on the border with Laos, at the very heart of the Himalayan corridor where tea first grew. Gedeng has a small area of ancient trees and new cultivated

areas. Mansa's tea bushes grow at 820 to 2,000 metres (2,690 to 6,562 feet). Manzhuan Mountain has large areas of newly planted tea growing at 1,000 to 1,800 metres (3,281 to 5,906 feet). Yibang Mountain is home to several different varietals of mostly old trees growing at 850 to 1,900 metres (2,789 to 6,234 feet) and also has some newer, small-scale, cultivated areas. Youle (also known as Jinuo) Mountain has 300 hectares of tea gardens at elevations from 570 to 1,650 metres (1,870 to 5,413 feet).

In 1962, Yiwu, Menghai, Nannou, Bulang, and Youle mountains in Xishuangbanna and Jingmai Mountain in Puerh Prefecture were named as the new group of six. Yiwu Mountain produces around 600,000 kilos (1.3 million pounds) of tea a year. Menghai Mountain has one of the oldest histories of tea growing and today has more than 260 hectares of old trees. Tea production on Nannou Mountain dates back to the Tang dynasty (618 to 907), and today, there are more than 660 hectares of old tea trees growing at 800 to 1,500 metres (2,625 to 4,921 feet). Bulang's tea cultivation area dates back 900 years or more and has more than 200 hectares of ancient trees. And Jingmai Mountain is thought to be the place where tea was first cultivated in Yunnan in 696 and has more than 650 hectares planted with tea.

Other important mountains are Ailao, Bada, Baoshan Banzhang, Bangwei, Jinggu, Mengsong, Nanqiao, Wuliang, and Yushou mountains, and historical locations include the Bangwei Village tree that is 1,800 years old; Zhenyuan, which was a famous stopping point on the Tea Horse Road; and Yongde County in Lincang Prefecture where there are more than 1,000 trees that are thought to be more than 1,000 years old. These include the *Camellia taliensis* (or *daliensis*) varietal, a wild relative of the tea plant that is used locally to make Puerh tea.

Taking into account the number of fresh-leaf options, the different processing methods, and the effects of aging and fermentation, Puerh teas are many and varied and may be made from any of the above tree or bush varietals grown in any of the different mountain regions, and sold as young or aged raw or young or aged ripe Puerh.

Ancient trees climbing tall and straight in a Yunnan forest. Photograph by David Collen; courtesy of *essenceoftea.com*

Country, State, or Province
Yunnan Province

Area Under Tea
401,300 hectares

Average Annual Production (Kilograms)
365.8 million

Terrain
A plateau region where 94% of the land is hilly. In the east, undulating mountains and karst hills divided by steep river ravines; in the north, high mountains; to the west, rugged, very steep mountains covered with thick forest vegetation, deep river, gorges, and canyons; and, in the south, thick tropical rain forests at lower altitudes. The high mountains are interspersed with very fertile flat basins.

Altitude
317 to 2,000 metres (1,040 to 6,561 feet)

Best Time to Visit
March to May, September, October

Main Varietals/Cultivars
More than 244 varietals and cultivars that include the following: Qiao Mu Da Ye Zhong (Old Tea Trees Big Leaf Varietal); Mengku Dayecha; Fangqing Dayecha; Menghai Dayecha; Yungkang; Hangye Baihao; Yunmei; Yungui; Aifeng; Yunkang; Yunxuan 9; Foxiangcha; Yuncha 1; Yuncha Chunyun; Yuncha Chunhao; Pingyun cultivars; Qianmei cultivars; Heitiaozicha; Niuzhaidachashu; Huangniheyecha; *Camellia taliensis*

Types of Tea Made
White, greens, jasmine greens, Puerh dark teas

Predominant Flavours; Tasting Notes
WHITE: thick, velvety, sweet, with suggestions of nuts, fruits, and spice
BLACK: rich, malty, sweet, with deep spicy notes and hints of liquorice, plums, and raisins
PUERH: *Sheng (Raw)*—when young, grassy and astringent; aged teas are complex, sweet, and mellow, with hints of tobacco, warm wood, and damp forests
Shou (Cooked)—earthy, peaty, mellow

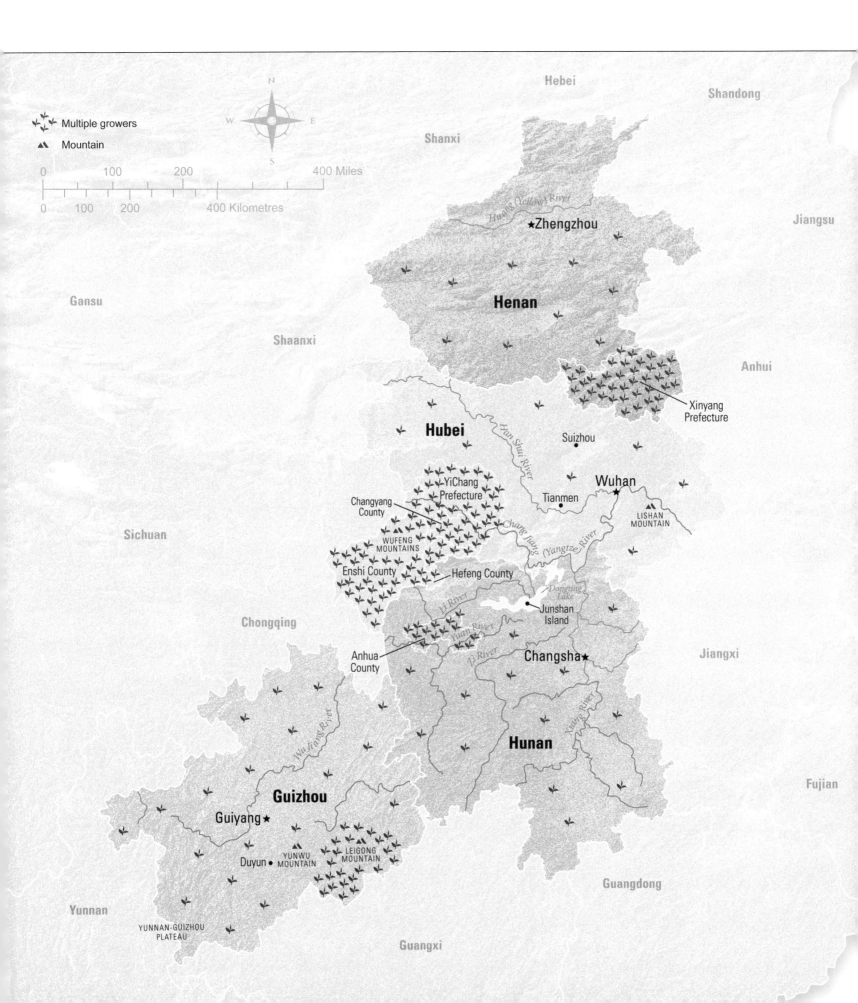

Multiple growers

▲ Mountain

0   100   200   400 Miles

0   100   200   400 Kilometres

Hebei

Shandong

Shanxi

Jiangsu

Huang (Yellow) River

★Zhengzhou

Gansu

Anhui

Shaanxi

Henan

Xinyang
Prefecture

Hubei

Han Shui River

Suizhou •

Wuhan★

YiChang
Prefecture

Tianmen •

▲▲
LISHAN
MOUNTAIN

Changyang
County

Chang Jiang (Yangtze) River

Sichuan

▲
WUFENG
MOUNTAINS

Enshi County

Hefeng County

Dongting
Lake

Junshan
Island

Ji River

Yuan River

Chongqing

Anhua
County

Zi River

Changsha★

Jiangxi

Guizhou

Hunan

Wu Jiang River

Xiang River

Fujian

Guiyang ★

Duyun •

▲
YUNWU
MOUNTAIN

▲
LEIGONG
MOUNTAIN

Guangdong

Yunnan

YUNNAN-GUIZHOU
PLATEAU

Guangxi

GUIZHOU

(CHINA)

The landscape of Guizhou is very similar to that of Guangdong, its conical karst hillocks, pinnacles, gorges, and high mountains rising from the plains like supernatural sculpted features. The high western reaches of the province lie on the Yunnan-Guizhou (Yungui) Plateau and are rich in zinc and selenium, while the east is lower and flatter towards the border with Hunan Province. The climate is subtropical with long, warm, humid summers and slightly cooler temperatures in the winter months. Cultivation and production are expanding rapidly here, and the tea bushes grow on neat terraced slopes surrounded by forests and along the banks of rivers and creeks. The region is particularly important for its green teas, including the heavily rolled Huo Qing Zhu Cha, a type of gunpowder tea. Producers also make white teas in Leigong Mountain in the Yungui Plateau, small amounts of oolong, and an increasing number of black teas that have a deep mellow flavour with hints of malt and chocolate.

GUIZHOU GREEN TEAS

Duyun Mao Jian (Fur Tip, Green Tip)

This green tea from Duyun City is said to have been a favourite of Ming Emperor Chongzhen (1627 to 1644) and so was designated a tribute tea. It is made from the youngest tiny buds and new leaves, which are covered with silvery down. They are panned, rolled, twisted, and dried using similar hand movements to those used to process Bi Luo Chun, and the tea is known locally as Yugou (Fish Hook) tea because of the appearance of the curled silver leaves and buds. The tea is also called Three Yellows tea because of its dry yellow leaves, the bright yellow of the wet leaves after brewing, and the yellow gold of the liquor. The aroma hints at spinach, and the flavour is lively with melon notes.

Guiding Yun Wu (Guiding Cloud Mist)

Made in Yun Wu Mountain in Guiding County at altitudes of 1,500 metres (4,921 feet), this was a tribute tea during the Qing dynasty. The almost constant cloud cover and mist conditions reduce the amount of sunlight and increase the levels of L-theanine amino acid in the teas, giving them a naturally sweet, umami character. The tea can be picked five times through the year, starting in April before Qing Ming. Processing is complicated, and fresh shoots of one downy bud and two leaves are lightly aired, then panned, twisted, kneaded, rubbed, and rolled. The steps are repeated several times as the tea dries in the wok, and at the end of the process, the leaves are very curly and have the same hooked appearance as Duyun Mao Jian. The flavour is mellow and smooth with honeyed notes.

TOP: Tea field in Guizhou Province where tea cultivation has been increasing over recent years. Photograph courtesy of Fujian Yuantai Tea Co., Ltd. ABOVE LEFT: Fresh leaf waiting to be carried to the factory. ABOVE RIGHT: Carrying the leaf back to the factory for processing. Photographs by David Collen; courtesy of *essenceoftea.com*

Country, State, or Province
Guizhou Province

Area Under Tea
459,400 hectares

Average Annual Production (Kilograms)
223.3 million

Terrain
In the west of the province, rugged terrain with high mountain peaks and deep gorges, karst hillocks, and strange rock formations. Flatter in the east and south.

Altitude
900 to 1,550 metres (2,953 to 5,085 feet)

Best Time to Visit
March to May, September, October

Main Varietals/Cultivars
Wu Chuan Da Shu Cha (Big-Tree-Tea from Wuchuan), an old varietal from Wuchuan County; Meitan Taicha; Qianmei

Types of Tea Made
Green

Predominant Flavours; Tasting Notes
GREEN: *Duyun Mao Jian (Fur Tip, Jade Tip)*—vegetal, spinach aroma and sweet, lively taste, with hints of melon; *Guiding Yun Wu (Guiding Cloud Mist)*—thin, curly leaves that brew a fragrant, mellow liquor with honeyed notes

HENAN

(CHINA)

In 1987, archaeologists found tea in excavated tombs in Xinyang's Gushi County dating back to 875 B.C., proving that the region's tea history dates back at least 2,300 years to the Zhou dynasty (1122 to 256 B.C.). Xinyang lies south of the Yellow River and is irrigated by a network of streams, small rivers, and plentiful rainfall, making the climate mild and misty.

HENAN GREEN TEA

Xinyang Mao Jian (Xinyang Hairy Tips or Xinyang Furry Tips)

With its pointed downy leaves, this green tea was originally called Mountain Tippy Tea but was renamed Xinyang Mao Jian when it won a gold medal at the 1914 Panama-Pacific International Exposition in San Francisco. The most tender teas are picked high up in the mountains from tea trees growing in an area known as "5 Mountains and 2 Pools." The tea is picked in mid-April, and the young, tender shoots of two tiny leaves and a bud are briefly withered and then panned to stop oxidation. The little bud sets are then pressed down briefly by hand against the hot wok, released, and stirred, and this pressing and stirring continues until all the tea is dried and the leaves are bright green, straight, and sharply pointed.

The Xinyang Mao Jian legend tells how a strange disease made everyone in Xinyang Village very ill and how a local girl searched everywhere for a cure. One day, she met an old man who told her that she must cross 99 mountains to find a special tree and, within 10 days, bring back some of its leaves to the village. She set off, crossed the mountains, and found the tree but was too exhausted to walk all the way back. The tree spirit took pity on her and changed her into a bird so that she could fly home with the leaves in her beak, and everyone in the village was cured with the brew made from the leaves. The now famous tea trees were propagated from leaf cuttings.

Country, State, or Province
Henan Province

Area Under Tea
153,800 hectares

Average Annual Production (Kilograms)
59.6 million

Terrain
Henan's tea area is located in the east of the province, which forms part of the North China Plain, the largest alluvial plain in eastern Asia.

Altitude
500 to 800 metres
(1,640 to 2,625 feet)

Best Time to Visit
late March, April, September, October

Main Varietals/Cultivars
Xinyang 10

Types of Tea Made
Green

Predominant Flavours; Tasting Notes
GREEN: *Xinyang Mao Jian (Xinyang Hairy Tips)*—the aroma of the jade green liquor is of warm summer meadows, and the taste is robust, sweet, and powerfully vegetal

HUBEI

(CHINA)

The name of this central, landlocked province means "north of the lake" and refers to Dongting Lake in Hunan Province, which lies to the south. The landscape is of high mountain ranges, the tributary streams and creeks, gorges, and dams of the Yangtze and Hanshui rivers, and so many lakes that Hubei is known as "the province of a thousand lakes." The province has very important historical links with tea, and Lishan Mountain, in the center of the province, is said to have been the birthplace of Shennong, the Father of Tea. (The other possible location is Hua in Shaanxi Province.) Shennong Cave is believed to mark the place where he lived, and a tributary of the Yangtze River running through Hubei is also named after him. In the north eastern Daba Mountain, the most famous landmark is Shennong Peak, and in the north western corner of the province lies Shennongjia Forestry District. Lu Yu, the Sage of Tea, was also born in Hubei's Tianmen City in 733.

The province is famous for its unusual steamed En Shi Yu Lu green tea, En Shi Cui Lu (En Shi Jade Green), Jade Cloud green, jasmine greens, gongfu black teas, and compressed dark teas. It also produces Keemun-style blacks, like those made in Anhui Province, but they are not considered to be as good.

HUBEI GREEN TEAS | *En Shi Yu Lu*
(En Shi Gyokuro, En Shi Jade Dew, En Shi Green Dew)

Until the rule of the Ming dynasty (1368 to 1644), China's green teas were prepared by steaming the fresh leaf to prevent oxidation. Under the Ming, a new method of applying dry heat was introduced and has been used by most Chinese producers ever since. However, in the Wufeng Mountains of Enshi Tuhia and Miao Autonomous Prefecture in south-west Hubei, the old steaming method is still used, and so, the tea is reminiscent of Japanese sencha, although the leaves have the appearance of a Chinese green tea and the character is milder and more mellow than most Japanese green teas. For the best En Shi Yu Lu teas, plucking begins as early as the middle of March and continues into April, depending on the region. The buds and leaves must be small, slender, very straight, and of uniform size and have the appearance of small pine needles. After steaming, the leaves are cooled and then rolled, rubbed, and shaped by hand on a special table, and gently heated to slowly reduce the water content. The rolling and heating are repeated until less than 5 percent water remains in the leaves. The tea is then cooled and ready for packing. The steaming process intensifies the green of the dry leaf and brings out the complex, deep, vegetal character, enhancing the slightly savoury character and nutty and floral notes of the tea.

Enshi's most famous tea garden is Wujiatai Tea Gardens in Xuan'en, which, in 1784, received a plaque from the Qing dynasty emperor Qianlong (1735 to 1796) to show his appreciation of the tea made there. Since that time, Wujiatai Tribute Tea has been one of China's famous teas. Enshi is also famous for its selenium-rich soil, which produces teas that contain high levels of selenium, a trace element that plays an active role in maintaining the body's mechanisms and strengthening the immune system. These teas include Greenwood Cui Feng, Wu Jia Tai, Enshi flower tea, and Qingjiang Jade.

Jade Cloud (Hubei Cloud or Rolling Cloud)

This mellow, refreshing green tea is produced at high altitudes in several of Hubei's high mountain areas, where the topmost peaks are constantly hidden by swirling clouds and the spring climate is cool and misty. The shady conditions mean that the teas have higher levels of chlorophyll and L-theanine, little astringency, and a mellow sweetness. The fresh leaves are panned, rolled, oven-baked, and roasted, and have a slightly savoury, toasted chestnut character with suggestions of spinach and meadow grass.

HUBEI BLACK TEAS | *Yi Hong Gongfu*

Hubei's skillfully made black teas, produced in Hefeng, Changyang, Enshi, and Yi Chang counties, have been exported to Western markets since they were first made in the 1850s. Between 1886 and 1888, some 15 million kilos (33 million pounds) are reported to have been sold to England, the United States, Russia, and Europe. The *Yi* in the name comes from the fact that these *hong cha* (red teas) travelled through Yi Chang County to

reach the port of Hankou for export. To make the tea, shoots consisting of one bud and one leaf are picked in the spring between Qing Ming on the 4th or the 5th of April and Gu Yu on the 20th of April, and then they are withered, rolled, oxidised, dried, and refined into different grades, of which the finest is Jin Ping A or Yihong Black Tea Grade 1. The top grades have fine, tight, tippy leaves that brew a bright, brilliant red liquor with a sweet aroma and brisk, mellow taste. Lower grades have coarser, uneven leaves and dull red liquors that are a little astringent and strong.

HUBEI DARK TEAS | *Lao Qing Cha (Hubei Hei Cha, Hubei Dark Tea)*

Hubei's dark tea is one of China's most important fermented teas, along with Puerh and Hunan Hei Cha. It is one of the teas that was transported hundreds of miles by camel and horse caravans to Tibet and into Mongolia. Sometimes called Qing Zhuan Cha (Green Brick Tea), it is made from a green-tea base that is dampened with steam and pile-fermented, then compressed and aged in warm, humid conditions for several years until the cake of tea darkens to a greenish-brown and the grassy green taste mellows and sweetens. Hubei bricks are usually rectangular and are often embossed with an image or inscription on one side and marked into squares or smaller rectangles on the underside to allow easy breaking of the cake for brewing.

Hubei also produces Mi Zhuan dark tea made from fully oxidised broken black tea, which, instead of being pile-fermented, is aged naturally. The cakes are usually flatter and thinner than Lao Qing Cha and brew a deep red liquor that is strong and mellow.

Country, State, or Province
Hubei Province

Area Under Tea
310,700 hectares

Average Annual Production (Kilograms)
197 million

Terrain
A land of lakes and rivers, dams, reservoirs, and high mountains with jagged peaks bathed in white cloud. The highest peak, Dashennongjia, known as "The Roof of Central China," climbs to 3,053 metres (10,016 feet).

Altitude
700 to 1,200 metres (2,296 to 3,973 feet)

Best Time to Visit
late March, April, September, October

Main Varietals/Cultivars
Yichang Dayecha; E'cha; Yihongzao; Jingfeng; Jinxiang

Types of Tea Made
Green, black, dark compressed tea

Predominant Flavours; Tasting Notes
GREEN: *En Shi Yu Lu (En Shi Jade Dew)*—complex, deeply vegetal, nutty, and slightly savoury, with floral notes
Jade Cloud (Hubei Cloud or Rolling Cloud)—slightly savoury, with toasted chestnut character and suggestions of spinach and meadow grass
BLACK: *Yi Hong Gongfu*—bright, brilliant red liquor with a sweet aroma and brisk, mellow taste
DARK: *Lao Qing Cha (Hubei Hei Cha, Hubei Dark Tea)*—grassy and green when young; more mellow and sweet when aged

HUNAN

(CHINA)

Hunan, which means "south of the lake," is so called because of its position south of Dongting Lake, the vast stretch of water that lies in the far north of the province. Tea production here dates back at least 1,800 years to the early part of the Han dynasty (206 B.C. to A.D. 220). Hunan tea found its way into other parts of China along the trade routes that connected Hunan and Fujian with Beijing, and on through the Great Wall to Mongolia, Siberia, and Russia. And as Puerh teas became popular in Tibet, Hunan also made compressed tea for transportation to Lhasa. The province is still famous for its dark teas, made in Anhua County for those long overland journeys, and Hunan is also renowned for Junshan Yin Zhen yellow, Xiangxi Guzhang Maojian green, and black teas that include Black Mao Feng, Wu Ling Mountain black, and Monkey Picked Golden Hunan.

An old stone bridge across a river in Hunan's Anhua dark-tea district. © Qiu Jun Song

HUNAN YELLOW TEA | *Junshan Yin Zhen*
(Silver Needle from Gentleman Mountain)

Although the name suggests that this is a silver-needle white tea, it is in fact a yellow tea from Junshan Island, which lies in the middle of Dongting Lake. Although tea bushes grow all around the edges of the lake, only the teas that actually grow on the island are allowed to bear the name. The tea has been famous since the days of the Tang dynasty (618 to 907) and is believed to have been chosen by Tang Princess Wencheng as part of her trousseau when she left China to marry the Tibetan King Songtsan Gampo in 641.

Junshan Island is often completely wrapped in mist because of the humidity rising from the lake, and the bushes love the low temperatures and damp, shady conditions. Plucking takes place seven to 10 days before and after Qing Ming, depending on the weather, when the new buds measure less than 30 millimetres (1.2 inches) and contain four or five tightly furled rudimentary buds. The tea is panned in batches of approximately 300 grams (10.5 ounces), first at 100° to 120°C (212° to 248°F), then at 80°C (176°F), to soften the leaves and reduce the water content by 30 percent. The leaves are then taken out of the wok, allowed to cool for four or five minutes, then heated over charcoal for about 20 minutes at 50° to 60°C (122° to 140°F) until the water content is reduced to 50 percent. After cooling, the tea is wrapped in thick paper in parcels of 1.5 kilos (3.3 pounds) and stored inside a pot for one or two days to ferment lightly. This smothering *men-huang* process reduces the tea's grassy notes. The tea is then unwrapped, heated again to stabilise the leaves' chemical content and reduce the water content to 20 percent, wrapped for another day, then dried again to reduce the moisture content to below 5 percent. The dried buds are yellow-green, straight, and downy, and when brewed in a tall glass, they gradually absorb water and drift to the bottom of the glass. Because they remain upright with their tips pointing upwards, Lu Yu referred to it as Bai He Lin or "White Crane Tail Feathers," and it is sometimes also called "Silent Bamboo Forest."

HUNAN BLACK TEA | *Monkey Picked Golden Hunan*

Grown at altitudes over 1,220 metres (4,003 feet), the best Golden Monkey black teas are made from just the downy buds, which give the dry leaf its wiry golden appearance. Producers make this and similar black teas, with names such as Black Bud Black Tea, Black Mao Feng, and Black Needle, throughout the province.

Tea bushes growing alongside kumquat bushes. Photograph courtesy of Fujian Yuantai Tea Co., Ltd.

HUNAN DARK TEAS | *Hunan Anhua Dark Tea*

Anhua County has been making logs and bricks of dark tea for approximately 400 years for transportation to Mongolia and Tibet. The logs are made in four sizes. Qian Liang is 152 centimetres (60 inches) long, has a diameter of around 20 centimetres (8 inches), and weighs 36.25 kilos (79.92 pounds); Bai Liang is 63.5 centimetres (25 inches) long, is just over 10 centimetres (4 inches) in diameter, and weighs 3.625 kilos (8 pounds); Qi Liu Liang is approximately 20 centimetres (8 inches) long, about 7.5 centimetres (3 inches) in diameter, and weighs 0.5 kilos (1.1 pounds); and Qi Liang is 20 centimetres (8 inches) long, 5 centimetres (2 inches) in diameter, and weighs 0.362 kilos (0.8 pounds). The earliest production was of Bai Liang (also called Hu Juan Cha). Manufacture of Qian Liang began in the 1820s during the Qing dynasty, stopped around 1950, but is back in production today. The teas, which are quite rough and contain stalks and coarse leaves, are either sold as whole logs or are sliced into smaller disks that are wrapped individually for sale.

Hunan dark teas differ from Puerh dark teas both because of the different processing and the different tea varietals and cultivars used (in Yunnan, native assamica; in other provinces, local sinensis varietals or cultivars). The fermentation in the teas also varies because of the different molds and fungi involved. In Yunnan, the main fungus is *Aspergillus niger*; in Hunan, the microbes of the main fungus, *Eurotium cristatum*, cause tiny yellow specks of Jin Hua, or Golden Flower, mold to grow on the tea, particularly in Hunan Zhuan, a dark brick tea.

To make Anhua dark tea, fresh leaves are withered, then panned at 260° to 300°C (500° to 572°F), then rolled while still hot to break the cells and squeeze out the juices. The leaves are then piled 60 to 100 centimetres (24 to 39 inches) deep and covered with a wet cloth to keep in the heat and the moisture and to provoke fermentation. After 24 hours of fermentation, the leaves are rolled again to break the cells by a further 30 percent to assist the fermentation process during storage, and then the leaves are dried. Finally, the tea is steamed and packed inside tubes of different sizes crafted from dried bamboo leaves and then stored in controlled conditions to age and allow the Jin Hua (Golden Flower) to grow on the tea.

Hunan Tian Jian | Another dark tea made in Anhua County, Hunan Tian Jian is a loose tea that is much easier to brew than the log teas. The freshly plucked green leaves are withered, panned, piled while still hot and damp, allowed to ferment, then dried over smoking pinewood. Before all the moisture has been dried out of the leaves, the tea is packed into boxy rectangular bamboo baskets and left to slowly continue fermenting. After a few years in the baskets, the tea brews a bright amber-orange liquor that is complex, clean, crisp, and fruity with smoky pine resin notes and suggestions of stewed plums and whole raw almonds.

Fu Cha | Also called Fu Zhuan Cha or Mongolian Diet Tea, Fu Cha dark tea has been in production since 1860. *Zhuan* means "brick," and rather than being compressed into log shapes, the tea comes in rectangular blocks. Like Qian Liang, Fu Cha is not a fancy tea and is made from older, rougher leaves and stalks.

TOP: Bags packed with fermented tea awaiting further processing that will turn it into different types of dark tea such as Qian Liang tea. Photograph courtesy of China Tea Hunan Anhua First Tea Factory Co., Ltd. RIGHT: Dried bamboo leaves are stitched together to prepare the top of the bamboo sleeve into which Anhua dark tea is pushed, then compressed and aged. © Qiu Jun Song (OPPOSITE PAGE) TOP LEFT: Gently steamed maocha is fed into the prepared bamboo sleeves inside which it will be left for years to ferment. TOP FAR RIGHT: Workers use all their force to shape and tighten the bamboo sleeve around the maocha before closing the top. BOTTOM: Once the tea is safely packed into the bamboo sleeve, the workers use their feet to roll and compress the tea so that it forms a solid cylinder of tea. © Qiu Jun Song

Country, State, or Province
Hunan Province

Area Under Tea
132,800 hectares

Average Annual Production (Kilograms)
172.355 million

Terrain
82% of the province is mountainous, and the landscape is of peaks and ridges, valleys, gorges, and ravines. Wuling Mountain range consists of quartzite sandstone pillars and peaks. The tea grows on vast, open, flat, or gently sloping fields and on steep terraced slopes.

Altitude
1,220 metres (4,002 feet)

Best Time to Visit
late March, April, September, October

Main Varietals/Cultivars
An Hua Yun Tai Shan Da Ye Zhong (Anhua Cloud Platform Mountain Big Leaf Varietal), local varietal of Da Ye Zhong; Gaoyaqi; Zhuyeqi; Baihaozao; Jianbohuang 13; Dajianye; Jianghua Kucha; Donghuzao; Rucheng Baimaocha; Chengbu Dongcha; Gaoqiaozao; Xiangbolü; Taoyuan Daye; Mingfeng; Bixiangzao; Anmingzao; Fuhao; Fufeng; Xianghongcha; Xiangfeicui; Yusun; Huangjincha

Types of Tea Made
White, black, dark

Predominant Flavours; Tasting Notes
YELLOW: *Jun Shan Yin Zhen (Silver Needle from Gentleman Mountain)*—pale yellow liquor that is fragrant and mellow
BLACK: *Monkey Picked Golden Hunan*—robust, oaky, often with hints of cocoa, caramelised sugar, and toasted grain
DARK: *Hunan Anhua Dark Tea*—woody, earthy, sometimes hints of pine from the pine fires used to dry the tea
Hunan Tian Jian—complex, clean, crisp, and fruity, with smoky pine resin notes and suggestions of stewed plums
Fu Cha—mild woody aroma and intense flavour with hints of dates

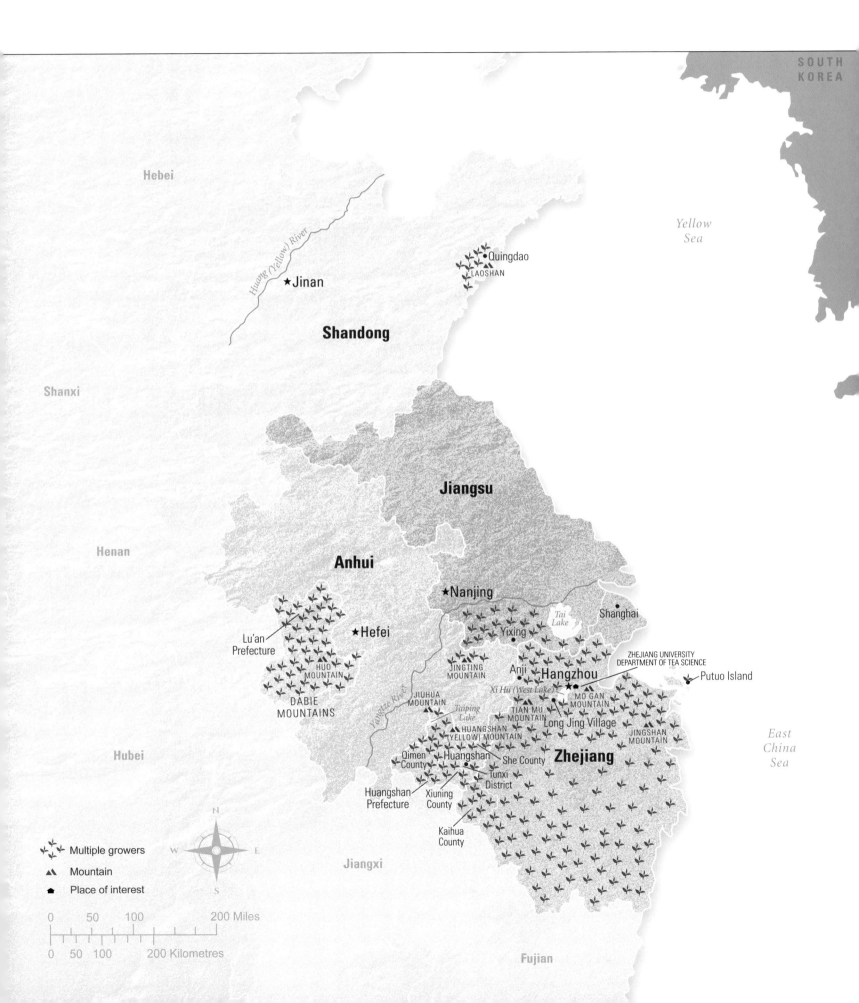

SOUTH
KOREA

Hebei

Huang (Yellow) River

*Yellow
Sea*

★Jinan

Shandong

•Quingdao
LAOSHAN

Shanxi

Henan

Jiangsu

Anhui

★Nanjing

Shanghai

*Tai
Lake*

Lu'an
Prefecture

★Hefei

Yixing

ZHEJIANG UNIVERSITY
DEPARTMENT OF TEA SCIENCE

HUO
MOUNTAIN

JINGTING
MOUNTAIN

Anji
Hangzhou

Putuo Island

Xi Hu (West Lake)

MO GAN
MOUNTAIN

DABIE
MOUNTAINS

Yangtze River

JIUHUA
MOUNTAIN

*Taiping
Lake*

TIAN MU
MOUNTAIN

Long Jing Village

JINGSHAN
MOUNTAIN

*East
China
Sea*

HUANGSHAN
(YELLOW) MOUNTAIN

Hubei

Qimen
County

Huangshan

She County

Zhejiang

Tunxi
District

Huangshan
Prefecture

Xiuning
County

Kaihua
County

Multiple growers

Mountain

Place of interest

N
W   E
S

0   50   100   200 Miles

0 50 100   200 Kilometres

Jiangxi

Fujian

ANHUI

(CHINA)

Long before Anhui Province was formed in 1666, this part of China was an important tea-growing region. It is believed that cultivation began here during the Song dynasty (960 to 1279) and burgeoned under the Ming emperors from the 14th to the 17th century when seedling bushes were planted on the steep slopes of granite mountains whose peaks disappear into blankets of billowing white clouds. From the 7th century, tea was exported from here to other parts of China, and the region became famous for its green teas.

Three main regions of the province are important for tea. The Dabie Mountains to the north of the Yangtze River are included in China's Jiangbei tea region; Jiuhuashan and Huangshan lie south of the Yangtze and are grouped in the Jiangnan tea region. Jiuhuashan is one of China's four famous Buddhist mountains (the others are Wutaishan, Emeishan, and Putuoshan); Huangshan, the famous Yellow Mountain with its heavily forested slopes, is known in China as Number One Mountain Under Heaven and is a UNESCO World Heritage Site. It covers 154 square kilometres (59 square miles), and the 99 peaks within the range are said to resemble the petals of a lotus flower. The most famous of the highest peaks are Lotus Peak, Bright Summit, and Celestial or Capital of Heaven Peak, which all climb to more than 1,800 metres (5,906 feet). Anhui's climate is mild and humid with plenty of rain during the warmer months, and the constant cloud cover shades the tea plants from scorching sun during the hot summer months. In the winter, temperatures drop low enough to bring snow to the topmost rocky outcrops.

Tourists love Huangshan for its natural beauty, hot springs, streams, waterfalls, unusual rock formations, and tall pines that grow at the very top of the mountains. Tea lovers revere it for its famous teas— Huangshan Mao Feng, Taiping Hou Kui, and Liu An Gua Pian green teas; Huoshan Huang Ya yellow; and Keemun black.

Huang Shan Mountain in Anhui Province, famous for its green and yellow teas and for Keemun (Qimen) black tea. Photograph courtesy of Wenli Guo

ANHUI GREEN TEAS | *Huangshan Mao Feng*
(Yellow Mountain Fur Peak or Yellow Mountain Hairy Peak)

Mao Feng is made in other parts of China, but the most famous and most valued comes from Anhui's Huangshan (Yellow Mountain). The name is from the tiny white hairs that cover the buds and young leaves of the local xiao zhu ye zhong varietal and because, after processing, the dry leaves resemble the sharp peak of a mountain. Since the 16th century, Buddhist monks are thought to have produced a green tea here called Huangshan Yun Wu (Cloud and Mist), which was recognized as China's finest tea during the Qing dynasty (1644 to 1912). Then, in 1875, local tea farmer Xie Zheng-an selected young buds from bushes growing in Fuxi and improved the processing to make a tea that was suitable for export. His methodology is now recognized as the correct traditional way to make Huangshan Mao Feng, and the original Yun Wu name is used today for the premium grade of Mao Feng. Zheng-an is said to have become very wealthy from sales of this special tea.

According to one of the many Mao Feng legends, a young girl called Luo Xiang, who lived in Huangshan, was so beautiful that several men dreamed of marrying her. She chose Shi Yong, a young man whom she loved, but one day, a village tyrant seized her and locked her up as his concubine. She managed to escape but found that the cruel tyrant had murdered Shi Yong. When she discovered his body, she wept so much that her tears turned him into a tea bush.

The best Mao Feng teas are picked only once a year, in late March and early April before Qing Ming, when new shoots of one tiny leaf and a white downy bud are carefully plucked and processed by hand. After a short wither at room temperature, the leaves are turned in a hot wok to evenly de-enzyme them and prevent oxidation. The temperature of the wok is then reduced and handfuls of leaves are rapidly scooped up from the wok about 60 times a minute, rolled between the hands, and dropped back into the pan without allowing them to scorch or burn. This rolling and drying continues until all the leaves are yellowish-green, very slightly twisted, pointed, and still showing their covering of little white hairs. Some Mao Feng are not rolled and twisted but keep the same straight, flat appearance they had when plucked. Next, the leaves are dried—sometimes in the wok with constant hand movements to stop them from burning, sometimes using the old traditional method of roasting the tea in bamboo baskets set over glowing charcoal.

Although the best Mao Feng are hand-made from one leaf and a bud, hand-plucked and hand-processed Mao Feng made from two small leaves and a bud can also be good quality. Some that are carefully machine-processed on a large scale in modern factories are also high-grade teas. Lower-grade Mao Feng is picked by hand later in the season and is processed by machine. The cheapest, lowest grades are harvested and processed by machine.

Taiping Hou Kui (Taiping Monkey King)

Taiping Hou Kui translates literally as Taiping Peaceful Monkey Leader. One version of the tea's legend explains how the villagers in the mountains where this tea was made long ago did not get along with the local monkeys because they used to destroy the farmers' crops. One day, a young monkey went missing, and although his father searched and searched, his son could not be found anywhere. The father monkey grew so tired from his relentless search that he collapsed, exhausted, in the mountains. A local farmer, Wang Laoer, found the father monkey and took him to his house to treat him with herbal remedies, and when the father monkey recovered, he was so grateful that he offered to organize the monkeys to help Wang pick his tea when the season came around. So Wang named his tea Taiping Monkey King. Some say that Taiping teas date back to the Qing dynasty, and the best are grown around the high remote village of Hou Keng in Taiping Prefecture in the foothills of Huangshan (Yellow Mountain) at the southern end of Taiping Lake.

The name of the tea can also be translated as "tea made by Mr. Wang Kui Cheng who lived in Hou Keng Village in Taiping County," and Wang is said to have invented the manufacturing process. In the distant past, the local villagers made tea from the local varietal, the long-leafed Shi De Ye, whose spear-shaped leaves and buds can measure up to 15 centimetres (6 inches). Because of the shape, the tea was called simply Jian-cha (or "pointy tea"). The tea was pressed by hand on paper and dried in bamboo baskets, and although it was a good tea, Wang thought he could improve the tea and added an extra step to the processing. To keep the leaves attractively long and straight during processing and to develop more flavour during the rolling process, he laid the bud sets side by side on a wire mesh, covered them with another mesh to hold them firm, and then rolled them flat using a home-made roller. The tea was very successful and became known as Taiping Hou Kui.

The nearby villages of Hou Gang and Xian Jia also produce Taiping teas, but they are not considered to be as good and sell for lower prices than those from Hou Keng Village. Early in the morning, the village women go out into the fields with their baskets and pick the fresh shoots of two leaves wrapped around one long bud. The best time for picking is between Gu Yu (Grain Rain) on the 20th of April and Li Xia, the beginning of summer, on the 6th of May. After that date, only low grades are made. The tea must be picked early in the morning and be sent to the factory or processing unit by 10 a.m. Each family in the village has a small manufacturing unit, inside which is a wok or locally made panning machine (or both), a rolling table, and a wooden oven or charcoal dryers. The different villages employ slightly different methods of processing to achieve the flat needles of green tea that look a little like a longer, larger version of Long Jing (Dragon Well). The most expensive, from Hou Keng Village, are called Nie Jian ("handmade") and are made in very small quantities at a time by panning the leaf shoots in a deep wok to stop oxidation, then spreading them thinly on a small round bamboo basket that is set over a series of charcoal fires at different temperatures. While the leaves slowly dry, they are pressed by hand to flatten them, then covered with a cloth and pressed again, then allowed to cool, and finally roasted several times, for a few minutes each roast, to remove most of the remaining water content in the leaves. Li Jian processing is carried out using wire mesh screens, but the teas are rolled with mechanical rollers rather than by hand. After panning, the tea is spread out in a single layer on a wire mesh. A second wire mesh is placed on top so that the leaves are pressed flat between the two layers of wire. On the rolling table, the mechanical roller is brought down and moved across the leaves until they are very flat, and then the entire frame of wire mesh with the tea inside goes into the oven. Because the tea leaves are pressed on wire mesh during processing, each long, flat, dry leaf set carries a very visible criss-cross pattern. The Bu Jian method covers the leaf with wet paper while mechanical rollers press down on the leaves.

To brew Taiping Hou Kui, use a tall glass or deep pot to accommodate the long leaves. The aroma of the pale green liquor carries suggestions of orchids, and the taste is complex, sweet, and nutty with floral overtones.

Liu An Gua Pian (Little Melon Seed)

In his *Cha Ching*, written during the days of the Tang dynasty (618 to 907), Lu Yu referred to Liu An Gua Pian as a superior tea. The name translates as "sunflower seed slice" because of the long, curled shape of the fresh green leaves, but over time, the Chinese name was abbreviated to Gua Pian, which means "watermelon slice," and so today, confusingly, the tea is known as Little Melon Seed. It comes from the Da Bie Mountains in Anhui's Liu An County and is made from a local cultivar called Da Guazi (Large Sunflower Seed) or from the small-leafed San Hao Xiao Ye Zhong cultivar. Some Liu An Gua Pian teas are today made by machine, but the best are handpicked and hand-processed.

Because the leaves for this tea must be a little larger than some spring teas, the pluckers wait for the second harvest in mid-April and pick single open leaves with a small amount of stem from just below the new growth on the shoot. They do not pick the buds. Because the leaves have been left on the bush slightly longer than usual, they are a little more mature and a slightly darker green. Once the fresh leaf has arrived in the factory, the stems are removed very carefully so as not to tear the leaves, and the tea is briefly withered in the shade. At least two people are needed to make this tea, and they sit in front of two hot woks at different temperatures. In larger factories, tea makers will sit in pairs at a bank of woks. The tea is placed in the wok and then moved quickly from the hot wok to the cooler wok to prevent the leaf from scorching, then back to the hotter wok. This is repeated up to 60 times. The tea makers use long brushes to move the teas around against the hot metal, and this stirring gradually gives the leaves their characteristic long, furled shape. From the woks, the leaf is transferred to bamboo baskets, which are placed repeatedly over a low charcoal fire for two or three seconds at a time. Each time the basket is lifted off the fire, the leaves are turned, and the basket is set back over the heat. This is repeated, sometimes a hundred times, until the leaf is quite dry. In a factory where several baskets of tea are being dried at the same time, the repeated movement to lift them in turn on and off the fire is like a carefully choreographed dance.

The tea has a floral sweetness and a slight nuttiness reminiscent of toasted pumpkin.

Tunxi Green (Tun Xi, Tunlu, Twankey Tea)

Also known as Tunlu, this historical green tea was first made in the 7th century, and when trade between China and Europe began in the 17th century, it was one of the teas that found its way to the West, where it was often called Twankey tea. It is made in Tunxi District and four neighbouring counties—She and Xiuning (Anhui Province), Kaihua (Zhejian Province), and Wuyuan (Jiangxi Province)—in the Huangshan area at elevations ranging from 90 to 610 metres (295 to 2,001 feet). To make the tea, new shoots of one, two, or three leaves and a bud are handpicked, panned to stop oxidation, rolled until the leaves are curved like eyebrows, then roasted over charcoal fires or baked in ovens. Because of their elliptical form, Tunxi teas are classed as Zhen Mei or Chun Mei (Precious Eyebrow) teas, and different grades are Precious Eyebrow, Tribute, Needle, First Rain, and Green Flake. The slender leaves yield a bright amber-green liquor that is fresh and mellow and has a pleasant lingering aftertaste.

Jingting Lu Xue (Jingting Green Snow Tea)

This tea from Jingting Mountain (often called Poem Mountain since the Chinese great poet Li Bai wrote verses about it) was classed as a famous tribute tea in the days of the Eastern Jin dynasty (317 to 420). It was lost during the Qing dynasty (1644 to 1912), but production started again in 1978. Some stories say that the name comes from the snowstorm effect that the downy green leaves make as they swirl in the cup or glass. But the traditional legend tells of how a kind and clever girl called Lu Xue picked fresh leaves here every day so that she could brew tea for her paralysed mother. The tea grew only in very high, steep places in the mountain, and one day, she fell from the cliff while trying to reach the bushes. The leaves she already had in her basket tumbled out and fell like snowflakes to the ground, and where they landed, tea bushes sprang up. The valley was filled with new tea plants, making it easier for local people to pick the tea without risking the danger of climbing the rocky mountain slopes. To remember the kind girl, the tea was named Jingting Lu Xue.

Young downy shoots are harvested in early April, and after withering, they are panned and rolled lengthways to become slightly furled like little birds' tongues. The taste is aromatic, fresh, and brisk.

OTHER GREEN TEAS FROM ANHUI PROVINCE

Other Anhui green teas include Yongxi Houqing, a gunpowder-style tea from Yongxi Village; Song Luo, a curled green from Song Luo Mountain in Xiuning County; and Dafang green (also called Zhupu Da Fang and Zhuye Da Fang) from She County.

ABOVE LEFT: The long fresh leaves of the local varietal that grows in and around Taiping Village and used to make Taiping Hou Kui green tea.
ABOVE RIGHT: To make Taiping Hou Kui, the fresh leaves are placed between two tight-fitting layers of fine wire mesh and are then rolled to develop the flavour of the tea. The criss-cross pattern of the wires can often be seen on the dry leaves. Photographs courtesy of Wenli Guo

ANHUI YELLOW TEA

Huoshan Huang Ya (Yellow Flower or Mount Huo Yellow Sprout)

This yellow tea is said to date back to the Tang dynasty (618 to 907) and was a tribute tea under the Ming (1368 to 1644) and Qing (1644 to 1912) dynasties. Made on Huo Mountain (Amber Mountain or Mountain of Fire), the processing method is said to have been lost in the 1940s and then re-created in 1972. Very small quantities are made each year by qualified tea masters. The bud sets are picked in the early spring. Whereas most yellow teas are heaped or wrapped to trap steam and cause light fermentation, Huoshan Huang Ya is steamed three times, and between each steaming, it is left lying for several hours indoors while light fermentation changes the leaves from vivid green to golden yellow. The buds are downy and straight and brew to give a rich, nutty aroma and flavour with a slightly roasted vegetal character.

ANHUI BLACK TEA

Qimen Mao Feng (Qimen Hong Mao Feng, Keemun Black Tea)

Produced in the south-eastern corner of Anhui Province, just west of Huangshan, Qimen tea was first made in the late 19th century. The inventor of Anhui's only black tea, Yu Gan Chen, grew up in a tea-making family in Anhui but spent much of his working life in Fujian Province. He became aware of the wealth that the increasing export of black teas was bringing to tea makers in that region, so when he retired and went home to Qimen County in 1875, he set up a black-tea manufacturing unit, plucked tea shoots from the local bushes, and made black tea according to the process he had seen in Fujian. Although in those days, the Chinese did not often drink black tea, Keemun became a favourite of the imperial family and was soon being exported to the United States and Britain. In 1913, it won a gold prize in Italy, and won gold again at the 1915 Panama-Pacific International Exhibition in San Francisco. In 1940, Keemun was recorded as the most expensive tea sold in the United States, and it is still an American favourite, drunk straight or often used as the base for American breakfast blends. In the 1980s, Deng Xiaoping, China's leader from 1978 to 1992, promoted it to help increase sales, and it is still quite popular amongst Chinese people.

The best Keemun blacks are made from the same small-leafed local varietal xiao zhu ye zhong that is used to make Huangshan Mao Feng green, and it gives the black tea a delicate sweetness. But other varietals and cultivars are also used, and they give their own individual character to the tea. Shoots of one or two leaves and a bud are picked from early to mid-April and are withered in the sun or under shade for several hours. They are then withered indoors for five to eight hours, rolled to break the leaf cells, and placed on bamboo baskets. Cloths are placed over the tea while it oxidises for three to five hours, and the tea is then dried twice for about 15 minutes each time. Qimen producers have recently started to make Keemun tea with very young shoots picked earlier in the spring, and this gives an even better-quality tea. The tea is also called Qi Men Hong or Qi Hong, and different grades are Keemun Hao Ya (Premium), which often contains silver tips; Keemun Xin Ya, a high-grade tippy tea made from early spring-picked buds; Keemun Ya Grade A and B; Keemun Mao Feng, which is lightly rolled so that it has the same neat, slightly twisted appearance as some Mao Feng greens and a sweet, smooth character; and Keemun Congou (from the term *gongfu*, meaning "made with careful skill"), which has thin, tight, very neat strips of leaf.

ANHUI DARK TEA

Anhui's Liu An Basket Tea is made in Liu An (or Lu'an) County, which lies to the north-west of Shanghai. It is made from Liu An Gua Pian green tea that is steamed and pressed into small bamboo baskets lined with bamboo leaves to stop the tea leaves from falling out. Smaller baskets hold around 500 grams (17.6 ounces) of tea, larger baskets hold around 18 kilos (40 pounds). Six baskets are then stacked and tied together and left to age in caves or warehouses for a minimum of 10 years. Younger Liu An dark teas are slightly astringent and green, while older teas can have a slightly musty aroma and a mellower, smooth character.

TOP: New buds on the shoots of wild bushes that grow on Huang Shan (Yellow Mountain). ABOVE: The finished leaf of Taiping Hou Kui (Taiping Monkey King) green tea. Photographs courtesy of Wenli Guo

Country, State, or Province
Anhui Province

Area Under Tea
170,000 hectares

Average Annual Production (Kilograms)
113.2 million

Terrain
The north is flat plains; the centre of the province is undulating hills; land on either side of the Yangtze River in the centre of the province is low-lying and flat; the south is hilly.

Altitude
400 to 1,400 metres (1,312 to 4,593 feet)

Best Time to Visit
Late March, April, September, October

Main Varietals/Cultivars
Huang Shan Da Ye; Huangshanzhong; Shi Da Ye (for Taiping Huo Kui); Yang Shu Lin Zhong (Aspen Forest Varietal), bred from Da Ye Zhong; Huangshan Zaoye; Huangjincha; Da Hua Ping Jin Ji Zhong (varietal from the village of Jinji of the community of Dahuaping), found locally around Huoshan; Dushan small-leaf tea cultivar for Lu An Gua Pian; Huoshan Jinjizhong; Qimenzhong and Zu Ye Zhong cultivar for Qimen Mao Feng; Shifocui; Wancha 91; Wannong 95; Shuchazao; Wannong 111; Yangshulin 783; Qingyang Tianyuncha; Songluozhong; Xiangcheng Jianyezhong; Yongxi Liuyezhong; Bohao; Mingzhou 12; Shifoxiang; Xianyuzao

Types of Tea Made
Greens, yellow, black

Predominant Flavours; Tasting Notes
GREEN: *Huangshan Mao Feng*—floral aroma of orchids and magnolia; sweet, clean flavour with no bitterness.
Traditional Roasted Mao Feng—very slight hint of charcoal
Taiping Huo Kui (Taiping Monkey King)—orchid aroma and smooth, sweet taste, with very little grassiness or astringency
Liu An Gua Pian (Little Melon Seed)—velvet smooth with a hint of charcoal on the first infusion but cleaner, crisper, more floral, and sweeter on the second and third steep
Tunxi Green—is fresh and mellow, with a pleasant lingering aftertaste
Jingting Lu Xue (Jingting Green Snow)—aromatic, fresh, and brisk
YELLOW: *Huoshan Huangya (Yellow Flower or Mount Huo Yellow Sprout)*—a rich, nutty aroma and flavour with a slightly roasted vegetal character
BLACK: *Qimen Mao Feng (Keemun)*—subtle, fruity, complex, and sweet with hints of light brown sugar and honey

JIANGSU

(CHINA)

During the Tang dynasty (618 to 907), Jiangsu was famous for a green tribute tea made here and for the pottery-making tradition that dates back 5,000 years to Neolithic days. The Tang government moved the main centre of tea production from Sichuan into Jiangsu just south of the Yellow River, close to Yixing whose kilns have been making teapots from the local zisha clay since the 16th century. The region is made up of flat plains dotted with countless lakes, rivers, and canals, and the climate is subtropical and humid with moderate rainfall. Jiangsu is famous for Bi Luo Chun green tea and also produces jasmine pearl teas.

JIANGSU GREEN TEA | *Bi Luo Chun (Green Spring Snail or Green Snail Spring)*

Bi Luo Chun, one of China's most famous green teas, is made on Dongting Mountain on Dongting Island in Tai Lake. It was originally known as Astounding Fragrance, but a Qing emperor renamed it Bi Luo Chun and made it an imperial tea. The tea's name is for the rich green of the leaves (Bi), the small snails that the curly spirals of dry leaf resemble (Luo), and spring when the tea is picked (Chun). To make the tea, shoots of one leaf and a bud are picked in the very early spring, and any remaining older leaves and stalk are carefully removed. The tea is then put into a hot wok and turned constantly against the hot metal to fix the green and to start drying out some of the moisture content. For about 40 minutes, the tea is repeatedly rolled and lifted to release the steam. The leaf becomes greener, and the down on the buds becomes whiter. The wok temperature is then reduced, and the tea maker takes up handfuls of the tea and rolls it round and round between the hands for about five seconds, drops the tea back down into the wok, and takes up another handful to roll. This rolling and releasing continues until all the tea has been rolled into tight spirals and the leaves are dry. In some larger factories, a panning machine is used to de-enzyme the tea and then workers roll the tea in heated baskets, but the best teas are made using traditional hand movements while the tea is in the wok.

The pale gold liquor has a sweet, honeyed aroma and a sweet, fruity, floral, and nutty taste with hints of asparagus and young leafy green vegetables such as spinach or baby kale.

A tea field in Jiangsu Province, famous for Bi Luo Chun (Green Snail Spring) green tea, made on Dongting Mountain.
Photograph courtesy of Fujian Yuantai Tea Co., Ltd.

Country, State, or Province
Jiangsu Province

Area Under Tea
34,000 hectares

Average Annual Production (Kilograms)
14 million

Terrain
Low-lying flat plains with average altitudes of 50 metres (160 feet); many lakes, rivers, and canals

Altitude
293 metres (961 feet)

Best Time to Visit
late March, April, September, October

Main Varietals/Cultivars
Yixingzhong; Xicha; Sucha 120; Dongtingchun

Types of Tea Made
Green, jasmine pearl

Predominant Flavours; Tasting Notes
GREEN: *Bi Luo Chun (Green Spring Snail)*— complex, nutty, and smooth, with fruity and floral notes

SHANDONG

(CHINA)

Shandong, China's most northerly tea-producing province, is home to the famous Taoist mountain Laoshan, the "cradle of Taoism." Qin dynasty (221 to 206 B.C.) emperors travelled to the mountain during the 2nd century B.C. to visit the supernatural beings that were said to live there, and Tang emperor Xuanzong (712 to 756) believed that herbs found growing among Laoshan's peaks would bring him eternal life. As Okakura Kakuzo wrote of tea in 1906 in his *Book of Tea*, "The Taoists claimed it as an important ingredient of the elixir of immortality." It was perhaps not herbs but tea that the emperor was seeking.

During its most famous Taoist days, there were nine palaces, eight temples, and 72 nunneries here, and the monks who lived here are thought to have been the first to grow tea. Taoism teaches an appreciation of the simplicity of life and an acceptance of the wider universe and our place within it. For the early Taoists, drinking tea created harmony between the universe and the tea drinker, and the tea ceremony was thought of as a quiet, calm time of meditation that focused on a combination of truth, kindness, and the beauty of nature. For centuries, this philosophy has been the cornerstone of tea drinking in China, Korea, and Japan and has had a profound influence on tea drinkers in many other cultures. Teas grown on Laoshan have a special significance for anyone who appreciates these connections.

Waiting for the leaf to fully oxidise to make black tea. Photograph courtesy of The Chinese Tea Company, London

With its towering peaks that face the Yellow Sea and its misty, humid climate, Laoshan produces some excellent black and green teas, including Laoshan green and Rizhao Xueqing green, Laoshan black, and Laoshan oolongs, which give creamy liquors that taste of freshly cut grass, soybeans, asparagus, and green beans. Local residents of the area say that it is the *yin* of the Yellow Sea and the *yang* of the granite mountains that give Laoshan teas their special character.

SHANDONG GREEN TEA | *Laoshan Green Teas*

For the very best of these teas, the new spring shoots are harvested early in the morning and then left to air-dry for about three to five hours on bamboo baskets placed indoors or in a shady place outdoors. They are then turned in the panning machine to prevent oxidation and inspected for any damaged leaves or twigs, which are removed by hand. The tea is then rolled by hand or machine to curl the leaves and work the flavour. The leaf is then inspected again, and any substandard leaves are removed. The tea is tumbled in the panning machine, removed, and inspected, and the panning and inspection process continues for 60 to 90 minutes until all the tea is dry. A final inspection ensures that the leaves are uniform and perfectly rolled and dried.

During the warmer part of the year, from spring to autumn, some farmers keep their bushes shaded in tunnels of light tarpaulin to protect them from the glare of the sun. The shade ensures that the leaves develop high levels of L-theanine amino acid and chlorophyll, thereby yielding liquors that are sweet, mellow, and umami with chestnut notes. The spring teas are delicate while summer teas are surprisingly thick, velvety, and full of flavour.

SHANDONG BLACK TEA | *Laoshan Black*

Some producers have installed modern equipment to produce orthodox black teas, but the smaller scale farmers use more traditional, rustic methods. Once the tea has been picked and withered, the leaves are rolled and then allowed to oxidise slowly in the sun for three days. To dry the leaves, they are tumbled in a hot panning machine, then sorted and quality-inspected before packing. The slow oxidation brings out rich, chocolatey, toasted cereal notes.

Country, State, or Province
Shandong Province

Area Under Tea
36,500 hectares

Average Annual Production (Kilograms)
21.5 million

Terrain
Very varied topography in this coastal region facing the Yellow Sea. Most of the area is mountainous, and at 1133 metres (3717 feet), Mount Laoshan is the second highest peak in Shandong.

Altitude
600 metres (1,968 feet)

Best Time to Visit
late March, April, September, October

Main Varietals/Cultivars
Luohan 1

Types of Tea Made
Black, green

Predominant Flavours; Tasting Notes
GREEN: *Laoshan Green*—sweet, velvety
BLACK: *Laoshan Black*—rich, chocolatey, with toasted cereal notes, honeyed sweetness, and suggestions of ripe fruits

ZHEJIANG

(CHINA)

Zhejiang is known as "the land of silk and tea" and has been famous for its green teas since the 3rd century. In the 8th century, Lu Yu praised the green teas made in Guzhu in his *Cha Jing*, and he is said to have taken some to the imperial court. The emperor was also impressed, and a royal tea garden was laid out on the lower slopes of Mount Guzhu, famous today for Guzhu Zisun green tea.

The province is a land of mountains and hills with flatter valleys and plains along the coast and rivers. With the Yangtze Delta in the north, the extensive coastline and a number of large lakes, including West Lake (Xi Hu) just inland from Hangzhou, and South Lake to the south-west of Shanghai, the region has a humid subtropical climate with a short winter and plenty of rain. Tea is the most important product, and Zhejiang is China's leading green tea-producing region and exports to some 60 countries. It has always been famous for its wide variety of green teas, including Long Jing, Zhu Cha (Gunpowder), and Chun Mee (Precious Eyebrows, rolled to give each leaf an eyebrow shape). Since 1978, the industry has focused on restoring its historical teas, creating new types, and improving quality. The most famous teas today are Long Jing (Dragon Well) from the West Lake area; Anji Bai Cha from Anji County; Mao Feng (Fur Peak); Huiming green from Chimu Mountain; Yunwu green; Songyang Yinhou green from Songyan; Wuyang Chunyu (Wu Yang Spring Rain) green, created in the 1990s in Wuyi County in Central Zhejiang; Mogan Huangya yellow tea; and Jiuqu Hingmei black, developed in the late 19th century for export to Europe and the United States.

ZHEJIANG GREEN TEAS | *Long Jing (Dragon Well)*

Long Jing's history goes back to the Qing dynasty when Emperor Kangxi (1661 to 1722) is said to have visited the Hu Gong Temple on Shifengshan (Lion Peak Mountain) in West Lake, where he was offered a cup of green tea. He found it so delicious that he gave the 18 tea bushes growing in front of the temple imperial status. Those original trees still grow there today, and the small amount of tea produced from them each spring fetches extremely high prices. Another story, from the Song dynasty (960 to 1279), tells how the emperor visited the Long Jing tea area to watch the tea being made and, while there, learned that his mother had fallen ill. He rushed home with some of the tea in his pocket. When he arrived home, his mother was intrigued by the wonderful aroma. The liquor he brewed from the leaves cured her, and so he granted the bushes imperial status. The tea is said to have been named after a nearby well that contained rather dense water, and whenever it rained, the swirling pattern of the lighter rainwater mingling with the heavier well water created an impression of a dragon.

The West Lake scenic area stretches for 60 square kilometres (23 square miles), and the lake itself covers 5.6 square kilometres (2 square miles). Five legendary villages produce authentic Long Jing tea today. They are Shifeng, Long Jing, Yunxi, Hupao, and Meijiawu. Shifeng is the original tea garden on Shifeng Mountain. Long Jing Village teas are second best to Shifeng. Yunxi Village, third best, lies high up on Yunxi Mountain and is continuously swathed in swirling clouds and mist. A stream winds through the village, and some believe that the stream is the dragon and the tea trees are his claws. Hupao is fourth in quality but receives more attention because of its proximity to Running Tiger Spring, a popular tourist spot. Meijiawu Village makes a lot of tea, but it is not considered such high quality. Teas made in these five locations include the village name, as with Shifeng Long Jing, Meijiawu Long Jing, and so on. Teas from places outside the original growing area are sold as Zhejiang Long Jing. "Fake" Long Jings are also made in Yunnan, Guizhou, Guangdong, and Sichuan. Bai Dragon Well Tea is produced in Zhejiang's Anji County and is not an authentic Dragon Well.

Most Long Jing growers have planted the new Long Jing No. 43 cultivar, which buds more than a week earlier than the traditional cultivar and is a crossbreed of several varietals planted centuries ago. Long Jing teas should be picked before Qing Ming on the 4th or the 5th of April. New shoots of one bud and one or two leaves that are just beginning to open are picked by hand, and 60,000 buds are needed to make 1 kilo (2.2 pounds) of tea. The little bud sets are air-dried on bamboo baskets in a cool place for between six and 12 hours, depending on how much water is in the leaves and on the ambient humidity and temperature, and they are carefully turned from time to time. When the leaves are ready, they are put into a wok and moved against the hot metal to kill the enzymes and stop oxidation. The heat of the wok is increased, and the leaves are then repeatedly lifted in handfuls from the wok and allowed to drop back again as the water evaporates. As the leaves soften, they are pressed briefly against the wok, then repeatedly lifted, dropped, and pressed.

The tea must not burn or dry too quickly, and the little needles of tea must be even and neat. It takes about six hours to make half a kilo (1.1 pounds) of tea.

As with the manufacture of many of China's specialty teas, the processing of Long Jing is being increasingly mechanised. Some companies combine mechanical and hand processing and de-enzyme their leaves in large batches in special panning machines with a convex paddle that emulates the traditional hand movements, but then hand-finish the leaf in woks so that the tea maker can control the movement of the tea and the temperature of the metal surface. The dry leaves of Long Jing should be very neat and regular, flat, yellowish green, sleek, and shiny.

A view of Long Jing (Dragon Well) Village near Hangzhou where the humidity from West Lake (Xi Hu) creates a perfect environment for the tea bushes to grow. Photograph courtesy of The Chinese Tea Company, London

Anji Bai Cha (Anji White Tea)

Despite its name, Anji Bai Cha is a green tea that, during the Song dynasty, was the favourite of Emperor Huizong (1100 to 1125). He noted that the tea plant from which it was made was "extremely rare" and of "superior quality." Production gradually died out but started again in 1982 when a single bush of the original varietal was discovered in Anji County. More bushes have since been propagated, and the tea is now available, although only in limited quantities. During the first spring growth, the Anji Bai varietal makes very little chlorophyll, and so, the new leaves are very pale. The tea also contains high levels of the amino acid L-theanine, giving the liquors a sweet floral character. By the end of April, the leaves produce more chlorophyll and are a darker green.

The pale green-white shoots of one long bud and one or two long leaves are handpicked before Qing Ming, sometimes as early as the 12th of March, and during withering, the buds and leaves turn to a pale yellowish green. They are then de-enzymed, rolled, and dried by hand in a wok, or shaken back and forth in a mechanised rectangular box with slanted metal compartments that moves quickly from side to side. After drying, the leaves look like long, tight, pale yellow-green pine needles, and liquors have sweet floral notes with citrus hints and suggestions of orchids and chestnuts.

Guzhu Zi Sun (Guzhu Mountain Purple Bamboo Shoot)

This was a tribute tea in the Tang dynasty (618 to 907), and Lu Yu wrote that Guzhu Mountain was the best place to cultivate tea and said that the local varietals were the best for making tea. The tea takes its name from the purplish colour of the slender leaves and buds that look just like young bamboo shoots. The tea grows wild on the slopes of Mount Guzhu in the north-west of Zhejiang where lush groves of bamboo, gingko trees, and other native plants and trees provide shade for the tea bushes. Small shoots of one bud and one leaf must be picked carefully between Qing Ming, on the 4th or the 5th of April, and Gu Yu, on the 20th or the 21st of April, and plucking from the uneven wild bushes—some quite low, some growing to shoulder height or higher—is hard work. The tea is withered for one or two hours, then panned by hand in woks, the tea master wearing a glove on the right hand and the left hand left bare in order to check the temperature of the wok. The little shoots are then cooled, dried in an electric oven, and baked for two or three hours on bamboo baskets set over charcoal that burns at a low temperature without any smoke. According to the size of the dry leaves, the different grades range from top-grade Zi Sun to Qiya (Flag Bud) and Queshe (Sparrow Tongue). The liquor is crystal clear and has a silky mouthfeel and a sweet, floral taste with suggestions of bamboo and sweet macadamia nuts.

Tian Mu Qing Ding (Heavenly Blue Peak)

A tribute tea during the Ming dynasty, this green tea is made in Tian Mu Mountain in Lin'an County, a major tea-producing region where forests of bamboo grow. At one time, the tea was thought to have been lost but is now back in production. New shoots of one bud and one or two small leaves are picked during only a short period in March or early April (depending on the weather), briefly withered, and then processed by skilled tea masters who turn the leaf in woks to de-enzyme the tea, allow the little shoots to cool, and then bake them on bamboo baskets set over charcoal to remove most of the remaining water content. The dry leaves are straight and downy and a deep green in colour. The aroma and taste of the smooth, pale yellow-gold liquor is elegant, fragrant, clean, and sweet.

Putuo Fo Cha (Buddha's Tea from Putuo Island, or Buddha Summit Cloud and Mist Tea)

The monks of Puji Temple on Mount Putuo have been making tea here since the days of the Tang dynasty, and during the Qing dynasty (1644 to 1912), the tea was selected as a tribute tea. Mount Putuo on Putuo Island is said to be the birthplace of Guan Yin, Goddess of Mercy, and is one of China's four sacred Buddhist mountains. The tea bushes grow on the southern slopes of the mountain and are harvested in small quantities each year. Dressed in their golden robes, the monks harvest tea shoots of one bud and the first two leaves after Qing Ming, wither it in the shade, and stir-fry it to prevent oxidation. Then, as the leaf dries against the hot metal of the wok, handfuls of leaf are rolled between the palms of the hands to twist and curl the tea, and are then dropped back into the wok. This lifting, rolling, and releasing is repeated until all the tea is twisted, and the tea is then baked until dry. The curled dry leaves are a wonderful mixture of green-gold, emerald green, and jade green and are covered with silvery down. They yield a clear yellow-gold liquor that is sweet and floral with light vegetal notes and suggestions of ripe peaches.

Jingshan Cha (Jing Mountain Tea)

In the 8th century, this was a monastery tea made by the monks of Jing Shan Buddhist Monastery. Like all of China's teas until the 13th and 14th century, Jingshan tea was a steamed green tea and was among the first teas to be taken home by Japanese monks who had been studying at Jingshan. Production of the tea died out as processing methods changed, and the monastery's importance declined during the Cultural Revolution. In the 1970s, work to restore Jingshan began, and the tea is now being made again but as a panned tea. The pan-frying, rolling, and roasting gives dry leaves that are downy and curled and liquors that are brisk and spicy.

Zhu Cha (Gunpowder)

Gunpowder tea dates back to the Tang dynasty and was one of the first teas to be exported to Europe and America in the 17th century. Named for its appearance resembling lead shot, it is traditionally made by stir-frying the tea, then rolling each individual leaf between the hands to make a small, tight ball. The smaller the leaf, the smaller the pellet of tea, and grades vary from pinhead (often called Temple of Heaven) to pea head. Today, most gunpowder teas are made in woks with a paddle that turns and twists the leaf as it dries, or in large tumblers with paddles inside, and the dried pellets of tea are never as neat as hand-rolled Zhu Cha.

ZHEJIANG YELLOW TEA | *Mo Gan Huang Ya (Mo Gan Mountain Yellow Tea)*

Mo Gan Mountain, part of the Tian Mu Mountain range, is famous for its springs and waterfalls, misty clouds, and bamboo forests. It lies in the north-east of the province, approximately 200 kilometres (124 miles) south-west of Shanghai, and the tea bushes grow happily in the shady, misty conditions. Only a few tea masters know how to make this yellow tea, so it is made in small quantities. The best shoots are picked around Gu Yu on the 20th of April, later than most spring teas, and are withered for two or three hours. Then the tea is fried in a very hot wok at around 300°C (572°F), with three or four tea masters taking turns for just a few seconds at a time over the intense heat to move the tea around on the hot metal. The tea is pan-fried for one minute, then taken out of the wok and placed on a bamboo basket, where it is hand-rolled. The tea is then wrapped in a cloth and pressed flat, and the bag of tea is placed on a bamboo cylindrical basket set over charcoal. Every half hour, the cloth is opened, the leaves are shaken and mixed and re-wrapped, and the parcel of tea is placed back over the charcoal. Finally, the leaves are dried. The very skillful process takes approximately 10 hours to complete, and the teas are expensive. The dry leaves are yellow-green and lightly curled. The liquor is yellow-gold and has a mellow richness and a sweet lingering aftertaste.

ZHEJIANG BLACK TEA

Jiu Qu Hong Mei (Long Jing Black, Red Plum Black Tea)

Some say this tea was first made from the buds and leaves of Long Jing tea bushes in the 1850s; others claim that it dates back to 1926. The tea is made from shoots of two leaves and a bud picked before Qing Ming from bushes growing at around 500 metres (1,640 feet) on Da Hu Mountain on the outskirts of Hangzhou. It is sometimes called Red Plum Black because of both the colour and the sweet, fruity, plummy aroma and flavour of the liquor. The very attractive, wiry, dry, black leaves display occasional golden tips and brew a beautiful amber liquor that has a honeyed, fruity aroma, is sweet and smooth, and carries notes of ripe berries and plums, sweet apples and hints of pine and orchid.

Country, State, or Province
Zhejiang Province

Area Under Tea
196,700 hectares

Average Annual Production (Kilograms)
176 million

Terrain
More than 70% of the province is hills and mountains, with plains in the coastal area; rich in lakes, rivers, forests, and bamboo groves.

Altitude
850 to 1,300 metres (2,789 to 4,265 feet)

Best Time to Visit
late March, April, September, October

Main Varietals/Cultivars
Jiukenzhong; Longjing 43; Longjing Changye; Yingshuang; Cuifeng; Jingfeng; Biyun; Zhenong 12; Juhuachun; Hanlü; Qingfeng; Zhongcha 102; Chunyu; Maolü; Shuigucha; Jiaming 1; Pingyun; Zhenong 121; Bifeng; Tengcha; Longjingzhong; Zhenong 25; Huangyezao; Rui'an Baimaocha; Rui'an Qingmingzao; Taixiangzi; Meifeng; Shuangfeng; Baiye 1; PIngyang Tezaocha; Yingoucha; Xiangshanzao 1; Huang Jinya; Qiannianxue

Types of Tea Made
Green, black

Predominant Flavours; Tasting Notes
GREEN: *Long Jing (Dragon Well)*—delicate and sweet, with gentle citrus notes, reminiscent of asparagus, peapods, sometimes sweet corn, hazelnuts, and chestnuts
Anji Bai Cha (Anji White Tea)—delicate, buttery, soothing, suggestions of green spring vegetables, pine nuts, and an orchid sweetness
Guzhu Zi Sun (Guzhu Mountain Purple Bamboo Shoot)—clean, with a little bitterness and a lingering sweet aftertaste
Tian Mu Qing Ding (Heavenly Blue Peak)—delicate but deep and intriguing, vibrant, sweet, and slightly nutty
Putuo Fo Cha (Buddha's Tea from Putuo Island, Buddha Summit Cloud and Mist Tea)—mild, flowery, sweet, with lingering hints of maltiness in the finish
Jingshan Cha (Jing Mountain Tea)—fresh, mild, and fruity, with a sweet aftertaste
Zhu Cha (Gunpowder)—intense, powerfully vegetal, slightly astringent, and sometimes a little smoky
YELLOW: *Mo Gan Huangya (Mo Gan Mountain Yellow Tea)*—mellow richness and sweet lingering aftertaste
BLACK: *Jiu Qu Hong Mei (Red Plum Classic)*—strong, honeyed, fruity, malty, with hints of ripe berries and plums, sweet apples, hints of pine and orchid

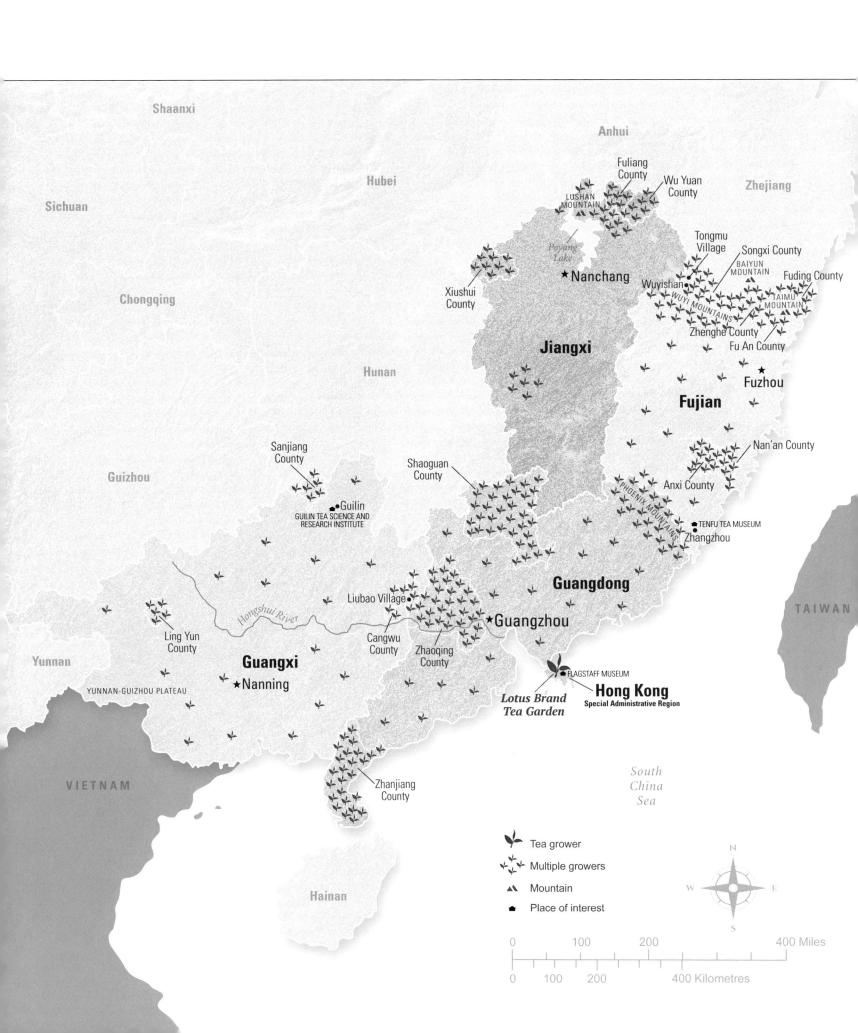

Shaanxi

Anhui

Hubei

Fuliang
County
Wu Yuan
County

Zhejiang

Sichuan

LUSHAN
MOUNTAIN

Tongmu
Village

Songxi County

Chongqing

*Poyang
Lake*

★Nanchang

BAIYUN
MOUNTAIN

Fuding County

TAIMU
MOUNTAIN

Hunan

Xiushui
County

Wuyishan

WUYI MOUNTAINS

Jiangxi

Zhenghe County

Fu An County

★
Fuzhou

Fujian

Guizhou

Sanjiang
County

Shaoguan
County

Nan'an County

Guilin

GUILIN TEA SCIENCE AND
RESEARCH INSTITUTE

PHOENIX MOUNTAINS

Anxi County

Guangxi

TENFU TEA MUSEUM

Zhangzhou

Guangdong

Hongshui River

Liubao Village

Yunnan

Ling Yun
County

Guangxi

★Nanning

Cangwu
County

Zhaoqing
County

★Guangzhou

FLAGSTAFF MUSEUM

Hong Kong
Special Administrative Region

TAIWAN

YUNNAN-GUIZHOU PLATEAU

*Lotus Brand
Tea Garden*

VIETNAM

*South
China
Sea*

Zhanjiang
County

Hainan

🌱 Tea grower

🌿 Multiple growers

▲ Mountain

⬠ Place of interest

N

W   E

S

0   100   200   400 Miles

0   100   200   400 Kilometres

FUJIAN

(CHINA)

China's south-eastern province of Fujian is a land of high mountains and hills, fast-running rivers and swirling rapids that sweep past rocky gorges, dense pine forests, and steep terraced slopes of tea. The region's high mountains, plentiful rainfall, and temperate, humid climate create a perfect environment for tea cultivation. A stone tablet, the Lian Hua Cha Jin (Lotus Flower Tea Dress), dated 376, placed at the top of Lotus Flower Peak in Nan'an County, bears witness to the fact that tea was grown here more than 1,600 years ago, and Lu Yu wrote in the Tang period (618 to 907) that tea grew in Jianzhou and Fuzhou districts. During the Song dynasty (960 to 1279), Jiangzhou became an important centre for the production of compressed tea, and for hundreds of years, Fuzhou has been famous for jasmine cultivation and the production of jasmine teas.

When trade with Europe started, it was from ports on the coast of Fujian, as well as from Canton, that tea was shipped, first to Holland and later to London and America. The local Amoy dialect passed its name for tea, *té*, to the Dutch, who passed it on to the English and other European nations. The first black, and possibly oolong, teas were made here to meet the growing demand for teas that did not lose their quality during the long sea voyage to foreign markets.

Fujian produces the largest share of China's tea and, from more than 330 different varietals, makes a wide range of white, green, jasmine green, oolong, and black teas. From the Wuyi Mountains come smoky Lapsang Souchongs, Bohea Lapsangs, and Jin Jun Mei black teas and dark rock oolongs such as Da Hong Pao (Big Red Robe), Rou Gui (Cassia), and Shui Xian (Narcissus or Water Sprite) oolongs. Anxi County is famed for its aromatic Iron Goddess of Mercy oolongs, while white teas come mainly from Fuding, Zhenghe, and Songxi counties and from Jianyang District.

White tea was produced for the first time here during the Song dynasty and was a favourite of the emperor. Earlier records from the 8th century show that it was made in Fuding County using buds plucked from the local small-leafed Xiao Bai (Small White) varietal. The Da Bai (Big White) varietal is thought to have been discovered in 1857, and farmers then started using its fat, silvery buds to make Yin Zhen (Silver Needles) and Bai Mu Dan (White Peony). Today, Fujian's white teas are made from Fuding Da Bai, Zhenghe Da Bai, Xiao Bai, Shui Xian (Narcissus), and Fu Ding Da Hao bushes. According to season and varietal, they are classified as Bai Hao Yin Zhen (Silver Needles), Bai Mu Dan (White Peony), Gong Mei (Tribute Eyebrow), and Shou Mei (Long Life or Longevity Eyebrow). The buds of these teas are silvery-white due to the covering of the fine white hairs (the Bai Hao or Pekoe) that protect the delicate new buds from harsh weather and insect attack while they are developing. To produce good white teas, they must be plucked and dried very carefully. If they are dried too quickly, the moisture in the leaves cannot evaporate evenly, so careful management of heating and ventilation in drying rooms and during the final baking stage is crucial.

Organic white tea plantation on Yushan Dao (Yushan Island) in Ningde, Fujian Province. Photograph courtesy of The Chinese Tea Company, London

Bai Hao Yin Zhen (Silver Needle)

The finest Bai Hao Yin Zhen is made using just the fleshy buds of Da Bai bushes picked in late March or early April, before Qing Ming. The buds must be very carefully picked so as not to bruise or damage the cells, and the finest of these needle-style teas show minimal oxidation. Legends tell how, in China's past, the tea was snipped from the shoot with small golden scissors and caught in a golden bowl so that no fingers could crush the tender buds. After slow natural drying, the buds should still be downy, silver, and plump.

Bai Mu Dan (White Peony)

Most Da Bai white teas are made from the Da Bai varietal but are plucked a little later in April. White Peony is made from one bud and one or two open leaves. During the natural withering, the open leaves spontaneously oxidise very slowly, and the dry leaves are a mixture of silvery buds and green or green-brown open leaves. This is considered a second-grade tea and is much cheaper than Bai Hao Yin Zhen.

Gong Mei (Tribute Eyebrow)

This looks a little like Bai Mu Dan, but because it is generally made from the buds and leaves of the small-leafed Xiao Bai varietal, the dry leaves are smaller and thinner than teas made from the Da Bai. It is considered a third-grade tea and is therefore cheaper. Liquors are usually quite dark amber and taste stronger than Bai Mu Dan teas.

Shou Mei (Long Life Eyebrow)

Also known as Longevity Eyebrow or Longevity Eyebrow King, most Shou Mei teas are plucked from Da Bai bushes later in the season than Bai Hao Yin Zhen and Bai Mu Dan. The leaves are therefore bigger and darker. Once dried, they are a mixture of silvery buds and large green, brown, deep plum, and almost black leaves that yield a stronger, less refined flavour than Bai Mu Dan. This is classified as a fourth-grade white tea.

Many villages in Fujian Province make green teas that are not sold outside China, such as Dingfeng Hao, Gushan Baiyan, and Meilan Chun from Fuzhou and Lianfeng Dahao from Minqing County. Famous greens include Bai Mao Hou (White Monkey Paw), Taimu Qu Hao (Taimu Spring Equinox), and Xue Ya (Snow Bud). Large quantities of Fujian green tea are used to make jasmine greens.

Bai Mao Hou (White Monkey Paw)

Bai Mao Hou is made in Taimu Mountain in Zhenghe County in the north of the province. The new shoots of two leaves and a downy bud are picked in late March from the same Da Bai varietal that is used for Bai Hao Yin Zhen and Bai Mu Dan. The leaves are withered to reduce 30 percent of their water content, panned, and then rolled to develop the flavour and give the tea its characteristic curly, tangled, downy appearance that is said to look like a monkey's paw. The liquor is pale yellow with a marine aroma suggestive of seaweed, and the taste is delicate, subtle, and sweet with hints of nuts and cooked vegetables.

Lu Xue Ya (Green Snow Bud)

Taimu Mountain is also home to Lu Xue Ya tea, which is made from bushes that grow in dense forest where heavy rain and thick fog make cultivation and harvesting very difficult. The tea is named for the snowy white down on the buds and leaves. Picked in the early spring, the dry leaves yield a pale yellow liquor with twinkling hints of green, and the taste is surprisingly strong and slightly astringent with just the merest hint of roasted chestnuts.

Mo Li Hua Cha (Jasmine Green)

Scenting teas with flowers became fashionable under the Ming dynasty (1368 to 1644). The Ming loved flowers and encouraged the production of scrolls, embroidery, porcelains, and jewellery decorated with floral designs. Inexpensive flower-scented teas became popular among the Chinese middle classes, and flowers that contained a high level of essential oil, such as orchids, osmanthus, rose, orange, and jasmine, were preferred. The traditional technique allowed one part flowers to three parts tea and alternated layers of tea and flowers in a porcelain pot that was then sealed with bamboo leaves. The pot was heated to help the tea absorb the flower aroma, and the contents were then tipped out and left to cool.

Jasmine was probably introduced to China during the 2nd century B.C., and cultivation spread during the second half of the 17th century. By the beginning of the 20th century, the area around Fuzhou City had become famous as a producer of huge quantities of jasmine flowers, and jasmine tea became one of the region's specialties. Today, Fuzhou is home to 1,200 hectares of tea gardens, and its jasmine fields yield 110 million kilos (242.5 million pounds) of flowers every year. The best jasmine teas are made using green teas that are picked in the early spring from the most tender new shoots, processed, and then carefully stored until the jasmine harvest in June, July, or August, depending on the jasmine varietal. Some jasmine teas are made with loose green tea, others with little pearls of tea, each containing two or three tiny whole shoots, rolled by hand, and in the best factories, wrapped in tissue paper while the tea dries.

When harvesting the jasmine during the summer months, it is important to pick the flowers at exactly the right moment to capture mature blossoms that are about to open and that contain plenty of oil. On the way to the factory, the flowers heat up and, once inside, must be cooled and slightly withered to lose some of their water content. The mature flower buds are separated from immature buds and stems. When the flowers open in the evening, they are layered with the tea. To scent 100 kilos (220 pounds) of tea, 100 kilos (220 pounds) of flowers are required, and the tea is usually scented five times or more, each time with a slightly smaller quantity of fresh flowers. Once the layers are complete, the tea and flowers are mixed together and left for five or six hours. Heat builds up in the heaped tea, so it is raked to a thinner layer to allow it to cool. It is then heaped again and left for a further five or six hours. At the end of the second heaping, the flowers are removed by hand before the tea is gently dried. The next and subsequent scentings take place in exactly the same way but with a slightly different temperature being allowed to build up in the heap of tea and flowers. Each scenting takes 11 to 12 hours. Jasmine teas are also produced in Zhejiang, Sichuan, Guanxi, and Hunan.

The word *oolong* means "black dragon" and was probably adopted because of the long curls and twists of dark oolong leaves that so often have the appearance of snarling dragons. Fujian produces two different styles of oolong in different parts of the province. The Wuyi Mountains, a UNESCO World Heritage Site since 1999, are famous for their dark, open-leafed rock oolongs, while Anxi County in the south of the province produces the popular Tie Guan Yin and other ball-rolled oolongs.

The volcanic Wuyi Mountain Range impresses visitors with its walls of red sandstone rock that rise along river banks and beside tea gardens like sculpted flat-topped pillars covered with forest trees and shrubs. The drama of the landscape is heightened by the deep gorges where the clear waters of Nine-Bend River twist and turn between the cliffs, passing the ruins of ancient temples and monasteries, a subtropical rainforest, and rocks inscribed in bright red paint with verses of poetry.

During the days of the Han, Wuyi was designated one of China's sacred mountains. Tang ruler Emperor Xuanzong (712 to 756) banned fishing and the felling of trees in the 8th century, the Yuan dynasty (1271 to 1368) established the imperial tea garden here, and after 1302, Wuyi tea was the only tea drunk by the imperial family. By the time the Ming took control of China in 1368, the Wuyi Mountains were famous for their compressed cake teas. But in its efforts to wipe out corruption in the tea trade, the new administration banned all manufacture of compressed teas and encouraged the production of loose-leaf teas. Factories were raided, machinery was removed, and the tea makers in the Wuyi area were badly affected. To adjust to the new rules, Fujian's tea farmers started experimenting with new processes, and somewhere along the way, accidentally or on purpose, leaves were left to oxidise, maybe for a short time, maybe for longer, then they were rolled in the usual way by hand and roasted over charcoal fires. This produced new styles of tea that looked and tasted very different from the cake teas that had previously been popular. Those partially oxidised, experimental teas were China's first oolongs, and it is on account of the area's

rocky terrain that Wuyi oolongs are called "rock teas" or Yan Cha. The special terroir gives the teas a mineral, wet-stone character that is often referred to as petrichor, a word created in 1964 from Greek *petra*, meaning "stone," and *ichor*, the fluid that runs through the veins of the gods in Greek mythology. The Chinese use the poetic term *yan yun* (literally "rock-rhyme") for the rocky aroma and rich mineral sweetness that lingers in the aftertaste.

Wuyi Rock Oolongs

Among the many different tea plant varietals that are grown in Wuyi, four are considered more important than the others. The Si Da Ming Cong (four big famous bushes) are Da Hong Pao (Big Red Robe), Tie Luo Han (Iron Monk Warrior), Shui Jin Gui (Golden Water Tortoise), and Bai Ji Guan (White Cockscomb). Other important varietals are Rou Gui (Cassia or Cinnamon) and Shui Xian (Narcissus or Water Sprite), which is closely related to the oolong varietals grown on Phoenix Mountain in Guangdong Province. To make Wuyi oolongs, shoots of three or four open leaves are plucked by hand after Gu Yu in mid-April. They are then sun-withered, taken indoors for further partial oxidation, and tumbled and shaken to lightly bruise the leaves until they are 40 to 50 percent oxidised. They are panned, rolled, and dried, and then all the stalks are removed by hand, leaving single leaves that are roasted over charcoal to give the characteristic

Four Da Hong Pao mother bushes grow high up on a rocky ledge, and only designated tea masters are allowed to pluck the leaves.
Photograph courtesy of The Chinese Tea Company, London

dark, twisted dry leaves that have a complex, fruity, toasty flavour. Different grades are available according to the level of roasting that takes place as the final stage of the manufacturing process. The charcoal roasting reduces the water content of the leaves, so that they retain their quality, and provokes a change in the amino acids and sugars in the leaf, giving the tea a more complex, caramelised character that deepens and enriches the flavour. Low heat retains the deep green and plummy red colour of the leaves and brings out the floral aromas of the tea. A medium heat darkens the leaves more, develops fruity flavours of peaches, apricots, and prunes and gives the liquor a yellow-gold hue. A high roast darkens the leaves to a charcoal black and yields a dark amber liquor with a more toasty, burnt sugar, caramelised character with hints of cocoa nibs and molasses. Some roasting is carried out today in electric ovens, but the results come a poor second to traditional charcoal roasting.

Da Hong Pao (Big Red Robe)

One of the Si Da Ming Cong varietals, Da Hong Pao (the name of both the varietal and the tea made from it) is often called the king of tea. One legend says that it came to fame when tea made from its leaves cured the sick mother of a Ming dynasty emperor, who then sent a large red robe to honour and protect the bushes. Six (some say four) of the original bushes (three different varietals) still grow on a high cliff face in Jiulongke in Wuyi, and visitors come from near and far to pay their respects. Only authorised tea masters are allowed to pluck the new shoots of these mother bushes each spring, and the tiny harvest yields less than 400 grams (0.88 pounds) of made tea. The tea is always very expensive and has in the past sold for over US$1 million per kilo (2.2 pounds). It is one of China's most sought-after teas and is reserved for very special guests. Over the last 400 years, since the bushes came to fame, cuttings from the original mother bushes have been cultivated, and high-quality Da Hong Pao oolongs are made each year by master craftsmen using leaves from the new generations of Da Hong Pao bushes.

Tie Luo Han (Iron Monk Warrior or Iron Apostle)

Legend says that the Tie Luo Han varietal, another of the Si Da Ming Cong, was found growing in a cave in one of Wuyi's 99 cliffs and that the tea was made for the first time by a warrior monk with dark skin the colour of iron. It is thought to be the oldest of the rock oolongs, dating back to the days of the Northern Song dynasty (960 to 1126), and the green-brown, twisty, curled leaves yield a strong, rich amber liquor that has a lightly toasty character with layers of floral notes, lychee, and baked almonds.

Shui Jin Gui (Golden Water Tortoise, Golden Marine Turtle)

The legend of this third Si Da Ming Cong varietal says that in the days of the Qing dynasty, a flood washed the original Shui Jin Gui tea tree from Tian Xin Temple at the top of Niu Lan Keng in the Wuyi Mountains further down the mountain to Lei Shi Temple, where the monks found it and planted it. When the monks from the Tian Xin Temple later discovered it growing there, a dispute over the ownership of the tea tree went on for more than a century until it was decided that the gods had been responsible for moving the tea bush and so it should stay where it had come to rest at Lei Shi Temple. Because water was involved and because of the rounded shape of the bush, the tea was named Golden Water Turtle. The dark, curled leaves brew to give an amber-green liquor that is strong, rich, and fruity.

Bai Ji Guan (White Cockscomb or White Rooster)

Oolongs made from this Si Da Ming Cong varietal are the rarest of the rock oolongs and are made in very small quantities. The fresh leaves are pale yellowish-white rather than green, and the dry leaves are less heavily roasted than other rock oolongs. The dark amber liquor is sweet, fruity, and honeyed with a lingering maltiness and suggestions of dark chocolate. The tea is said to have been named by a monk in memory of a courageous rooster that sacrificed its life while protecting its chicks from a predatory eagle.

Rou Gui (Cassia or Cinnamon Oolong)

Tea made from the Rou Gui varietal is sweet and rich with natural dry cinnamon notes and is becoming more and more popular in China and in international markets. Known also as Wuyi Cassia Oolong and Yu Gui Oolong, it is 40 to 50 percent oxidised with large, crinkled brown leaves and a sweet, spicy, woody aroma. Its liquor is malty, spicy, and sweet with hints of charcoal and cocoa.

Shui Xian (Narcissus or Water Sprite)

This varietal is closely related to the bushes that grow in Phoenix Mountain in Guangdong Province where teas made from it are known as Dan Cong oolongs. Shui Xian's other names include Lao Cong Shui Xian (Old Bush Water Sprite) and Wu Yi Old Bush Shui Xian. Wuyi Shui Xian oolongs are fragrant and floral with suggestions of lychee, ripe grapes, and vanilla as well as darker hints of cocoa nibs and molasses.

Other rock oolongs from Wuyi include Bai Sui Xiang (100-Year Fragrance), Fo Shou (Buddha's Hand), Qi Zhong (Strange Varietal), Qi Lan (Rare Orchid), and Xiao Hong Pao (Small Red Robe).

ANXI OOLONGS

Anxi County, in the south of Fujian Province, has been producing tea for more than 1,000 years and is perhaps most famous for Tie Guan Yin (Iron Goddess of Mercy), which originated in the mountain village of Xiping. But also famous are its Se Chung balled oolongs, including Bai Ya Qi Lan (White Sprout Rare Orchid), Huang Jin Gui (Golden Cassia or Golden Osmanthus), Yong Chun Fo Shou (Buddha's Hand), and Mao Xie (Hairy Crab). The literal translation of the term *Se Chung* is "colourful variety," but it is used today to refer to all oolongs made in the Anxi region with the exception of Tie Guan Yin. The best teas are made in the spring and the autumn and are less heavily oxidised than Wuyi's dark oolongs. After sun withering, bruising and tumbling, light oxidation, and panning, they are rolled inside cloth bags many times until each leaf shoot is tightly wound to a neat little nugget.

Tie Guan Yin (Iron Goddess of Mercy)

Tie Guan Yin oolongs are made from the tea varietal of the same name. It is also written Ti Kwan Yin, Ti Kuan Yin, Tiet Kwun Yum, or Tit Kwun Yum, and is translated as Iron Buddha, Iron Goddess Oolong, and Tea of the Iron Bodhisattva. The tea dates back to 1720 or 1730, and its legend tells of a tea farmer who, on his way to his tea garden each day, walked past a neglected and rundown shrine with an iron statue of the goddess Guan Yin, the Goddess of Mercy. Out of respect for the goddess, he put fresh flowers on the altar, lit incense, and kept the shrine clean and tidy. Several months later, the statue appeared to him in a dream and told him that if he looked behind the shrine the next morning, he would find treasure. All he found was a tea shoot, which he planted in his tea garden and named after the goddess. When he made tea from its leaves, the teas were deliciously fragrant with orchid and hyacinth notes, and his plant became famous. He shared cuttings of the bush with his neighbours, and they, too, started making their own Tie Guan Yin teas.

The teas are cultivated at altitudes between 300 and 1,000 metres (984 and 3,281 feet) and give four harvests each year—one in the spring, two in the summer, and one in the autumn—and the spring and autumn teas are considered the best. Some people prefer the spring teas, which are stronger and have a light floral aroma; others choose the autumn teas, which have a more powerful aroma and a more buttery character. During processing, some teas are very lightly oxidised, while others are allowed to oxidise for longer. At the end of the normal balled-oolong manufacturing process, the teas are dried, and then all the stalks are removed by hand so that when brewed, single leaves open to reveal their red-brown edges where oxidation has taken place. This removal of stems is done either by the producer in the factory or by the merchant who buys the tea, and the task must be carried out on a dry day so that the tea does not absorb too much humidity before being packed for sale. As an additional step, the teas are sometimes baked to give a warm, complex flavour profile. Traditional Tie Guan Yin is quite heavily baked. More moderately baked types are becoming more popular, and the more modern, lightly oxidised, aromatic teas are very lightly baked so that they retain an almost green character. The colour and flavour profile of the different grades and types of Tie Guan Yin vary according to the different levels of oxidation and baking. The lightly oxidised teas, which dominate the market today, are extremely aromatic and give floral liquors with hints of sappy spring flowers such as hyacinth, lily of the valley, and narcissus; the lightly oxidised and more moderately baked teas give a mellow, slightly roasted aroma and a smooth, fresh, floral flavour; and the traditional heavily baked teas have a very floral aroma and give liquors that are sweet and fruity with complex toasty notes.

Mao Xie (Hairy Crab) Oolong

This wonderfully aromatic, floral balled oolong from the town of Da Ping in Anxi County takes its name from the fine hairs on the underside of the leaves that make the tightly rolled balls of tea look a little like the Chinese freshwater mitten crab with its hairy claws. The name Mao Xie is used for both the made tea and the cultivar, which has thick leaves with gently serrated edges. Shoots of one bud and two or three leaves are picked and processed as balled oolongs, and after drying, the tight pellets of tea retain an attractive mix of dark and light jade green. The little nuggets open when brewed to yield a rounded, buttery liquor with good body, a sweet floral aroma, and hints of ripe peaches, gardenia, jasmine, orchids, and honey in the flavour. Like other balled oolongs, the tea is sometimes baked after manufacture to give more complex toasty notes with hints of dried fruit.

The dark, twisted, oxidised leaf of a rock oolong from the Wuyi Mountains.
Photograph courtesy of The Chinese Tea Company, London

FUJIAN BLACK TEAS

Fujian's best-known black tea is Tanyang Gongfu from Tanyang Village, Fu An County, in Baiyun Mountain. First produced in 1851, it is made from the Da Bai (Big White) varietal grown at 1,200 metres (3,937 feet) and is named for the tangle of golden buds and twisted leaves that resemble a monkey's claws. The premium grade is often sold as Tanyang Jin Hou (Golden Monkey), which has black leaves mingled with golden buds and yields a bright red liquor. The aroma is of cocoa and caramel, and the taste is honeyed with hints of cocoa, walnuts, and roasted sweet potato. Other black teas are Bailin Gongfu from Taimu Mountain, made from the Da Bai varietal or the local Xiao Zhong small-leafed varietal; and Zhenghe Gongfu from Jin Ping Village in Zhenghe County, made from the Da Bai varietal and first produced in 1874. These Gongfu teas, whose name indicates that they are made with great skill, have become very popular since the 1980s. Fujian is also famous for its smoky teas, Lapsang Souchong, Bohea Lapsang, and the new Jin Jun Mei.

Zhengshan Xiao Zhong (Lapsang Souchong)

There are two possible explanations for Lapsang Souchong's name. One suggests that it is a derivation of the Chinese *lāpùshān xiăozhŏng*, meaning "small-leafed varietal" from Lapu Mountain, Lapu perhaps being the local dialect for the particular mountain area in the Wuyi Mountains range. The other says that perhaps *Lapsang* derives from *lei xun*, meaning "smoke-scented," and *xiaozhong* means "small-leaf varietal."

There are also two stories that try to explain the origin of this smoky tea. The tea originates from Tongmu Village and is thought to have been developed during the days of the Ming dynasty (1368 to 1644). Before the Ming took control of the country, Chinese teas were compressed, but the Ming forbade this because of what they said were corrupt practices and insisted that tea was made loose. Factories were raided and equipment removed, and many of the Wuyi Mountain producers shut down their operations for 150 years or so. When production started again, mistakes were made in processing and, instead of making the traditional green tea, the leaves were partially or fully oxidised, and what we know today as a black tea probably started as a Wuyi oolong as tea producers experimented with new processing techniques. The tea was dried over fires of locally grown pinewood, which gave the tea a lightly smoked character. Another legend says that during the time of the Qing (1644 to 1912), the Chinese army used a tea factory as their resting place one night and slept on the freshly picked tea that was waiting to be de-enzymed, rolled, and dried. When the soldiers left the next morning, the workers wondered what they could do with the spoiled leaf that had oxidised and was tainted with the smell of the soldiers. One factory worker suggested roasting the tea over pine rather than the usual bamboo in order to hide the bad smell of the damaged tea. But it is much more likely that during the normal drying of the tea over fires of young, sappy local pine, the leaves absorbed a little smoke and created a tea that Western customers seemed to enjoy. Over time, producers increased the amount of smoke, and the original lightly smoked teas developed a smokier character.

Harvesting begins in May after all the buds have opened and shoots of two or three mature leaves, without buds, are plucked. They are withered and rolled into tight strips, oxidised, and put through a first drying stage. Then, they are placed on bamboo baskets ready to finish drying over smoking pinewood. Inside each Lapsang factory is an enclosed two-floor drying area. The lower room contains smouldering pinewood, and the smoke drifts up to the upper room through small gaps in the ceiling. The baskets of tea sit on rafters in the upper room, slowly drying and absorbing the smoky aroma. Levels of smokiness are adjusted by burning younger, sappy wood or older, dryer wood. The teas give a rich red liquor and have a smoky aroma and flavour with hints of dried longan, the succulent, juicy Chinese fruit Dragon Eye, which tastes of dark chocolate and toasted raisins when dried.

Bohea Lapsang

The name, which appears in 18th-century British and American tea merchants' records to mean "black tea," is a westernization of Wuyi, where the teas originated. Traders and sailors were told the name of the region, misunderstood or mispronounced it, and brought it back home as "Voui" or "Bohea." In 1699, John Ovington, chaplain to King William III, wrote in his *Essay upon the Nature and Qualities of Tea:* "The first Sort is Bohea, or as the Chinese have it, Voui, which is the little Leaf inclining to black and generally tinges the Water brown, or of a reddish colour." And Twinings' sales ledgers for 1715 and 1716 contain the following entries: "Mrs Bankes (of Kingston Hall) ½ pound bohea at 18/-; Mr Edward Stanley 12 lb finest bohea tea at 18/-; Mr Stoughton 1lb Bohea tea & a canister." Porcelain and earthenware tea jars made by English potteries for the storage of the dry leaf often carried the word *Bohea* for black tea and *Hyson* for green.

Bohea Lapsang is a lightly smoked version of Lapsang Souchong and is made today to replicate the original 17th- and 18th-century black (perhaps they were oolong) teas that absorbed a small amount of smoke during the normal drying process.

Jin Jun Mei (Golden Beautiful Eyebrow)

Created in 2005 by Jiang Yuan Xun, general manager of Wuyi Zhengshan Tea Company, this is one of China's most expensive black teas and sells for thousands of U.S. dollars per kilo (2.2 pounds). Jiang Yuan Xun apparently chanced upon some wild tea bushes growing in the Wuyi National Nature Reserve at an altitude of over 1,800 metres (5,906 feet) and picked the small leaf buds to make this new-style, very high-grade tea. One day each spring, before Qing Ming, 20 pluckers work together to gather 50,000 buds to make just 500 grams (17.6 ounces) of tea. The tea is made in Tongmu Village where Lapsang Souchong was first made, but instead of being heavily smoked in Lapsang style, this tea is carefully withered, hand-rolled, oxidised, and then fired over dried, well-seasoned pinewood. The beautiful, twisted, tippy leaves brew to give a rich, dark amber liquor that breathes the aroma of cocoa and caramel and the flavours of creamy butterscotch, lychee, and roses.

ABOVE: The beautiful gold-tipped leaf and coppery liquor of Jin Jun Mei. Photograph courtesy of Thomas Kasper, Siam Teas OPPOSITE PAGE: Tongmu Village in the Wuyi Mountains where the first Lapsang tea was made during the Ming dynasty (1368 to 1644). Photograph ©2017 Victoria Wu and Meimei Fine Teas (*meimeitea.com*). Used here with permission.

Country, State, or Province
Fujian Province

Area Under Tea
246,700 hectares

Average Annual Production (Kilograms)
380 million

Terrain
Mountains and hills cover 80% of Fujian; a stunningly beautiful landscape of rivers, forests, tea gardens, and granite mountains that rise from the ground like great towers of rock; the Wuyi Mountains in the north-west are famous for virgin forest, volcanic peaks, and grotesque karst rock formations.

Altitude
280 to 1,525 metres (919 to 5,003 feet)

Best Time to Visit
late March, April, September, October

Main Varietals/Cultivars
Da Bai (Big White); early sprouting Fuding Dabaicha (FD); Fuding Dahaocha; Fu'an Dabaicha; Zhenghe Dabaicha; Xiao Bai; Bai Sha; Da Hong Pao (Big Red Robe); Tie Luo Han (Iron Monk Warrior); Shui Jin Gui (Golden Water Tortoise); Bai Ji Guan (White Cocksomb); Rou Gui (Cassia or Cinnamon); Shui Xian (Narcissus, or Water Sprite); Da Ye Wulong; Tie Guan Yin; Wuyi Caicha cultivar for Jin Jun Mei; Jinmudan; Huangmeigui; Zimudan; Chunlan; Dangui; Ruixiang; Xiapu Chunbolü; Huangqi; Mingke; Yuemingxiang; Baxiancha; Fuyun; Huangdan; Maoxie; Meizhan; Zaofengchun; Foshu; Zhaoyang; Baiya Qilan; Jiulong Dabaicha; Fengyuanchun; Xinrencha; Xiapu Yuanxiaolü; Jiulongpao; Zaochunhao; Zimeigui

Types of Tea Made
White, green, jasmine green, dark oolongs, Tie Guan Yin balled oolongs, black, smoky Lapsang Souchongs, lightly smoked Bohea Lapsang

Predominant Flavours; Tasting Notes
WHITE: *Bai Hao Yin Zhen (Silver Needle)*—delicate, vegetal, with hints of nuts and melon
Bai Mu Dan (White Peony)—mellow, hints of cucumber, slightly floral
Gong Mei (Tribute Eyebrow)—less delicate, stronger, slightly earthy
Shou Mei (Long Life Eyebrow)—stronger, less refined, sweet
GREEN: *Bai Mao Hou (White Monkey Paw)*—delicate, smooth, sweet
Lu Xue Ya (Green Snow Bud)—sweet, floral, with hints of oatmeal, asparagus, and honey
Mo Li Hua Cha (Jasmine Green)—fragrant, delicate, exotic, sweet
OOLONG: *Rock Oolongs*—complex, floral, peachy, and sweet, with hints of apricots and plums, sometimes spicy and with warm, dark, roasted cocoa and molasses notes (See text for different rock oolongs.)
Tie Guan Yin (Iron Goddess of Mercy)—powerful orchid notes, lightly astringent, with hints of honey and toasted nuts
Mao Xie (Hairy Crab)—rounded, buttery liquor with good body, a sweet floral aroma, and hints of ripe peaches, gardenia, jasmine, orchids, and honey in the flavour
BLACK: *Zheng Shan Xiao Zhong (Lapsang Souchong)*—smoky, with pine notes and hints of spice and prunes
Bohea Lapsang—less smoky, more subtle than Lapsang Souchong
Jin Jun Mei (Golden Beautiful Eyebrow)—robust, malty, spicy, honey-sweet, with subtle hints of dark chocolate, toasted grain, oranges, and caramelised sugar

GUANGDONG

(CHINA)

Guangdong's hilly coastline is the longest of all China's provinces, and the region has been important for trade with foreign merchants since the days of the Roman Empire. The province's tea history is thought to date back to the 12th century when a Song emperor hid in Guangdong's mountains while fleeing south from the Mongols. While there, he brewed tea from leaves plucked from old trees growing nearby, found the liquor delicious, and named it Phoenix Tea because of the pointed beak–shaped dry leaves. Since it was discovered or planted during the Song dynasty, the varietal of the plant was named Song-zhong, and Phoenix Mountain (Fenghuangshan) became famous for its oolong teas. In the days of the Ming dynasty, the tea became a tribute tea.

Guangdong's climate is tropical in the lower-lying coastal areas and subtropical monsoon in the mountains. It enjoys long, warm summers with plentiful rainfall between April and September, and temperatures that rarely fall below 12°C (53.6°F). Oolong manufacture began here around 300 years ago, and the province is today China's third most important region for oolong production after the Wuyi Mountains and Anxi County. Almost all the Phoenix oolongs are produced in Wudongshan (Wu Dong Mountain), which is one of the many peaks in the Phoenix range and has high altitudes, good soil, and the oldest trees.

The province also makes black teas such as Shaoguan Mao Feng and Guangdong Da Ye Qing, and Da Ye Qing yellow tea.

Gathering leaf to make dark Phoenix oolong teas from the ancient trees in Phoenix Mountain.
Photograph courtesy of Canton Tea Company

GUANGDONG OOLONGS | *Guangdong Feng-huang Dan Cong Oolongs (Phoenix Oolongs from a Single Tree)*

Deep in Phoenix Mountain are groves of ancient tea trees, each containing clumps of large bushes or small trees of a different individual varietal. Each varietal is thought to descend from the original Shui Xian varietal (found both here and in the Wuyi Mountains), but each has developed its own DNA over the centuries through natural mutation. The oldest Shui Xian tree found here is thought to be more than 900 years old. There are many tea gardens in Phoenix Mountain where cloned younger bushes grow alongside older, semi-wild trees, and the best-quality teas are from the higher altitudes and the older trees. Some of the oldest, most precious trees are protected by perimeter fencing.

Until the middle of the 20th century, it was common to harvest and process the leaves of each single tree separately in order to maintain its individual character, so Phoenix Mountain trees came to be known as Dan Cong or "single tree" teas. In some places, this controlled harvest continues, but the tiny amounts of tea (500 grams [17.6 ounces] or less) made from 500- to 900-year-old trees do not become available outside China. The name *Dan Cong* has today become a generic term for all oolongs made in Phoenix Mountain, and the different varieties are becoming more and more widely available as tea lovers learn to appreciate their powerful fragrances and complex toasty and floral flavours.

Some Phoenix Dan Cong tea bushes and trees grow at altitudes between 1,000 and 1,500 metres (3,281 or 4,921 feet), and the plants flourish in the rocky environment where they can push their roots into the rich red soil between the solid rock. The air here is warm and humid, and a thick, misty fog entirely envelops Phoenix Mountain most of the time. Since the Phoenix trees and bushes grow on such rocky ground, the liquors often have a similar mineral, wet-rock character to Wuyi oolongs.

The leaf shoots of the various Feng-huang Shui Xian varietals have medium-sized, long, oval leaves with a sharp tip and contain a high level of aromatic ingredients including linalool, which gives the tea floral and spicy notes, and geraniol, which has a rose-like scent. The best teas are made in the late spring when the leaves are fully open but do not give a bitter flavour. To pluck the new shoots, pickers must climb tall ladders to reach the high branches of the old trees. They gather shoots of two or three fully open leaves with no bud. The fresh leaf is quickly sun-withered for 20 or 30 minutes, then cooled and withered indoors. The leaves are shaken on bamboo baskets and tumbled in bamboo drums to provoke oxidation. As the bruised parts of the leaves change from green to reddy-brown, the aroma develops from grassy and green to sweet, flowery, or fruity. When the desired level of oxidation has been reached, the tea is panned and rolled by hand or in rolling machines until the leaves become long, twisted strips, and then the mass of leaves is carefully loosened by hand and spread thinly on bamboo baskets. The tea is partially dried in ovens, and then comes the final charcoal drying that is crucial to giving the teas their complex toasty notes and layers of powerful floral fragrances and rich hints of ripe autumn fruit. The charcoal drying takes place in two stages. During the first stage, the temperature of the smouldering charcoal is high, and the leaves are dried for approximately 40 minutes; during the second stage, the temperature is cooler, and the leaves dry for approximately 20 minutes. The teas are then left on the baskets with no heat to finish drying. Different manufacturers use different roasting temperatures and timings depending on the thickness and size of the leaves, but it is important not to give the teas a burnt flavour but to enhance the natural floral, spicy, or fruity notes. When the roasting has been completed, any stems and poor-quality leaves are removed by hand.

There are some 13 well-known and more than 90 less well-known varietals that still grow here, and the most famous mountain within the Phoenix range is Wudongshan, home to more than 3,000 bushes that are over 100 years old. The teas have powerful flower or spice fragrances and are named accordingly:

— Mi Lan Dan Cong *(Honey Orchid)*

— Feng-huang Shui Xian
(Phoenix Narcissus or Phoenix Water Sprite)

— Yu Lan Xiang *(Magnolia Blossom Fragrance)*

— Huang Zhi Xiang
(Gardenia or Orange Blossom Fragrance)

— Jiang Hua Xiang *(Ginger Flower Fragrance)*

— Rou Gui Xiang *(Cinnamon Fragrance)*

— Gui Hua Xiang *(Osmanthus Fragrance)*

— You Hua Xiang *(Pomelo Flower Fragrance)*

— Mi Lan Xiang *(Honey Orchid Fragrance)*

— Xing Ren Xiang *(Almond Fragrance)*

— Zhi Lan Xiang *(Irises and Orchids Fragrance)*

GUANGDONG GREEN TEAS

Guangdong is not noted for its green tea but does produce an ancient tea called Gulao or Kooloo, which is said to date back to the 6th century and is named for the city of Gulao in the south-west of the province, where the climate is warm and misty year-round. Fresh leaves are gathered from the tea bushes that grow here and are processed as a green tea by panning, rolling, and drying in the sun. They are then roasted in a hot panning machine at approximately 300°C (572°F), and this gives the leaves a burnt character. When brewed, they give a red-brown liquor that has a slightly burnt flavour and a surprising sweet aftertaste.

GUANGDONG YELLOW TEA | *Guangdong Da Ye Qing*

Dating back to the days of the Ming dynasty, this yellow tea is a Guangdong specialty made from the broad-leaf assamica varietal (Da Ye) that grows in Shaoguan and Zhaoqing counties and in the city of Zhanjiang. The freshly hand-plucked shoots are withered, panned, rolled, and piled to provoke light fermentation and reduce the tea's natural grassy taste. The dry leaves are yellowish-green, large, fat, and tight with buds that are covered in furry down. They brew to give a clear yellow liquor with a smooth, mellow flavour.

GUANGDONG BLACK TEAS

In the 19th century, Guangdong exported large amounts of black tea to Europe, but today, very few tea producers make black teas here. The best known are Shaoguan Mao Feng and Guangdong Ying De Hong.

Shaoguan Mao Feng

Also called Guangdong Mao Feng, this is a relatively new black tea manufactured in the style of green Mao Feng. Some are made from the Jin Xuan cultivar (famous in Taiwan for aromatic oolongs) that grows here at high altitude near Shaoguan city. Others are made from large-leafed assamicas that have been growing in Guangdong for about 30 years. The tea liquors are bright orange-amber and are sweet and aromatic with hints of fig, molasses, honey, and raisins and have a long, sweet, mellow aftertaste.

Guangdong Ying De Hong
(Guangdong Black, Ying De Black, Ying Hong)

Leaf shoots of two leaves and a bud are picked from the Ying Hong No. 9 cultivar, developed by the Guangdong Tea Research Institute from the assamica broad-leafed varietal and first planted in 1956. Production is in April and May each year and only about 50 kilos (110 pounds) are made. The golden buds and leaves are lightly curled and yield a bright amber liquor that has a sweet nut and cocoa aroma with hints of honey, chocolate, and pepper in the taste.

TOP LEFT: A small orthodox roller. Photograph courtesy of The Chinese Tea Company, London TOP RIGHT: Fresh leaves for Chao Zhou, a rare dark oolong, are plucked from wild bushes growing in the Feng Huang Mountains, then withered and oxidised on bamboo baskets © Qiu Jun Song ABOVE: Tea plants in Guangdong picked to make the province's famous Ying De black tea. Photograph courtesy of Fujian Yuantai Tea Co., Ltd.

Country, State, or Province
Guangdong Province

Area Under Tea
51,300 hectares

Average Annual Production (Kilograms)
79.2 million

Terrain
The high mountains in the north of the province include Phoenix Mountain, where groves of old trees grow on steep, rocky slopes. Some of the tea trees are planted on neatly terraced slopes where the rich red of the soil contrasts strikingly with the bright green of the tea bushes.

Altitude
300 to 1,500 metres (974 to 4,921 feet)

Best Time to Visit
Late March, April, September, October

Main Varietals/Cultivars
Fenghuang Shui Xian (Phoenix Water Sprite); Fenghuang Dan Cong; Fenghuang Huangzhixiang Dan Cong; Danxia; Jin Xuan; Da Ye assamica; Lechang Baimaocha; Lingtou Dan Cong; Xiuhong; Wulinghong; Yunda Danlü; Hongyan; Bai Mao; Lechang Bai Mao; Liannan Dayecha; Ying Hong 9; Huangye Shuixian; Heiye Shuixian

Types of Tea Made
Yellow, green, black, and dark

Predominant Flavours; Tasting Notes
YELLOW: *Guangdong Da Ye Qing*—smooth and mellow
GREEN: *Kooloo*—slightly burnt flavour, with sweet aftertaste
DARK OOLONG: *Feng-huang Dan Cong (Phoenix Dan Cong)*—each of the many Dan Congs has its own flavour profile, usually flowery, occasionally spicy, and always with roasted notes that result from the charcoal drying stage that finishes the process *(See text for more details.)*
BLACK: *Shaoguan Mao Feng*—smooth, sweet, and fruity, with hints of raisins
Guangdong Ying De Hong (Guangdong Black)—subtle, honey-sweet, smooth, and mellow, with suggestions of raisins, honey, chocolate, and peppery spiciness

GUANGXI

(CHINA)

Guangxi, officially known as Guangxi Zhuang Autonomous Region, lies on the southern side of the ancient Yungui Plateau that stretches through Yunnan and into Guizhou Province. In the north of the province, high mountains climb to 1,800 metres (5,906 feet), while in the south, altitudes are just above sea level. The landscape is a strange mixture of plains and karst hills, some pointed, some smooth and humped, others with sculptural craggy peaks. These mounds and peaks descend from ancient coral reefs that turned to limestone over thousands of years and were gradually dissolved by rain and carbon dioxide, leaving curious protuberances rising from the land.

Although not as important for tea as neighbouring provinces, Guangxi is best known for its Liubao dark teas made from the region's native small-leafed varietal. A variety of other teas is made from the new large-leafed Ling Yun Bai Hao cultivar (*C. sinensis* var. *pubilimba* cv. Lingyun-baimaocha), which was developed in Guangxi in 1985 from a tea tree found growing in Ling Yun County. It is now widely cultivated as a smaller, sturdy bush in Guangxi and Guizhou provinces and is used to make a number of green, osmanthus- and jasmine-scented greens, yellow, oolong, and black teas. The best known are Ling Yun Bai Hao Yinzhen downy green tea, a single bud tea that looks like a white Yin Zhen but undergoes panning to stop oxidation rather than the slow air drying that is normal for white tea; Ling Luo Chun green with a curled downy dry leaf that yields a bright, fragrant, yellow-green liquor with suggestions of chestnuts; Guangxi Lingyun Bai Mao Cha green; Ling Chun Mao Jian green; Ling Chun Huang Da Cha yellow; Golden Bud black tea; and 100-year-old black.

The Guilin Tea Science and Research Institute, founded here in 1965, has a bank of more than 300 tea seeds and manages a 42-hectare organic tea garden where 250 different varietals and cultivars are grown. The garden produces 82 million kilos (180.7 million pounds) of hand-plucked, hand-processed tea annually and combines tea cultivation with scientific research into growing and manufacturing different types of tea.

GUANGXI GREEN TEA | *Green Needle*

Green Needle tea is produced in Sanjiang in northern Guangxi, in misty, subtropical organic tea gardens that lie at altitudes of between 700 and 1,000 metres (2,297 to 3281 feet) above sea level. The tea was, until recently, consumed only locally, but it is now more readily available outside Guangxi. It is made from just new buds that are still clothed in their downy winter jackets and the long, thin, jade needles of tea shine green through the silver hairs. The liquor is delicate, mild, and smooth with a subtle nutty character.

GUANGXI BLACK TEA | *Guangxi 100-Year Black Tea*

The tea is named from the fact that it is made from 100-year-old wild tea trees growing in the mountains of Sanjiang in northern Guangxi. Until a few years ago, the local villagers used the large leaves for cooking and to make tea oil. They are now looking after the trees more carefully in order to improve the yield and increase production of this special tea. In an area where large-scale cultivation of tea is developing rapidly, these old wild trees are extremely valuable for the production of a quality tea. The whole dry leaves are long and twisted, with plenty of golden buds, and they give a bright amber liquor with a smooth, sweet, fruity smell and flavour.

GUANGXI DARK TEA | *Liubao Hei Cha (Liubao Dark Tea)*

Originally made at the end of the 18th century in Liubao Village, Wuzhou City, Cangwu County, this fermented tea is today made in several parts of the province. It is similar to a Shu (ripe, ripened, or cooked) Puerh tea in that the traditional processing involves the manufacture of a green tea that is heaped under wet cloths to provoke bacterial fermentation. The idea of making ripe Puerh in Yunnan Province in 1972 developed from this Guangxi process, and whereas Puerh was originally a raw fermented tea and ripe Puerh was developed later, Liubao's history was the reverse. Original Liubao tea was always a ripe tea, but today, because of the influence and popularity of Puerh, it is now also made as a raw tea that is lightly steamed and fermented more slowly and more naturally. The young raw teas give an amber liquor that is astringent and spicy but, with aging, develops a similar flavour profile to the traditional Liubao heaped and fermented teas and tastes smoother and mellower.

To make traditional Liubao, shoots of three or four leaves and a bud are harvested, panned quickly at a high temperature to prevent oxidation, and rolled. While still warm and wet, the leaves are piled in a layer 15 to 25 centimetres (6 to 10 inches) thick and covered with a wet cloth to keep in the heat and the water content in the leaves (a process called *wo dui*,

ABOVE LEFT: New shoots with a pink tinge on bushes in the Liu Bao area. ABOVE RIGHT: New cuttings growing in semi-shaded conditions in Liubao.
Photographs courtesy of Cangwu Liubao Tea Co., Ltd.

which translates as "wet piling") for around 20 days in a controlled humid environment. Once the tea has fermented to the required level, it is rolled again and dried over pinewood to reduce the moisture content to around 15 percent. The tea is then sorted and blended, wet heaped again for 7 to 10 days, then steamed for about 30 minutes, and compressed into bricks or more commonly packed loose into bamboo baskets that each hold between 35 kilos (77 pounds) and 50 kilos (110 pounds). The tea is then stored in the factory for at least 180 days before being moved to an underground cave where it remains for at least a year in 55 to 75 percent humidity and an average temperature of 20° to 28°C (68° to 82.4°F). After a year in these conditions, it is moved to a brick-and-wood-built warehouse at ground level where it is stored for at least another year in warmer, dryer conditions. By the time the tea is ready to be retailed, it is at least 3 years old and probably between 8 and 10 years old, so Liubao tea is never "young" or "fresh." In the past, the tea was aged in Guangxi Province or was exported to merchants in Hong Kong who stored and aged it there, or it was exported to Malaysia where it was drunk by labourers who worked in the very deep tin mines there. Liubao tea is said to warm the body and cure diseases, and workers in the cold damp mines at around 600 metres (1,969 feet) underground refused to take a job anywhere that did not supply them with Liubao tea.

The place in which the tea has been aged affects the final character of the tea, and Liubao connoisseurs can tell the difference between Hong Kong Liubao and a Wuzhou Liubao aged in Guangxi or Malaysia. In Hong Kong in the past, traders sped up the fermentation process by alternately storing the tea in a very humid location and a drier location. Malaysia and Guangxi are both very warm and humid throughout the long tropical summer, and this creates ideal aging conditions. The most important molds active in Liubao tea are *Aspergillus niger*, the same fungus that activates Puerh tea, and *Eurotium cristatum*, which causes little yellow speckles called Jin Hua (Golden Flower) to grow on the tea. This is said to improve the digestion and aid absorption of starch and protein, but inhibit the absorption of fat.

Today, processing varies from place to place and may be of the traditional ripe Liubao type or the modern raw type. Liubao teas are today sold loose or compressed into disks, cakes, bricks, nest-shaped *tuo*, or packed inside tubes of bamboo leaves tied four times at intervals to create five small balls of compressed tea. Like raw Puerh, the longer Liubao tea is stored, the better it tastes.

LEFT: Pickers gathering fresh leaf to make Liubao dark tea. TOP: Ornate gateway into the Liubao Town. ABOVE: Cangsong Liubao Tea factory, built in 1955, is the oldest Liubao factory and still produces Liubao dark tea. Photographs courtesy of Cangwu Liubao Tea Co., Ltd.

Country, State, or Province
Guangxi Province

Area Under Tea
69,300 hectares

Average Annual Production (Kilograms)
60 million

Terrain
Karst hills with strange, surreal, sometimes grotesque formations, mountains covered with forest, lakes, rivers, waterfalls, and caves.

Altitude
Up to 1,800 metres (6,000 feet)

Best Time to Visit
Late March, April, September, October

Main Varietals/Cultivars
Qiao Mu Da Ye Zhong (Old Tea Trees Big Leaf Varietal); Lingyun Baimaocha; Guihong; Guilü 1; Guire; Yaoshan Xiulü; Guixiang 18

Types of Tea Made
Black, green, jasmine green, osmanthus green, yellow, white, dark compressed tea

Predominant Flavours; Tasting Notes
GREEN: *Needle*—delicate, mild, and smooth with a subtle nutty character *Osmanthus*—delicate, sweet, and peachy
YELLOW: smooth, mellow
BLACK: *100-Year Black*—smooth, sweet, and fruity
DARK: *Liubao Hei Cha (Liubao Dark Tea)*—clean, smooth, sweet, and thick, with hints of pine smoke and betel nut

HONG KONG

(CHINA)

In 1945, British-born Brook Bernacchi, lawyer and politician, settled in Hong Kong and worked as a member of the Hong Kong Bar Association. During the war, he had served in the Royal Marines in Ceylon and Burma and was inspired to try growing tea. So, in 1949, he bought a stretch of land on Ngong Ping Plateau on Lantau Island behind the Po Lin Monastery. The land he acquired was barren, bleak, and totally undeveloped, but he planted trees and shrubs and, in 1948, established a 50-hectare tea garden on the slopes around the house that he had inherited with the land. He named the house (built in the early 1890s and previously home to an order of nuns) All Knowing Lotus and called the tea garden The Lotus Brand Tea Plantation. The teas were sold in Hong Kong and in England for teabags. Production continued, with a Taiwanese tea master in charge, until 1994 when the tea master died and the factory was closed.

Bernacchi died in 1996, and the house and garden were closed up. Part of the garden was sold in the 1990s to a neighbour and the remaining area stood idle until, in 2010, Bernacchi's grandson Stefan Oechsner, who spent his childhood here, opened it up again and began slowly refurbishing the tea bushes. The surviving tea had been struggling amongst the acacia trees that surround the house and covers less than a hectare today. In the humid climate of Hong Kong, plants grow very fast and soon become a tangled jungle, overwhelming smaller plants that struggle for light and space. Oechsner has been clearing the land and filling the gaps with newly propagated tea bushes. He made his first batch of tea in 2013, and the results encouraged him to focus on the manufacture of dark, Phoenix-style oolongs. In addition to teas made at the new Lotus Brand tea garden, his re-launched Lotus Brand Tea Company also sells a selection of quality China teas.

Country, State, or Province
Hong Kong Special Administrative Region

Area Under Tea
Less than a hectare on Ngong Ping Plateau on Lantau Island

Average Annual Production (Kilograms)
Not yet known

Terrain
Lantau Island is the largest island in Hong Kong. Ngong Ping Plateau, reached by cable car or bus, is surrounded by steep, forested mountain slopes.

Altitude
457 metres
(1,500 feet)

Best Time to Visit
late March, April, September, October

Main Varietals/Cultivars
Not yet known

Types of Tea Made
Dark oolongs

Predominant Flavours; Tasting Notes
OOLONG:
Lotus Oolong—light, fruity, and complex

JIANGXI

(CHINA)

The hilly province of Jiangxi is surrounded by mountain ranges and has a subtropical climate with high humidity and very wet summers. It is home to Poyang Lake, China's largest freshwater lake, to the west of which is Lushan, the province's most famous tea mountain. Lushan covers an area of 30,200 hectares and is important for its ancient temples and villas, its archaeological sites, ancient stone inscriptions, and natural beauty. In the north-east of the province lies the city of Jingdezhen, an important centre of porcelain manufacture since the days of the Han, 1,800 years ago, and one of China's 24 famous cities of historical and cultural interest. Jiangxi started exporting its fine porcelains in the 3rd century, and it was Jingdezhen's blue-and-white porcelain tea wares that reached Europe in the early 17th century. An anonymous American writer explained how the export trade to the West worked: "The china-ware is brought from the country (Ching-tê Chên) plain, and painted according to fancy in the city (Canton) . . . They are great copyists and we have several sets of China to order with the family coat of arms."

Jiangxi's most famous green teas are Lushan Yun Wu (Lu Mountain Cloud and Mist), Wu Yuan Ming Mei (Wu Yuan Lady's Eyebrows), and Ning Hong Gongfu black. It also produces Lan Xiang Xian Zhi (Orchid Fairy Twig), Chun Mee (Precious Eyebrows), and Zhu Cha (Gunpowder) greens; jasmine-scented teas; white teas; and Keemun-style blacks similar to those produced in Anhui Province.

Bushes used for making Ning Hong black tea (often called the "King of Tea" by Chinese experts) that has a slightly sweet character with hints of caramel and chocolate. Photographs courtesy of Fujian Yuantai Tea Co., Ltd.

JIANGXI GREEN TEAS

Lushan Yun Wu (Lu Mountain Cloud and Mist)

Lushan National Park is a UNESCO Geopark, and green tea has been produced in Lu Mountain for more than 1,800 years. Lu Yu mentioned how delicious he found Lushan tea in his *Cha Ching* in the 8th century, and during the Song dynasty, it was designated a tribute tea. A poem written in the Song period reads, "Lushan Yunwu Tea. Strong taste. Daring Fragrance. Drinking for a long time will beget good health and longevity." The tea's name comes from the thick cover of cloud and mist that envelops the mountain throughout the year, nourishing and shading the plants. The humidity gives them the water they need, and the shady conditions cause more chlorophyll and amino acids to develop in the leaves, giving the teas their intense green colour and sweet character.

The land on Lushan is rough and rocky, and the old bushes, rounded like small humps, grow in low patches between the boulders. In recent years, the government has been encouraging the tea growers here to plant a newer cultivar, which has larger leaves and downy buds and flushes earlier in the spring. But the older plants give better teas and so still dominate. Teas picked early in the spring from the old varietal have more silver down on the dry leaves, while teas picked a little later are drier-looking and have less downy covering. Lushan Yun Wu, made from the new cultivar growing lower down the mountain, has paler, slightly larger leaves.

Plucking standards are very strict, and up to 40 percent of fresh leaf is rejected and used to make other teas. The best of the teas are made from tiny shoots of one bud and one or two leaves that are harvested before Qing Ming. Some producers use machinery to process the leaves, but the best teas are handmade. First, the leaves are panned in a wok, and the tea is moved back and forth against the hot metal, lifted to separate the leaf and release the heat and steam, dropped back into the wok, and moved back and forth again. The constant movement continues until the leaves are soft enough for rolling, and then, one handful of tea at a time is lifted out of the wok and rubbed between the hands, with one hand remaining still and the other moving back and forth to rub the tea. After several seconds of rubbing, the tea is dropped back into the wok, and the process is repeated again and again until all the tea has been rolled. To remove the last moisture, the tea is scattered thinly and evenly on a wire frame and baked in an oven.

Wu Yuan Ming Mei (Wu Yuan Lady's Eyebrows)

Also mentioned by Lu Yu, Wu Yuan's green tea is said to have been a favourite tea of the Song dynasty (960 to 1279) and was a tribute tea for the Ming (1368 to 1644) and Qing (1644 to 1912). Grown amongst the ridges and peaks of the mountains in Wu Yuan County, plucking standards demand very young bud shoots picked in the early spring on sunny days after the fog has lifted. The leaves are then withered briefly in the shade, panned to prevent oxidation, and rubbed, rolled, and dried in the wok using similar hand movements to those used for Lushan Yun Wu. The tea is then given a final bake to remove any excess moisture. The dry leaves are curved like green eyebrows with a covering of fine downy hairs.

JIANGXI BLACK TEA

Ning Hong Gongfu (Ning Prefecture Black Tea)

Made in Xiushui County, production of this black tea began during the early 19th century, and by the 1890s, the province was exporting 7.5 million kilos (16.5 million pounds) to foreign markets that often then sold it as Qimen (Keemun) tea. The bushes grow in Jiangxi's typically humid and foggy conditions, and bud shoots about 3 centimetres (just over 1 inch) long are very carefully handpicked, withered, rolled, oxidised, dried, sorted, and fired. The dry leaves are long, straight, and tightly twisted with a high level of golden tips, and liquors are coppery red and strong enough to take a little milk.

Country, State, or Province
Jiangxi Province

Area Under Tea
93,000 hectares

Average Annual Production (Kilograms)
50.35 million

Terrain
60% of the province is hills and mountains, with sloping land running down towards Poyang Lake in the north

Altitude
500 to 1,500 metres (1,640 to 4,921 feet)

Best Time to Visit
Late March, April, September, October

Main Varietals/Cultivars
Damianbai; Shangmeizhouzhong; Ningzhouzhong; Gancha

Types of Tea Made
Green, jasmine green, white, black

Predominant Flavours; Tasting Notes
WHITE: fragrant, delicate, mellow, with sweet vegetal taste
GREEN: *Lu Shan Yun Wu (Lu Mountain Cloud and Mist)*—complex, buttery, sweet, deep, with hints of young spinach and hazelnuts
Wu Yuan Ming Mei (Wu Yuan Lady's Eyebrows)—smooth, sweet, mellow, fruity, and floral
BLACK: *Ning Hong Gongfu (Ning Prefecture Black Tea)*—sweet, with caramel notes and hints of chocolate and roasted barley

TOP: Steep terraces where the bushes for Ning Hong Gongfu (Jiangxi's famous black tea) are cultivated. ABOVE: Bushes used for making black tea in the area around the city of Fuliang. Fuliang was previously called Jingdezhen, famous for porcelain manufacture and, by the time of the Tang dynasty (618 to 907), an important tea distribution centre.
Photographs courtesy of Fujian Yuantai Tea Co., Ltd.

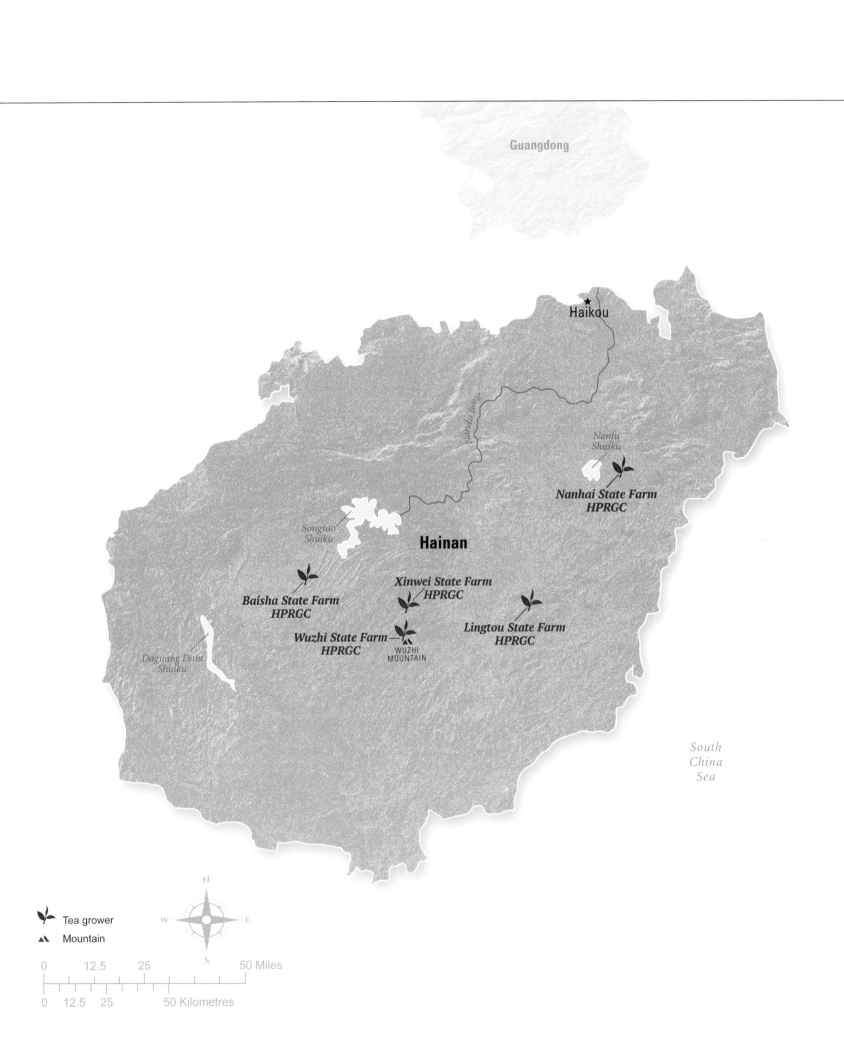

Guangdong

★ Haikou

Nandu Jiang

Nanfu Shuiku

Nanhai State Farm HPRGC

Songtao Shuiku

Hainan

Daguang Dam Shuiku

Baisha State Farm HPRGC

Xinwei State Farm HPRGC

Lingtou State Farm HPRGC

Wuzhi State Farm HPRGC

WUZHI MOUNTAIN

South China Sea

🌱 Tea grower

▲ Mountain

N
W   E
S

0   12.5   25   50 Miles

0   12.5   25   50 Kilometres

HAINAN

(CHINA)

Hainan is a group of 200 islands off China's south coast and, with its mild temperatures and plentiful rainfall, is well suited to the mass production of tea from low-growing bushes that yield well. The province's black tea production has been increasing since the 1960s, due to the work of the Hainan Reclamation Tropical Crops Development Co., Ltd. (HRTCD), which controls more than 460,000 hectares of agricultural land and has been developing the tea industry here. HRTCD, a stock company held by Hainan Provincial Reclamation Group Corp. (HPRGC), was established in 1960 under China's Ministry of Foreign Trade and Economic Cooperation, and in addition to improving production and processing techniques, it has developed several new tea cultivars (including Qilan, Fuding Dabai, Haiyan #2, and Haiyan #18) and has imported scientific and technological expertise. It has also introduced tea-processing machinery for large-scale manufacture of black CTC teas, and the province has become a major exporter of these teas to Europe, the United States, and Southeast Asia. At the company's five gardens (Nanhai, Baisha, Xinwei, Lingtou, and Wuzhi state farms) in the Wuzhi Mountains, the annual harvest starts two or three months earlier than in more northerly regions, and instead of eight harvests a year, Hainan has 10 harvests.

Hainan also produces orthodox black and green teas, the best known of which are Baisha Green, Wuzhi (Five Finger) Mountain Green, Hainan Lychee-flavoured black, and Xiang Lan Vanilla black, flavoured with the orchid *Vanilla planifolia* grown by Hainan's smallholders.

HAINAN GREEN TEA | *Wuzhi (Five Finger) Mountain Green*

For 500 years, tea has been produced on Wuzhi Mountain, which is shrouded in thick misty fog that shades the tea bushes from the sun for more than 200 days a year. This provokes the development of higher levels of chlorophyll and L-theanine in the leaves, which gives the tea liquors less astringency and more velvety umami sweetness. The bright green dry leaves are taut, straight, and wiry.

Country, State, or Province
Hainan Province

Area Under Tea
700 hectares

Average Annual Production (Kilograms)
4.41 million

Terrain
Island province off China's south coast, tropical forest; the five peaks of Wuzhi Mountain point towards the sky like the fingers of an upturned hand. The peaks are often shrouded in mist and clouds, and waterfalls cascade down through the forests.

Altitude
Around 1,700 metres (5,577 feet)

Best Time to Visit
late March, April, September, October

Main Varietals/Cultivars
Hainan Daye

Types of Tea Made
Green, some orthodox black, CTC black

Predominant Flavours; Tasting Notes
GREEN: *Wuzhi (Five Finger) Mountain Tea*—smooth, mild, and fragrant
BLACK: aromatic, thick, and mellow

CHINA

Taiwan Strait

East China Sea

Taipei ★ *Danshui River*

Taoyuan County

New Taipei City

Wenshan District

Hsinchu County

▲▲ LALA SHAN

Cho-shui River

Miaoli County

Yilan County

▲▲ HSUEHSHAN

Taichung County

Ta Chia River

▲ LISHAN

Nantou County

▲ SHAN LIN SI

Changhua County

Hualien County

Hsi-Lo River

Yunlin County

Taiwan

DONG DING

▲ ALISHAN

Chiayi County

▲ YU SHAN

▲▲ WUHE SHAN

Philippine Sea

Tainan County

Kaohsiung County

Taitung County

Laonang River

South China Sea

Nanzizian River

Pingtung County

🌿🌿 Multiple growers

▲ Mountain

0   12.5   25   50 Miles

0 12.5 25   50 Kilometres

TAIWAN

While the current geopolitical status of Taiwan may be the subject of great international debate, the quality and uniqueness of its teas set this self-governing island state apart from other tea-producing regions of the world. Mainland Chinese settled here in the 14th century, and when Portuguese traders sailed past in 1542, they recorded in their ship's log that they had seen an *Ilha Formosa*, or "Beautiful Island." So, the land became known as Formosa, and teas from here often still bear the ancient name. The Dutch East India Company established a colony here in 1624 and used it as a base for their trade with Japan. The Dutch *Diary of Batavia Town*, written in 1645, records that "Tea trees are also found here in Taiwan…" (the name derived from Tayouan, a coastal sandbar in Tainan, and was originally used to refer to that region, but by the 17th century, was in use to mean the entire island), and the colonisers explored the possibility of cultivating tea but were ousted by the Chinese in 1661 before they could do so. In 1682, the Qing dynasty (1644 to 1912) made Formosa a county of Fujian Province, and in 1885, it became an independent Chinese province. Meanwhile, settlers from Fujian and other regions along China's east coast set up home on the island and, in 1697, also recorded that wild tea trees had been found in the mountains and that the leaves were used to make an infusion. From around 1796, more new immigrants arrived with tea bushes and seeds from the Wuyi Mountains in Fujian, which they planted in the mountains around Taipei.

Large-scale production did not start until the 1860s when British merchant John Dodd and his Chinese assistant Lee Chun-sheng brought more seedlings from Anxi County in Fujian, lent the local people money to help them establish farms, and promised to buy all the fresh leaf they harvested. He sent the tea to Amoy on the mainland for processing and sold the dried teas in Macao for a good price. In 1868, he introduced a professional tea maker to Formosa, built a factory to manufacture oolong teas, and in 1869, sold around 100,000 kilos (more than 220,000 pounds) to merchants in New York. Formosa oolongs began to acquire an international reputation, and this encouraged other foreign traders to establish offices in Taipei. After the Japanese took control in 1895, they developed the island's infrastructure, organised and expanded the tea industry, and promoted Taiwan oolong and green teas at world trade fairs. They also established testing and research facilities, developed some of the cultivars that are still widely grown today, and experimented with the production of black tea. The first of Formosa's black teas were exported to Russia and Turkey in 1908, and in 1926, assamica varietals from India were planted in Nantou County. By 1934, exports of black tea had reached 3.29 million kilos (7.25 million pounds), overtaking green and oolong as the island's main tea export.

In 1945, the Chinese took back control of the island and introduced their method of processing green tea, by panning rather than steaming. Producers started making gunpowder and Chun Mee teas, learning the necessary skills from professionals from the mainland, and these green teas were exported to Algeria, Morocco, other parts of North Africa, and Afghanistan. As Chinese producers took over those markets, the Taiwanese imported Japanese machinery, learned how to make steamed aracha, and sold the teas to Japan for refining and blending.

Between 1965 and 1968, annual exports rose from 1 million kilos (2.2 million pounds) to 7 million kilos (15.4 million pounds) and, in 1973, reached a peak of 12 million kilos (26.5 million pounds), the output of 120 producers.

In the 1980s, Taiwan grew wealthier, and domestic tea consumption began to take precedence over exports. The government supported farmers by removing the tax on tea, allowing producers to sell direct to brokers (most of whom were based in Taipei), or to customers abroad, and instead of large-scale controlled industry, tea farming now became a small-scale, family-run agribusiness. The Taiwanese could now afford quality teas and developed a taste for high-mountain oolongs that have made the island so famous. Since then, the business has boomed. Tea has replaced other crops such as pineapples, bamboo, and coffee, and tea farmers have become relatively wealthy. Most of the teas are still produced for the local market.

Shan Ling Xi Mountain in Nantou County, famous for jade oolongs that have a powerful sweet aroma and a floral character with subtle mineral notes.
Photograph courtesy of Thomas Shu, Ambassador of Taiwan Tea

One or two of Taiwan's teas are made only in particular regions, but the majority of the teas are ball-rolled oolongs that are made throughout the island using the same methods. Some producers also make lightly oxidised Bao Zhongs (Pouchongs), Oriental Beauty oolongs, some green, and an increasing quantity of black teas. In most regions, there are four picking seasons.

1. *Spring flush* (late March in low-altitude areas, April in high elevations) Bao Zhong (Pouchong), oolong, and green teas

2. *Summer flush* (June, July, early August) oolong, Oriental Beauty, green, and black teas

3. *Autumn flush* (mid-August to mid-October) oolong and black teas

4. *Winter flush* (mid-October to late March) oolong and green teas

Bao Zhong (Baozhong, Pouchong) | These are regarded as *Ching Cha* (pure tea). The leaf is 8 to 12 percent oxidised, and although some people sell them as green teas, they are actually very lightly oxidised oolongs. They are grown at 1,000 to 1,300 metres (3,281 to 4,265 feet) where catechin levels in the leaf are lower and L-theanine levels are higher. Processing takes approximately 24 hours and involves the usual steps of oolong manufacture, but sun withering is only 10 to 15 minutes, and oxidation is also shorter to capture the tea's special sweet, floral character. The leaf is then gently rolled to develop the flavour and then dried. The dry leaves have the same large, twisted shape as those of China's dark Wuyi or Phoenix oolongs but, instead of being dark brown, are a rich blue-green and have an intense, sweet, floral aroma reminiscent of sweet peas and orchids. The name *Bao Zhong* means "wrapped kind" because, traditionally, the teas were wrapped for sale in 150-gram lots inside square packages made of two pieces of rectangular paper, closed with a seal and the maker's name.

High Mountain (Gaoshan) Oolongs | Taiwan's Gaoshan teas are grown above 1,000 metres (3,281 feet) in mountain ranges where the air is very clear, and the misty humidity, regular rainfall, and wide difference in temperature between day and night produce teas that are particularly aromatic, rich, sweet, creamy, and very floral. The majority of the high-mountain areas are in Nantou and Chiayi Counties, and the most famous teas come from Alishan, Wushan, Lishan, Shan Lin Xi, and Yushan. The jade oolong teas are harvested twice a year, in spring and winter, and made in the usual way, using shoots of three or four leaves and a bud that are only 10 to 15 percent oxidised. The stalks are not removed at the end of the process. The limited quantity of these excellent-quality teas makes them the most expensive of the island's oolongs.

Jade (Ball-Rolled) Oolongs | Shoots of three or four leaves and a bud, still attached to the stalk, are sun-withered for approximately two hours (in areas where sunshine is unpredictable, some farmers use artificial ultraviolet light in their withering rooms), withered indoors, with intermittent shaking and tumbling, oxidised to approximately 20 to 30 percent, panned, and rolled. Batches of tea are then packed tightly inside cotton cloths and rolled for about 20 minutes. The tea is then taken out, panned briefly, repacked into the cotton cloths, tightened, and rolled again. This unpacking, panning, rebagging, and rolling continues repeatedly until each shoot has been scrunched into a tight, jade-green nugget of tea.

Milk Oolongs | Teas made from the Jin Xuan (Jin Suang) cultivar at altitudes of 200 to 1,525 metres (656 to 5,003 feet) sometimes have a natural creamy, silky character with powerful orchid notes; these are known as "milk" oolongs. To capture this very desirable character, farmers have found that, whereas they normally pluck shoots of four open leaves and a bud, for milk oolongs, they need to pick three fully open leaves and a bud. If they wait for the fourth leaf to open, they have found that they tend to lose the milky, buttery aroma and flavour. During the withering stage of manufacture, the farmer must be careful to make sure that the leaves do not oxidise too little or too much. Because these milky oolongs have become very popular in recent years, some farmers and wholesalers add milk flavouring or essence to give the teas an artificial buttery, milky character that is not as subtle and special as the flavour of the real milk oolongs.

Muzha Tie Guan Yin | This tea is named after the Muzha area in the Wenshan District of Taipei where it is produced. Tie Guan Yin tea plants were brought into Taiwan in large numbers in the early part of the 20th century by the Muzha Tealeaves Group. Founded by the Zhang family in the 1920s, two of the brothers went to Anxi County in Fujian to bring the varietal back home. The new tea bushes were planted on a hill in Muzha, and the Zhang family started to make Tie Guan Yin balled oolongs. Today, the Muzha tea farms cover more than 110 hectares and more than 60,000 kilos (132,277 pounds) of Tie Guan Yin are made each year. The shoots are harvested four or five times a year, and the production method, which takes approximately 20 hours, is a little different from that used to make other Taiwan balled oolongs. The 40 percent level of oxidation is higher than the usual 20 to 30 percent, and the tea goes through more stages of bagging and rolling, hand rolling, and gentle roasting than other balled oolongs. The wet leaves have a very wrinkled surface, and the aroma and flavour profile is quite different from that of Tie Guan Yins from Anxi County. The lightly roasted teas are refined and smooth but crisp, with a warm, sweet fruitiness and floral notes; the medium-roasted teas have a smooth, honeyed character with a toasty nuttiness and suggestions of ripe melon; the more heavily roasted and aged teas are rich, mellow, and woody, with hints of molasses, dried figs, prunes, honey, and caramel, and a lingering sweet aftertaste.

Baked (Amber) and Aged Oolongs | The dark colour of baked balled oolongs is not because of a heavy level of oxidation (most are only 20 to 30 percent oxidised), but because of the post-manufacture baking or roasting that is carried out over charcoal or, more often today, by electricity. This slow process reduces the level of caffeine and gives the teas a toasty, caramelised character. The baking is sometimes carried out at the tea factory, or in ovens in merchants' stores where the teas are often baked to order, or in small baking ovens that are available for home or office use. Sometimes, the teas are stored for two or three years and baked again, then stored for several years to mature. The final character of the brewed tea depends on the varietal or cultivar used to make the oolong, the level of roasting, and how well the roasting has been carried out. For example, roasted oolongs made from the Jin Xuan cultivar can be creamy and smooth with a complex, spicy, and honeyed toastiness in the lower notes , while medium-roasted Dong Ding oolongs made from the Qing Xin cultivar retain their powerful floral notes but develop a rich creaminess with hints of dried fruits, toasted nuts, honey, and roasted barley.

Oriental Beauty | This can only be made each year if little leafhoppers (*Jacobiasca formosana*, known as jassids or thrips) infest the tea bushes and nibble the leaves while they are still growing. As the leaf cells are broken, oxidation starts; at the same time, the bushes manufacture enzymes (monoterpene diol and hotrienol) to fend off the insects. The teas made after the infestation are honey-sweet and peachy.

The tea was first made one summer, in the early 19th century when the tea farmers in Beipu, Hsinchu County, noticed that their crop had been attacked by jassids, thought the crop was ruined, and so decided not to pluck the new shoots. One farmer, however, made his tea as usual, and when he took it to market, a local merchant found it so good that he paid double the normal price. Because the farmer bragged about this to his neighbours, they named the tea Peng Feng Cha or Phong-fûng Chhà, or Bragger's Tea. The tea is produced in low-lying areas where the insects visit each summer, and very small shoots of two leaves and a bud are picked in June or July after the insect attack. Only 40 to 50 percent of the crop is harvested, so very small quantities are available each year. The shoots are sun-withered, shaken, tumbled, and withered indoors until 60 to 65 percent oxidised, and then they are panned, rolled very gently to avoid crushing and breaking the fragile leaf, and dried. The finished tea is made up of delicate whole shoots with plum-brown leaves and silvery buds. Other names are Dongfang Meiren, White Tip Oolong, Champagne Oolong, Imperial Oolong, Eastern Beauty, Bai Hao Oolong, Pekoe Oolong, and Wu Se Cha (Five Colour Tea) for the five different colours (brown, yellow, red, green, and silver) that are evident in the dry leaf.

Taitung Oolong | It took several years of research and development to perfect this highly oxidised balled oolong, known as Orange Pearl and nicknamed Cognac Formosa Oolong. It is produced on the island's Pacific Coast, and the process involves extensive withering, 70 to 80 percent oxidation, and the usual panning, wrapping, rolling, and drying to create small, neat, dark brown nuggets flecked with bronze and amber. It is made from the Jin Xuan or the Chin Shin cultivar, and the liquor has an intensely fruity character with powerful, sweet, caramelised orange notes.

Brandy Oolong and Formosa Bonita | Made from the Ruby 18, Hong Yun 21, Chin Shin, and Jin Xuan cultivars, these are a new category of dark Taiwanese oolongs. Developed over decades, the Ruby 18 cultivar was at first called Ching Sing ES18 but is now commonly referred to by its much more attractive and memorable name Ruby 18. The dark oolongs made from it are 80 to 90 percent oxidised and give brandy-coloured infusions that are sweet, rich, honeyed, and peachy, sometimes malty, with hints of toasted almonds and a lingering toasty note typical of dark oolongs.

Taiwan Black Teas | Black tea production in Taiwan dates back to the first decade of the 20th century when the first black varieties were made in Nantou County using assamica plants brought in from India. Black tea became an important export, and in the 1970s, the government of Nantou County promoted their black teas as Sun Moon Lake Black, which became very famous, and the tea gardens

TOP: Plucking leaf to make Oriental Beauty in Hsinchu County. MIDDLE: Rolling large cotton bags of lightly oxidised tea shoots for jade oolongs. The tea is repeatedly panned, bagged, and rolled until each shoot has been twisted and tightened into a neat little nugget. BOTTOM: During the manufacture of Formosa Bonita dark oolong, the leaves are left to oxidise up to 80 or 90 percent. Photographs courtesy of Thomas Shu, Ambassador of Taiwan Tea

in Ruisui Village in Hualien County focused almost entirely on the manufacture of black teas. Today, the most important areas for black tea manufacture are Ruisui, Puli in Nantou County, and Taitung County. Some producers use the original assamica bushes, but most use the new Ruby 18 and Hon Yun 21 cultivars to make small quantities of deliciously spicy, smooth, rich black teas. Another new small-leafed cultivar, Number 19 (known as Blue Heart), has been developed and patented by local tea farmer Mr. Kang and recognised by the Taiwan Tea Research and Extension Station. It gives black teas with a malty, sweet, smooth profile with a suggestion of ripe peaches.

Honey Black | These teas are made in Hualien on the Pacific Coast after little leafhoppers have nibbled the leaves while they are still growing on the plant (in the same way that they do for Oriental Beauty oolong). These full-bodied black teas have a natural fruity sweetness with hints of honey, cinnamon, and malt.

TAIWANESE VARIETALS AND CULTIVARS

As well as working to improve cultivation, processing, technology, and education, Taiwan's Tea Research and Extension Station (TRES) has developed many new cultivars for the production of oolong and black teas using the different varietals and cultivars introduced to the island over the last 300 years. Those include Shan Cha wild trees, plants from Fujian Province introduced by immigrants in the 18th century, the Chin Sing cultivar from China introduced between 1855 and 1875, and manipuri assamica and jaipuri assamica plants introduced by the Japanese in the 1920s for the manufacture of black teas. Taiwan's teas are often sold by the name of the cultivar they are made from.

Chin Sing (Qing Xin, Chin-hsin, Chin Cing, Luanze) | This is the most widely used cultivar in Taiwan and is particularly popular for the production of high-mountain oolongs and Bao Zhongs that develop complex sweet flavours and aromas during

Eco-farming in Taiwan is gaining momentum and tea farmers are turning more and more towards organic farming methods. Photograph courtesy of Thomas Shu, Ambassador of Taiwan Tea

slow growth at high altitudes. It has low resistance to insect attack but is popular for the quality teas it produces.

Chin Sing Dahpan (Qing Xin Dah Pan, Chin-hsin Dah Pan)
Closely related to Chin Sing, this cultivar is believed to have been brought from Fujian. It is the most popular one for making Oriental Beauty and is also used for Bao Zhongs and high-mountain oolongs. The best of its teas are fragrant, honey-sweet, and peachy.

Jin Xuan (Jin Suang, Jin Shuen) | Developed in the 1970s and released for planting in 1981, Jin Suang (Golden Day Lily) is very popular for buttery, creamy Gaoshan oolongs. Naturally milky, unflavoured "milk" oolongs are made from this cultivar. (Some producers actually enhance the tea's natural milky character by adding flavouring to the teas.) The cultivar grows well at lower elevations, yields faster (by 20 percent or more) than other types, and has good resistance to disease.

Si Ji Chun | Also called "Four Seasons Like Spring" or "Evergreen," this cultivar is named for its ability to flush five or six times a year. This was not developed by TRES but was found by chance in northern Taiwan in 1981 and is thought to be a natural hybrid of two Chin Sing varietals (Chin Sing and Chin Sing Dahpan). It thrives at mid-elevation in Nantou County and gives oolongs and Bao Zhongs an intensely fruity character.

Tsui Yu (Cui Yu, Tzuiyu, Tai Cha No 13) | Developed by TRES in the 1980s, Tsui Yu grows well at lower altitudes and is popular for jade oolongs, Oriental Beauty, and Bao Zhongs. It yields well and gives delicate floral aromas.

Ruby 18 | Released for planting in 1999, this popular new "Red Jade" cultivar took 48 years to develop. It is a cross between Taiwan's native wild assamica trees and the assamica bushes imported by the Japanese. Ruby 18 is cultivated in Yuchi

Township near Sun Moon Lake where Taiwan's black teas were first grown in the early 20th century from plants imported by the Japanese in 1925. It gives rich, malty oolongs and assertive, sweet, fruity, and aromatic black teas, with hints of spice and liquorice.

Hon Yun 21 (Red Rhythm) | This is a new hybrid, crossbred from Keemun and an assamica from Kyang in Nepal. It makes black teas that are low in tannin, smooth, and honey-sweet, with a fruity cherry tang.

Tie Guan Yin | Introduced from China to the north of Taiwan in 1875, this is still only grown in the Muzha region near Taipei to make delicate Tie Guan Yin oolongs. The bushes are now quite old and are likely to gradually be replaced by new higher-yielding cultivars that give more fragrant, floral jade oolongs.

Shan Cha (Mountain Tea) | Taiwan's wild tea trees, which appear to be closely related to the assamica, grow in misty, shady forests in the south, east, and central areas of the country, at elevations between 650 and 1,500 metres (2,133 and 4,921 feet). These wild trees are now protected as "national treasures" in four areas and were used to develop the Ruby 18 cultivar. Shan Cha black teas are subtle, sweet, floral, and fruity.

The Ruby 18 tea cultivar, which took 48 years to develop before being released to farmers in 1999. Photograph courtesy of Thomas Shu, Ambassador of Taiwan Tea

Taiwan is a land of high mountains with peaks that climb to altitudes of nearly 4,000 metres (13,000 feet). Tea grows on the high slopes and in the foothills and plains of the Chung-yang Range that runs 270 kilometres (170 miles) from Taipei in the north to the Hengchun Peninsula in the south. The subtropical climate in the north and the warmer tropical conditions in the south, the cool misty mornings, long sunny days, and plentiful rainfall in the warmer months are ideal for tea cultivation. The tea regions are divided into five major districts. Northern Taiwan (Taipei City, New Taipei City, and Yilan County), Tao-Chu-Miao (Taoyuan, Hsinchu, and Miaoli counties), Mid and Southern Taiwan (Nantou, Yunlin, Chaiyi, Tainan, Kaohsiung, Pingtung counties), Pacific Ocean Coast (Hualien and Taitung counties), and the High Mountain Tea District (Central Mountain Range tea areas over 1,000 metres [3,281 feet] in Hsuehshan, Lishan, San Lin Si, and Alishan).

NORTHERN TAIWAN DISTRICT | *New Taipei City, Taipei City, and Yilan County*

This region is famous for its Bao Zhong (Pouchong), amber oolongs, and green teas. New Taipei City (previously Taipei County) is the oldest of Taiwan's tea areas, and the Wenshan region, which includes Shiding, Wulai, Hshintien, and Pinglin, is the home of beautiful, dark blue-green Bao Zhong teas. Pinglin, considered the tea capital of Wenshan, has 106 tea farms, and approximately 90 percent of the township's residents work in the tea industry. Farmers in Sansia Township are Taiwan's only manufacturers of Long Jing–type green teas in the spring, and some growers also manufacture Oriental Beauty in June or July. Most of the north-eastern area of Yilan County is relatively low-lying, but the high misty slopes of La La Shan (Beautiful Mountain), on the border with Taoyuan County, produce excellent teas, the best of which are made in the spring before the summer rains begin.

TAO-CHU-MIAO DISTRICT | *Taoyuan, Hsinchu, and Miaoli counties*

Most of the gardens in Hsinchu County are located in the foothills of the Xueshan and Dabajian Mountains, and Beipu Township is famous as the birthplace of Oriental Beauty oolongs. This district still focuses on the production of those delicious teas and also makes black and green teas. *Taoyuan* means "peach garden," named for the many peach trees that grow there, and the region's teas grow prolifically on flatter, lower-lying plateaux surrounded by high mountain peaks. The Taiwan Tea Research and Extension Station (TRES) is located here and carries out research into tea breeding, cultivation, mechanisation, management, and manufacturing. The region is home to the Hakka people who migrated to Taiwan from China during the 18th century. Traditional Hakka tea, Lei Cha, is prepared by pounding together green or oolong tea, roasted peanuts, and sesame seeds, adding a little hot water and mixing all the ingredients to a paste, then adding more hot water to make a kind of soup.

MID AND SOUTHERN TAIWAN DISTRICT | *Nantou, Yunlin, Chiayi, Tainan, Kaohsiung, and Pingtung counties*

This district is famous for its jade oolongs and, in particular, for Tung Ting (Dong Ding) oolongs from Lu Gu (Deer Valley) in Nantou County. These classic jade oolongs used to be the most popular of Taiwan's high-mountain jade oolongs. They fell from favour for a while but are now becoming very popular again. They are 20 to 25 percent oxidised and are roasted for 40 minutes at the end of the manufacturing process. Dong Ding Mountain (Frozen Peak) is almost constantly hidden in a blanket of foggy mist and produces teas that have a very sweet and flowery flavour. There is a tea culture museum in Lu Gu, and farmers associations organise regular tea competitions here. In Yuchi Township, in the centre of Nantou County, lies Sun Moon Lake (Ri Yue Tan), where black teas have been made since

1925 when the Japanese planted assamica bushes here. In the south of Nantou, growers on Yu Shan (Jade Mountain) produce low-grown oolongs from the thick, juicy leaves of the plants that grow here. Mingjian Township is Taiwan's most mechanised and automated tea region, and although teas from here are produced in large quantities, the quality is good.

The west coast of Yunlin is mostly low-lying, and the tea is machine-harvested six times a year, from early spring through to November. Most of Kaohsiung tea is made in the Namasia (previously San Ming) District, which is nestled in the Nan Tzu Hsien River Valley. The high slopes of Namasia's mountains are misty and cool, and the humid air and marked drop in temperature from day to night produce high-quality teas, the best of which are made in spring and winter.

Pingtung County is a low-lying region close to the sea on the southern tip of the island. And the local *gangkou (kungko)* ("harbour" or "sea") teas are made from local bushes that were introduced here from China's Fujian Province and, over time, developed thick leaves as they adapted to the local soil, weather conditions, and salty sea air. These teas have strong and sometimes slightly astringent liquors.

PACIFIC OCEAN COAST | *Hualien and Taitung counties*

This region produces Ruby 18 black, Honey Black (made from leaves that have been bitten by leafhoppers), greens, pomelo-scented oolongs, and Formosa Bonita oolongs. The most famous of the high-plateau east-coast region in Taitung is the Luye Terrace area, previously called Luliao, where tea grows on 400 hectares of steep hillsides. The tea gardens were developed in the 1960s in the Gaotai District around Longtian and Yongan villages, and the Taitung branch of the Taiwan Tea Research and Extension Station was also set up here. So that visitors can take full advantage of the beautiful scenery, the 94-hectare Luye Tourist Tea Plantation is run as a "recreational" farm where tourists may stay overnight, learn about tea cultivation and processing, and buy the local teas from the nearby shops. As a result of the success of tea-growing in the region, many farmers in Taifeng have switched from the cultivation of daylilies to tea.

In Hualien County, the Wuhe Terrace area was once a major coffee-growing district but, in the 1970s, was developed for tea cultivation. To honour Dr. Qian Tianhe, whose work improved the quality of the tea here, Wuhe teas are referred to as "Tianhe Tea." Around 30 or 40 families grow black tea here today and make excellent-quality, intensely aromatic teas that are prized by connoisseurs around the world. A few years ago, the farmers found that the leaves of their tea bushes were being nibbled by little leafhoppers, as happens in Beipu Township where Oriental Beauty was first made, and when they processed their usual black teas, they found that it had a special peachy-honey flavour. After experimenting with the processing, their Honey-Touched or Honey Peach Black Tea (Mi Xiang Hong Cha) is now very popular in speciality tea markets.

HIGH MOUNTAIN TEA DISTRICT | *Gaoshan areas in the Central Mountain Range, including Hsuehshan (Xueshan), Lishan, Shan Lin Si, and Alishan*

Famous for their exquisite jade oolongs, these areas now also produce Formosa Bonita. Prize-winning Shan Lin Si oolongs are produced in the Long Feng canyon of Shan Lin Si Mountain, Nantou County. Teas in Lishan (Pear Mountain), Taichung County, are cultivated at altitudes of between 1,700 and 2,650 metres (5,577 to 8,694 feet), where winter snow and chilly spring days with sunny mornings and misty afternoons create ideal conditions. Lishan oolongs are now so acclaimed around the world that more and more of the mountain areas are being developed for tea cultivation. The Tsuei Luan region, first planted in 1990 on 3 hectares, now has 130 hectares under tea. At the highest elevations, the tea is harvested twice a year, in spring and winter; at lower altitudes, the tea is picked three times each year. Alishan climbs to 2,190 metres (7,185 feet) in the eastern part of Chiayi County and is famous for its floral, creamy oolongs grown in the high, misty conditions where longer winters and wide differences between daytime and night-time temperatures mean slower growth and more complex flavours. Farmers value both Chin Sing and Jin Suang cultivars to produce their prize-winning oolongs.

TOP: Neat little buds gathered from bushes at a Taiwanese eco-farm. MIDDLE: Withering leaves for the manufacture of Oriental Beauty, Taiwan's sweet and fruity dark oolong that is also marketed as White Tip Oolong or Champagne Oolong. BOTTOM: Delivering fresh leaf for the manufacture of Oriental Beauty.
Photograph courtesy of Thomas Shu, Ambassador of Taiwan Tea

Country, State, or Province
Taiwan

Number of Gardens
12,000 to 15,000 family farms, some very small, some large estates

Main Districts or Gardens
Chiayi County, Hualien County, Hsinchu County, Kaohsiung County, Miaoli County, Nantou County, Pingtung County, Taichung County, Taitung (Taidong) County, New Taipei City (previously Taipei County), Taipei City, Taoyuan County, Yilan County, Yunlin County

Area Under Tea
Taiwan: 11,906 hectares

Chiayi County:
1,819 hectares

Hualien County:
139 hectares

Hsinchu County:
361 hectares

Kaohsiung County:
165 hectares

Miaoli County:
281 hectares

Nantou County:
6,510 hectares

Pingtung County:
19 hectares

Taichung County:
412 hectares

Taitung (Taidong) County:
213 hectares

New Taipei City (previously Taipei County):
756 hectares

Taipei City: 131 hectares

Taoyuan County:
565 hectares

Yilan County:
143 hectares

Yunlin County:
387 hectares

Average Annual Production (Kilograms)
Taiwan: 15.2 million

Chiayi County: 2.1 million

Hualien County: 103,000

Hsinchu County: 381,000

Kaohsiung County:
178,000

Miaoli County: 344,000

Nantou County:
10.127 million

Pingtung County: 16,000

Taichung County: 340,000

Taitung (Taidong)
County: 148,000

New Taipei City (previously Taipei County): 413,000

Taipei City: 83,000

Taoyuan County: 486,000

Yilan County: 102,000

Yunlin County: 372,000

Terrain
Chiayi County: Bordered by mountains on one side and sea on the other; an area of lakes, woodland, waterfalls, plains, hills and seascapes.

Hualien County: The Pacific Ocean lies to the east, and the central mountains to the west; tea fields stretch for miles over vast Wuhe Terrace area, surrounded by lakes, forests, and mountain peaks.

Hsinchu County: Coastal region with Taiwan Straits to the west and the Xueshan and Dabajian Mountains to the east; a mix of tablelands and mountains.

Kaohsiung County: Very unspoilt mountainous region with views of Yu Shan; highest peak is Mount Xinwangling at 2,481 metres (8,140 feet)

Miaoli County: Facing the Taiwan straits, this region has very little flat land and the hills run from the northwest coast to the foothills of the Hsuehshan mountains

Nantou County: Landlocked mountainous, agricultural region with recreational farms; 41 mountains over 3,000 metres (9843 feet) high; a landscape of steep slopes, lakes, ponds and rivers

Pingtung County: Long, narrow area of fertile farmland, plains, and rivers bordered by coast to the west and mountains to the north and east

Taichung County: Rocky cliffs of Lishan Mountain, the most famous peak here; Lishan sits at the heart of central Taiwan; highlands, steep cliffs, deep canyons, rivers, and forests.

Taitung (Taidong) County: Relatively isolated and under-developed low-lying region on south-east coast.

New Taipei City (previously Taipei County) & Taipei City: Volcanic, steep, mountainous area; hills are covered with terraced rows of tea that grows in soil that is rich with oganic matter; close to the ocean but the Shimen hills protect the plants from salty sea air.

Taoyuan County: Low alluvial plains, hills and mountains, interspersed with plateaus; thousands of square miles of arable land; lakes, nature reserves, caves, and mountain forests on the higher ground

Yilan County: Virgin forest, ancient cypress trees, wildlife sanctuaries, and tea gardens on very steep misty slopes of La La Mountain

Yunlin County: Flatlands of the Chianin Plain with the Taiwan Straits to the west and the foothills of Ali Shan to the east

Altitude
Chiayi County: 1,600 metres

Hualien County: 200 metres

Hsinchu County: 450 metres

Kaohsiung County: 800 to 1,200 metres

Miaoli County: 450 metres

Nantou County: 300 to 2200 metres

Pingtung County: 100 metres

Taichung County: 1,700 to 2,600 metres

Taitung (Taidong) County: 400 metres

New Taipei City (previously Taipei County) & Taipei City: 200 to 800 metres

Taoyuan County: Up to 1,300 metres

Yilan County: 102,000 metres

Yunlin County: 300 metres

Production Period
Taiwan: Late March to November

Best Time to Visit
March, April, September, October

Main Varietals/ Cultivars
Chiayi County: Jin Xuan, Si Ji Chun (Four Seasons)

Hualien County: Shan Cha, Jin Xuan, Qing Xin, Si Ji Chun, Cui Yu

Hsinchu County: Jin Xuan, Qing Xin Da Pan

Kaohsiung County: Shan Cha, Jin Xuan

Miaoli County: Qing Xin Da Pan, Qing Xin, Qing Xin Da Mao

Nantou County: Qing Xin, Jin Xuan, Cui Yu, Si Ji Chun, Zhu Shan, Shan Cha, Asamudaye

Pingtung County: Original Wuyi varietal imported in 1790s (Pingtung used to be known as Taiwan Tea Gene Bank.); Jin Suang

Taichung County: Qing Xin, Shui Xian

Taitung (Taidong) County: Jin Xuan, Cui Yu

New Taipei City (previously Taipei County) & Taipei City: Qing Xin, Jin Xuan, Cui Yu, Si-ji Chun, Damanzhong

Taoyuan County: Si Ji Chun, Ruby 18 (Hong Yu)

Yilan County: Qing Xin

Yunlin County: Jin Xuan, Si Ji Chun

Types of Tea Made
Chiayi County: High-mountain oolongs, Ali Shan oolong

Hualien County: Black

Hsinchu County: Oriental Beauty, oolongs

Kaohsiung County: Oolong, black

Miaoli County: Oriental Beauty

Nantou County: High-mountain oolong, Dong Ding oolong, Jin Xuan oolong, Cui Yu oolong, Qing Xin oolong, Four Seasons Spring oolong, Shan Lin Xi oolong, black

Pingtung County: Kang-Ko Cha (Gangkou, Kingko) jade oolongs; farmers now also making baked and aged oolongs

Taichung County: High-Mountain Li Shan and Da Yu Ling oolongs, black

Taitung (Taidong) County: Jade oolongs, Oriental Beauty

New Taipei City (previously Taipei County) & Taipei City: Bao Zhong, Tie Guan Yin oolong, Baked Tie Guan Yin oolong, Bi Luo Chun–type green, Long Jing–type green

Taoyuan County: Bao Zhong, oolongs, Ruby Brandy oolong, green, black

Yilan County: Oolongs from La La Mountain

Yunlin County: Ball-rolled oolongs

Predominant Flavours; Tasting Notes
Chiayi County: OOLONG: *Ali Shan*—floral complex, and sweet, reminiscent of orchids and lilies

Hualien County: BLACK: *Wuhe*—strong, roasty, sweet, and malty, with sometimes musky, bitter-sweet, and citrus notes and hints of dark chocolate *Honey Peach*—smooth, silky, honeyed, and peachy

Hsinchu County: OOLONG: *Oriental Beauty*—velvet smooth, honey sweet, with summer fruits such as apricot and nectarine, and a flowery, slightly mineral finish

Kaohsiung County: OOLONG: *Oriental Beauty*—fragrant, sweet, floral BLACK: *Namasia Pa Kung Fu*—multi-layered, rich

Miaoli County: OOLONG: *Oriental Beauty*—reminiscent of ripe fruits and flowers in full bloom, richly honeyed, with hints of pine

Nantou County: OOLONG: *Dong Ding*—sweet, fruity, and nutty, with suggestions of caramel and chestnuts

Shan Ling Xi—smooth and very floral SUN BLACK: *Moon Lake*—complex, floral, woodsy, spicy, with hints of oranges

Pingtung County: OOLONG: *Gangkou*—strong, slightly bitter, biscuity with nuances of the sea

Taichung County: OOLONG: *Li Shan*—light, floral, fresh, with hints of melon, pears, lemons, and hazelnuts *Da Yu Ling*—strong, floral, fragrant, and sweet BLACK: *Shan Cha*—smooth, slightly tart, with peachy notes.

Taitung (Taidong) County: OOLONG: *Jade*—fragrant, fruity, reminiscent of pear, honey, apricot, and peach *Oriental Beauty*—smooth, sweet, honeyed, fresh, and crisp

New Taipei City (previously Taipei County) & Taipei City: OOLONG: *Bao Zhong*—creamy, soft, floral *Tie Guan Yin*—complex, smooth, fruity *Baked Tie Guan Yin*—mellow, spicy, toasty, hints of dried apricots, cinnamon, and candied fruits GREEN: *Bi Luo Chun-type*—delicate, velvet smooth, nutty, with hints of young bamboo shoots *Long Jing-type*—smooth, sweet, vegetal, with hints of melon and fresh-mown grass

Taoyuan County: OOLONG: *Brandy*—a rich and malty tea BLACK: *Ruby 18*—strong, with spicy notes and hints of tropical fruits, cinnamon, wintergreen, and camphor

Yilan County: OOLONG: *La La Shan*—rich, aromatic, and foral, reminiscent of sweet pea blossoms

Yunlin County: OOLONG: floral, delicate and fruity

INDIA

On the 31st of December 1600, Queen Elizabeth I awarded a Royal Charter to a group of London merchants, granting them a monopoly on the trading of all goods from the Orient. The company struggled initially in the spice trade and engaged in frequent hostilities in the Indian Ocean with the Portuguese and the Dutch. Then, with the encouragement of James I and the patronage of the Mughal emperor Mirza Nur-ud-din Beig Mohammad Khan Salim (known by his imperial name Jahangir), the company made India its trading base, and by 1690, factories had been built at strategic points around the Indian coastline, including Surat, Madras, Bombay, and Calcutta. The most important goods traded were cotton, silk, indigo dye, saltpeter, and tea. The Honourable East India Company's power steadily increased until, by the 1760s, it had become not simply a powerful association of traders, but also the representative of the British Crown in India.

The amount of tea being consumed throughout Britain by the middle of the 18th century had grown rapidly, and the merchants in London were wholly dependent for their supplies on China, the only large commercial producer at that time. But relations between the two countries had become strained due to the high price of tea and the fact that the Chinese had little use for any British goods. The only product purchased in exchange by the Chinese was the opium grown in Assam by the East India Company and dispatched to China via a devious and obscure system of brokers and shipping agents in the belief that the Chinese emperor would perhaps never find out that it was British grown. Disputes over the trade eventually led to the outbreak of the first Opium War in March 1839.

Pickers at Khongea Tea Estate in Assam, owned by the Prakash family who also own Glenburn Tea Estate in Darjeeling. Photograph courtesy of the Prakash family from Khongea Tea Estate

In 1764, mindful of the growing difficulties, the company's court of directors began to explore the possibility of growing tea somewhere outside China, preferably on British territory. Ten years later, in 1774, a consignment of tea seeds was sent to Calcutta where the new governor-general, Lord Warren Hastings, arranged for some to be planted at the botanic garden, sending others on to Bhutan for experimental cultivation there. At the same time, Sir Joseph Banks, director of the Royal Botanical Gardens at Kew in England, was asked to prepare a report on the possibility of cultivating new crops, including tea, in the colonies. Banks clearly understood the relevance of tea to British life and described it as "an article of the greatest national importance." He recommended the north-east of India as a suitable area for its cultivation and advised that "the Mountains of Bartan afford in a short distance all the climates that are found in the cooler parts of the Empire of China and consequently every variety necessary for the production of the Green Teas." Banks even suggested that Chinese labour should be imported into India for the purpose, saying, "the inhabitants of Canton are now in the habit of Shipping themselves on board our India-men whenever hands are wanted." He further suggested that favourable terms should be offered to encourage tea growers from Canton and Hunan to emigrate to India and set up in business there.

In 1823, Robert Bruce, a trader and explorer from Scotland, visited Upper Assam to meet Bessa Gaum, chief of the Singhpo people, because he had heard that tea was grown there and that the leaves were eaten as a vegetable with garlic and infused in hot water to make a drink. Sadly, Bruce died the following year. In 1832, Lieutenant Andrew Charlton of the Assam Light Infantry sent news to Calcutta that he had come across the tea plant growing wild in Assam. He wrote, "The tea tree grows in the vicinity of Saddiya, most remote of the British possessions towards the east, in Assam, and adjacent to the Burmah territory; some of the natives of Suddiya are in the habit of drinking an infusion of the dried leaves, but they do not prepare them in any particular manner. Although the leaves are devoid of any fragrance, in their green state, they acquire the smell and taste of Chinese tea when dried. The tree bears a flower very like that of the wild rose, but much smaller." In 1833, Robert Bruce's brother Charles Alexander Bruce, who had retired from the Royal Navy and taken up employment with the East India Company in Assam, brought the native tea plant to the notice of the authorities and explained how the local Khamti people plucked the leaves, tore them into small pieces, removed any fibres, boiled the leaf, and finally, squeezed the wet mass into a ball that was left to dry in the sun and stored for later use.

Despite these sightings of the plant and evidence of local tea consumption, when samples of the Assam plant were sent for examination by experts, they were declared to be "camellias" and not the true tea plant at all. But the search now began in earnest for a suitable region in which to grow British tea, and in 1834, Lord William Henry Cavendish Bentinck, governor-general of India (1828 to 1835), set up a tea committee that was tasked with investigating the possibilities of cultivating and manufacturing tea in India. Later that year, a member of the committee, G. J. Gordon, was sent to China to obtain a supply of young plants and seeds and to recruit Chinese workers who knew how to cultivate the plant and process the leaf. In early 1835, some 80,000 tea seeds from China arrived at Calcutta Botanic Garden where they were propagated, and towards the end of 1835, 20,000 seedlings were sent for trials in Assam, 20,000 to Kumaon in the North-West Province, and 2,000 to Madras. Of the 20,000 sent to Assam, only 8,000 survived the journey and those struggled badly in the intense heat of the Assamese jungle.

By this time, a visit to Assam by members of the committee had provided enough evidence to convince the botanists that the tea bushes found there were indeed true tea plants. But the government team still insisted that only the imported Chinese variety was suitable for commercial cultivation. The experimental Chinese varietals did indeed thrive on the higher slopes of Kumaon, but only 500 plants survived the heat and humidity of low-lying Assam. Meanwhile, Charles Bruce was appointed Superintendent of Tea Culture and was charged with overseeing the new nurseries. Bruce had also discovered remote tracts of tea bushes growing wild in the forests of Sadiya in Upper Assam, and with the first Chinese tea makers to arrive in the region, he spent days travelling through dense jungle from one patch of tea to another to collect the fresh leaf and transport it back to the new experimental gardens for processing. He kept detailed notes of everything he learned from the Chinese about propagation, cultivation at different altitudes, when and how to pluck the fresh shoots, the number of workers required to complete the various tasks, and how to manufacture both green and black tea. He wrote at the end of his report to the committee in June 1839, "In looking forward to the unbounded benefit the discovery of this plant will produce to England, to India, to Millions, I cannot but thank God for so great a blessing to our country."

In November 1838, 12 chests of black tea, made from the wild Assam tea plants that had been steadfastly rejected by the tea committee, arrived in London. The tea from four of those chests was distributed to East India Company directors and other interested persons, while eight were put up for sale in the London auction on the 10th of January 1839, valued by the experts at a price of between 1 shilling and 10 pence (equivalent to 9 pence today) and 2 shillings (equivalent to 10 pence today). In fact, the entire lot went to a Captain Pidding, proprietor of "Howqua" blend, at extraordinary prices of between 20 and 34 shillings per pound (around £568 to £965 per pound in today's values). Having proved that tea could be successfully grown in India, private enterprise took over from government experimentation, and the industry in Assam grew rapidly through the 1830s and '40s. The 1840s saw expansion into Chittagong and Sylhet (both today situated in Bangladesh), and in the mid-1850s, new gardens were established in Kangra in the north, around the small hill-town of Darjeeling in the north-east, and in Travancore and the Nilgiri Hills in the south-west.

Country, State, or Province
India

Number of Gardens
More than 50,558 estates, plus at least 150,000 smallholders

Main Districts or Gardens
In the north: Arunachal Pradesh, Assam, Bihar, Darjeeling, Dooars and Terai, Kangra, Kumaon (in Uttarakhand), Manipur, Meghalaya, Mizoram, Nagaland, Sikkim, and Tripura;

In the south-west: the Nilgiri Hills in Kerala and Tamil Nadu (including the smaller regions of Anamallais, Karnataka, Munnar, Travancore, and Wayanad)

Area Under Tea
Approximately 565,000 hectares

Average Annual Production (Kilograms)
1.25 billion

LEFT: Risheehat Tea Estate, Darjeeling. OPPOSITE PAGE, TOP: Assamica two leaves and a bud. Photographs by John O'Hagan; ©Hoffman Media OPPOSITE PAGE, BOTTOM: Jacaranda trees on a tea estate in the Nilgiri Hills, Southern India. Photograph by Indi Khanna; © Tea 'n' Teas

ASIA

Indus River

Himachal
Pradesh

Uttarakhand

New Delhi ★

Ganges River

Tropic of Cancer

INDIA

Sikkim

DOOARS

Arunachal Pradesh

TERAI

Bihar

Brahmaputra River

Assam

Nagaland

Meghalaya

Manipur

Tripura

West
Bengal

Mizoram

Bay of
Bengal

Wainganga River

Godavari River

Krishna River

Arabian
Sea

WESTERN GHATS

Karnataka

THE NIGRILIS

Tamil
Nadu

Kerala

ANAMALLAIS

Travancore

INDIAN
OCEAN

Tea grower

Multiple growers

N
W   E
S

0   125   250   500 Miles

0   125   250   500 Kilometres

The winding roads and steep slopes of the organic Risheehat
Tea Estate in Darjeeling. Photograph by John O'Hagan; © Hoffman Media

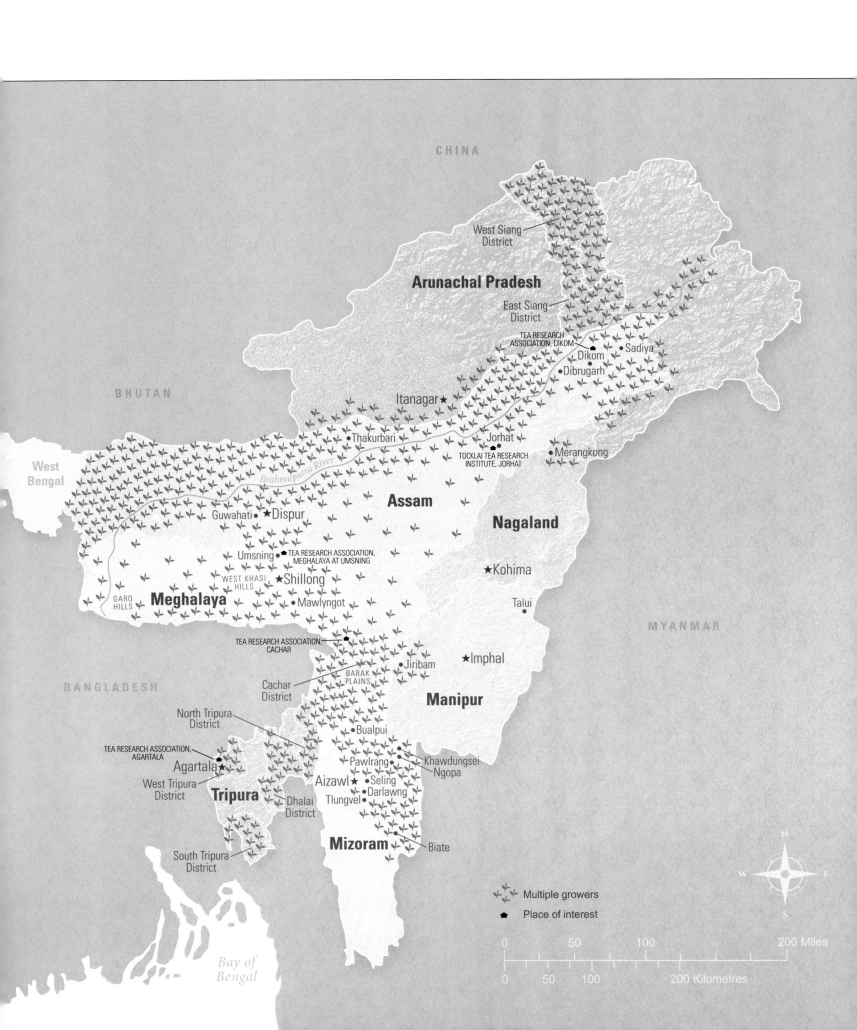

CHINA

West Siang
District

Arunachal Pradesh

East Siang
District

TEA RESEARCH
ASSOCIATION, DIKOM
• Dikom   • Sadiya
• Dibrugarh

Itanagar ★

BHUTAN

• Thakurbari

Jorhat
• Merangkong

Brahmaputra River

TOCKLAI TEA RESEARCH
INSTITUTE, JORHAT

West
Bengal

Assam

Nagaland

Guwahati • ★ Dispur

Umsning • ■ TEA RESEARCH ASSOCIATION,
MEGHALAYA AT UMSNING

★ Kohima

WEST KHASI
HILLS   ★ Shillong

GARO
HILLS   Meghalaya   • Mawlyngot

Talui •

MYANMAR

TEA RESEARCH ASSOCIATION,
CACHAR

★ Imphal

BANGLADESH

BARAK
PLAINS

• Jiribam

Cachar
District

Manipur

North Tripura
District

• Bualpui

TEA RESEARCH ASSOCIATION,
AGARTALA
Agartala ★

Pawlrang •   • Khawdungsei
            Ngopa

West Tripura
District

Aizawl ★   • Seling

Tripura   • Dhalai
District

Tlungvel •   • Darlawng

South Tripura
District

Mizoram   • Biate

N

W ✦ E

S

🌿🌿 Multiple growers

⬟ Place of interest

Bay of
Bengal

0   50   100   200 Miles

0   50   100   200 Kilometres

ARUNACHAL PRADESH

(INDIA)

Arunachal Pradesh is India's most northerly state and borders with Bhutan to the west, Tibet to the north, Myanmar to the east, and Assam and Nagaland to the south. Its name means "land of the dawn-lit mountains," but it is also known as the Orchid State of India and Paradise of the Botanists, and the mountains are home to pine and fir trees, rhododendrons, maples, orchids, and bamboo. In the past, tea was only one of many important crops, but since the beginning of the 21st century, production has been increasing, and it is today India's fifth-largest tea-growing state. In some cases, farmers have been persuaded to give up opium production and plant tea instead on small farms of between 1 and 5 hectares. In 2014, the Tocklai Tea Research Institute at Jorhat in Assam opened a new base at Itanagar as a centre for the expansion of tea production and to provide training for tea farmers. Until these recent developments, most of the state's tea was low-grown along the border with Assam, and most of the fresh leaf was processed in the Assam factories. In the new areas on the steep slopes of the state's higher mountains in East Siang and West Siang, some of the growers have propagated plants using seed collected from wild tea bushes growing along the border with Myanmar; others are growing clonal bushes. Altitudes are similar to those in Darjeeling, and with advice and support from the research team, it is hoped that in the future, Arunachal Pradesh will be able to produce high-quality teas with the delicate flavour of high-grown Darjeelings.

The local people also use leaf plucked from the old wild trees to make "bamboo tea." The harvested leaf is withered in the sun, pan-fried, and then packed into tubes of fresh bamboo and wrapped in banana leaves. The bamboo tubes of tea are then roasted over an open fire, steamed, and stored for six months for the flavour to develop.

Country, State, or Province
Arunachal Pradesh

Number of Gardens
40 registered large gardens, 32 registered small gardens, 20 factories, and 4,500 smallholders

Area Under Tea
Approximately 2,000 hectares

Average Annual Production (Kilograms)
Approximately 23.2 million (This is the total production for Arunachal Pradesh, Bihar, Manipur, Mizoram, Nagaland, Tripura, and Uttarakhand.)

Terrain
Agricultural region of deep valleys and highland plateaux climbs from the plains of Assam up to ridges and spurs at 3,000 metres (10,000 feet)

Altitude
60 to 1,600 metres (200 to 5,250 feet)

Production Period
March to October/November

Best Time to Visit
Early spring/late autumn

Main Varietals/Cultivars
New assamica cuttings propagated from wild trees growing along the Burmese border, sinensis

Types of Tea Made
Darjeeling-style black orthodox, green

Predominant Flavours; Tasting Notes
BLACK: bright red liquors, delicate Darjeeling character combined with Assam strength, aromatic
GREEN: fragrant, pungent

ASSAM

(INDIA)

The name for India's largest tea-producing region, Assam, derives from the Ahom tribe who invaded the Brahmaputra Valley in the 13th century. The name *Ahom* is thought to come from an earlier word, *Acham*, which means "undefeated" or "conqueror," and over time, with the introduction of Sanskrit to the area, *Acham* became *Asama*. It is also possible that it was the landscape of low, wide plains that gave the province its name because in Bodo, the native language of early settlers in Assam, the word *Ha-com* means "low-lying" or "flat, level land."

Until 1825, the region, an area measuring some 805 kilometres (500 miles) in length and 97 kilometres or so (60-plus miles) across, was ruled by a number of different dynasties, but by the late 18th century, the British East India Company was involved both commercially and militarily in the region. By 1833, Assam was part of the British Empire. Once the East India Company had proved that the cultivation and manufacture of tea was possible here, the directors handed over their experimental gardens to private companies. The first of these, the Assam Company, was inaugurated on the 12th of February 1839, and the directors immediately employed Charles Bruce as superintendent of the company's northern division of tea gardens, and hired local Assamese and Chinese workers to clear jungle and build boats, huts, and store houses. Having recognised that they needed to cultivate the local assamica tea varietal here, the jungle was burnt back in areas where wild bushes were growing abundantly, and within a year, the tea bushes had started to grow again. And where small tracts of tea had already been established, tall jungle trees were pruned back to allow in the light, and the waste areas between the patches of tea were filled with young bushes grown from locally collected seed or with 2- or 3-year-old plants that were transplanted from more remote locations. But more seeds were needed, and in 1847, Robert Fortune was employed by the Horticultural Society to travel to China to gather *Camellia sinensis* var. *sinensis* seeds and young plants. He disguised himself in Chinese garb, learnt Mandarin, collected around 13,000 tea seeds, and recruited Chinese workers to travel to India to teach the British how to manufacture tea.

As the importance of Assam tea grew, more and more land was planted, and by 1862, there were 160 tea gardens in Assam owned by 57 companies. In 1863, the First Inland Emigration Act introduced terms and conditions to protect workers, and the Bengal Act III of 1865 added further controls to protect workers' rights and appointed protector/inspectors to monitor the gardens. In 1881, the Indian Tea Association was set up, and the first Indian tea auction took place in Calcutta.

The Belseri Tea Estate, which covers 1500 acres, and is one of the largest organic tea gardens in northern Assam. Photograph by John O'Hagan; © Hoffman Media

Assam was very important for the early development of tea-making methodology and for the invention of the machinery that allowed the production of mass volumes of tea for the British market. The first machine for rolling tea was invented in 1868, and soon, steam engines, boilers, and dryers were being built in Britain and shipped to India for installation in the factories. Once the tea had been made, it was packed into lead-lined wooden chests, which were then loaded on riverboats ready for the slow six-week journey down to Calcutta and onward to London. In the 1930s, the introduction of the heat-sealed, paper fibre tea bag in the United States and the mass production of the first tea bags totally changed the way in which tea was manufactured, blended, packed, and brewed. The idea of the teabag was to offer the public a fast-brewing, convenient alternative to loose-leaf tea, and the machinery that was invented to pack the bags required small particles of broken leaf. As the demand for tea bags grew, the industry could not keep pace, so a new manufacturing process was invented specifically to produce smaller particles of tea to fill those bags. The new "Cut, Tear, and Curl" (CTC, in some parts of the world this is called "Crush, Tear, and Curl") machines came into use in Assam in the early 1930s. In 1958, the Rotorvane

machine, designed to twist and break the leaf before it went into the CTC machines, was introduced, and the Assam factories experimented with the two machines in order to perfect the new manufacturing methodology. Most Assam factories are currently capable of both orthodox and CTC manufacture, and switch from one to the other as demand varies around the world.

Assam is today the world's second-largest tea-producing region after China. The low-lying, fertile province lies in the north-eastern corner of India, bordered to the north by Bhutan and the Indian state of Arunachal Pradesh in the Himalayan foothills, to the east by the states of Nagaland and Manipur (and beyond that Myanmar), to the west by Darjeeling, and to the south by the state of Meghalaya and Bangladesh. It is a land of earthquakes and thunderstorms, floods and fog, strong winds and heavy downpours of rain. Spring is a time of showers and warm, oppressive afternoons; summer months are cloudy, sultry, and very humid; and autumn and winter are cooler, calmer, and more stable. The tea gardens stretch for mile after mile over gently sloping plains on both sides of the Brahmaputra River, which tumbles down into the province through Arunachal Pradesh from its origins in Tibet. Tea is crucial to the economy of the state and the country, and earns approximately 50 percent

LEFT: Bags of made CTC black tea at Belseri Tea Estate; the factory makes both CTC and orthodox organic black teas. Photograph by John O'Hagan; © Hoffman Media
RIGHT: Pickers ready to carry their baskets of tea back to the factory at Khongea Tea Estate in the upper reaches of Assam. Photograph courtesy of the Prakash family from Khongea Tea Estate

of the Indian tea industry's foreign exchange. The bushes grow in three main areas of the province—the Brahmaputra Valley (the largest of the three, covering 71.7 percent of the state), the Barak plains, and the Hill range—which together produce 51 percent of India's tea and one-sixth of all the tea grown around the world. Shade trees, usually leguminous varieties chosen for their ability to fix nitrogen from the atmosphere and add it back into the air and the soil, afford the bushes some protection from the intense glare of the sun. Their presence also helps to increase tea yields, improves the size and weight of the tea shoots, helps to aerate and reduce water loss from the soil, and increases the circulation of nutrients around the roots of the bushes.

Most of the tea gardens are today owned by large Indian companies, but the number of independent farmers has increased since the 1990s when unemployed young people started to grow tea as a way of earning a living. About 5,270,000 local people (17 percent of the population) are employed in the tea industry, working in the gardens, the factories, or related jobs such as transportation, marketing, warehousing, etcetera. As in Darjeeling and other parts of India, the majority of the families live on the tea estates in housing provided by the owners.

In the past, all Assam tea was plucked by hand, but a shortage of labour in the 1980s meant that some mechanical harvesting, using shears, had to be introduced. In 2013, successful trials were carried out with a new type of selective mechanical harvesting machine (developed in Australia by Geoff Williames), which cleverly replicates selective hand-plucking and therefore facilitates much finer plucking than is achieved by other mechanical harvesters and allows the picking of larger quantities than can be harvested by hand-pluckers.

In recent years, the economy of Assam has not developed as fast as in other parts of India, and the tea industry has suffered, with some gardens closing down. The major problems have been a lack of modernisation and investment in infrastructure, political unrest, competition from other parts of the world, low yields, plant disease and pest attacks, higher production costs, too little rain water for spraying, and rising water levels in rivers leading to the abandonment of some tracts of land. Climate change currently presents the biggest challenge, and warmer temperatures and shifts in rainfall patterns are causing a rise in pest attacks, crop losses, higher production costs, a drop in tea quality, and slight changes in the character of the teas.

LEFT: Assam tea bushes are shaded from glaring sun by shade trees, which are usually leguminous species that harness nitrogen to benefit the tea.
RIGHT: Assam pluckers typically carry their tea baskets on the top of their heads or support them with straps that pass over the head. Photographs by John O'Hagan; © Hoffman Media

THE TEAS OF ASSAM AND THEIR SEASONS

Assam is a seasonal area, and the bushes develop new leaves only from March through to late November or early December. The bushes are *Camellia sinensis* var. *assamica*, the large-leafed varietal of the tea bush that loves low-lying, hot, humid locations where plentiful rainfall nourishes them and encourages fast growth. The assamica is particularly well suited to the manufacture of black teas, and the majority of the crop is processed as traditional Assam black tea, although some estates also make small quantities of white and green teas. In the cooler winter months, when temperatures drop to between 6°C and 8°C (43°F to 46°F), the plants stop flushing and wait for the first warmth and spring rain to form new shoots. The early buds and young leaves that are gathered in March and April give black teas that are fresh, slightly grassy, and astringent. These are rarely sold as self-drinkers but are usually blended with teas harvested later in the year in order to offer a smoother, sweeter flavour that is more representative of the Assam character. Assam's best second flush teas are harvested in May and June and are manufactured either as orthodox or CTC teas, depending on the demands of the world market. Through the summer months, with heavy monsoon rains and temperatures over 37°C (98.6°F), the bushes grow much faster and the wonderful quality of the second flush teas is partially lost. These teas are usually blended as single-origin Assam teas or are sold in bulk to tea companies around the world who mix them with teas from other origins to create breakfast blends, house blends, or flavoured teas.

The even, twisted, dark brown leaves of the second flush orthodox teas are often mingled with "golden tips," the paler, younger buds that are evidence of careful plucking and manufacture. Because of the high quantity of tip, the best teas are sometimes marketed as Tippy Assam or Assam Gold. The CTC teas are stronger, punchier, and more robust but have the same sweet, smooth, malty character as the orthodox teas. Because of a growing demand for green tea, in India and around the world, some Assam producers now also make both orthodox and CTC green varieties, and some gardens also produce elegant needle-style white teas made from just the tightly furled buds.

Country, State, or Province
Assam

Number of Gardens
50,000 gardens, 52,000 smallholders, and 160 bought-leaf factories

Area Under Tea
312,210 hectares, including 65,000 hectares of smallholdings

Average Annual Production (Kilograms)
618 million

Terrain
Vast, flat alluvial plains on both sides of the Brahmaputra River

Altitude
45 to 60 metres (148 to 197 feet)

Production Period
March to November

Best Time to Visit
Early spring/late autumn

Main Varietals/Cultivars
Assamicas

Types of Tea Made
Mainly black CTC and orthodox, some green and white

Predominant Flavours; Tasting Notes
BLACK: *Orthodox*—dark amber liquors; subtle, rounded malty flavour, with hints of raisins, toasted grains, caramelised sugar and honey
CTC—coppery red liquors, punchy, full-bodied, robust, with roasted malty note and sometimes suggestions of raspberry jam
GREEN: amber liquors, with soft, grassy notes and hints of young green wood
WHITE: sweet, floral, with malty notes

MANIPUR

(INDIA)

The name of this small state, which lies to the south of Assam, means "Jewel City," and it is a beautiful region with gently rolling hills, green valleys, thick forests, lakes, and waterfalls. Local farmers grow rubber, coffee, a little tea, oranges, cardamom, and basic food crops such as rice, maize, and potatoes. At Talui in the north of the state, the local people make green tea, which is handpicked and dried in the sun.

The Manipur Plantation Crops Corporation Limited started growing tea at Manipur Tea Estate, Jiribam, in 1981–82, and until they could build their own factory, the fresh leaf was transported to Jirighat Tea Estate in Assam. In the early years, it was hoped that tea would become an important income-generating crop here, but the industry was badly neglected, the construction of the processing factory was never finished, and it was not until 2004 that attempts were made to revive the garden with investment from the state government. In 2015, an inspection of the Manipur Tea Estate by the state government agricultural team concluded that the garden could generate income if the state "could focus more on the estate." The Tea Board has encouraged village farmers to grow tea and 484 smallholder growers with plots covering a total of 1,362.61 hectares are now registered.

Hand plucking new leaf shoots from assamica bushes. Photograph by John O'Hagan; © Hoffman Media

Country, State, or Province
Manipur

Number of Gardens
484 smallholder farmers who grow tea organically and make tea as a cottage industry

Area Under Tea
1,362.61 hectares registered

Average Annual Production (Kilograms)
Approximately 23.2 million (This is the total production for Arunachal Pradesh, Bihar, Manipur, Mizoram, Nagaland, Tripura, and Uttarakhand.)

Terrain
A mix of hills and flat land, but difficult to cultivate; erratic seasons with intense rain so more forest cover

Altitude
500 metres (1,640 feet) or less

Production Period
March to November

Best Time to Visit
Early spring/late autumn

Main Varietals/Cultivars
Assamicas

Types of Tea Made
Small quantities of black orthodox and CTC

Predominant Flavours; Tasting Notes
Poor quality, rather plain

MEGHALAYA

(INDIA)

Meghalaya, whose name means "abode of clouds," used to be part of Assam but, since January 1972, has been a separate state that occupies 22,429 square kilometres (8,660 square miles) between Assam to the north and east and Bangladesh to the south and west. Although this subtropical region was recommended in the early 19th century by the East India Company as an eminently suitable tea-growing region, it was not developed as tea land until 1974 when the Tea Board of India recognised its potential. The Board's report suggested that assamica seedlings should be transplanted to the low, flat plains that border Assam, and that sinensis varietals from Darjeeling should be planted on the high, misty slopes of the Garo Hills and West Khasi Hills, at elevations between 914 and 1,676 metres (2,999 and 5,499 feet). All the tea is certified organic.

The state's Department of Agriculture has two farms at Umsning and Upper Shillong and markets its high-quality black and green orthodox teas under the brand name Meg Tea. There are also small private plots farmed by smallholders, village grower societies, and several large private farms. Lakyrsiew Tea Estate, owned by Nayantara and Geert Linnebank, covers 25 acres on the outskirts of Shillong and produces small quantities of white teas in the summer, green orthodox, and beautiful seasonal black orthodox teas in Darjeeling style. Sohryngkham Estate's Sharawn brand includes black and green teas. A group of 20 farmers from Mawlyngot Village runs a cooperative to market their green, black, and white teas under the brand name Urlong Tea. And Anderson Tea Estate sells a blend of CTC and orthodox black teas. Before tea was planted here, villagers grew potatoes, sweet potatoes, millet, and sesame, but tea cultivation has increased earnings and opened up international markets, and buyers love the light floral character of the high-grown teas and the sweet caramel maltiness of the low-grown teas.

There is also now an advisory centre in Meghalaya—one of six in North India run by the Tea Research Association (TRA)—and this gives routine extension advice on planting, plant husbandry, agronomy, etcetera, to help farmers improve their work.

Country, State, or Province
Meghalaya

Number of Gardens
35 estates

Area Under Tea
2,000 hectares

Average Annual Production (Kilograms)
600,000

Terrain
Rain-soaked mountains (in some parts, the wettest place on earth) with high plateaux and long stretches of valley between; numerous rivers, waterfalls and gorges

Altitude
914 to 1,676 metres (3,000 to 5,500 feet)

Production Period
March to October

Best Time to Visit
Early spring/late autumn

Main Varietals/Cultivars
Assamicas on the lower plains, sinensis from Darjeeling on the higher hills

Types of Tea Made
Mainly orthodox black, a small amount of green, white—all organic

Predominant Flavours; Tasting Notes
BLACK: amber liquors, malty, softened by subtle honey note, deep and rich with toffee or chocolate notes
GREEN: complex, delicate, muscatel grape notes
WHITE: *LaKyrsiew*—smooth and sweet

MIZORAM

(INDIA)

The name of Mizoram, which borders Tripura, Assam, Manipur, Myanmar, and Bangladesh, means "land of the hill people." In the 1990s, a Scientific and Commercial Tea Plantation programme was established in the region by setting up Small Tea Grower societies in each village. The scheme now involves a total of around 697 small-scale farmers growing tea on a total of 1,934.34 hectares in Biate, Ngopa, Pawlrang, North-East Bualpui, Khawdungsei, Tlungvel, Darlawng, and Seling. They receive grants and subsidies from the Tea Board for the purchase of plants, vehicles to deliver the tea to the factory, nylon carrying bags, etc., and sell their fresh leaf into the factory, which was built with funding from the Tea Board. The Tea Board has also registered nine tea estates that together grow tea on 391 hectares. Mizoram is also home to F. K. Tea Estate, a private tea garden located just north of the town of Ngopa, in the north of the state. The company's black tea is marketed as Mizo Tea, and there are plans to install new machinery to make green and other types of tea.

CTC black tea is made in huge quantities in most regions of Assam and in small quantities in Mizoram. Photograph by John O'Hagan; © Hoffman Media

Country, State, or Province
Mizoram

Number of Gardens
9 estates and some 697 smallholder farmers

Area Under Tea
1,934.34 hectares under small-scale farmers; 391 hectares under tea estates

Average Annual Production (Kilograms)
Approximately 23.2 million (This is the total production for Arunachal Pradesh, Bihar, Manipur, Mizoram, Nagaland, Tripura, and Uttarakhand.)

Terrain
A region of rugged rolling hills, rivers, and lakes; steep slopes and occasional flatter plains in the valleys

Altitude
Approximately 1,678 metres (5,505 feet)

Production Period
March to October

Best Time to Visit
Early spring/late autumn

Main Varietals/Cultivars
Assamicas

Types of Tea Made
Black orthodox, CTC

Predominant Flavours; Tasting Notes
Strong

NAGALAND

(INDIA)

Nagaland lies in the north-eastern corner of India and shares a border with Assam to the north-west, Manipur to the south, and Myanmar to the east. When India was partitioned in 1947, the area remained part of Assam, but in 1963, it became a separate state. It is one of the country's smallest states, mostly made up of mountains but with lower land along the border with Assam's Brahmaputra Valley. The region has a monsoon climate with heavy rains through the warm summer months and temperatures that drop low enough for frost in winter. Farmers have been growing small quantities of tea since the 19th century, but the total area planted has been increasing steadily since 1995. Since the beginning of the 21st century, tea cultivation has become a viable industry, and on the 18th of February 2001, the Indian Express wrote, "Tea cultivation in Nagaland of late has become a reality and there is much enthusiasm among planters after various studies revealed that the land here is suitable for quality tea production." Development of the tea industry here has advanced in response to a demand for more tea but a shortage of land suitable for cultivation in the traditional areas such as Assam, Dooars, Terai, and Arunachal Pradesh. Smallholder farmers in the area have been encouraged to turn away from timber production and slash-and-burn (*jhum*) agricultural practices and to plant tea instead. The Tea Board of India provided technical and financial support, and the Nagaland State Department of Land Resources supplied planting material and paid for training for interested villagers. In the past, the fresh leaf was taken into Assam for processing, which involved a long journey and incurred a tax, but now, there is a factory at Merangkong. The Nagaland Empowerment of People through Economic Development, an Indo-Canadian project, is also developing sustainable development by encouraging smallholder farmers to cultivate tea as well as their other crops.

Country, State, or Province
Nagaland

Number of Gardens
3 estates, plus smallholder farmers who make tea as a cottage industry

Main Districts or Gardens
Mopungchukit, Sayeang, Chaying

Area Under Tea
1,362.61 hectares registered

Average Annual Production (Kilograms)
Approximately 23.2 million (This is the total production for Arunachal Pradesh, Bihar, Manipur, Mizoram, Nagaland, Tripura, and Uttarakhand.)

Terrain
20% of the state is covered with forests; rich flora and fauna; often foggy, heavy rain and some sunshine: fine clay, and loamy clay soils

Altitude
No details available

Production Period
Late March to October

Best Time to Visit
Early spring/late autumn

Main Varietals/Cultivars
Assamicas

Types of Tea Made
Hand-made orthodox black and small amounts of white

Predominant Flavours; Tasting Notes
BLACK: plain to medium quality
WHITE: deep flavour, with smooth hints of raisins and toasted grains

TRIPURA

(INDIA)

There are 58 large tea estates in Tripura, in the districts of Dhalai and South, North, and West Tripura. Approximately 1,500 registered growers and 11 co-operative gardens also grow tea. Two of the co-operatives each have their own factories.

Much of the tea in Tripura is hand picked by smallholder farmers and sold into factories on nearby estates. Photograph by John O'Hagan; © Hoffman Media

Country, State, or Province
Tripura

Number of Gardens
58 large estates, plus 1,500 smallholders and 11 cooperative gardens

Area Under Tea
More than 4,000 hectares

Average Annual Production (Kilograms)
Approximately 23.2 million (This is the total production for Arunachal Pradesh, Bihar, Manipur, Mizoram, Nagaland, Tripura, and Uttarakhand.)

Terrain
Hilly areas interspersed with narrow, well-watered alluvial plains; most of the agricultural land is in the west and south of the state; a wet area with high rainfall

Altitude
939 metres (3,081 feet) or less

Production Period
March to October

Best Time to Visit
Early spring/late autumn

Main Varietals/Cultivars
Assamicas

Types of Tea Made
Orthodox black, small amounts of green

Predominant Flavours; Tasting Notes
Plain to medium quality

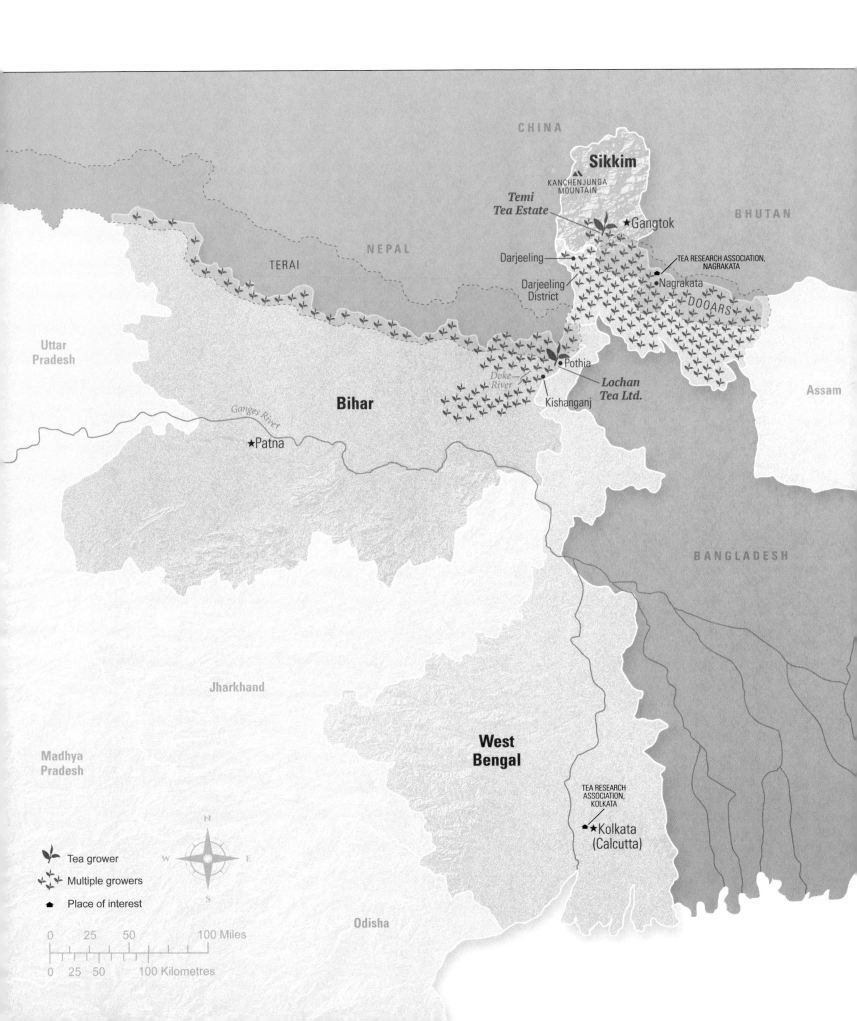

CHINA

Sikkim

KANCHENJUNGA
MOUNTAIN

*Temi
Tea Estate*

BHUTAN

★ Gangtok

Darjeeling

TEA RESEARCH ASSOCIATION,
NAGRAKATA

Darjeeling
District

● Nagrakata

DOOARS

NEPAL

TERAI

*Doke
River*

● Pothia

Assam

*Lochan
Tea Ltd.*

Uttar
Pradesh

Kishanganj

Bihar

Ganges River

★ Patna

BANGLADESH

Jharkhand

Madhya
Pradesh

**West
Bengal**

TEA RESEARCH
ASSOCIATION,
KOLKATA

★ Kolkata
(Calcutta)

🌿 Tea grower

N

🌿 Multiple growers

W ─── E

⬠ Place of interest

S

Odisha

0   25   50   100 Miles

0   25   50   100 Kilometres

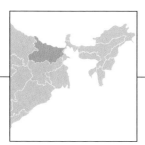

BIHAR

(INDIA)

In 1975, the Indian government started encouraging tea cultivation in Bihar in an effort to halt the mass migration of people from this very dry area of north eastern India to more fertile regions. An area of four blocks of the Kishanganj District (Pothia, Thakurganj, Bahadurganj, and Kishanganj itself) was declared a "non-traditional tea growing area" by the Indian Tea Board in June 1999, and financial help was offered to tea growers who were prepared to establish tea gardens, create jobs, and therefore offer the prospect of a better life for the people who live here. The efforts of the new farmers were helped by the diversion of water from a hydroelectric plant in Bengal into the very dry Doke River (also spelt Dauk, Dahuk, and Dohuk) that runs through Bihar. A significant rise in the level of the river created a more reliable source of water for the tea plants and a sizeable area in the district of Kishanganj is now planted with lush green fields of tea owned by thousands of large and small growers. They sell their leaf into five bought-leaf factories, one of which is a cooperative factory owned by the provincial government. These processing units cannot cope with all the leaf grown here, and while another factory is being built, about 25 percent of green leaf is sold into factories in West Bengal. In 2015, the Tea Board of India appointed two tea development officers in Kishanganj and Thakurganj areas to oversee the accurate assessment of area, crop, and land holding in the region, and financial support is also being offered to farmers to help them form self-help groups (SHG) and build their own mini processing factories.

Most of the tea is processed as CTC black tea, but Rajiv Lochan of Lochan Tea Ltd. established a 100-hectare organic tea garden here on the banks of the Doke in the village of Pothia in 1998, and makes beautiful handmade white, green, oolong, and orthodox black teas that are very popular in foreign markets, particularly in Canada, the United States, and China. Profits from sales go to improve the lives, houses, and educational opportunities for the workers, and a percentage is also donated to the Indus Foundation, a nonprofit organization for the betterment of the country's future and which is planning to set up a number of primary schools.

Country, State, or Province
Bihar

Number of Gardens
2 large estates, 5 processing factories, and 10,000 smallholders

Area Under Tea
4,046.85 hectares

Average Annual Production (Kilograms)
Approximately 23.2 million (This is the total production for Arunachal Pradesh, Bihar, Manipur, Mizoram, Nagaland, Tripura, and Uttarakhand.)

Terrain
Vast stretches of fertile plains divided into two halves by the River Ganges

Altitude
47 metres (154 feet)

Production Period
Mid-February to December

Best Time to Visit
Early spring/late autumn

Main Varietals/Cultivars
Assamicas

Types of Tea Made
Black CTC and orthodox black, green, white, and oolong from Doke Tea Garden

Predominant Flavours; Tasting Notes
BLACK: *CTC*—rich burgundy liquors, robust, strong
Doke Tea Estate Orthodox—complex, buttery, malty, with suggestions of molasses and grape
GREEN: *Doke Tea Estate*—lightly earthy, with notes of cherry and citrus zest
OOLONG: *Doke Tea Estate*—amber liquor, complex, smooth, fruity, rich, with malt and jasmine notes
WHITE: *Doke Tea Estate*—golden liquor, clean, smooth, sweet, and creamy, with notes of peach blossom and dried apricot

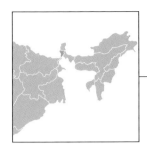

DARJEELING

(INDIA)

Two legends explain Darjeeling's name. The first, of Tibetan heritage, tells how the *dorge* (meaning "thunderbolt" or "sceptre") of Indra, the deity revered among the Himalayan foothills, struck the earth at this place or *ling*. A second, more prosaic tale says that before the British were given the territory in 1835, the narrow strip of mountainous land was home to only a Buddhist monastery and a small cluster of some 20 simple huts. The welfare of the monks and the residents of this modest village was the responsibility of the monastery's lama, a priest by the name of Dorge. Since it was his duty to collect any revenue from the area and deliver it to the King of Sikkim, the place was listed in the register as Dorge Ling, or "village governed by Dorge."

The region around Darjeeling was once a part of the ancient Kingdom of Sikkim but was seized by the Nepalese in the late 18th century. In 1814, the British won a two-year war with Nepal over border disputes and, in 1816, forced them to hand back the territory to Sikkim. After a visit in the 1820s, Governor-General Sir William Bentinck decided that it was an ideal location for a sanitarium, a fact that was recorded by the King of Sikkim when, in gratitude for British support, he signed the land over to the British in 1835:

"Since the climate of Darjeeling is cool, the Governor-General is desirous of occupying it, because, Government servants suffering from sickness and ill-health can regain their health after a period of rest in the hills. Therefore, I King of Dezzong (Sikkim), am by this document presenting to the Governor-General, out of esteem and friendship, the land to the south of the Greater Rangnit (River Rangeet)."

Ambootia Organic and Biodynamic Tea Estate, which sits at an altitude of around 950 to 1,450 metres (1,039 to 1,586 feet) and has a view of snow-capped Mount Kenchanjunga in the distance.
© Ambootia Tea Group

Two government employees, Lieutenant Napier (later Lord Napier of Magdala) and Dr. Archibald Campbell of the Indian Medical Service were sent to develop the area. Campbell became the first superintendent of the sanitarium in 1839 and planted a few China tea seeds in his garden at an altitude of 2,134 metres (7,001 feet). He found that the plants grew well and others followed his example. When Sir Joseph Dalton Hooker, the great British botanist and explorer, visited the area in 1848, he wrote, "The tea-plant succeeds here admirably, and might be cultivated at a great profit, and be of advantage in furthering a trade with Tibet." By 1853, according to a letter written by Campbell to the Board of Revenue in Calcutta, there were "upwards of 2,000 plants now growing on different elevations from 7,000 to 2,000 feet, and of different ages, from twelve years to seedlings of a few months."

With such encouraging results, the government began to seriously promote the cultivation of tea and, under the Waste Land Bill, divided available land into plots of approximately 250 acres and sold them at affordable prices. Most of the development took place on the lower slopes since many people considered the more elevated altitudes too high for the plants' welfare. The first garden was planted at Alubari in 1856, and by 1857, several thousand acres of jungle had been cleared, between 50 and 60 hectares had been planted with at least 1,000 kilos (2,205 pounds) of tea seeds, and six tea nurseries had been established to provide further supplies of seed. The "uninhabitable mountain," which in 1840 accommodated only 30 mean and humble dwellings, now boasted 70 buildings that included two churches, a convent, a cemetery, a hospital, a dispensary, a jail, a school, a hotel, and various cottages, lodges, and smarter residences. As the population grew, roads were built, steam railways were introduced, telegraph wires were connected, and places of entertainment were opened. Darjeeling had become a town, and the Darjeeling tea industry was firmly established.

The labour force that plucked the fresh tea shoots, pruned the bushes, weeded the gardens, and worked in the factories to manufacture the tea was at first made up of local people from the Lepcha and Bhutia tribes. As the number of gardens increased, other workers were brought in from the surrounding areas so that, eventually, there were Tibetans, Nepalese, Sikkimese, Kashmiris, Rajbanshis, Peshawaris, Mechis, Afghans, and Nagpuris living and working on the plantations. By 1866, the region had 39 tea gardens yielding 196,405.5 kilos (433,000 pounds) of tea; in 1870, 56 gardens on 11,000 acres of land were yielding 771,107 kilos (1.7 million pounds) of tea. Between 1866 and 1874, the number of gardens trebled and the amount of tea produced multiplied tenfold. The annexation of Terai by the British in 1850 expanded the potential area for tea cultivation, and the first gardens were laid out there in 1861. As the industry developed, electricity was introduced, and mechanised rollers, sorters, and dryers took over some of the hard manual work. By the time India gained independence in 1947, Darjeeling teas had become famous all over the world, and 102 gardens covering almost 18,500 hectares were producing 14 million kilos (31 million pounds) of tea each year.

Until India achieved independence, the ownership of approximately 90 percent of the plantations remained firmly in the hands of the European tea companies, but by 1956, a large proportion had been sold to Indian owners. Changes of ownership and management of a tea garden can result in an initial decline in the consistency of tea quality as the new team familiarises itself with the particular topography and character of the plantation, the seasonal fluctuations and weather patterns, and the workforce. In the 1950s, the situation was compounded by a number of other factors: a general lack of experience amongst the new owners and management, fierce competition at the tea auctions, a drop in yield from aging tea bushes, and new pressures arising from the newly won power of the Communist Party. As increasing numbers of plantation workers joined unions, labour relations also worsened, and the acute financial crisis resulting from this period of intense change led to the closure of many tea estates. In the 1980s, as political dissent worsened, the plantations had to cope with agitation, violence, and strikes caused by growing demands from the Gorkha National Liberation Front (GNLF) for a separate state of Gorkhaland. Although peace was restored after the introduction in 1988 of the Darjeeling Gorkha Hill Council (which was given a degree of autonomy to govern the district), fresh demands since then have brought further disruption to the region. Transportation strikes can hold up the movement of tea from the plantations down to the ports, and unrest amongst the workforce sometimes hampers the daily routine of the gardens. There have even been some extreme situations—for example, the assassination of Gorkha leader Madan Tamang in May 2010—when some hill subdivisions have been completely shut down for periods of time. In June 2017, demands by the Gorkha Janmukti Morcha (GJM) for a separate Gorkha state led to strikes, violence, the torching of trucks, and some deaths amongst protesters in the towns and rural areas.

In 1964, with troubled labour relations rumbling in the background, the government started to address the question of low yield and quality by setting up the Tea Research Association (TRA), with Tocklai Experimental Station (established in 1911) at the centre of the programme of research for north-east India. The scientists were tasked with developing cloned plants from carefully selected mother bushes that were well suited to the conditions of the different growing areas. To date, Tocklai has released 30 clonal plants and 14 hybrid seeds for use by the industry, and extensive replanting in Darjeeling has helped to improve both yield and quality there. In recent years, however, the region has also been challenged by the devastating effects of climate change. Whilst landslides and erosion of the steep hillsides caused by heavy monsoon rain have always been a fact of life, more recent changes in weather patterns have added to the situation. The prized First and Second Flush teas depend on the slow growth of the plants in cool, relatively dry spring weather. But if temperatures stay too low or rise too sharply in March and April or if too much rain falls too early or for too long, the regular pattern of growth is unsettled and the subtle fragrance and quality of these early teas is lost. A drought that began in 2009 and the prolonged excessive rainfall in the spring of 2010 meant that production dropped from an average outturn of 14 million kilos (30.9 million pounds) to only 7 million kilos (15.4 million pounds), the lowest in Darjeeling's history.

Although ownership of the Darjeeling tea industry remains almost totally in the hands of private companies, the government maintains control by legislation and through the Tea Board of India, set up in 1953. Working in close collaboration with the Darjeeling Planters' Association, the Tea Board has introduced measures designed to protect Darjeeling tea's worldwide reputation and prevent teas from other regions being sold as Darjeeling. This included, in 1986, creating and trademarking a Darjeeling logo to be used on packets and boxes as a guarantee that the contents are entirely from the region. In 2004, Darjeeling Tea was registered as geographical indication (GI) and the Tea Board's definition of Darjeeling tea states that it is "tea which has been cultivated, grown, produced, manufactured, and processed in tea gardens in the hilly areas of Sadar Sub-Division . . . which, when brewed, has a distinctive, naturally occurring aroma and taste with light tea liquor and the infused leaf of which has a distinctive fragrance."

The Darjeeling tea industry currently employs some 52,000 people on a permanent basis and a further 15,000 during the plucking season. As in many tea-growing countries, the majority of the families who care for the plants, pluck the tea, and process it in the factories actually live on the plantations. The plantation owner is required by law to provide free housing, subsidised rations of cereals, medical and maternity care, and crèches. Previously, the tea garden also provided primary education, but this has subsequently been taken over by the government. Because the workforce is composed of numerous ethnic groups, an individual tea estate may additionally provide different community centres, places of worship, shops, and sports facilities to cater for the workers' varied needs.

All estates today are unionised, and whilst owners and managers expect occasional strikes when wage negotiations are due, the relationship between employer and employee is for the most part good. The smooth running of the individual gardens is thanks largely to the crucial role played by the estate manager. Throughout Darjeeling's history, the estate manager has been responsible for every aspect of daily life—from the quality of the tea to the financial success of the garden and the welfare of the workers. It is a multifarious role that includes resolving disputes, solving crimes, settling arguments, administering justice, and generally being available at all times of day and night to make vital decisions about tea manufacture or to listen to workers' grievances.

The factory manager, who works closely with the estate manager, must also be an expert in all aspects of tea manufacture and is a valuable asset to the successful production of quality tea. The factory manager needs to understand how fresh leaf and the fine details of manufacturing vary day by day, week by week, season by season. Manufacturing good Darjeeling tea demands different skills from those needed to make good Assam or Nilgiri tea, and the factory manager will have experience, understanding, and knowledge built up over years spent working in the region. The factory manager uses a wealth of technical expertise to bring out the best in the freshly plucked leaf and to decide how to adjust the manufacturing method to suit the time of year, the ambient temperature, the level of humidity, and the type of tea to be made. Local knowledge is crucial, and expert tea makers tend to remain in a particular region for the duration of their working life because the skills required to produce good teas there are unique.

Pickers in Darjeeling have to climb the steep slopes several times a day in order to fill their baskets and then deliver the fresh leaf to mustering points where the tea is weighed. Photographs by John O'Hagan; © Hoffman Media

The new shoots are carefully picked and then taken to the factory as quickly as possible for processing. ABOVE LEFT: © Ambootia Tea Group ABOVE RIGHT: Photograph by John O'Hagan; © Hoffman Media

The workers start their day at about 6 a.m. and make their way to the factory or plucking area either on foot or in buses provided by the estate owner. Plucking (which was traditionally carried out by women in Darjeeling, but now also involves men) starts at 7 a.m. and finishes around 3 p.m. The day is punctuated by tea and lunch breaks that are taken wherever the pluckers are on the estate. When the baskets are full, the fresh leaf gathered by each plucker is weighed, and the weight is recorded to ensure that the worker is paid the correct amount. A tariff to be paid for a minimum quantity of leaf is set by the Tea Board, depending on the area and season, and any amount of leaf over the required weight earns a bonus. The harvested leaf is collected from a mustering point two or three times each day and transported to the factory, which is either on the estate itself or in the neighbouring area.

Darjeeling's 88 estates (the total number changes from time to time as gardens are merged or divided) range in size from 40 to 970 hectares. Some of the land on each estate is given over to jungle in order to help prevent soil erosion and landslides and to retain the natural balance of biodiversity. Leopards and tigers are occasionally seen on the estates, and monkeys and a wide variety of birds, including birds of prey, live wild on the edges of the cultivated areas. The ownership of estates in Darjeeling falls into three main categories: groups of estates owned by large corporations, which sometimes have interests outside tea; single estates owned by individuals or families; and single estates owned by worker co-operatives. Takeovers by the latter in the 1990s were prompted by a severe decline in the value of tea estates and the fact that some owners simply abandoned unviable properties and left resident families with no livelihood. Since 2014, Ambootia Tea Estate has been buying sick, failing, and abandoned tea gardens in order to provide work for the communities living there and to refurbish the estates and turn them into viable organic and biodynamic gardens that take care of the tea bushes and the environment, and provide a sustainable future for the workers. In 2017, the Ambootia Group owned 17 gardens in Darjeeling and Assam, and was planning to eventually own a total of 21 gardens.

As well as operating as full-time tea estates, some gardens now also offer excellent tourist activities such as walking, canoeing, tennis, bird-watching, cycling, swimming, and tours to other interesting locations. Bungalows have been refurbished and modernised to provide comfortable accommodation in the style of a small country house hotel, and visitors can enjoy good food and wine as well as the peace and quiet of the spectacular countryside.

Darjeeling teas are defined by the season in which they are made. The floral green First Flush teas of spring give way to the bolder and balanced Second Flush teas of summer before the rains wash away much of the flavour of the Monsoon teas, and finally, the tea year ends with the gentle aromas and textures of the Autumnal teas. The seasons are expressed very vividly in Darjeeling teas, and it may be the variety as well as the incredible flavours and tastes associated with Darjeeling teas that makes them a favourite with connoisseurs.

To understand the area's famous First Flush and Second Flush teas, it is significant to know that many of Darjeeling tea bushes are descended from or, in some cases, still are the tea plants bought from China in the 19th century by the British. Others are the assamicas acquired by early planters who used whatever supplies of seed or cuttings were available, and hybrids and new clones are also now being planted. But some gardens value their original Chinese stock so much that they have established seed orchards in order to propagate a plentiful supply of new sinensis plants.

As well as the individual characteristics of the tea species and the particular varietals that grow in the region, other factors play a part in shaping the unique taste and aroma of Darjeeling tea. The cool weather and high altitude slow the plants' growth and concentrate flavour. Processing methods vary from season to season to capture the fresh, fruity notes in the tea, and the landscape itself also varies. Even on one estate, the altitude can vary by 1,000 metres (3,281 feet) or more, and the steep slopes planted with tea face in different directions, varying their exposure to wind, rain, and sun. Teas made on different days and during different seasons vary greatly, and with each flush in Darjeeling lasting a month or more, there is a wide variety of style, character, and quality in the teas produced by each estate.

On clear days, the snow-capped mountains of the Himalayan foothills and in particular Mount Kanchenjunga, the world's third-highest peak, can be seen in the distance. Occasionally, in winter, snow falls here, and the temperature drops to below 0°C (32°F); but even on warmer days, the crystal-clear skies make it seem colder than the thermometer indicates. The low temperatures from November to March stop new leaf growth and allow the tea bushes a complete rest after producing new leaf shoots during the warmer months. The first warm sunshine in mid- to late February encourages the first new growth, and by March, the tea bushes have started to slowly develop the first new leaf shoots at the tip of each stem, called the "flush." The teas made in the spring are therefore known as First Flush teas, and they are among the first new teas produced each year in the world's seasonal tea regions and should ideally be enjoyed very fresh within six months of production as they tend to quickly lose their aroma and flavour.

Whereas until the 1970s, First Flush Darjeeling teas were fully oxidized to give a brown dry leaf, the fashion since then has been for very green, lightly oxidized First Flush teas, and manufacturing has been adapted to meet market demands. Instead of withering the fresh leaf until the traditional 35 percent of their water content has been evaporated, the leaf for the modern, greener First Flush teas is "hard withered" to remove up to 63 to 65 percent of the moisture in the leaves. The tea is then lightly rolled in orthodox rollers and allowed to oxidise only very briefly, and sometimes not at all, before being dried. The hard wither inhibits oxidation, and this, combined with a very short period of oxidation between rolling and drying, gives a leaf that, in its dry state and after brewing, remains predominantly green with only hints of brown where very slight oxidation has taken place. This method of processing also captures the very fresh, slightly grassy and fruity character that modern Darjeeling lovers demand. Because these teas do not go through the classic stages of black tea processing, which normally involves full oxidation, it is hard to categorise them as black teas, but nor can they be classified as green or oolong. So, they are now commonly referred to as "hard-wither" teas. The same style of manufacture is found in the production of some Nilgiri Frost teas that often have a flaky, green dry leaf resulting from this hard-wither style of manufacture.

By late May and into June each year, Darjeeling's Second Flush teas are being produced. These early summer teas, which are rolled harder and oxidised for longer, produce a stronger, darker tea. Although still not fully oxidised—giving dry tea that mingles silver buds with flecks of dark green and purple and darker brown leaves—when brewed, these teas give a darker, reddish liquor that has a rounded, fruity, sometimes spicy and woody character, with notes of ripe peaches and muscatel grapes and hints of summer flowers.

After the Second Flush comes the hot, rainy monsoon period, from late June to early September. Up to 2 metres (6.5 feet) of rain can fall during this time, and it is easy to see why Darjeeling is said to mean "Land of the Thunderbolt." Thunderstorms and torrential rains often cause chaos and landslides in the region. Despite the extreme weather, tea production continues through this wet season, and the combination of summer heat and rain makes the new shoots grow faster. The tea bushes often need to be plucked every eight to 10 days, but unfortunately, the tea loses its distinctive concentration of flavour and aroma and seems diluted by the rains. The large volumes of Monsoon tea are generally used in Darjeeling blends, to which a skilful blender can add a little of the more fragrant flushes to produce a tea with typical Darjeeling character. And because the fresh leaf does not suit the manufacture of high-value traditional Darjeeling teas, some factories now make darker, open-leafed oolongs at this time of the year, often in the style of Taiwanese Oriental Beauty oolongs, which share the sweet muscatel characteristics that the best Darjeeling oolongs often have. The reason for this diversification is mainly financial because the oolongs can

TOP LEFT: A mustering point where the tea is weighed, and kept dry and out of the sun. Photograph by John O'Hagan; © Hoffman Media
TOP RIGHT: Pluckers with full baskets of tea at Ambootia Tea Estate. © Ambootia Tea Group RIGHT: A balance of vegetation on the plunging hillsides of Darjeeling is important for the local ecology and to help protect against landslides. Photograph courtesy of Angela Pryce

command good prices at a time of year when the quality and prices of traditional Darjeeling Monsoon teas fall.

As the dry weather returns, so does the quality of the Autumnal teas in late September and October. Less easy to obtain than the First and Second Flush teas, Autumn Flushes are also often used in blends but the best of them deserve to find wider appreciation. The best are less astringent than First and Second Flushes, and the coppery liquors harmonize warm, sweet, aromatic spiciness with hints of autumn leaves and slightly earthy notes.

As well as making delicious oolongs, some Darjeeling estates also produce high-quality white teas that have a smooth, delicate fruitiness and floral sweetness, and fetch high prices in the specialty world market.

Country, State, or Province	Main Varietals/ Cultivars
Darjeeling	Sinensis from China, assamicas from Assam
Number of Gardens 88 gardens and 72 factories	**Types of Tea Made** Black orthodox, green, white, and oolong
Area Under Tea 8.1 million hectares	**Predominant Flavours; Tasting Notes**
Average Annual Production (Kilograms) 18.3 million	BLACK: *First Flush*—delicate, refined, slightly grassy, floral, with hints of apricots and peaches *Second Flush*—delicate, nutty, woody, fruity, with hints of ripe muscatel grapes, less grassy than First Flush teas *Monsoon*—plain, duller than spring teas *Autumnal*—full-flavoured, rounded, woody, sweet, fruity
Terrain Steep hills and deep valleys, waterfalls and rivers, with views in the distance of the high peaks of the Himalayas and Mount Kanchenjunga	
Altitude 600 to 2,000 metres (1,969 to 6,562 feet)	GREEN: pale amber liquors, aromatic and floral taste and aroma WHITE: pale golden liquors, complex, sweet, flowery character OOLONG: complex, floral, and fruity, with suggestions of muscatel grapes, dried fruits, peaches, and honey
Production Period Late March to October	
Best Time to Visit Spring/autumn	

DOOARS AND TERAI

(INDIA)

While the high slopes of Darjeeling were developing as a dynamic new tea-growing region in the 1850s, planters were also encouraged to try planting at lower elevations in the foothills and plains of Terai and Dooars. Terai is a made up of a belt of lowland plains that run from east to west between northern India and southern Nepal; Dooars is a vast area of foothills and floodplains that extends to the south of Darjeeling from West Bengal into Assam. James White, who had previously established Singel Tea Estate near Kurseong in Darjeeling, planted out the first garden in Terai, New Chumpta, in 1862. The first Dooars garden was Gazeldubi. By the mid-1870s, there were 13 estates located at altitudes ranging from 90 to 1,750 metres (295 to 5,741 feet) in a landscape of tropical forests and open plains, tumbling streams, and wide, meandering rivers. Situated at much lower elevations than Darjeeling, the climate is milder and the plucking season longer, starting with the first March rains and ending in late November or early December.

The industry thrived here until the end of the 20th century, with the mainly black teas reaching markets in the USSR, Pakistan, and Iraq. But the breakup of the USSR and the war in Iraq led to a severe decline in exports. The problem was exacerbated by increased wages, rising production costs, and out-of-date equipment and infrastructure. By 2014, few of the 158 gardens in Dooars were doing well and 40 or so of the estate owners were looking for buyers. Even the large companies were seeing a worrying drop in profits, and planters were looking to central and state government for financial relief measures to help the ailing industry in this important region that produces one-third of India's tea. Rising temperatures and insufficient rain continued to create further problems, and strikes over wages in 2015 added to disruptions in production.

The factories here make mostly CTC and orthodox black teas, which have a bright, smooth, sweet, and full-bodied character. The First Flush Dooars teas are quite fragrant while the Second Flush are more vibrant and mouth-filling. Terai teas tend to be spicier and sweeter. Some producers also make very good-quality Darjeeling-type spring teas with greenish-brown dry leaves that deliver a bright liquor with just a hint of astringency, delicate fruity and pleasant woody notes, and sweet lingering pine notes in the aftertaste. And white teas from Terai can be nutty and sweet.

Country, State, or Province
India

Number of Gardens
158 estates

Main Districts or Gardens
Dooars and Terai

Area Under Tea
97,280 hectares

Average Annual Production (Kilograms)
226 million

Terrain
Tea gardens intermingle with forests; countless rivers and streams on the flat floodplains of Dooars and marshy grasslands and gentle hills of Terai

Altitude
90 to 1,750 metres (295 to 5,741 feet)

Production Period
March to late November

Best Time to Visit
Spring/autumn

Main Varietals/Cultivars
Assamicas

Types of Tea Made
Black orthodox and CTC, and a few white teas

Predominant Flavours; Tasting Notes
BLACK: bright, smooth, full-bodied and sweet
FIRST FLUSH: fragrant, woody, fruity and sweet
WHITE: *Terai*—nutty and sweet

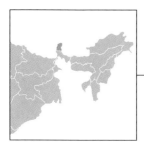

SIKKIM

(INDIA)

Sikkim is a tiny state hidden way in the Himalayas north of Darjeeling. Its ice-capped peaks create the border with Tibet and Bhutan, and the world's third-highest mountain, Kangchenjunga, soars to 8,586 metres (28,169 feet) on the border with Nepal. The only large tea estate here is Temi Tea Garden, which was established in 1969 by the government at Ravangla in South Sikkim. Seedling stock from Darjeeling was planted on a gently sloping hill, and the views of surrounding villages and hillsides are stunningly beautiful, especially in winter when the landscape is splashed with the pink of the cherry trees in full blossom. The estate is run by a tea board set up by the government of Sikkim, and provides employment for more than 600 local families. Since 2008, the garden has been fully organic and produces orthodox black teas similar to those of Darjeeling, which sell abroad and locally. Until the first decade of the 21st century, the number of smallholder farmers growing tea here was declining, but the Sikkim Commerce and Industries Department identified tea production as a way of developing the region and has actively encouraged farmers to increase cultivation of tea, cardamom, and oranges. Temi Tea Estate has been helping with this by providing seedling plants and technical support.

The organic Temi Tea Estate is the only tea garden in Sikkim. Photograph by Aaron Leonart and Raghav Ramesh; © Temi Tea Estate Sikkim

Country, State, or Province
Sikkim

Number of Gardens
1 (Temi Tea Garden) and smallholders

Area Under Tea
177 hectares

Average Annual Production (Kilograms)
100,000

Terrain
Gentle slopes and wooded valleys below the high peaks of the Himalayas

Altitude
2,133 metres (7,000 feet)

Production Period
Late March to October

Best Time to Visit
Spring/autumn

Main Varietals/ Cultivars
Sinensis

Types of Tea Made
Darjeeling-style black orthodox

Predominant Flavours; Tasting Notes
BLACK ORTHODOX: similar to Darjeeling flushes with the same delicate character in early spring, more rounded second flush, plainer in the monsoon, and fruity with warm woody notes in autumn

Jammu and Kashmir

PAKISTAN

**Dharmsala
Tea Company**

**Manjhee Valley
Tea Estate**

DHAULADHAR
MOUNTAINS
Kangra•
Nagrota• •Palampur
Bhawarna•

Wah Tea Estate

Pong
Reservoir

Kangra District

Beas River

Spiti River

Himachal Pradesh

CHINA

Sutlej River

Govind Sagar

★Shimla

**Nauti
Tea Factory**

Yamuna River

Ganges River

Dehradun
District

Garhwal Division

Rudraprayag
District

Alaknanda River

Gori River

★Dehradun

Chamoli
District

Pithoragarh
District

Bageshwar
District

Uttarakhand

UTTARAKHAND
TEA DEVELOPMENT BOARD,
DHARANAULA, ALMORA

**Kausani
Tea Factory**

Ramganga River

Almora District

**Ghorakhal
Tea Factory**

Kumaon Division
Nainital
District

Champawat
District

Punjab

🌿 Tea grower

🌿 Multiple growers

🔷 Place of interest

0   25   50   100 Miles

0   25   50   100 Kilometres

N
W   E
S

**Champawat
Tea Estate**

NEPAL

Udham Singh Nagar
District

Uttar Pradesh

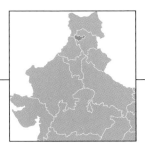

KANGRA

(INDIA)

Kangra District, hemmed in on either side by the Chamba and Mandi districts of India's north-west state of Himachal Pradesh, is India's smallest tea region. Known as "The Valley of the Gods," the region lies on the foothills of the perennially snow-covered Himalayan peaks of the Dhauladhar range, pine forests, and gushing streams that run down through the foothills to join the Ganges. It was here in 1849 that Dr. William Jameson, superintendent of the botanical gardens in Peshawar, carried out a survey to discover if this was a suitable area for tea cultivation and, in 1852, having decided that the lower slopes of the Dhauladhar range of mountains were ideal, organized for the first young Chinese tea varietals to be planted in government gardens at Kangra, Nagrota, and Bhawama. By 1892, 3,642 hectares had been planted on estates owned by British, European, and local planters. Kangra's tea became popular in India, Europe, and Central Asia, and until the late 20th century, its green teas were sold in large quantities to Afghanistan.

Then, in 1905, the area suffered the devastating effects of an earthquake, which killed 20,000 people, demolished 100,000 buildings, and wrecked the tea gardens and factories. Many of the planters departed, leaving local residents to continue small-scale cultivation of the tea, but the region never fully recovered, and today, most of the tea is grown on smallholder gardens, each of which is generally less than 2 hectares. Between 1964 and 1983, the state government helped to set up four cooperative tea factories at Bir, Palampur, Baijnath, and Sidhbari to which the local smallholder farmers could sell their fresh leaf. But these gradually became unviable, and by 2002, only the Palampur factory was still open. Then, the Tea Board of India decided to offer financial support and training to the tea farmers and at the same time encouraged successful tea growers and tea professionals from other parts of India to become involved and offer support. In addition to a large number of smallholders who cultivate approximately 2,000 hectares of rather rough bushes, a few private enterprises (Wah, Manjhee Valley, and Dharmsala estates) are now running successfully, and Kangra is once again recognised as an important Indian tea region.

The valley, which is also home to the Dalai Lama, experiences a similar climate to Darjeeling, and the growing season lasts from March to October. The bushes are all hardy, cold-resistant sinensis cultivars propagated from the original plants that were brought here in the 1850s, and manufacture of both black and green teas is all orthodox, with some teas being rolled by hand. The tiny first-flush shoots, gathered in the spring, are withered for longer than usual and rolled very lightly, giving teas that are floral, rounded, and fragrant with none of the astringency of Darjeeling teas.

The tea fields of Kangra with the Himalayas in the background. Photograph by Indi Khanna; © Tea 'n' Teas

Country, State, or Province
Kangra

Number of Gardens
3 private estates
and smallholders on
96% of cultivated land

Main Districts or Gardens
Wah, *Manjhi Valley*,
and *Dharmsala* estates

Area Under Tea
2,000 hectares of
smallholder farms, plus
3 private enterprises

**Average Annual
Production (Kilograms)**
800,000

Terrain
Some flat fields, some
gentle slopes in the Kangra
Valley, surrounded by the
snow-capped peaks of the
Dhauladhar Mountain range

Altitude
1,500 metres (4,921 feet)

Production Period
Late March to October

Best Time to Visit
Spring/autumn

Main Varietals/Cultivars
Sinensis from China

Types of Tea Made
Black orthodox, green

**Predominant Flavours;
Tasting Notes**
BLACK: *Large-Leaf
Orthodox*—amber liquors,
subtle, sweet
Broken-Leaf Orthodox—
bright red liquors, robust,
brisk taste
GREEN: light green liquors,
fresh, delicate, woody
flavour and aroma

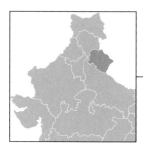

UTTARAKHAND

(INDIA)

In the 1820s, the East India Company planted experimental tea seedlings in Kumaon, Uttarakhand, when directors of the company were exploring the possibility of growing tea in the Indian Himalayas. Although the baby plants grew well here, the region was deemed unsuitable because of its distance from any ports, and so the idea of developing this as a tea region was abandoned. But the plants were left to grow wild, and cultivation on a small scale by local villagers continued until the 1990s when the state government set up a project to create jobs and improve the standards of living in this remote rural area. In 2004, the government of Uttarakhand set up the Uttarakhand Tea Development Board to further develop the state's tea industry, and since then, tea gardens have been established in Almora, Bageshwar, Champawat, Chamoli, Nainital, Pithoragarh, and Rudraprayag districts. The number of smallholder farmers has also increased, and four processing factories have been built: Ghorakhal Tea Factory in Nainital, Kausani Tea Factory in Bageshwar District, Champawat Tea Factory in Champawat, and Nauti Tea Factory in Chamoli. The mainly black tea is sold in the Kolkata auctions.

In Kumaon Division in the 1930s, a group of families from Sri Lanka arrived with a plan to rehabilitate the tea plants and revitalize the industry here. Then, in 2015, with funding raised through Kickstarter, American tea entrepreneurs Raj Vable and Keith Pennington also started working in the division to develop commercial tea production here with seeds provided by Indi Khanna of Tea 'n' Teas, based in the Nilgiris. Their goal is to train more farmers to grow tea and to create a sustainable model that brings employment and a better quality of life to the villagers. Their company, Young Mountain Tea, partnered with Avani, a local nonprofit organization, to create 400 jobs for 60 households in three villages with the aim of producing 2,000 pounds (907 kilos) of tea per year. The tea is grown organically, intercropped with plants that are used to make natural dyes used by local weavers (supported by Rashmi Bharti of Avani) who make scarves, shawls, and jackets. The tea is processed at the nearest government-run factory, managed by Desmond Birkbeck, the grandson of one of the original Sri Lankan families, and Young Mountain Tea Company sells organic-certified orthodox black and white teas made with leaf plucked from the 150-year-old bushes that grow on Birkbeck's Champawat Tea Estate. The typical signature flavour of the teas that grow here is fruity and green with hints of honeydew melon and cucumber.

Country, State or Province
Uttarakhand

Number of Gardens
8 estates, plus smallholder farmers and 4 factories

Area Under Tea
Not yet known

Average Annual Production (Kilograms)
Approximately 23.2 million (This is the total production for Arunachal Pradesh, Bihar, Manipur, Mizoram, Nagaland, Tripura, and Uttarakhand.)

Terrain
Very mountainous with high snow-topped peaks all around and rivers running down into the valleys from their source in Tibet; rich soil and great diversity of plants and wild life

Altitude
Some growers at 1,100 to 1,900 metres (3,609 to 6,234 feet); the majority at 1,400 to 1,700 metres (4,593 to 5,576 feet)

Production Period
March to October

Best Time to Visit
Spring/autumn

Main Varietals/Cultivars
Original assamicas and new seeds from the Nilgiris

Types of Tea Made
Black orthodox and white

Predominant Flavours; Tasting Notes
BLACK: fragrant, with light body and vegetal finish
WHITE: fruity and green, with hints of honey-dew melon, cucumber, and honeysuckle

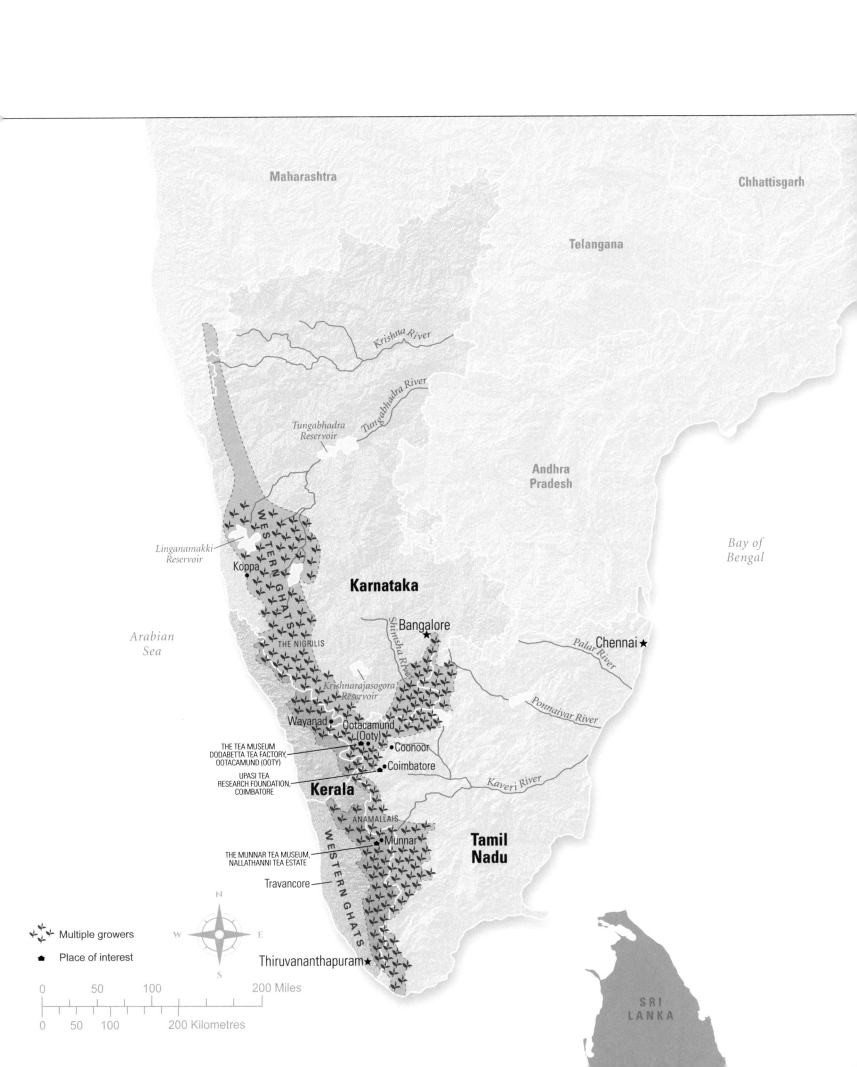

Maharashtra

Chhattisgarh

Telangana

Krishna River

Tungabhadra River

Tungabhadra
Reservoir

Andhra
Pradesh

Bay of
Bengal

Linganamakki
Reservoir

WESTERN GHATS

Koppa

Karnataka

Arabian
Sea

THE NIGRILIS

Shimsha River

Bangalore

Chennai ★

Palar River

Krishnarajasogora
Resrvoir

Ponnaiyar River

Wayanad

Ootacamund
(Ooty)

THE TEA MUSEUM
DODABETTA TEA FACTORY,
OOTACAMUND (OOTY)

Coonoor

Coimbatore

UPASI TEA
RESEARCH FOUNDATION,
COIMBATORE

Kaveri River

Kerala

ANAMALLAIS

Tamil
Nadu

THE MUNNAR TEA MUSEUM,
NALLATHANNI TEA ESTATE

Munnar

Travancore

WESTERN GHATS

Multiple growers

Place of interest

N
W   E
S

Thiruvananthapuram ★

0   50   100   200 Miles

0   50   100   200 Kilometres

SRI
LANKA

THE NILGIRIS

(SOUTHERN INDIA)

Nilgiris translates as "Blue Mountains" (*neelum* means "blue," and *giri* means "mountain"), and the mountains were so named because of the violet-blue Neelakurinji bushes that blossom here once every 12 years. The plateau lies at the southern end of the Western Ghats in southern India, a region of high rolling hills covered in natural wild forest and grassland punctuated by vast lakes, small trickling streams, and swirling rivers that water the land on their way down to the plains below. In the 1850s, the government initiated the planting of eucalyptus and acacia trees, pines, conifers, and cypresses, and these now grow throughout the region. The area is home to tigers, elephants, wild boars, monkeys, panthers, leopards, bison, porcupines, deer, mongeese, wild peacocks, and large sambar deer with their spreading antler crowns.

The Nilgiri mountain area came under British control in 1789, and 30 years later, in 1819, two British civil servants discovered the comfortably cool climate and beautiful landscape of these rolling hills. Kotagiri became a popular place of residence for Europeans, and Ootacamund, today a busy town known affectionately as Ooty, developed as a summer hill resort with sanatarium and guesthouses, and eventually became the seat of government for Madras. Once the East India Company had proved that tea could be cultivated on Indian soil and the first Assam gardens had started producing large quantities of tea, the Nilgiris became the centre for trials in southern India. The first experimental plantings were carried out at a farm in Ketti in 1835, and in 1843, Kannahutty Tea Estate was established by M. D. Cockburn, coffee planter and district collector for Salem in Tamil Nadu. The more concentrated development of the area began with the creation of Thiashola and Dunsandle tea estates in 1859, and the gradual growth of the tea industry here continued through the second half of the 19th century, with further large-scale expansion taking place between 1904 and 1911. When India became independent from Britain, many of the estates were acquired by local private companies. As the industry grew and the quantities of tea being produced increased, tea auctions were set up in several local towns. In 1947, the first auction took place in Cochin, and this is now the most important of India's auctions after Kolkata and Guwahati in Assam. Coonoor's first auction took place in 1963 and Coimbatore's in 1981. Today, roughly 70 percent of Nilgiri teas are sold through these auction centres.

The area was badly affected when Russia started buying very large quantities of Nilgiri teas at the auctions. The producers knew that they could sell the Russian buyers just about every particle of tea they produced, no matter how good or bad, so there was a general drop in the quality of Nilgiri teas. When the Russian market collapsed in the 1990s, the Nilgiri factories found it hard to recover economically and difficult to regain the quality of the teas they had been making before the Soviet boom. Today, the large private tea estates account for approximately 30 percent of production, while the majority of the tea is grown by smallholder farmers who cultivate their own small pieces of land, usually less than 1 hectare, and sell their fresh leaf into bought-leaf factories, or to the factories on the large estates. The number of smallholder farmers has been steadily increasing over recent years due to an increase in tea prices. There are also state-owned tea gardens and co-operative factories. Of the 130 million kilos (286.6 million pounds) of tea made in the Nilgiris, smallholder tea accounts for some 80 million kilos (176.3 million pounds). Most of the tea is CTC black, but some factories also produce orthodox black teas. And to combat a recent drop in CTC prices that has resulted from the large quantities of CTC teas being made by countries such as Argentina and Vietnam, some Nilgiri producers are now making speciality white, green, and black teas that fetch better prices on the world market. Nilgiri includes the smaller tea areas of Anamallais, Karnataka, Munnar, Travancore, and Wayanad and is India's second-largest tea-producing region after Assam.

THE TEAS OF NILGIRI AND SOUTHERN INDIA

The tea bushes grow here at some of the highest elevations in the world. The altitudes, rich soil, and generous rainfall make this a high-yielding area of teas that are fruity, mellow, and well balanced. As in Sri Lanka, the high-grown teas are the finest and most fragrant and have subtle fruity notes, with sometimes a hint of the perfume from the eucalyptus and cypress trees that grow here. They are usually sold as single-origin or single-estate teas. The mid-grown teas are of medium quality, and the teas that grow on the lower slopes are generally stronger, with a mellow aroma and brisk, bright liquors. The lower-grown teas are often blended or used as a base for flavoured teas. Nilgiri teas do not cloud as they cool down and so are particularly suitable for the preparation of iced teas.

ABOVE LEFT: Tea bushes shaded by silver oak trees on the steep slopes of the Nilgiri Hills. Photograph courtesy of *camellia-sinensis.com* ABOVE RIGHT: A tea plucker at work in the Nilgiri Hills, where the bushes flush all year. Photograph by Jane Pettigrew OPPOSITE PAGE: A view of the Nilgri tea gardens with silver oak shade trees. Photograph by Indi Khanna; © Tea 'n' Teas

Since southern India is close to the equator, the tea bushes flush year-round, but the character improves during the dryer periods of the year. The wettest times of the year are when rain arrives with the south-west monsoon from June to September and with the north-east monsoon from October to mid-December. During the colder period in late January and February, rainfall is moderate, but temperatures can drop close to 0°C (32°F) and sometimes as low as -7°C (19°F). The daytime sunshine is very strong and can warm the air to between 16°C and 20°C (61°F to 68°F). At night, frost settles on the bushes and burns the leaves, severely damaging the plants. Some estates lose 20 percent of their tea area, and the frost-burned bushes can take two or three months to recover. The only effective way to control the damage is to spread grass or hay over the plucking table in the frost-prone areas so that the frost settles on that and not on the tea shoots. Since the damaged bushes cannot be plucked, a limited quantity of leaf is harvested from other tea plants that have not been severely affected by the cold weather. However, the low temperatures stress the plants and cause a change in the tea, and instead of their usual mellow briskness, the liquors from these "frost teas" are well structured and fine and have a very special, green spring freshness and a smooth, barley-sugar sweetness. This is partly due to the metabolites (pyruvate, acetaldehyde, and ethanol) that accumulate in the leaves due to the stressful conditions, and partly due to the manufacturing process that is adjusted to bring out the best in these teas. The leaves are withered for much longer than normal in order to reduce the water content by 65 percent, and this makes the withered leaves much drier than usual, causing dry particles to flake off during the rolling process, and giving the teas their fresh green character.

Like Darjeeling tea, Nilgiri orthodox tea is registered with its own geographic indication (GI).

ANAMALLAIS | Anamallais is a small region of tropical rainforest wedged on the Valparai Plateau between Tamil Nadu and Kerala, just across the hills from the High Ranges. The name means "Elephant Mountains," and it was once important for its coffee plantations established by the British in the 1850s. In the late 1800s, tea was planted where coffee once grew (before being attacked by the same rust fungus that killed Ceylon's coffee bushes), and there are now approximately 12,000 hectares under tea. Four protected wildlife sanctuaries surround the undulating fields of tea—Indira Gandhi Wildlife Sanctuary, Chinnar Wildlife Sanctuary, Eravikulam National Park, and Parambikulam Wildlife Sanctuary—and coffee and cardamom also grow well here. Elephants and black panthers wander freely through these grassy hills, and it is not uncommon to see sambar, civet cats, and lion-tailed macaques. Elevations range from 900 to 1,600 metres (2,953 to 5,249 feet), and the teas give golden liquors that are bright and strong, brisk and vibrant, with a complex intensity of floral and biscuity (slightly sweet cookie) notes.

KARNATAKA | Karnataka was formerly Mysore State, which was created as a new state in 1956 and renamed in 1971. It is an important coffee region that was developed in the 1840s, but tea was also planted here. Today, there are some 2,140 hectares of the tea bushes at an altitude of 1,524 metres (5,000 feet). The tea is scattered amongst spice groves, cashew nut gardens, rubber plantations, and vast areas of coffee, and elephants and tigers wander the forests where teak, ebony, and rosewood trees grow. At Koppa, to the north-west of Bangalore, there is an important Regional Tea Centre, which was set up in 1986 to advise and train tea planters in general areas of tea cultivation such as crop production and disease control. The centre is also important for its work in the screening of tea clones and irrigation. Karnataka teas yield golden liquors that are much less strong and complex than some of the other southern teas. They are fragrant and balanced and have medium body and moderate briskness.

MUNNAR | Also referred to as the High Ranges, Munnar was once a favourite British hill resort in the Western Ghats and is still today one of India's most popular holiday destinations. Its name means "Three Rivers," and the land here is watered by the Madhurapuzha, Nallathanni, and Kundaly rivers that tumble down through the virgin forest, open grasslands, and green valleys where buffalo, bison, spotted deer, tigers, leopards, and monkeys roam wild.

The first Munnar tea was planted at Parvathi Tea Estate (now part of Sevenmullay Estate) in the 1870s by Scottish planter A. H. Sharp. In 1895, Messrs Finlay Muir & Company purchased 33 tea gardens here and, at the same time, bought nine estates in the Anamallais. The Kanan Devan Hills Produce Company was formed in 1897 (today, the Kanan Devan Hills Plantations Company), and by 1915, there were 16 factories operating. A severe monsoon hit the region in 1924, causing landslides and heavy flooding, which destroyed housing, stole lives, and badly damaged the tea bushes, but large-scale replanting was carried out after the disaster and the area has continued to thrive. In 1964, Indian conglomerate Tata Group joined forces with Finlay to develop a range of value-added teas, and in 1983, Finlay sold all its interests in the area to Tata Tea Ltd, which today owns 16 estates.

Munnar tea estates, among the highest in the world at 2,600 metres (8,530 feet), nestle in a circular valley that dips like a shallow bowl into the plateau close to the town of Munnar. The teas from these unusually high gardens give liquors that are golden amber, clean, strong, and brisk with malty, biscuity (slightly sweet cookie) notes and hints of fruit and a lingering sweetness in the aftertaste.

Photograph by Indi Khanna; © Tea 'n' Teas

TRAVANCORE | Travancore was once the summer retreat of the maharaja of Travancore who had two palaces here. Development of coffee plantations began in the 1850s and '60s, but when the coffee rust fungus attacked the bushes in 1875, the planters turned to tea. The first tea estate, Penshurst, was laid out in the Peermade Hills that same year by F. M. Parker. In 1897, the Travancore Tea Estate Company was established, vast new areas of land were cleared of trees, and seedling tea bushes were planted. By 1906, there were 3,237.48 hectares under tea, but the overdevelopment of the region and the increased deforestation led to soil erosion, flooding, and landslides, and in 1913, the Travancore government introduced legislation to limit the amount of development in the area.

The area today comprises Peermade, Vagamon, Thekkady, and Vandiperiyar, and 14,000 hectares are planted with tea at elevations of between 300 and 2,500 metres (984 and 8,202 feet). Annual production amounts to 20 million kilos (44 million pounds) of mainly black teas that are balanced and fragrant and have good body and briskness. However, as in other parts of India, the tea industry here has suffered in recent years from the low price and oversupply of tea on the world market, rising costs of production, low productivity, weak management, and the fact that most of the growers are smallholder farmers who sell their leaf into bought-leaf factories.

WAYANAD | Wayanad lies in the north-east of Kerala State, and its rolling hills are clothed in evergreen forests and plantations growing tea, rubber, coffee, and spices, especially cardamom. The first tea garden established here in 1874 was New Hope Estate in Ouchterlony Valley. In 1880, rumours spread claiming that there was gold in the hills in this part of the Western Ghats. A number of large companies purchased coffee and tea estates in Cherambadi, Devala, and Pundalur, and other businesses, particularly mining companies, rapidly bought up land. But there was no gold, and the speculators' dreams crashed. At the same time, coffee, which had been an important crop here, also failed due to the coffee rust fungus that had devastated the bushes in Sri Lanka. Tea was seen as a safe and sensible alternative, and the first of the new gardens, Wentworth Estate, was established in 1897. The area today has many tea plantations at altitudes ranging from 850 to 1,400 metres (2,789 to 4,593 feet) and covering a total area of 5,470 hectares. Each year, the factories produce 16 million kilos (35 million pounds) of mainly full-bodied black teas that brew earthy, reddish liquors and have a mild and mellow character with biscuity (slightly sweet cookie) notes.

Country, State, or Province
Nilgiri Hills in Kerala and Tamil Nadu, including Anamallais, Karnataka, Munnar, Travancore, Wyanad

Number of Gardens
More than 200 large companies, 80,000 smallholders, 165 bought-leaf factories

Area Under Tea
66,175 hectares

Average Annual Production (Kilograms)
230 million, including—
Karnataka: 5 million
Kerala: 56 million
Tamil Nadu: 135 million

Terrain
Very high, smooth, rolling hills of tea gardens, forests, grasslands, part of a bio reserve, all framed by the high misty peaks of the Western Ghats

Altitude
2,286 to 2,438 metres (7,500 to 8,000 feet)

Production Period
All year, with a cold, frosty snap in January each year in some areas

Best Time to Visit
All year

Main Varietals/Cultivars
Mostly assamicas, a few original sinensis from China planted in 1850s

Types of Tea Made
Black CTC and orthodox, green, white

Predominant Flavours; Tasting Notes
BLACK: golden liquors, crisp, fragrant, aromatic, with delicate floral notes (See text for slight regional differences.)
GREEN: The best are sweet and vegetal, with hints of buttered spring greens and broccoli.
WHITE: The best are crisp and clean, with gentle citrus notes.

RUSSIA

CHINA

NORTH
KOREA

Sea of
Japan

Hokkaido

•Sapporo

Japan

Honshu

Ibaraki

Saitama

Gifu

SHIZUOKA GREEN
TEA MUSEUM OF
OCHANOSATO

Shiga

★Tokyo

★Seoul

BEAUTIFUL
TEA MUSEUM

South
Korea

Yellow
Sea

JIRI MOUNTAIN

Jeonnam
Province

Hadong County

Boseong
County

Fukuoka

Saga

Nagasaki

OSULLOC TEA MUSEUM

Jeju
Island

CHINA

East
China
Sea

Ryuku Islands

Okinawa

TOGANOO-SAN
KOSANJI TEMPLE

Okayama

Kyoto

Shimane

Yamaguchi

Uji

•Yokohama

Shizuoka

KANAYA TEA
RESEARCH STATION

TEA SCIENCE CENTER
UNIVERSITY OF SHIZUOKA

Aichi

Kakegawa

NATIONAL INSTITUTE OF
VEGETABLE AND TEA SCIENCE

Nara

Mie

Tokushima

HOSHINO
TEA MUSEUM

Shikoku

Kochi

Oita

Kumamoto

Kyushu

Miyazaki

MAKURAZAHI
TEA EXPERIMENT
STATION

Kagoshima

Multiple growers

Mountain

Place of interest

N

W   E

S

0   125   250   500 Miles

0   125 250   500 Kilometres

JAPAN

Tea first arrived in Japan in the first decade of the 9th century when Buddhist monks such as Eichu, Saichō, and Kūkai brought tea seeds with them when they returned from periods of study in Chinese monasteries. In 815, the *Nihon Koki* (*Later Chronicles of Japan*) recorded that Eichu invited Emperor Saga to the Bonshakuji Temple and served him a bowl of green tea. This was probably prepared from a brick of compressed green tea, popular at that time in China, and brewed by grinding the tea, mixing it with hot water, and adding salt, ginger, and other spices to the liquor. Saga must have enjoyed it because, less than two months later, he ordered tea to be planted in the capital and in the grounds of the imperial palace, and he commanded that he was to be presented with tea every year. However, after his death in 842, the custom of drinking tea at court declined, although the beverage remained popular in Buddhist shrines and temples where the priests often drank it for its medicinal properties.

In 1191, when the monk Eisai returned from studying in China, he introduced Zen, a new form of Buddhism, and a new style of tea. The Chinese were by now drinking powdered tea ground from dried green leaves and whipped into hot water with a bamboo whisk. Eisai wrote, "Tea leaves picked in the morning should be immediately steamed. Dry them during the day and roast them carefully on a roasting shelf through the night until the next day. . . . Tea should be made with very hot, clear water. The amount used should be two or three spoonfuls." This was the first time that matcha was drunk in Japan, and Eisai encouraged its consumption by explaining the health benefits in his *Kissayōjōki* (*Treatise on Tea Drinking for Health*), written in 1211: "Tea is the ultimate mental and medical remedy and has the ability to make one's life more full and complete." He added, "A medicine is for one disease only, but green tea is a kind of panacea that can prevent and treat all sort of ailments."

Eisai planted some of the seeds he had brought from China in the Kyushu area, and he also gave some to the priest Myoe Shonin, who planted them at his temple Kosanji in the Toganoo Mountains in Kyoto. When the seedlings had matured, Myoe transplanted them to Uji, and a stone monument at the gates of Uji's Manpukuji Temple records that, "From the hillside of Toganoo, a Horse was led and where it left its hoof prints, Seedlings were planted, One in each." The leaves plucked from the young bushes were processed by steaming, the method then used in China. During the 13th century, as well as being drunk in Buddhist temples to help the monks stay awake through long periods of prayer, tea also played an important role at banquets held by the ruling warrior class. After copious quantities of food and rice wine had been consumed, rather rowdy *tocha* tea contests were held during which participants were challenged to distinguish *honcha* (real tea from Toganoo) from *hicha* (teas from other areas).

In the 15th century, the meaning and style of tea drinking acquired a more spiritual role as influential Zen Buddhist tea masters developed *Chado* (The Way of Tea). Their quieter, more frugal, and rustic tea ritual revered the simple life of respectful self-control and appreciation of the imperfect, quiet beauty of the natural world. Promoted by legendary tea master Sen no Rikyu in the 16th century, the ceremonial preparation of whisked matcha now appealed not just to priests and monks in Buddhist temples but also to the aristocracy and to the newly wealthy merchant class. But matcha was too expensive for ordinary people, so they made do with a common tea, *hiboshu-bancha*, made from leaves that were boiled and dried in the sun.

In the 15th century, the Chinese method of panning rather than steaming the fresh leaves was introduced to tea makers in Kyushu, and while powdered whisked tea was still served as part of the Zen tea ceremony, panned loose-leaf teas were now widely drunk and continued to be popular until the 18th century. However, many of these teas were of very poor quality, and so, in 1738, Uji tea maker Nagatani Soen developed a new method to improve the taste and colour by steaming the tea before rolling and drying the leaves. The clear, bright green liquors had an attractively mild, sweet taste, and one famous tea merchant, Baisao, declared the tea to be "an incomparable beverage with an exquisite colour and an aroma of delectable freshness." Soon, the new *sencha* tea was being made and consumed all over Japan, and other types of steamed green tea were also developed. In the 1830s, Kahei Yamamoto, a tea grower in Uji, refined the method of shading the bushes before plucking the shoots to make *gyokuro*, and the same technique was used to produce *tencha* (to make matcha). The intense sweetness of these new teas and their increasing availability gave tea a new appeal to a wider audience, including ordinary people as well as the upper classes.

In 1859, Japanese teas began to find their way into a wider market when Japanese ports were opened for trade with America. The change came about because the American whaling industry needed ports to put into for supplies and protection from storms while working in the seas around Japan. The Japanese government signed a friendship and trade agreement with America (and shortly afterwards with Holland, Russia, Britain, and France), and the port of Yokohama was opened. As the whaling trade died out soon after, the ships involved sailed back home laden not with whale oil but with Japanese tea, and by 1869, American tea merchants were importing a quarter of their tea from Japan. Japan's new relationship with the United States and other industrialised countries encouraged a desire to catch up with the West, and from the 1880s, new tea-processing machinery and production methods were introduced. And while the West was learning to love Japan's teas, the Japanese themselves were also drinking more tea. The cultivation of tea was encouraged, and instead of being grown in remote mountain regions, large plantations were now laid out on lower flatter land. Output steadily increased, domestic consumption rose, and by the 1920s, Japan exported a record total of more than 20 million kilos (44 million pounds).

As well as green tea, Japan also started manufacturing black tea for export to compete with origins such as India and Ceylon, and to serve consumers in the country's popular western cafés called *kissatens*. Traditional tea ceremony schools also changed and went from being the bastion of upper-class male culture, controlled by the aristocracy and warrior class, to places where wealthy middle-class women could refine their skills of etiquette while learning about Japanese culture and art. Today, approximately 1 million people, mainly women, attend tea ceremony schools on a regular basis.

Through the 20th century, the Japanese tea business became a highly developed, computerised industry, and this allowed the country to produce high-quality teas at affordable prices for the domestic market. In the 1980s and '90s, the industry also pioneered ready-to-drink teas and the technology to dispense them hot or cold from machines on street corners. These teas now account for around half of the country's tea market and outsell other convenience drinks. Ninety-seven percent of all the teas produced are consumed in Japan, and tea is also widely used in the food industry in cakes, confectionery, savoury snacks, ice creams, and noodles. Japanese consumers are amongst the most health conscious in the world and see green tea as beneficial to their general well-being. Whether they eat tea, drink it from a bottle or a can, or start their day with a shot of matcha, tea is a central part of Japanese life.

THE CULTIVATION OF JAPANESE TEA

Eisai is said to have planted his Chinese tea seeds in Seburisan in Saga Prefecture on the island of Kyushu. Myoe Shonin also raised seedlings in Uji in Kyoto Prefecture, and the cultivation of tea gradually spread to Yamato in Nara Prefecture, Iga and Ise in Mie Prefecture, and the old province of Musashi around Tokyo. The bushes were planted individually (rather than in organised rows as they are today) in the gardens around Buddhist temples. The idea of shading the tea developed in the 16th century, at first to make sencha, but then this became the traditional technique for producing matcha and gyokuro. The reduction of light inhibits photosynthesis in the leaves and causes their chemical composition to change. The level of bitter catechins is reduced while the amount of chlorophyll, caffeine, theophylline (a muscle relaxant), and L-theanine amino acid are increased. The teas are less bitter, sweeter, and more intensely umami in character. Originally, the plants were shaded by spreading straw or reeds directly onto the top of the bushes. Today, *tana* shading is created by erecting a wire or trellis frame 1.8 to 2.1 metres (6 to 7 feet) above the tea garden and covering it with black netting or plastic canvas. This cuts out 90 percent of the sunlight and is used for the production of tencha for matcha and gyokuro. *Jikagise* shading wraps each row of bushes in netting that sits just above the bushes. This cuts out 50 percent of the light and is used more often by small farmers and for the production of *kabusecha* shaded teas (*kabuse* means "nets").

As the industry developed in the second half of the 19th century, Japan was the first country to introduce the use of plucking shears and these allowed pluckers to harvest the crop between five and 10 times faster. Today, the finest high-grade senchas, gyokuros, and tenchas are still picked by hand, but most harvesting is carried out by machines. These include portable machines operated by one or two people, self-propelled machines that are walked or ridden, and machines that run on rails. Hand-pluckers collect between 10 and 15 kilos (22 to 33 pounds) per person per day; shear pluckers, 100 to 200 kilos (220 to 441 pounds); two-person portable hedge-trimmer machines, between 700 and 1,000 kilos (1,543 to 2,205 pounds); ride-on machines, between 4,000 and 5,000 kilos (8,818 to 11,023 pounds); and a harvester running on rails, between 2,000 and 3,000 kilos (4,409 to 6,614 pounds) per day. The use of mechanical harvesting depends on the location of individual farms. In higher regions where tea grows on steep slopes, the tea is mainly handpicked or harvested with hedge trimmers. On lower, flatter land, large farms are equipped with ride-on mechanical harvesters and machines that run on tracks.

Most farms today are family run and cover an average of 4 to 6 hectares, while some large companies cultivate larger plantations of between 6 and 20 hectares. The majority of bushes are relatively young, but some ancient bushes can still be found. Trees that are 200 to 300 years old still grow in Gifu Prefecture around Kasuga Village; Ureshino in Saga Prefecture has a 400-year-old tree with 10 trunks growing up from the base; and an old tree with a diameter of 0.67 metres (2.2 feet) and 4.1 metres (13.5 feet) tall grows in Kirishima-shi, Kagoshima Prefecture. In the south-west of Japan, wild native plants called *yamacha* appear to date back to the earliest cultivation of tea in Japan when tea seeds from China were planted. A study led by Professor Minoru Hashimoto, of the Faculty of Agriculture at Meijo University, suggested that these native plants may have been cultivated secretly during the 12th and 13th centuries to avoid paying taxes imposed on farmers by government. And a 2002 study concluded that modern Japanese cultivars are closely related to yamacha bushes and were probably bred from them. Native bushes are referred to as *zairai* plants, and because they are an inconsistent mix of different varietals, with different leaf shapes and sizes and different flavours, they have gradually been replaced by new cultivars. However, they are considered by some farmers to be of value since they have deep roots, are resistant to insect attack, and brew teas that perhaps have the true original character of Japanese tea.

As in China, the best teas are harvested in the spring from late April to mid-May, the second harvest takes place in late June, the third in late July and early August, and the fourth and last harvest of the year takes place in mid-September. Shaded teas are only produced from the earlier harvests and account for a very small proportion of the total tea output. The covering that is erected around the tea plants to create a shaded environment also affords protection from frost, an annual hazard in this seasonal growing region. Frost damages the new buds and can mean huge financial losses for the farmer. So, in the past, the plants were protected with a layer of straw (the origin of the idea of shading the tea), but today, warm air fans are erected on masts standing 6 to 8 metres (20 to 26 feet) high at intervals across the tea field; or water sprinklers are used to prevent desiccation in the plants and render them less vulnerable to frost. The sprinklers are also used to spray pesticides when required. The high use of pesticides is of current concern and makes some of Japan's teas difficult to sell into the international market.

The fact that the ocean is never more than 121 kilometres (75 miles) away from any tea-growing location in Japan gives the teas their characteristic marine character with strong vegetal hints of seaweed. Altitude also plays its part, and although Japanese teas grow at relatively low altitudes compared to China and India, elevations of around 600 to 700 metres (1,969 to 2,297 feet) in some regions are enough to give the teas a better aroma and a more intense flavour. The highest tea garden in Japan is situated at 1,050 metres (3,445 feet) in Umegashima in Shizuoka.

JAPANESE TEAS

In general, Japanese tea producers in the different regions of the country make the same types of green tea (*ryokucha*), so for example, tea lovers can enjoy sencha green tea made in Shizuoka in the east, in Uji in the centre of the country, or in Kyushu in the south. This does not mean that those sencha teas will all taste the same since the cultivar, the terroir, and the tea maker's individual processing styles also play a part in creating the particular character of each region's teas. Nor does it mean that every type of tea can be found in every region, for producers in certain areas often focus on particular types. But unlike China or India, where certain regions are known for specific teas, most of Japan's teas are made throughout the country using the same manufacturing techniques.

A group of tea pickers in Japan. Photograph courtesy of Sasuki Green Tea Co., Ltd.

DIFFERENT TYPES OF JAPANESE TEA AND HOW THEY ARE MADE

Aracha (Crude Tea) | *Aracha* is the rough, unrefined tea that results from the steaming, rolling, and drying processes used to make Japanese green tea. It contains leaves of different sizes, dusty particles, stalks, stems, and leaf veins. It is usually sold at auction to merchants and wholesalers who sort the tea and use the different components for different blends. It is sometimes drunk by the tea farmers themselves and is occasionally offered for direct sale by tea farms. Aracha is often kept in cold storage by the producers or wholesale merchants and is refined at different times through the year to meet customers' demands.

To make aracha, the freshly picked tea is brought to the factory and stored in cool humid air for between three and six hours. It then goes into a steaming machine for 30 to 45 seconds (called *asamushi* or *futsumushi*, meaning lightly steamed) or one to two minutes for *fukamushi* (deeply steamed tea). During the steaming, the heat deactivates the enzymes that would otherwise allow oxidation to take place in the leaves. The leaves become intensely green, very supple, and contain approximately 75 percent water. Next, the tea passes into a drying roller in which the leaves are twisted and dried in hot air for about 45 minutes to reduce the water content to around 50 percent. The leaves are then rolled without heat for about 20 minutes in order to break the cells and work the juices evenly through the leaves. The next stage is to roll the tea again in hot air to lower the water content to 30 percent, and then the tea is dried to 13 percent moisture while the leaves are pressed and shaped for about 40 minutes. Finally, the flat needles of tea pass through a dryer for another 30 minutes to reduce the moisture to 5 percent. The resulting tea is a mix of large and small pieces of leaf, stalk, stems, and fibre.

In the past, the different processes were carried out by hand using the *temomi* method. Said to have been invented by a Zen priest in 1400, the tea was rolled on a table called a *hoiro*, under which a furnace created the heat required to dry the tea. The tea master rolled the tea for about four hours on the warm table until all the leaves were long, thin, and dry. In the 1800s, several schools of handmade teas encouraged the process, and by 1905, the temomi method had become the accepted process and produced shiny, dark green needles. Temomi is still used today by small organisations wishing to preserve the old processing method, but most Japanese tea is today manufactured in large factories, and aracha is manufactured in automated machines operated by computers. In smaller factories, the tea is moved from one process to the next by hand. The finished aracha is sold to wholesalers who refine it, separating stalks from leaves and buds, to make sencha, bancha, kukicha, mecha, etcetera, depending on the season of the harvest and the style of the leaf.

Asamushicha | A lightly steamed tea, most often used to refer to sencha.

Awabancha | A dark tea from Fukuoka and Tokushima made from bancha that is boiled, rubbed or rolled, pressed into a barrel, and sealed. Anaerobic fermentation takes place due to lactic acid bacteria in the tea. Before use, the tea is dried in the sun for a day.

Bancha | Bancha, 24.7 percent of Japan's tea, is made by the same process as sencha, first manufactured as aracha, but from lower-quality leaves of the first flush (*ichibancha*), or from the second flush (*nibancha*) or third flush (*sanbancha*). The leaves are rougher and bigger than quality sencha, contain fewer amino acids, and so taste less sweet and less intense. Bancha is often used to make inexpensive teas such as *genmaicha*, or is roasted to make *hojicha*. In the Kyoto region, some producers make a roasted tea, which is also called bancha. Outside Kyoto, the same roasted tea is known as Kyobancha. Brew the tea at 75°C (167°F).

Chumushicha | A green tea that is steamed for a longer time than a lightly steamed tea and a shorter time than a deeply steamed tea.

Fukamushicha | A green tea that is steamed for one to three minutes.

Genmaicha | Genmaicha is another inexpensive tea made with lower grades of green tea that are blended with rice (*genmai*) that has been soaked in water, steamed, dried, roasted, and cooled. During the roasting, some of the grains pop and produce popcorn-like pieces. Reputedly, genmaicha originated as a way of making expensive tea go further. Genmaicha is traditionally made using bancha, but it is also produced today using sencha, gyokuro, and hojicha. Its popularity is enhanced by its easy preparation and sweet nutty taste. Powdered matcha is sometimes added to the blend to make what is called *matcha-iri genmaicha*. Brew at around 82°C (180°F).

Goishicha | A fermented dark tea made in Kochi Prefecture on Shikoku Island. The tea leaves are steamed, layered, and covered to allow them to ferment. They are then placed in a barrel with a weight on top while the fermentation continues. The final stage is to dry the tea in the sun.

Gyokuro (Jade Dew) | Gyokuro is considered the very finest of Japanese green tea and accounts for only 0.3 percent of Japan's annual production. Like tencha, used to make powdered matcha, it is shaded for approximately three weeks before being harvested. This shading reduces the amount of light reaching the plants to 10 percent, and the leaves contain high levels of chlorophyll, caffeine, and L-theanine, which gives the tea its smooth, sweet umami taste.

To shade the tea as it grows, a frame is erected over the bushes and a covering of straw, bamboo mesh, black plastic, or nylon canvas is laid over the top to slightly reduce the light. Over the next few days, additional layers are added to gradually reduce the light to about 10 percent. The lack of light makes the plants develop long stems and long thin leaves as they strive upwards towards the small amount of light filtering through. After the leaves are plucked, gyokuro is processed in a similar way to sencha. First, the leaves are steamed, then heated and rolled to develop the flavour of the tea—first loosely, then more tightly to twist the leaves and develop the characteristic needle shape. Then, they are rolled without heat, rolled again in hot air, pressed, and finally dried until the water content is reduced to around 5 percent. The finished tea is a mix of small and large pieces of leaf, stalk, stems, and fibre, and this is sold to a wholesaler who carries out the refining process. The crude tea mixture has to be sorted to remove buds, flaky particles, and stems, leaving neat, blue-green needles of gyokuro. These are then graded and ready for blending. The removed buds, stalks, and stems are packaged separately as *gyokuro mecha*, *karigane*, and *konacha gyokuro-ko* (flakes and small particles). Gyokuro is best brewed using water at 50°C to 60°C (122°F to 140°F).

Hojicha | Hojicha is a roasted tea. Lower grades of steamed green teas such as bancha and *kukicha* are roasted over a high heat (between 170°C and 200°C [338°F to 392°F]) for a short time. First made in the 1920s, hojicha was traditionally roasted in a porcelain pot set over charcoal by tea merchants, but today, many producers make their own hojicha by roasting the leaves in a rotating hot drum. The leaves become reddish brown and contain less caffeine and fewer tannins, so the tea is milder and the roasting gives it a toasty, nutty, slightly caramelised note. It is often drunk after meals and before going to sleep and is popular amongst children and the elderly. Best brewed at 95°C (203°F).

Japanese Dark Tea | A few Japanese producers now make Puerh-style dark teas under carefully controlled, hygienic conditions. A crude aracha (a steamed equivalent to panned maocha in China) is moistened, pasteurised, dried and cooled, then inoculated with selected microbes such as *Aspergillus niger*, allowed to ferment, pasteurised again, blended with enzymes to enhance the aroma, pasteurised, and dried.

Kabusecha (Covered or Shaded Tea) | Kabuse teas are cultivated by putting covers directly over the tea bushes for 10 to 14 days before the tea is plucked—a shorter time than for the production of gyokuro. After harvesting, the tea is processed as aracha, which is then refined. The resulting green tea is intensely green and has characteristics of both gyokuro and sencha. Kabusecha makes up 3.1 percent of Japan's annual tea production. Brew the tea at 70°C (158°F).

Kamairicha | Kamairicha is made by panning rather than steaming and was once very common in Japan. But over the last 200 years, as steamed green teas have become more popular, kamairicha has become much rarer. The tea is processed in a *kama* (a pan like a wok), which is set into a wall at an angle of 45 degrees. The leaves are placed in the kama and turned with a brush or the hands against the hot metal in the same way that Chinese teas are panned. It is important that the leaves are moved continually to de-activate the enzymes without burning the leaves as they lose their water content. There are two styles of kamairicha. Kamairi

tamaryokucha (sometimes called kamaguri) is panned and the leaves are then rolled to produce curled dry leaves. Kamanobicha (pan-stretched tea) is panned but is then rolled in a special rotating drum called a *shimeiri-ki* to make flat sencha-style needles of dry tea. Kamairicha is best brewed at 90°C (194°C).

Karigane (Wild Goose) | Karigane is made from the *kuki*, or stalks, of gyokuro and the highest-quality sencha tea. The tea's unusual name is said to come from the fact that the dried tea leaves look like the logs in the sea on which migrating geese sometimes rest during their long journey. Brew at 70°C to 80°C (158°F to 176°F).

Konacha (Residual Green Tea) | Konacha is made from broken leaves and small particles from other teas, mainly sencha. The best-known konacha is *agari*, which is served in sushi restaurants. Unlike other Japanese green teas, it is usually brewed with water that is just below boiling.

Kukicha (Stalk Tea) | *Kuki* means "twig or stalk," and kukicha is composed mainly of stems and stalks that have been discarded during the refining of sencha. Kukicha can be a green tea or a roasted green tea. Both are considered to be lower in caffeine than Japanese leaf teas and have a delicious sweet character. Kukicha is sometimes called Bocha (stick tea) and is best brewed at 70°C to 80°C (158°F to 176°F).

Matcha | Although its origins are Chinese, modern-day matcha is a very different tea from the powdered teas first imported from China in the 12th century. Matcha is made by grinding tencha leaves to a fine powder. The highest-grade matchas are made from tencha from the Samidori, Okumidori, and Yabukita cultivars, which, as with the production of gyokuro, are grown under shade for about three weeks before being picked. The tea develops long, thin stems as it grows towards the limited light. In early May, the flush is picked by hand. The tea is then steamed, cooled, and dried, without going through the rolling and pressing stages used to make sencha and bancha. The unrefined tea is stored in refrigerated conditions and is refined in small quantities as required to make matcha.

To turn the tencha into matcha, the tea is cut to uniform-size pieces, and all the veins and stalks are blown from the tea by powerful fans. The remaining tea is then sifted, cut again, and dried to intensify the aroma and flavour. Electrostatic rollers remove any remaining veins and stems, and the different qualities of tencha are then blended. To turn tencha to matcha, the tea is fed into traditional hand-turned or electrically powered stone mills that very slowly grind the tea to a very fine, bright emerald-green powder. One mill grinds approximately 40 grams of matcha an hour, and because matcha degrades quickly once it comes into contact with the air, it is packed in quantities of 40 grams or less, often in air-tight foil bags which are sealed tightly inside small tins with a double lid, or in small, air-tight, single-serve sachets like those used for sugar in the service industry.

Matcha is whisked into hot water during the Japanese Tea Ceremony, but is also very popular today as an everyday tea, and is also used in many foods, sweets, and drink products. Tencha, which accounts for 2.7 percent of Japanese production, is almost never drunk as a leaf tea but is ground to make matcha. To prepare matcha, sieve the fine green powder into the mixing bowl to ensure there are no lumps, add a little hot water, just under boiling, and mix with a bamboo whisk to make a paste, then add more water and whisk to a froth. A battery-operated whisk can be used instead of a bamboo whisk.

Mecha | Mecha is made up of the small buds of the early tea harvests that are separated out during the sencha refining process. It is often strong in taste and flavour and needs careful, short brewing at 90°C (194°F) so that the liquor does not become bitter.

Ryokucha | This just means "green tea."

Sencha | Sencha is the country's most popular green tea and accounts for 63.4 percent of all Japan's tea. It is refined from aracha and can be made in two styles: asamushi (or futsumushi), which involves a light 30- to 45-second steaming, and fukamushi (deep steaming), which involves steaming the leaves for one or two minutes. The longer steaming gives the leaves an intense green and yields liquors with more body and less astringency, and also slightly reduces the caffeine in the tea. Senchas can range from very expensive, high-grade teas to inexpensive, lower grades.

ABOVE LEFT: Examining green leaf as it comes out of the steaming machine where the leaves are de-enzymed to stop oxidation. Photograph courtesy of Sasuki Green Tea Co., Ltd. TOP RIGHT AND ABOVE RIGHT: Electrically operated grinding machines that reduce the dried tencha leaf to very fine matcha powder.
© Aiya Europe GmbH

To make sencha, aracha is refined in a finishing factory. The tea is separated by machines into different-sized pieces, then fired to reduce the moisture level, enhance the aroma, and reduce the grassy character of the tea. Any stalks are removed by static electricity, and finally, different batches of sencha are blended to produce teas that meet customers' requirements. Sencha teas are often a blend of teas from different regions and different cultivars. Teas grown at high altitudes have a stronger aroma, while low-grown teas are lighter in flavour. Sencha is best brewed at around 75°C (167°F).

Shincha | Shincha is the first flush or *ichibancha* (first tea) that is picked in late April and early May. Because it is the very first growth after the period of winter dormancy, the leaves contain high levels of L-theanine, and have a sweet, umami character. Most producers release shincha for sale as soon as it has been made, without refining or blending, because it captures the unique aroma and flavour of the spring harvest. Because shincha usually has a high moisture content, it does not keep its quality and flavour as well as blended sencha. Brew at around 75°C (167°F).

Tamaryokucha (also known as guricha or mushiguri) | Tamaryokucha is a refreshing green tea made by steaming, but instead of rolling the leaves into flat sencha-like needles, the tea is dried while being turned in hot air inside a revolving drum. As it dries, it becomes lightly curved or curled. Tamaryokucha is mainly produced in Kyushu and accounts for 3.4 percent of Japan's annual production. Brew at 80°C (176°F).

Tencha | Green tea that is used to make matcha. The bushes are grown under shade, like gyokuro, for the last 21 days before harvesting. The tea is processed in the same way as gyokuro but without rolling the leaves. Before grinding into matcha powder, all the veins and stalks are removed, using powerful fans and leaving flat pieces of intensely green leaf, which can be ground to high-quality matcha.

Wakoucha or Kocha (Japanese Black Tea) | Interest in black tea over the past 20 or 30 years has prompted Japanese tea growers to manufacture black tea instead of, or as well as, the traditional green. It is not the first time that Japanese producers have produced black tea. During the late 19th century, growers were encouraged by the government to make black teas in order to compete with India and Ceylon (now Sri Lanka) as an important exporter of black teas to Europe and the United States. They were not successful, but today, instead of trying to replicate the character of teas from other origins, Japanese tea makers focus on giving their black teas a distinctly Japanese flavour profile. And so, using favourite Japanese tea cultivars such as Yabukita, Benifuki, Benihomare, and Benihikari, today's Japanese orthodox black teas yield bright coppery liquors that are mild, sweet, and elegant with fragrant floral notes that are becoming popular in international markets as well as in Japan.

LEFT: New shoots of bushes used to make tencha for matcha, growing under shade, which increases the level of L-theanine amino acid in the leaves. MIDDLE: Freshly picked leaf being steamed inside a Japanese factory. Photograph courtesy of Sasuki Green Tea Co., Ltd. RIGHT: Before whisking matcha into hot water, the powder is often sieved to ensure a smooth liquor. © Aiya Europe GmbH

The breeding of new cultivars in Japan began in the 19th century when private farmers started crossbreeding established bushes. In 1932, the government started breeding new cultivars, and in 1953, the Asatsuyu (Morning Dew) was one of the first to be registered. Many new types have since been bred from it. During the 1970s, tea consumption began to increase as Japan became wealthier, but farmers could not meet the growing demand, so cultivation increased and mechanical harvesting was improved. Machine-plucking requires plants to yield well and grow evenly so that harvesters can collect shoots of regular height with the same number of leaves. The Yabukita cultivar proved suitable and became very popular but was prone to insect attack and demanded high inputs of fertiliser. So, other new cultivars were developed and over 80 are now used, although Yabukita still dominates. Work continues to create new plants to suit changing conditions and shifts in Japanese tastes.

Yabukita (north [kita] of the bamboo bush [yabu]) | The Yabukita cultivar was developed close to Shizuoka City in 1908 when Hikosaburo Sugiyama cleared a bamboo grove in order to extend his tea nursery and planted some tea seeds there. When they had grown, he chose the best two bushes, planted one on the north of the grove (Yabukita) and one on the south (Yabu Minami). Yabukita proved cold resistant, high yielding, and rich in the velvety umami taste so prized in Japanese green teas. It was tested at the Shizuoka industrial tea laboratory in 1954, registered in 1956, and soon became the most popular cultivar in the country. At one time, Yabukita accounted for almost 90 percent of Japanese plants, but today, it is less widely used. It accounts for 93 percent of the plants cultivated in the Shizuoka region where it originated. It is also widely grown in Mie (86 percent), Fukuoka (75 percent), Saitama (72 percent), Kyoto (69 percent), and Kagoshima (37 percent). The Yabukita spring flush is usually between April and mid-May, depending on the environment.

Yutakamidori | The name of Japan's second most popular cultivar means "lush green," and the teas are noted for their intense green colour and sweet flavour. It was developed from the Asatsuyu cultivar at the National Institute of Vegetable and Tea Science in Shizuoka, was registered in 1966, and is now mainly cultivated in Kagoshima and Miyazaki regions. It buds five days earlier than Yabukita and is often shaded to make gyokuro, kabuse, or fukamushi-style sencha.

Sayamakaori | This is a natural cross from Yabukita plants and was registered in 1971, intended for the production of sencha. It is easy to cultivate and is cold and frost resistant, so it grows well in the colder northern regions. It is harvested two or three days earlier than Yabukita, is rich in catechins, and has a powerful aroma and taste.

Saemidori | Saemidori is a high-quality green tea cultivar created by crossbreeding Yabukita with the Asatsuyu cultivar and was registered in 1990. It was named "clear green" because of the brilliant green liquors that it yields. It buds several days before Yabukita and gives teas with low astringency and an even higher umami level than Yabukita. It is not frost resistant and is more suitable for warmer areas such as Kyushu, where it is grown to make gyokuro and fukamushi sencha.

Okumidori | Okumidori, a cross developed in Shizuoka between a native wild zairai varietal and Yabukita, was registered in 1974, and is another high-quality cultivar originally intended for the production of sencha, but is now also used for shaded teas such as tencha (used to make matcha) and gyokuro. It shares characteristics and is sometimes blended with Yabukita. Its liquors have low astringency and a fresh fragrant character. It buds about a week after Yabukita, an advantage in places where early frosts can damage other cultivars. Okumidori is found throughout Japan, including in southern areas of Kyushu.

Gokou | Gokou cultivar was developed from a wild varietal local to the Uji area in Kyoto Prefecture and was registered in the 1950s. It buds a little later than Yabukita but has similarly high yields. Gokou has an excellent fragrance and, when shaded, produces umami-rich teas, so it is suitable for quality gyokuro and matcha. In Uji, most shaded teas are made using the Gokou or Ujihikari cultivars and these are used elsewhere in Japan, but others such as Saemidori and Samidori are also common for gyokuro and matcha.

Benihikari, Benihomare, and Benifuuki | These were developed to make black teas, called red in Asia, which explains their names—Red Light (Benihikari), Red Honour (Benihomare), and Red Wealth (Benifuuki). They are sometimes used to make green teas because greens and oolongs from these cultivars are known to contain high levels of methylated epigallocatechin gallate (EGCG), thought to reduce allergic reactions.

Benihikari was developed in the 1950s at the Makurazaki Tea Experiment Station, Kagoshima, from a pure assamica cultivar called Benikaori and a sinensis cultivar called Cn1. It was registered in 1969 and is mainly used for black tea since the green tea it produces is very astringent.

Benihomare was cultivar No. 1 when registration began in 1953. It is a pure assamica cultivar, selected from seedlings brought back from India by Tada Motokichi, who tried in the late 19th century to find cultivars outside Japan that were suitable for black tea. It is late-budding and low-yielding but is resistant to cold and produces a highly regarded, rich black tea.

Benifuuki, registered in 1993, was created by crossing the assamica Benihomare with Makura Cd86, a Darjeeling sinensis cultivar. It is high-yielding, buds shortly after Yabukita and is used to make a high-quality black tea with pleasing astringency and hints of its Darjeeling ancestry.

TOP: Fields of tea in the Kakegawa region of Shizuoka; the symbol for tea can be seen formed from bushes at the top of the hillside in the background.
TOP LEFT: Feeding fresh green leaves into a steaming machine in order to de-enzyme the tea and stop oxidation. Photograph courtesy of Sasuki Green Tea Co., Ltd.
ABOVE LEFT: In the Kakegawa region of Shizuoka, dried grasses are used to mulch and fertilise the bushes. Photograph courtesy of Asako Steward, City of Kakegawa
ABOVE RIGHT: Shaded bushes for the production of tencha (for matcha) and gyokuro. © Aiya Europe GmbH

Tea is grown in almost all of Japan's prefectures, except in the north, where temperatures are too cold. Although most producers make the most widely drunk sencha, each region specialises in particular teas, sometimes because of their tea history, sometimes because of local conditions. The most important areas are Shizuoka, Kagoshima and Mie, which together produce 67 percent of the country's tea.

Aichi | Aichi lies on the southern coast of Honshu, Japan's main island, surrounded by the other important tea-growing areas of Shizuoka, Gifu, and Mie. It is Japan's largest producer of matcha, mainly in Nishio, which grows roughly 70 percent of the country's tencha. Tea was first planted in Nishio in the 13th century when Shoichi Kokushi brought tea seeds from China and planted them at the Jisso-ji Temple. The teas quickly acquired fame around Japan for their quality and fragrance. In the 19th century, Jundo Adachi, head priest at the Koju-in Temple, brought seeds from Uji and introduced matcha production. Nishio was soon recognised as the most important region for the production of ceremonial-grade matcha. Aiya Corporation has been producing matcha here since 1888 and exports 30 percent of its total production. In Nishio's neighbouring Okazaki City, stone masons craft the stone mills required to grind tencha to produce matcha and quality of the stone and the mills helped the development of Nishio as a producer of very fine matcha.

Gifu | The best-known teas from Gifu Prefecture are grown in the mountain village of Shirakawa, which lies in a sheltered valley amongst the highest peaks of Mount Haku in the Ryōhaku Mountains. Snowy winters, high altitudes, and mountain mists give the teas, grown here for more than 400 years, their powerful aroma and sweet, lightly astringent character.

Kyoto | Kyoto Prefecture's wider tea region includes the prestigious Uji District, and tea is also grown in Wazuka. Uji's tea history dates back to the 13th century when the priest Myoe, after first planting seeds at Toganoo near Kobe, decided on Uji's Obaku area near Kyoto as a more suitable location because of its misty conditions and lack of frost. Uji tea gradually became famous and in the 14th century, the shogun Ashikaga Yoshimitsu (1358 to 1408) established Uji-shichi-meien (Seven Excellent Tea Gardens of Uji), and encouraged more farmers to grow tea. Tea made in Toganoo at this time was referred to as honcha, or "real tea," while teas from other regions were known as hicha, but the excellent quality and taste of Uji teas soon meant that they replaced Toganoo teas as honcha. Sen no Rikyu, who perfected and promoted *chanoyu*, or "way of tea," is said to have regularly visited Uji to taste the teas and hold tea ceremonies there, and his patronage further increased the popularity and fame of Uji tea. Then in 1738, a tea maker by the name of Soen Nagatani introduced a new processing method to make sencha. Until this point, the emperor and the nobility had been drinking expensive matcha, made from shaded tencha, while poorer people could only afford to drink cheap, roasted, low-grade hojicha. And while only a few producers had previously been licenced to make matcha, Nagatani's new technique meant that more local farmers could produce good-quality, loose-leaf green teas that were available to everyone. His new process, which involved steaming the freshly picked leaves for 30 to 45 seconds, then passing the tea through various drying and rolling steps, became the standard sencha process and is still used today. In Nagatani's time, the hand-processing took four hours to make 4 kilos (8.8 pounds) of dried tea. Each year, the prized first crop of shincha, designated for the emperor, was packed in jars and carried on foot from Uji to the capital Edo (now called Tokyo), a journey that took 12 to 14 days. In 1835, gyokuro was developed by Kahei Yamamoto, sixth-generation owner of the now famous green tea company Yamamotoyama, which grows tea both in Japan and Australia. Yamamoto went to Uji to study the method of processing tencha and found that the tea farmers protected their tea bushes from frost by erecting a covering of straw. When he tried to replicate this technique, he found that the tea, which he named *tamanotsuyu*, tasted sweeter. Shigejuro Eguchi developed the method further and named the resulting tea gyokuro. Today, the best gyokuro comes from Yame in Fukuoka Prefecture, Kyushu.

By the middle of the 19th century, Uji teas were recognised as the best in the country and, by the Meiji period from 1868 to 1912, was the only tea drunk at the imperial palace. Uji sencha was also amongst the green teas shipped to America when Japanese ports were opened to trade in the 1860s. The Port of Yokohama, south of Tokyo, became the centre of this new trade, and tea companies built tea-processing factories here to dry-roast the teas in a wok or in a basket placed over a brazier and remove the stems before they were shipped. Labels in English from packages shipped at that time state "pan-fired," in a wok, or "basket fired," over a brazier.

As Uji tea became more famous and more popular in the early part of the 19th century, other districts around Kyoto were developed for tea cultivation. These included Wazuka, which had been growing tea since the 13th century when a high-ranking priest had chosen it as a suitable place to plant seeds and make tea for the imperial family. Today, around 300 families grow tea on small farms that together cover some 600 hectares in Soraku District. The neat rows of tea hug the contours of the steep slopes, surrounded by dense forest in the mountains that lie between Nara and Kyoto. The mountain dew that settles on the tea in the early morning is said to contribute to the quality of Wazuka teas. The area produces approximately 47 percent of Kyoto's green teas and, because of a growing interest in matcha, processes more tencha than ever before. But because teas from the wider Kyoto area are usually sold as Uji teas, Wazuka's name is not well known outside the region.

Because many of the Kyoto region's teas are shaded teas, fewer Yabukita plants are grown, and the most popular cultivars are Gokou, Samidori, Asahi, Uji-hikari, and Saemidori. When Japanese teas are sold, any blend that contains 50 percent Kyoto tea is sold as Uji tea, even if the teas actually come from Mie, Nara, Shiga, or Wazuka.

Nara | Before Kyoto became Japan's capital city in 794, Nara had been the seat of power from 710. It was then called Yamato, so the teas made in the prefecture are often referred to as Yamato cha. The city had been the centre of Buddhism from the 7th century, and as tea seeds arrived from China in the 13th century and were planted in the gardens of Buddhist temples, Nara's Buddhist history merged with that of tea. The region's tea gardens developed along the Nabari River in Tsukigase, and the teas were transported by boat to Kyoto and Osaka. Today, tea bushes still grow here, and local producers make high-quality green and black teas. Many of the local plants are the zairai native varietal that is thought to have developed from the original Chinese plants, and the teas made from their leaves have high levels of L-theanine and an aromatic orchid character. Nara craftsmen also make bamboo and wooden utensils required for matcha tea preparation and have been producing 120 different styles of bamboo whisk for more than 500 years. The material used, the shape, and the number of spines varies according to the individual schools of tea and the type of tea to be drunk (thick *koicha* or thin *usucha*).

Kyushu | Situated in the south of Japan, closer to China than other parts of the archipelago, the island of Kyushu was the first region to become aware of tea as Buddhist priests journeyed to and from China. After Eisai planted seeds in Saga Prefecture, tea cultivation spread to Fukuoka, Kagoshima, Kumamoto, Miyazaki, Nagasaki, and Oita. By the 1760s, Saga's green teas were being exported through the port of Nagasaki to Holland. Kyushu has kept many of its old tea-making traditions that were established in the days when the Japanese first learnt how to make tea from the Chinese, and the region specialises in the manufacture of panned kamairicha and steamed, rolled tamaryokucha, which has been made here for 500 years. Saga's coastal district of Ureshino, whose name means "fields of happiness," is famous for tamaryokucha; Kumamoto Prefecture, on the west coast, makes mostly kamairicha; and Miyazaki and Oita prefectures, on Kyushu's east coast, are also both famous for the production of kamairicha. Kyushu grows so many different cultivars today, with fewer Yabukita plants than anywhere else in the country, that the region produces a very wide spectrum of teas and tea flavours.

Kagoshima Prefecture is Kyushu Island's most important region, producing 30 percent of the country's total output, and is second in importance to Shizuoka. The prefecture's largest cultivation area runs from Minamikyushu City to Makurazaki where around 40 percent of the region's tea is grown. A priest from Uji is thought to have been the first to plant tea here in the 14th century. In the Edo period from 1603 to 1867, the Shimazu family, who controlled Kagoshima's Satsuma Province, encouraged the cultivation of tea here, and production gradually increased, although the majority of the teas were of poor quality. So, in the 19th century, Kagoshima growers created an association that aimed to improve the quality of the teas being made in the region. However, it was not until the 1950s that quality improved, after local tea growers had spent time studying cultivation and processing methods in Shizuoka. They introduced the Yabukita cultivar, and in the late 1980s, local government improved quality further by strengthening the Kagoshima Tea Research Station and the Tea Growers Association. Although the region produces such large quantities, the quality is not always as high as elsewhere in Japan. Most of Kagoshima teas are sold as aracha to merchants and wholesalers in Shizuoka for refining and blending.

As this southerly region is the warmest part of Japan, many of the cultivars now grown here bud early and allow an earlier first harvest than elsewhere in the country. Most of the landscape of the southern central region is made up of open plains, where the tea is cultivated on wide, flat fields on large farms of between 6 and 20 hectares and is harvested by ride-on machines or harvesters running on tracks. Because this is such an open, sunny area, many farmers shade their bushes here before the harvest in order to increase the sweetness of the liquors. In the north of the prefecture, the teas are cultivated on small family farms in the cooler temperatures of the mountain slopes.

In Fukuoka's Yame tea district, tea bushes scramble up the steep slopes of the Minou mountain foothills at altitudes of 400 to 700 metres (1,312 to 2,297 feet). The local sencha, called Yamecha, is produced in Hoshino Village, where the shady and foggy climate, the altitude, and the difference in temperature between night and day make the tea grow slowly and produce complex, sweet, umami flavours. Yame is the most important region in Japan for the production of top-quality gyokuro. In Miyazaki Prefecture, in addition to making traditional kamairicha, some producers are now also manufacturing excellent, flavoury black teas from the Meiryoku cultivar, a cross between Yabukita and Yamatomidori, registered in 1986, as well as roasted oolongs made from the Minami Sayaka cultivar that have a natural sweetness and warmth. Also in Miyazaki, the green tea company Ito En has been collaborating with Miyakonojo Agricultural Cooperative since 2001 in its Program for Revitalising Tea-Growing Regions. The objectives of the project are to improve production efficiency, offer training and support for tea growers, and produce raw materials suitable for use in Ito En's range of bottled tea products. A similar project with Ito En is being run with the government of Oita Prefecture. Kitsuki in Oita was once a major producer of black tea, but when the government liberalised the importation of black teas in 1971, the growers switched to green. The Yabakei region in northern Oita has recently reclaimed and developed large areas of farmland for tea cultivation.

Tea also grows at altitudes of 200 to 400 metres (656 to 1,312 feet) on Mount Kirishima, whose name, Mist Island, derives from the fact that the top of the mountain appears as an island in a sea of low misty cloud. It is one of Japan's hundred famous mountains, and the warm days and cold nights intensify the floral sweetness of the tightly rolled, deep green needles of sencha, the shiny and intense green gyokuro, and the bright emerald-green matcha produced here. And Nagasaki, Japan's 11th most important producer, makes some senchas but specialises in their local version of curled tamaryokucha, which they call Sonogicha. It was from the port of Nagasaki that Japanese green teas were shipped to America in the 1860s.

Mie | Since the 12th century, tea has been grown in Mie Prefecture in central Honshu. It is the country's third-largest producer, after Shizuoka and Kagoshima, and accounts for

8.5 percent of annual output. The region specialises in the production of shaded teas such as gyokuro and tencha for matcha, and also makes a large quantity of deep-steamed fukamushi senchas as well as unrefined aracha for use in the food industry to make such products as ice cream and confectionery. Mie produces more kabusecha, grown mostly in the north of the prefecture, than any other region in Japan; fukamushi is made in the south. All of these different green teas from Mie are referred to as Isecha, meaning "teas from Ise," a city in central Mie and the site of the Ise Grand Shrine, the most important sacred Shinto shrine in Japan. The area around Suizawa Village, Yokkaichi City, is particularly famous for the tea that grows at the foot of Mount Kamagatake in the Suzuka Quasi-National Park. The vast tea gardens here are dotted with warm air fans to help protect the plants from frost. In 2000, the Mie Prefecture Tea Industry Council instigated a movement to ensure that Mie tea is compliant with safety standards, use of agro-chemicals, and traceability. Some gardens grow their tea organically in areas where the use of chemicals is prohibited.

Saitama | An ancient document from the 1350s referred to tea from Kawagoe, the old name for the modern Sayama area in Saitama Prefecture. Although famous in the 14th century, tea cultivation declined, and Sayamacha almost totally disappeared. In the early 1800s, three men from Sayama—Yoshizumi Yoshikawa, Morimasa Murano, and Han'emon Sashida—decided to try and revive the old tradition of tea-making in the area and developed a new technique of processing, called Sayama Biire, which first steamed and then panned the fresh leaves before rolling and drying them. By 1819, they were selling their teas to a Tokyo tea merchant, Sayamacha became more and more popular, and cultivation in Saitama began to expand. In the 1870s, large quantities of the teas were exported to America and the name became well known in international markets. Production here reached its peak in the 1960s and '70s but, since then, has dropped.

Today, the region produces approximately 6.3 percent of Japan's tea, which is grown on small farms by families who have been making tea here for hundreds of years. Some still hand-roll their tea on a hoiro table using the traditional temomi method. Saitama is very cold and prone to frost, and over time, the local tea bushes developed very thick leaves that could survive the low temperatures. In the 1950s, the varietal was used to develop the new Sayamamidori cultivar, registered in 1953, which produces green teas that contain high levels of catechins (polyphenols that act as antioxidants in the body) and so brew liquors that can be rather astringent and are not as good as teas from Shizuoka and Uji cultivars. However, the cultivar is very well suited to the manufacture of floral, rich, sweet, black, and oolong teas. One local tea maker, Keichiro Shimizu, found that if he made tea from leaves harvested on a warm, sunny day, the liquors tasted sweeter, so in 1980, he introduced sun-withering to his processing. Today, he spreads the leaves under the shade of plastic netting and allows them to lightly oxidise for two hours, withers them indoors for three hours, then pan-fires and rolls them to produce an unusual Bao Zhong that is sweet and mild and very floral.

Shiga | Tea seeds were first planted in Shiga in 805 by the monk Saicho when he returned from China, and teas grown here are generally referred to as Omi-cha. The district is most famous for its high-quality, intense, sweet, and full-bodied Asamiya sencha teas, which have won many awards over the centuries. They are grown at 300 to 450 metres (98 to 1,476 feet) around Shigaraki town where the local soil is rich in potassium and calcium and has been used for hundreds of years for the manufacture of Shigaraki ware pottery tea bowls. These vessels gradually replaced the wooden bowls that ordinary people previously used to drink tea. The simplicity and natural beauty of Shigaraki bowls harmonised with the philosophy of *wabi-suki*, the belief in the importance of a simple and humble appreciation of natural beauty and the most basic principles of *chanoyu*, the way of tea.

Shizuoka | Shizuoka's tea gardens date back to 1241 when the monk Shoichi Kokushi planted tea seeds here. The region's teas became famous when the Tokugawa shogunate, which ruled Japan from 1603 to 1867, made Shizuoka its power base and chose to drink the local tea rather than the more famous Uji teas. Today, the region is the most important in the country and produces 37.9 percent of the country's tea on 40.3 percent of the total cultivated area. It is known for its high-quality green teas and specialises in sencha and sencha fukamushi. It was in Kakegawa, in the hills south of Shizuoka City, that the deep-steaming method was developed in the late 1950s as a way of producing good-quality, flavoury teas from lower-quality leaf. The longer deep steam of one to two minutes breaks down the cells in the leaf more than a shorter steam treatment and gives the tea a stronger, more intensely vegetal character.

Kakegawa's tea bushes are cultivated by the traditional method of *chagusaba* (semi-natual grasslands), which dates back thousands of years to a time when much of the Japanese landscape was given over to the cultivation of grasses that were used for roofing and as organic fertiliser. Today, the grasses are fertilised between July and October, then harvested in late autumn and left to dry in the fields. They are then cut down into shorter lengths and, between November and January, spread in layers 15.24 to 20.32 centimetres (6 to 8 inches) thick as a mulch between the tea bushes and around their roots. This ensures that the soil stays moist and warm; that weeds cannot grow amongst the tea bushes; that the grasses decompose to become an organic fertiliser, which introduces micro-organisms to the soil and improves soil quality; that the grass prevents any soil erosion; and gradually, over time, that the layers of the beneficial mulch enrich the soil to a depth of at least 1 metre (3.28 feet) below the surface.

This method of farming results in very high-quality green teas, and to make Kakegawa fukamushicha (deeply steamed teas), the leaves (which are a little tougher than leaves from bushes grown in other areas) are steamed for 150 seconds instead of the

TOP: Temomi processing involves rolling the tea by hand on a hoiro table. This can take around eight hours. BOTTOM: Drying the rolled tea on the hoiro table, which is gently heated, traditionally by charcoal or, more recently, by gas or electricity. Photographs courtesy of Asako Steward, City of Kakegawa

normal one or two minutes. The length of steaming varies according to the condition of the plucked leaves, which is affected by the season, the humidity, the amount of sunshine, and other factors relating to terroir. Teas picked in the later part of the year are tougher than leaves gathered in the spring and so need to be steamed for slightly longer. The extra steaming breaks down the fibres in the leaves and more easily extracts L-theanine (the amino acid that gives tea its sweet, umami character), the healthful catechins, and other ingredients such as beta-carotene, vitamin E, and chlorophyll. After steaming, the manufacturing process continues in the same way as for sencha, and the tea is dried, rolled, and shaped in automated machines. But whereas sencha has a well-balanced aroma, umami, and astringency, Kakegawa fukamushicha brews a deep, rich aroma and a sweet, mellow taste with no astringency or bitterness. The dry leaves of these teas tend to be darker in colour, yellower than other senchas, and include a higher proportion of small particles as well as longer needles of rolled leaf. This means that the tea liquors are cloudier than sencha liquors and have more small particles deposited in the bottom of the tea bowl.

The Shizuoka region also makes gyokuro, guricha, kamairicha, and black tea, and the majority of tea produced in other regions is sent here for refining and blending. Most of Shizuoka's tea is produced on small family farms on the plains of Makinohara and Kakegawa and in the more mountainous areas of Kawane, Hon-yama, and Tenryu. The region's high-quality teas benefit from the thick fog that drifts in from the ocean, creating shady, humid conditions, and from the significant variations in temperature from day to night during the growing season. The change from warm, humid days to harsh, chilly nights stresses the plants so that they develop more enzymes in the leaves and yield liquors that are intense, sweet, and umami in character. The area is also important because of its coastal location and easy access to nearby ports. It is the largest commercial centre for tea and is also at the heart of research and development. Mechanical harvesters were developed here and much of the research into tea and health has been carried out at Shizuoka Prefectural Research Institute of Agriculture and Forestry Tea Research Centre and at the University of Shizuoka's new Tea Science Centre that was opened in April 2014.

Note: The figures and percentages quoted in the above text vary from year to year.

Country, State, or Province
Japan

Number of Gardens
Approximately 28,116 farmers

Main Districts or Gardens
Aichi (Nihio region), *Gifu, Kyoto* (Uji, Wazuka), *Kyushu* (Saga, Fukuoka, Kagoshima, Kumamoto, Miyazaki, Nagasaki, and Oita), *Mie, Nara, Saitama, Shiga, Shizuoka*

Area Under Tea
37,770 hectares, including—
Aichi: 489 hectares
Gifu: 554 hectares
Kyoto: 1,400 hectares
Kyushu: 13,604 hectares
Mie: 2,850 hectares
Nara: 655 hectares
Saitama: 666 hectares
Shiga: 377 hectares
Shizuoka: 16,500 hectares

Average Annual Production (Kilograms)
Approximately 82 million, including—
Aichi: 884,000
Gifu: 571,000
Kyoto: 3.02 million
Kyushu: 35.6 million
Mie: 7.13 million
Nara: 1.76 million
Saitama: 37,000
Shiga: 685,000
Shizuoka: 32.2 million

Terrain
Aichi: Fertile valleys along the eastern banks of the Yahagi River; cool mountain environment where the low temperatures help give teas their sweetness

Gifu: Sheltered valley in the lower reaches of the heavily forested mountains; near the point where several rivers converge into the Shirakawa River

Kyoto: Mountainous region with red soil that is rich in nutrients

Kyushu: Japan's earliest flushing region due to the warm spring season; flat, low-lying fields in the south with volcanic soil rich in minerals, and mild sea breezes; mountains in the north of the region, with misty, mountain fog

Mie: Sazuka Mountains in the north-west, Nunobuki Mountains in the south, coastline to the east, inland plains, natural parkland and forests; less urban than many Japanese prefectures

Nara: Rich soil on the gentle slopes the Tsukigase region of the Yamato Plateau

Saitama: Wide alluvial plains to the north and north-west of Tokyo (The soil of the Musashino Plateau is rich in volcanic ash and is ideal for tea growing.)

Shiga: Misty, hilly region on the Shigaraki Plateau with nutrient-rich soil; dramatic changes in temperature from day to night

Shizuoka: Located between Mount Fuji and the Pacific Coast, the region has a long rocky coastline with mountains overlooking the bays and beaches; inland plains of rich volcanic soil, punctuated by lakes, rivers and hot springs; often shrouded in thick foggy mists

Altitude
Aichi: 500 to 600 metres (1,640 to 1,969 feet)

Gifu: 600 metres (1,969 feet)

Kyoto: 200 to 500 metres (656 to 1,640 feet)

Kyushu: 200 to 600 metres (656 to 1,969 feet)

Mie: 200 to 600 metres (656 to 1,969 feet)

Nara: 200 to 500 metres (656 to 1640 feet)

Saitama: 30 metres (98 feet)

Shiga: 300 to 450 metres (984 to 1,476 feet)

Shizuoka: 200 to 1,050 (656 to 3,444 feet)

Production Period
Late April to October, depending on region

Kyushu: Earlier harvest than elsewhere because of warmer climate

Best Time to Visit
May to October

Main Varietals/Cultivars
Aichi: Asahi, Yabukita, Yamanoibuki, Ujihikari, Ujimidori, Okumidori

Gifu: Zairai, Yabukita, Okumidori

Kyoto: 69% Yabukita, plus Gokou, Samidori, Asahi, Ujihikari, Saemidori, Meiryoku, Benifuuki, zairai, Sayamakaori, Tsuyuhikari, Yamanoibuki, Sakimidori

Kyushu: 37% Yabukita, 28% Yutakamidori, plus Zairai, Asanoka, Asatsuyu, Saemidori, Okumidori, Meiryoku, Minama Sayake, Okuyutaka, Tsuyuhikari, Fujikaori, Shimamidori, Kanayamidori

Mie: 86% Yabukita, plus Asatsuyu, Sayamakaori

Nara: Yabukita, zarai wild varietal, Gokou, Benifuuki

Saitama: 72% Yabukita, plus Sayamakaori, Hokumei, Fukimidori

Shiga: Yabukita Benifuuki, Okumidori,

Saemidori, Sayamakaori, Sayamamidori, Okuhikari, Asatsuyu

Shizuoka: 93% Yabukita, plus Harumidori, Inzatsu, Sofu, Yamakai, Koshun, Mariko, Okumidori, Kondowase, Kanayamidori, Okuyutaka, Sayamakaori

Types of Tea Made
Aichi: Tencha for matcha, shincha, sencha

Gifu: Sencha

Kyoto: Sencha, gyokuro, matcha, kabusecha

Kyushu: Matcha, sencha, gyokuro, bancha, panned bancha, hojicha, kukicha, genmaicha, kabusecha, kamairicha, tamaryokucha, black

Mie: Isecha including shincha, sencha, gyokuro, kabusecha; tencha for matcha; aracha; black

Nara: Sencha, bancha, kabusecha, black

Saitama: Shincha, sencha, kamairicha, oolong, black

Shiga: Asamiya sencha

Shizuoka: Mainly sencha and fukamushi sencha, also top-quality gyokuro, bancha, hojicha, genmaicha, tencha for matcha

Predominant Flavours; Tasting Notes
The character of the different teas depends on the cultivar used as well as the different local conditions.

Aichi:
GREEN: *Matcha*—rich, deep flavour, and fragrant aroma
Shincha—fruity, umami, full-bodied
Sencha—brisk, full-bodied, with hints of brine and fresh-cut grass

Gifu:
GREEN: *Sencha*—powerful, sweet, with a little astringency

Kyoto:
GREEN: *Sencha*—depending on cultivar, sweet, floral, mellow, often dense and umami, sometimes with a hint of pine, toasted nuts, asparagus, and mashed potato
Gyokuro—sweet, fragrant, fruity, buttery, low astringency
Matcha—intense, vibrant, mellow, aromatic, sweet, umami, with hints of grass

Kyushu:
GREEN: *Matcha*—invigorating, slightly tart, but generally sweet and warming
Sencha—rich, sweet, grassy, slightly astringent, can be velvet smooth, honeyed with suggestions of kiwi
Gyokuro—deep, vegetal, strong, fresh, smooth, with hints of the ocean
Kabusecha—light, mild, less astringent than sencha
Tamayrokucha—slightly astringent, with sweet buttery notes and hints of fruits and toasted nuts
Kamairicha—yellow liquor, smooth, sweet, floral, with hints of aniseed and exotic fruits
Bancha—panned early spring bancha from Miyazake is balanced, sweet, very vegetal, and grassy; other banchas are strong, grassy, quite astringent
Hojicha—fresh, with toasty, caramelised character
OOLONG: *From Minami Sayaka Cultivar*—dark amber liquors, robust, full flavour, sweet, smooth, warming
BLACK: *From Meiryoku Cultivar*—clean, rich, flavoury
Oita—fragrant and floral, with hints of spice

Mie:
GREEN: *Shincha*—fresh, crisp and sweet *Sencha*—subtle, flowery, fragrant, soft, fresh, and sweet
Gyokuro—sweet, mellow, umami
Kabusecha—complex, sweet, and umami, with a hint of astringency
Matcha—intense, deep, sweet
BLACK: bright and vibrant, strong enough to take a little milk

Nara:
GREEN: *Sencha*—deep, rich, refreshing, flowery, with a slightly grassy character
BLACK: refreshing and intense, strong enough to take a little milk

Saitama:
GREEN: *Shincha*—deeply vegetal, rich, umami, buttery, hints of broccoli, buttered spinach, and ripe pears
Sencha—thick, robust, rich, and sweet
Kamairicha—subtle, light, slightly floral
OOLONG: fragrant, floral, fruity, sweet
BLACK: rich, sweet, complex, fragrant, medium strong

Shiga:
GREEN: *Sencha*—intense, sweet and full-bodied, with lingering sweet aftertaste

Shizuoka:
GREEN: *Sencha*—smooth, flowery, refreshing
Fukamushi Sencha—vegetal, sweet and intense
Gyokuro—delicate, mellow, refreshing, sweet, with hints of seaweed
Bancha—mild and sweet, with a little astringency
Hojicha—rich, full-bodied, warming, nutty, sometimes with hints of cinnamon
Matcha—deep and complex, initially bitter, but with a sweet aftertaste

SOUTH KOREA

Buddhist monks, returning from study in China, brought tea to Korea in the 6th or 7th century, and in 828, King Heundok acquired seeds from China. Tea ceremonies became part of state and royal occasions, and for Buddhists, the tea ceremony was a meditation. In temples, green tea was offered to statues of the Buddha and to the spirits of ancestors, revered leaders, and monks.

In the 14th century, Confucianism replaced Buddhism, temples were destroyed, and tea culture was suppressed. Some monks returned to civilian life, while others fled to remote mountain temples to secretly continue their tea traditions. In the 1590s, the Japanese occupied the country and wreaked further devastation, and tea disappeared from Korean life until the early 19th century when philosopher and poet Jeong Yak-Yong re-awakened interest and became known as Dasan, meaning "the Mountain of Tea." He taught The Way of Tea (later known as Panyaro). His most famous student, the Buddhist monk Choui Uisun, transcribed a Chinese tea encyclopaedia and, in 1837, composed the "Dongdasong," Korea's greatest hymn to tea.

In 1905, the country came under Japanese rule and Korean culture was repressed, but once again, Buddhist monks continued to practise The Way of Tea in their mountain temples. After independence in 1945, the monk and Buddhist scholar the Venerable Hyo-dang Choi Beom-sul, who had been very active in the independence movement, planted new tea bushes, taught tea across the country, and wrote *Hanguk-ui Dado* (The Korean Way of Tea), outlining the history and culture of Korean tea. He introduced Panyaro (Dew of Enlightening Wisdom), a new style of tea and Zen ceremony, and in 1976–77, founded the Korean Association for the Way of Tea. The Panyaro Institute, run today by Tea Master Chae Won-Hwa, teaches the naturalness, simplicity, moderation, firmness, flexibility, and gratitude of tea. Today, Korea's tea culture is strong, with academic courses, festivals, and conferences creating new interest across the land.

The Korean Tea Ceremony, or *darye* (etiquette for tea), which is thought to date back at least 1,000 years. Photograph courtesy of Ryu Seunghoo

Tea is grown in four southern regions: Boseong, Hadong's Jirisan, Jeonnam, and Jeju Island. Most of the teas are green (*nokcha*), and some producers also make semi-oxidised Hwang-cha and oxidised black tea. The green teas are named by the time of harvest. The best-quality teas, hand-plucked before the 20th of April, are called Woojeon (before the rain tea), and their tiny new buds give delicate, brothy, sweet, buttery liquors. The second grade, Sejak (small sparrow, also called *dumul-cha*, meaning "second-flush tea"), is made with slightly larger buds and leaves handpicked between the 20th of April and the 5th of May. The liquors are gold-green, the aroma complex and nutty, and the flavour rich and sweet with hints of passion fruit and tangerine. The third harvest, Jungjak (medium sparrow), is handpicked about 10 days after the start of summer when the buds have opened into leaves and yield jade liquors that are full-bodied and fragrant, sometimes sweet and spicy with suggestions of warm hay. The fourth harvest is Daejak (large sparrow), made from the coarser, machine-picked, late-summer leaves that give plainer teas for tea bags. Other terms used are *Gamnong* ("sweet harvest," the first April flush) and *Jaksul* ("sparrow's tongue"), which describes the April bud teas that look just like little sparrows' tongues. Korean manufacturing processes vary slightly from those of other tea regions. To make green tea, Puch'o-cha, the leaves are lightly steamed, pan-fired in large woks or panning machines, cooled, and alternately rolled (by hand on bamboo mats or in machines), and pan-dried. The alternate rolling and drying is repeated multiple times to develop the required flavour and aroma. Panyaro tea, developed by the Venerable Hyo-dang, is made by the *chung-ch'a* method, which consists of plunging the fresh leaves into near-boiling water, draining them, and then pan-firing. The leaves are then rolled, shaped, and pan-dried. Small quantities of Japanese-style steamed green and matcha teas are also made.

Korean powdered tea is like Japanese matcha and is also sometimes called Malcha. Sometimes the bushes are shaded artificially for a few days (a shorter time than in Japan) or sometimes naturally by cloud and mist or overhanging trees, so the shading is not so concentrated. Because longer shading makes the tea sweeter, Korean powdered tea is less sweet and umami than Japanese matcha and has a more bitter and grassy character.

Semi-oxidised Hwang-cha (also called Bu-Bun Balhyo Cha—*balhyo* means "oxidised"), an oolong tea, was developed in the 1970s by Yang Won Suh, designated 34th Grand Master of Traditional Korean Foods for his work in the field of Hwang-cha and matcha and founder of the Hankook Tea Company. To make Hwang-cha, the leaves are withered and lightly oxidised, panned, rolled, 50 to 60 percent oxidised inside linen cloths, and dried. The teas have a wonderful toasty character with hints of roasted squash and an amazing dark chocolate finish.

Korean black tea (Balyo cha or Hong cha, "red tea") is handpicked, lightly roasted, oxidised, partially dried, rolled, dried for three to four hours (during which time the tea continues to oxidise), and finally, roasted again. The teas are very complex and buttery and often have chocolate and vanilla notes with layers of toasty nuttiness, sweet fruits and jam, honey, and rose geranium.

Korean dark tea, Tteokcha (Tteok-cha, Ddok-cha, Ttok-cha, Chung Tae Jeon, and also in the past called *byeongcha*, meaning cake tea), probably introduced from China before 500, is made by steaming, pounding, and shaping the green tea leaves by hand into small cakes of different shapes (rounds, squares, rectangles, hexagons, octagons, flowers, and so on) or by forming the leaves into a coin-shaped cake with a hole in the middle by pressing them into a round mould. The little cakes are then allowed to age and ferment for several years. The little holes in the coin cakes are used to string several together for storage. To prepare for brewing, a cake of tea is roasted over charcoal, then broken, and simmered in boiling water. The teas are usually fragrant and fruity with spicy, woody, or earthy notes and hints of liquorice, with slight astringency and a sweet, peaty, caramelised sugar finish.

Boseong | Historical records indicate that tea was first grown and processed here around 369 B.C. In 494 B.C., Buddhist monks cultivated a tea garden in Mundeog-myeonin in Boseong County, and old tea trees still grow there today on more than 3 hectares. Tea was also listed in a 1478 record of local products, was presented as a gift to the king, and was often used to pay taxes. During the Japanese occupation of 1910 to 1945, formal gardens were established on 30 hectares of steep mountain slopes, but the tea was not considered a success and the plants were abandoned after the Japanese left. In 1957, the Daehan Tea Produce Company Ltd. (founded by Yeong-Seop Jang) purchased 50 hectares of the tea land, upgraded its Boseong Tea Plantation in 1994 as a tourist resort, and today farms 120 hectares.

In the 1970s, heavy frosts damaged many of the bushes and reduced the cultivated area to 241 hectares. In 1973, cultivation expanded again to 590 hectares and Boseong accounted for 74 percent of the country's total tea area. Since then, more land has been planted, the industry has become more organised, and in 1996, Boseong County created a 10-year tea-cultivation plan. The region is today Korea's largest tea-growing region and manufactures 40 percent of the country's tea. The weather is warm, humid, and often misty, with plenty of rain in summer, and millions of tea bushes flourish on the elegantly curving contours of the hills. The fresh shoots are hand-plucked and processed in 74 factories, 50 percent of which are privately owned, while 50 percent are owned by the county or the state and managed by local families.

Honam Tea Estates, established by Hankook in 1981, at the southernmost tip of the mainland. ©Hankook Tea Company

The Boseong Green Tea Festival is held every year in early May, and visitors tour the tea fields, pick and process tea, and enjoy performances of the tea ceremony.

Hadong | Hadong is Korea's oldest cultivated tea region—although old wild tea bushes still grow in other southern parts of the country—and the gardens of ancient Buddhist temples are home to tea trees planted many centuries ago. Korea's *Samguk Sagi* (History of the Three Kingdoms) tells of "Daeryeom, an envoy to Tang China, who brought back tea seeds, and the king ordered them planted near Mt. Jiri." The seeds were smuggled out of China in the seams of Daeryeom's clothing during King Heungdeok's reign (828), and since the king ordered the planting here, Hadong tea is known as "The King's Tea." During the 9th century, the Zen monk Jingam cared for the bushes at Ssanggyesa Temple, and cultivation increased steadily through the Hwagae Valley. In the 19th century, the monk Cho-ui wrote, "Hwagae is the place with the biggest tea plantation, one about 40–50 ri," (approximately 15 to 20 kilometres [9.3 to 12.4 miles]). He explained that people in the region picked tea leaves, dried them in the sun, then boiled them in water to make a "turbid, reddish in colour brew bitter and astringent."

Until the 1950s, the bushes were abandoned, and many continued to grow wild. But after the Korean War, seeds collected from the old bushes were planted on the steep southern slopes of Jirisan (Mount Jiri). The local farmers produce handmade green teas that account for 36 percent of the country's tea. The temperate, humid climate here is perfect for the production of delicate green teas, with plentiful rain and spring temperatures varying between 5°C and 20°C (41°F and 68°F).

The Tea Culture Center is located at the foot of Jiri Mountain, adjacent to the tea-farming area and Ssanggyesa Temple, and works to promote Hadong green tea and tea culture. Each year in May, the Hadong Wild Tea Cultural Festival is held here.

Jeju Island | This semi-tropical, volcanic island lies in the Korea Strait to the south of the mainland and is South Korea's fastest-developing tea region. It is possible that the Japanese planted the first tea here in the early 20th century during trials to find the best region for tea production, and today, the bushes grow in the foothills of Halla Mountain. Commercial cultivation did not start until 1980 when Seo Seong Hwan (founder in 1945 of AmorePacific, South Korea's largest beauty products company) established the Dolsongi Tea Garden on the lower slopes of Mount Halla. Seong Hwan hoped to re-establish South Korea's traditional tea culture and began producing green tea under the brand name Osulloc, which means "first flush tea" in old Korean. The conditions here—volcanic soil, the humid and subtropical climate, with cool, dry winters and hot, humid summers—are ideally suited to tea-growing. Osulloc now owns three tea estates—Dolsongi, Hannam, and Seogwang—which produce 24 percent of the country's total output.

Seong Hwan recognised the antioxidant benefits of tea as a botanical, and Osulloc green teas as also used as an ingredient in a range of AmorePacific skincare products. AmorePacific runs the company's chain of tea houses on the mainland and Jeju Island as well as the Osulloc Tea Museum at the Seogwang Tea Garden near Seogwangdawon. The *O* in Osulloc translates as both "of" and "to appreciate and enjoy."

Other large companies on the island also mass-produce green teas, some of which are sold into the domestic market and into North America. A few of the gardens here hand-pluck the fresh leaf shoots, while most use hedge-trimmer or Japanese tractor harvesters. The majority of the teas are processed in Japanese automated machines by steaming rather than by the traditional steaming and panning method, and the liquors are clean and pure rather like Japanese senchas.

Jeonnam | This beautiful growing region is located in the south-west where there are mountains running along the coast, mountainous islands just off the coast, rivers, bamboo forests, and gently sloping fields of tea. The yellow soil is famous for its iron, magnesium, and calcium carbonate content, and Korean celadon and white porcelain were first made in this region. It is cooler here than in the country's other tea regions and is particularly suited to the production of powdered green teas (like Japanese matcha) as well as Korea's other green teas. As in Japan, the bushes are shaded before being harvested around Ipha, which marks the first day of summer at the beginning of May.

Tea fields in Boseong, often referred to as South Korea's green tea capital. Photograph courtesy of Ryu Seunghoo

Pouring tea during the Korean Tea Ceremony. Photograph courtesy of Ryu Seunghoo

Country, State or Province
South Korea

Number of Gardens
Countless small farms, some large estates, wild tea, and Buddhist temples with tea fields
Boseong: 1,363 family gardens, 74 factories
Jeju Island: Three Osulloc estates, plus other large companies
Jeonnam: 121 registered tea companies/farms plus many unregistered micro-growers, farms, and Buddhist temples with tea fields and wild tea bushes
Jiri Mountain:
2,000 small farms

Main Districts or Gardens
Boseong in South Joella Province; Jeonnam in South Joella Province; Jeju Island; Jiri Mountain in Hadong in South Gyeongsang Province

Area Under Tea
Approximately 2,500 hectares, Including—
Boseong: 1,147.7 hectares
Jeju Island:
More than 132 hectares
Jeonnam: 2,150 hectares
Jiri Mountain:
More than 1,043 hectares

Average Annual Production (Kilograms)
Approximately 3.5 million

Terrain
Boseong: Smooth, swooping hills and valleys of neatly terraced tea, often very misty
Jeju Island: Gently sloping wide fields of tea around the foot of volcanic Halla Mountain
Jeonnam: Partially mountainous with some flat coastal plains; abundant rainfall and the warmest of South Korea's weather; plenty of water from a number of rivers; fertile soil
Jiri Mountain: Steep, rough rocky hillsides where the tea grows amongst bamboo; famous for its cherry blossom festival in spring

Altitude
Boseong: 140 to 160 metres (459.3 to 525 feet) plus some wild tea growing in the hills at just over 200 metres (656 feet)

Jeju Island: Sea level to 500 metres (1,640 feet)

Jeonnam:
Under 200 metres (656 feet)

Jiri Mountain: Mostly under 200 metres (656 feet)

Production Period
Late April to August or September

Best Time to Visit
April to September

Main Varietals/Cultivars
Sinensis varietals from China

Types of Tea Made
Green, matcha, brown rice green tea, Hwang-Cha (semi-oxidised), black, dark fermented teas

Predominant Flavours; Tasting Notes
GREEN: depending on season, sweet, brothy, umami, slightly grassy, nutty with hints of broccoli, passion fruit, tangerine, and mango
Green Powdered Tea (like matcha)—grassy and astringent, a little tart, less rich, smooth, and sweet than Japanese matcha
OOLONG:
Hwang-cha—complex, toasty, with powerful notes of roasted squash and pumpkin, and a dark chocolate finish
BLACK: chocolate, vanilla aroma, buttery, supple, round, creamy, floral, toasty, nutty, with hints of vanilla, chocolate, fruit, jam, honey, and back notes of rose geranium
DARK: Subtle confectionery note and hints of liquorice with an earthy dryness; slightly astringent with treacle and molasses in the finish and lingering peaty notes in the aftertaste

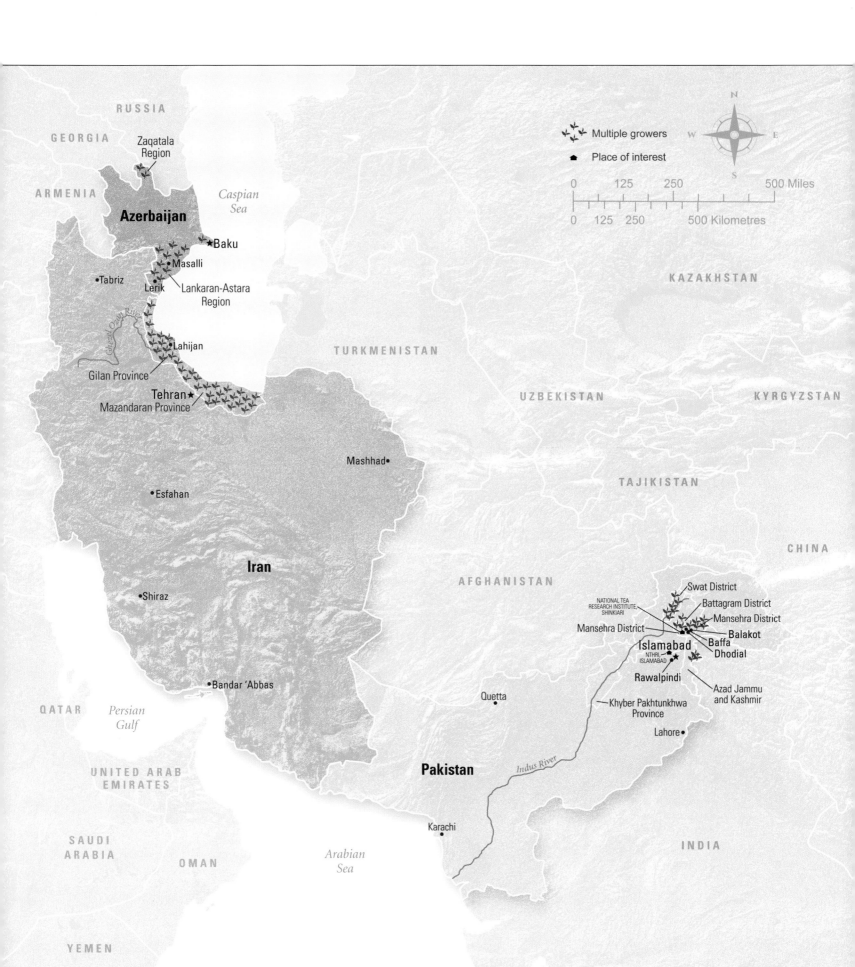

RUSSIA

GEORGIA

Zaqatala
Region

ARMENIA

Azerbaijan

*Caspian
Sea*

★Baku

•Masalli

•Tabriz

Lerik

Lankaran-Astara
Region

Ghezel Ozan River

•Lahijan

Gilan Province

Tehran★

Mazandaran Province

Iran

•Mashhad•

•Esfahan

•Shiraz

•Bandar 'Abbas

QATAR

*Persian
Gulf*

UNITED ARAB
EMIRATES

SAUDI
ARABIA

OMAN

*Arabian
Sea*

YEMEN

KAZAKHSTAN

UZBEKISTAN

KYRGYZSTAN

TURKMENISTAN

TAJIKISTAN

CHINA

AFGHANISTAN

Swat District

NATIONAL TEA
RESEARCH INSTITUTE,
SHINKIARI

Battagram District

Mansehra District

Mansehra District

Balakot

Baffa

Dhodial

Islamabad

NTHRI,
ISLAMABAD

Rawalpindi

Azad Jammu
and Kashmir

•Quetta

Khyber Pakhtunkhwa
Province

Lahore•

Pakistan

Indus River

•Karachi

INDIA

Multiple growers

Place of interest

N
W   E
S

0   125   250   500 Miles

0   125   250   500 Kilometres

AZERBAIJAN

During the 1880s, the Lankaran-Astara region with its subtropical climate was identified as a suitable tea-growing region. In 1896, landowner M. O. Novoselov planted 2,000 bushes on one hectare of his land and, in 1912, wrote in the journal *Russkiye Subtropiki* ("Russian Subtropics") that conditions here were suitable for the cultivation of tea and other subtropical plants. In 1920, Azerbaijan became part of the Soviet Union, and the government rapidly increased production. In 1931, a second tea estate was established, and in 1937, an independent trust, Azerbaijan Chay, was set up to manage the developing industry and organise training abroad for new employees. Through the 1950s, some 36,000 hectares of land were drained, water reservoirs were built, irrigation systems were constructed, and the industry expanded. Between 1970 and 1980, the tea fields were extended to a total of 13,400 hectares, water supplies were improved, high-level training continued, new processing factories were built, and the output of black tea peaked at 8.2 million kilos (more than 18 million pounds).

Plans in the 1980s aimed to increase annual production to 20 million kilos (44 million pounds) by the year 2000. But in 1991, just as the state-owned industry was about to be privatised, the USSR collapsed, production in Azerbaijan quickly declined, and the total cultivated area fell to just 7,000 hectares. In 2006, in collaboration with the German government, Azerbaijan set up a project to revive the tea sector by improving quality control, upgrading equipment in factories, increasing technical skills, and organising training. In 2010, Gilan Holdings rehabilitated two of the former estates and built a new factory, and has plans to restore more of the old gardens. In 2011, the Astarachay factory, designed by a South Korean company and creating jobs for 1,000 people, opened in the south with capacity to produce around 11,000 kilos (24,251 pounds) per day. Almost all the tea grows in the subtropical climate of Lankaran-Astara in the south, at Lankaran, Masalli, Lerik, Baku, and Astara, and in the north-west, the Zaqatala region has one factory.

Country, State, or Province
Azerbaijan

Number of Gardens 14

Main Districts or Gardens
Zaqatala in the north,
Lankaran-Astara in the south

Area Under Tea
Zaqatala: 60 hectares

Lankaran-Astara: 844 hectares

Average Annual Production (Kilograms)
Zaqatala: 2,500

Lankaran-Astara:
Approximately 7 million

Terrain
Zaqatala: Ganykh Ayrichay Valley amongst the southern slopes of the Caucasus between Georgia and the Russian state of Dagestan

Lankaran-Astara: Low-lying subtropical region of Astara climbing up to the higher slopes of Lerik, a mountain area between the Iranian border in the Talysh Mountains and the Lankaran lowland plain

Altitude
Zaqatala: 600 metres (1,968 feet)

Lankaran-Astara:
5 to 1,096 metres (16 to 3,596 feet)

Production Period
May to September

Best Time to Visit
May to September

Main Varietals/Cultivars
Sinensis varietals from Darjeeling, China, and Japan; Kolkhida varietal tea seeds from Georgia

Types of Tea Made
Black orthodox

Predominant Flavours; Tasting Notes
BLACK: *Brokens*—medium quality, strong
Large and Whole Leaf—complex with some astringency, sweet, hints of raisins

IRAN

When Iran became an Islamic country, coffee replaced alcohol as the everyday beverage, but it was expensive and gradually gave way to China tea brought into the country by Persian merchants trading along the Silk Road, and in the early 19th century, tea from India was also imported. In 1899, Kashef Al Saltaneh, Iranian ambassador to India, learnt from growers in India how to cultivate and manufacture tea, and in 1901, he imported 3,000 seedling plants from Kangra in northern India to establish Persia's own plantations. The young plants were nurtured in Lahijan, close to the Caspian Sea, and cultivation quickly expanded into the surrounding region of Gilan and neighbouring Mazandaran. The first factory was built in 1934.

Until the first decade of this century, the industry thrived, and tea was grown by approximately 42,000 smallholders on private plots of 0.5 to 50 hectares in the plains and adjacent hillsides in the north of the country. Farmers sold their fresh leaf into 107 factories, which processed around 62 million kilos (136.6 million pounds) of mainly black orthodox tea a year. Since 2005, the market has been very badly affected by the vast quantities of tea (almost 55 percent of total consumption) being smuggled into the country, and as a result, several factories have closed down, and growers and pluckers have lost their jobs. The industry has also been affected by drought, poverty, mismanagement, and late payments to farmers by state-owned factories, and quality and quantity have continued to fall. By 2015, the amount of harvested leaf had dropped by 40 percent, and fewer than 100 factories were still operating, 10 of which were manufacturing green tea to meet a growing demand from abroad. The best of the larger orthodox grades are produced in the spring and are sold loose, while the smaller dust and fannings grades are mainly used in teabags. Iran exports its black teas to 17 countries, and green tea sales are increasing to Germany, the UAE, Canada, Russia, Azerbaijan, Georgia, Tajikistan, and Turkmenistan.

An Iranian tea field. Photograph courtesy of Vahid Saleem

Country, State, or Province
Iran

Number of Gardens
105 factories

Main Districts or Gardens
Gilan Province: 90%
Mazandaran Province: 10%

Area Under Tea
32,000 hectares

Average Annual Production (Kilograms)
31.2 million

Terrain
Northern slopes of the Elburz Mountains along the Caspian Sea; very productive land on flat coastal plains and steep rugged slopes at low atitudes

Altitude
4 to 400 metres
(13 to 1,312 feet)

Production Period
May to late October

Best Time to Visit
late March to June

Main Varietals/Cultivars
Sinensis varietals from Kangra in north India

Types of Tea Made
Black orthodox, small amounts of CTC, some green

Predominant Flavours; Tasting Notes
BLACK: *Orthodox Large Leaf Grades*—some are brisk and robust; some are smooth and light with gentle hints of honey; some have a peppery character
Orthodox Dusts and Fannings—rather plain

PAKISTAN

The Pakistan Tea Board first tried to cultivate tea in 1958 at Baffa, Mansehra District, but the project was abandoned. In 1964, the West Pakistan Agricultural Development Corporation established a trial plot of irrigated tea at Misriot Dam, Rawalpindi, but both climate and soil proved unsuitable. After the 1971 separation from East Pakistan (now Bangaladesh), a feasibility study into tea-growing was carried out with the help of Chinese specialists. In 1986, the National Tea Research Institute was established on 20 hectares at Shinkiari in Mansehra District with a 12-hectare tea garden, a 5-hectare nursery, a soil laboratory, and a miniature processing unit. Five Chinese varietals were planted on smallholder fields in Mansehra, Battagram, and Swat districts and Balakot in Khyber Pakhtunkhwa Province; 60,000 hectares of suitable land were identified; and plans were made to popularise tea cultivation and train farmers in plucking and small-scale green tea processing. In the mid-1980s, a green tea factory was built with finance from the Pakistan Science Foundation and equipped with machinery from China. The first black tea–processing factory was built in 2001 with Chinese assistance, and a total of 245 hectares of smallholder plots, each about half a hectare, were planted. Research into processing and the mechanisation of tea for profitability continues at what is now the National Tea & High Value Crop Research Institute (NTHRI).

In 1986, Unilever Pakistan also started growing tea for its own black tea bag blends, established a Tea Experimental Station, planted 542 hectares of smallholder plots in Mansehra, trained farmers to use mechanical shears, and built a CTC factory at Dhodial. Since 2010, a few other private companies have acquired land for tea cultivation in Azad Jammu and Kashmir State on 15- or 30-year leases and are now growing tea, but government plans to expand tea production through a public-private scheme that offered financial support to new growers has since collapsed.

A view of Pakistan's National Tea & High Value Crops Research Institute in Shinkiari.
Photograph courtesy of Dr. Abdul Waheed

Country, State, or Province
Pakistan

Number of Gardens
3 factories (*Tea Board:* 2; *Unilever:* 1); and 1,500 to 1,600 smallholders (*Tea Board:* 200 to 300; *Unilever:* 1,300), plus a few new private growers

Main Districts or Gardens
Tea Board: Mansehra, Battagram, and Swat districts in Khyber Pakhtunkhawa Province; Azad Jammu and Kashmir State
Unilever: Mansehra
Azad Jammu and Kashmir State

Area Under Tea
60 to 80 hectares in Khyber Pakhtunkhawa Province, approximately 1,600 hectares in Azad Jammu and Kashmir

Average Annual Production (Kilograms)
28,000 to 29,000—
NTHRI: 20,000 black, 5,000 green; *Unilever:* 3,000 to 4,000; *Azad Jammu and Kashmir:* Not yet known

Terrain
Plains and valleys, lakes and rivers in foothills of the Himalayas close to Kashmir border

Altitude
Approximately 1,000 to 1,500 metres (3,281 to 4,921 feet)

Production Period
April to October

Best Time to Visit
April to October

Main Varietals/Cultivars
Chinese cultivars from Kenya and South Carolina (USA)

Types of Tea Made
Black orthodox, CTC, green

Predominant Flavours; Tasting Notes
BLACK: thick, coloury, strong, sweet

CHINA

CHINA

NEPAL

BHUTAN

INDIA

Kachin
State

Panchagarh
District

Sylhet

Surma Rvr.

Kushiyara Rvr.

BANGLADESH
TEA RESEARCH INSTITUTE

INDIA

Brahmaputra Rvr.

Padma Rvr.

★ Dhaka

Bangladesh

Irrawaddy (Ayeyarwady) Rvr.

Chittagong

Myanmar

Mandalay
Sagaing

Shan
State

LAOS

Bay of
Bengal

Thanlwin Rvr.

Rangoon ★

THAILAND

Andaman
Sea

Gulf of
Thailand

Multiple growers

Place of interest

N

W   E

S

0   125   250   500 Miles

0   125   250   500 Kilometres

BANGLADESH

The pioneer tea garden of Bangladesh was established in the hills of Chittagong in 1840, and commercial cultivation began in 1854 at Malnicherra in Sylhet. The area developed as part of the Indian tea industry, and when India was partitioned in 1947, 103 tea estates covering 28,734 hectares became part of East Pakistan, renamed Bangladesh in 1971, after the Bangladesh War of Independence. In 1952, the Pakistan Tea Association was set up to coordinate the industry, and in 1960, with a growing domestic demand for tea, the government legislated for a mandatory increase of land under tea of 3 percent per year. By 1970, 153 tea gardens covered 42,685 hectares and production had risen from 19.01 million kilos (41.9 million pounds) in 1960 to 31.38 million kilos (69.18 million pounds). However, during the civil war, the industry suffered enormous damage. Tea plants and factories were neglected, experienced staff left, and tea yields and quality fell dramatically.

In 1980, the government initiated the Bangladesh Tea Rehabilitation Project, and by 2006, 163 gardens were producing 53.41 million kilos (117.7 million pounds) of black tea. In 2013, with annual production at 66.26 million kilos (146.7 million pounds) and domestic consumption totalling more than 64 million kilos (141 million pounds), the Tea Board introduced a 12-year Strategic Development Plan, Vision 2021. The aim was to increase production to 100 million kilos (220 million pounds) by 2025, improving yields and quality, raising the workers' standard of living, and boosting exports. In 1980, exports had peaked at 31 million kilos (68.3 million pounds) but then dropped to only 850,000 kilos (1.87 million pounds) in 2013, and by 2014, 10.62 million kilos (23.4 million pounds) were being imported each year. The country is expected to soon disappear from the list of exporting countries.

Bangladesh is a low-lying country, very prone to flooding, and tea is grown in the north-eastern district of Greater Sylhet, which borders Assam, in Chittagong on the west coast, and in Panchagarh in the north-west, a new tea-growing area that has been developed since 2000. The industry is divided into three main categories. Category A includes 27 estates, the majority of which are owned by three sterling companies—Duncan Brothers, Deundi Tea Company, and The New Sylhet Tea Estate; Category B includes estates owned by the government, Bangladeshi companies, and private individuals; Category C includes a few small estates that are owned by individual families. The industry provides employment for a total of 133,000 people, of which approximately 50 percent are women, and with all other related jobs such as transportation, blending, packaging, marketing, etc., the number employed is 500,000. Tea contributes approximately 1 percent of total Gross Domestic Product and has made a positive contribution to the preservation of ecological balance and soil conservation in the hilly regions and to the safety and security of forest animals and birds.

The country faces severe meteorological challenges such as very uneven rainfall, cloud outburst, and drought. From December to March, the weather is sometimes so dry that plants die due to stress if there is no rain the following autumn. In the wet season, many estates suffer from water-logging, especially in the peripheral districts where the catchment areas have been converted into paddy fields. The majority of the teas are granular CTC black teas, which are sold through the Chittagong auction to export customers that include the UAE, Australia, Canada, China, the UK, Indonesia, India, Jordan, Japan, Korea, Kuwait, Sri Lanka, Mauritius, Malaysia, Nigeria, Nepal, New Zealand, Pakistan, Saudi Arabia, and the United States. Increasing quantities of green, white, oolong, and orthodox black teas are manufactured at the Kazi & Kazi estate in Panchagarh for export to speciality markets, and Duncan Brothers have orthodox machinery at two of their factories.

The Bangladesh Tea Research Institute (BTRI), established in 1957 at Sreemangal as the Pakistan Tea Research Station, carries out research into climate change, pest management, soil rehabilitation, and the standardisation of cultivation practices such as planting, pruning, and plucking. One of its most important roles is to develop new, high-yielding, quality clones, and so far, 17 new clones have been developed to suit local conditions. BTRI also provides farmer training and is a central source of information on technology and processing. Despite these developments, production has not increased significantly since 2004, and to meet the targets set out in Vision 2021, 9,705 hectares of old and ailing, low-yielding bushes need to be replaced with new clones, and more available land needs to be developed. However, the projected expansion may not now be possible since the potential tea area has been squeezed by unplanned road development, and the creation of dams for irrigation to other crops, which has disturbed the flow of streams and rivers.

GREATER SYLHET

Until partition in 1947, Sylhet was part of Assam, and the first tea garden in the area was set up in 1854 in the Surma River valley by British company Duncan Brothers. The region, which includes Moulvibazar and Habiganj districts, enjoys the country's best tea-growing climate, with cool air in winter and warm temperatures in summer. The land is watered by countless streams that feed into the Surma and Kushiara rivers, and the area enjoys regular rainfall brought in on humid winds that precipitate their moisture over the tea fields. Farms in the area grow oranges, pineapples, jackfruits, and lemons, and in Habiganj District, many gardens have planted rubber and other fruit crops to bring the unused land under cultivation.

CHITTAGONG

Chittagong, in the south of the country, is the commercial and industrial capital of Bangladesh, and the Chittagong tea auctions were set up here in 1949. The tropical monsoon climate brings dry, cool days from November to March, very hot and dry pre-monsoon weather in April and May, and warm, cloudy, wet monsoon conditions from June to October. In 2007, the Bangladesh Tea Board launched a sustainable tea smallholding project on unused land in the Bandarban District of the Chittagong Hill Tracts. With financial help from the European Union, the Tea Board distributed a new high-yielding cultivar to local farmers to help them establish small tea gardens, increase earnings, and improve their living standards. However, the project has not been as successful as expected because of restricted root space for the plants.

PANCHAGARH

This relatively new tea region lies in the north of the country along the border with Darjeeling. The climate here is subtropical or temperate, and temperatures and rainfall are lower than in the tropical southern parts of the country. The cooler air and drier conditions produce better-quality teas than are grown in Sylhet. When the region was developed in 2000, 118 hectares were planted, and since then, the tea area has expanded and is now farmed by 405 small-scale farmers, 15 medium-scale farmers, and 5 large tea estates. In 2013, a record quantity of 1.46 million kilos (3.2 million pounds) was produced, an increase of 27.48 percent since 2012, and production is steadily rising year on year. Several nurseries have been established to supply seedlings to new growers, and the hope is that the new industry will provide employment for small and marginal farmers and women, raise earnings, allow farmers to send their children to school, increase tea exports, and enhance the local economy.

Panchagarh had never been cultivated before the new tea estates and smallholder plots were developed, so the soil was free from pesticides and chemical fertilisers. Kazi & Kazi Tea Estate Limited, one of the new companies in the district, decided to grow tea organically here and has now acquired organic certification from Japan, Switzerland, and the United States. It is the country's first organic tea garden and is optimistic about the future of Panchagarh tea. The Kazi & Kazi factory at Rawshanpur manufactures orthodox black, green, white, and oolong teas as well as black CTC, and sells them locally under the Kazi & Kazi brand name and internationally as Teatulia Organic Teas, named after the Tetulia district where they are grown.

Tea growing beneath shade trees in Bangladesh. Photograph courtesy of Professor Mohammed Ataur Rahman

Country, State, or Province
Bangladesh

Number of Gardens
More than 163, including—
Greater Sylhet: 134
Chittagong: 24 gardens, plus smallholders
Panchagarh: 5 large estates plus around 420 smallholders

Main Districts or Gardens
Greater Sylhet, Chittagong, Panchagarh

Area Under Tea
Greater Sylhet: 98,000 hectares

Chittagong: Around 15,459 hectares including smallholders

Panchagarh: 1,838 hectares, including smallholder farms

Average Annual Production (Kilograms)
66 million

Terrain
Greater Sylhet: Hillocks and basins with low-lying flood plain at the centre

Chittagong: Low hills and fertile valleys filled by deposits of sand and clay washed down from the hills

Panchagarh: The fertile alluvial Surma Valley with terraces and slopes of tea and forest irrigated by Surma River

Altitude
Greater Sylhet:
Approximately 35 metres (115 feet)

Chittagong:
30 metres (98 feet)

Panchagarh:
46 metres (150 feet)

Production Period
March to December

Best Time to Visit
February, March, late October, November

Main Varietals/Cultivars
Assamica varietals and new cultivars: BT1-BT16 developed by the Bangladesh Tea Research Institute (BTRI) BT13 and 14 for drought resistance, TV23 for high yield

Types of Tea Made
Black CTC, orthodox black, green, oolong, and white

Predominant Flavours; Tasting Notes
Greater Sylhet:
BLACK: *CTC*—bright, strong, sometimes slightly spicy

Chittagong:
BLACK: *CTC*—bright, strong, sometimes slightly spicy

Panchagarh:
BLACK: *CTC*—better quality than other regions;
Kazi & Kazi Orthodox—dark golden liquor, full-bodied, with subtle strength and flavour and hints of spice, malt, and sometimes black cherry
GREEN: *Kazi & Kazi*—light, slightly grassy, with hints of green bell peppers
WHITE: *Kazi & Kazi*—soft, light, with hints of nectarines, melon, and peach blossom;
OOLONG: *Kazi & Kazi*—golden liquor, full-bodied, hints of butterscotch and spice, with floral and citrus notes

MYANMAR

Legend says that tea was introduced to Myanmar (then Burma) during the days of the Bagan Kingdom that ruled the country from the 9th to the 13th century. During a royal tour of his kingdom, King Alaung Sithu (1113 to 1160) is said to have presented tea seeds to the Ta'ang (Palaung) people in northern Shan State where the seedlings flourished. Some tea horticulturalists say that Myanmar has its own species of the large-leafed *Camellia sinensis* var. *assamica*, which they call *Camellia arrawadimis* after the country's Ayeyarwady River, and suggest that this is the original source of the tea plant.

Northern Shan State became the centre of tea cultivation and, today, produces 65 percent of the country's tea. The best, most tender shoots, picked in late March and early April, are used to make *laphet*, a pickled tea, which accounts for 17 percent of production. The rest of the crop is processed to make green (52 percent of production) and black tea (31 percent), and a few producers make small quantities of balled oolongs. Some semi-wild tea trees grow in more remote areas away from the villages, perhaps left from the days when the local Palaung people did not prune the bushes for fear of killing them, but instead cut them down for fuel after 10 years of harvesting. Today, the leaves and buds from those old trees are used to make compressed Puerh-style teas or are sold into Yunnan Province, China, for the manufacture of Puerh teas there.

Since Myanmar was a British colony until 1948, efforts to expand the tea industry and increase exports were impeded by Britain's emphasis on Indian and Ceylon teas. Since independence, most of Myanmar's tea has been consumed domestically or sold to China to make Puerh tea. Shan State has a long history of poppy cultivation for opium, and in 2003, in efforts to eradicate the crop, the Ministry for Progress of Border Areas financed and promoted the cultivation of tea and other cash crops. In 2007, the Myanmar Tea Association met with a delegation of tea producers and traders from Assam to discuss how the Indian growers could assist with technology and knowledge to increase productivity and quality. It provided training in pest control, soil conservation, and farming systems. However, by giving up high-earning opium cultivation, many smallholder farmers fell into poverty, and in 2011, opium production increased by 14 percent. Since 2011, tea farmers have also been facing financial and social problems because of a sharp decline in the market, an influx of untaxed tea from China, high costs, low tea prices, and military conflict in the region between the Myanmarese army and local ethnic groups. In 2014, Shan's tea area was also being disrupted by the construction of new roads and pipelines, around 80 of the 100 factories had closed down, and some tea farmers had left the region to look for work elsewhere. Several NGOs have recently become involved to help fight poverty, provide education, and work with the Tea Association to increase productivity, improve quality, and provide farmer training.

The Myanmarese name for tea is *laphet*, and ancient stories say that this derives from the day the king gifted the first tea seeds to his people in the north of the country. They apparently did not know that they should receive the king's gift with two hands (*lat neh phet*) and so took it with only one (*lat teh phet*). Tea was, therefore, named *lat te' phet*, ("one hand plant"), and this became *laphet*. The word is also used for the pickled tea, eaten as a salad, that is considered Myanmar's national dish. To manufacture laphet, young, fresh leaves are steamed for five minutes, packed into hollow bamboo stems or wooden boxes, and pressed using heavy weights before being buried in pots and left for several months to ferment. The tea is then sorted and repacked into sacks inside which the fermentation process continues. When served as a salad, the fermented leaf is mixed with roasted peanuts, toasted sesame seeds, fried garlic, green chilli, dried shrimp, and various vegetables.

Country, State, or Province
Myanmar

Number of Gardens
Around 20 factories and smallholder farmers

Main Districts or Gardens
Southern Shan State, Sagaing and Mandalay in the centre of the country, Kachin State on the northern border with China

Area Under Tea
320,000 hectares (240,000 of that in Shan State)

Average Annual Production (Kilograms)
20 million

Terrain
Shan State is a hilly plateau with steep slopes of tea in all directions; Sagaing and Mandalay are dry and hilly with rich red soil; Kachin is an area of heavily forested highlands, with valleys running down into the Ayeyarwady River.

Altitude
1,525 to 2,130+ metres (5,000 to 7,000+ feet)

Production Period
Late March to November

Best Time to Visit
April to October

Main Varietals/ Cultivars
Mainly assamicas, some very old, wild trees, var. *lasiocalyx cambod* tea, *Camellia arrawadiensis*

Types of Tea Made
Black CTC, black orthodox, green (mostly handmade), oolong, and compressed Puerh-style teas

Predominant Flavours; Tasting Notes
BLACK: *CTC*—dark, rich, astringent, slightly earthy, with a slight smokiness
GREEN: light, vibrant, refreshing, with vegetal notes and a hint of citrus
OOLONG: intense aroma, sweet, floral liquor with hint of raspberries and apples, and a suggestion of caramel
DARK: *Compressed Puerh-Style*—often astringent with hints of apples and grapes, reminiscent of young Chinese raw Puerhs

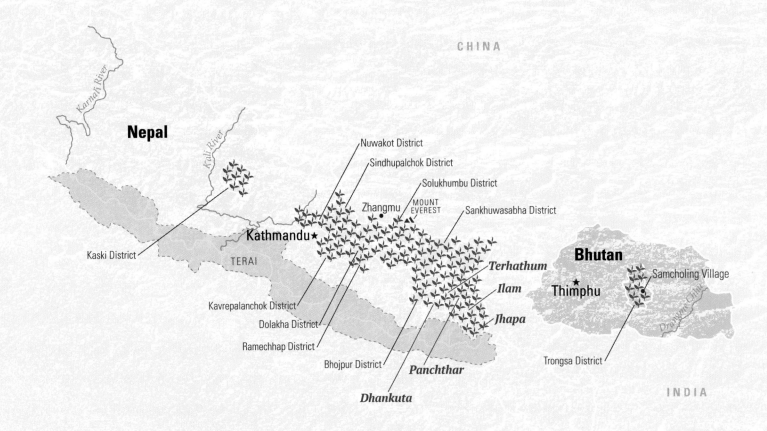

CHINA

Nepal

Nuwakot District

Sindhupalchok District

Solukhumbu District

Zhangmu

MOUNT
EVEREST

Sankhuwasabha District

Kathmandu★

Bhutan

Samcholing Village

Thimphu
★

Kaski District

TERAI

Terhathum

Ilam

Kavrepalanchok District

Jhapa

Dolakha District

Ramechhap District

Bhojpur District

Panchthar

Trongsa District

INDIA

Dhankuta

INDIA

BANGLADESH

Multiple growers

Mountain

0   25   50   100 Miles

0 25 50   100 Kilometres

N

W   E

S

BHUTAN

In 1774, Warren Hastings, British governor-general of Bengal, sent some tea seeds to George Bogle, British emissary in Bhutan, with instructions to plant them as part of British research into the possibility of growing tea in the Himalayas. In the 1940s, the Second King of Bhutan is thought to have planted *Camellia sinensis* seeds and saplings from China and India near the old Palace of Samcholing. In 2000, assamicas from India were introduced by the District Forestry sector, but the bushes were largely ignored by the locals. Then in 2008, Korean specialists from Jinju National University (now Gyeongnam National University of Science and Technology) and growers from Hadong, Korea, identified the plants and explained the health benefits of green tea and Bhutan's potential for cultivation. With financial support from the university, six local farmers planted new tea bushes, two other farmers rehabilitated existing plants, and research was carried out into plucking patterns, yield, processing, production, and the flavour of teas made from both plant types. Before embarking on mass cultivation, B. B. Rai, coordinator for the School Agriculture Program at the Ministry of Agriculture and Forests, carried out further research and published his findings in *Journal of Renewable Natural Resources Bhutan* in 2012.

In 2009, processing equipment (a roller, a panning machine, and a roasting pan) was purchased with South Korean financial support, and by 2012, approximately 40 farmers were growing tea on plots of 0.2 to 1.2 hectares, both in Samcholing Village and in the wider area of Drakteng Gewog, Trongsa District. A nursery was established, training courses were run by the Agriculture Ministry and Jinju University, and the tea area was expanded. An increasing quantity of green tea was sold locally and to tourists, and the aim is to eventually export it to Japan, Korea, the United Arab Emirates, and the United States (indeed, small quantities are now exported to In Pursuit of Tea in the USA). At first, the tea was processed by hand in the farmers' houses, but in 2012, a three-storey Green Tea House, which includes a processing and packing factory equipped with some machinery for rolling and drying, guesthouse, shop, office, and tearoom, was built with funding from the government and Gyeongnam University and is now managed by the farmers. Tea production has increased steadily and sales of Druk Samcholing Green Tea rose from 700 packets of 50 grams (1.76 ounces) in 2012 to 7,000 packets in 2015, and the annual income of the farmers has risen substantially as a result of this new tea industry.

Country, State, or Province
Bhutan

Number of Gardens
27 smallholders

Main Districts or Gardens
Samcholing Village, Trongsa District, Central Bhutan

Area Under Tea
About 47 acres with 75 acres planned

Average Annual Production (Kilograms)
Upwards of 400 and increasing

Terrain
Very steep terraced hills around Trongsa, the location of the 2nd King's winter palace, today a monastery school

Altitude
1,400 to 1,800 metres (4,593 to 5,900 feet)

Production Period
April to October

Best Time to Visit
April, May, October, November

Main Varietals/Cultivars
95% sinensis, 5% assamica, growing organically

Types of Tea Made
Whole-leaf green

Predominant Flavours; Tasting Notes
GREEN: delicate, light, sweet, and fruity

NEPAL

Home to Mount Everest, Nepal is a land of high snow-capped summits, valleys bathed in swirling misty clouds, vast lakes whose waters sparkle in the sunlight, and terraced green slopes. Most of the country's tea grows in the low plains of Terai and at high altitudes in Ilam in the eastern part of the country where the tea fields adjoin those of Darjeeling and Sikkim.

The history of the commercial development of tea estates in Nepal dates back to bushes grown from seeds given by the Chinese emperor to Jung Bahadur Rana, prime minister of the country from 1846 to 1856 and again from 1857 to 1877. Some stories say that Rana instructed his governor-general Colonel Gajraj Singh Thapa to plant the seeds and that Thapa established the first garden in 1863 in the district of Ilam at elevations ranging from 914 to 2,286 metres (2,999 to 7,500 feet), and a second in 1865 at Soktim in the low-lying region of Jhapa in Terai. Another story suggests that it was Thapa who was inspired to plant the first tea in Nepal after visiting Darjeeling and seeing how well the plants were thriving there. The first factory was built in 1873, but until 1951, Nepal was ruled by the autocratic Rana dynasty and remained isolated from the rest of the world, often in a state of turmoil and tyranny, economic instability, and corruption, and so, the tea industry did not develop in the way it had in India in Darjeeling and Assam. When the Rana dynasty came to an end, the country opened its borders, and investment from outside the country helped the industry to develop. In 1959, the first private estate was established at Bhudhakaran in Jhapa. Meanwhile, the Ilam garden was expanded by the government into seven gardens and, in 1966, became the Nepal Tea Development Corporation (NTDC).

Ilam, Nepal's high growing region that borders Darjeeling. Photograph by Rocky Prajapati; Courtesy of nepaliteatraders.com

Between the downfall of the Rana regime in 1951 and the 1970s, most of the freshly plucked leaf was sold to factories in Darjeeling. In 1978, a second Nepali factory opened at Soktim. In 1982, King Birendra Bir Bikram Shah designated five districts—Jhapa, Ilam, Dhankuta, Terhathum, and Panchthar—as "Tea Zones," and smallholder farmers in those districts were encouraged to grow more tea. The 1992 National Tea Policy focused on improving production and processing methods, marketing and promotion, training, and the development of ancillary industries. The National Tea Policy of 2000 encouraged private investment, made more land available for planting, provided training for farmers, created systems to increase exports, initiated a programme of marketing, and privatised the NTDC. So, whereas before 1980, the industry was government controlled, now more private estates and factories opened and a number of NGOs became involved in working with rural communities to build sustainable tea businesses and help eradicate poverty. In October 1998, the Himalayan Orthodox Tea Producers Association (HOTPA) was set up, and in June 2003, the Himalayan Tea Producers Cooperative Ltd. (HIMCOOP) was established by HOTPA to help producers of high-quality, speciality teas to sell them into the international market. The organisation currently represents 20 factories and estates that produce a variety of white, green, black, and oolong teas. The Nepal Tea Planters Association (NTPA) markets CTC teas in Terai, HOTPA deals with high-grown orthodox teas, and the Specialty Tea Association of Nepal (STAN) markets speciality teas.

Today, there are 140 registered estates, 18,000 smallholders, 40 bought-leaf factories, and a growing number of village cooperatives made up of farmers who have pooled their land and are in the process of acquiring grants of up to 50 percent from the government to assist with the purchase of equipment. The industry throughout the country provides employment for 100,000 people, and more jobs are becoming available in new tea areas that are being developed in Dolakha, Kavrepalanchok, Sindhupalchok, Nuwakot, and Ramechhap in central Nepal, Bhojpur in the east, Solukhumbu and Sankhuwasabha on the northern border with Tibet, and Kaski in the west. The low-grown teas are all CTC and sell into the domestic market or foreign markets such as the Commonwealth of Independent States (CIS), India, and Pakistan, while the estates at higher elevations make orthodox black and speciality teas for niche markets in the UK, Europe, the United States, Australia, and Japan. Exports total between 4 and 5 million kilos (8.8 and 11 million pounds) per year—approximately 43 percent of total production—and that is increasing by 15 percent annually.

Throughout Nepal, the farmers work with a deep respect for the land, for nature, for their fellow humans, and for the teas they make, and it is this focus that is helping to build the speciality business here. However, the industry is still held back by political instability, the lack of reliable roads, the fact that it is a landlocked country with no ports, and the difficulty, with so many smallholders in so many remote districts, of devising a coordinated production and marketing strategy.

Nepal's tea seasons are like those of Darjeeling. The first flush is harvested from March to late April, and the teas are refined and delicate with hints of lemon, apricots, and peaches; the second flush is gathered from mid-May to mid-July and yields liquors that are rounded, muscatel, fruity, and mellow; the monsoon late-summer teas are stronger, full-bodied, and honey-sweet; and the autumnal teas, plucked in October and November, are tangy, spicy, and sweet.

ILAM

Ilam lies in the subtropical-temperate climate of the hills of the Mahabharata Range in the Eastern Development Region. Mountain streams and thick forests of fir, birch, and pine surround the tea fields. Some of the country's best-known and most successful estates are located here. Ilam Tea Estate, established in 1863, is the oldest; Maloom Tea Estate opened in 1993 and buys leaf from smallholders; Kanyam Tea Estate covers 240 hectares; Maipokhari and Sandakphu (the latter of which is the first and only factory to employ a female manager and female finance officer) are the district's highest gardens; Ilam Tea Producers PVT Ltd (ITPL) has two factories at Altabare and Ilam and a production capacity of about 2 million kilos (4.4 million pounds) per year; Sunderpani is an organic co-operative of 300 smallholders who process their leaf at the Kanchanjangha Tea Factory, certified organic in the 1990s; and there are 15 or so tea farmers' processing units. All the factories make high-quality orthodox black, hand-rolled black, white, green, and oolong teas and account for 85 percent of the country's total orthodox output.

DHANKUTA

Like Ilam, Dhankuta is situated in the Eastern Development Region where the hills rise from around 300 to 2,500 metres (984 to 8,202 feet). The lower slopes are warm and humid, whereas the higher districts are misty and cool and sometimes covered with snow in winter. In the north-west of the region, the Raniban Forest is dense with pine trees and rhododendrons, while in the open areas, farmers grow rice, maize, millet, citrus fruits, vegetables, ginger, and tea. The three most important gardens here are Guranse, Jun Chiyabari, and Kuwapani, which grow their own tea and also buy fresh leaf from smallholders. Guranse, established in 1990 on 250 hectares using organic Chinese clonal plants, buys from 73 smallholders in remote areas and processes 30,000 kilos (66,139 pounds) of organic black tea per year. In the Hile hills bordering Darjeeling, Jun Chiyabari Tea Garden opened in 2000 on 50 hectares that were planted with cultivars from Nepal, Darjeeling, Taiwan, and Japan. Kuwapani Tea Garden's 40.47 hectares were planted in 2001 with sinensis varietals from Darjeeling, and the tea is processed to make orthodox black and white speciality teas.

JHAPA

The district of Jhapa covers 1,606 square kilometres (620 square miles) of low-lying alluvial plains in Nepal's Terai region and borders Ilam to the north and India's Bihar to the south and east. *Jhapa* means "canopy," and the area was once covered with extensive, thick forest. In 1988, the Agricultural Development Bank set up the Small Farmer Development Program to help lift villagers out of poverty. This was then handed over to the local farmers and renamed the Small Farmers Cooperative Ltd

(SFCL). There are currently 13 SFCLs in Jhapa, some of which grow rice and some tea. The tea bushes cover half of the country's total tea land, and production is almost exclusively CTC, with a few factories making small quantities of orthodox black teas. Jhapa manufactures some 16 million kilos (35.3 million pounds) of black tea for the domestic market and for export customers such as India and Pakistan. The major estates are Giribandhu, Burne, Tokla, Himalaya Tea Garden, and Sattighatta.

PANCHTHAR

Panchthar lies in Nepal's Eastern Development Region in an area of high biodiversity close to the Singalila National Park. It shares a border with Sikkim and Darjeeling, and the green contours on both sides of the frontier merge into fields of tea that extend as far as the eye can see. Farmers here grow cardamom, medicinal plants, and tea. The tea bushes grow at altitudes ranging from 1,800 to 2,000 metres (5,906 to 6,562 feet). Pathivara Tea Estate was established in 1984 in a stunning location facing the spectacular white peaks of Mount Kumbhakarna. After being abandoned during the Maoist insurgency of the 1990s, the plantation and factory were refurbished in 2012. In 1980, Kanchanjangha Tea Estate and Research Centre was founded as a farmer cooperative in the foothills of Mount Kangchenjunga in Ranitar Village. One hundred farmers pooled their land, started growing tea on 94 hectares, and now produce high-quality organic orthodox teas. The estate, which lies at 1,300 to 1,800 metres (4,265 to 5,906 feet), runs training programmes on such topics as pest control, cultivation, processing, and environmental issues; finances a scholarship programme to fund education for local children; has rebuilt the local primary school; and is building eco-houses powered by solar energy.

TERHATHUM

This is the smallest of the main growing regions, with around 616 smallholder farmers who grow tea on approximately 231 hectares of land, which yields 46,000 kilos (101,413 pounds) a year. Until 2013, they sold their green leaf to the factories located in nearby Dhankuta District, but as this was not the most viable arrangement for the smallholders, two farmers started a trial with mini tea manufacture, and a second mini factory was constructed to allow growers to process their tea near their farms.

Country, State, or Province
Nepal

Number of Gardens
140 estates, 40 bought-leaf factories, 18,000 smallholders, and village cooperatives

Main Districts or Gardens
Ilam, Dhankuta, Jhapa, Panchthar, Terhathum

Area Under Tea
16,718 hectares

Average Annual Production (Kilograms)
18.3 million

Terrain
The low-growing plains of Terai are flat, marshy grasslands with forest; the hill areas are similar to Darjeeling and Sikkim, with rolling hills and valleys covered with tea and other cash crops.

Altitude
In Terai, 67 to 300 metres (220 to 984 feet); in the hills, 1,300 to 2,000 metres (4,265 to 6,562 feet)

Production Period
In hill areas, late March to November; in the Terai plains, February to late November

Best Time to Visit
Late March to November

Main Varietals/Cultivars
Mainly sinensis from Darjeeling; assamicas mainly from Assam in Terai; cultivars from Japan, Taiwan, and China in a few areas; some seeds from Yunnan for possible Puerh-style tea production; seeds from other countries for research and development

Types of Tea Made
Black orthodox and CTC, white, green, oolong

Predominant Flavours; Tasting Notes
BLACK: *CTC*—rich, brisk, full-bodied, and strong with a subtle aroma
High-Grown First Flush Orthodox—similar to Darjeeling First Flush, refined, slightly grassy, delicate with hints of lemon, apricots, and peaches
High-Grown Second Flush Orthodox—rounded, muscatel, fruity, mellow
High-Grown Monsoon Orthodox—stronger, full-bodied, and honey-sweet
High-Grown Autumnal Orthodox—tangy, spicy, and sweet
Other Speciality Black Teas—smooth, rich, sweet, mellow with caramel and malty notes
GREEN: bright, fresh, sweet, mild
OOLONG: sometimes sweet and earthy, or mellow and sweet, or rich and complex
WHITE: crisp, fresh, elegant, with nutty or citrus notes

TOP: Sandakphu Tea Factory in Sandakphu Village, Ilam, established by Chandra Bhushan and and his wife, Twistina, to provide a processing facility for local smallholder growers. MIDDLE: Inside Sandalphu Tea Factory where small machines allow local growers to make small batches of high quality teas. BOTTOM: Tea pickers gathering leaf in Ilam.
Photographs by Rocky Prajapati; Courtesy of *nepaliteatraders.com*

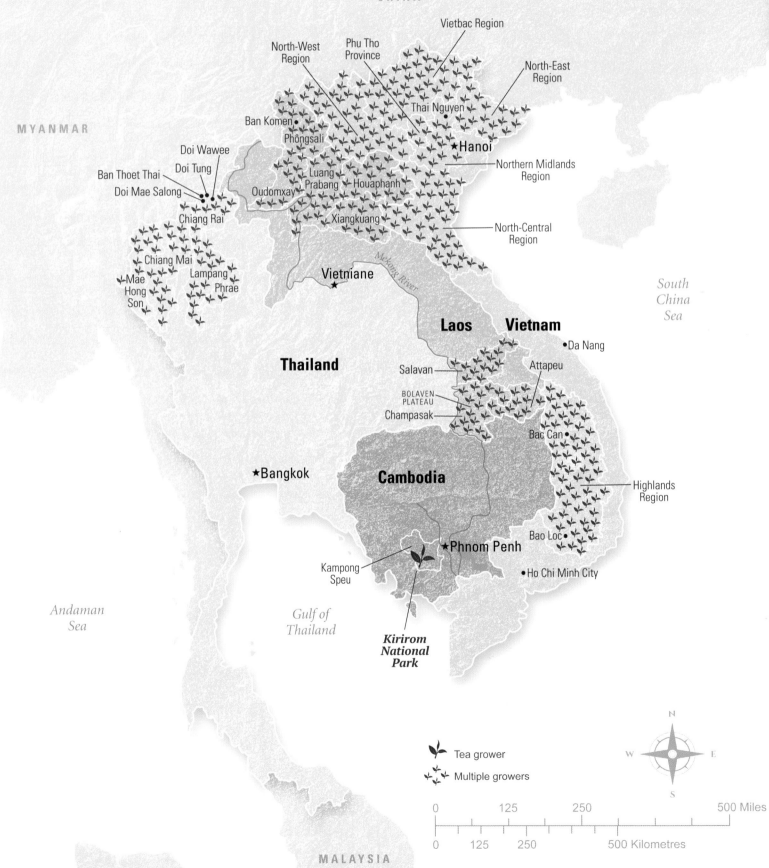

CHINA

MYANMAR

Vietbac Region

Phu Tho
Province

North-West
Region

North-East
Region

Ban Komen •

Phôngsali

Thai Nguyen

Doi Wawee

★Hanoi

Doi Tung

Ban Thoet Thai

Northern Midlands
Region

Luang
Prabang

Houaphanh

Doi Mae Salong

Oudomxay

Chiang Rai

Xiangkuang

North-Central
Region

Chiang Mai

Lampang

Mekong River

Mae
Hong
Son

Phrae

Vietniane
★

Laos

Vietnam

Thailand

• Da Nang

Salavan

Attapeu

BOLAVEN
PLATEAU

Champasak

Bac Can •

★Bangkok

Cambodia

Highlands
Region

Bao Loc •

★Phnom Penh

Kampong
Speu

• Ho Chi Minh City

Andaman
Sea

Gulf of
Thailand

Kirirom
National
Park

South
China
Sea

 Tea grower

Multiple growers

N

W   E

S

0   125   250   500 Miles

0   125   250   500 Kilometres

MALAYSIA

CAMBODIA

Of the three main branches of the *Camellia sinensis* family (*Camellia sinensis* var. *sinensis*, *Camellia sinensis* var. *assamica*, and *Camellia sinensis* var. *cambodiensis*, also known as *Camellia sinensis parviflora*), the Cambodian variety is the least used for commercial cultivation. However, since the Cambodian variety is well known, it is strange that Cambodia is not today a tea-producing country. However, perhaps things were different in the past, for in Mondulkiri Province in the east of the country lies a village called Chomka Te, which translates literally as "Tea Plantation." No tea grows there today, but the name indicates that this must once have been a tea-producing area.

There are also the remains of a tea garden in Kirirom National Park, two hours outside Phnom Penh. In this cool, quiet location once stood the summer mansion of King Sihanouk, king of Cambodia 1941 to 1955 and 1993 to 2004, and he gave the area the name *Kirirom*, meaning "mountain of joy." Today, only the ruins of the mansion remain, but this is also the former location of a tea garden. In 1962, an area of 300 hectares was made available by the king, and tea plants were donated by Zhou Enlai, China's Prime Minister from 1949 to 1976. Once the Khmer Rouge, who ruled from 1975 to 1979, had fled, a private investor continued the cultivation of tea, and 500 people lived and worked here until the manager died in 2000. During the 1995 inauguration of the park, King Sihanouk referred in his speech to the tea garden, and in 1996, 1,500 hectares of the park, including the tea plants, were sold to a local investor who claimed he planned to develop the tea garden. However, in 1997, the Rasmei Kampuchea newspaper reported that he had in fact sold the land and destroyed the tea garden. Some of the plants still grow wild and are harvested on a small scale by local people, and one former tea garden employee, Kim Loan, still makes tea and sells it beside the road to park visitors.

Country, State, or Province
Cambodia

Number of Gardens 1

Main Districts or Gardens
Kirirom National Park,
Kampong Speu Province

Area Under Tea
Originally 300 hectares,
but now only a few wild
bushes left

**Average annual
production (Kilograms)**
Tiny quantities
made by locals

Terrain
High plateau at eastern end
of Cardamom Mountains,
wildlife sanctuary with pine
forests, waterfalls, and rapids

Altitude
670 metres (2,200 feet)

Production Period
All year

Best Time to Visit
November to April

Main Varietals/Cultivars
Camellia sinensis var.
parviflora, a sub-variety of
Camellia sinensis var. *sinensis*
(Some believe this to be a
hybrid of the Chinese and
Assam varietals that may
have developed naturally
or by tea growers.)

Types of Tea Made
Green

**Predominant Flavours;
Tasting Notes**
Not yet known

LAOS

Until the late 19th century, parts of northern Laos were within Chinese borders, but a Sino-French treaty of 1895 transferred Phôngsali and Muang Sing to French Laos. The country remained a French protectorate until 1953. Until around 2010, there was no structured tea industry, and producers faced the challenge of lack of technology, low world prices, low domestic tea consumption, competition from imported teas, and high rates of interest. But now, a rudimentary tea association with government and producer representatives has been established, and several international non-government organisations (NGOs) are running projects to increase production, improve quality and sustainability, and raise prices. Today, tea cultivation is expanding, with government support in some areas to replace opium farming, and small factories are being built, farmer-training programmes are being organised, and routes to international markets are being established. The majority of tea is grown in the north, and more than 95 percent of teas produced here are sold to China. Small areas have recently also been developed in the south.

NORTHERN REGIONS

Just as China's Yunnan Province is famous for its ancient tea trees, so the mountainous forests of northern Laos are home to tea trees dating back over 1,000 years, and sections of the old Tea Horse Road are said to have run through Laos. The same assamica varietals that thrive in Yunnan have grown into tall trees here in the misty, cool winters and rainy, humid summers. The spring harvest from the ancient trees is almost all processed as maocha and sold across the border into China to make Puerh teas, and some are now also being sold to foreign buyers. Later harvests from the forest trees and from recently planted family-owned tea

Ban Komen, where villagers gather fresh leaf from ancient assamica tea trees to make green teas and maocha for Puerh-style teas. Photograph courtesy of Dominic Smith

farms are mostly processed as green teas, which, made from the assamica varietal, can be rather bitter.

Most of the tea is cultivated by smallholder farmers who have little access to electricity and, therefore, process by hand. The use of pesticides and fertilisers is banned by local government, so all the teas are naturally organic. As well as supplying Chinese manufacturers with raw tea for Puerh, growers also make smoky Bang Laa (bamboo tea). To process this, green tea is made by the normal method, lightly steamed, and then packed tightly inside fresh bamboo tubes. The bamboo is baked over a wood stove; then, the compressed cylinders of tea are taken out of the bamboo and bundled in fours and tied with strips of bamboo ready for sale.

Until 1999, there were no processing factories in the region, and local farmers depended on the cultivation of rice and other crops, rather than tea, to earn a living. They made tea for their own consumption and very little reached the market. In 1999, the first Chinese-owned factory was built in Ban Komen in collaboration with the local people, and since then, more Chinese and Malaysian investors have built factories. In 2013, Chinese investors began the development of a new processing factory that has the capacity to process 5 million kilos (11 million pounds) a year and is expected to produce better-quality tea for Chinese buyers.

SOUTHERN REGIONS

In the 1920s and '30s, the French established tea gardens on the Bolaven Plateau, in the provinces of Champasak, Attapeu, and Salavan, but the farms were abandoned over the following 50 years, mainly because producers did not have any access to markets. In 1986, the Association for the Support to Lao Farmers' Communities (ASDSP) was set up in France to help make credit more available to farmers and to provide irrigation systems. It acts as an umbrella organization to unite two co-operatives, Lao Farmers' Products (LFP) and Batieng Products, which work in partnership with the producers to market tea and other local products. In 2001, Batieng Products built a tea factory at the foot of the Bolaven Plateau and encouraged farmers to stop cutting down their tea trees. It also supports agricultural diversification and pays a fair price for the organic tea.

Country, State, or Province
Laos

Number of Gardens
Northern Regions: Mainly family smallholder, cottage processors, and a few small estates

Southern Regions: 200+ families

Main Districts or Gardens
Northern Regions: Provinces of Phôngsali, Oudomxay, Luang Prabang, Xiangkouang, and Houaphanh

Southern Regions: Provinces of Champasak, Attapeu, and Salavan on the Bolaven Plateau

Area Under Tea
2,710 hectares

Average Annual Production (Kilograms)
Northern Regions: 3 million

Southern Regions: 3.013 million

Terrain
Northern Regions: High jagged mountains, thick primary forests, remote villages, often foggy or misty

Southern Regions: Cool fertile plateau with volcanic soil, thick jungle, waterfalls and rivers gushing down into the Mekong Valley

Altitude
Northern Regions: 450 to 2,000 metres (1,476 to 6,560 feet)

Southern Regions: 800 to 1,350 metres (2,600 to 4,400 feet)

Production Period
March to November

Best Time to Visit
March to September

Main Varietals/ Cultivars
Northern Regions: Wild assamica trees and cultivated bushes developed from them

Southern Regions: Cuttings from wild assamicas growing in northern Laos and Myanmar

Types of Tea Made
Northern Regions: Maocha for Puerh-type teas; bamboo green tea (Bang Laa)

Southern Regions: Orthodox black, green, and oolongs

Predominant Flavours; Tasting Notes
Northern Regions:
GREEN: *Maocha*— bitter, astringent
Bang Laa—smoky

Southern Regions:
BLACK: woody, fruity, sometimes with hints of malt, spice and tobacco
GREEN: buttery and intense; sometimes nutty, earthy, or smoky; sometimes with floral overtones
OOLONGS: aromatic with suggestions of red berries and citrus fruits

THAILAND

For hundreds of years, tea has grown wild in Thailand's northern hills, in similar conditions to those in Vietnam, Laos, Myanmar, and Assam. In 1941, a farmer by the name of Prasit Poomchusri planted tea on his land in Chiang Mai (today, Raming Tea), but large-scale commercial cultivation only started in the late 1980s when the government and the king, Bhumibol Adulyadej Rama IX, encouraged tea-growing in northern Thailand, where criminal gangs had previously been engaged in opium production, gem and drug smuggling, and black marketing. The new interest in tea cultivation was helped by the fact that, in the 1950s, a number of Chinese (who had been supporters of Chinese General Chiang Kai Shek's failed resistance movement against Mao Zedong's Cultural Revolution) had settled in Doi Mae Salong and Doi Wawee in Chang Rai, northern Thailand, and began to use their traditional skills to cultivate tea as the Royal Development Project gained momentum. In 1994, seedling stock was imported from China and Alishan in Taiwan, in particular the Taiwanese oolong cultivars Jin Xuan and Ruan Zhi, and were given to local farmers in Chiang Rai Province where 7,200 hectares are now planted. Machinery, expertise, and training were also brought in from Taiwan, and from the mid-1990s, the industry expanded around the villages of Doi Tung (administration centre and focus of the Royal Development Project), Doi Mae Salong, Doi Wawee, and Ban Hin Taek. Doi Mae Salong is today especially noted for its green teas, jade oolongs, darker oolongs similar in character to Taiwanese Oriental Beauty, and scented varieties such as jasmine and osmanthus flavoured teas.

Tea cultivation is categorised as wild Shan tea (assamicas found mostly in the far northern Himalayan foothills), traditional tea gardens around villages, and commercial estates, recently developed and mostly in Chiang Mai and Chiang Rai. Imported sinensis varietals and cultivars are used for the production of green teas, flavoured greens, and Taiwanese-style balled oolongs. The assamicas are used for black tea and some green, but more than 50 percent of the assamica leaf is used to make *miang*, a fermented "chewing" tea, traditionally made in Chiang Mai (where the majority of the assamica verietals grow) by fermenting steamed leaves for about three months. A little like Myanmar's laphet, the leaves are eaten alone or flavoured with salt, sugar, or ginger. Locally, the word *miang* also refers to the assamica varietal.

Tea drinking in Thailand is increasing, and around 85 percent of production is now consumed domestically. The country's favourite *cha yen* (cold tea) is a thick, sweet blend of black tea, star anise, yellow food colouring, and condensed and evaporated milk, poured over ice.

TOP: Tea growing in the north of Thailand. Photograph courtesy of tea explorer Dani Lieuthier MIDDLE LEFT: Tea cultivation in Doi Wawee, one of the most important tea regions in northern Thailand. MIDDLE RIGHT: Tea shop in a village in northern Thailand. Photographs courtesy of Thomas Kasper, Siam Teas BOTTOM: Bamboo drums inside which withered leaf for oolongs is gently tumbled to bruise the cells and provoke oxidation. Photograph courtesy of tea explorer Dani Lieuthier

Country, State, or Province
Thailand

Number of Gardens
Some small factories, and many family producers growing in their own small tea gardens

Main Districts or Gardens
Northern Thailand in the provinces of Chiang Rai, Chiang Mai, Mae Hong Son, Lampang, Phrae

Area Under Tea
16,000 hectares

Average Annual Production (Kilograms)
Approximately 40 million

Terrain
Some flat fields, some very steep terraced slopes in foothills of northern Thailand

Altitude
1,200 to 1,800 metres
(3,937 to 5,905 feet)

Production Period
All year

Best Time to Visit
November to early April/May

Main Varietals/Cultivars
Native assamicas, and sinensis varietals and cultivars from China and Taiwan, including the Jin Xuan cultivar and Ruan Zhi No. 17

Types of Tea Made
Balled oolongs, green, flavoured green, small quantities of black, miang (chewing tea)

Predominant Flavours; Tasting Notes
OOLONG: complex fragrance, sweet, floral, reminiscent of orchids and lilies
GREEN: mellow
BLACK: rich, nutty, chocolaty
BLACK: *Miang*—tart, sour, slightly smoky

VIETNAM

It is impossible to know when the leaves of tea plants were first plucked and processed in Vietnam. The northern states share a border with China's Yunnan Province, often called the "Cradle of Tea" and where tea trees dating back at least 3,000 years are prized by the local people and still plucked to make expensive Puerh teas. Perhaps Vietnamese tea trees have flourished here for the same length of time. Legends tell how tea grew here during the reign of the Hung kings, who ruled the country from 2879 B.C. to 258 B.C., and tea drinking has certainly been a part of daily life in these northern mountains for centuries. Villagers gathered leaves from the wild trees that grew in the surrounding forests, boiled the leaves in water, and drank the brew as an everyday beverage.

Commercial cultivation of tea began with the arrival of the French at the end of the 19th century. Vietnam became a French protectorate in 1883, and almost as soon as it had taken power, the colonial administration started exploring the possibility of growing tea in various regions. In 1885, surveys were conducted along the Da and Mekong rivers, and the first estate of 60 hectares was laid out in 1890 in Tinh Cuong, Phu Tho, to the north-west of Hanoi in the central northern part of the country. In 1918, the Phu Tho Research Centre of Agri-Forestry was set up in Phu Ho District, and cultivation and processing techniques employed in Indonesia and Sri Lanka were developed using equipment imported from England. In 1923, the first factory for processing black tea was built in Phu Ho district, and green, black, and local speciality teas were exported to France and other parts of Western Europe. In 1927, a second research station was opened at

Local villagers pluck leaf in northern Vietnam where tea is made from both ancient wild trees and new cultivated bushes. Photograph courtesy of Dominic Smith

Bau Can, Gia Lai Province, in the southern central region, and a third was opened in Bao Loc District, Lam Dong Province, in the south in 1931. By 1945, 13,585 hectares had been planted, production totalled 6 million kilos (13.2 million pounds), and export of the teas to France and North Africa continued.

During the First Indochina War (1946 to 1954) and the Vietnam War (1955 to 1975), most of the cultivated tea areas were abandoned. In the late 1970s, the USSR funded a rehabilitation programme, and new processing factories were equipped with Russian and Chinese machinery. Cooperatives were also set up, and the restored tea research station at Phu Ho worked to improve cultivation techniques and develop new cultivars. Close ties with Russia ensured a strong market for the country's black tea, but the collapse of the USSR and instability in Eastern Europe in the 1990s meant a decline in export markets and severe problems for the industry. From 1995, joint ventures with Japan, Taiwan, Iraq, and the UK and the introduction of advanced technologies led to an increase in production levels, yields, and quality. Between 2005 and 2013, 12 new high-yielding varietals and cultivars were introduced, the tea area increased from 95,600 hectares in 2001 to 131,200 hectares in 2009, and the country exported 136,000 metric tons (136 million kilos [299.8 million pounds]) compared to 52,100 (52.1 million kilos [114.86 million pounds]) in 2000.

Vietnam's tea industry is export driven, with around 84 percent of production sold into 110 foreign markets. But prices remain low, mainly because of the tea's poor quality in some regions and because the industry does not yet have adequate structures and capital to facilitate improvements and establish a sustainable supply chain. Overuse of pesticides is an ongoing problem and has lost the country its German markets, and attempts to advance Rainforest Alliance are hampered by the difficulty of controlling smallholder output. More and more private companies are becoming involved, and foreign investment is helping to mechanise the large-scale manufacture of green teas and new categories such as oolongs. But there is a divide between those who believe in the preservation of traditional tea making and tea varieties and those who favour the production of new types in order to raise prices and increase future possibilities of exporting into the international market.

The government is committed both to preserving traditional teas and to increasing the country's position in the global market. In 2011, it invested more than 100 billion Dong to promote Vietnam's teas at the first International Festival of Tea in Thai Nguyen, and a second festival was held in 2013. By 2020, the government aims to open up another 150,000 hectares; increase yields; introduce new cultivars; improve quality, health, and safety management; and gain certification for some of the teas. Vietnam is seeking foreign investment, and big estate companies continue to show an interest but are deterred by a lack of both proper trade organisations and discipline in the industry. In some areas, NGOs are working with farmers to create co-operatives, organise training, teach price-negotiation skills, and help raise export prices.

Vietnam has six tea regions: North-West, Vietbac, North-East, Central Highlands, Northern Midlands, and North-Central. Some farmers process and sell their tea into the open market; other contract farmers are affiliated with estate-based factories and must sell only to that factory. Fresh leaf is sold to factories owned by the state, private Vietnamese companies, or joint ventures with foreign companies. About 53 percent of the tea is orthodox and (since 1994) CTC black, 45 percent is green and oolong, 2 percent is yellow or other specialties. Some producers have switched to green manufacture to meet a growing export demand for cheap CTC for making extracts for bottled teas. Most of the traditional greens are consumed domestically. Oolong teas, made from cultivars imported from Taiwan, have been manufactured since the 1990s, mainly by Taiwanese companies, in the Highlands and in North-West Region. Export of the country's teas is handled by joint-venture companies, foreign companies, and national companies, of which state-run Vietnam National Tea Corporation (Vinatea) is the biggest, although it is less prominent now than it once was.

NORTH-WEST REGION

The tea-growing provinces of Son La, Lai Chau, and Dien Bien lie amongst steep mountains, craggy gorges, and sweeping river valleys. The weather during the winter months here can be very cold, misty, and damp, with temperatures of 1°C (34°F) in January, and summer months that are much cooler and fresher than in more southerly regions. Thousands of tea trees have been growing here along the border with China and Laos for hundreds of years, and no one knows if they were planted, perhaps by the French, or seeded themselves in conditions similar to those in other parts of the ancient tea-growing foothills of the Himalayas. The local people call the trees "immortal," revere them as symbols of vitality and endurance, and consider that teas made from their leaves are beneficial for health and strength. The average height of these Tuyet trees is 10 to 15 metres (33 to 49 feet), and villagers clamber up into the branches, often with bare feet, to gather the plump buds and young leaves. Because the trees are old and grow organically, pushing their roots deep into the soil to find water and nutrients, the new buds form very slowly and are harvested only three or four times between April and October. Each year, one tree yields only 7 or 8 kilos (15 to 17.6 pounds) of fresh leaf, which is processed to give just 1.5 kilos (3.3 pounds) of Shan Tuyet green tea. The buds retain their covering of tiny white hairs, so they are often called Tra Shan Tuyet or Snowy Shan Tea. The teas are of high economic value to the region, and local government has encouraged investment in new tea areas. The region is also well suited to the production of oolong teas, and bushes are now being cultivated by co-operatives, by several enterprises and joint ventures with Taiwan and Japan, and by a few foreign-funded companies. Each cultivation area has a processing factory, and the made tea is sent to packing factories for blending and marketing.

VIETBAC REGION

The land in this region, which includes the provinces of Ha Giang, Yen Bai, Tuyen Quang, Lao Cai, Bac Can, and Cao Bang, is a complex mix of rugged high mountains, vast tracts of forests, terraced slopes of tea, lakes, swamps, rivers, and rice paddy fields in the valleys. Like the North-West Region, the climate is subtropical, and temperatures at higher altitudes range from 20°C (68°F) in summer to 0°C (32°F) in winter, with persistent drizzle. In the lowland areas, tea farming is intensive and involves the use of plant protection agents. In the highland forest areas, at altitudes between 400 and 1,000 metres (1,300 and 3,280 feet), ancient tea trees grow organically. Local villagers harvest the leaves of these trees to make Shan Tuyet green tea. Production of these organic teas is helping to protect the northern rainforests and increase the economic success of the region. The Shan Tuyet varietal is able to resist cold, damp conditions and is well suited to these northerly mountain regions. It has therefore been propagated for cultivation in the newly developed areas of tea for the production of black as well as green teas, and many of the factories here produce good-quality, tippy orthodox black teas.

Tea cultivation on a more industrial scale in Vietbac has been increased in recent years to help reduce poverty and create a more sustainable economy. However, widespread use of fertilisers and other plant protection agents was harming the environment, reducing the value of the teas and making them hard to sell. So, in 2013, farmers began to work with VietGAP (Vietnamese Good Agricultural Practices), a code of farming standards published by the country's Ministry of Agriculture and Rural Development, which sets safety standards requiring a reduction in the use of chemicals and the introduction of more sustainable agricultural practices. In November 2013, the first garden achieved VietGAP standards, and the project, involving 2,000 households, has been extended across the region. As a result, productivity has increased, prices have gone up, and the teas are finding their way into new markets.

The Northern Midlands provinces of Thai Nguyen, Phu Tho, Hoa Binh, Ha Tay, Hanoi, and Vinh Phuc cover 70 percent of the northern growing regions and produce most of Vietnam's tea. The terrain here is a mix of limestone mountains, caves containing stalactite and stalagmite formations that lure thousands of tourists every year, rocky cliffs, vast lakes, and plains running down to the Red River Delta. Wild trees were harvested in Phu Tho and Thai Nguyen long before the arrival of the French in the 1880s, when vast commercial estates were planted out to produce black tea for the European market and green for North African consumers. When the country gained independence, the government established more gardens and co-operatives, most of which have since been taken over by private tea producers and joint stock companies.

Thai Nguyen is the heart of Vietnam's tea production. Tea bushes grow in the shelter of the steep mountains, and high levels of rainfall and the warm, humid climate give the teas their exceptional quality. In the hills of Phu Tho Province, one of the country's poorest areas, several experimental tea projects began in 2009 to replace old gardens with new plants, reduce the use of chemicals to improve soil fertility, develop new areas, and build new factories. Today, more than 15,000 families grow tea on more than 9 percent of the cultivated land, and the recent agricultural development programmes have improved living standards.

Other districts in these provinces produce thousands of tons of green, black, oolong, and jasmine tea every year and have the potential to increase production further. To help improve the economic situation of thousands of families, foreign joint ventures and non-profit organisations are helping to plant new areas with high-yielding varietals and cultivars to produce teas that will achieve organic and other certifications to meet international standards. The region produces mostly black and green tea for domestic consumption and export.

ABOVE LEFT: Ancient tea trees in the very far north-west of Vietnam, close to the border with China's Yunnan Province. Photograph courtesy of Dominic Smith
ABOVE RIGHT: Plucking tea in Vietnam. Photograph courtesy of Angela Pryce

HIGHLANDS REGION

This region includes the southern provinces of Lam Dong, Gia Lai, and Kon Tum, and production dates back to the 1890s when the French established tea fields and factories here. From the 1930s, Lam Dong produced large quantities of black tea for export to Western Europe and, in the late 1970s, to Russia. But after the collapse of the USSR, the market for black tea collapsed, and the region now produces green, oolong, white, aged Puerh–style teas, lotus, jasmine, and Shan Tuyet green teas as well as some orthodox and CTC black teas. Taiwanese companies introduced oolong tea production in the 1990s, and experts from Taiwan have also taught producers to make Bao Zhong–style teas. Lam Dong is today the largest tea region in the country, has steadily increased its growing area to 23,876 hectares, and now accounts for around 192 million kilos (423.28 million pounds) of tea a year—27 percent of the country's tea output. By 2015, 20 companies had achieved VietGAP safety certification standards.

NORTH-EAST REGION

Tea grows in the mountainous provinces of Quang Ninh, Lang Son, and Bac Giang, another of the country's poorest regions, partly because of the remoteness of the villages. In 2014, Quang Ninh entered into an agricultural partnership with Taiwan, which includes plans to increase tea cultivation, build a new factory, and increase exports. Lang Son's tea grows in the valleys and along the banks of the Ky Cung and Thuong rivers. Bac Giang's tea plants are in poor condition, farming methods are out of date, yields are very low, bushes need replacing with higher-yielding varietals, and smallholder farmers receive very low prices for their crop.

NORTH-CENTRAL REGION

Tea production in this coastal region of Thanh Hoa, Nghe An, and Ha Tinh provinces is concentrated in the mountains of Nghe An. The majority of teas produced are CTC black teas and small-grade greens for teabags. Improvements in technology, training, equipment, and infrastructure have increased production, quality, exports, prices, and living standards, and many farmers have switched from other crops, such as corn and cassava, to tea.

Lotus Tea | Lotus tea is unique to Vietnam and is said to have been created for King Tu Duc, who ruled from 1848 to 1883. During the late afternoon each day in June, when the lotus flowers bloom, the king's servants rowed small quantities of green tea to the lotus flowers growing in the royal lake. They gently opened the blossoms and placed a small quantity of tea inside each, closed the petals around the tea, and bound them to keep the tea safe. Early the next day, they returned to collect the tea and to scoop up the morning drops of dew that had collected on the lotus leaves, and this was used to brew the tea for the king.

Today, the flavouring process is carried out in family homes, and the lotus flowers are gathered from Hanoi's West Lake. To flavour 1 kilo (2.2 pounds) of tea, 1,500 blossoms are required, and the tea is flavoured five times, using 300 flowers each time. Once the outer and inner petals of 300 flowers have been removed, the stamens that carry the pollen are collected and sifted. The tea is then layered with the pollen in a large pan for two days, and then the mix is wrapped in packages of wax paper and the parcels are tied around the outside of a large pan of warm water. The packets of tea and the pan of water are wrapped up inside brown paper and a thick blanket in a bamboo basket for 12 hours. The white pollen stamens are then removed by hand, and the flavouring process is repeated four more times over 15 days, using a fresh batch of 300 flowers each time. The tea has a crisp, clean, aniseed flavour with just a slight hint of vanilla and is often drunk at Tet, Vietnamese New Year. Since there is a limited quantity of lotus flowers available each year and the flavouring of the tea is demanding and time-consuming, only 30 Hanoi families still make this very special tea.

**Country, State,
or Province**
Vietnam

Number of Gardens
700 processing
companies, plus
smallholders

**Main Districts
or Gardens**
North-West Region:
(Provinces of Son La, Lai
Chau, Dien Bien)

Vietbac Region:
(provinces of Ha Giang,
Yen Bai, Tuyen Quang, Lao
Cai, Bac Can, Cao Bang)

Northern Midlands Region:
(Provinces of Thai Nguyen,
Phu Tho, Hoa Binh, Ha Tay,
Hanoi, Vinh Phuc)

Highlands (Provinces
of Lam Dong, Gia Lai,
Kon Tum)

North-East Region
(Provinces of Quang Ninh,
Lang Son, Bac Giang)

North-Central Region
(Provinces of Thanh Hoa,
Nghe An, Ha Tinh)

Area Under Tea
135,300 hectares,
of which 70% is
smallholder farms

North-West Region:
17,200 hectares

Vietbac Region:
41,000 hectares

Northern Midlands Region:
35,000 hectares, including
15,000 family plots

Highlands:
26,000 hectares

North-East Region:
2,000 hectares

North-Central Region:
11,000 hectares

**Average Annual
Production (Kilograms)**
175 million

Terrain
North-West Region:
Rugged hills in the
mountains bordering
China's Yunnan Province

Vietbac Region:
Steep slopes in rugged
high mountains

Northern Midlands Region:
Plains and mountain
slopes amongst high
mountain ranges, deep
valleys or gorges

Highlands: A complex
mix of plateaux, high
peaks, and flat valleys

North-East Region:
High mountains in
poor remote areas

North-Central Region:
Coastal area

Altitude
North-West Region: 500
to 2,200 metres
(1,640 to 7,217 feet)

Vietbac Region:
200 to 1,000 metres
(650 to 3,280 feet)

Northern Midlands Region:
400 to 2,000 metres
(1,300 to 6,560 feet)

Highlands:
850 to 1,500 metres
(2,788 to 4,920 feet)

North-East Region:
300 to 900 metres (980
to 2,950 feet)

North-Central Region:
1,600 metres (5,249 feet)

Production Period
March to November
in more southerly
regions, April to
October in the north

Best Time to Visit
February to April,
August to October

**Main Varietals/
Cultivars**
North-West Region:
Old, semi-wild assamicas,
Camellia sinensis var.
cambodiensis, new
Taiwanese varietals,
imported assamicas

Vietbac Region:
Ancient assamica
trees, known as Shan
Tuyet, and new plants
propagated from the
ancient trees

Northern Midlands Region:
Ancient wild trees and
new cultivated bushes,
assamica varietals
introduced from India

Highlands:
Sinensis imported from
China, assamicas imported
from India, and native
Shan tea, plus oolong
cultivars from Taiwan

North-East Region:
Sinensis from China

North-Central Region:
Hybrid varieties LDP1
and LDP2 have very
good drought tolerance
and have replaced
older bushes.

Types of Tea Made
North-West Region:
Mainly black orthodox
and CTC, green, oolongs

Vietbac Region:
Green, black orthodox

Northern Midlands Region:
Green, black, oolong

Highlands:
Black orthodox; black
CTC; green; oolong;
roasted oolong; small
quantities of Pouchong;
aged Puerh-style teas;
lotus, jasmine, and Shan
Tuyet green teas

North-East Region:
Green, oolong

North-Central Region:
Mainly black CTC

**Predominant Flavours;
Tasting Notes**
North-West Region:
GREEN: bright, sweet,
sometimes a little
astringent
Shan Tuyet—a little
bitter at first but with a
sweet aftertaste
JADE OOLONGS: buttery,
floral, with hints of
gardenia and cinnamon

Vietbac Region:
GREEN: medium bodied
and lightly astringent
with grassy, mineral
notes and hints of roses
and toasted nuts
Shan Tuyet—sweet, with
soft floral notes and
hints of dried fruits
BLACK: crisp, rich, malty
with a hint of molasses

Northern Midlands Region:
GREEN: *Thai Nguyen*—
fragrant and flowery, with
hints of toasted nuts and
grains, fennel, fresh-cut
grass, and passionfruit
Phu To—medium bodied,
lightly astringent, with
grassy, mineral notes
and hints of roses and
toasted nuts

Highlands:
BLACK: *Orthodox*—
coppery liquor, rich, sweet
CTC—bright, strong
GREEN: light, sweet,
smooth
OOLONG: light, sweet,
silky, floral, with
suggestions of brown
sugar and citrus
ROASTED OOLONG: hints
of orchid, baked apple,
brown sugar, sweet cream
or butter, honey, vanilla

North-East Region:
GREEN: mild, sweet
OOLONG: soft, sweet

North-Central Region:
BLACK: *CTC*—strong,
fresh, mellow with
flowery notes

TAIWAN

CHINA

MYANMAR

VIETNAM

LAOS

THAILAND

CAMBODIA

*Philippine
Sea*

Manila★

Philippines

*South
China
Sea*

•Cebu

Davao•

Sulu Sea

•
Zamboanga City

*Gulf of
Thailand*

MOUNT KINABALU ▲▲ **Sabah
Tea Gardens**

BRUNEI

Celebes Sea

Simalungun

Malaysia
Cameron Highlands

Malaysia

Medan•

★Kuala
Lumpur

•Pontianak

Indonesia

Sulawesi

•Ambon

North
Sumatra

Banda Sea

•Palembang

Makassar•

Java Sea

South
Sumatra

Pekalongan

Jakarta Tegal

Timor Sea

West Java

Central Java

Wanayasa Garut

East Java

PENGALENGAN
PLATEAU

N

🌿 Tea grower

W E

🌿 Multiple growers

S

▲▲ Mountain

OCEANIA

0   125   250   500 Miles

0 125 250   500 Kilometres

INDONESIA

Tea was introduced to the islands of Indonesia by the Dutch, who arrived here in the 16th century in their quest to find supplies of nutmeg, cloves, and pepper. The Dutch East India Company established the city of Batavia (now Jakarta) as company headquarters and shipped back to Holland all the tea, silk, spices, porcelain, and other valuable goods they purchased in Japan, China, and Java.

It is thought that the first tea seeds were brought from Japan to Tijgersgracht in Batavia in 1684 by Andreas Cleyer, a German botanist and trader, but these were not intended for commercial cultivation. In the early 18th century, local people planted seeds from China on their own land to make tea for their own consumption. In 1824, seeds were planted at the Lands Plantentuin te Buitenzorg (now Bogor Botanical Garden), and by 1827, larger-scale operations were underway at the Cisurupan Experimental Plantation in Garut and Wanayasa, both in West Java. The first commercial plantation was established by tea expert Jacobus Isidorus Loudewijk Levian Jacobson in 1828, and the first 200 cases of Java-grown black teas were shipped to Holland and auctioned in Amsterdam in 1835. In 1877, Ceylon seeds were planted at Gambung Plantation in West Java, and gradually, the original Chinese plants were replaced with assamica varietals. In 1910, a plantation was established at Simalungun in Sumatra, and by 1942, Indonesia was the fourth-largest tea producer in the world. But during World War II, more than half of the plantations were seriously damaged, factories were abandoned, and plants were left to grow wild.

In the late 1980s, the Ministry of Agriculture of Indonesia introduced a programme of recovery, and the country is today the eighth-largest producer in the world. However, tea contributes only 0.5 percent of foreign currency earnings each year and is far less important than palm oil and rubber, and tea production has been declining over the past decade. This comes as a result of competition from increased production in Vietnam, reductions in available planting area, old technology, poor planting stock, low yields, poor farming methods, lack of capital and expertise, rising wages, and infrastructure weaknesses. To help boost the industry, the Tea Board is currently coordinating the National Agribusiness Rescue Movement, which aims to improve productivity and quality on 57,000 hectares of smallholder land, organise an effective promotion and marketing programme, create a better business climate, and improve the welfare of smallholders in the longer term.

Just under half the land planted is cultivated by smallholders on plots of between 0.8 and 2 hectares. State ownership accounts for 32 percent of tea land, while 22 percent is owned by large private companies. The state-owned estates grow their own leaf and process it as 82 percent black tea (mainly orthodox and small quantities of CTC) and 18 percent green tea. Most of the leaf is plucked by hand, but shears are used in hotter, wetter periods when the bushes are flushing faster, and one of the state-owned estates uses hedge trimmers. A few producers also make oolongs, which fetch good prices in export markets. The leaf grown by the smallholders is sold into the private factories where around 90 percent is processed as green tea (often later perfumed with jasmine flowers) and the remaining 10 percent as black tea. In the past, the smallholders' dependence on payment from processing factories meant low prices for the growers and no control over earnings. But in 2014, the first factory owned and managed by a smallholder, the Rakyat Iroet Tea Factory, was opened at Garut in West Java, and the government and Tea Board are supporting the scheme to build 20 more of these farmer-owned factories.

The most important growing regions are Central Java, West Java, and North Sumatra, and small amounts of tea grow in East Java, West Sumatra, South Sumatra, and Sulawesi. The best 20 percent of the teas are grown in the West Javan high-mountain areas at altitudes over 1,200 metres (3,937 feet); 50 percent are mid-grown at between 800 and 1,200 metres (2,625 and 3,937 feet), while 30 percent are low-grown at elevations of between 500 and 800 metres (1,640 and 2,625 feet). The best of the black teas are strong, full-bodied, and fruity. The plainer black and green teas are sold for blending as loose or tea bag teas, or for use in ready-to-drink (RTD) products. Around 65 percent of Indonesian tea is exported to Russia, the United Kingdom, Malaysia, Pakistan, Germany, the United States, Poland, and the Netherlands.

WEST JAVA

West Java is the heartland of the Indonesian tea industry and accounts for 77 percent of land under tea and 70 percent of production. The best teas are from the Pengalengan Plateau. West Java also produces bulk green teas, which are scented with jasmine in reprocessing factories located in Pekalongan and Tegal on the north coast in Central Java where the jasmine plants are cultivated. One or two of the gardens, such as Harendong Green Farm, have planted sinensis varietals that flourish in the cool, humid air of the high mountains. Producers here make a wide range of high-quality green, oolong, white, and black teas for domestic and international markets.

CENTRAL JAVA

Java is of volcanic origin, and the volcanic soil, high altitudes, and tropical climate are perfect for tea growing. Most of the tea produced in the region is jasmine green, the most popular tea amongst local consumers. It is drunk hot and sweet in glasses filled from large kettles, or purchased as Teh Botol, a chilled, bottled jasmine tea introduced as Teh Cap Botol by the SOSRO brand in the 1940s.

NORTH SUMATRA

Indonesia's largest island, Sumatra is the second most important of the country's tea regions in terms of the quantity of tea produced. Until the 1990s, most of the plants were more than 75 years old, and some 2,000 hectares have since been planted with high-yielding clones produced by vegetative propagation. Sumatra produces mainly black teas, which are popular as self-drinkers but are also used in breakfast blends to add their smooth, warm strength.

TOP: Pluckers at the organic Harendong Tea Estate in the high mountains of West Java. ABOVE: Harendong Tea Factory, which makes green, oolong, white, and black teas. Photographs courtesy of Harendong Tea Estate

Country, State, or Province
Indonesia

Number of Gardens
Approximately 35 private, 7 state-owned; 100,000 smallholders

Main Districts or Gardens
West Java, Central Java, North Sumatra

Area Under Tea
120,222 hectares, including approximately 27,381 private; 37,728 state-owned; 55,176 smallholders

Average Annual Production (Kilograms)
Approximately 130 million, including—
West Java: 101.8 million
Central Java: 9.27 million
North Sumatra: 12.9 million

Terrain
West Java: Valley basin lying amongst rainforest in the volcanic highlands of West Java

Central Java: Hilly tea gardens on the high plain of Central Java

North Sumatra: Vast expanses of tea growing in fertile volcanic soil on the lower slopes of Sumatra's highlands

Altitude
West Java:
1,200 to 1,500 metres (3,937 to 4,921 feet)

Central Java:
800 to 2,050 metres (2,625 to 6,726 feet)

North Sumatra:
250 to 750 metres (800 to 2,400 feet)

Production Period
All year

Best Time to Visit
April to September

Main Varietals/ Cultivars
90% assamicas, 10% sinensis

Types of Tea Made
West Java: Black orthodox, balled oolongs, various grades of green orthodox that are often used as a base for jasmine tea

Central Java:
Jasmine green

North Sumatra:
Mainly black orthodox

Predominant Flavours; Tasting Notes
West Java:
BLACK ORTHODOX: high-quality teas, bright clear liquor, a sweet, woodsy aroma and taste, sometimes with hints of cedarwood; peak-season teas have a more delicate, malty, caramel character with floral and fruity notes
GREEN: delicate, mild, refreshing, sweet, with floral notes and sometimes hints of grapefruit
BALLED OOLONGS: silky, honeyed, with hints of roasted chestnuts and walnuts

Central Java:
GREEN: *Jasmine*—light, delicate, perfumed with jasmine blossoms

North Sumatra:
BLACK: sweet, sometimes nutty, and full-bodied but low in tannin

MALAYSIA

The Cameron Highlands, known today as Malaysia's "Green Bowl," were discovered in 1885 by William Cameron, government surveyor during British rule. The first planter to grow tea here was British businessman John Archibald Russell, who recognised that the equatorial climate, rolling hills, gently dipping valleys, well-drained soil, regular rainfall, and long hours of sunshine were ideal for tea cultivation. In 1929, he and Ceylon tea planter A. B. Milne established the first BOH Tea Plantation. Today, two companies—BOH and the Bharat Group—grow tea on the lush green plateau in the Titiwangsa Mountains in Pahang, surrounded by lofty peaks that disappear into curling white clouds. And on the island of Borneo, Sabah Tea Gardens grow tea in the foothills of Mount Kinabalu. Malaysia's tea bushes are kept to a height of only 46 centimetres (18 inches) by hard pruning every three years, and most of the tea is harvested mechanically. Shears are used to cut shoots from the sides of the bushes, and hedge-trimmer machines skim off the shoots from the top. Current challenges to all tea producers here include changing weather patterns, a shortage of labour, and the fact that more land is being given over to oil palm plantations, which are easier and cheaper to run. In 2014, the Malaysia External Trade Development Corporation (MATRADE) encouraged tea exporters to market their products into the United Arab Emirates (UAE), one of the world's biggest importers of tea, in order to help revive and strengthen the country's tea industry.

ABOVE: The tearoom at BOH Tea Estate extends out over the tea garden and gives visitors an uninterrupted view of the estate and the surrounding landscape. OPPOSITE PAGE: The BOH Tea Estate, owned by BOH Plantations Sdn Bhd, in the Cameron Highlands. Photographs courtesy of BOH Plantations

BOH PLANTATIONS SDN BHD TEA

BOH's name was inspired by "Bohea," the English pronunciation of Wuyi, China's famous tea mountains in Fujian Province, and the word that came to mean "black tea" to British and American tea drinkers in the 17th and 18th centuries. Today, BOH owns three gardens in the Cameron Highlands—Fairlie, Sungei Palas, and the original garden at Habu—and a fourth at Bukit Cheeding in Selangor near Kuala Lumpur, which also has a packing facility. The teas are blended and packed here for the domestic market and for customers in the United States, United Arab Emirates, Japan, Singapore, Brunei, and various European countries. BOH's tea gardens cover a total area of 1,200 hectares (almost 52 percent of the country's land under tea), and the company produces 4 million kilos (8.8 million pounds) of tea every year, which is approximately 70 percent of Malaysia's tea. The CEO of the company is Caroline Russell, John Archibald Russell's granddaughter. (Nerada Tea in Australia is a subsidiary independent company.) BOH teas include an assertive, strong black tea with hints of cocoa and raisins, and a light, delicate green tea. The Sungei Palas garden also has a tea centre where visitors can enjoy views out over the tea fields, learn about tea and tea manufacture, taste the different teas, and buy retail packs to take home.

BHARAT GROUP

The Bharat Group, a multi-business conglomerate founded in Malaysia in 1910 by Indian entrepreneur Shuparshad Bansal Agarwal, started growing tea in the Cameron Highlands in 1933. When Agarwal died in 1937, his brothers took over and expanded the business, launching its first branded tea, Chop Rusa, in 1952 and acquiring the Shalimar Tea Estate and factory in 1963. Today, Bharat has four estates and grows tea on 1,600 acres, produces 70,000 kilos (154,324 pounds) of green leaf per week and manufactures black teas, fresh and clean greens, mild whites, flavoured teas, and a range of bottled teas. In 2002, the company's first Cameron Valley Tea House opened near Tanah Rata, and three more have subsequently opened, including one in Kuala Lumpur.

SABAH TEA GARDENS

Sabah Tea Gardens, Malaysia's only organic tea producer, was opened by the government in 1984. It is situated at the foothills of Mount Kinabalu, Malaysia's highest peak, on the island of Borneo in the East Malaysian state of Sabah where the tea bushes are surrounded by the trees of a 130-million-year old rainforest. In 1997, Yee Lee Corporation Berhad acquired the estate and now produces black and flavoured teas. The company also has a restaurant; offers accommodation in long houses, cottages, a guesthouse, and a campsite; and welcomes visitors who wish to learn more about tea.

On the steep slopes of the BOH estate, the crop is harvested about every three weeks using shears, which can bring in around 120 kilograms per day per plucker. Photographs courtesy of BOH Plantations

Country, State, or Province
Malaysia

Number of Gardens 9

Main Districts or Gardens
Cameron Highlands, Pahang;
Sabah, Borneo

Area Under Tea
Approximately 2,533 hectares

**Average Annual
Production (Kilograms)**
Approximately 5.4 million

Terrain
Cameron Highlands: Hill station in the chain of mountains running down the spine of Malaysia; as well as tea estates, there are jungles, forests, nature reserves, and strawberry farms.

Sabah: Dominated by the high peaks of Mount Kinabalu, an oval-shaped granite mountain often swathed in misty cloud; surrounded by tropical rainforest and close to Poring hot springs and Kinabalu National Park

Altitude
Cameron Highlands:
693 to 1,930 metres
(2,273 to 5,850 feet)

Sabah: 693 metres (2,273 feet)

Production Period
All year

Best Time to Visit
All year

Main Varietals/Cultivars
Assamicas

Types of Tea Made
Black orthodox: whole leaf, brokens, fannings, and dusts; green; white

**Predominant Flavours;
Tasting Notes**
BLACK:
Large Grades—golden, honey-coloured liquors, strong, sweet
Small Black Grades—darker liquors, robust, strong, full-bodied
GREEN: delicate, light, clean
WHITE: mild and delicate

PHILIPPINES

Sometime in the 1980s, the Philippines Bureau of Plant Industry planted the country's first tea seeds from Ceylon at its experimental station in Baguio in the north of the country, perhaps with a view to growing tea commercially, but this did not happen. Then, in the 1990s, during a visit to Baguio, farmer Leodegario Garcia became aware of the mature bushes, collected 500 grams (17.6 ounces) of seeds, and took them home to La Paz in Zamboanga City, in the south. He potted the seeds in protective plastic bags, and when 85 percent sprouted, he initiated a programme of research and concluded that Zamboanga was ideal for tea cultivation. The strip of flat land on the east coast lies just north of the equator and has a tropical climate that brings plenty of warm humid air throughout the year and high levels of rain from May to October. Garcia proposed large-scale cultivation of the Ceylon plants to the government, but his suggestion was turned down due to lack of funds.

Then, in 2011, Dante de Lima, director of the Department of Agriculture's High Value Commercial Crops Development Program (HVCDP), became involved in the project, and as a result, the government allocated 725,000 pesos to establish the Organic Tea Production and Commercialization Project. The Department of Agriculture is now working in collaboration with the Alternative Center for Organizational Reforms and Development, Inc. (ACORD) to encourage tea-growing in La Paz. The project is managed by Orlando Telmo, superintendent of La Paz Experiment Station and Seed Farm, a research station for hill farming. Telmo is conducting research and development, has established two tea nurseries to produce seedlings from leaf cuttings taken from the original Ceylon tea plants, has set up two demonstration tea farms, and runs training for new tea farmers. The aim of the scheme is to create new possibilities for local hill farmers, generate income, create jobs, and contribute to the environmental and economic stability of the region.

Country, State, or Province
Philippines

Number of Gardens
Smallholder farms planned

Main Districts or Gardens
La Paz in the south of the country

Area Under Tea
2 nurseries and 2 demonstration farms

Average Annual Production (Kilograms)
Not yet known

Terrain
Soft rolling land surrounded in the distance by rugged hills with steep slopes that climb to altitudes of 1,000 to 1,500 metres (3,281 to 4,921 feet)

Altitude
933 metres (3,060 feet)

Production Period
May to October

Best Time to Visit
November to April

Main Varietals/Cultivars
Assamica varietals from Sri Lanka

Types of Tea Made
Not yet known

Predominant Flavours; Tasting Notes
Not yet known

INDIA

Gulf of
Mannar

INDIAN
OCEAN

Deduru Oya

Sri Lanka

Mahaweli Ganga

Madara Oya

Kandy

CEYLON
TEA MUSEUM

Nuwara
Eliya

Uda Pussallawa

Colombo★

Kelani Ganga

Dimbula

Kalu Ganga

Uva

TEA RESEARCH
INSTITUTE, SRI LANKA

Kirindi Oya

INDIAN
OCEAN

Sabaragamuwa

Ruhuna

N

W   E

S

Multiple growers

Place of interest

0   12.5   25   50 Miles

0 12.5 25   50 Kilometres

SRI LANKA

In 1815, the island of Ceylon came under the control of the British who decided to cultivate coffee here. They employed local workers to clear vast areas of jungle and construct necessary buildings, and brought Tamils from southern India to work on the new plantations. In 1796, a Captain Percival had learned that "the tea plant has also been discovered native in the forests," and in 1816, the Reverend Ringletaube, recently arrived in Ceylon, wrote, "In the garden of Mr Cripp, Master Attendant at Colombo, I am told grows the tea plant. Were you to offer that you would introduce the culture of this most valuable plant in Ceylon, somewhere near Colombo… perhaps the offer would take." In 1839, tea seeds from Assam were planted at the Royal Botanic Gardens in Kandy, and a few young bushes raised there were transplanted to the Oliphant estate in Nuwara Eliya. Two German brothers, Maurice and Gabriel Worms, also acquired cuttings from China and planted them amongst the coffee bushes on their Rothschild and Sogama estates near Kandy.

In 1869, a coffee rust fungus, *Hemileia vastatrix*, destroyed the coffee bushes and caused the collapse of the island's coffee industry. Some planters gave up and returned home to Britain; some planted *Cinchona*, cardamom, cocoa, or rubber; and some decided to try growing tea. Three years earlier, at G. and J. A. Hadden's Loolecondera coffee estate, recently arrived Scottish employee James Taylor had already been put in charge of sowing experimental tea seeds, and in 1867, he established the first plantation on 7.7 hectares of the estate. Once the bushes were established, Taylor had begun to experiment with manufacturing methods and, in 1870, had sent his first samples of tea for sale on the Kandy market. By 1872, he had built a fully equipped factory that included a rolling machine of his own invention and, a year later, had dispatched 23 pounds (10.4 kilos) of black tea to London where it was sold at auction, valued at 3 shillings and 9 pence a pound.

Taylor's success now encouraged others to plant tea, and by 1875, 437 hectares of tea had been planted with seed from India. By the mid-1890s, coffee had almost totally disappeared from the Central Highlands, and new tea factories were being built. Some Sinhalese and Europeans purchased land on which to grow tea, but the majority of the new gardens were British-owned, with labour provided by the Tamils who had previously worked on the coffee plantations. In 1890, newcomer Thomas Lipton started growing tea to sell direct through his chain of very successful grocery stores in Britain. The low price of his teas and his famous slogan "Direct from the tea garden to the teapot" captured public attention, and his name became synonymous with good-quality, low-priced Ceylon tea. Local growers and brokers decided it was now time to set up Ceylon's own tea auctions in order to sell the increasing volumes available to buyers around the world. The first sale was held on the 30th of July 1883, at the offices of Somerville & Co., one of Colombo's leading tea brokers, and by 1894, the Ceylon Chamber of Commerce had become the auctions' home.

Until the late 1890s, all Ceylon tea was black, but some of the factories started producing green varieties to meet a growing demand from North America and continued to produce green teas until 1936. Meanwhile, the quantities of black tea exports continued to rise, and with the majority of the profits going to the UK-based British companies, discontent amongst the Sinhalese people began to grow and strengthened a movement for independence. On February 4, 1948, the British colony became an independent self-governing member of the Commonwealth. In 1972, Ceylon became a republic called Sri Lanka, but the Ceylon tea industry chose to keep its famous name for marketing and publicity purposes.

After independence, the tea industry continued much as before, but with the threat of nationalisation of the estates, some sterling companies sold out or diverted funds to their interests in other countries, thus causing a gradual decline in the condition of the Ceylon tea factories and gardens. Tea yields, efficiency, and production all suffered, and by the time nationalisation of

the plantations began in 1971, tea bushes on at least two-thirds of the estates were neglected, buildings were run down, and the standard of workers' living conditions was well below acceptable levels. In 1971, the government introduced a Land Reform Act, imposing a limit of 20.24 hectares per person as the maximum area of agricultural land that any individual could own. In 1975, a second wave of land takeover by the state further changed the structure of the plantation sector. British control was finally broken, and the larger tea estates were put under the control of two government bodies, Sri Lanka State Plantation Corporation (SLSPC) and Janatha Estate Development Board (JEDB). By 1990, the government owned 502 estates, almost all managed by the SLSPC or the JEDB and producing 65 percent of all Sri Lanka's tea. The long-term effects of putting civil servants in charge were disastrous and almost all the plantations ran at a loss. In 1990, the government began another major restructuring and invited private tea companies to become more involved in the management of the plantations while ownership remained in government hands.

In the 1980s, in an effort to increase profits, some producers began, with subsidies from the Sri Lanka Tea Board, to convert their factories from orthodox to CTC, but quickly realised that the quality of the teas was being lost and so decided to retain their traditional orthodox methodology. Also in the '80s, the Tea Board introduced the now famous lion logo, which appears on packs of tea that contain 100 percent quality Ceylon tea. The aim of the logo is to boost recognition of Ceylon tea and to protect its reputation in the world market. The Tea Board requires that any packets carrying the logo must be packed in Sri Lanka by Ceylon tea companies; foreign importers and blenders who pack their tea elsewhere are not allowed to apply it to their packaging.

TOP: Passenger train running through Holyrood Tea Estate in Dimbula. FAR LEFT: Leaf cuttings grown by vegetative propagation to produce new clonal plants. MIDDLE LEFT: Poronuwa Estate in Ratnapura District in the low-growing Ruhuna tea region. NEAR LEFT: Black tea oxidising at Great Western Tea Estate, owned by Dilmah. Photographs courtesy of Dilmah Tea

Since Sri Lanka is close to the equator, the tea bushes grow throughout the year from sea level up to 2,000 metres (7,000 feet) in the southern central mountains. The tea bushes hug the slopes and contours of the steep hills in a landscape where waterfalls and rivers, rocky outcrops, and thick woodland punctuate the lush green of the tea. The plants that thrive here were grown from a mixed stock of Chinese seeds and cuttings imported in the 1870s and Assam seeds propagated and planted as the industry expanded in the 1880s. Many of the old plants were replaced with new higher-yielding cloned cultivars, but since these do not go on producing for as long and are less robust, many estates have retained the original bushes planted in the 19th century.

The seven tea areas—Ruhuna, Sabaragamuwa, Kandy, Dimbula, Uva, Uda Pussellawa, and Nuwara Eliya—are divided by altitude and region, and the teas from each have their own very individual character. "Low-grown" teas are cultivated below 600 metres (2,000 feet); "mid-grown" or "mid-country" teas are from altitudes of 600 to 1,200 metres (2,000 to 4,000 feet); and "high-grown" teas are produced above 1,200 metres (4,000 feet). Within those divisions by altitude, there are variances in the exact altitudes of some gardens.

Although Sri Lanka is not seasonal, the character of the teas is affected by changing weather patterns through the year. Two monsoons have a marked effect on teas growing on each side of the north-south mountain range. One that sweeps down from the north-east of the island brings rain from December to March to the teas growing on the eastern side of the mountains; the other, from the south-west, brings rain to the western slopes from June to September. During the drier period in each region, the bushes grow more slowly and therefore yield "peak season" high-quality teas.

Out of 649 factories, 610 produce orthodox black teas, 27 process CTC blacks (which account for approximately 7 percent of production), 11 factories in the mid-grown and high-grown districts make green teas, and one manufactures instant tea. Around 370,842 smallholders cultivate a total of 118,275 hectares, mostly in the low-growing districts of Ruhuna. Their plots range from less than 1 hectare to 2 hectares, and a few cultivate bigger plots of more than 50 hectares. The majority of the processing factories are also in the low-growing regions of Ruhuna and Sabaragamuwa.

RUHUNA | The first tea estates were established here in the early 1900s, and the area was previously categorised as two regions—Galle and Ruhuna. It is today divided into four sub districts: Ratnapura/Balangoda, Deniyaya, Matara, and Galle. Although protected from the full force of the south-west monsoon by the Sinharaja Forest Reserve, the land still receives a generous quantity of rain, and the warmth and humidity encourage the bushes to grow robustly throughout the year. The area is mainly farmed by smallholder families, who sell their leaf into the local factories. The region is most famous for its beautiful large-leafed Orange Pekoes and Tippy Flowery Orange Pekoes. During rolling, only light pressure is applied, and this produces large neat twists of wiry, jet-black, sometimes tippy, leaf, which is particularly popular in western Asia, the Middle East, and CIS countries.

SABARAGAMUWA | This is Sri Lanka's largest tea-growing region on the western and south-western slopes of the Central Highlands where the alluvial soil is richly fertile. Although the gardens lie at low elevations, the teas are different in character from low-grown teas produced in other parts of the world. In the north-western part of the region, the liquors have a light aromatic quality similar to those of Kandy teas. Teas from the south-western area are lighter and slightly sweeter with a dry mouth character. On the eastern slopes, where the monsoon and Cachan wind that affect Uva teas have an influence on the character of the teas, liquors are dark yellow-brown during the rainy season, more reddish in the dry months, and the large Orange Pekoe–grade leaves yield teas that are bright and strong.

KANDY | Kandy is divided into two sub districts: Pussellawa/ Hewaheta and Matale. The town of Kandy is the former capital, and the tea bushes that grow nearby are the oldest on the island, planted on land that was originally laid out with coffee in the early 19th century. When the British took over the governance of the country in 1815, this was the centre of their operations. The botanical gardens were established here, and it was at the Loolecondera coffee estate in the District of Hewaheta near Kandy where James Taylor first planted tea seeds from Assam. The section he planted is today known as No. 7 field.

The Kandy area, part of the Central Province of the island, is what is termed the mid-grown or mid-country region. The majority of the tea hills slope gently upwards around the town on the western side of the central mountains and so are affected by the wet and dry seasons and the fierce winds associated with the south-west monsoon. During the cooler, drier months at the beginning of the year, the plants grow more slowly and yield the peak-season, quality teas. The Kandy factories produce a wide range of tea styles, from CTC tea for teabags to whole and broken-leaf orthodox teas. Kandy teas are known for their strength, body, and bright coppery brew, although the altitude of each garden affects the character in the cup. The smaller-leafed higher-grown teas give a lighter liquor while large-leafed varieties from the lower slopes have a slightly stronger character. One or two estates in the region make Chinese-style green teas such as gunpowder and Chun Mee.

UDA PUSSELLAWA | Uda Pussellawa is divided into two sub-districts: Maturata and Ragala/Halgranoya. There is very little habitation here, and the area is almost entirely covered with tea bushes and the Hakgala Strict Nature Reserve, where rare plant species thrive and leopards roam free through the forests and occasionally onto the tea estates. The region lies north-east of Nuwara Eliya and north of Uva and so is affected by the north-east monsoon winds that give peak-season Uva teas their

TOP: Craighead Tea Estate in the mid-grown Kandy tea region where tea growing was established in 1867. Photograph courtesy of Dilmah Tea
ABOVE: Pickers waiting for their tea to be weighed at Radella Tea Estate in Dimbula, Sri Lanka. Photograph by John O'Hagan; © Hoffman Media

characteristic mentholated character. Most of the rain here falls during the monsoon from November to January. Hakgala has 211 days of rain every year on average, so the area has a climate that is often misty and wet. During the very dry period between the monsoons, the teas grow more slowly and so develop their peak quality from July to September. But because of its position, the region is also affected by the south-west monsoon winds, which leave the land very dry during the first four months of the year. Uda Pussellawa therefore enjoys two quality seasons each year. During the wetter months, the teas have a dark amber liquor and a strong vibrant taste; during the drier, cooler months of July, August, and September, the teas from the higher elevations in Ragala/Halgranoya have medium body, good strength, a hint of roses in the aroma, and a rosy hue to the liquor. The teas from Maturata, to the east of Nuwara Eliya, are subtle, strong, and less delicate than those from the higher slopes.

DIMBULA | Dimbula is divided into six sub-districts: Bogawantalawa, Dickoya, Kotagala, Maskeliya, Nanu Oya, and Talawakelle.

The high-growing Dimbula region was the first to be developed after the coffee crop failed in the late 1860s, and the tea gardens sweep across the western slopes of the mountains. When the pioneer planters found that Dimbula teas had a wonderfully fragrant character, more and more land was cleared to allow the establishment of new gardens. The area is named after the valley that is surrounded by the slopes and high plateaux of the various Dimbula sub-districts.

Because Dimbula lies on the western side of the mountains, it is affected by the heavy rains of the south-west monsoon from May until September. The teas from this wet, misty season are full-flavoured and aromatic. When the days are crisp and cool and the nights cold and windy during the first few months of the year, the peak-quality teas range from full-bodied, bright, fresh, and clean to delicate, light, and fragrant. Sometimes, the liquors carry hints of oak, cypress, spice, citrus fruits, or jasmine. The higher the altitude at which the bushes grow, the fresher and brighter the teas. Teas from Bogawantalawa are full of bright flavour throughout the year; teas from the lower slopes of Dickoya are rounded and fresh; Kotagala teas have strength and body; Maskeliya produces teas with hints of summer roses and a satisfyingly full flavour; and bushes in Nanu Oya and Talawakelle yield lighter, more fragrant teas.

Dilmah's Radella Tea Estate, in the Dimbula region, is well known for its high-quality green tea. Photograph by John O'Hagan; © Hoffman Media

UVA | Uva is divided into eight sub-districts: Malwatte/ Welimada, Demodera/Hali-Ela/Badulla, Passara/Lunugala, Madulsima, Ella/Namunukula, Banderawela/Poonagala, Haputale, and Koslanda/Haldummulla.

Uva is hidden away high on the south-eastern side of the mountains, and the journey up to the tea gardens is long and slow. This eastern side of the Central Highlands is drenched by the rains of the north-east monsoon from December to March, but during July, August, and September, the cool, dry Cachan wind gusts through the valleys and rocky gorges up to the higher slopes, sucking up the air and moisture in its path. As a result of the powerful wind, the growth of the tea bushes slows, the normal photosynthesis in the leaves is disrupted, and the warmth of the daylight hours and the cold night temperatures cause the teas to develop a unique "quality-season" mentholated character that is reminiscent of wintergreen, a medicinal plant used to ease aching muscles and joints, rheumatic symptoms, fevers, and sore throats. If too much rain falls during this prized quality season, the teas fail to develop the highly individual taste and aroma. The manufacturing process is changed slightly during the peak season and producers focus on the smaller broken-leaf grades that concentrate the very special flavour of these teas.

The teas from the different Uva districts vary slightly in flavour and strength. Koslanda/Haldummulla's teas are strong, and Demodera/Hali-Ela/Badulla also yield quite strong flavoury teas, while Haputale produces more rounded, delicate teas. Some Uva factories make CTC black teas as well as the traditional range of orthodox teas, and a few producers, particularly in Idalgashinna in Badulla, make a range of green teas.

NUWARA ELIYA | Nuwara Eliya is not divided, as the other areas are, into smaller districts.

The little town of Nuwara Eliya, developed by the British in the first half of the 19th century as a cool hill station retreat for British civil servants, is situated at 1,868 metres (6,128 feet) above sea level. The tea grows on the gentle slopes of a wide oval mountain valley in the island's highest tea region where temperatures sometimes drop low enough to allow frost to form. Sitting at the very top of the Central Highland Range, the region is exposed to the effects of both the north-east and the south-west monsoons and so has two peak-quality seasons— in January and February and again in August and September. During processing, the withered leaves develop a slightly orange hue, and liquors are golden and clear with an exquisite aroma and flavour that carry the scent of the wild mint, cypress, and eucalyptus trees that grow here. The finest teas are considered to be the large, whole-leaf Orange Pekoe grades that have a subtle, lightly mentholated character.

ABOVE LEFT: Oxidising black tea at Imboolpitiya Tea Estate factory in the Kandy region. ABOVE RIGHT: Withering troughs at Houpe Tea Estate in the foothills of the Balangoda Hills in Ratnapura. The estate is famous for its black teas. Photographs courtesy of Dilmah Tea

Country, State, or Province
Sri Lanka

Number of Gardens
Approximately 714 factories, including 116 high-grown, 119 mid-grown, 429 low-grown, plus 370,000 smallholders

Main Districts or Gardens
Dimbula, Kandy, Nuwara Eliya, Ruhuna, Sabaragamuwa, Uda Pussellawa, Uva

Area Under Tea
222,000 hectares

Average Annual Production (Kilograms)
328 million

Terrain
Dimbula: Western side of the Central Highlands south of Kandy, gardens sweep steeply upwards through peaks and mountain passes

Kandy: Slopes of tea in the hills and valleys around Kandy on the western side of the Central Highlands

Nuwara Eliya: Gentle slopes of a wide valley in a rugged mountainous region at the top of the highlands

Ruhuna: Low-lying, slopes in the steamy, grassy, coastal plains, amongst forest reserves, nature reserves, thick jungle, and salt marshes

Sabaragamuwa: Hills and valleys where fast-running streams and waterfalls have in the past brought down gemstones such as rubies and moonstones. Gem mines are nearby.

Uda Pussellawa: Eastern slopes of the highlands amongst forests and nature reserves

Uva: Remote region on the steep south-eastern slopes of the highlands

Altitude
Sri Lanka: Varies from sea level up to 2,286 metres (7,500 feet)

Dimbula: 1,066 to 1,524 metres (3,500 to 5,000 feet)

Kandy: 600 to 1,200 metres (2,000 to 4,000 feet)

Nuwara Eliya: Up to 2,286 metres (7,500 feet)

Ruhuna: Sea level to 600 metres (2,000 feet)

Sabaragamuwa: Sea level to around 800 metres (2,500 feet)

Uda Pussellawa: 950 to 1,600 metres (3,000 to 5,000 feet)

Uva: 914 to 1,524 metres (3,000 to 5,000 feet)

Production Period
All year

Best Time to Visit
Any time, but to avoid monsoons, January to April or mid-July to September

Main Varietals/Cultivars
Mixed sinensis from China and assamicas from Assam, plus new cultivars

Types of Tea Made
Dimbula: Black orthodox, needle-style white

Kandy: Black orthodox and CTC, some Chinese-style green

Nuwara Eliya: Black orthodox, needle-style white

Ruhuna: Tippy black orthodox, some needle-style white

Sabaragamuwa: Black orthodox

Uda Pussellawa: Black orthodox

Uva: Black orthodox, needle-style white

Predominant Flavours; Tasting Notes
Dimbula:
BLACK: golden-orange liquors, full of flavour and aroma; during dry months at the beginning of the year, the teas are bright, fresh, lively, with hints of oak, cypress, spice, and citrus
WHITE: smooth, gentle, sweet, with hints of honey-dew melon

Kandy:
BLACK: lower gardens give strong liquors; teas from higher gardens are more subtle and delicate
GREEN: light brown liquors with grassy aroma, slightly spicy, with a citrus note and refreshing finish

Nuwara Eliya:
BLACK: pale amber liquors, delicate, aromatic, refined, fruity, with hints of citrus and spice
WHITE: pale liquors, delicate, light taste

Ruhuna:
BLACK: rich red liquors, strong, with thick juicy sweetness
WHITE: pale gold liquor, sweet and floral, with very light hints of grassiness

Sabaragamuwa:
BLACK: coppery red liquors, similar to Ruhuna teas but less thick and juicy, sweet, with hints of caramelised sugar

Uda Pussellawa:
BLACK: during wetter months, dark amber liquors with a strong vibrant taste; during the dryer cooler months of July, August, and September, medium body, good strength, a hint of roses in the aroma, and a rosy hue to the liquor

Uva:
BLACK: bright coppery liquors, strong, mellow, smooth; during dryer months of July, August, and September, the teas develop a mentholated, medicinal character
WHITE: smooth, mild, buttery, and slightly nutty

Nerada Tea Estate in Queensland, Australia.
Photograph courtesy of Nerada Tea

CHAPTER 7

OCEANIA

THE BRITISH INTRODUCED TEA DRINKING TO AUSTRALIA DURING THE 18TH CENTURY, AND ALFRED BUSHELL ESTABLISHED THE FIRST TEA RETAIL STORE IN QUEENSLAND IN 1883. BUSHELL LATER EXPANDED THE FAMILY BUSINESS ALL OVER THE COUNTRY AND INTO NEW ZEALAND.

The idea of growing tea in Australia developed in the late 19th century when the Cutten Brothers established the first plants at Bingil Bay in Queensland. The project was abandoned in 1918 when the devastating Mackay cyclone destroyed the crop. Allan Maruff made the next attempts in the 1950s. Maruff started a tea nursery in Innisfail and, in 1958, purchased land that is today Nerada Tea Estates.

Australia governed Papua New Guinea from 1906 to 1975, and in the 1930s, the Australian Department of Agriculture, Stock and Fisheries decided to plant an experimental tea plot with 90,000 assamica varietals on undeveloped swampland in the Wahgi Valley, Western Highlands Province. In the 1960s, after a small factory had been constructed, the government decided to expand tea cultivation on 3,000 hectares of land, with the goal of setting up large estates with their own factories, and smallholder producers who would sell fresh leaf to those factories. Today, WR Carpenter (PNG) Group of Companies is the country's only remaining tea producer.

Tea probably was introduced to New Zealand during the late 18th century when British sealers traded sealskins to the Chinese in exchange for tea, spices, oils, and fabrics. And when British missionaries began to settle here in the early 19th century, they would have brought a supply of dry leaf with them. Once introduced, tea followed much the same path as it did in Britain: China tea was replaced by teas from India and Ceylon as cheaper supplies from those regions became more available. Today, tea is grown at the Zealong Tea Estate near Hamilton on North Island.

Zealong Tea Estate in Hamilton, North Island, New Zealand.
Photograph courtesy of Zealong Tea Estate

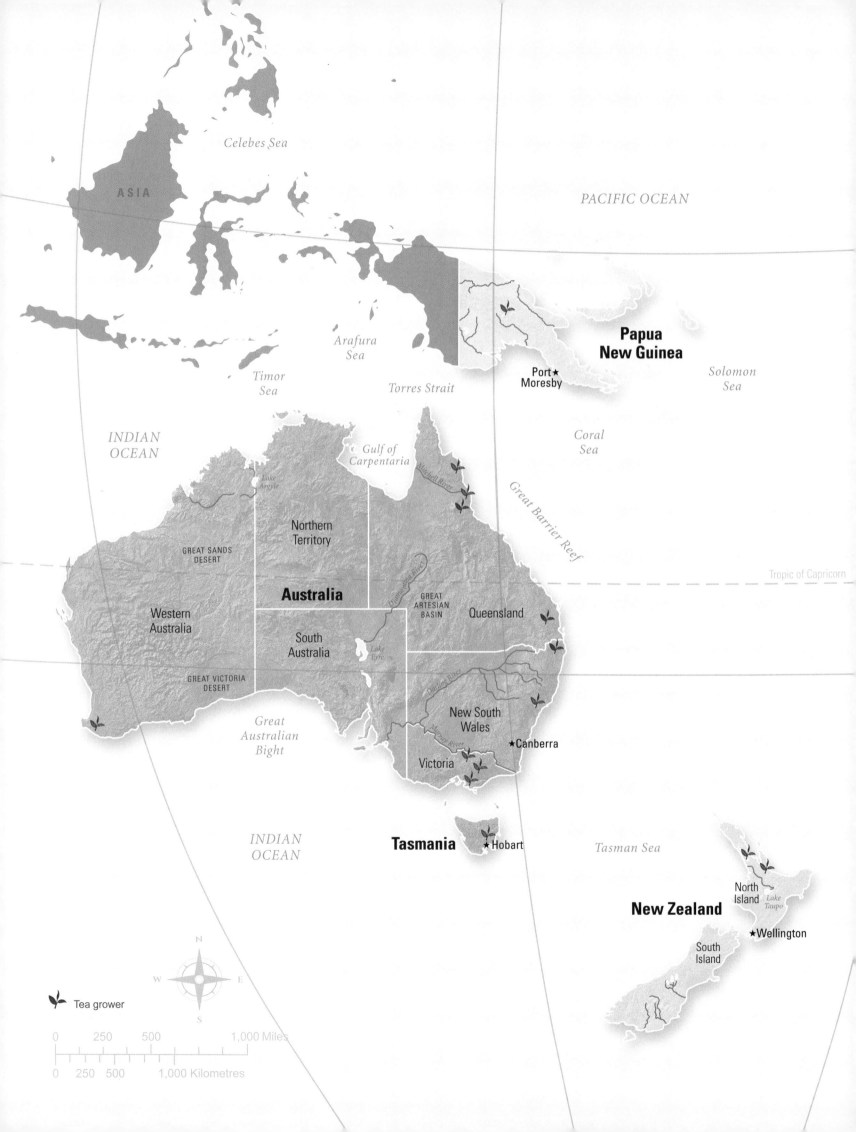

ASIA

Celebes Sea

PACIFIC OCEAN

Arafura
Sea

Timor
Sea

Torres Strait

**Papua
New Guinea**

Port ★
Moresby

*Solomon
Sea*

INDIAN
OCEAN

Gulf of
Carpentaria

Coral
Sea

Lake
Argyle

Great Barrier Reef

Northern
Territory

Mitchell River

Tropic of Capricorn

GREAT SANDS
DESERT

Australia

Diamantina River

GREAT
ARTESIAN
BASIN

Queensland

Western
Australia

South
Australia

Lake
Eyre

GREAT VICTORIA
DESERT

Darling River

New South
Wales

Great
Australian
Bight

Murray River

★Canberra

Victoria

INDIAN
OCEAN

Tasmania

★ Hobart

Tasman Sea

North
Island

Lake
Taupo

New Zealand

★Wellington

South
Island

N

W E

S

🌱 Tea grower

0   250   500   1,000 Miles

0   250 500   1,000 Kilometres

Madura Teas Estate in New South Wales.
Photograph courtesy of Madura Tea Estates, *maduratea.com.au*

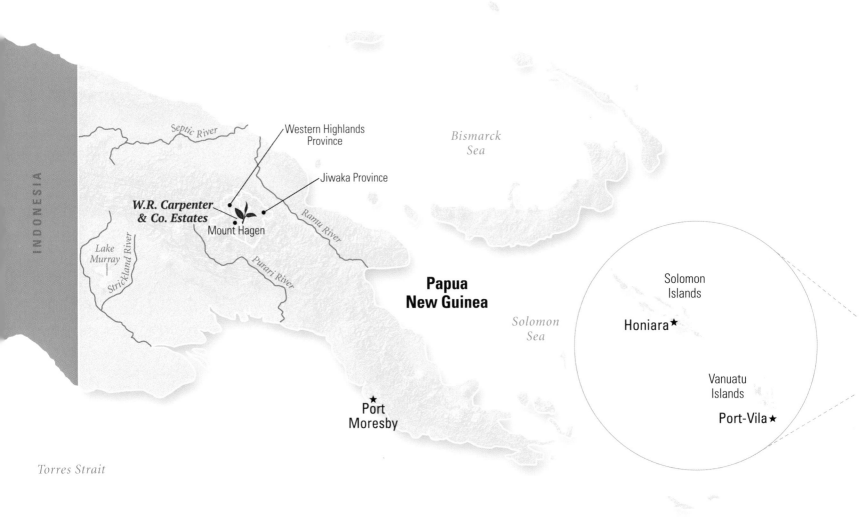

PACIFIC OCEAN

INDONESIA

Septic River

Western Highlands
Province

Jiwaka Province

**W.R. Carpenter
& Co. Estates**

Mount Hagen

Ramu River

*Bismarck
Sea*

*Lake
Murray*

Strickland River

Purari River

**Papua
New Guinea**

*Solomon
Sea*

Solomon
Islands

Honiara ★

Vanuatu
Islands

Port-Vila ★

★
Port
Moresby

Torres Strait

*Coral
Sea*

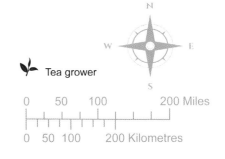

Tea grower

| 0 | 50 | 100 | | 200 Miles |

| 0 | 50 | 100 | | 200 Kilometres |

PAPUA NEW GUINEA

From 1906 until 1975, Papua New Guinea was administered by Australia, and it was the Australian Department of Agriculture that decided in the 1930s to cultivate 90,000 assamica varietals on swampland in Western Highlands Province. In 1962, a small factory was built, the first tea was exported, and the good quality and promising yields prompted the government to develop large estates with factories and smallholder farms here on 3,000 hectares of land. But the smallholders preferred to grow coffee and vegetables, so six foreign-owned estates dominated the new industry. By the late 1970s, these were producing 80 percent of the country's tea. Five smaller estates were also now growing tea in the Western Highlands and in Simbu Province, and smallholder tea accounted for less than 3 percent of total crop. During the 1970s, the industry expanded, but this growth was not sustained. By 1997, only 50 percent of the developed land was still being cultivated.

Today, W.R. Carpenter & Co. Estates is the only remaining producer and grows tea on four estates covering a total of 1,800 hectares in the Wahgi Valley in Jiwaka Province, a new province carved from Western Highlands Province. The estates at Kudjip, Kindeng, Aviamp, and Minjigina, all dating back to the 1960s and '70s, were planted with varietals propagated from the original 1930s seeds. The country lies close to the equator, so its climate is warm; it receives plenty of rain through the year—a total of about 2,540 millimetres (100 inches); and the rich volcanic soil is ideal for the plants. The bushes grow unshaded and without pesticides at elevations of 1,500 metres (4,921 feet) and are mechanically harvested throughout the year. Because the land is wet and soft, some mechanical harvesters proved to be too heavy, so small, lightweight Japanese-built machines are used. Carpenters produces nine grades of bright, strong, colour black CTC tea, which are exported to Australia, New Zealand, North America, Malaysia, Singapore, Russia, Fiji, the Solomon Islands, and the Vanuatu Islands.

Country, State, or Province
Papua New Guinea

Number of Gardens
4

Main Districts or Gardens
Around Mount Hagen in the Waghi Valley, Jiwaka Province

Area Under Tea
1,800 hectares

Average Annual Production (Kilograms)
7 million

Terrain
Wide, undulating fields with volcanic soil in the foothills of the Western Highlands

Altitude
1,500 metres (5,000 feet)

Production Period
All year

Best Time to Visit
May to October

Main Varietals/Cultivars
Assamicas from Malaysia via Queensland, Australia

Types of Tea Made
9 grades of CTC black tea

Predominant Flavours; Tasting Notes
BLACK: bright, strong, colour

INDONESIA

PAPUA
NEW GUINEA

*Arafura
Sea*

*Timor
Sea*

Torres Strait

*Coral
Sea*

INDIAN
OCEAN

Gulf of
Carpentaria

**Daintree Tea
Company**

**Nerada Tea
Plantation**

**Nucifora Tea
Plantation**

*Lake
Argyle*

Northern
Territory

GREAT SANDS
DESERT

Great Barrier Reef

Queensland

Diamantina River

GREAT
ARTESIAN
BASIN

Western
Australia

Australia

**Arakai
Tea Estate**

Brisbane.

South
Australia

*Lake
Eyre*

Darling River

**Madura
Tea Estate**

GREAT VICTORIA
DESERT

•Perth

New South
Wales

Kumitaro Co. Ltd.

*Great
Australian
Bight*

•Adelaide

Murray River

★Canberra

Southern Forest Tea

INDIAN
OCEAN

Victoria

Ito En

**Alpine Tea
Company**

**Two Rivers
Green Tea**

N

W   E

S

Tasmania

★Hobart

🌱 Tea grower

**Tasmanian
Green Tea**

| 0 | 125 | 250 | | 500 Miles |
| 0 | 125 | 250 | | 500 Kilometres |

AUSTRALIA

Tea-growing pioneers in the 20th century recognised that the high cost of labour to hand pluck tea would make Australian-grown tea too expensive, so research at the South Johnstone Research Station in North Queensland in the 1970s and 1980s focused on the viability of mechanical harvesting. With promising results, interest in tea farming grew; further areas were planted out; and by 1999, some 12 commercial projects had been established—10 in Queensland and two in New South Wales. Further research showed that soil, weather conditions, and water supplies were suitable. This, coupled with a threefold increase in tea consumption across the country due to the tea and health message, prompted more farmers to consider tea as a viable crop.

At the turn of the millennium, new developments in Victoria and New South Wales were being driven by Japanese tea companies Ito En and Kunitaro Co., Ltd., which were looking for new territories on which to grow green tea. They chose Australia because it offered conditions similar to those in some of Japan's most famous growing regions. In June 2000, the Australian Green Tea Growers Association (AGTGA) was established to bring all aspects of the developing industry under one umbrella. By 2013, tea farming was well established in New South Wales, Queensland, Tasmania, and Victoria. And in Western Australia, new growers Maria and Ron Kemp started harvesting tea at their family farm in Northcliffe in 2015 and sell their Southern Forest sencha and matcha to local stores.

NEW SOUTH WALES

(AUSTRALIA)

KUNITARO CO., LTD. | *Gosford*

In 1998, the New South Wales Department of Primary Industries entered into a partnership with Japanese Kunitaro Co., Ltd., with the aim of growing tea near Gosford, just north of Sydney. After successful trials, Kunitaro established a 5-hectare plantation at Mungrove Mountain in 2004, which was gradually increased to 10 hectares. A small cooperative-style factory was built at Somersby for crude processing, with the leaf then being sent to Japan for refining and finishing, and in 2017, it also started producing matcha. In 2018, the estate was certified organic JAS (Japanese Organic Standard).

Because of this highly successful project, several universities, private food research institutes, and the government's Department of Primary Industries became involved in the research and funding of other tea-growing activities. By 2017, more than 20 trial plantations had been established all over New South Wales, and more farmers were waiting to plant seedlings in anticipation of further factory-supported cooperatives.

MADURA TEA ESTATE | *Clothiers Creek*

Madura Tea Estate was established in 1978 on the outskirts of Murwillumbah in the Tweed Valley. Third-generation former Ceylon tea planter Michael Grant Cook and his wife, Norma, purchased a disused dairy farm and planted tea seedlings brought in from Tanzania. Madura (Tamil for "paradise") is set amongst a beautiful rainforest and has an abundance of rivers and streams.

The Cooks chose the location not simply for its beauty but because the flat terrain suited mechanical harvesting and because its climate and topography are very similar to those of Assam. Summers are hot and humid, while winters are cold with occasional frosts. His plan was to grow, process, taste, blend, and pack Madura tea at the estate, but he also imported quality world teas to create a range of suitable blends. In the 1980s, Madura was the first company to successfully introduce green tea to the Australian market.

The Cooks sold the farm in 1992 to four local families, and in 2000, they built a tea-packing facility that now employs more than 50 staff. The 250,000 tea bushes are mechanically harvested every eight to 10 days to make green tea that is blended with Asian teas, and a black that is mixed with Ceylon and South Indian teas to create Madura's Premium, English Breakfast, and Earl Grey blends.

Madura Tea Estate, which introduced the first green tea to the Australian market in the 1980s and now sells a range of green, white, and black teas and flavoured blends. Photographs courtesy of Madura Tea Estates, *maduratea.com.au*

Country, State, or Province
New South Wales

Number of Gardens
2

Main Districts or Gardens
Kunitaro Co., Ltd., Gosford Central Coast Region

Madura Tea Estate:, Tweed Valley

Area Under Tea
Kunitaro Co., Ltd.:
12.5 hectares at Mangrove Mountain, 1 hectare at Somersby, plus smallholders (Somersby used for cuttings, not crop)

Madura Tea Estate:
12 hectares

Average Annual Production (Kilograms)
Kunitaro Co., Ltd.:
65,000

Madura Tea Estate:
17,000 to 18,000

Terrain
Kunitaro Co., Ltd.:
Very gently sloping land; popular agricultural area for citrus, grapes, and grain

Madura Tea Estate:
Flat, low-lying coastal region with volcanic soil

Altitude
Kunitaro Co., Ltd.:
300 metres (984 feet)

Madura Tea Estate:
30.48 metres (100 feet)

Production Period
Kunitaro Co., Ltd.:
September or October to late April or early May

Madura Tea Estate:
Late September to June

Best Time to Visit
All year

Main Varietals/Cultivars
Kunitaro Co., Ltd.:
Japanese varietals, mainly Yabukita and Sayamakaori, imported from Japan and Tasmania

Madura Tea Estate:
Assamica varietals from Tanzania

Types of Tea Made
Kunitaro Co., Ltd.:
Japanese-style green

Madura Tea Estate:
Black, green CTC, white

Predominant Flavours; Tasting Notes
Kunitaro Co., Ltd.:
GREEN: sweet, intense, umami

Madura Tea Estate:
BLACK: strong, bright, full-bodied
GREEN: fresh, smooth
WHITE: light and delicate

QUEENSLAND

(AUSTRALIA)

ARAKAI TEA ESTATE | *Bellthorpe*

The Collins family established this farm in 1999 and for the first few years grew rainforest trees and avocados. Then, they became aware of the increasing collaboration between tea farmers in Victoria and large Japanese tea companies and began to consider growing tea. The family turned to farmers in Japan, Taiwan, and China for advice on cultivation, harvesting, and processing and, in 2011, planted 4,720 plants grown from six Japanese cultivars.

Today, 12,500 plants thrive on 1 hectare of rich acidic Queensland soil surrounded by timber trees that provide protection from the wind. The fresh shoots are harvested mechanically every five or six weeks, using a self-made bicycle-based, motorised plucking and pruning machine, and the leaves are processed to make different seasonal black and Japanese-style steamed green teas. In 2015, the year of their first harvest, the Collinses won Best Australian Green Tea, Best Australian Black Tea, and Best Green Tea from among international entrants in the Australian Tea Masters' Golden Leaf Awards at the first Australian International Tea Expo in Melbourne.

DAINTREE TEA COMPANY | *Diwan*

The Daintree Tea Company, located on the Cubbagudta Plantation in the heart of the Daintree Wilderness area of North Queensland, was established in 1978 by the Nicholas family. *Cubbagudta* means "rainy place" in the language of the local Kuku Yalanji Aboriginal people, and the tea farm, situated on the fringes of the Daintree Rainforest, enjoys 4 metres (13 feet) of rain every year. The bushes are harvested approximately every two weeks, and the leaf is transported to the estate factory and processed into black tea. The dry, choppy leaf is sold as single-origin unblended Daintree tea. Other tea companies in the UK, Europe, New Zealand, North America, Japan, and China also buy and blend the leaves.

NERADA TEA PLANTATION | *Sunnybank Hills*

On the 1st of April 1882, four brothers—James, Herbert, Leonard, and Sidney Cutten—discovered Bingil Bay in the Cairns Highlands of North Queensland and established a timberworks, where they also grew tropical plants, including tea. Regular cyclones and severe drought over the next 40 years gradually killed the various crops, and in 1918, the brothers abandoned the farm. In 1958, Allan Maruff established a tea industry in the area by collecting seed and cuttings from the Cuttens' old bushes and planting them on 129 hectares in the Nerada Valley. By 1968, 80 acres of tea were thriving there, and in 1970, with a group of engineers, Maruff invented a 5-tonne harvester and joined forces with local trading company Burns Philp to build a processing factory. However, tea prices at the time were not high enough to sustain the company, and in 1972, the factory and tea estate closed down.

In 1969, local businessman Rod Taylor had formed a consortium, Tea Estates of Australia (TEA), and had also started growing tea on a neighbouring 200-acre property. TEA then acquired Nerada Tea Estate's assets, joined the two tea estates together, and in 1974, launched the Nerada Tea brand in the Queensland market. The area under tea was expanded with seed from Africa and Malaysia, and today, the Nerada factory processes 6 million kilos (13.2 million pounds) of fresh leaf every year. The shoots are scooped off the bushes mechanically every seven to 20 days and turned into black CTC tea. Nerada is a subsidiary independent company of BOH Plantations Sdn Bhd in Malaysia.

NUCIFORA TEA PLANTATION | *East Palmerston*

Established in 1985, Nucifora Tea Plantation sits just outside Innisfail at the base of the World Heritage Wooroonooran National Park in the District of Palmerston. Sybbie Nucifora raises beef cattle, and when the Nucifora family decided to also grow tea, they battled green ants and raspberry canes to harvest 4,000 kilos (8,818 pounds) of tea seed from an old abandoned tea farm nearby. These were planted on 60 hectares of land in this wet, tropical, rich agricultural region of North Queensland. In the warm, sunny climate and with average annual rainfall of 4,000 millimetres (157 inches), the tea grows happily alongside the cattle. The fresh shoots of two leaves and a bud are gathered every 21 days by a mechanical harvester that is a cross between a lawnmower and a vacuum cleaner. They are then processed to make small-leafed black tea for tea bags and a large-leaf grade for the speciality market.

TOP: Processing machinery at Nerada Tea Plantation, Queensland. ABOVE: Nerada Tea Estate where tea grows on more than 1,000 acres. Photographs courtesy of Nerada Tea

Mechanical harvesters work 24 hours a day at Nerada Tea Estate to gather 4,000 kilograms (8,818 pounds) of fresh leaf an hour.

Photographs courtesy of Nerada Tea

Country, State, or Province
Queensland

Number of Gardens 4

Main Districts or Gardens
Arakai Estate, Bellthorpe

Daintree Tea, Daintree Wilderness

Nerada Tea, Nerada Valley

Nucifora Tea, East Palmerston

Area Under Tea
Arakai Estate: 1 hectare

Daintree Tea: 72 hectares

Nerada Tea: 400 hectares

Nucifora Tea: 60 hectares

Average Annual Production (Kilograms)
Arakai Estate: 1,000

Daintree Tea: 20,000 to 40,000

Nerada Tea: 1.5 million

Nucifora Tea: 200,000

Terrain
Arakai Estate: Gently sloping, wide fields with rich volcanic soil; the farm includes 300 acres of native forest, 500 avocado trees, and commercial plantations of timber (including some native rainforest species)

Daintree Tea: Undulating, flat, open fields with red volcanic soil

Nerada Tea: Vast open flat fields with rich volcanic soil on the Atherton Tablelands

Nucifora Tea: Gently sloping pastureland on the fringe of the coastal forest of the Coral Sea

Altitude
Arakai Estate:
580 metres (1,903 feet)

Daintree Tea:
50 metres (164 feet)

Nerada Tea:
760 metres (2,493 feet)

Nucifora Tea:
250 metres (820 feet)

Production Period
Arakai Estate: September to April

Daintree Tea: August to April

Nerada Tea: November to May

Nucifora Tea: All year

Best Time to Visit
May to September

Main Varietals/Cultivars
Arakai Estate: 6 Japanese cultivars: Yabukita, Sayamakaori, Meirokyu, Yutaka Midori, Fushin, Okumidori

Daintree Tea: Origin not known

Nerada Tea: Seeds from Africa and Malaysia, and seeds from plants imported from India in the 1880s

Nucifora Tea: Assamicas

Types of Tea Made
Arakai Estate: First-flush green teas processed in Taiwanese style; first-flush black; green and black teas from late spring, summer, and autumn harvests

Daintree Tea: Black CTC

Nerada Tea: Black CTC

Nucifora Tea: Black

Predominant Flavours; Tasting Notes
Arakai Estate: First-flush teas are aromatic and sweet; later-season greens are smooth and buttery, with floral notes and hints of citrus; the later-season blacks have a chocolate and chestnut aroma like a dark oolong, and a complex vibrant taste with floral hints and a soft finish

Daintree Tea:
BLACK: mild, smooth, with slightly earthy character

Nerada Tea:
BLACK: full-bodied with a slightly malty character

Nucifora Tea:
BLACK: rich, smooth, full-bodied, slightly earthy with hints of green wood and raisins

TASMANIA

(AUSTRALIA)

TASMANIAN GREEN TEA | *Hobart*

In 1988, the Tasmanian Department of Primary Industries in Hobart imported the first Japanese tea plants (Sayamakaori, Yabukita, and Okuhikaori cultivars) into Tasmania to assess the island's suitability for tea cultivation. With Gordon Brown in charge, the plants were sent out for cultivation at five sites around Tasmania. Salty sea air, waterlogged soil, and frost in the different locations killed off the majority of the plants, but those growing at Scottsdale did well. After successful sampling, the Japanese decided to grow tea not in Tasmania, but in Victoria and New South Wales. With a new passion for the tea plants, Brown and his wife, Jane, were disappointed by the ending of the Tasmanian project and so decided to cultivate the leftover plants on 1,000 square metres (10,764 square feet) of their own land. They processed their first green tea in 1999 and expanded the garden to 4,000 square metres (43,056 square feet), but they constantly have to replant because of persistent attacks by wallabies, bandicoots, and rabbits. Small birds choose the tea bushes as a safe haven in which to build their nests, and native hens also shelter, nest, and raise their families under the branches. Westerly winds crossing to and from New Zealand and the southern tip of South America keep the Tasmanian air free of pollutants.

Gordon Brown at his Tasmanian tea garden, which was developed using left-over plants from early trials in the 1980s that investigated the possibility of growing tea in Australia. Photograph courtesy of Gordon Brown, Dry Ideas

Country, State, or Province
Tasmania

Number of Gardens
1

Main Districts or Gardens
Tasmania Green Tea, Hobart

Area Under Tea
0.4 hectares

Average Annual Production (Kilograms)
400

Terrain
Gently sloping fields on undulating country in a valley just south of Hobart

Altitude
200 metres (656 feet)

Production Period
Mid-November to early April

Best Time to Visit
December to February

Main Varietals/ Cultivars
Japanese Sayamakaori and Yabukita

Types of Tea Made
Japanese-style green

Predominant Flavours; Tasting Notes
GREEN: brisk, clean, with hints of seafood and fresh-mown grass

VICTORIA

(AUSTRALIA)

ITO EN | *Wangaratta*

In the early 1990s, Japanese tea growers began to look for safe, reliable sources of green tea outside Japan. After considering China, New Zealand, Africa, and South America as potential locations, Ito En settled on Australia because it was thought to offer the best resources, soil, climate, expertise, and supporting industries. And they chose Victoria because it lies on the same latitude as Japan's Shizuoka Prefecture. In 1994, Ito En Australia Pty Ltd was incorporated, and in 2001, cuttings were brought in from Tasmania's research crop to establish a commercial garden. The Ito En factory opened in October 2004, a serendipitous time when local tobacco farmers were looking for an alternative crop. Ito En's tea is grown by 14 contracted growers, each working an average of 20 acres, and is sold to the Ito En processing plant at Wangaratta in the Ovens Valley, North Victoria.

The bushes took eight years to mature, and drought, spring frost, and beetles are the crop's biggest enemies. The tea is harvested three or four times a year, using Japanese hedge-trimmer harvesters, and most of the leaf is processed as *aracha*, a crude form of steamed green tea. It is then vacuum-packed, put into cold storage, and exported to Japan for final processing. A small amount is refined in Australia and sold into the local market. Some of the farmers buy back the processed tea to pack and sell under their own brand names. Below are details of two of these farms.

ALPINE TEA COMPANY | *Tawonga*

Tea grows on 4 hectares of Davide and Erin Angelini's 50-hectare property at Tawonga in Victoria's Alpine National Park. They produce 25,000 kilograms (55,116 pounds) of fresh leaf per hectare per year, which is grown on contract for Ito En and is processed as steamed green tea at the Japanese company's factory in Wangaratta.

Davide, whose parents were tobacco farmers here until 1995, became interested in tea cultivation when Ito En began talking to farmers in Victoria in 2000. In 2001, he planted 60,000 18-month-old Yabukita cultivar plants brought in from Ito En's nursery in Thornton, Victoria, and after eight years, the farm was in full production.

During the first few years, frost killed about 30 percent of the plants. Davide created an overhead sprinkler system that gives frost protection and irrigation, with the water coming from the Kiewa River using pumps and irrigation powered by solar panels. The sprinkler system was so successful that it is now installed on all the farms working with Ito En in Victoria. Ito En advisers visit the farms regularly and provide a harvesting machine when required.

Some of the teas Ito En processes come back to the farm, and the Angelinis sell about 1,500 kilograms (3,307 pounds) of the shincha, sencha, and hojicha each year under the Alpine Tea Company brand. They also sell their powdered matcha to the local Beechworth's Bridge Brewers for the production of the brewery's Mayday Hills Green T IPA (India Pale Ale) that was released in January 2017.

TWO RIVERS GREEN TEA | *Alexandra*

The Two Rivers Green Tea estate takes the name from its location at the junction of the Goulburn and Acheron rivers in north-east Victoria, about 150 kilometres (93 miles) from Ito En's processing plant in Wangaratta. William Leckey's 360-hectare sheep and cattle farm, Heatherly, was established by his parents in the 1920s. In the 1990s, Leckey began looking for a crop that would suit the local soil. At the same time, Japanese tea company Ito En was looking for perfect tea-growing conditions outside Japan and, in 2000, started looking for potential growers in Victoria. In 2001, Leckey planted his first 170,000 tea seedlings on 12 hectares of his estate. The crop—harvested every 45 to 55 days four times a year using a mechanical Japanese Kawasaki harvester—is processed by Ito En at Wangaratta for sale in Japan, Australia, and around the world. Some of the tea, which varies according to season, now comes back to Heatherly to be packed and sold as the Two Rivers Green Tea brand. Leckey, who knew nothing about tea cultivation in 2000, is now president of the Australian Green Tea Growers Association.

Country, State, or Province
Victoria

Number of Gardens
Approximately 8 farms, plus Ito En's processing factory

Contracted farmers include:
Alpine Tea Company, Two Rivers Green Tea, Matthew Van Helvoirt, George Barel, Andrew Pederic, Mauro Stafani, Collin Walker, and David Cooper

Main Districts or Gardens
Ito En, Wangaratta

Alpine Tea Company, Tawonga

Two Rivers Green Tea, Alexandra

Area Under Tea
Ito En: 68.5 hectares of contracted growers' farms; 50.5 hectares of smallholder farms

Alpine Tea Company: 4 hectares

Two Rivers Green Tea: 12 hectares

Average Annual Production (Kilograms)
Ito En: 327,000

Alpine Tea Company: 100,000 of fresh leaf that is processed at Ito En's factory in Wangaratta

Two Rivers Green Tea: 195,000 of fresh leaf (43,000 of made tea)

Terrain
Alpine Tea Company:
Wide, gently sloping fields in the the upper reaches of the Kiewa Valley at Tawonga, against a backdrop of mountains

Two Rivers Green Tea: Vast, wide paddocks on free-draining river flats surrounded by gentle hills

Altitude
Alpine Tea Company:
320 metres (1,050 feet)

Two Rivers Green Tea:
200 metres (656 feet)

Production Period
Alpine Tea Company:
Late October to late February

Two Rivers Green Tea:
Normally three harvests from early October to mid-February; or four harvests from early October to early April

Best Time to Visit
December to February

Main Varietals/Cultivars
Alpine Tea Company:
Japanese cultivar Yabukita

Two Rivers Green Tea:
Japanese cultivars: Sayamakaori, Yabukita, Okuhikaori

Types of Tea Made
Ito En: Japanese-style green teas: shincha, sencha, hojicha

Alpine Tea Company: Japanese-style steamed green teas, processed by Ito En: First Harvest, sencha, hojicha

Two Rivers Green Tea: Japanese-style green teas, processed by Ito En: shincha, sencha, hojicha, genmaicha

Predominant Flavours; Tasting Notes
Ito En:
GREEN: creamy, light, balanced, with hints of sweet grasses, bell pepper, and green beans

Alpine Tea Company:
GREEN:
Shincha—sweet, mild, and brothy
Sencha—gently astringent, refreshing, with hints of freshly cut grass
Hojicha—woody and nutty with a honeyed aroma

Two Rivers Green Tea:
GREEN:
First-flush shincha—intense, strong, and sweet
Sencha—light and sweet
Hojicha—toasty and nutty, with caramel notes
Genmaicha—nutty, with a sweet, light finish

The Purangi
Tea Collection

Coromandel
Peninsula

Auckland

Waikato River

Hamilton

Zealong
Tea Estate, Ltd.

Lake
Taupo

North
Island

★Wellington

South
Island

Tasman Sea

SOUTHERN ALPS

New Zealand

Waitaki River

PACIFIC OCEAN

Clutha River

Mataura River

Tea grower

0   50   100   200 Miles

0   50 100   200 Kilometres

NEW ZEALAND

In 1882, a letter from an "Old Settler" published in New Zealand's *The Press* told readers, "A company is being promoted in Scotland to carry on tea and silk farming in New Zealand." Nothing happened until 1979, when the government backed trials to assess whether tea might make a viable alternative crop to tobacco. Yabukita cultivars were planted on 115 hectares at Motueka, near Nelson, where smallholders farmed plots of 1 to 6 hectares and owned a single-line processing plant. By 1999, only six of the 38 farmers were still growing tea on 20 hectares. Harsh frosts in late November three years running killed the harvest; cold winds, rain, and sandblasting by the wind coming off the ocean caused further damage; attempts at vegetative propagation failed, probably because of root disturbance and incorrect irrigation; and a thin ozone layer above South Island allowed too much UV light through to the plants, thus turning the fresh leaf a yellowish colour rather than vibrant green and giving a dried leaf that was brown rather than green.

THE PURANGI TEA COLLECTION | *Auckland*

In 1993, the Thames Valley Coromandel Business Development Board, based near Auckland, funded an investigation at Purangi Estate Limited into the culture and manufacture of tea. Although the research work was thorough and wide ranging, the project never took off. However, the Purangi Tea Collection survives as an archival collection of 66 different assamica sub-varietals and plants of Cambodian origin at Purangi Estate on the Coromandel Peninsula.

ZEALONG TEA ESTATE, LTD. | *Hamilton*

In 1996, the Chen family emigrated from Taiwan to the Hamilton area of North Island, and when they discovered that ornamental camellias grew well in the area, Tzu Wan Chen and his son Vincent decided to try growing tea here. They purchased 15 acres of land, previously a dairy farm, sought out the best tea bushes in Taiwan, and imported 1,500 leaf cuttings packed in wet paper. Only 130 survived 10 months in quarantine, but this natural selection gave very robust stock for propagating new plants for the existing estate. The original surviving cuttings still grow in Vincent's back garden.

In 2000, a 10-acre tea garden was established, and in 2004, a factory was built and equipped with government-approved machinery from Taiwan, but oolong processing methods had to change to meet legal requirements. In Taiwan, sunshine plays an important part in the development of sweet floral notes during the initial outdoor withering of the freshly harvested leaves. New Zealand ministry officials would not allow this outdoor stage of the processing to take place, and today the tea has to be withered inside greenhouses where conditions can be controlled to meet health and safety requirements. The Chens also placed particular focus on traceability and organic standards. Research at Zealong has shown how terroir affects the way the tea plant adapts to local conditions—the leaves of Zealong's plants are thicker and wider than those of the parent plants, and caffeine and nutrient levels vary from those found in the original bushes in Taiwan.

The first Zealong teas were launched in 2009, and in 2012, the farm moved to a new site at nearby Gordonton that is planted with 1.2 million tea bushes across 48 hectares of certified-organic land. These yield 100 tons of handpicked fresh leaf shoots that are processed by a combination of traditional and new manufacturing methods from Japan, other parts of Asia, and Europe. The aim is to eventually have 2 million plants in the ground and to manufacture 40,000 or 50,000 kilos (88,185 or 110,231 pounds) of tea a year. In 2014–15, a 900-square-metre (9,688-square-foot) factory and a conference centre were constructed, and the remaining 4 hectares are given over to a plant nursery, the Tea House restaurant, pavilion, lake, and visitor centre.

TOP: Zealong Tea Estate near Hamilton on North Island. The sun deck of the estate's Tea House restaurant can be seen in the foreground.
LEFT: Native birds at Zealong Tea Estate help organic cultivation by controlling the number of insects. RIGHT: Giant Chinese teapots and tea bowls at the entrance to Zealong Tea Estate. Photographs courtesy of Zealong Tea Estate

Country, State, or Province
New Zealand

Number of Gardens
1

Main Districts or Gardens
Zealong Tea Estate, Ltd., Hamilton, Waikato

Area Under Tea
48 hectares

Average Annual Production (Kilograms)
20,000

Terrain
Almost-flat, open field

Altitude
40 metres (130 feet)

Production Period
November to March

Best Time to Visit
Late November to March

Main Varietals/Cultivars
Taiwanese varietals

Types of Tea Made
Black, oolong, green

Predominant Flavours; Tasting Notes
GREEN: smooth, silky, floral with hints of toasted chestnuts and a subtle, sweet finish
PURE OOLONG: sweet, fresh, aromatic, and buttery
AROMATIC OOLONG: clear and aromatic with a hint of fruits and flowers
DARK OOLONG: rich, deep, nutty, with a hint of charcoal and dark chocolate but no bitterness
BLACK OOLONG: full-bodied, fruity, with a sweet, honeyed undertone and smooth, silky finish

PLACES OF INTEREST

AFRICA

Kenya

Tea Research Institute (TRI)
Off Kericho-Nakuru Road,
P.O. Box 820 — 20200
Kericho
kalro.org/tea

Malawi

Tea Research Foundation of
Central Africa (TRFCA)
P.O. Box 51
Mulanje
trfca.net

Mauritius

Bois Cheri Tea Factory
and Tea Museum
Bois Cheri Road
Bois Cheri
saintaubin.mu

Tanzania

Tea Research Institute
of Tanzania (TRIT)
P.O. Box 2177
Dar es Salaam

ASIA

Bangladesh

Bangladesh Tea Board
171–172 Baizid
Bostami Road
Nasirabad, Chittagong

Bangladesh Tea Research
Institute (BTRI)
Srimangal-3210
Moulvibazar, Sylhet
btri.gov.bd

Tea Resort & Museum
(Bangladesh Tea Board)
Sreemangal-Bhanugach
Road
Sreemangal 3210
Moulvibazar

China

Guilin Tea Research
Institute
17# Jingji Road
Guangxi
guilintea.com

Flagstaff House
Museum of Tea Ware
10 Cotton Tree Drive
(Inside Hong Kong Park)
Central, Hong Kong
hk.art.museum

National Tea Museum
Long Jing (Dragon Well)
Village
West Lake
Zhejiang

Tea Research Institute,
Chinese Academy of
Agricultural Sciences
(TRI, CAAS)
No. 9, Meilin South Road
Xihu District
Hangzhou 310008
tricaas.com/English/

Tenfu Tea Museum
Zhangzhou, Fujian
museum.tenfu.com

Zhejiang University
Department of Tea Science
866 Yuhang Tang Road
Hangzhou
Zhejiang 310058

India

Darjeeling Tea Research &
Management Association
(NITM)
P.O. Kadamtala
Siliguri – 734011
Darjeeling, West Bengal

The Munnar Tea Museum
Nullatanni Estate
Munnar, Idukki District
Kerala 685612

National Tea Research
Foundation (NTRF)
Tea Board
14, B. T. M. Sarani,
9th Floor
Kolkata 700001

Tea Museum
Dodabetta Tea Factory
Dodabetta Road
Ootacamund
The Nilgiris, Tamil Nadu
teamuseumindia.com

Tea Research Association
113, Park Street, 9th Floor
Kolkata – 700016
tocklai.org

Tea Research Association
P.O. Silcuri – 788 118
Cachar, Assam

Tea Research Association
P.O. Dikom – 786 101
Assam

Tea Research Association
Tocklai Tea Research Institute
P.O. Jorhat – 785008
Assam

Tea Research Association
P.O. Thakurbari – 784 503
Assam

Tea Research Association
c/o Tea Development Centre
Directorate of Horticulture
Lumnongrim
Dewlieh, Umnsing District
Meghalaya 793105

Tea Research Centre
P.O. Kanjaban – 799 006
Agartala, Tripura

Tea Research Association
P.O. Bengdubi – 734 424
Darjeeling, West Bengal

Tea Research Association
P.O. Nagrakata – 735 225
West Bengal

Tea Research Association
15 Coochbeher Road
P.O. Darjeeling – 734 101
West Bengal

UPASI Tea Research
Foundation
Nirar Dam BPO,
Valparai – 642 127
Coimbatore, Tamil Nadu

Uttarakhand Tea
Development Board,
Zila Panchayat Building,
Dhranaula
Almora 263 601
Uttarakhand
utdb.uk.gov.in

Japan

Hoshino Tea Museum
10816-5 Hoshino-mura
Yame-gun, Fukuoka

Kanaya Tea Research Station
2769 Shishidoi
Kanaya, Shimada
Shizuoka 428-8501

PLACES OF INTEREST

Makurazaki Tea
Research Station
87 Seto
Makurazaki
Kagoshima 898-0087

NARO Institute of
Vegetable and Tea
Science (NIVTS)
360 Kusawa
Ano, Tsu
Mie 514-2392
naro.affrc.go.jp

Shizuoka Green Tea
Museum of Ochanosato
3053-2 Kanaya Fujimicho
Shimada
Shizuoka 428-0034

Tea Research Centre
(Shizuoka Prefectural
Research Institute of
Agriculture and Forestry
University of Shizuoka)
1706-11 Kurasawa
Kikugawa City
Shizuoka Prefecture
439-0002

Tea Science Centre
University of Shizuoka
52-1 Yada
Suruga-ku
Shizuoka 422-8526
*sfns.u-shizuoka-ken.ac.jp/
sfnseng/teachers/page037.
html*

Pakistan

National Tea and High
Value Crops Research
Institute (NTHRI)
Park Road
Islamabad - 44000
*parc.gov.pk/index.php/en/
nthri-introduction*

National Tea Research
Institute
N35/AH4 Karakoram
Highway
Baffa
North-West Frontier

South Korea

Beautiful Tea Museum
19-11 Insa-dong
Jongno-gu, Seoul-si

Hadong Tea
Culture Center
571-25 Ssanggye-ro
Hwagae-myeon
Hadong-gun
Gyeongsangnam-do
hadongteamuseum.org

Osulloc Tea Museum
15 Sinhwayeoksa-ro
Andeok-myeon
Seogwipo, Jeju-do
osulloc.com/kr/en/museum

Sri Lanka

Ceylon Tea Museum
Hantana Road
(3 kilometres
from Kandy)
Hantana, Kandy 20000

Tea Research Institute
Sri Lanka
Talawakelle
tri.lk

Taiwan

Lugu Tea Culture Center
No. 231, Section 1,
Zhongzheng Road
Lugu Township
Nantou County 558

The Pinglin Tea Museum
No. 19-1
Shuisongqikeng
Pinglin District
New Taipei City 232

Taiwan Black Tea Museum
No. 73, Zhongshan Road
Guanxi Township
Hsinchu County

Tea Research and Extension
Station (TRES)
Yangmei, Taoyuan
*tres.gov.tw/eng/show_
index.php*

EUROPE

The Netherlands

Coffee and Tea Museum
Amsterdam
Geels & Co.-
Koffiebranderij
en Theehandel
Kikkertweg 22
1521 RG Wormerveer
geels.nl

Russia

Tea Museum
Boyarsky pereulok d. 2
Moscow 107078

United Kingdom

The Cutty Sark
King William Walk
Greenwich
London SE10 9HT
rmg.co.uk/cutty-sark

Tea Trail London
teatrail.london

The Twining Teapot Gallery
Norwich Castle Museum
and Art Gallery
24 Castle Meadow
Norwich, Norfolk NR1 3JU
*museums.norfolk.gov.uk/
norwich-castle*

Twinings
216 Strand
London WC2R 1AP

NORTH AMERICA

United States

Boston Tea Party Ships
& Museum
306 Congress Street
Boston, Massachusetts
02210
bostonteapartyship.com

Charleston Tea Plantation
6617 Maybank Highway
Wadmalaw Island,
South Carolina 29487
charlestonteaplantation.com

OCEANIA

Australia

Bygone Beautys Treasured
Teapot Museum
20-22 Grose Street
Leura
New South Wales 2780
Blue Mountains
bygonebeautys.com.au

New Zealand

Gypsy Rose Tea Museum
319 Gloucester Street
Taradale, Napier
gypsyroseteamuseum.webs.com/

INDEX

INDEX

INDEX

JANE PETTIGREW'S WORLD OF TEA

Author: Jane Pettigrew
Editor: Lorna Reeves
Art Director: Cailyn Haynes
Copy Editor: Meg Lundberg
Maps Illustrator: Karissa Brown
Cartographer: Melissa Langston
Maps Production Assistant: Samantha Sullivan

(Cover)
Photographer: Marcy Black Simpson
Stylist: Sidney Bragiel
Tea plants: *TeaHawaii.com*